# Classes, Power,
# and Conflict

# [Classes, Power, and Conflict]

## Classical and Contemporary Debates

Edited by
Anthony Giddens and David Held

University of California Press
Berkeley • Los Angeles

University of California Press
Berkeley and Los Angeles, California
© 1982 by
The Regents of the University of California
Printed in the United States of America
2 3 4 5 6 7 8 9

Designer: Janet Wood
Compositor: Innovative Media
Printer: Vail-Ballou
Binder: Vail-Ballou
Text: Bembo

Library of Congress Cataloging in Publication Data
Main entry under title:
Classes, power, and conflict.
Includes bibliographies.
1. Social classes.    2. Social conflict.
3. Labor and laboring classes.    4. Elite (Social
sciences)    5. Power (Social sciences)    I. Giddens,
Anthony.    II. Held, David.
HT675.C55      305.5      81-23122
ISBN 0-520-04489-4      AACR2
ISBN 0-520-04627-7 (pbk.)

# Contents

## II. Contemporary Theories of Class and Class Conflict

## III. Classes, Elites, and the State

## IV. Technology, Conflict, and the Labour Market

# Preface

In this book we have sought to provide a comprehensive introduction to current debates in class analysis. Recent years have seen a strong resurgence of interest in problems of class theory and in its application to the study of the industrialised societies today. In providing a source book for those interested in these problems, we have tried to resist two tendencies which seem to us to be misplaced. On the one hand, we want to break away from the tendency to obscure issues of class analysis by swamping them in more diffuse, unhistorical accounts of 'stratification'. Such has been the tendency of many authors who have written from non-Marxist positions or have assumed a strongly anti-Marxist stance. On the other hand, however, we wish to avoid the implication that either Marx or self-professed 'Marxists' have said all there is to say of any importance about questions of class and class conflict. We hold that Marx's writings do indeed contain ideas of essential significance, which continue to be as relevant today as they ever were to the analysis of the structural properties of the industrialised societies. But neither of us believes that an unreconstructed version of Marxism has any hope of coming to terms with a twentieth-century world that is very different from the one which Marx anticipated.

In a field in which there is a vast range of literature available, any selection has an arbitrary element to it. In including only three major 'classical' thinkers, we were guided by the supposition that a fairly substantial coverage of a few key writers is preferable to a superficial glimpse of the ideas of a large number. Therefore, we have not included materials from authors who in anyone's lexicon have made major contributions to class analysis: Trotsky, Lukács, Gramsci, and many others. There are other *lacunae*. We had originally planned to include a section on class and social mobility and one dealing at some length with imperialism, capitalism, and the contemporary 'world system'. We had to forego these because of considerations of space, but in an ideal world they would have appeared rather prominently in this book.

We should perhaps emphasise that we have selected contributions which we consider to be of basic importance for contemporary debates in the field of class analysis. Many of the issues in this field are necessarily highly contentious. In offering introductions to each section of the book, we have tried to keep our critical impulses under tight rein, attempting to give an accurate representation of the ideas developed by the various authors. Some of our prejudices probably creep through, and it is as well to declare here that inclusion of articles in the book does not of course imply that we are always in agreement with the views which they contain.

Section One offers an introduction to the writings of Marx, Lenin, and Weber, the individuals who to a very large extent have defined the terms of reference of class analysis. The second section contains a selection of key contributions to current debates about the theory of class and class conflict. The papers in Section Three explore the intersection of class and power and the relevance of class analysis for the comprehension of contemporary political life. Section Four raises questions concerning the relation between hierarchy, work discipline, and the labour process; while Section Five sets out in some detail central considerations for the understanding of social beliefs and ideology. The sixth section contains articles which examine the importance of the study of gender and patriarchy for an adequate grasp of power and social structure. The penultimate section raises equally significant considerations about race and the nature of urban space. The relevance of many of the issues raised for the analysis of East European societies are then explored in the last section. Finally, the reader should note that in the preparation of this volume it was necessary to cut some contributions so that a large variety of materials could be included. Our cuts are indicated by three dots in the text.

A number of colleagues have given valuable advice which has helped us in deciding the organisation and coverage of this book. We should like to thank in particular the following people: Gavin Mackenzie, Maurice Zeitlin, Harold Wilensky, Elizabeth Garnsey, John Barber, Kevin Bonnett, Michelle Stanworth, and Jane Morgan. Particular thanks are due to our editors, Grant Barnes at the University of California Press and John Winckler at Macmillan.

Cambridge and York
April 1981

# · I ·
# Classical Views

# Introduction

## Marx: Class Relations and Capitalism

Marx's texts remain the fundamental resources with which anyone interested in the theory of classes and capitalist development must begin. Although the concepts of class and class conflict are integral to the whole of Marx's work, he never managed to complete a comprehensive formulation of them. Many of Marx's writings—including *Capital* itself—remained unfinished. Some of his most important and influential ideas are stated only in an incomplete way. As a consequence, any selection from Marx's writings tends to have a fragmentary character. Matters are further complicated by scholarly debates over how far Marx's 'early' works, especially *The Economic and Philosophical Manuscripts,* embody views which Marx later discarded.

These issues help to fuel the continuing and involved interpretative debates in which Marx's writings have long been entangled. Such debates often have a scholastic quality to them, but they also raise questions of great importance for class analysis today, many of which are discussed in the contributions which follow in this book. It is probably no longer possible to provide even a summary description of Marx's views of class and class conflict which would command the agreement of everyone. So the thumbnail sketch which we offer here should be read with this in mind.

According to Marx, class divisions are not found in all forms of society: classes are a creation of history and in the future will again disappear. The earliest, and smallest, types of society (which Marx usually refers to as 'tribal societies') are classless. This is because, in such types of society, there is no surplus production and no private property. In tribal societies production is based upon communal resources—appropriated through hunting and gathering or through agriculture—and the fruits of productive activity are distributed through the community as a whole. Class divisions only arise when a surplus is generated, such that it becomes possible for a class of nonproducers to live off the productive activity of others. Those who are able to gain control of the means of production (in precapitalist societies this is above all *land*) form a dominant or ruling class both economically and politically. Class relations for Marx are thus necessarily exploitative and imply divisions of interest between ruling and subordinate classes. Class divisions are moreover inherently conflictual and frequently give rise to active class struggle, this being in Marx's view the chief 'motor' of historical development.

Marx distinguishes several types of class society in European history: ancient society (Greece and Rome), medieval feudalism, and capitalism. As class societies, they all share elements in common; but capitalism has certain very distinctive features as compared with the prior types. Marx spent a good deal of his career working out what these features are; and in analysing the trajectory of development of capitalist society that would lead to the creation of a socialist order in which classes would be transcended. In *The Economic and Philosophical Manuscripts* (1844), from which the first two extracts are taken, Marx's ideas are as yet only developed in a fairly rudimentary way; nonetheless, they contain the outlines of a critical analysis of capitalism that carries formidable intellectual penetration and moral fervour. Taking over the concept of *alienation* from Hegel, Marx strips it of the epistemological connotations it had in the writings of that author and applies it to examining the consequences of the emergence of the capitalist class system.

Marx's account of the alienation of the worker in capitalist production may seem on initial acquaintance to be both vague and abstract. It becomes much less so when understood as a first attempt to specify some of the contrasts between capitalism and prior types of productive system. The political economists—the early founders of economics—Marx argues, have already demonstrated that the class system of capitalism is based upon one predominant class relationship: that between capital and wage labour. 'Capitalists' are those who own the factories and machines which increasingly replace land as the primary means of production. Wage labour, or 'wage workers', represent a class of propertyless workers, who have been expropriated from control of their means of production. As capitalism matures, the vast majority of the population become wage workers, who have to sell their labour power to the owners of capital in order to secure a livelihood. But the political economists have failed both to examine the origins of this class system, which has emerged out of the dissolution of feudalism, and have analysed capitalism purely from the point of view of the capitalist.

When we study the development of capitalism from the perspective of the worker, Marx says, we see a very different picture from the rosy view of prosperity typically painted in political economy. Marx was not an admirer of peasant production, the dominant form of production in feudalism. Peasant production yields little of the material abundance unleashed by the advent of capitalism. But, although not the legal owner of his plot of land, the enserfed peasant was still largely in control of the process of production itself. The peasant worker controlled the rhythms of the working day and the nature of the labour process. Such is not the case, however, with the wage worker in the workshop or factory. The wage worker sells his or her labour power to the capitalist employer and thereby forfeits control over the labour process, which is organised by the employer. In speaking of the 'alienation' of labour, Marx is attempting to describe the implications of this loss of control, whereby basic aspects of the production process become 'alien' impositions upon the worker. The worker becomes alienated from the labour task itself; from the products of his or her labour, which are sold on the market by the employer; from fellow labourers; and from human 'species being'. 'Species being' refers to the distinctive characteristics of the human being, as compared with the other animals. Because they are not merely driven by instincts, human beings do not adapt in a passive fashion to their environment, as the animals do. Human beings must actively and creatively master their environment to survive; creativity and control of one's circumstances are thus an intrinsic part of what it is to be 'human'. A worker in a factory, routinely doing dull and unrewarding tasks from hour to hour, is reduced to merely adapting passively to the environment—in Marx's evocative phrase, 'the animal becomes human and the human becomes animal'.

In the course of his later writings, Marx gave this analysis a more substantive historical backdrop and developed his own views with much greater precision. A major transition in Marx's thought occurs with his adoption of the notion of 'surplus value'. From the 1850s onwards, this concept occupies the central position in his analysis and critique of the capitalist class system. This analysis retains strong ties to Marx's early diagnosis of the nature of 'alienated labour', but in *Capital* the term 'alienation' is rarely used.

Why did Marx accord the concept of 'surplus value' such importance? The answer is bound up with his continuing preoccupation with criticising the writings of the political economists. According to political economy, the worker selling labour power to the capitalist gets full value in return in the form of wages. Such a conception effectively conceals the class character of capitalism because it seems as if the exchange between worker and employer is on an equal footing and there is no exploitation involved. In disclosing the origins of surplus value, Marx identifies the main axis of capitalist class relations by showing how capital is able to exploit wage labour. In common with other commodities, the value of labour power is determined by the amount of labour time necessary for its production. In the case of labour power—the 'brain and muscle' supplied by the worker—this amount of labour time represents how much the capitalist has to pay the worker for that worker's services. Surplus value is generated by the amount of labour time left over when the employer has recouped the cost of the wages of the worker. In a working day of ten hours, if the cost of paying the worker is recovered after six hours' work, the remaining four hours' production is appropriated by the capitalist as surplus value. Surplus value is the source of profit, the key element in a capitalist economy, since production for profit is the driving force of capitalist enterprise.

Marx's analysis of the dynamics of capitalist production is integrally connected with his interpretation of the changes that will produce a socialist order.

Two processes are involved in his analysis of the transformation of capitalism into socialism. On the level of the economy, a set of changes occur whereby the foundations of capitalist production are progressively undermined 'from within', that is, as a result of its own maturation over time. Capitalism is an internally contradictory system of production that cannot operate in a stable fashion. The most basic contradiction of the capitalist economy is that although founded upon 'private appropriation'—the search for profit on the part of capitalist entrepreneurs—it is in fact inherently the most 'socialised' form of order that human beings have ever created. For a capitalist economy involves the cooperation and mutual dependence of everyone in a way foreign to prior types of society. In prior types of production of an agrarian character, the peasant is largely self-sufficient as a producer working a specific plot of land. But with the development of capitalism, all of us become dependent upon a multiplicity of goods produced by others, exchanged on the market. 'Socialism', as a series of political ideas and as an emergent type of society, represents an acknowledgement of the inherently socialising character of capitalist production.

The economic changes that tend to undermine competitive capitalism in favour of an emerging socialist order, as described by Marx, are complex. But one main factor involved is the fluctuating nature of the capitalist economy, a concrete expression of its contradictory character. Capitalism is prone to cycles of boom and depression. In periods of depression or crisis, large firms tend to expand at the expense of smaller ones, which are thrust out of business. The growth of large firms is part of a process of an increasing 'concentration' of economic life. Concentration of economic activity tends to go along with what Marx calls the increasing 'centralisation' of the economy; this refers primarily to the expansion of the activities of banks and other financial organisations, partly operating through the state, in coordinating economic life as a whole. Taken together, concentration and centralisation progressively make manifest the necessarily social nature of capitalist production, undermining the mechanisms of individualistic entrepreneurial competition. This is an incipient form of socialism, coming into being with the very movement of capitalist production.

As part and parcel of these developments, however, according to Marx, we find the intensification of class struggle. The rise of labour movements, directed to the objective of achieving a socialist society, forms the main political medium whereby the changes described above are 'pushed further', are actualised in a socialist revolution. The nature of class struggle in capitalism is best explained in terms of the capitalist labour contract. The capitalist labour contract, as we saw above, involves the sale of labour power to employers in exchange for a monetary wage; in entering such a contract, the worker sacrifices control over the labour task and other aspects of the context of production. The rise of labour movements is first of all founded upon the attempts of workers to achieve a measure of 'defensive control' of the workplace. A primary means of resisting the power of employer and management is via the collective withdrawal of labour or its threat—the strike. The involvement of workers in such struggles leads to the formation of local unions and thence to the unification of labour movements upon a national level and to their extension into the political sphere. The existence of parliaments and recognition of the formal right to organise political parties in the apparatus of bourgeois democracy permit the formation of labour parties that increasingly challenge the dominant order. Through such political mobilisation, the revolution is made—a process which Marx apparently believed could be a peaceful transition in certain countries with strong democratic traditions but was likely to involve violent confrontations elsewhere.

## Lenin: Class, Revolution, and the State

As the leader of the first successful revolution explicitly affiliated to Marxist ideas, Lenin of course has secured an enduring place in history. He was not a thinker of Marx's stature, but his ideas have of course taken on concrete expression in the development of the Soviet Union (although just how far the Soviet Union today is 'Leninist', or rather the outcome of the policies pursued by Stalin, is a matter of fierce controversy). Much of the distinctiveness of Lenin's contributions to Marxist thought derives precisely from the fact that he was involved in promoting revolutionary activity in a 'backward'—though rapidly developing—country, Russia. In contradistinction to many of his Marxist contemporaries, Lenin believed it possible to achieve a socialist revolution in Russia even while it remained a predominantly peasant society. Hence much of his written work consists in polemical interchanges with those who held different views about the possibilities of revolution. Although Lenin's views changed with different stages of political struggle, he often took the position that successful revolutionary activity, particularly in a country which lacked a strongly developed industrial sector, necessitated the 'professional' leadership of a disciplined cadre of revolutionaries.

In assuming this stance, he directed his critical attacks against those who held that working-class movements should engage in 'spontaneous' revolutionary activity, based upon workers' own appraisals of the potentialities of achieving political change. According to Lenin, left to their own devices, labour movements tend to produce only reformist ideas. To achieve a more radical outlook, they need the leadership that can only be supplied by intellectuals, trained to take a 'broader view' and educated in the theory of socialism; such leaders are generally 'defectors' from the bourgeois class, who choose to take the side of the working class. These ideas are worked out in their most succinct form in *What Is to Be Done?*, a manifesto for political action. Socialism, Lenin claims, is not a set of ideas that has emerged from labour movements themselves; it is a creation of intellectuals, introduced into class struggle from the outside. Here Lenin states his famous theory of the limitations of 'trade union consciousness'. This in effect questions the intrinsic connection that Marx drew between the formation of the working class, unions, and the extension of class conflict to the political sphere in the formation of socialist parties. Lenin argues that the relation between industrial and political conflict is more complicated than this. 'Left to themselves', workers will form unions and struggle against employers to secure greater returns from the labour contract and will also attempt to pressure the government to pass various sorts of welfare legislation. But revolution and socialism are not a natural outgrowth of these processes.

It is easy to see how these views fitted with the thesis—which Lenin turned into an active accomplishment—that socialist revolution was possible in 'backward' Russia. For Lenin stressed the need for active intervention in history to achieve socialist goals, placing much more emphasis upon revolutionary leadership than upon the level of development of industrial capitalism as such. This viewpoint remains now as controversial as it was in Lenin's own day. Critics have argued that Lenin's conception of the 'vanguard party' is an autocratic principle that has contributed to the formation of a bureaucratic state in the Soviet Union, a system far from the classless order Marx anticipated.

Lenin was himself however much concerned with analysing the nature of the state and its relations to classes and to socialism. *The State and Revolution* represents his most systematic statement on these issues. The book was written in the summer of 1917, when the 'February Revolution', which instituted a bourgeois parliamentary constitution, had taken place and just prior to the 'October Revolution' that was to sweep Lenin's party to power. It considers the question of how far the state is a 'neutral' organisation, which can be taken over by a revolutionary party and turned to its own ends, or how far alternatively the state is intrinsically wedded to the interests of the capitalist class. If the second of these alternatives is the case, the state cannot simply be adopted by the socialist party assuming power, but has to be much more radically attacked or 'smashed' if a classless society is to be brought into being.

Basing his views upon an interpretation of comments by Marx and Engels on the state, Lenin asserts that the state is a product or expression of class antagonisms. The state (in all types of class society) is the apparatus whereby the dominant class is able to secure its rule. It follows that the state is essentially a repressive agency, concerned with the suppression of the interests of subordinate classes in society. Capitalist states differ from prior types of state because they characteristically involve parliamentary democracy. Parliamentary democracy supposedly permits the representation of the interests of the population as a whole. However, according to Lenin, it is as much a form of direct class rule as other, seemingly much more despotic state systems. This is so for two reasons. First, access to parliament is controlled by capitalist interests. The 'real essence of bourgeois parliamentarianism', in Lenin's words, is 'to decide every few years which member of the ruling class is to repress and crush the people through parliament'. Second, parliament is in any case more of a debating forum than anything else: the real policies of government are forged in the civil service bureaucracy, which is not accountable to the people. The reality of parliamentary government is bureaucratic power, the 'state machine', which serves the interests of the ruling class.

The implications of all this for socialism, in Lenin's view, are clear. The state, and its bureaucratic underpinning, must be dramatically transformed as part and parcel of the achievement of a classless society. Although Lenin talks of 'smashing' or 'destroying' the state with the advent of a socialist order, he is careful to separate his ideas from those he sees as implied in anarchism. Anarchists, he claims, wish to destroy any form of centralised authority altogether. But this ambition is incompatible with a society in which there is to be the planned coordination of production in the service of the needs of the commu-

nity. The false democracy characteristic of capitalism must be replaced by genuinely representative democratic bodies, in which the mass of the population
would be directly and continuously involved. In the early stages of socialism,
this would be a state—a proletarian state, or what Marx referred to as the
'dictatorship of the proletariat'. It would still maintain repressive elements,
directed this time not against the majority of the working population but against
the remnants of the bourgeois order. As these are dissolved, a phenomenon
which involves an extended process, the repressive features of the state will
begin to drop away. This follows directly from Lenin's conception of the state as
an expression of class relationships. In a society where privately owned capital
has ceased to exist, there are no longer any classes, and therefore the repressive,
bureaucratic state has no longer any foundation for its continuance. The state
'withers away'.

## Weber: Classes, Status Groups, and Bureaucratic Domination

To Max Weber, ideas such as these seemed excessively naïve and dangerously
misleading. Although Weber drew very substantially upon Marx's writings, he
did so in a critical vein. His interpretation of past history is in some respects very
different from Marx; so are both his characterisation of contemporary capitalism and his prognosis about the likely destiny of socialist societies. The optimis-
tic and progressive philosophy of history that informs the writings of Marx and
of Lenin is replaced in Weber's work by a much more sombre interpretation of
the future of humanity.

Some of the most important differences between Weber's views and those of
Marx are the following. First, the concepts of class and class conflict do not
occupy as important a role in Weber's thought as in that of Marx. That class
struggles have frequently occurred in different phases of history, Weber accepts;
and he agrees with much of what Marx has to say about the specific significance
of class conflict between capital and wage labour in industrial capitalism. But
class conflict is not for Weber the main 'motor' of historical change. Conflicts
between states, ethnic communities, and what Weber calls 'status groups' have
been at least as important.

Second, Weber sees capitalism as a distinctively *Western* phenomenon in its
origins, incorporating distinctive values and modes of activity that are divergent
from those generated by other civilisations. The most important feature of this
'Western-ness' is what Weber refers to as the 'rationalised' character of capitalist
production, something which stretches well beyond economic enterprise itself.
Rationalisation is a phenomenon which permeates each of the major institutions
of capitalist society. 'Rationalisation' is not an unambiguously formulated concept in Weber's writings. But in its core meaning it refers to the extension of
calculative attitudes of a technical character—epitomised in scientific reason and
given substantive expression in the increasing role that science and technology
play in modern life.

Third, Weber sees the increasing spread of bureaucracy as an inevitable
accompaniment of the rationalised character of capitalist society. When Marx
and Lenin wrote about 'bureaucracy', they had in mind the civil service, the

bureaucratic apparatus of the state. But Weber applies the concept of bureaucracy much more broadly, to characterise all forms of large-scale organisation: the state, to be sure, but also business firms, unions, political parties, universities, hospitals, and so on. Weber agrees with Marx and Lenin that bureaucracy is essentially undemocratic because bureaucrats are not accountable to the mass of the population affected by their decisions. But (1) the problem of bureaucratic domination is much more pervasive than they imagined, and (2) there is, according to Weber, no way of transcending bureaucratic domination save by limiting the spread of bureaucracy. In particular, there can be no question of 'transcending the state' in the manner anticipated by Marx and Lenin. The arrival of a socialist society, in Weber's view, will have quite the contrary consequence to that predicated by socialist thinkers: the further extension of bureaucratic domination.

Weber's formulation of the concepts of class and class conflict, like that of Marx, remained unfinished. There are two versions of his ideas to be found in his work, both of which are included here. 'Class, Status, and Party' is the earlier of the two and the fuller exposition. Weber distinguishes three main axes of the distribution of power in society, of which class relationships form one. His concept of class has some affinities with that of Marx but in other ways contrasts with Marx's usage. In assessing these similarities and differences, it is not enough merely to compare what he writes in 'Class, Status and Party', as many commentators have done, with Marx's analyses. Weber's conceptual discussion in the essay must be related to his broader writings in sociology and economic history, such as are contained in the other sources we have included from Weber's work in this book.

According to Weber, following Marx, class is first and foremost an 'objective' feature of economic relations, founded upon property relations. Weber accepts that the emergence of modern capitalism involved the formation of a mass of propertyless wage workers, who sell their labour to owners of capital in order to sustain a livelihood. He did not, however, accept the theory of surplus value, drawing instead mainly upon 'marginalist' economics, thus conceptualising class differently from Marx. According to Weber, classes consist of aggregates of individuals who share similar sets of "life chances" in labour and commodity markets. Classes are not groups, although group action may be taken on the basis of common class interests. Weber did not believe in the likelihood, or the desirability, of proletarian revolution and, consequently, tends to present a more diversified view of conflicts in capitalist societies than Marx. Coordinated action that is taken on a class basis is often cross-cut by power relations deriving from two other forms of group solidarity: those involved with 'status groups' and political parties. Status groups are founded upon relationships of consumption rather than production and take the form of 'styles of life' that separate one group from another. According to Weber's view, status groups, in the shape of feudal estates, or castes in India, have been prominent elements in all precapitalist societies. While tending to be overshadowed by class relations in modern capitalism, status group affiliations by no means lose their significance.

Weber's discussion of the independent importance of party formation has to be connected to his interpretation of the nature of the modern state. Marx's view of the state, which was never developed in detail, emphasised a conception of the state as the expression of class struggles (see, however, the articles collected in Section Three below). Weber, on the other hand, sees the state as based upon its capability of monopolising the legitimate control of the means of violence within a given territory. The modern state is a nation-state in embattled relations with other nation-states. Sentiments of ethnic community or of 'nationalism' for Weber become of major significance in the nation-state. Ethnically based, or nationalist, parties are forms of political mobilisation that do not necessarily follow class lines.

In concluding this preface to the 'classics', we have to expand upon the themes of rationalisation and bureaucracy in Weber's work. Weber's writings in respect of these issues can be read as a direct challenge to those who foresee the possibility of creating socialist societies that are not bureaucratic tyrannies. Although some writers, particularly those of a more orthodox Marxist persuasion, are prone to dismiss rather cursorily Weber's pessimistic appraisals of the modern world, it surely is the case that they pose problems of major importance. It is useless to pretend that these problems can be just pushed to one side.

The easiest way to get some insight into the standpoint Weber developed and how it contrasts with that of Marx—and Lenin—is to return to the idea of the expropriation of the worker with the emergence of capitalism. As we have noted, Weber agrees with Marx in accepting that the formation of a propertyless labour force is a distinguishing feature of capitalism. But he generalises the idea of the 'expropriation of the worker from control of the means of production' beyond the sphere of industry, relating it to the general expansion of bureaucracy in the modern world. The 'expropriation of the worker', Weber argues, is actually characteristic of all bureaucratic organisations and is a process that is irreversible. The alienation of the worker—loss of control over the instruments and process of labour—here becomes an ineluctable element of the centralisation of administration. Individuals at the lower levels in bureaucratic organisations inevitably lose control of the work they do, which is determined by those in the higher echelons. Bureaucracy, according to Weber, forms a 'steel-hard cage' in which the vast majority of the population are destined to live out a large part of their lives. This is the price, he argues, we pay for living in a technically highly developed civilisation.

# · 1 ·

# Karl Marx

Selections from *The Economic and Philosophical Manuscripts, The German Ideology, The Poverty of Philosophy, The Manifesto of the Communist Party, The Eighteenth Brumaire of Louis Bonaparte,* Preface to *A Contribution to the Critique of Political Economy,* 'Value, Price, and Profit', and *Capital,* vols. 1 and 2

## Labour and Alienation

The outstanding achievement of Hegel's *Phenomenology* [Hegel's *Phenomenology of Spirit*—eds.]—the dialectic of negativity as the moving and creating principle—is, first, that Hegel grasps the self-creation of man as a process, objectification as loss of the object, as alienation and transcendence of this alienation, and that he, therefore, grasps the nature of *labour,* and conceives objective man (true, because real man) as the result of his *own labour.* The *real,* active orientation of man to himself as a species-being, or the affirmation of himself as a real species-being (i.e. as a human being) is only possible so far as he really brings forth all his *species-powers* (which is only possible through the co-operative endeavours of mankind and as an outcome of history) and treats these powers as objects, which can only be done at first in the form of alienation. . . .

For the present, let us make these preliminary observations: Hegel's standpoint is that of modern political economy. He conceives *labour* as the *essence,* the self-confirming essence of man; he observes only the positive side of labour, not its negative side. Labour is *man's coming to be for himself* within *alienation,* or as an *alienated* man.

*The Economic and Philosophical Manuscripts,* pp. 202–03

Political economy begins with the fact of private property; it does not explain it. It conceives the *material* process of private property, as this occurs in reality, in general and abstract formulas which then serve it as laws. It does not *comprehend* these laws; that is, it does not show how they arise out of the nature of private property. Political economy provides no explanation of the basis for the distinction of labour from capital, of capital from land. When, for example, the relation of wages to profits is defined, this is explained in terms of the interests of capitalists; in other words, what should be explained is assumed. Similarly, competition is referred to at every point and is explained in terms of external conditions. Political economy tells us nothing about the extent to which these external and apparently accidental conditions are simply the expression of a necessary development. . . .

Let us not begin our explanation, as does the economist, from a legendary primordial condition. Such a primordial condition does not explain anything; it merely removes the question into a grey and nebulous distance. It asserts as a fact or event what it should deduce, namely, the necessary relation between two things; for example, between the division of labour and exchange. In the same way theology explains the origin of evil by the fall of man; that is, it asserts as a historical fact what it should explain.

We shall begin from a *contemporary* economic fact. The worker becomes poorer the more wealth he produces and the more his production increases in power and extent. The worker becomes an ever cheaper commodity the more goods he creates. The *devaluation* of the human world increases in direct relation to the *increase in value* of the world of things. Labour does not only create goods; it also produces itself and the worker as a *commodity,* and indeed in the same proportion as it produces goods.

This fact simply implies that the object produced by labour, its product, now stands opposed to it as an *alien being,* as a *power independent* of the producer. The product of labour is labour which has been embodied in an object and turned into a physical thing; this product is an *objectification* of labour. The performance of work is at the same time its objectification. The performance of work appears in the sphere of political economy as a *vitiation* of the worker, objectification as a *loss* and as *servitude to the object,* and appropriation as *alienation.*

So much does the performance of work appear as vitiation that the worker is vitiated to the point of starvation. So much does objectification appear as loss of the object that the worker is deprived of the most essential things not only of life but also of work. Labour itself becomes an object which he can acquire only by the greatest effort and with unpredictable interruptions. So much does the appropriation of the object appear as alienation that the more objects the worker produces the fewer he can possess and the more he falls under the domination of his product, of capital.

All these consequences follow from the fact that the worker is related to the *product of his labour* as to an *alien* object. For it is clear on this presupposition that the more the worker expends himself in work the more powerful becomes the world of objects which he creates in face of himself, the poorer he becomes in his inner life, and the less he belongs to himself. It is just the same as in religion. The more of himself man attributes to God the less he has left in himself. The worker puts his life into the object, and his life then belongs no longer to himself but to the object. The greater his activity, therefore, the less he possesses. What is embodied in the product of his labour is no longer his own. The greater this product is, therefore, the more he is diminished. The *alienation* of the worker in his product means not only that his labour becomes an object, assumes an *external* existence, but that it exists independently, *outside himself,* and alien to him, and that it stands opposed to him as an autonomous power. The life which he has given to the object sets itself against him as an alien and hostile force.

Let us now examine more closely the phenomenon of *objectification;* the worker's production and the *alienation* and *loss* of the object it produces, which is involved in it. The worker can create nothing without *nature,* without the *sensuous external world.* The latter is the material in which his labour is realized, in which it is active, out of which and through which it produces things.

But just as nature affords the *means of existence* of labour, in the sense that labour cannot *live* without objects upon which it can be exercised, so also it provides the *means of existence* in a narrower sense; namely the means of physical existence for the *worker* himself. Thus, the more the worker *appropriates* the external world of sensuous nature by his labour the more he deprives himself of *means of existence,* in two respects: first, that the sensuous external world becomes progressively less an object belonging to his labour or a means of existence of his labour, and secondly, that it becomes progressively less a means of existence in the direct sense, a means for the physical subsistence of the worker.

In both respects, therefore, the worker becomes a slave of the object; first, in that he receives an *object of work,* i.e. receives *work,* and secondly, in that he receives *means of subsistence.* Thus the object enables him to exist, first as a *worker* and secondly, as a *physical subject.* The culmination of this enslavement is that he can only maintain himself as a *physical subject* so far as he is a *worker,* and that it is only as a *physical subject* that he is a worker.

(The alienation of the worker in his object is expressed as follows in the laws of political economy: the more the worker produces the less he has to consume; the more value he creates the more worthless he becomes; the more refined his product the more crude and misshapen the worker; the more civilized the product the more barbarous the worker; the more powerful the work the more feeble the worker; the more the work manifests intelligence the more the worker declines in intelligence and becomes a slave of nature.)

*Political economy conceals the alienation in the nature of labour in so far as it does not examine the direct relationship between the worker (work) and production.* Labour certainly produces marvels for the rich but it produces privation for the worker. It produces palaces, but hovels for the worker. It produces beauty, but deformity for the worker. It replaces labour by machinery, but it casts some of the workers back into a barbarous kind of work and turns the others into machines. It produces intelligence, but also stupidity and cretinism for the workers.

*The direct relationship of labour to its products is the relationship of the worker to the objects of his production.* The relationship of property owners to the objects of production and to production itself is merely a *consequence* of this first relationship and confirms it. We shall consider this second aspect later.

Thus, when we ask what is the important relationship of labour, we are concerned with the relationship of the *worker* to production.

So far we have considered the alienation of the worker only from one aspect; namely, *his relationship to the products of his labour.* However, alienation appears not merely in the result but also in the *process of production,* within *productive activity* itself. How could the worker stand in an alien relationship to the product of his activity if he did not alienate himself in the act of production itself? The product is indeed only the *résumé* of activity, of production. Consequently, if the product of labour is alienation, production itself must be active alienation—the alienation of activity and the activity of alienation. The alienation of the object of labour merely summarizes the alienation in the work activity itself.

What constitutes the alienation of labour? First, that the work is *external* to the worker, that it is not part of his nature; and that, consequently, he does not fulfil himself in his work but denies himself, has a feeling of misery rather than well-being, does not develop freely his mental and physical energies but is physically exhausted and mentally debased. The worker, therefore, feels himself at home only during his leisure time, whereas at work he feels homeless. His work is not voluntary but imposed, *forced labour.* It is not the satisfaction of a need, but only a *means* for satisfying other needs. Its alien character is clearly shown by the fact that as soon as there is no physical or other compulsion it is avoided like the plague. External labour, labour in which man alienates himself, is a labour of self-sacrifice, or mortification. Finally, the external character of work for the worker is shown by the fact that it is not his own work but work for someone else, that in work he does not belong to himself but to another person.

Just as in religion the spontaneous activity of human fantasy, of the human brain and heart, reacts independently as an alien activity of gods or devils upon the individual, so the activity of the worker is not his own spontaneous activity. It is another's activity and a loss of his own spontaneity.

We arrive at the result that man (the worker) feels himself to be freely active only in his animal functions—eating, drinking and procreating, or at most also in his dwelling and in personal adornment—while in his human functions he is reduced to an animal. The animal becomes human and the human becomes animal.

Eating, drinking and procreating are of course also genuine human functions. But abstractly considered, apart from the environment of human activities, and turned into final and sole ends, they are animal functions.

We have now considered the act of alienation of practical human activity, labour, from two aspects: (1) the relationship of the worker to the *product of labour* as an alien object which dominates him. This relationship is at the same time the relationship to the sensuous external world, to natural objects, as an alien and hostile world; (2) the relationship of labour to the *act of production* within *labour.* This is the relationship of the worker to his own activity as something alien and not belonging to him, activity as suffering (passivity), strength as powerlessness, creation as emasculation, the *personal* physical and mental energy of the worker, his personal life (for what is life but activity?), as an activity which is directed against himself, independent of him and not belonging to him. This is *self-alienation* as against the above-mentioned alienation of the *thing.*

We have now to infer a third characteristic of *alienated labour* from the two we have considered.

Man is a species-being not only in the sense that he makes the community (his own as well as those of other things) his object both practically and theoretically, but also (and this is simply another expression for the same thing) in the sense that he treats himself as the present, living species, as a *universal* and consequently free being.

Species-life, for man as for animals, has its physical basis in the fact that man (like animals) lives from inorganic nature, and since man is more universal than an animal so the range of inorganic nature from which he lives is more universal. Plants, animals, minerals, air, light, etc. constitute, from the theoretical aspect, a part of human consciousness as objects of natural science and art; they are man's spiritual inorganic nature, his intellectual means of life, which he must first prepare for enjoyment and perpetuation. So also, from the practical aspect, they form a part of human life and activity. In practice man lives only from these natural products, whether in the form of food, heating, clothing, housing, etc. The universality of man appears in practice in the universality which makes the whole of nature into his inorganic body: (1) as a direct means of life; and equally (2) as the material object and instrument of his life activity. Nature is the inorganic body of man; that is to say nature, excluding the human body itself. To say that man *lives* from nature means that nature is his *body* with which he must remain in a continuous interchange in order not to die. The statement that the physical and mental life of man, and nature, are interdependent means simply that nature is interdependent with itself, for man is a part of nature.

Since alienated labour: (1) alienates nature from man; and (2) alienates man from himself, from his own active function, his life activity; so it alienates him from the species. It makes *species-life* into a means of individual life. In the first place it alienates species-life and individual life, and secondly, it turns the latter, as an abstraction, into the purpose of the former, also in its abstract and alienated form.

For labour, *life activity, productive life,* now appear to man only as *means* for the satisfaction of a need, the need to maintain his physical existence. Productive life is, however, species-life. It is life creating life. In the type of life activity resides the whole character of a species, its species-character; and free, conscious activity is the species-character of human beings. Life itself appears only as a *means of life*.

The animal is one with its life activity. It does not distinguish the activity from itself. It is *its activity*. But man makes his life activity itself an object of his will and consciousness. He has a conscious life activity. It is not a determination with which he is completely identified. Conscious life activity distinguishes man from the life activity of animals. Only for this reason is he a species-being. Or rather, he is only a self-conscious being, i.e. his own life is an object for him, because he is a species-being. Only for this reason is his activity free activity. Alienated labour reverses the relationship, in that man because he is a self-conscious being makes his life activity, his being, only a means for his *existence*.

The practical construction of an *objective world,* the *manipulation* of inorganic nature, is the confirmation of man as a conscious species-being, i.e. a being who treats the species as his own being or himself as a species-being. Of course, animals also produce. They construct nests, dwellings, as in the case of bees, beavers, ants, etc. But they only produce what is strictly necessary for themlves or their young. They produce only in a single direction, while man produces universally. They produce only under the compulsion of direct physical needs, while man produces when he is free from physical need and only truly produces in freedom from such need. Animals produce only themselves, while man reproduces the whole of nature. The products of animal production belong directly to their physical bodies, while man is free in face of his product. Animals construct only in accordance with the standards and needs of the species to which they belong, while man knows how to produce in accordance with the standards of every species and knows how to apply the appropriate standard to the object. Thus man constructs also in accordance with the laws of beauty.

It is just in his work upon the objective world that man really proves himself as a *species-being*. This production is his active species-life. By means of it nature appears as *his* work and his reality. The object of labour is, therefore, the *objectification of man's species-life;* for he no longer reproduces himself merely intellectually, as in consciousness, but actively and in a real sense, and he sees his own reflection in a world which he has constructed. While, therefore, alienated labour takes away the object of production from man, it also takes away his *species-life,* his real objectivity as a species-being, and changes his advantage over animals into a disadvantage in so far as his inorganic body, nature, is taken from him.

Just as alienated labour transforms free and self-directed activity into a means, so it transforms the species-life of man into a means of physical existence.

Consciousness, which man has from his species, is transformed through alienation so that species-life becomes only a means for him. (3) Thus alienated labour turns the *species-life of man,* and also nature as his mental species-property, into an *alien* being and into a *means* for his *individual existence.* It alienates from man his own body, external nature, his mental life and his *human* life. (4) A direct consequence of the alienation of man from the product of his labour, from his life activity and from his species-life, is that *man* is *alienated* from other *men.* When man confronts himself he also confronts *other* men. What is true of man's relationship to his work, to the product of his work and to himself, is also true of his relationship to other men, to their labour and to the objects of their labour.

In general, the statement that man is alienated from his species-life means that each man is alienated from others, and that each of the others is likewise alienated from human life.

Human alienation, and above all the relation of man to himself, is first realized and expressed in the relationship between each man and other men. Thus in the relationship of alienated labour every man regards other men according to the standards and relationships in which he finds himself placed as a worker.

We began with an economic fact, the alienation of the worker and his production. We have expressed this fact in conceptual terms as *alienated labour,* and in analysing the concept we have merely analysed an economic fact.

Let us now examine further how this concept of alienated labour must express and reveal itself in reality. If the product of labour is alien to me and confronts me as an alien power, to whom does it belong? If my own activity does not belong to me but is an alien, forced activity, to whom does it belong? To a being *other* than myself. And who is this being? The *gods?* It is apparent in the earliest stages of advanced production, e.g., temple building, etc. in Egypt, India, Mexico, and in the service rendered to gods, that the product belonged to the gods. But the gods alone were never the lords of labour. And no more was *nature.* What a contradiction it would be if the more man subjugates nature by his labour, and the more the marvels of the gods are rendered superfluous by the marvels of industry, the more he should abstain from his joy in producing and his enjoyment of the product for love of these powers.

The *alien* being to whom labour and the product of labour belong, to whose service labour is devoted, and to whose enjoyment the product of labour goes, can only be *man* himself. If the product of labour does not belong to the worker, but confronts him as an alien power, this can only be because it belongs to *a man other than the worker.* If his activity is a torment to him it must be a source of *enjoyment* and pleasure to another. Not the gods, nor nature, but only man himself can be this alien power over men.

Consider the earlier statement that the relation of man to himself is first *realized, objectified,* through his relation to other men. If he is related to the product of his labour, his objectified labour, as to an *alien,* hostile, powerful and independent object, he is related in such a way that another alien, hostile, powerful and independent man is the lord of this object. If he is related to his own activity as to unfree activity, then he is related to it as activity in the service, and under the domination, coercion and yoke, of another man.

Every self-alienation of man, from himself and from nature, appears in the relation which he postulates between other men and himself and nature. Thus religious self-alienation is necessarily exemplified in the relation between laity and priest, or, since it is here a question of the spiritual world, between the laity and a mediator. In the real world of practice this self-alienation can only be expressed in the real, practical relation of man to his fellow men. The medium through which alienation occurs is itself a *practical* one. Through alienated labour, therefore, man not only produces his relation to the object and to the process of production as to alien and hostile men; he also produces the relation of other men to his production and his product, and the relation between himself and other men. Just as he creates his own production as a vitiation, a punishment, and his own product as a loss, as a product which does not belong to him, so he creates the domination of the non-producer over production and its product. As he alienates his own activity, so he bestows upon the stranger an activity which is not his own.

We have so far considered this relation only from the side of the worker, and later on we shall consider it also from the side of the non-worker.

Thus, through alienated labour the worker creates the relation of another man, who does not work and is outside the work process, to this labour. The relation of the worker to work also produces the relation of the capitalist (or whatever one likes to call the lord of labour) to work. *Private property* is, therefore, the product, the necessary result, of *alienated labour,* of the external relation of the worker to nature and to himself.

*Private property* is thus derived from the analysis of the concept of *alienated labour;* that is, alienated man, alienated labour, alienated life, and estranged man.

We have, of course, derived the concept of *alienated labour (alienated life)* from political economy, from an analysis of the *movement of private property.* But the analysis of this concept shows that although private property appears to be the basis and cause of alienated labour, it is rather a consequence of the latter, just as the gods are *fundamentally* not the cause but the product of confusions of human reason. At a later stage, however, there is a reciprocal influence.

Only in the final stage of the development of private property is its secret revealed, namely, that it is on one hand the *product* of alienated labour, and on the other hand the *means* by which labour is alienated, *the realization of this alienation.*

*The Economic and Philosophical Manuscripts,* pp. 120–31

## The Universality of Class and Class Struggle[1]

The history of all hitherto-existing society[2] is the history of class struggles.

Freeman and slave, patrician and plebeian, lord and serf, guild-master[3] and journeyman, in a word, oppressor and oppressed, stood in constant opposition to one another, carried on an uninterrupted, now hidden, now open fight, a fight that each time ended, either in a revolutionary re-constitution of society at large, or in the common ruin of the contending classes.

In the earlier epochs of history, we find almost everywhere a complicated arrangement of society into various orders, a manifold gradation of social rank. In ancient Rome we have patricians, knights, plebeians, slaves; in the Middle Ages, feudal lords, vassals, guild-masters, journeymen, apprentices, serfs; in almost all of these classes, again, subordinate gradations.

The modern bourgeois society that has sprouted from the ruins of feudal society has not done away with class antagonisms. It has but established new classes, new conditions of oppression, new forms of struggle in place of the old ones.

*The Manifesto of the Communist Party,* pp. 108–09

---

[1] By bourgeoisie is meant the class of modern Capitalists, owners of the means of social production and employers of wage-labour. By proletariat, the class of modern wage-labourers who, having no means of production of their own, are reduced to selling their labour-power in order to live. [*Note by Engels to the English edition of 1888.*]

[2] That is, all *written* history. In 1847, the pre-history of society, the social organization existing previous to recorded history, was all but unknown. Since then, Haxthausen discovered common ownership of land in Russia, Maurer proved it to be the social foundation from which all Teutonic races started in history, and by and by village communities were found to be, or to have been the primitive form of society everywhere from India to Ireland. The inner organization of this primitive Communistic society was laid bare, in its typical form, by Morgan's crowning discovery of the true nature of the *gens* and its relation to the *tribe.* With the dissolution of these primaeval communities society begins to be differentiated into separate and finally antagonistic classes. I have attempted to retrace this process of dissolution in *Der Ursprung der Familie, des Privateigentums und des Staats* [*The Origin of the Family, Private Property and the State*], 2nd edition, Stuttgart 1886. [*Note by Engels to the English edition of 1888.*]

[3] Guild-master, that is, a full member of a guild, a master within, not a head of a guild. [*Note by Engels to the English edition of 1888.*]

In the Middle Ages the citizens in each town were compelled to unite against the landed nobility to save their skins. The extension of trade, the establishment of communications, led the separate towns to get to know other towns, which had asserted the same interests in the struggle with the same antagonist. Out of the many local corporations of burghers there arose only gradually the burgher *class*. The conditions of life of the individual burghers became, on account of their contradiction to the existing relationships and of the mode of labour determined by these, conditions which were common to them all and independent of each individual. The burghers had created the conditions insofar as they had torn themselves free from feudal ties, and were created by them insofar as they were determined by their antagonism to the feudal system which they found in existence. When the individual towns began to enter into associations, these common conditions developed into class conditions. The same conditions, the same contradiction, the same interests necessarily called forth on the whole similar customs everywhere. The bourgeoisie itself, with its conditions, develops only gradually, splits according to the division of labour into various fractions and finally absorbs all propertied classes it finds in existence[1] (while it develops the majority of the earlier propertyless and a part of the hitherto propertied classes into a new class, the proletariat) in the measure to which all property found in existence is transformed into industrial or commercial capital. The separate individuals form a class only insofar as they have to carry on a common battle against another class; otherwise they are on hostile terms with each other as competitors. On the other hand, the class in its turn achieves an independent existence over against the individuals, so that the latter find their conditions of existence predestined, and hence have their position in life and their personal development assigned to them by their class, become subsumed under it. This is the same phenomenon as the subjection of the separate individuals to the division of labour and can only be removed by the abolition of private property and of labour itself.

*The German Ideology*, p. 82

The owners merely of labour-power, owners of capital, and landowners, whose respective sources of income are wages, profit and ground-rent, in other words, wage-labourers, capitalists and landowners, constitute then three big classes of modern society based upon the capitalist mode of production.

In England, modern society is indisputably most highly and classically developed in economic structure. Nevertheless, even here the stratification of classes does not appear in its pure form. Middle and intermediate strata even here obliterate lines of demarcation everywhere (although incomparably less in rural districts than in the cities). However, this is immaterial for our analysis . . . the continual tendency and law of development of the capitalist mode of production is more and more to divorce the means of production from labour, and more and more to concentrate the scattered means of production into large groups, thereby transforming labour into wage-labour and the means of pro-

---

[1] [Marginal note by Marx:] To begin with it absorbs the branches of labour directly belonging to the State and then all + [more or less] ideological estates.

duction into capital. And to this tendency, on the other hand, corresponds the independent separation of landed property from capital and labour, or the transformation of all landed property into the form of landed property corresponding to the capitalist mode of production.

The first question to be answered is this: What constitutes a class?—and the reply to this follows naturally from the reply to another question, namely: What makes wage-labourers, capitalists and landlords constitute the three great social classes?

At first glance—the identity of revenues and sources of revenue. There are three great social groups whose members, the individuals forming them, live on wages, profit and ground-rent respectively, on the realisation of their labour-power, their capital, and their landed property.

However, from this standpoint, physicians and officials, e.g., would also constitute two classes, for they belong to two distinct social groups, the members of each of these groups receiving their revenue from one and the same source. The same would also be true of the infinite fragmentation of interest and rank into which the division of social labour splits labourers as well as capitalists and landlords—the latter, e.g., into owners of vineyards, farm owners, owners of forests, mine owners and owners of fisheries. [Here the manuscript breaks off.]

*Capital*, vol. 3, pp. 885–86

### Classes in Capitalist Society

The bourgeoisie, historically, has played a most revolutionary part.

The bourgeoisie, wherever it has got the upper hand, has put an end to all feudal, patriarchal, idyllic relations. It has pitilessly torn asunder the motley feudal ties that bound man to his "natural superiors," and has left remaining no other nexus between man and man than naked self-interest, than callous "cash payment." It has drowned the most heavenly ecstasies of religious fervour, of chivalrous enthusiasm, of philistine sentimentalism, in the icy water of egotistical calculation. It has resolved personal worth into exchange value, and in place of the numberless indefeasible chartered freedoms, has set up that single, unconscionable freedom—Free Trade. In one word, for exploitation, veiled by religious and political illusions, it has substituted naked, shameless, direct, brutal exploitation.

The bourgeoisie has stripped of its halo every occupation hitherto honoured and looked up to with reverent awe. It has converted the physician, the lawyer, the priest, the poet, the man of science, into its paid wage-labourers.

The bourgeoisie has torn away from the family its sentimental veil, and has reduced the family relation to a mere money relation.

The bourgeoisie has disclosed how it came to pass that the brutal display of vigour in the Middle Ages, which Reactionists so much admire, found its fitting complement in the most slothful indolence. It has been the first to show what man's activity can bring about. It has accomplished wonders far surpassing Egyptian pyramids, Roman aqueducts, and Gothic cathedrals; it has conducted expeditions that put in the shade all former Exoduses of nations and crusades.

The bourgeoisie cannot exist without constantly revolutionising the instruments of production, and thereby the relations of production, and with them the whole relations of society. Conservation of the old modes of production in unaltered form, was, on the contrary, the first condition of existence for all earlier industrial classes. Constant revolutionising of production, uninterrupted disturbance of all social conditions, everlasting uncertainty and agitation distinguish the bourgeois epoch from all earlier ones. All fixed, fast-frozen relations, with their train of ancient and venerable prejudices and opinions, are swept away, all new-formed ones become antiquated before they can ossify. All that is solid melts into air, all that is holy is profaned, and man is at last compelled to face with sober senses, his real conditions of life, and his relations with his kind.

The need of a constantly expanding market for its products chases the bourgeoisie over the whole surface of the globe. It must nestle everywhere, settle everywhere, establish connexions everywhere.

The bourgeoisie has through its exploitation of the world–market given a cosmopolitan character to production and consumption in every country. To the great chagrin of Reactionists, it has drawn from under the feet of industry the national ground on which it stood. All old-established national industries have been destroyed or are daily being destroyed. They are dislodged by new industries, whose introduction becomes a life and death question for all civilised nations, by industries that no longer work up indigenous raw material, but raw material drawn from the remotest zones; industries whose products are consumed, not only at home, but in every quarter of the globe. In place of the old wants, satisfied by the productions of the country, we find new wants, requiring for their satisfaction the products of distant lands and climes. In place of the old local and national seclusion and self-sufficiency, we have intercourse in every direction, universal inter-dependence of nations. And as in material, so also in intellectual production. The intellectual creations of individual nations become common property. National one-sidedness and narrow-mindedness become more and more impossible, and from the numerous national and local literatures, there arises a world literature.

The bourgeoisie, by the rapid improvement of all instruments of production, by the immensely facilitated means of communication, draws all, even the most barbarian, nations into civilisation. The cheap prices of its commodities are the heavy artillery with which it batters down all Chinese walls, with which it forces the barbarians' intensely obstinate hatred of foreigners to capitulate. It compels all nations, on pain of extinction, to adopt the bourgeois mode of production; it compels them to introduce what it calls civilisation into their midst, *i.e.,* to become bourgeois themselves. In one word, it creates a world after its own image.

The bourgeoisie has subjected the country to the rule of the towns. It has created enormous cities, has greatly increased the urban population as compared with the rural, and has thus rescued a considerable part of the population from the idiocy of rural life. Just as it has made the country dependent on the towns, so it has made barbarian and semi-barbarian countries dependent on the civilised ones, nations of peasants on nations of bourgeois, the East on the West.

The bourgeoisie keeps more and more doing away with the scattered state of the population, of the means of production, and of property. It has agglomerated population, centralised means of production, and has concentrated property in a few hands. The necessary consequence of this was political centralisation. Independent, or but loosely connected provinces, with separate interests, laws, governments and systems of taxation, became lumped together into one nation, with one government, one code of laws, one national class-interest, one frontier and one customs-tariff.

The bourgeoisie, during its rule of scarce one hundred years, has created more massive and more colossal productive forces than have all preceding generations together. Subjection of Nature's forces to man, machinery, application of chemistry to industry and agriculture, steam-navigation, railways, electric telegraphs, clearing of whole continents for cultivation, canalisation of rivers, whole populations conjured out of the ground—what earlier century had even a presentiment that such productive forces slumbered in the lap of social labour? . . .

In proportion as the bourgeoisie, i.e., capital, is developed, in the same proportion is the proletariat, the modern working class, developed—a class of labourers, who live only so long as they find work, and who find work only so long as their labour increases capital. These labourers, who must sell themselves piecemeal, are a commodity, like every other article of commerce, and are consequently exposed to all the vicissitudes of competition, to all the fluctuations of the market.

Owing to the extensive use of machinery and to division of labour, the work of the proletarians has lost all individual character, and, consequently, all charm for the workman. He becomes an appendage of the machine, and it is only the most simple, most monotonous, and most easily acquired knack, that is required of him. Hence, the cost of production of a workman is restricted, almost entirely, to the means of subsistence that he requires for his maintenance, and for the propagation of his race. But the price of a commodity, and therefore also of labour, is equal to its cost of production. In proportion, therefore, as the repulsiveness of the work increases, the wage decreases. Nay more, in proportion as the use of machinery and division of labour increases, in the same proportion the burden of toil also increases, whether by prolongation of the working hours, by increase of the work exacted in a given time or by increased speed of the machinery, etc.

Modern industry has converted the little workshop of the patriarchal master into the great factory of the industrial capitalist. Masses of labourers, crowded into the factory, are organised like soldiers. As privates of the industrial army they are placed under the command of a perfect hierarchy of officers and sergeants. Not only are they slaves of the bourgeois class, and of the bourgeois State; they are daily and hourly enslaved by the machine, by the overlooker, and, above all, by the individual bourgeois manufacturer himself. The more openly this despotism proclaims gain to be its end and aim, the more petty, the more hateful and the more embittering it is.

The less the skill and exertion of strength implied in manual labour, in other words, the more modern industry becomes developed, the more is the labour of men superseded by that of women. Differences of age and sex have no longer any distinctive social validity for the working class. All are instruments of labour, more or less expensive to use, according to their age and sex. . . .

Of all the classes that stand face to face with the bourgeoisie today, the proletariat alone is a really revolutionary class. The other classes decay and finally disappear in the face of Modern Industry; the proletariat is its special and essential product.

The lower middle class, the small manufacturer, the shopkeeper, the artisan, the peasant, all these fight against the bourgeoisie, to save from extinction their existence as fractions of the middle class. They are therefore not revolutionary, but conservative. Nay more, they are reactionary, for they try to roll back the wheel of history. If by chance they are revolutionary, they are so only in view of their impending transfer into the proletariat, they thus defend not their present, but their future interests, they desert their own standpoint to place themselves at that of the proletariat.

The "dangerous class," the social scum, that passively rotting mass thrown off by the lowest layers of old society, may, here and there, be swept into the movement by a proletarian revolution, its conditions of life, however, prepare it far more for the part of a bribed tool of reactionary intrigue.

In the conditions of the proletariat, those of old society at large are already virtually swamped. The proletarian is without property; his relation to his wife and children has no longer anything in common with the bourgeois family-relations; modern industrial labour, modern subjection to capital, the same in England as in France, in America as in Germany, has stripped him of every trace of national character. Law, morality, religion, are to him so many bourgeois prejudices, behind which lurk in ambush just as many bourgeois interests.

All the preceding classes that got the upper hand, sought to fortify their already acquired status by subjecting society at large to their conditions of appropriation. The proletarians cannot become masters of the productive forces of society, except by abolishing their own previous mode of appropriation, and thereby also every other previous mode of appropriation. They have nothing of their own to secure and to fortify; their mission is to destroy all previous securities for, and insurances of, individual property.

All previous historical movements were movements of minorities, or in the interests of minorities. The proletarian movement is the self-conscious, independent movement of the immense majority, in the interests of the immense majority. The proletariat, the lowest stratum of our present society, cannot stir, cannot raise itself up, without the whole superincumbent strata of official society being sprung into the air.

Though not in substance, yet in form, the struggle of the proletariat with the bourgeoisie is at first a national struggle. The proletariat of each country must, of course, first of all settle matters with its own bourgeoisie.

In depicting the most general phases of the development of the proletariat, we traced the more or less veiled civil war, raging within existing society, up to the point where that war breaks out into open revolution, and where the violent overthrow of the bourgeoisie lays the foundation for the sway of the proletariat.

Hitherto, every form of society has been based, as we have already seen, on the antagonism of oppressing and oppressed classes. But in order to oppress a ass, certain conditions must be assured to it under which it can, at least, continue its slavish existence. The serf, in the period of serfdom, raised himself to membership in the commune, just as the petty bourgeois, under the yoke of feudal absolutism, managed to develop into a bourgeois. The modern labourer, on the contrary, instead of rising with the progress of industry, sinks deeper and deeper below the conditions of existence of his own class. He becomes a pauper, and pauperism develops more rapidly than population and wealth. And here it becomes evident, that the bourgeoisie is unfit any longer to be the ruling class in society, and to impose its conditions of existence upon society as an over-riding law. It is unfit to rule because it is incompetent to assure an existence to its slave within his slavery, because it cannot help letting him sink into such a state, that it has to feed him, instead of being fed by him. Society can no longer live under this bourgeoisie, in other words, its existence is no longer compatible with society.

The essential condition for the existence, and for the sway of the bourgeois class, is the formation and augmentation of capital; the condition for capital is wage-labour. Wage-labour rests exclusively on competition between the labourers. The advance of industry, whose involuntary promoter is the bourgeoisie, replaces the isolation of the labourers, due to competition, by their revolutionary combination, due to association. The development of Modern Industry, therefore, cuts from under its feet the very foundation on which the bourgeoisie produces and appropriates products. What the bourgeoisie, therefore, produces, above all, is its own grave-diggers. Its fall and the victory of the proletariat are equally inevitable.

*The Manifesto of the Communist Party,* pp. 111–119

### Proletarianization of the Middle Class

The lower strata of the middle class—the small tradespeople, shopkeepers, and retired tradesmen generally, the handicraftsmen and peasants—all these sink gradually into the proletariat, partly because their diminutive capital does not suffice for the scale on which Modern Industry is carried on, and is swamped in the competition with the large capitalists, partly because their specialized skill is rendered worthless by new methods of production. Thus the proletariat is recruited from all classes of the population.

*The Manifesto of the Communist Party,* p. 115

### The Political Marginalization of the Peasantry

The small-holding peasants form a vast mass, the members of which live in similar conditions but without entering into manifold relations with one another. Their mode of production isolates them from one another instead of bringing them into mutual intercourse. The isolation is increased by France's bad means of communication and by the poverty of the peasants. Their field of production, the small holding, admits of no division of labour in its cultivation, no application of science and, therefore, no diversity of development, no variet of talent, no wealth of social relationships. Each individual peasant family is almost self-sufficient; it itself directly produces the major part of its consumption and thus acquires its means of life more through exchange with nature than in intercourse with society. A small holding, a peasant and his family; alongside them another small holding, another peasant and another family. A few score of these make up a village, and a few score of villages make up a Department. In this way, the great mass of the French nation is formed by simple addition of homologous magnitudes, much as potatoes in a sack form a sack of potatoes. In so far as millions of families live under economic conditions of existence that separate their mode of life, their interests and their culture from those of the other classes, and put them in hostile opposition to the latter, they form a class. In so far as there is merely a local interconnection among these small-holding peasants, and the identity of their interests begets no community, no national bond and no political organisation among them, they do not form a class. They are consequently incapable of enforcing their class interests in their own name, whether through a parliament or through a convention. They cannot represent themselves, they must be represented. Their representative must at the same time appear as their master, as an authority over them, as an unlimited governmental power that protects them against the other classes and sends them rain and sunshine from above. The political influence of the small-holding peasants, therefore, finds its final expression in the executive power subordinating society to itself.

*The Eighteenth Brumaire of Louis Bonaparte*, pp. 478–79

## The Ideology of Class Domination

The ideas of the ruling class are in every epoch the ruling ideas, i.e. the class which is the ruling *material* force of society, is at the same time its ruling *intellectual* force. The class which has the means of material production at its disposal, has control at the same time over the means of mental production, so that thereby, generally speaking, the ideas of those who lack the means of mental production are subject to it. The ruling ideas are nothing more than the ideal expression of the dominant material relationships, the dominant material relationships grasped as ideas; hence of the relationships which make the one class the ruling one, therefore, the ideas of its dominance. The individuals composing the ruling class possess among other things consciousness, and therefore think. Insofar, therefore, as they rule as a class and determine the extent and compass of an epoch, it is self-evident that they do this in its whole range, hence among other things rule also as thinkers, as producers of ideas, and regulate the production and distribution of the ideas of their age: thus their ideas are the ruling ideas of the epoch. For instance, in an age and in a country where royal power, aristocracy, and bourgeoisie are contending for mastery and where, therefore, mastery is shared, the doctrine of the separation of powers proves to be the dominant idea and is expressed as an "eternal law."

The division of labour, . . . as one of the chief forces of history up till now, manifests itself also in the ruling class as the division of mental and material labour, so that inside this class one part appears as the thinkers of the class (its active, conceptive ideologists, who make the perfecting of the illusion of the class about itself their chief source of livelihood), while the others' attitude to these ideas and illusions is more passive and receptive, because they are in reality the active members of this class and have less time to make up illusions and ideas about themselves. Within this class this cleavage can even develop into a certain opposition and hostility between the two parts, which, however, in the case of a practical collision, in which the class itself is endangered, automatically comes to nothing, in which case there also vanishes the semblance that the ruling ideas were not the ideas of the ruling class and had a power distinct from the power of this class. The existence of revolutionary ideas in a particular period presupposes the existence of a revolutionary class; about the premises for the latter sufficient has already been said above. . . .

If now in considering the course of history we detach the ideas of the ruling class from the ruling class itself and attribute to them an independent existence, if we confine ourselves to saying that these or those ideas were dominant at a given time, without bothering ourselves about the conditions of production and the producers of these ideas, if we thus ignore the individuals and world conditions which are the source of the ideas, we can say, for instance, that during the time that the aristocracy was dominant, the concepts honour, loyalty, etc. were dominant, during the dominance of the bourgeoisie the concepts freedom, equality, etc. The ruling class itself on the whole imagines this to be so. This conception of history, which is common to all historians, particularly since the eighteenth century, will necessarily come up against the phenomenon that increasingly abstract ideas hold sway, i.e. ideas which increasingly take on the form of universality. For each new class which puts itself in the place of one ruling before it, is compelled, merely in order to carry through its aim, to represent its interest as the common interest of all the members of society, that is, expressed in ideal form: it has to give its ideas the form of universality, and represent them as the only rational, universally valid ones. The class making a revolution appears from the very start, if only because it is opposed to a *class,* not as a class but as the representative of the whole of society; it appears as the whole mass of society confronting the one ruling class.[1] It can do this because, to start with, its interest really is more connected with the common interest of all other non-ruling classes, because under the pressure of hitherto existing conditions its interest has not yet been able to develop as the particular interest of a particular class. Its victory, therefore, benefits also many individuals of the other classes which are not winning a dominant position, but only insofar as it now puts these individuals in a position to raise themselves into the ruling class. When the French bourgeoisie overthrew the power of the aristocracy, it thereby made it possible for many proletarians to raise themselves above the proletariat, but

---

[1][Marginal note by Marx:] Universality corresponds to (1) the class versus the estate, (2) the competition, world-wide intercourse, etc., (3) the great numerical strength of the ruling class, (4) the illusion of the *common* interests (in the beginning this illusion is true), (5) the delusion of the ideologists and the division of labour.

only insofar as they become bourgeois. Every new class, therefore, achieves its hegemony only on a broader basis than that of the class ruling previously, whereas the opposition of the non-ruling class against the new ruling class later develops all the more sharply and profoundly. Both these things determine the fact that the struggle to be waged against this new ruling class, in its turn, aims at a more decided and radical negation of the previous conditions of society than could all previous classes which sought to rule.

This whole semblance, that the rule of a certain class is only the rule of certain ideas, comes to a natural end, of course, as soon as class rule in general ceases to be the form in which society is organised, that is to say, as soon as it is no longer necessary to represent a particular interest as general or the "general interest" as ruling.

*The German Ideology*, pp. 64–66

## Political Economy: Labour-Power and the Theory of Value

By labour-power or capacity for labour is to be understood the aggregate of those mental and physical capabilities existing in a human being, which he exercises whenever he produces a use-value of any description.

But in order that our owner of money may be able to find labour-power offered for sale as a commodity, various conditions must first be fulfilled. The exchange of commodities of itself implies no other relations of dependence than those which result from its own nature. On this assumption, labour-power can appear upon the market as a commodity, only if, and so far as, its possessor, the individual whose labour-power it is, offers it for sale, or sells it, as a commodity. In order that he may be able to do this, he must have it at his disposal, must be the untrammelled owner of his capacity for labour, *i.e.*, of his person. He and the owner of money meet in the market, and deal with each other as on the basis of equal rights, with this difference alone, that one is buyer, the other seller; both, therefore, equal in the eyes of the law. The continuance of this relation demands that the owner of the labour-power should sell it only for a definite period, for if he were to sell it rump and stump, once for all, he would be selling himself, converting himself from a free man into a slave, from an owner of a commodity into a commodity. He must constantly look upon his labour-power as his own property, his own commodity, and this he can only do by placing it at the disposal of the buyer temporarily, for a definite period of time. By this means alone can he avoid renouncing his rights of ownership over it.

The second essential condition to the owner of money finding labour-power in the market as a commodity is this—that the labourer instead of being in the position to sell commodities in which his labour is incorporated, must be obliged to offer for sale as a commodity that very labour-power, which exists only in his living self.

In order that a man may be able to sell commodities other than labour-power, he must of course have the means of production, as raw material, implements, &c. No boots can be made without leather. He requires also the means of subsistence. Nobody—not even "a musician of the future"—can live upon future products, or upon use-values in an unfinished state; and ever since the first moment of his appearance on the world's stage, man always has been, and must still be a consumer, both before and while he is producing. In a society where all products assume the form of commodities, these commodities must be sold after they have been produced, it is only after their sale that they can serve in satisfying the requirements of their producer. The time necessary for their sale is superadded to that necessary for their production.

For the conversion of his money into capital, therefore, the owner of money must meet in the market with the free labourer, free in the double sense, that as a free man he can dispose of his labour-power as his own commodity, and that on the other hand he has no other commodity for sale, is short of everything necessary for the realisation of his labour-power.

The question why this free labourer confronts him in the market, has no interest for the owner of money, who regards the labour-market as a branch of the general market for commodities. And for the present it interests us just as little. We cling to the fact theoretically, as he does practically. One thing, however, is clear—Nature does not produce on the one side owners of money or commodities, and on the other men possessing nothing but their own labour-power. This relation has no natural basis, neither is its social basis one that is common to all historical periods. It is clearly the result of a past historical development, the product of many economic revolutions, of the extinction of a whole series of older forms of social production. . . .

We must now examine more closely this peculiar commodity, labour-power. Like all others it has a value. How is that value determined?

The value of labour-power is determined, as in the case of every other commodity, by the labour-time necessary for the production, and consequently also the reproduction, of this special article. So far as it has value, it represents no more than a definite quantity of the average labour of society incorporated in it. Labour-power exists only as a capacity, or power of the living individual. Its production consequently pre-supposes his existence. Given the individual, the production of labour-power consists in his reproduction of himself or his maintenance. For his maintenance he requires a given quantity of the means of subsistence. Therefore the labour-time requisite for the production of labour-power reduces itself to that necessary for the production of those means of subsistence; in other words, the value of labour-power is the value of the means of subsistence necessary for the maintenance of the labourer. Labour-power, however, becomes a reality only by its exercise; it sets itself in action only by working. But thereby a definite quantity of human muscle, nerve, brain, &c., is wasted, and these require to be restored. This increased expenditure demands a larger income. If the owner of labour-power works to-day, to-morrow he must again be able to repeat the same process in the same conditions as regards health and strength. His means of subsistence must therefore be sufficient to maintain him in his normal state as a labouring individual. His natural wants, such as food, clothing, fuel, and housing, vary according to the climatic and other physical conditions of his country. On the other hand, the number and extent of his so-called necessary wants, as also the modes of satisfying them, are themselves the product of historical development, and depend therefore to a great extent on the degree of civilisation of a country, more particularly on the conditions under which, and consequently on the habits and degree of comfort in which, the class of free labourers has been formed. In contradistinction therefore to the case of other commodities, there enters into the determination of the value of labour-power a historical and moral element. Nevertheless, in a given country, at a given period, the average quantity of the means of subsistence necessary for the labourer is practically known.

The owner of labour-power is mortal. If then his appearance in the market is to be continuous, and the continuous conversion of money into capital assumes this, the seller of labour-power must perpetuate himself, "in the way that every living individual perpetuates himself, by procreation." The labour-power withdrawn from the market by wear and tear and death, must be continually replaced by, at the very least, an equal amount of fresh labour-power. Hence the sum of the means of subsistence necessary for the production of labour-power must include the means necessary for the labourer's substitutes, *i.e.,* his children, in order that this race of peculiar commodity-owners may perpetuate its appearance in the market.

In order to modify the human organism, so that it may acquire skill and handiness in a given branch of industry, and become labour-power of a special kind, a special education or training is requisite, and this, on its part, costs an equivalent in commodities of a greater or less amount. This amount varies according to the more or less complicated character of the labour-power. The expenses of this education (excessively small in the case of ordinary labour-power), enter *pro tanto* into the total value spent in its production.

The value of labour-power resolves itself into the value of a definite quantity of the means of subsistence. It therefore varies with the value of these means or with the quantity of labour requisite for their production. . . .

The minimum limit of the value of labour-power is determined by the value of the commodities, without the daily supply of which the labourer cannot renew his vital energy, consequently by the value of those means of subsistence that are physically indispensable. If the price of labour-power falls to this minimum, it falls below its value, since under such circumstances it can be maintained and developed only in a crippled state.

*Capital,* vol. 1, pp. 167–73

What is the *value* of a commodity? How is it determined?

At first sight it would seem that the value of a commodity is a thing quite *relative,* and not to be settled without considering one commodity in its relations to all other commodities. In fact, in speaking of the value, the value in exchange of a commodity, we mean the proportional quantities in which it exchanges with all other commodities. But then arises the question: How are the proportions in which commodities exchange with each other regulated?

We know from experience that these proportions vary infinitely. Taking one single commodity, wheat, for instance, we shall find that a quarter of wheat exchanges in almost countless variations of proportion with different commodities. Yet, *its value remaining always the same,* whether expressed in silk, gold, or any other commodity, it must be something distinct from, and independent of, these *different rates of exchange* with different articles. It must be possible to express, in a very different form, these various equations with various commodities.

Besides, if I say a quarter of wheat exchanges with iron in a certain proportion, or the value of a quarter of wheat is expressed in a certain amount of iron, I say that the value of wheat and its equivalent in iron are equal *to some third thing,* which is neither wheat nor iron, because I suppose them to express the same magnitude in two different shapes. Either of them, the wheat or the iron, must, therefore, independently of the other, be reducible to this third thing which is their common measure.

To elucidate this point I shall refer to a very simple geometrical illustration. In comparing the areas of triangles of all possible forms and magnitudes, or comparing triangles with rectangles, or any other rectilinear figure, how do we proceed? We reduce the area of any triangle whatever to an expression quite different from its visible form. Having found from the nature of the triangle that its area is equal to half the product of its base by its height, we can then compare the different values of all sorts of triangles, and of all rectilinear figures whatever, because all of them may be resolved into a certain number of triangles.

The same mode of procedure must obtain with the values of commodities. We must be able to reduce all of them to an expression common to all, distinguishing them only by the proportions in which they contain that identical measure.

As the *exchangeable values* of commodities are only *social functions* of those things, and have nothing at all to do with their *natural* qualities, we must first ask, What is the common *social substance* of all commodities? It is *Labour*. To produce a commodity a certain amount of labour must be bestowed upon it, or worked up in it. And I say not only *Labour,* but *social Labour.* A man who produces an article for his own immediate use, to consume it himself, creates a *product,* but not a commodity. As a self-sustaining producer he has nothing to do with society. But to produce a *commodity,* a man must not only produce an article satisfying some *social* want, but his labour itself must form part and parcel of the total sum of labour expended by society. It must be subordinate to the *Division of Labour within Society.* It is nothing without the other divisions of labour, and on its part is required to *integrate* them.

If we consider *commodities as values,* we consider them exclusively under the single aspect of *realised, fixed,* or, if you like, *crystallised social labour.* In this respect they can *differ* only by representing greater or smaller quantities of labour, as, for example, a greater amount of labour may be worked up in a silken handkerchief than in a brick. But how does one measure *quantities of labour?* By the *time the labour lasts,* in measuring the labour by the hour, the day, etc. Of course, to apply this measure, all sorts of labour are reduced to average or simple labour as their unit.

We arrive, therefore, at this conclusion. A commodity has a *value,* because it is a *crystallisation of social labour.* The *greatness* of its value, of its *relative* value, depends upon the greater or less amount of that social substance contained in it; that is to say, on the relative mass of labour necessary for its production. The *relative values of commodities* are, therefore, determined by the *respective quantities or amounts of labour, worked up, realised, fixed in them.* The *correlative* quantities of commodities which can be produced in the *same time of labour* are *equal.* Or the value of one commodity is to the value of another commodity as the quantity of labour fixed in the one is to the quantity of labour fixed in the other.

I suspect that many of you will ask, does then, indeed, there exist such a vast, or any difference whatever, between determining the values of commodities by *wages,* and determining them by the *relative quantities of labour* necessary for their production? You must, however, be aware that the *reward* for labour, and *quantity* of labour, are quite disparate things. Suppose, for example, *equal quantities of labour* to be fixed in one quarter of wheat and one ounce of gold. I resort to the example because it was used by Benjamin Franklin in his first Essay published in 1729, and entitled, *A Modest Enquiry into the Nature and Necessity of a Paper Currency,* where he, one of the first, hit upon the true nature of value. Well. We suppose, then, that one quarter of wheat and one ounce of gold are *equal values* or *equivalents,* because they are *crystallisations of equal amounts of average labour,* of so many days' or so many weeks' labour respectively fixed in them. In thus determining the relative values of gold and corn, do we refer in any way whatever to the *wages* of the agricultural labourer and the miner? Not a bit. We leave it quite *indeterminate how* their day's or week's labour was paid, or even whether wages labour was employed at all. If it was, wages may have been very unequal. The labourer whose labour is realised in the quarter of wheat may receive two bushels only, and the labourer employed in mining may receive one-half of the ounce of gold. Or, supposing their wages to be equal, they may deviate in all possible proportions from the values of the commodities produced by them. They may amount to one-half, one-third, one-fourth, one-fifth, or any other proportional part of the one quarter of corn or the one ounce of gold. Their *wages* can, of course, not *exceed,* not be *more* than the values of the commodities they produced, but they can be *less* in every possible degree. Their *wages* will be *limited* by the *values* of the products, but the *values of their products* will not be limited by the wages. And above all, the values, the relative values of corn and gold, for example, will have been settled without any regard whatever to the value of the labour employed, that is to say, to *wages.* To determine the values of commodities by the *relative quantities of labour fixed in them,* is, therefore, a thing quite different from the tautological method of determining the values of commodities by the value of labour, or by *wages.* This point, however, will be further elucidated in the progress of our inquiry.

In calculating the exchangeable value of a commodity we must add to the quantity of labour *last* employed the quantity of labour *previously* worked up in the raw material of the commodity, and the labour bestowed on the implements, tools, machinery, and buildings, with which such labour is assisted. For example, the value of a certain amount of cotton-yarn is the crystallisation of the quantity of labour added to the cotton during the spinning process, the quantity of labour previously realised in the cotton itself, the quantity of labour realised in the coal, oil, and other auxiliary substances used, the quantity of labour fixed in the steam engine, the spindles, the factory building, and so forth. Instruments of production properly so-called, such as tools, machinery, buildings, serve again and again for a longer or shorter period during repeated processes of production. If they were used up at once, like the raw material, their whole value would at once be transferred to the commodities they assist in producing. But as a spindle, for example, is but gradually used up, an average calculation is made, based upon the average time it lasts, and its average waste of wear and tear during a certain period, say a day. In this way we calculate how much of the value of the spindle is transferred to the yarn daily spun, and how much, therefore, of the total amount of labour realised in a pound of yarn, for example, is due to the quantity of labour previously realised in the spindle. For our present purpose it is not necessary to dwell any longer upon this point.

It might seem that if the value of a commodity is determined by the *quantity of labour bestowed upon its production,* the lazier a man, or the clumsier a man, the more valuable his commodity, because the greater the time of labour required for finishing the commodity. This, however, would be a sad mistake. You will recollect that I used the word "*Social* labour," and many points are involved in this qualification of *"Social."* In saying that the value of a commodity is determined by the *quantity of labour* worked up or crystallised in it, we mean *the quantity of labour necessary* for its production in a given state of society, under certain social average conditions of production, with a given social average intensity, and average skill of the labour employed. When, in England, the power-loom came to compete with the hand-loom, only one half of the former time of labour was wanted to convert a given amount of yarn into a yard of cotton or cloth. The poor hand-loom weaver now worked seventeen or eighteen hours daily, instead of the nine or ten hours he had worked before. Still the product of twenty hours of his labour represented now only ten social hours of labour, or ten hours of labour socially necessary for the conversion of a certain amount of yarn into textile stuffs. His product of twenty hours had, therefore, no more value than his former product of ten hours.

If then the quantity of socially necessary labour realised in commodities regulates their exchangeable values, every increase in the quantity of labour wanted for the production of a commodity must augment its value, as every diminution must lower it.

If the respective quantities of labour necessary for the production of the respective commodities remained constant, their relative values also would be constant. But such is not the case. The quantity of labour necessary for the production of a commodity changes continuously with the changes in the productive powers of the labour employed. The greater the productive powers of labour, the more produce is finished in a given time of labour: and the smaller the productive powers of labour, the less produce is finished in the same time. If, for example, in the progress of population it should become necessary to cultivate less fertile soils, the same amount of produce would be only attainable by a greater amount of labour spent, and the value of agricultural produce would consequently rise. On the other hand, if with the modern means of production, a single spinner converts into yarn, during one working day, many thousand times the amount of cotton which he could have spun during the same time with the spinning wheel, it is evident that every single pound of cotton will absorb many thousand times less of spinning labour than it did before, and, consequently, the value added by spinning to every single pound of cotton will be a thousand times less than before. The value of yarn will sink accordingly.

Apart from the different natural energies and acquired working abilities of different peoples, the productive powers of labour must principally depend:

Firstly. Upon the *natural* conditions of labour, such as fertility of soil, mines, and so forth;

Secondly. Upon the progressive improvement of the *Social Powers of Labour,* such as are derived from production on a grand scale, concentration of capital and combination of labour, subdivision of labour, machinery, improved methods, appliance of chemical and other natural agencies, shortening of time and space by means of communication and transport, and every other contrivance by which science presses natural agencies into the service of labour, and by which the social or co-operative character of labour is developed. The greater the productive powers of labour, the less labour is bestowed upon a given amount of produce; hence the smaller the value of this produce. The smaller the productive powers of labour, the more labour is bestowed upon the same amount of produce; hence the greater its value. As a general law we may, therefore, set it down that:—

*The values of commodities are directly as the times of labour employed in their production, and are inversely as the productive powers of the labour employed. . . .*

Now suppose that the average amount of the daily necessaries of a labouring man require *six hours of average labour* for their production. Suppose, moreover, six hours of average labour to be also realised in a quantity of gold equal to 3*s.* Then 3*s.* would be the *Price,* or the monetary expression of the *Daily Value* of that man's *Labouring Power.* If he worked daily six hours he would daily produce a value sufficient to buy the average amount of his daily necessaries, or to maintain himself as a labouring man.

But our man is a wage labourer. He must, therefore, sell his labouring power to a capitalist. If he sells it at 3*s.* daily, or 18*s.* weekly, he sells it at its value. Suppose him to be a spinner. If he works six hours daily he will add to the cotton a value of 3*s.* daily. This value, daily added by him, would be an exact equivalent for the wages, or the price of his labouring power, received daily. But in that case *no surplus value or surplus produce* whatever would go to the capitalist. Here, then, we come to the rub.

In buying the labouring power of the workman, and paying its value, the capitalist, like every other purchaser, has acquired the right to consume or use the commodity bought. You consume or use the labouring power of a man by making him work as you consume or use a machine by making it run. By paying the daily or weekly value of the labouring power of the workman, the capitalist has, therefore, acquired the right to use or make that labouring power work during the *whole day or week.* The working day or the working week has, of course, certain limits, but those we shall afterwards look more closely at.

For the present I want to turn your attention to one decisive point.

The *value* of the labouring power is determined by the quantity of labour necessary to maintain or reproduce it, but the *use* of that labouring power is only limited by the active energies and physical strength of the labourer. The daily or weekly *value* of the labouring power is quite distinct from the daily or weekly exercise of that power, the same as the food a horse wants and the time it can carry the horseman are quite distinct. The quantity of labour by which the *value* of the workman's labouring power is limited forms by no means a limit to the quantity of labour which his labouring power is apt to perform. Take the example of our spinner. We have seen that, to daily reproduce his labouring power, he must daily reproduce a value of three shillings, which he will do by working six hours daily. But this does not disable him from working ten or twelve or more hours a day. But by paying the daily or weekly *value* of the spinner's labouring power, the capitalist has acquired the right of using that labouring power during *the whole day or week*. He will, therefore, make him work say, daily, *twelve* hours. *Over and above* the six hours required to replace his wages, or the value of his labouring power, he will, therefore, have to work *six other hours,* which I shall call hours of *surplus labour,* which surplus labour will realise itself in a *surplus value* and a *surplus produce.* If our spinner, for example, by his daily labour of six hours, added three shillings' value to the cotton, a value forming an exact equivalent to his wages, he will, in twelve hours, add six shillings' worth to the cotton, and produce a *proportional surplus of yarn.* As he has sold his labouring power to the capitalist, the whole value or produce created by him belongs to the capitalist, the owner *pro tem.* of his labouring power. By advancing three shillings, the capitalist will, therefore, realise a value of six shillings, because, advancing a value in which six hours of labour are crystallised, he will receive in return a value in which twelve hours of labour are crystallised. By repeating this same process daily, the capitalist will daily advance three shillings and daily pocket six shillings, one-half of which will go to pay wages anew, and the other half of which will form *surplus value,* for which the capitalist pays no equivalent. It is this *sort of exchange between capital and labour* upon which capitalistic production, or the wages system, is founded, and which must constantly result in reproducing the working man as a working man, and the capitalist as a capitalist.

*The rate of surplus value,* all other circumstances remaining the same, will depend on the proportion between that part of the working day necessary to reproduce the value of the labouring power and the *surplus time* or *surplus labour* performed for the capitalist. It will, therefore, depend on the *ratio in which the working day is prolonged over and above that extent,* by working which the working man would only reproduce the value of his labouring power, or replace his wages.

'Value, Price, and Profit', pp. 202–13

## Working Class Organization and Political Struggle

The first attempts of workers to *associate* among themselves always take place in the form of combinations.

Large-scale industry concentrates in one place a crowd of people unknown to one another. Competition divides their interests. But the maintenance of wages, this common interest which they have against their boss, unites them in a common thought of resistance—*combination.* Thus combination always has a double aim, that of stopping competition among the workers, so that they can carry on general competition with the capitalist. If the first aim of resistance was merely the maintenance of wages, combinations, at first isolated, constitute themselves into groups as the capitalists in their turn unite for the purpose of repression, and in face of always united capital, the maintenance of the association becomes more necessary to them than that of wages. This is so true that English economists are amazed to see the workers sacrifice a good part of their wages in favour of associations, which, in the eyes of these economists, are established solely in favour of wages. In this struggle—a veritable civil war—all the elements necessary for a coming battle unite and develop. Once it has reached this point, association takes on a political character.

Economic conditions had first transformed the mass of the people of the country into workers. The combination of capital has created for this mass a common situation, common interests. This mass is thus already a class as against capital, but not yet for itself. In the struggle, of which we have noted only a few phases, this mass becomes united, and constitutes itself as a class for itself. The interests it defends become class interests. But the struggle of class against class is a political struggle.

In the bourgeoisie we have two phases to distinguish: that in which it constituted itself as a class under the regime of feudalism and absolute monarchy, and that in which, already constituted as a class, it overthrew feudalism and monarchy to make society into a bourgeois society. The first of these phases was the longer and necessitated the greater efforts. This too began by partial combinations against the feudal lords.

Much research has been carried out to trace the different historical phases that the bourgeoisie has passed through, from the commune up to its constitution as a class.

But when it is a question of making a precise study of strikes, combinations and other forms in which the proletarians carry out before our eyes their organization as a class, some are seized with real fear and others display a *transcendental* disdain.

An oppressed class is the vital condition for every society founded on the antagonism of classes. The emancipation of the oppressed class thus implies necessarily the creation of a new society. For the oppressed class to be able to emancipate itself it is necessary that the productive powers already acquired and the existing social relations should no longer be capable of existing side by side. Of all the instruments of production, the greatest productive power is the revolutionary class itself. The organization of revolutionary elements as a class supposes the existence of all the productive forces which could be engendered in the bosom of the old society.

Does this mean that after the fall of the old society there will be a new class domination culminating in a new political power? No.

The condition for the emancipation of the working class is the abolition of every class, just as the condition for the liberation of the third estate, of the bourgeois order, was the abolition of all estates[1] and all orders.

The working class, in the course of its development, will substitute for the

---

[1]Estates here in the historical sense of the estates of feudalism, estates with definite and limited privileges. The revolution of the bourgeoisie abolished the estates and their privileges. Bourgeois society knows only *classes*. It was, therefore, absolutely in contradiction with history to describe the proletariat as the "fourth estate." [*Note by F. Engels to the German edition, 1885.*]

old civil society an association which will exclude classes and their antagonism, and there will be no more political power properly so-called, since political power is precisely the official expression of antagonism in civil society.

Meanwhile the antagonism between the proletariat and the bourgeoisie is a struggle of class against class, a struggle which carried to its highest expression is a total revolution. Indeed, is it at all surprising that a society founded on the opposition of classes should culminate in brutal *contradiction,* the shock of body against body, as its final *dénouement?*

Do not say that social movement excludes political movement. There is never a political movement which is not at the same time social.

It is only in an order of things in which there are no more classes and class antagonisms that *social evolutions* will cease to be *political revolutions.* Till then, on the eve of every general reshuffling of society, the last word of social science will always be:

*"Le combat ou la mort; la lutte sanguinaire ou le néant. C'est ainsi que la question est invinciblement posée."*

The Poverty of Philosophy, pp. 172–75

## The Structure of Social Transformation

The first work which I undertook to dispel the doubts assailing me was a critical re-examination of the Hegelian philosophy of law; the introduction to this work being published in the *Deutsch-Französische Jahrbücher* issued in Paris in 1844. My inquiry led me to the conclusion that neither legal relations nor political forms could be comprehended whether by themselves or on the basis of a so-called general development of the human mind, but that on the contrary they originate in the material conditions of life, the totality of which Hegel, following the example of English and French thinkers of the eighteenth century, embraces within the term "civil society"; that the anatomy of this civil society, however, has to be sought in political economy. The study of this, which I began in Paris, I continued in Brussels, where I moved owing to an expulsion order issued by M. Guizot. The general conclusion at which I arrived and which, once reached, became the guiding principle of my studies can be summarised as follows. In the social production of their existence, men inevitably enter into definite relations, which are independent of their will, namely relations of production appropriate to a given stage in the development of their material forces of production. The totality of these relations of production constitutes the economic structure of society, the real foundation, on which arises a legal and political superstructure and to which correspond definite forms of social consciousness. The mode of production of material life conditions the general process of social, political and intellectual life. It is not the consciousness of men that determines their existence, but their social existence that determines their consciousness. At a certain stage of development, the material productive forces of society come into conflict with the existing relations of production or—this merely expresses the same thing in legal terms—with the property relations within the framework of which they have operated hitherto. From forms of development of the productive forces these relations turn into their fetters. Then begins an era of social revolution. The changes in the economic foundation lead sooner or later to the transformation of the whole immense superstructure. In studying such transformations it is always necessary to distinguish between the material transformation of the economic conditions of production, which can be determined with the precision of natural science, and the legal, political, religious, artistic or philosophic—in short, ideological forms in which men become conscious of this conflict and fight it out. Just as one does not judge an individual by what he thinks about himself, so one cannot judge such a period of transformation by its consciousness, but, on the contrary, this consciousness must be explained from the contradictions of material life, from the conflict existing between the social forces of production and the relations of production. No social order is ever destroyed before all the productive forces for which it is sufficient have been developed, and new superior relations of production never replace older ones before the material conditions for their existence have matured within the framework of the old society. Mankind thus inevitably sets itself only such tasks as it is able to solve, since closer examination will always show that the problem itself arises only when the material conditions for its solution are already present or at least in the course of formation. In broad outline, the Asiatic, ancient, feudal and modern bourgeois modes of production may be designated as epochs marking progress in the economic development of society. The bourgeois mode of production is the last antagonistic form of the social process of production—antagonistic not in the sense of individual antagonism but of an antagonism that emanates from the individuals' social conditions of existence—but the productive forces developing within bourgeois society create also the material conditions for a solution of this antagonism. The prehistory of human society accordingly closes with this social formation.

Preface to *A Contribution to the Critique of Political Economy,* pp. 20–22

Finally, from the conception of history we have sketched we obtain these further conclusions: (1) In the development of productive forces there comes a stage when productive forces and means of intercourse are brought into being, which, under the existing relationships, only cause mischief, and are no longer productive but destructive forces (machinery and money); and connected with this a class is called forth, which has to bear all the burdens of society without enjoying its advantages, which, ousted from society, is forced into the most decided antagonism to all other classes; a class which forms the majority of all members of society, and from which emanates the consciousness of the necessity of a fundamental revolution, the communist consciousness, which may, of course, arise among the other classes too through the contemplation of the situation of this class. (2) The conditions under which definite productive forces can be applied are the conditions of the rule of a definite class of society, whose social power, deriving from its property, has its *practical*-idealistic expression in each case in the form of the State; and, therefore, every revolutionary struggle is directed against a class, which till then has been in power.[1] (3) In all revolutions

---

[1][Marginal note by Marx:] The people are interested in maintaining the present state of production.

up till now the mode of activity always remained unscathed and it was only a question of a different distribution of this activity, a new distribution of labour to other persons, whilst the communist revolution is directed against the preceding *mode* of activity, does away with *labour,* and abolishes the rule of all classes with the classes themselves, because it is carried through by the class which no longer counts as a class in society, is not recognised as a class, and is in itself the expression of the dissolution of all classes, nationalities, etc. within present society; and (4) Both for the production on a mass scale of this communist consciousness, and for the success of the cause itself, the alteration of men on a mass scale is, necessary, an alteration which can only take place in a practical movement, a *revolution;* this revolution is necessary, therefore, not only because the *ruling* class cannot be overthrown in any other way, but also because the class *overthrowing* it can only in a revolution succeed in ridding itself of all the muck of ages and become fitted to found society anew.

*The German Ideology,* pp. 94–95

## Sources

Karl Marx, *Capital,* vols. 1 and 3 (London: Lawrence & Wishart, 1972).

———, *The Economic and Philosophical Manuscripts,* in *Early Writings,* trans. and ed. T. B. Bottomore (London: C. A. Watts, 1963).

———, *The Eighteenth Brumaire of Louis Bonaparte,* in *Selected Works* (in three volumes).

———, *The Poverty of Philosophy* (New York: International Publishers, 1963).

———, Preface to *A Contribution to the Critique of Political Economy,* trans. S. W. Ryazanskaya, ed. M. Dobb (London: Lawrence & Wishart, 1971).

———, "Value, Price, and Profit," in Karl Marx and Friedrich Engels, *Selected Works* (New York: International Publishers, 1968).

Karl Marx and Friedrich Engels, *The German Ideology,* ed. and intro. C. J. Arthur (London: Lawrence & Wishart, 1970).

———, *The Manifesto of the Communist Party,* in *Selected Works* (in three volumes).

———, *Selected Works* (Moscow: Progress Publishers, 1969), 3 vols.

# · 2 ·

# V. I. Lenin:

Selections from *The Development of Capitalism
in Russia, What Is to Be Done?, The State and
Revolution,* and *A Great Beginning*

## The Emergence of Capitalism in Russia

As our starting-point in examining the present system of landlord economy we must take the system of that economy which prevailed in the epoch of serfdom. The essence of the economic system of those days was that the entire land of a given unit of agrarian economy, i.e., of a given estate, was divided into the lord's and the peasants' land; the latter was distributed in allotments among the peasants, who (receiving other means of production in addition, as for example, timber, sometimes cattle, etc.) cultivated it with their own labour and their own implements, and obtained their livelihood from it. The product of this peasants' labour constituted the necessary product, to employ the terminology of theoretical political economy; necessary—for the peasants in providing them with means of subsistence, and for the landlord in providing him with hands; in exactly the same way as the product which replaces the variable part of the value of capital is a necessary product in capitalist society. The peasants' surplus-labour, on the other hand, consisted in their cultivation, with *the same* implements, of the landlord's land; the product of that labour went to the landlord. Hence, the surplus-labour was separated then in space from the necessary labour: for the landlord they cultivated his land, for themselves their allotments; for the landlord they worked some days of the week and for themselves others. The peasant's allotment in this economy served, as it were, as wages in kind (to express oneself in modern terms), or as a means of providing the landlord with hands. The peasants' "own" farming of their allotments was a condition of the landlord economy, and its purpose was to "provide" not the peasant with means of livelihood but the landlord with hands.[1]

It is this system of economy which we call corvée [Russ.: barshchina] economy. Its prevalence obviously presumes the following necessary conditions: firstly, the predominance of natural economy. The feudal estate had to constitute a self-sufficing, self-contained entity, in very slight contact with the outside world. The production of grain by the landlords for sale, which developed particularly in the latter period of the existence of serfdom, was already a harbinger of the collapse of the old regime. Secondly, such an economy required that the direct producer be allotted the means of production in general, and land in particular; moreover, that he be tied to the land, since otherwise the landlord was not assured of hands. Hence, the methods of obtaining the surplus–product under corvée and under capitalist economy are diametrically opposite: the former is based on the producer being provided with land, the latter on the producer being dispossessed of the land.[2] Thirdly, a condition for such a system of economy was the personal dependence of the peasant on the landlord. If the landlord had not possessed direct power over the person of the peasant, he could not have compelled a man who had a plot of land and ran his own farm to work for him. Hence, "other than economic pressure," as Marx says in describing this economic regime, was necessary (and, as has already been indicated above, Marx assigned it to the category of *labour-rent; Das Kapital,* III, 2, 324). The form and degree of this coercion may be the most varied, ranging from the peasant's serf status to his lack of rights in the social estates. Fourthly, and finally, a condition and a consequence of the system of economy described was the extremely low and stagnant condition of technique, for farming was in the hands of small peasants, crushed by poverty and degraded by personal dependence and by ignorance. . . .

The corvée system of economy was undermined by the abolition of serfdom. All the main foundations of this system were undermined: natural economy, the self-contained and the self-sufficient character of the landed estate, the close connection between its various constituents, and the landlord's power over the peasants. The peasant's farm was separated from that of the landlord; the peasant was to buy back his land and become the full owner of it; the landlord, to adopt the capitalist system of farming, which, as has just been observed, has a diametrically opposite basis. But such a transition to a totally different system could not, of course, take place at once, and for two different reasons. First, the

---

[1] An extremely vivid description of this system of economy is given by A. Engelhardt in his *Letters from the Countryside* (St. Petersburg, 1885, pp. 556–557). The author quite rightly points out that feudal economy was a definite, regular and complete system, the director of which was the landlord, who allotted land to the peasants and assigned them to various jobs.

[2] In opposing the view of Henry George, who said that the expropriation of the mass of the population is the great and universal cause of poverty and oppression, Engels wrote in 1887: "This is not quite correct historically. . . . In the middle ages, it was not the expropriation of the people *from,* but on the contrary, their appropriation *to* the land which became the source of feudal oppression. The peasant retained his land, but was attached to it as a serf or villein, and made liable to tribute to the lord in labour and in produce" (*The Condition of the Working-Class in England in 1844,* New York, 1887, Preface, p. III).

conditions required for capitalist production did not yet exist. A class of people was required who were accustomed to work for hire; the peasant's implements had to be replaced by those of the landlord; agriculture had to be organised on the same lines as any other commercial and industrial enterprise and not as the business of the lord. All these conditions could only take shape gradually, and the attempts of some landlords, immediately after the Reform, to import machinery and even workers from abroad could not but end in a fiasco. The other reason why the transition to the capitalist conduct of affairs was not possible at once was that the old corvée system of economy had been undermined, but not yet completely destroyed. The peasants' farms were not entirely separated from those of the landlords, for the latter retained possession of very essential parts of the peasants' allotments: the "cut-off lands," the woods, meadows, watering places, pastures, etc. Without these lands (or easement rights) the peasants were absolutely unable to carry on independent farming, so that the landlords were able to continue the old system of economy in the form of labour-service. The possibility of exercising "other than economic pressure" also remained in the shape of the peasants' temporarily-bound status, collective responsibility, corporal punishment, forced labour on public works, etc.

Thus, capitalist economy could not emerge at once, and corvée economy could not disappear at once.

*The Development of Capitalism in Russia,* pp. 191–93

## The "Mission" of Capitalism

We still have, in conclusion, to sum up on the question which in literature has come to be known as that of the "mission" of capitalism, i.e., of its historical role in the economic development of Russia. Recognition of the progressiveness of this role is quite compatible (as we have tried to show in detail at every stage in our exposition of the facts) with the full recognition of the negative and dark sides of capitalism, with the full recognition of the profound and all-round social contradictions which are inevitably inherent in capitalism, and which reveal the historically transient character of this economic regime.

The progressive historical role of capitalism may be summed up in two brief propositions: increase in the productive forces of social labour, and the socialisation of that labour. But both these facts manifest themselves in extremely diverse processes in different branches of the national economy.

The development of the productive forces of social labour is to be observed in full relief only in the epoch of large-scale machine industry. Until that highest stage of capitalism was reached, there still remained hand production and primitive technique, which developed quite spontaneously and exceedingly slowly. The post-Reform epoch differs radically in this respect from previous epochs in Russian history. The Russia of the wooden plough and the flail, of the watermill and the hand-loom, began rapidly to be transformed into the Russia of the iron plough and the threshing machine, of the steam-mill and the power-loom. An equally thorough transformation of technique is seen in every branch of the national economy where capitalist production predominates. This process of transformation must, by the very nature of capitalism, take place in the midst of much that is uneven and disproportionate: periods of prosperity alternate with periods of crisis, the development of one industry leads to the decline of another, there is progress in one aspect of agriculture in one area and in another aspect in another area, the growth of trade and industry outstrips, the growth of agriculture, etc. A large number of errors made by Narodnik writers spring from their efforts to prove that this disproportionate, spasmodic, feverish development is not development. . . .

The socialisation of labour by capitalism is manifested in the following processes. Firstly, the very growth of commodity production destroys the scattered condition of small economic units that is characteristic of natural economy and draws together the small local markets into an enormous national (and then world) market. Production for oneself is transformed into production for the whole of society; and the greater the development of capitalism, the stronger becomes the contradiction between this collective character of production and the individual character of appropriation. Secondly, capitalism replaces the former scattered production by an unprecedented concentration both in agriculture and in industry. That is the most striking and outstanding, but not the only, manifestation of the feature of capitalism under review. Thirdly, capitalism eliminates the forms of personal dependence that constituted an inalienable component of preceding systems of economy. In Russia, the progressive character of capitalism in this respect is particularly marked, since the personal dependence of the producer existed in our country (and partly continues to exist to this day), not only in agriculture, but in manufacturing industry ("factories" employing serf labour), in the mining and metallurgical industries, in the fishing industry, etc. Compared with the labour of the dependent or bonded peasant, the labour of the hired worker is progressive in all branches of the national economy. Fourthly, capitalism necessarily creates mobility of the population, something not required by previous systems of social economy and impossible under them on anything like a large scale. Fifthly, capitalism constantly reduces the proportion of the population engaged in agriculture (where the most backward forms of social and economic relationships always prevail), and increases the number of large industrial centres. Sixthly, capitalist society increases the population's need for association, for organisation, and lends these organisations a character distinct from those of former times. While breaking down the narrow, local, social-estate associations of medieval society and creating fierce competition, capitalism at the same time splits the whole of society into large groups of persons occupying different positions in production, and gives a tremendous impetus to organisation within each such group. Seventhly, all the above-mentioned changes effected in the old economic system by capitalism inevitably lead also to a change in the mentality of the population. The spasmodic character of economic development, the rapid transformation of the methods of production and the enormous concentration of production, the disappearance of all forms of personal dependence and patriarchalism in relationships, the mobility of the population, the influence of the big industrial centres, etc.—all this cannot but lead to a profound change in the very character of the producers. . . .

*The Development of Capitalism in Russia*, pp. 602–06

## The Working Class and the Intelligentsia

In the very first literary expression of Economism[1] we observe the exceedingly curious phenomenon—highly characteristic for an understanding of all the differences prevailing among present-day Social-Democrats—that the adherents of the "labour movement pure and simple", worshippers of the closest "organic" contacts . . . with the proletarian struggle, opponents of any non-worker intelligentsia (even a socialist intelligentsia), are compelled, in order to defend their positions, to resort to the arguments of the *bourgeois* "pure trade-unionists". . . . This shows . . . that *all* worship of the spontaneity of the working-class movement, all belittling of the role of "the conscious element", of the role of Social-Democracy, *means, quite independently of whether he who belittles that role desires it or not, a strengthening of the influence of bourgeois ideology upon the workers.* All those who talk about "overrating the importance of ideology",[2] about exaggerating the role of the conscious element, etc., imagine that the labour movement pure and simple can elaborate, and will elaborate, an independent ideology for itself, if only the workers "wrest their fate from the hands of the leaders". But this is a profound mistake. To supplement what has been said above, we shall quote the following profoundly true and important words of Karl Kautsky on the new draft programme of the Austrian Social-Democratic Party[3]:

Many of our revisionist critics believe that Marx asserted that economic development and the class struggle create, not only the conditions for socialist production, but also, and directly, the *consciousness* [K. K.'s italics] of its necessity. And these critics assert that England, the country most highly developed capitalistically, is more remote than any other from this consciousness. Judging by the draft, one might assume that this allegedly orthodox-Marxist view, which is thus refuted, was shared by the committee that drafted the Austrian programme. In the draft programme it is stated: 'The more capitalist development increases the numbers of the proletariat, the more the proletariat is compelled and becomes fit to fight against capitalism. The proletariat becomes conscious' of the possibility and of the necessity for socialism. In this connection socialist consciousness appears to be a necessary and direct result of the proletarian class struggle. But this is absolutely untrue. Of course, socialism, as a doctrine, has its roots in modern economic relationships just as the class struggle of the proletariat has, and, like the latter, emerges from the struggle against the capitalist-created poverty and misery of the masses. But socialism and the class struggle arise side by side and not one out of the other; each arises under different conditions. Modern socialist consciousness can arise only on the basis of profound scientific knowledge. Indeed, modern economic science is as much a condition

---

[1] [The "economists," according to Lenin, defined the tasks of working class struggle purely in economic terms, e.g. the struggle for higher wages, and rejected the need for a Marxist party—eds.]

[2] Letter of the "Economists", in *Iskra* No. 12.

[3] *Neue Zeit*, 1901–02, XX, I, No. 3, p. 79. The committee's draft to which Kautsky refers was adopted by the Vienna Congress (at the end of last year) in a slightly amended form.

for socialist production as, say, modern technology, and the proletariat can create neither the one nor the other, no matter how much it may desire to do so; both arise out of the modern social process. The vehicle of science is not the proletariat, but the *bourgeois intelligentsia* [K. K.'s italics]: it was in the minds of individual members of this stratum that modern socialism originated, and it was they who communicated it to the more intellectually developed proletarians who, in their turn, introduce it into the proletarian class struggle where conditions allow that to be done. Thus, socialist consciousness is something introduced into the proletarian class struggle from without [*von aussen Hineingetragenes*] and not something that arose within it spontaneously [*urwüchsig*]. Accordingly, the old Hainfeld programme quite rightly stated that the task of Social-Democracy is to imbue the proletariat [literally: saturate the proletariat] with the *consciousness* of its position and the consciousness of its task. There would be no need for this if consciousness arose of itself from the class struggle. The new draft copied this proposition from the old programme, and attached it to the proposition mentioned above. But this completely broke the line of thought. . . .

Since there can be no talk of an independent ideology formulated by the working masses themselves in the process of their movement,[4] the *only* choice is—either bourgeois or socialist ideology. There is no middle course (for mankind has not created a "third" ideology, and, moreover, in a society torn by class antagonisms there can never be a non-class or an above-class ideology). Hence, to belittle the socialist ideology *in any way, to turn aside from it.in the slightest degree* means to strengthen bourgeois ideology. There is much talk of spontaneity. But the *spontaneous* development of the working-class movement leads to its subordination to bourgeois ideology, *to its development along the lines of the Credo programme;* for the spontaneous working-class movement is trade-unionism, is *Nur-Gewerkschaftlerei,* and trade-unionism means the ideological enslavement of the workers by the bourgeoisie. Hence, our task, the task of Social-Democracy, is *to combat spontaneity, to divert* the working-class movement from this spontaneous, trade-unionist striving to come under the wing of the bourgeoisie, and to bring it under the wing of revolutionary Social-Democracy. The sentence employed by the authors of the "Economist" letter published in *Iskra,* No. 12, that the efforts of the most inspired ideologists fail to divert the working-class movement from the path that is determined by the interaction of the material elements and the material environment *is* therefore *tantamount to renouncing socialism.* If these authors were capable of fearlessly, consistently, and thoroughly considering what they say, as everyone who enters the arena of literary and public activity should be, there would be nothing left for them but to "fold their useless arms over their empty breasts" and—surrender the field of action to the Struves and Prokopoviches, who are dragging the working-class

---

[4]This does not mean, of course, that the workers have no part in creating such an ideology. They take part, however, not as workers, but as socialist theoreticians, as Proudhons and Weitlings; in other words, they take part only when they are able, and to the extent that they are able, more or less, to acquire the knowledge of their age and develop that knowledge. But in order that working men *may succeed in this more often,* every effort must be made to raise the level of the consciousness of the workers in general; it is necessary that the workers do not confine themselves to the artificially restricted limits of *"literature for workers"* but that they learn to an increasing degree to master *general literature.* It would be even truer to say "are not confined", instead of "do not confine themselves", because the workers themselves wish to read and do read all that is written of the intelligentsia, and only a few (bad) intellectuals believe that it is enough "for workers" to be told a few things about factory conditions and to have repeated to them over and over again what has long been known.

movement "along the line of least resistance", i.e., along the line of bourgeois trade-unionism, or to the Zubatovs, who are dragging it along the line of clerical and gendarme "ideology".

Let us recall the example of Germany. What was the historic service Lassalle rendered to the German working-class movement? It was that he *diverted* that movement from the path of progressionist trade-unionism and cooperativism towards which it had been spontaneously moving. . . . To fulfil such a task it was necessary to do something quite different from talking of underrating the spontaneous element, of tactics-as-process, of the interaction between elements and environment, etc. *A fierce struggle against spontaneity* was necessary, and only after such a struggle, extending over many years, was it possible, for instance, to convert the working population of Berlin from a bulwark of the progressionist party into one of the finest strongholds of Social-Democracy. This struggle is by no means over even today (as might seem to those who learn the history of the German movement from Prokopovich, and its philosophy from Struve). Even now the German working class is, so to speak, split up among a number of ideologies. A section of the workers is organised in Catholic and monarchist trade unions; another section is organised in the Hirsch-Duncker unions, founded by the bourgeois worshippers of English trade-unionism; the third is organised in Social-Democratic trade unions. The last-named group is immeasurably more numerous than the rest, but the Social-Democratic ideology was able to achieve this superiority, and will be able to maintain it, only in an unswerving struggle against all other ideologies.

But why, the reader will ask, does the spontaneous movement, the movement along the line of least resistance, lead to the domination of bourgeois ideology? For the simple reason that bourgeois ideology is far older in origin than socialist ideology, that it is more fully developed, and that it has at its disposal *immeasurably* more means of dissemination.[5] And the younger the socialist movement in any given country, the more vigorously it must struggle against all attempts to entrench non-socialist ideology, and the more resolutely the workers must be warned against the bad counsellors who shout against "overrating the conscious element", etc. The authors of the Economist letter . . . inveigh against the intolerance that is characteristic of the infancy of the movement. To this we reply: Yes, our movement is indeed in its infancy, and in order that it may grow up faster, it must become imbued with intolerance against those who retard its growth by their subservience to spontaneity. Nothing is so ridiculous and harmful as pretending that we are "old hands" who have long ago experienced all the decisive stages of the struggle.

*What Is to Be Done?*, pp. 39–43

---

[5]It is often said that the working class *spontaneously* gravitates towards socialism. This is perfectly true in the sense that socialist theory reveals the causes of the misery of the working class more profoundly and more correctly than any other theory, and for that reason the workers are able to assimilate it so easily, *provided*, however, this theory does not itself yield to spontaneity, *provided* it subordinates spontaneity to itself. Usually this is taken for granted, but it is precisely this which *Rabocheye Dyelo* forgets or distorts. The working class spontaneously gravitates towards socialism; nevertheless, most widespread (and continuously and diversely revived) bourgeois ideology spontaneously imposes itself upon the working class to a still greater degree.

We have said that *there could not have been* Social-Democratic consciousness among the workers. It would have to be brought to them from without. The history of all countries shows that the working class, exclusively by its own effort, is able to develop only trade-union consciousness, i.e., the conviction that it is necessary to combine in unions, fight the employers, and strive to compel the government to pass necessary labour legislation, etc.[1] The theory of socialism, however, grew out of the philosophic, historical, and economic theories elaborated by educated representatives of the propertied classes, by intellectuals. By their social status, the founders of modern scientific socialism, Marx and Engels, themselves belonged to the bourgeois intelligentsia. In the very same way, in Russia, the theoretical doctrine of Social-Democracy arose altogether independently of the spontaneous growth of the working class movement; it arose as a natural and inevitable outcome of the development of thought among the revolutionary socialist intelligentsia. In the period under discussion, the middle nineties, this doctrine not only represented the completely formulated programme of the Emancipation of Labour group, but had already won over to its side the majority of the revolutionary youth in Russia.

*What Is to Be Done?*, pp. 31–32

## Class, Politics, and the State

### *The State as the Product of the Irreconcilability of Class Antagonisms*

What is now happening to Marx's doctrine has, in the course of history, often happened to the doctrines of other revolutionary thinkers and leaders of oppressed classes struggling for emancipation. During the lifetime of great revolutionaries, the oppressing classes have visited relentless persecution on them and received their teaching with the most savage hostility, the most furious hatred, the most ruthless campaign of lies and slanders. After their death, attempts are made to turn them into harmless icons, canonise them, and surround their *names* with a certain halo for the "consolation" of the oppressed classes and with the object of duping them, while at the same time emasculating and vulgarising the *real essence* of their revolutionary theories and blunting their revolutionary edge. At the present time, the bourgeoisie and the opportunists within the labour movement are co-operating in this work of adulterating Marxism. They omit, obliterate, and distort the revolutionary side of its teaching, its revolutionary soul. They push to the foreground and extol what is, or seems, acceptable to the bourgeoisie. All the social-chauvinists are now "Marxists"—joking aside! And more and more do German bourgeois professors, erstwhile specialists in the demolition of Marx, speak now of the "national-German" Marx, who, they aver, has educated the labour unions which are so splendidly organised for conducting the present predatory war!

In such circumstances, the distortion of Marxism being so widespread, it is

---

[1]Trade-unionism does not exclude "politics" altogether, as some imagine. Trade unions have always conducted some political . . . agitation and struggle.

our first task to *resuscitate* the real teachings of Marx on the state. For this purpose it will be necessary to quote at length from the works of Marx and Engels themselves. Of course, long quotations will make the text cumbersome and in no way help to make it popular reading, but we cannot possibly avoid them. All, or at any rate, all the most essential passages in the works of Marx and Engels on the subject of the state must necessarily be given as fully as possible, in order that the reader may form an independent opinion of all the views of the founders of scientific Socialism and of the development of those views, and in order that their distortions by the present predominant "Kautsky-ism"[1] may be proved in black and white and rendered plain to all.

Let us begin with the most popular of Engels' works, *Der Ursprung der Familie, des Privateigentums und des Staats,*[2] the sixth edition of which was published in Stuttgart as far back as 1894. We must translate the quotations from the German originals, as the Russian translations, although very numerous, are for the most part either incomplete or very unsatisfactory.

Summarising his historical analysis Engels says:

The state is therefore by no means a power imposed on society from the outside; just as little is it "the reality of the moral idea," "the image and reality of reason," as Hegel asserted. Rather, it is a product of society at a certain stage of development; it is the admission that this society has become entangled in an insoluble contradiction with itself, that it is cleft into irreconcilable antagonisms which it is powerless to dispel. But in order that these antagonisms, classes with conflicting economic interests, may not consume themselves and society in sterile struggle, a power apparently standing above society becomes necessary, whose purpose is to moderate the conflict and keep it within the bounds of "order"; and this power arising out of society, but placing itself above it, and increasingly separating itself from it, is the state.[3]

Here we have, expressed in all its clearness, the basic idea of Marxism on the question of the historical role and meaning of the state. The state is the product and the manifestation of the *irreconcilability* of class antagonisms. The state arises when, where, and to the extent that the class antagonisms *cannot* be objectively reconciled. And, conversely, the existence of the state proves that the class antagonisms *are* irreconcilable.

It is precisely on this most important and fundamental point that distortions of Marxism arise along two main lines.

On the one hand, the bourgeois, and particularly the petty-bourgeois, ideologists, compelled under the pressure of indisputable historical facts to admit that the state only exists where there are class antagonisms and the class struggle, "correct" Marx in such a way as to make it appear that the state is an organ for *reconciling* the classes. According to Marx, the state could neither arise nor maintain itself if a reconciliation of classes were possible. But with the petty-bourgeois and philistine professors and publicists, the state—and this frequently

---

[1]While Lenin in the earlier part of his career accorded with Kautsky's views, he later became extremely critical of Kautsky—eds.

[2]Friedrich Engels, *The Origin of the Family, Private Property, and the State,* London and New York, 1933—*Ed.*

[3]*Ibid.—Ed.*

on the strength of benevolent references to Marx!—becomes a conciliator of the classes. According to Marx, the state is an organ of class *domination,* an organ of *oppression* of one class by another; its aim is the creation of "order" which legalises and perpetuates this oppression by moderating the collisions between the classes. But in the opinion of the petty-bourgeois politicians, order means reconciliation of the classes, and not oppression of one class by another; to moderate collisions does not mean, they say, to deprive the oppressed classes of certain definite means and methods of struggle for overthrowing the oppressors, but to practice reconciliation.

For instance, when, in the Revolution of 1917, the question of the real meaning and role of the state arose in all its vastness as a practical question demanding immediate action on a wide mass scale, all the Socialist-Revolutionaries and Mensheviks suddenly and completely sank to the petty-bourgeois theory of "reconciliation" of the classes by the "state." Innumerable resolutions and articles by politicians of both these parties are saturated through and through with this purely petty-bourgeois and philistine theory of "reconciliation." That the state is an organ of domination of a definite class which *cannot* be reconciled with its antipode (the class opposed to it)—this petty-bourgeois democracy is never able to understand. Its attitude towards the state is one of the most telling proofs that our Socialist-Revolutionaries and Mensheviks are not Socialists at all (which we Bolsheviks have always maintained), but petty-bourgeois democrats with a near-Socialist phraseology.

On the other hand, the "Kautskyist" distortion of Marx is far more subtle. "Theoretically," there is no denying that the state is the organ of class domination, or that class antagonisms are irreconcilable. But what is forgotten or glossed over is this: if the state is the product of the irreconcilable character of class antagonisms, if it is a force standing *above* society and "increasingly separating itself from it," then it is clear that the liberation of the oppressed class is impossible not only without a violent revolution, *but also without the destruction* of the apparatus of state power, which was created by the ruling class and in which this "separation" is embodied. As we shall see later, Marx drew this theoretically self-evident conclusion from a concrete historical analysis of the problems of revolution. And it is exactly this conclusion which Kautsky—as we shall show fully in our subsequent remarks—has "forgotten" and distorted.

### Special Bodies of Armed Men, Prisons, etc.

Engels continues:

In contrast with the ancient organisation of the *gens,* the first distinguishing characteristic of the state is the grouping of the subjects of the state *on a territorial basis.* . . .

Such a grouping seems "natural" to us, but it came after a prolonged and costly struggle against the old form of tribal or gentilic society.

The second is the establishment of a *public force,* which is no longer absolutely identical with the population organising itself as an armed power. This special public force is necessary, because a self-acting armed organisation of the population has become impossible since the cleavage of society into classes . . . This public force exists in every state; it consists not merely of armed men, but of material appendages, prisons and repressive institutions of all kinds, of which gentilic society knew nothing. . . .[4]

Engels develops the conception of that "power" which is termed the state—a power arising from society, but placing itself above it and becoming more and more separated from it. What does this power mainly consist of? It consists of special bodies of armed men who have at their disposal prisons, etc.

We are justified in speaking of special bodies of armed men, because the public power peculiar to every state is not "absolutely identical" with the armed population, with its "self-acting armed organisation."

Like all the great revolutionary thinkers, Engels tries to draw the attention of the class-conscious workers to that very fact which to prevailing philistinism appears least of all worthy of attention, most common and sanctified by solid, indeed, one might say, petrified prejudices. A standing army and police are the chief instruments of state power. But can this be otherwise?

From the point of view of the vast majority of Europeans at the end of the nineteenth century whom Engels was addressing, and who had neither lived through nor closely observed a single great revolution, this cannot be otherwise. They cannot understand at all what this "self-acting armed organisation of the population" means. To the question, whence arose the need for special bodies of armed men, standing above society and becoming separated from it (police and standing army), the Western European and Russian philistines are inclined to answer with a few phrases borrowed from Spencer or Mikhailovsky, by reference to the complexity of social life, the differentiation of functions, and so forth.

Such a reference seems "scientific" and effectively dulls the senses of the average man, obscuring the most important and basic fact, namely, the break-up of society into irreconcilably antagonistic classes.

Without such a break-up, the "self-acting armed organisation of the population" might have differed from the primitive organisation of a herd of monkeys grasping sticks, or of primitive men, or men united in a tribal form of society, by its complexity, its high technique, and so forth, but would still have been possible.

It is impossible now, because society, in the period of civilisation, is broken up into antagonistic and, indeed, irreconcilably antagonistic classes, which, if armed in a "self-acting" manner, would come into armed struggle with each other. A state is formed, a special power is created in the form of special bodies of armed men, and every revolution, by shattering the state apparatus, demonstrates to us how the ruling class aims at the restoration of the special bodies of armed men at *its* service, and how the oppressed class tries to create a new organisation of this kind, capable of serving not the exploiters, but the exploited.

In the above observation, Engels raises theoretically the very same question which every great revolution raises practically, palpably, and on a mass scale of action, namely, the question of the relation between special bodies of armed men

---

[4] *Ibid.*—*Ed.*

and the "self-acting armed organisation of the population." We shall see how this is concretely illustrated by the experience of the European and Russian revolutions.

But let us return to Engels' discourse.

He points out that sometimes, for instance, here and there in North America, this public power is weak (he has in mind an exception that is rare in capitalist society, and he speaks about parts of North America in its pre-imperialist days, where the free colonist predominated), but that in general it tends to become stronger:

It [the public power] grows stronger, however, in proportion as the class antagonisms within the state grow sharper, and with the growth in size and population of the adjacent states. We have only to look at our present-day Europe, where class struggle and rivalry in conquest have screwed up the public power to such a pitch that it threatens to devour the whole of society and even the state itself.[5]

This was written as early as the beginning of the 'nineties of last century, Engels' last preface being dated June 16, 1891. The turn towards imperialism, understood to mean complete domination of the trusts, full sway of the large banks, and a colonial policy on a grand scale, and so forth, was only just beginning in France, and was even weaker in North America and in Germany. Since then the "rivalry in conquest" has made gigantic progress—especially as, by the beginning of the second decade of the twentieth century, the whole world had been finally divided up between these "rivals in conquest," *i.e.,* between the great predatory powers. Military and naval armaments since then have grown to monstrous proportions, and the predatory war of 1914–1917 for the domination of the world by England or Germany, for the division of the spoils, has brought the "swallowing up" of all the forces of society by the rapacious state power nearer to a complete catastrophe.

As early as 1891 Engels was able to point to "rivalry in conquest" as one of the most important features of the foreign policy of the great powers, but in 1914–1917, when this rivalry, many times intensified, has given birth to an imperialist war, the rascally social-chauvinists cover up their defence of the predatory policy of "their" capitalist classes by phrases about the "defence of the fatherland," or the "defence of the republic and the revolution," etc.!

### The State as an Instrument for the Exploitation of the Oppressed Class

For the maintenance of a special public force standing above society, taxes and state loans are needed.

Having at their disposal the public force and the right to exact taxes, the officials now stand as organs of society *above* society. The free, voluntary respect which was accorded to the organs of the gentilic form of government does not satisfy them, even if they could have it. . . .

Special laws are enacted regarding the sanctity and the inviolability of the officials. "The shabbiest police servant . . . has more authority" than the repre-

---

[5] *Ibid.*—Ed.

sentative of the clan, but even the head of the military power of a civilised state "may well envy the least among the chiefs of the clan the unconstrained and uncontested respect which is paid to him."[6]

Here the question regarding the privileged position of the officials as organs of state power is clearly stated. The main point is indicated as follows: what is it that places them *above* society? We shall see how this theoretical problem was solved in practice by the Paris Commune in 1871 and how it was slurred over in a reactionary manner by Kautsky in 1912.

As the state arose out of the need to hold class antagonisms in check; but as it, at the same time, arose in the midst of the conflict of these classes, it is, as a rule, the state of the most powerful, economically dominant class, which by virtue thereof becomes also the dominant class politically, and thus acquires new means of holding down and exploiting the oppressed class. . . .

Not only the ancient and feudal states were organs of exploitation of the slaves and serfs, but

the modern representative state is the instrument of the exploitation of wage-labour by capital. By way of exception, however, there are periods when the warring classes so nearly attain equilibrium that the state power, ostensibly appearing as a mediator, assumes for the moment a certain independence in relation to both. . . .[7]

Such were, for instance, the absolute monarchies of the seventeenth and eighteenth centuries, the Bonapartism of the First and Second Empires in France, and the Bismarck régime in Germany. . . .

In a democratic republic, Engels continues, "wealth wields its power indirectly, but all the more effectively," first, by means of "direct corruption of the officials" (America); second, by means of "the alliance of the government with the stock exchange" (France and America).

At the present time, imperialism and the domination of the banks have "developed" to an unusually fine art both these methods of defending and asserting the omnipotence of wealth in democratic republics of all descriptions. If, for instance, in the very first months of the Russian democratic republic, one might say during the honeymoon of the union of the "Socialists"—Socialist-Revolutionaries and Mensheviks—with the bourgeoisie, Mr. Palchinsky obstructed every measure in the coalition cabinet, restraining the capitalists and their war profiteering, their plundering of the public treasury by means of army contracts; and if, after his resignation, Mr. Palchinsky (replaced, of course, by an exactly similar Palchinsky) was "rewarded" by the capitalists with a "soft" job carrying a salary of 120,000 rubles per annum, what was this? Direct or indirect bribery? A league of the government with the capitalist syndicates, or "only" friendly relations? What is the role played by the Chernovs, Tseretelis, Avksentyevs and Skobelevs? Are they the "direct" or only the indirect allies of the millionaire treasury looters?

The omnipotence of "wealth" is thus more *secure* in a democratic republic, since it does not depend on the poor political shell of capitalism. A democratic republic is the best possible political shell for capitalism, and therefore, once

---

[6] *Ibid.—Ed.*
[7] *Ibid.—Ed.*

capital has gained control (through the Palchinskys, Chernovs, Tseretelis and Co.) of this very best shell, it establishes its power so securely, so firmly that *no* change, either of persons, or institutions, or parties in the bourgeois republic can shake it.

We must also note that Engels quite definitely regards universal suffrage as a means of bourgeois domination. Universal suffrage, he says, obviously summing up the long experience of German Social-Democracy, is "an index of the maturity of the working class; it cannot, and never will, be anything else but that in the modern state."

The petty-bourgeois democrats, such as our Socialist-Revolutionaries and Mensheviks, and also their twin brothers, the social-chauvinists and opportunists of Western Europe, all expect "more" from universal suffrage. They themselves share, and instil into the minds of the people, the wrong idea that universal suffrage "in the *modern* state" is really capable of expressing the will of the majority of the toilers and of assuring its realisation.

We can here only note this wrong idea, only point out that this perfectly clear, exact and concrete statement by Engels is distorted at every step in the propaganda and agitation of the "official" (*i.e.,* opportunist) Socialist parties. A detailed analysis of all the falseness of this idea, which Engels brushes aside, is given in our further account of the views of Marx and Engels on the "modern" state.

A general summary of his views is given by Engels in the most popular of his works in the following words:

The state, therefore, has not existed from all eternity. There have been societies which managed without it, which had no conception of the state and state power. At a certain stage of economic development, which was necessarily bound up with the cleavage of society into classes, the state became a necessity owing to this cleavage. We are now rapidly approaching a stage in the development of production at which the existence of these classes has not only ceased to be a necessity, but is becoming a positive hindrance to production. They will disappear as inevitably as they arose at an earlier stage. Along with them, the state will inevitably disappear. The society that organises production anew on the basis of a free and equal association of the producers will put the whole state machine where it will then belong: in the museum of antiquities, side by side with the spinning wheel and the bronze axe.[8]

It is not often that we find this passage quoted in the propaganda and agitation literature of contemporary Social-Democracy. But even when we do come across it, it is generally quoted in the same manner as one bows before an icon, *i.e.,* it is done merely to show official respect for Engels, without any attempt to gauge the breadth and depth of revolutionary action presupposed by this relegating of "the whole state machine . . . to the museum of antiquities." In most cases we do not even find an understanding of what Engels calls the state machine.

### The "Withering Away" of the State and Violent Revolution

Engels' words regarding the "withering away" of the state enjoy such popularity, they are so often quoted, and they show so clearly the essence of the usual

---

[8] *Ibid*—Ed.

adulteration by means of which Marxism is made to look like opportunism, that we must dwell on them in detail. Let us quote the whole passage from which they are taken.

The proletariat seizes state power, and then transforms the means of production into state property. But in doing this, it puts an end to itself as the proletariat, it puts an end to all class differences and class antagonisms, it puts an end also to the state as the state. Former society, moving in class antagonisms, had need of the state, that is, an organisation of the exploiting class at each period for the maintenance of its external conditions of production; therefore, in particular, for the forcible holding down of the exploited class in the conditions of oppression (slavery, bondage or serfdom, wage-labour) determined by the existing mode of production. The state was the official representative of society as a whole, its embodiment in a visible corporate body; but it was this only in so far as it was the state of that class which itself, in its epoch, represented society as a whole: in ancient times, the state of the slave-owning citizens; in the Middle Ages, of the feudal nobility; in our epoch, of the bourgeoisie. When ultimately it becomes really representative of society as a whole, it makes itself superfluous. As soon as there is no longer any class of society to be held in subjection; as soon as, along with class domination and the struggle for individual existence based on the former anarchy of production, the collisions and excesses arising from these have also been abolished, there is nothing more to be repressed, and a special repressive force, a state, is no longer necessary. The first act in which the state really comes forward as the representative of society as a whole—the seizure of the means of production in the name of society—is at the same time its last independent act as a state. The interference of a state power in social relations becomes superfluous in one sphere after another, and then becomes dormant of itself. Government over persons is replaced by the administration of things and the direction of the processes of production. The state is not "abolished," *it withers away*. It is from this standpoint that we must appraise the phrase "people's free state"—both its justification at times for agitational purposes, and its ultimate scientific inadequacy—and also the demand of the so-called Anarchists that the state should be abolished overnight.[9]

Without fear of committing an error, it may be said that of this argument by Engels so singularly rich in ideas, only one point has become an integral part of Socialist thought among modern Socialist parties, namely, that, unlike the Anarchist doctrine of the "abolition" of the state, according to Marx the state "withers away." To emasculate Marxism in such a manner is to reduce it to opportunism, for such an "interpretation" only leaves the hazy conception of a slow, even, gradual change, free from leaps and storms, free from revolution. The current popular conception, if one may say so, of the "withering away" of the state undoubtedly means a slurring over, if not a negation, of revolution.

Yet, such an "interpretation" is the crudest distortion of Marxism, which is advantageous only to the bourgeoisie; in point of theory, it is based on a disregard for the most important circumstances and considerations pointed out in the very passage summarising Engels' ideas, which we have just quoted in full.

In the first place, Engels at the very outset of his argument says that, in assuming state power, the proletariat by that very act "puts an end to the state as the state." One is "not accustomed" to reflect on what this really means. Generally, it is either ignored altogether, or it is considered as a piece of "Hegelian weakness" on Engels' part. As a matter of fact, however, these words express succinctly the experience of one of the greatest proletarian revolutions—the

---

[9]Friedrich Engels, *Anti-Dühring*, London and New York, 1933—*Ed.*

Paris Commune of 1871, of which we shall speak in greater detail in its proper place. As a matter of fact, Engels speaks here of the destruction of the bourgeois state by the proletarian revolution, while the words about its withering away refer to the remains of *proletarian* statehood *after* the Socialist revolution. The bourgeois state does not "wither away," according to Engels, but is "put an end to" by the proletariat in the course of the revolution. What withers away after the revolution is the proletarian state or semi-state.

Secondly, the state is a "special repressive force." This splendid and extremely profound definition of Engels' is given by him here with complete lucidity. It follows from this that the "special repressive force" of the bourgeoisie for the suppression of the proletariat, of the millions of workers by a handful of the rich, must be replaced by a "special repressive force" of the proletariat for the suppression of the bourgeoisie (the dictatorship of the proletariat). It is just this that constitutes the destruction of "the state as the state." It is just this that constitutes the "act" of "the seizure of the means of production in the name of society." And it is obvious that such a substitution of one (proletarian) "special repressive force" for another (bourgeois) "special repressive force" can in no way take place in the form of a "withering away."

Thirdly, as to the "withering away" or, more expressively and colourfully, as to the state "becoming dormant," Engels refers quite clearly and definitely to the period *after* "the seizure of the means of production [by the state] in the name of society," that is, *after* the Socialist revolution. We all know that the political form of the "state" at that time is complete democracy. But it never enters the head of any of the opportunists who shamelessly distort Marx that when Engels speaks here of the state "withering away," or "becoming dormant," he speaks of *democracy*. At first sight this seems very strange. But it is "unintelligible" only to one who has not reflected on the fact that democracy is *also* a state and that, consequently, democracy will *also* disappear when the state disappears. The bourgeois state can only be "put an end to" by a revolution. The state in general, *i.e.*, most complete democracy, can only "wither away."

Fourthly, having formulated his famous proposition that "the state withers away," Engels at once explains concretely that this proposition is directed equally against the opportunists and the Anarchists. In doing this, however, Engels puts in the first place that conclusion from his proposition about the "withering away" of the state which is directed against the opportunists.

One can wager that out of every 10,000 persons who have read or heard about the "withering away" of the state, 9,990 do not know at all, or do not remember, that Engels did not direct his conclusions from this proposition against the Anarchists *alone*. And out of the remaining ten, probably nine do not know the meaning of a "people's free state" nor the reason why an attack on this watchword contains an attack on the opportunists. This is how history is written! This is how a great revolutionary doctrine is imperceptibly adulterated and adapted to current philistinism! The conclusion drawn against the Anarchists has been repeated thousands of times, vulgarised, harangued about in the crudest fashion possible until it has acquired the strength of a prejudice, whereas the conclusion drawn against the opportunists has been hushed up and "forgotten"!

The "people's free state" was a demand in the programme of the German

Social-Democrats and their current slogan in the 'seventies. There is no political substance in this slogan other than a pompous middle-class circumlocution of the idea of democracy. In so far as it referred in a lawful manner to a democratic republic, Engels was prepared to "justify" its use "at times" from a propaganda point of view. But this slogan was opportunist, for it not only expressed an exaggerated view of the attractiveness of bourgeois democracy, but also a lack of understanding of the Socialist criticism of every state in general. We are in favour of a democratic republic as the best form of the state for the proletariat under capitalism, but we have no right to forget that wage slavery is the lot of the people even in the most democratic bourgeois republic. Furthermore, every state is a "special repressive force" for the suppression of the oppressed class. Consequently, *no* state is either "free" or a "people's state." Marx and Engels explained this repeatedly to their party comrades in the 'seventies.

Fifthly, in the same work of Engels, from which every one remembers his argument on the "withering away" of the state, there is also a disquisition on the significance of a violent revolution. The historical analysis of its role becomes, with Engels, a veritable panegyric on violent revolution. This, of course, "no one remembers"; to talk or even to think of the importance of this idea is not considered good form by contemporary Socialist parties, and in the daily propaganda and agitation among the masses it plays no part whatever. Yet it is indissolubly bound up with the "withering away" of the state in one harmonious whole.

Here is Engels' argument:

That force, however, plays another role (other than that of a diabolical power) in history, a revolutionary role; that, in the words of Marx, it is the midwife of every old society which is pregnant with the new; that it is the instrument with whose aid social movement forces its way through and shatters the dead, fossilised political forms—of this there is not a word in Herr Dühring. It is only with sighs and groans that he admits the possibility that force will perhaps be necessary for the overthrow of the economic system of exploitation—unfortunately! because all use of force, forsooth, demoralises the person who uses it. And this in spite of the immense moral and spiritual impetus which has resulted from every victorious revolution! And this in Germany, where a violent collision—which indeed may be forced on the people—would at least have the advantage of wiping out the servility which has permeated the national consciousness as a result of the humiliation of the Thirty Years' War. And this parson's mode of thought—lifeless, insipid and impotent—claims to impose itself on the most revolutionary party which history has known.[10]

How can this panegyric on violent revolution, which Engels insistently brought to the attention of the German Social-Democrats between 1878 and 1894, *i.e.,* right to the time of his death, be combined with the theory of the "withering away" of the state to form one doctrine?

Usually the two views are combined by means of eclecticism, by an unprincipled, sophistic, arbitrary selection (to oblige the powers that be) of either one or the other argument, and in ninety-nine cases out of a hundred (if not more often), it is the idea of the "withering away" that is specially emphasised. Eclecticism is substituted for dialectics—this is the most usual, the most widespread

---

[10] *Ibid.*—*Ed.*

phenomenon to be met with in the official Social-Democratic literature of our day in relation to Marxism. Such a substitution is, of course, nothing new; it may be observed even in the history of classic Greek philosophy. When Marxism is adulterated to become opportunism, the substitution of eclecticism for dialectics is the best method of deceiving the masses; it gives an illusory satisfaction; it seems to take into account all sides of the process, all the tendencies of development, all the contradictory factors and so forth, whereas in reality it offers no consistent and revolutionary view of the process of social development at all.

We have already said above and shall show more fully later that the teaching of Marx and Engels regarding the inevitability of a violent revolution refers to the bourgeois state. It *cannot* be replaced by the proletarian state (the dictatorship of the proletariat) through "withering away," but, as a general rule, only through a violent revolution. The panegyric sung in its honour by Engels and fully corresponding to the repeated declarations of Marx (remember the concluding passages of the *Poverty of Philosophy* and the *Communist Manifesto,* with its proud and open declaration of the inevitability of a violent revolution; remember Marx's *Critique of the Gotha Programme* of 1875 in which, almost thirty years later, he mercilessly castigates the opportunist character of that programme)—this praise is by no means a mere "impulse," a mere declamation, or a polemical sally. The necessity of systematically fostering among the masses *this* and just this point of view about violent revolution lies at the root of the *whole* of Marx's and Engels' teaching. The neglect of such propaganda and agitation by both the present predominant social-chauvinist and the Kautskyist currents brings their betrayal of Marx's and Engels' teaching into prominent relief.

The replacement of the bourgeois by the proletarian state is impossible without a violent revolution. The abolition of the proletarian state, *i.e.,* of all states, is only possible through "withering away."

*The State and Revolution,* pp. 7–19

### The Abolition of Classes

And what does the "abolition of classes" mean? All those who call themselves socialists recognize this as the ultimate goal of socialism, but by no means all ponder over its significance. Classes are large groups of people which differ from each other by the place they occupy in a historically determined system of social production, by their relation (in most cases fixed and formulated in law) to the means of production, by their role in the social organization of labour, and, consequently, by the mode of acquisition and the dimensions of the share of social wealth of which they dispose. Classes are groups of people one of which can appropriate the labour of another owing to the different places they occupy in a definite system of social economy.

Clearly, in order to abolish classes completely, it is not enough to overthrow the exploiters, the landlords and capitalists, not enough to abolish *their* rights of ownership; it is necessary also to abolish *all* private ownership of the means of production, it is necessary to abolish the distinction between town and country, as well as the distinction between manual workers and brain workers. This requires a very long period of time. In order to achieve this an enormous step forward must be taken in developing the productive forces; it is necessary to overcome the resistance (frequently passive, which is particularly stubborn and particularly difficult to overcome) of the numerous survivals of small production; it is necessary to overcome the enormous force of habit and conservatism which are connected with these survivals.

The assumption that all "working people" are equally capable of doing this work would be an empty phrase, or the illusion of an antediluvian, pre-Marxist socialist; for this ability does not come of itself, but grows historically, and grows *only* out of the material conditions of large-scale capitalist production. This ability, at the beginning of the road from capitalism to socialism, is possessed by the proletariat *alone*. It is capable of fulfilling the gigantic task that confronts it, first, because it is the strongest and most advanced class in civilized societies; secondly, because in the most developed countries it constitutes the majority of the population, and thirdly, because in backward capitalist countries, like Russia, the majority of the population consists of semi-proletarians, i.e., of people who regularly live in a proletarian way part of the year, who regularly earn a part of their means of subsistence as wage-workers in capitalist enterprises.

Those who try to solve the problems involved in the transition from capitalism to socialism on the basis of general talk about liberty, equality, democracy in general, equality of labour democracy, etc. (as Kautsky, Martov and other heroes of the Berne yellow International do), thereby only reveal their petty-bourgeois, philistine nature and ideologically slavishly follow in the wake of the bourgeoisie. The correct solution of this problem can be acquired only by concrete study of the specific relations between the specific class which has conquered political power, namely, the proletariat, and the whole non-proletarian, and also semi-proletarian, mass of the toiling population—relations which do not take shape in fantastically harmonious, "ideal" conditions, but in the real conditions of the frantic resistance of the bourgeoisie which assumes many and diverse forms.

The vast majority of the population—and all the more so of the toiling population—of any capitalist country, including Russia, have thousands of times experienced, themselves and through their kith and kin, the oppression, the robbery and every sort of outrage and insult perpetrated by capital. The imperialist war, i.e., the slaughter of ten million people in order to decide whether British or German capital was to have supremacy in plundering the whole world, intensified, increased and deepened these ordeals exceedingly, and made the people realize their meaning. Hence the inevitable sympathy displayed by the vast majority of the population, particularly the working masses, for the proletariat, because it is, with heroic courage and revolutionary ruthlessness, overthrowing the yoke of capital, overthrowing the exploiters, suppressing their resistance, and shedding its blood to pave the road for the creation of the new society, in which there will be no room for exploiters.

Great and inevitable as may be their petty-bourgeois waverings and vacillations back to bourgeois "order," under the "wing" of the bourgeoisie, the non-proletarian and semi-proletarian mass of the toiling population cannot but recognize the moral and political authority of the proletariat, which is not only overthrowing the exploiters and suppressing their resistance, but is building a new and higher social bond, a social discipline, the discipline of class-conscious and united working people, who know no yoke and no authority except the authority of their own unity, of their own, more class-conscious, bold, solid, revolutionary and steadfast vanguard.

In order to achieve victory, in order to build and consolidate socialism, the proletariat must fulfill a two-fold or dual task: first, it must, by its supreme heroism in the revolutionary struggle against capital, win over the entire mass of the working and exploited people; it must win them over, organize them and lead them in the struggle to overthrow the bourgeoisie and utterly suppress its resistance, of whatever kind. Secondly, it must lead the whole mass of the working and exploited people, as well as all the petty-bourgeois strata, onto the road of new economic construction, onto the road to the creation of a new social bond, a new labour discipline, a new organization of labour, which will combine the last word in science and capitalist technology with the mass association of class-conscious workers creating large-scale socialist production.

The second task is more difficult than the first, for it cannot possibly be fulfilled by single acts of heroic fervour; it requires the most prolonged, most persistent and most difficult mass heroism in *plain, everyday* work. But this task is more essential than the first, because, in the last analysis, the deepest source of strength for victories over the bourgeoisie and the sole guarantee of the durability and permanence of these victories can only be a new and higher mode of social production, the substitution of large-scale socialist production for capitalist and petty-bourgeois production.

*A Great Beginning*, pp. 13–16

## Sources

V. I. Lenin, *The Development of Capitalism in Russia* (Moscow: Progress Publishers, 1964).

_____, *A Great Beginning* (Peking: Foreign Languages Press, 1977), also in his *Selected Works* (Moscow: Progress Publishers, 1968).

_____, *The State and Revolution* (New York: International Publishers, 1971); also in *Selected Works*.

_____, *What Is to Be Done?* (Moscow: Progress Publishers, 1947).

# Max Weber

Selections from *Economy and Society,* vols. 1 and 2; and
*General Economic History*

### The Distribution of Power: Class, Status, Party

#### *Economically Determined Power and the Status Order*

The structure of every legal order directly influences the distribution of power, economic or otherwise, within its respective community. This is true of all legal orders and not only that of the state. In general, we understand by "power" the chance of a man or a number of men to realize their own will in a social action even against the resistance of others who are participating in the action.

"Economically conditioned" power is not, of course, identical with "power" as such. On the contrary, the emergence of economic power may be the consequence of power existing on other grounds. Man does not strive for power only in order to enrich himself economically. Power, including economic power, may be valued for its own sake. Very frequently the striving for power is also conditioned by the social honor it entails. Not all power, however, entails social honor: The typical American Boss, as well as the typical big speculator, deliberately relinquishes social honor. Quite generally, "mere economic" power, and especially "naked" money power, is by no means a recognized basis of social honor. Nor is power the only basis of social honor. Indeed, social honor, or prestige, may even be the basis of economic power, and very frequently has been. Power, as well as honor, may be guaranteed by the legal order, but, at least normally, it is not their primary source. The legal order is rather an additional factor that enhances the chance to hold power or honor; but it cannot always secure them.

The way in which social honor is distributed in a community between typical groups participating in this distribution we call the "status order." The social order and the economic order are related in a similar manner to the legal order. However, the economic order merely defines the way in which economic goods and services are distributed and used. Of course, the status order is strongly influenced by it, and in turn reacts upon it.

Now: "classes," "status groups," and "parties" are phenomena of the distribution of power within a community.

### Determination of Class Situation by Market Situation

In our terminology, "classes" are not communities; they merely represent possible, and frequent, bases for social action. We may speak of a "class" when (1) a number of people have in common a specific causal component of their life chances, insofar as (2) this component is represented exclusively by economic interests in the possession of goods and opportunities for income, and (3) is represented under the conditions of the commodity or labor markets. This is "class situation."

It is the most elemental economic fact that the way in which the disposition over material property is distributed among a plurality of people, meeting competitively in the market for the purpose of exchange, in itself creates specific life chances. The mode of distribution, in accord with the law of marginal utility, excludes the non-wealthy from competing for highly valued goods; it favors the owners and, in fact, gives to them a monopoly to acquire such goods. Other things being equal, the mode of distribution monopolizes the opportunities for profitable deals for all those who, provided with goods, do not necessarily have to exchange them. It increases, at least generally, their power in the price struggle with those who, being propertyless, have nothing to offer but their labor or the resulting products, and who are compelled to get rid of these products in order to subsist at all. The mode of distribution gives to the propertied a monopoly on the possibility of transferring property from the sphere of use as "wealth" to the sphere of "capital," that is, it gives them the entrepreneurial function and all chances to share directly or indirectly in returns on capital. All this holds true within the area in which pure market conditions prevail. "Property" and "lack of property" are, therefore, the basic categories of all class situations. It does not matter whether these two categories become effective in the competitive struggles of the consumers or of the producers.

Within these categories, however, class situations are further differentiated: on the one hand, according to the kind of property that is usable for returns; and, on the other hand, according to the kind of services that can be offered in the market. Ownership of dwellings; workshops; warehouses; stores; agriculturally usable land in large or small holdings—a quantitative difference with possibly qualitative consequences; ownership of mines; cattle; men (slaves); disposition over mobile instruments of production, or capital goods of all sorts, especially money or objects that can easily be exchanged for money; disposition over products of one's own labor or of others' labor differing according to their various distances from consumability; disposition over transferable monopolies of any kind—all these distinctions differentiate the class situations of the propertied just as does the "meaning" which they can give to the use of property, especially to property which has money equivalence. Accordingly, the propertied, for instance, may belong to the class of rentiers or to the class of entrepreneurs.

Those who have no property but who offer services are differentiated just as much according to their kinds of services as according to the way in which they make use of these services, in a continuous or discontinuous relation to a recipient. But always this is the generic connotation of the concept of class: that the kind of chance in the *market* is the decisive moment which presents a common condition for the individual's fate. Class situation is, in this sense, ultimately market situation. The effect of naked possession *per se,* which among cattle breeders gives the non-owning slave or serf into the power of the cattle owner, is only a fore-runner of real "class" formation. However, in the cattle loan and in the naked severity of the law of debts in such communities for the first time mere "possession" as such emerges as decisive for the fate of the individual; this is much in contrast to crop-raising communities, which are based on labor. The creditor-debtor relation becomes the basis of "class situations" first in the cities, where a "credit market," however primitive, with rates of interest increasing according to the extent of dearth and factual monopolization of lending in the hands of a plutocracy could develop. Therewith "class struggles" begin.

Those men whose fate is not determined by the chance of using goods or services for themselves on the market, e.g., slaves, are not, however, a class in the technical sense of the term. They are, rather, a status group.

### Social Action Flowing from Class Interest

According to our terminology, the factor that creates "class" is unambiguously economic interest, and indeed, only those interests involved in the existence of the market. Nevertheless, the concept of class-interest is an ambiguous one: even as an empirical concept it is ambiguous as soon as one understands by it something other than the factual direction of interests following with a certain probability from the class situation for a certain average of those people subjected to the class situation. The class situation and other circumstances remaining the same, the direction in which the individual worker, for instance, is likely to pursue his interests may vary widely, according to whether he is constitutionally qualified for the task at hand to a high, to an average, or to a low degree. In the same way, the direction of interests may vary according to whether or not social action of a larger or smaller portion of those commonly affected by the class situation, or even an association among them, e.g., a trade union, has grown out of the class situation, from which the individual may expect promising results for himself. The emergence of an association or even of mere social action from a common class situation is by no means a universal phenomenon.

The class situation may be restricted in its efforts to the generation of essentially *similar* reactions, that is to say, within our terminology, of "mass behavior." However, it may not even have this result. Furthermore, often merely amorphous social action emerges. For example, the "grumbling" of workers known in ancient Oriental ethics: the moral disapproval of the work-master's conduct, which in its practical significance was probably equivalent to an increasingly typical phenomenon of precisely the latest industrial development, namely, the slowdown of laborers by virtue of tacit agreement. The degree in which "social action" and possibly associations emerge from the mass behavior of the members of a class is linked to general cultural conditions, especially to those of an intellectual sort. It is also linked to the extent of the contrasts that have already evolved, and is especially linked to the transparency of the connections between the causes and the consequences of the class situation. For however different life chances may be, this fact in itself, according to all experience, by no means gives birth to "class action" (social action by the members of a class). For that, the real conditions and the results of the class situation must be distinctly recognizable. For only then the contrast of life chances can be felt not as an absolutely given fact to be accepted, but as a resultant from either (1) the given distribution of property, or (2) the structure of the concrete economic order. It is only then that people may react against the class structure not only through acts of intermittent and irrational protest, but in the form of rational association. There have been "class situations" of the first category (1), of a specifically naked and transparent sort, in the urban centers of Antiquity and during the Middle Ages; especially then when great fortunes were accumulated by factually monopolized trading in local industrial products or in foodstuffs; furthermore, under certain conditions, in the rural economy of the most diverse periods, when agriculture was increasingly exploited in a profit-making manner. The most important historical example of the second category (2) is the class situation of the modern proletariat.

### Types of Class Struggles

Thus every class may be the carrier of any one of the innumerable possible forms of class action, but this is not necessarily so. In any case, a class does not in itself constitute a group *(Gemeinschaft)*. To treat "class" conceptually as being equivalent to "group" leads to distortion. That men in the same class situation regularly react in mass actions to such tangible situations as economic ones in the direction of those interests that are most adequate to their average number is an important and after all simple fact for the understanding of historical events. However, this fact must not lead to that kind of pseudo-scientific operation with the concepts of class and class interests which is so frequent these days and which has found its most classic expression in the statement of a talented author, that the individual may be in error concerning his interests but that the class is infallible about its interests.

If classes as such are not groups, nevertheless class situations emerge only on the basis of social action. However, social action that brings forth class situations is not basically action among members of the identical class; it is an action among members of different classes. Social actions that directly determine the class situation of the worker and the entrepreneur are: the labor market, the commodities market, and the capitalistic enterprise. But, in its turn, the existence of a capitalistic enterprise presupposes that a very specific kind of social action exists to protect the possession of goods *per se,* and especially the power of individuals to dispose, in principle freely, over the means of production: a certain kind of legal order. Each kind of class situation, and above all when it rests upon the power of property *per se,* will become most clearly efficacious when all other determinants of reciprocal relations are, as far as possible, eliminated in their significance. It is in this way that the use of the power of property in the market obtains its most sovereign importance.

Now status groups hinder the strict carrying through of the sheer market principle. In the present context they are of interest only from this one point of view. Before we briefly consider them, note that not much of a general nature can be said about the more specific kinds of antagonism between classes (in our meaning of the term). The great shift, which has been going on continuously in the past, and up to our times, may be summarized, although at a cost of some precision: the struggle in which class situations are effective has progressively shifted from consumption credit toward, first, competitive struggles in the commodity market and then toward wage disputes on the labor market. The class struggles of Antiquity—to the extent that they were genuine class struggles and not struggles between status groups—were initially carried on by peasants and perhaps also artisans threatened by debt bondage and struggling against urban creditors. For debt bondage is the normal result of the differentiation of wealth in commercial cities, especially in seaport cities. A similar situation has existed among cattle breeders. Debt relationships as such produced class action up to the days of Catilina. Along with this, and with an increase in provision of grain for the city by transporting it from the outside, the struggle over the means of sustenance emerged. It centered in the first place around the provision of bread and determination of the price of bread. It lasted throughout Antiquity and the entire Middle Ages. The propertyless flocked together against those who actually and supposedly were interested in the dearth of bread. This fight spread until it involved all those commodities essential to the way of life and to handicraft production. There were only incipient discussions of wage disputes in Antiquity and in the Middle Ages. But they have been slowly increasing up into modern times. In the earlier periods they were completely secondary to slave rebellions as well as to conflicts in the commodity market.

The propertyless of Antiquity and of the Middle Ages protested against monopolies, pre-emption, forestalling, and the withholding of goods from the market in order to raise prices. Today the central issue is the determination of the price of labor. The transition is represented by the fight for access to the market and for the determination of the price of products. Such fights went on between merchants and workers in the putting-out system of domestic handicraft during the transition to modern times. Since it is quite a general phenomenon we must mention here that the class antagonisms that are conditioned through the market situations are usually most bitter between those who actually and directly participate as opponents in price wars. It is not the rentier, the share-holder, and the banker who suffer the ill will of the worker, but almost exclusively the manufacturer and the business executives who are the direct opponents of workers in wage conflicts. This is so in spite of the fact that it is precisely the cash boxes of the rentier, the share-holder, and the banker into which the more or less un-earned gains flow, rather than into the pockets of the manufacturers or of the business executives. This simple state of affairs has very frequently been decisive for the role the class situation has played in the formation of political parties. For example, it has made possible the varieties of patriarchal socialism and the frequent attempts—formerly, at least—of threatened status groups to form alliances with the proletariat against the bourgeoisie.

### Status Honor

In contrast to classes, *Stände (status groups)* are normally groups. They are, however, often of an amorphous kind. In contrast to the purely economically determined "class situation," we wish to designate as *status situation* every typical component of the life of men that is determined by a specific, positive or nega-tive, social estimation of *honor.* This honor may be connected with any quality shared by a plurality, and, of course, it can be knit to a class situation: class distinctions are linked in the most varied ways with status distinctions. Property as such is not always recognized as a status qualification, but in the long run it is, and with extraordinary regularity. In the subsistence economy of neighborhood associations, it is often simply the richest who is the "chieftain." However, this often is only an honorific preference. For example, in the so-called pure modern democracy, that is, one devoid of any expressly ordered status privileges for individuals, it may be that only the families coming under approximately the same tax class dance with one another. This example is reported of certain smaller Swiss cities. But status honor need not necessarily be linked with a class situation. On the contrary, it normally stands in sharp opposition to the preten-sions of sheer property.

Both propertied and propertyless people can belong to the same status group, and frequently they do with very tangible consequences. This equality of social esteem may, however, in the long run become quite precarious. The equality of status among American gentlemen, for instance, is expressed by the fact that outside the subordination determined by the different functions of business, it would be considered strictly repugnant—wherever the old tradition still prevails—if even the richest boss, while playing billiards or cards in his club would not treat his clerk as in every sense fully his equal in birthright, but would bestow upon him the condescending status-conscious "benevolence" which the German boss can never dissever from his attitude. This is one of the most important reasons why in America the German clubs have never been able to attain the attraction that the American clubs have.

In content, status honor is normally expressed by the fact that above all else a specific *style of life* is expected from all those who wish to belong to the circle. Linked with this expectation are restrictions on social intercourse (that is, inter-course which is not subservient to economic or any other purposes). These restrictions may confine normal marriages to within the status circle and may lead to complete endogamous closure. Whenever this is not a mere individual and socially irrelevant imitation of another style of life, but consensual action of this closing character, the status development is under way. . . .

## Ethnic Segregation and Caste

Where the consequences have been realized to their full extent, the status group evolves into a closed caste. Status distinctions are then guaranteed not merely by conventions and laws, but also by religious sanctions. This occurs in such a way that every physical contact with a member of any caste that is considered to be lower by the members of a higher caste is considered as making for a ritualistic impurity and a stigma which must be expiated by a religious act. In addition, individual castes develop quite distinct cults and gods.

In general, however, the status structure reaches such extreme consequences only where there are underlying differences which are held to be "ethnic." The caste is, indeed, the normal form in which ethnic communities that believe in blood relationship and exclude exogamous marriage and social intercourse usually associate with one another. As mentioned before [ch. VI:$vi$:6], such a caste situation is part of the phenomenon of pariah peoples and is found all over the world. These people form communities, acquire specific occupational traditions of handicrafts or of other arts, and cultivate a belief in their ethnic community. They live in a diaspora strictly segregated from all personal intercourse, except that of an unavoidable sort, and their situation is legally precarious. Yet, by virtue of their economic indispensability, they are tolerated, indeed frequently privileged, and they live interspersed in the political communities. The Jews are the most impressive historical example.

A status segregation grown into a caste differs in its structure from a mere ethnic segregation: the caste structure transforms the horizontal and unconnected coexistences of ethnically segregated groups into a vertical social system of super- and subordination. Correctly formulated: a comprehensive association integrates the ethnically divided communities into one political unit. They differ precisely in this way: ethnic coexistence, based on mutual repulsion and disdain, allows each ethnic community to consider its own honor as the highest one; the caste structure brings about a social subordination and an acknowledgement of "more honor" in favor of the privileged caste and status groups. This is due to the fact that in the caste structure ethnic distinctions as such have become "functional" distinctions within the political association (warriors, priests, artisans that are politically important for war and for building, and so on). But even pariah peoples who are most despised (for example, the Jews) are usually apt to continue cultivating the belief in their own specific "honor," a belief that is equally peculiar to ethnic and to status groups. . . .

## Economic Conditions and Effects of Status Stratification

. . . We have seen above that the market and its processes knows no personal distinctions: "functional" interests dominate it. It knows nothing of honor. The status order means precisely the reverse: stratification in terms of honor and styles of life peculiar to status groups as such. The status order would be threatened at its very root if mere economic acquisition and naked economic power still bearing the stigma of its extra-status origin could bestow upon anyone who has won them the same or even greater honor as the vested interests claim for themselves. After all, given equality of status honor, property *per se* represents an addition even if it is not overtly acknowledged to be such. Therefore all groups having interest in the status order react with special sharpness precisely against the pretensions of purely economic acquisition. In most cases they react the more vigorously the more they feel themselves threatened. Calderon's respectful treatment of the peasant, for instance, as opposed to Shakespeare's simultaneous ostensible disdain of the *canaille* illustrates the different way in which a firmly structured status order reacts as compared with a status order that has become economically precarious. This is an example of a state of affairs that recurs everywhere. Precisely because of the rigorous reactions against the claims of property *per se*, the "parvenu" is never accepted, personally and without reservation, by the privileged status groups, no matter how completely his style of life has been adjusted to theirs. They will only accept his descendants who have been educated in the conventions of their status group and who have never besmirched its honor by their own economic labor.

As to the general *effect* of the status order, only one consequence can be stated, but it is a very important one: the hindrance of the free development of the market. This occurs first for those goods that status groups directly withhold from free exchange by monopolization, which may be effected either legally or conventionally. For example, in many Hellenic cities during the "status era" and also originally in Rome, the inherited estate (as shown by the old formula for placing spendthrifts under a guardian) was monopolized, as were the estates of knights, peasants, priests, and especially the clientele of the craft and merchant guilds. The market is restricted, and the power of naked property *per se,* which gives its stamp to class formation, is pushed into the background. The results of this process can be most varied. Of course, they do not necessarily weaken the contrasts in the economic situation. Frequently they strengthen these contrasts, and in any case, where stratification by status permeates a community as strongly as was the case in all political communities of Antiquity and of the Middle Ages, one can never speak of a genuinely free market competition as we understand it today. There are wider effects than this direct exclusion of special goods from the market. From the conflict between the status order and the purely economic order mentioned above, it follows that in most instances the notion of honor peculiar to status absolutely abhors that which is essential to the market: hard bargaining. Honor abhors hard bargaining among peers and occasionally it taboos it for the members of a status group in general. Therefore, everywhere some status groups, and usually the most influential, consider almost any kind of overt participation in economic acquisition as absolutely stigmatizing.

With some over-simplification, one might thus say that classes are stratified according to their relations to the production and acquisition of goods; whereas status groups are stratified according to the principles of their *consumption* of goods as represented by special styles of life. . . .

As to the general economic conditions making for the predominance of stratification by status, only the following can be said. When the bases of the acquisition and distribution of goods are relatively stable, stratification by status is favored. Every technological repercussion and economic transformation threatens stratification by status and pushes the class situation into the foreground. Epochs and countries in which the naked class situation is of predominant significance are regularly the periods of technical and economic transformations. And every slowing down of the change in economic stratification leads, in due course, to the growth of status structures and makes for a resuscitation of the important role of social honor.

## Parties

Whereas the genuine place of classes is within the economic order, the place of status groups is within the social order, that is, within the sphere of the distribution of honor. From within these spheres, classes and status groups influence one another and the legal order and are in turn influenced by it. *"Parties"* reside in the sphere of power. Their action is oriented toward the acquisition of social power, that is to say, toward influencing social action no matter what its content may be. In principle, parties may exist in a social club as well as in a state. As over against the actions of classes and status groups, for which this is not necessarily the case, party-oriented social action always involves association. For it is always directed toward a goal which is striven for in a planned manner. This goal may be a cause (the party may aim at realizing a program for ideal or material purposes), or the goal may be personal (sinecures, power, and from these, honor for the leader and the followers of the party). Usually the party aims at all these simultaneously. Parties are, therefore, only possible within groups that have an associational character, that is, some rational order and a staff of persons available who are ready to enforce it. For parties aim precisely at influencing this staff, and if possible, to recruit from it party members.

In any individual case, parties may represent interests determined through class situation or status situation, and they may recruit their following respectively from one or the other. But they need be neither purely class nor purely status parties; in fact, they are more likely to be mixed types, and sometimes they are neither. They may represent ephemeral or enduring structures. Their means of attaining power may be quite varied, ranging from naked violence of any sort to canvassing for votes with coarse or subtle means: money, social influence, the force of speech, suggestion, clumsy hoax, and so on to the rougher or more artful tactics of obstruction in parliamentary bodies.

The sociological structure of parties differs in a basic way according to the kind of social action which they struggle to influence; that means, they differ according to whether or not the community is stratified by status or by classes. Above all else, they vary according to the structure of domination. For their leaders normally deal with its conquest. In our general terminology, parties are not only products of modern forms of domination. We shall also designate as parties the ancient and medieval ones, despite the fact that they differ basically from modern parties. Since a party always struggles for political control *(Herrschaft)*, its organization too is frequently strict and "authoritarian." Because of these variations between the forms of domination, it is impossible to say anything about the structure of parties without discussing them first. Therefore, we shall now turn to this central phenomenon of all social organization.

Before we do this, we should add one more general observation about classes, status groups and parties. The fact that they presuppose a larger association, especially the framework of a polity, does not mean that they are confined to it. On the contrary, at all times it has been the order of the day that such association (even when it aims at the use of military force in common) reaches beyond the state boundaries. This can be seen in the [interlocal] solidarity of interests of oligarchs and democrats in Hellas, of Guelphs and Ghibellines in the Middle Ages, and within the Calvinist party during the age of religious struggles; and all the way up to the solidarity of landlords (International Congresses of Agriculture), princes (Holy Alliance, Karlsbad Decrees [of 1819]), socialist workers, conservatives (the longing of Prussian conservatives for Russian intervention in 1850). But their aim is not necessarily the establishment of a new territorial dominion. In the main they aim to influence the existing polity.

'Class, Status, and Party', *Economy and Society,* vol. 2, pp. 926–40

## Status Groups and Classes

### Class Situation and Class Types

"Class situation" means the typical probability of

1. procuring goods
2. gaining a position in life and
3. finding inner satisfactions,

a probability which derives from the relative control over goods and skills and from their income-producing uses within a given economic order.

"Class" means all persons in the same class situation.

a) A "*property* class" is primarily determined by property differences,

b) A "*commercial* class" by the marketability of goods and services,

c) A "*social* class" makes up the totality of those class situations within which individual and generational mobility is easy and typical.

Associations of class members—class organizations—may arise on the basis of all three types of classes. However, this does not necessarily happen: "Class situation" and "class" refer only to the same (or similar) interests which an individual shares with others. In principle, the various controls over consumer goods, means of production, assets, resources and skills each constitute a *particular* class situation. A *uniform* class situation prevails only when completely unskilled and propertyless persons are dependent on irregular employment. Mobility among, and stability of, class positions differs greatly; hence, the unity of a social class is highly variable.

### Property Classes

The primary significance of a positively privileged property class lies in

$\alpha$) its exclusive acquisition of high-priced consumers goods, β) its sales monopoly and its ability to pursue systematic policies in this regard,

γ) its monopolization of wealth accumulation out of unconsumed surpluses,

δ) its monopolization of capital formation out of savings, i.e., of the utilization of wealth in the form of loan capital, and its resulting control over executive positions in business,

ε) its monopolization of costly (educational) status privileges.

I. Positively privileged property classes are typically *rentiers,* receiving income from:

   a) men (the case of slave-owners),

   b) land,

   c) mines,

   d) installations (factories and equipment),

   e) ships,

   f) creditors (of livestock, grain or money),

   g) securities.

II. Negatively privileged property classes are typically

   a) the unfree (see under "Status Group"),

   b) the declassed (the *proletarii* of Antiquity),

   c) debtors,

   d) the "paupers".

In between are the various "middle classes" *(Mittelstandsklassen),* which make a living from their property or their acquired skills. Some of them may be "commercial classes" (entrepreneurs with mainly positive privileges, proletarians with negative ones). However, not all of them fall into the latter category (witness peasants, craftsmen, officials).

The mere differentiation of property classes is not "dynamic," that is, it need not result in class struggles and revolutions. The strongly privileged class of slave owners may coexist with the much less privileged peasants or even the declassed, frequently without any class antagonism and sometimes in solidarity (against the unfree). However, the juxtaposition of property classes *may* lead to revolutionary conflict between

1. land owners and the declassed or

2. creditor and debtors (often urban patricians versus rural peasants or small urban craftsmen).

These struggles need not focus on a change of the economic system, but may aim primarily at a redistribution of wealth. In this case we can speak of "property revolutions" *(Besitzklassenrevolutionen).*

A classic example of the lack of class conflict was the relationship of the "poor white trash" to the plantation owners in the Southern States. The "poor white trash" were far more anti-Negro than the plantation owners, who were often imbued with patriarchal sentiments. The major examples for the struggle of the declassed against the propertied date back to Antiquity, as does the antagonism between creditors and debtors and land owners and the declassed.

## Commercial Classes

The primary significance of a positively privileged commercial class lies in

α) the monopolization of entrepreneurial management for the sake of its members and their business interests,

β) the safeguarding of those interests through influence on the economic policy of the political and other organizations.

  I. Positively privileged commercial classes are typically *entrepreneurs:*

    a) merchants,

    b) shipowners,

    c) industrial and

    d) agricultural entrepreneurs,

    e) bankers and financiers, *sometimes* also

    f) professionals with sought-after expertise or privileged education (such as lawyers, physicians, artists), or

    g) workers with monopolistic qualifications and skills (natural, or acquired through drill or training).

  II. Negatively privileged commercial classes are typically *laborers* with varying qualifications:

    a) skilled

    b) semi-skilled

    c) unskilled.

In between again are "middle classes": the self-employed farmers and craftsmen and frequently:

  a) public and private officials

  b) the last two groups mentioned in the first category [i.e., the "liberal professions" and the labor groups with exceptional qualifications].

## Social Classes

Social classes are

  a) the working class as a whole—the more so, the more automated the work process becomes,

  b) the petty bourgeoisie,

  c) the propertyless intelligentsia and specialists (technicians, various kinds of white-collar employees, civil servants—possibly with considerable social differences depending on the cost of their training),

d)  the classes privileged through property and education.

The unfinished last part of Karl Marx's *Capital* apparently was intended to deal with the issue of class unity in the face of skill differentials. Crucial for this differentiation is the increasing importance of semi-skilled workers, who can be trained on the job in a relatively short time, over the apprenticed and sometimes also the unskilled workers. Semi-skilled qualification too can often become monopolistic (weavers, for example, sometimes achieve their greatest efficiency after five years). It used to be that every worker aspired to be a self-employed small businessman. However, this is less and less feasible. In the generational sequence, the rise of groups a) and b) into c) (technicians, white-collar workers) is relatively the easiest. Within class d) money increasingly buys *everything,* at least in the sequence of generations. In banks and corporations, as well as in the higher ranks of the civil service, class c) members have a chance to move up into class d).

Class-conscious organization succeeds most easily

a)  against the immediate economic opponents (workers against entre-preneurs, but *not* against stockholders, who truly draw "unearned" incomes, and also *not* in the case of peasants confronting manorial lords);

b)  if large numbers of persons are in the same class situation,

c)  if it is technically easy to organize them, especially if they are con-centrated at their place of work (as in a "workshop community"),

d)  if they are led toward readily understood goals, which are imposed and interpreted by men outside their class (intelligentsia).

### Status and Status Group (Stand)

"Status" *(ständische Lage)* shall mean an effective claim to social esteem in terms of positive or negative privileges; it is typically founded on

a)  style of life, hence

b)  formal education, which may be

  α)  empirical training or

  β)  rational instruction, and the corresponding forms of behavior,

c)  hereditary or occupational prestige.

In practice, status expresses itself through

  α)  connubium,

  β)  commensality, possibly

  γ)  monopolistic appropriation of privileged modes of acquisition or the abhorrence of certain kinds of acquisition,

  δ)  status conventions (traditions) of other kinds.

Status *may* rest on class position of a distinct or an ambiguous kind. However, it is not solely determined by it: Money and an entrepreneurial position are not in themselves status qualifications, although they may lead to them; and the lack of property is not in itself a status disqualification, although this may be a reason for it. Conversely, status may influence, if not completely determine, a class position without being identical with it. The class position of an officer, a civil servant or a student may vary greatly according to their wealth and yet not lead to a different status since upbringing and education create a common style of life.

A "status group" means a plurality of persons who, within a larger group, successfully claim

a) a special social esteem, and possibly also

b) status monopolies.

Status groups may come into being:

a) in the first instance, by virtue of their own style of life, particularly the type of vocation: "self-styled" or occupational status groups,

b) in the second instance, through hereditary charisma, by virtue of successful claims to higher-ranking descent: hereditary status groups, or

c) through monopolistic appropriation of political or hierocratic powers: political or hierocratic status groups.

The development of hereditary status groups is generally a form of the (hereditary) appropriation of privileges by an organization or qualified individuals. Every definite appropriation of political powers and the corresponding economic opportunities tends to result in the rise of status groups, and vice-versa.

Commercial classes arise in a market-oriented economy, but status groups arise within the framework of organizations which satisfy their wants through monopolistic liturgies, or in feudal or in *ständisch*-patrimonial fashion. Depending on the prevailing mode of stratification, we shall speak of a "status society" or a "class society." The status group comes closest to the social class and is most unlike the commercial class. Status groups are often created by property classes.

Every status society lives by conventions, which regulate the style of life, and hence creates economically irrational consumption patterns and fetters the free market through monopolistic appropriations and by curbing the individual's earning power. More on that separately.

*Economy and Society*, vol. 1, pp. 302 07

## The Expropriation of Workers from the Means of Production

The expropriation of the individual worker from ownership of the means of production is determined by purely *technical* factors in the following cases: (a) if the means of production require the services of many workers, at the same time or successively; (b) if sources of power can be rationally exploited only by using them simultaneously for many similar types of work under a unified control; (c) if a technically rational organization of the work process is possible only by combining many complementary processes under continuous common super-vision; (d) if special technical training is needed for the management of co-ordinated processes of labor which, in turn, can only be exploited rationally on a large scale; (e) if unified control over the means of production and raw materials creates the possibility of subjecting labor to a stringent discipline and hence of controlling the speed of work and of attaining standardization of effort and of product quality.

These factors, however, do not exclude the possibility of appropriation by an organized group of workers, a producers' co-operative. They necessitate only the separation of the *individual* worker from the means of production.

The expropriation of workers *in general,* including clerical personnel and technically trained persons, from possession of the means of production has its *economic* reasons above all in the following factors: (a) The fact that, other things being equal, it is generally possible to achieve a higher level of economic ration-ality if the management has extensive control over the selection and the modes of use of workers, as compared with the situation created by the appropriation of jobs or the existence of rights to participate in management. These latter conditions produce technically irrational obstacles as well as economic irration-alities. In particular, considerations appropriate to small-scale budgetary admin-istration and the interests of workers in the maintenance of jobs ("livings") are often in conflict with the rationality of the organization. (b) In a market econ-omy a management which is not hampered by any established rights of the workers, and which enjoys unrestricted control over the goods and equipment which underlie its borrowings, is of superior credit-worthiness. This is particu-larly true if the management consists of individuals experienced in business affairs and with a good reputation for "safety" derived from their continuous conduct of business. (c) From a historical point of view, the expropriation of labor has arisen since the sixteenth century in an economy characterized by the progressive extensive and intensive expansion of the market system on the one hand, because of the sheer superiority and actual indispensability of a type of management oriented to the particular market situations, and on the other because of the structure of power relationships in the society.

In addition to these general conditions, the effect of the fact that enterprise has been oriented to the exploitation of market advantages has in the following ways favored such expropriation: (a) because it put a premium on capital ac-counting—which can be effected in the technically most rational manner only with full appropriation of capital goods to the owner—as against any type of economic behavior with less rational accounting procedures; (b) because it put a premium on the purely commercial qualities of the management, as opposed to the technical ones, and on the maintenance of technical and commercial secrets; (c) because it favored a speculative business policy, which again requires expro-priation. Further, and in the last analysis quite regardless of the degree of techni-cal rationality, this expropriation is made possible, (d) by the sheer bargaining superiority which in the labor market any kind of property ownership grants vis-à-vis the workers, and which in the commodity markets accrues to any business organization working with capital accounting, owned capital equipment and borrowed funds vis-à-vis any type of competitor operating on a lower level of rationality in methods of calculation or less well situated with respect to capital and credit resources. The fact that the maximum of *formal* rationality in capital accounting is possible only where the workers are subjected to domination by entrepreneurs, is a further specific element of *substantive* irrationality in the modern economic order. Finally, (e), a further economic reason for this expropriation is that free labor and the complete appropriation of the means of production create the most favorable conditions for discipline. . . .

The expropriation of *all* the workers from the means of production may in practice take the following forms: (1) Management is in the hands of the administrative staff of an organization. This would be true very particularly also of any rationally organized socialist economy, which would retain the expropriation of all workers and merely bring it to completion by the expropriation of the private owners. (2) Managerial functions are, by virtue of their appropriation of the means of production, exercised by the owners or by persons they appoint. The appropriation of control over the persons exercising managerial authority by the interests of ownership may have the following forms: (a) Management by one or more entrepreneurs who are at the same time owners—the immediate appropriation of entrepreneurial functions. This situation, however, does not exclude the possibility that a wide degree of control over the policies of management may rest in hands outside the enterprise, by virtue of their powers over credit or financing—for instance, the bankers or financiers who finance the enterprise; (b) separation of managerial functions from appropriated ownership, especially through limitations of the functions of owners to the appointment of management and through shared free (that is, alienable) appropriation of the enterprise as expressed by shares of the nominal capital (stocks, mining shares). This state, which is related to the purely personal form of appropriation through various types of intermediate forms, is rational in the *formal* sense in that it permits, in contrast to the case of permanent and hereditary appropriation of the management itself of accidentally inherited properties, the selection for managerial posts of the persons best qualified from the point of view of profitability. But in practice it may mean a number of things, such as: that control over the managerial position may come, through appropriation, into the hands of "outside interests" representing the resources of a budgetary unit, or mere wealth *(Vermögen)*, and seeking above all a high rate of income; or that control over the managerial position comes, through temporary stock acquisitions, into the hands of speculative "outside interests" seeking gains only through the resale of their shares; or that disposition over the managerial position comes into the hands of outside business interests, by virtue of power over markets or over credit, such as banks or "financiers," which may pursue their own business interests, often foreign to those of the organization as such.

We call "outside interests" those which are not primarily oriented to the long-run profitability of the enterprise. This may be true of any kind of budgetary "wealth" interests. It is particularly true, however, of interests which consider their control over the plant and capital goods of the enterprise or of a share in it not as a permanent investment, but as a means of making a purely short-run

speculative profit. The types of outside interest which are most readily reconciled with those of the enterprise—that is, its interests in present *and* long-run
profitability—are those seeking only income *(rentiers)*.

The fact that such "outside" interests can affect the mode of control over
managerial positions, even and especially when the highest degree of *formal*
rationality in their selection is attained, constitutes a further element of *substantive* irrationality specific to the modern economic order. These might be entirely
private "wealth" interests, or business interests which are oriented to ends
having no connection whatsoever with the organization, or finally, pure gambling interest. By gaining control of shares, all of these can control the appointment of the managing personnel and, more important, the business policies
imposed on this management. The influence exercised by speculative interests
outside the producing organizations themselves on the market situation, especially that for capital goods, and thus on the orientation of the production of
goods, is *one* of the sources of the phenomena known as the "crises" of the
modern market economy.

*Economy and Society,* vol. 1, pp. 137–40

## Power and Bureaucracy

### *The Political Irrelevance of Functional Indispensability*

The democratization of society in its totality, and in the *modern* sense of the term,
whether actual or perhaps merely formal, is an especially favorable basis of
bureaucratization, but by no means the only possible one. After all, bureaucracy
has merely the [limited] striving to level those powers that stand in its way in
those concrete areas that, in the individual case, it seeks to occupy. We must
remember the fact which we have encountered several times and which we shall
have to discuss repeatedly: that "democracy" as such is opposed to the "rule" of
bureaucracy, in spite and perhaps because of its unavoidable yet unintended
promotion of bureaucratization. Under certain conditions, democracy creates
palpable breaks in the bureauratic pattern and impediments to bureaucratic
organization. Hence, one must in every individual historical case analyze in
which of the special directions bureaucratization has there developed.

For this reason, it must also remain an open question whether the *power* of
bureaucracy is increasing in the modern states in which it is spreading. The fact
that bureaucratic organization is technically the most highly developed power
instrument in the hands of its controller does not determine the weight that
bureaucracy as such is capable of procuring for its own opinions in a particular
social structure. The ever-increasing "indispensability" of the officialdom,
swollen to the millions, is no more decisive on this point than is the economic
indispensability of the proletarians for the strength of the social and political
power position of that class (a view which some representatives of the proletarian movement hold). If "indispensability" were decisive, the equally "indispensable" slaves ought to have held this position of power in any economy where
slave labor prevailed and consequently freemen, as is the rule, shunned work as
degrading. Whether the power of bureaucracy as such increases cannot be

decided *a priori* from such reasons. The drawing in of economic interest groups or other non-official experts, or the drawing in of lay representatives, the establishment of local, interlocal, or central parliamentary or other representative bodies, or of occupational associations—these *seem* to run directly against the bureaucratic tendency. How far this appearance is the truth must be discussed in another chapter, rather than in the framework of this purely formal and typological *(kasuistisch)* discussion. In general, only the following can be said here:

The power position of a fully developed bureaucracy is always great, under normal conditions overtowering. The political "master" always finds himself, vis-à-vis the trained official, in the position of a dilettante facing the expert. This holds whether the "master," whom the bureaucracy serves, is the "people" equipped with the weapons of legislative initiative, referendum, and the right to remove officials; or a parliament elected on a more aristocratic or more democratic basis and equipped with the right or the *de facto* power to vote a lack of confidence; or an aristocratic collegiate body, legally or actually based on self-recruitment; or a popularly elected president or an "absolute" or "constitutional" hereditary monarch.

*Economy and Society,* vol. 2, pp. 990–92

## Open and Closed Social Relationships

A social relationship, regardless of whether it is communal or associative in character, will be spoken of as "open" to outsiders if and insofar as its system of order does not deny participation to anyone who wishes to join and is actually in a position to do so. A relationship will, on the other hand, be called "closed" against outsiders so far as, according to its subjective meaning and its binding rules, participation of certain persons is excluded, limited, or subjected to conditions. Whether a relationship is open or closed may be determined traditionally, affectually, or rationally in terms of values or of expediency. It is especially likely to be closed, for rational reasons, in the following type of situation: a social relationship may provide the parties to it with opportunities for the satisfaction of spiritual or material interests, whether absolutely or instrumentally, or whether it is achieved through co-operative action or by a compromise of interests. If the participants expect that the admission of others will lead to an improvement of their situation, an improvement in degree, in kind, in the security or the value of the satisfaction, their interest will be in keeping the relationship open. If, on the other hand, their expectations are of improving their position by monopolistic tactics, their interest is in a closed relationship.

There are various ways in which it is possible for a closed social relationship to guarantee its monopolized advantages to the parties. (a) Such advantages may be left free to competitive struggle within the group; (b) they may be regulated or rationed in amount and kind, or (c) they may be appropriated by individuals or sub-groups on a permanent basis and become more or less inalienable. The last is a case of closure within, as well as against outsiders. Appropriated advantages will be called "rights." As determined by the relevant order, appropriation may be (1) for the benefit of the members of particular communal or associative groups (for instance, household groups), or (2) for the benefit of individuals. In the latter case, the individual may enjoy his rights on a purely personal basis or in such a way that in case of his death one or more other persons related to the holder of the right by birth (kinship), or by some other social relationship, may inherit the rights in question. Or the rights may pass to one or more individuals specifically designated by the holder. These are cases of hereditary appropriation. Finally, (3) it may be that the holder is more or less fully empowered to alienate his rights by voluntary agreement, either to other specific persons or to anyone he chooses. This is alienable appropriation. A party to a closed social relationship will be called a "member"; in case his participation is regulated in such a way as to guarantee him appropriated advantages, a privileged member *(Rechtsgenosse)*. Appropriated rights which are enjoyed by individuals through inheritance or by hereditary groups, whether communal or associative, will be called the "property" of the individual or of groups in question; and, insofar as they are alienable, "free" property.

The apparently gratuitous tediousness involved in the elaborate definition of the above concepts is an example of the fact that we often neglect to think out clearly what seems to be obvious, because it is intuitively familiar.

1. (a) Examples of communal relationships, which tend to be closed on a traditional basis, are those in which membership is determined by family relationship.

   (b) Personal emotional relationships are usually affectually closed. Examples are erotic relationships and, very commonly, relations of personal loyalty.

   (c) Closure on the basis of value-rational commitment to values is usual in groups sharing a common system of explicit religious belief.

   (d) Typical cases of rational closure on grounds of expediency are economic associations of a monopolistic or a plutocratic character.

   A few examples may be taken at random. Whether a group of people engaged in conversation is open or closed depends on its content. General conversation is apt to be open, as contrasted with intimate conversation or the imparting of official information. Market relationships are in most, or at least in many, cases essentially open. In the case of many relationships, both communal and associative, there is a tendency to shift from a phase of expansion to one of exclusiveness. Examples are the guilds and the democratic city-states of Antiquity and the Middle Ages. At times these groups sought to increase their membership in the interest of improving the security of their position of power by adequate numbers. At other times they restricted their membership to protect the value of their monopolistic position. The same phenomenon is not uncommon in monastic orders and religious sects which have passed from a stage of religious proselytizing to one of restriction in the interest of the maintenance of an ethical standard or for the protection of material interests. There is a similar close relationship between the extension of market relationships in the interest of increased turnover on the one hand, their monopolistic restriction on the other. The promotion of linguistic uniformity is today a natural result of the interests of publishers and writers, as opposed to the earlier, not uncommon, tendency for status groups to maintain linguistic peculiarities or even for secret languages to emerge.

2. Both the extent and the methods of regulation and exclusion in relation to outsiders may vary widely, so that the transition from a state of openness to one of regulation and closure is gradual. Various conditions of participation may be laid down; qualifying tests, a period of probation, requirement of possession of a share which can be purchased under certain conditions, election of new members by ballot, membership or eligibility by birth or by virtue of achievements open to anyone. Finally, in case of closure and the appropriation of rights within the group, participation may be dependent on the acquisition of an appropriated right. There is a wide variety of different degrees of closure and of conditions of participation. Thus regulation and closure are relative concepts. There are all manner of gradual shadings as between an exclusive club, a theatrical audience the members of which have purchased tickets, and a party rally to which the largest possible number has been urged to come; similarly, from a church service open to the general public through the rituals of a limited sect to the mysteries of a secret cult.

3. Similarly, closure within the group may also assume the most varied forms. Thus a caste, a guild, or a group of stock exchange brokers, which is closed to outsiders, may allow to its members a perfectly free competition for all the advantages which the group as a whole monopolizes for itself. Or it may assign every member strictly to the enjoyment of certain advantages, such as claims over customers or particular business opportunities, for life or even on a hereditary basis. This is particularly characteristic of India. Similarly, a closed group of settlers *(Markgenossenschaft)* may allow its members free use of the resources of its area or may restrict them rigidly to a plot assigned to each individual household. A closed group of colonists may allow free use of the land or sanction and guarantee permanent appropriation of separate holdings. In such cases all conceivable transitional and intermediate forms can be found. Historically, the closure of eligibility to fiefs, benefices, and offices within the group, and the appropriation on the part of those enjoying them, have occurred in the most varied forms. Similarly, the establishment of rights to and possession of particular jobs on the part of workers may develop all the way from the "closed shop" to a right to a particular job. The first step in this development may be to prohibit

the dismissal of a worker without the consent of the workers' representatives. The development of the "works councils" [in Germany after 1918] might be a first step in this direction, though it need not be. . . .

The most extreme form of permanent appropriation is found in cases where particular rights are guaranteed to an individual or to certain groups of them, such as households, clans, families, in such a way that it is specified in the order either that, in case of death, the rights descend to specific heirs, or that the possessor is free to transfer them to any other person at will. Such a person thereby becomes a party to the social relationship so that, when appropriation has reached this extreme within the group, it becomes to that extent an open group in relation to outsiders. This is true so long as acquisition of membership is not subject to the ratification of the other, prior members.

4. The principal motives for closure of a relationship are: (a) The maintenance of quality, which is often combined with the interest in prestige and the consequent opportunities to enjoy honor, and even profit; examples are communities of ascetics, monastic orders, especially, for instance, the Indian mendicant orders, religious sects like the Puritans, organized groups of warriors, of *ministeriales* and other functionaries, organized citizen bodies as in the Greek states, craft guilds; (b) the contraction of advantages in relation to consumption needs *(Nahrungsspielraum);*[1] examples are monopolies of consumption, the most developed form of which is a self-subsistent village community; (c) the growing scarcity of opportunities for acquisition *(Erwerbsspielraum)*. This is found in trade monopolies such as guilds, the ancient monopolies of fishing rights, and so on. Usually motive (a) is combined with (b) or (c).

*Economy and Society,* vol. 1, pp. 43–46

## The Meaning and Presuppositions of Modern Capitalism

Capitalism is present wherever the industrial provision for the needs of a human group is carried out by the method of enterprise, irrespective of what need is involved. More specifically, a rational capitalistic establishment is one with capital accounting, that is, an establishment which determines its income yielding power by calculation according to the methods of modern bookkeeping and the striking of a balance. The device of the balance was first insisted upon by the Dutch theorist Simon Stevin in the year 1698.

---

[1] Weber's term here is *Nahrungsspielraum.* The concept refers to the scope of economic resources and opportunities on which the standard of living of an individual or a group is dependent. By contrast with this, *Erwerbsspielraum* is a similar scope of resources and economic opportunities seen from the point of view of their possible role as sources of profit. The basic distinction implied in this contrast is of central importance to Weber's analysis. . . .

It goes without saying that an individual economy may be conducted along capitalistic lines to the most widely varying extent; parts of the economic provision may be organized capitalistically and other parts on the handicraft or the manorial pattern. Thus at a very early time the city of Genoa had a part of its political needs, namely those for the prosecution of war, provided in capitalistic fashion, through stock companies. In the Roman empire, the supply of the population of the capital city with grain was carried out by officials, who however for this purpose, besides control over their subalterns, had the right to command the services of transport organizations; thus the leiturgical or forced contribution type of organization was combined with administration of public resources. Today, in contrast with the greater part of the past, our everyday needs are supplied capitalistically, our political needs however through compulsory contributions, that is, by the performance of political duties of citizenship such as the obligation to military service, jury duty, etc. A whole epoch can be designated as typically capitalistic only as the provision for wants is capitalistically organized to such a predominant degree that if we imagine this form of organization taken away the whole economic system must collapse.

While capitalism of various forms is met with in all periods of history, the provision of the everyday wants by capitalistic methods is characteristic of the occident alone and even here has been the inevitable method only since the middle of the 19th century. Such capitalistic beginnings as are found in earlier centuries were merely anticipatory, and even the somewhat capitalistic establishments of the 16th century may be removed in thought from the economic life of the time without introducing any overwhelming change.

The most general presupposition for the existence of this present-day capitalism is that of rational capital accounting as the norm for all large industrial undertakings which are concerned with provision for everyday wants. Such accounting involves, again, first, the appropriation of all physical means of production—land, apparatus, machinery, tools, etc. as disposable property of autonomous private industrial enterprises. This is a phenomenon known only to our time, when the army alone forms a universal exception to it. In the second place, it involves freedom of the market, that is, the absence of irrational limitations on trading in the market. Such limitations might be of a class character, if a certain mode of life were prescribed for a certain class or consumption were standardized along class lines, or if class monopoly existed, as for example if the townsman were not allowed to own an estate or the knight or peasant to carry on industry; in such cases neither a free labor market nor a commodity market exists. Third, capitalistic accounting presupposes rational technology, that is, one reduced to calculation to the largest possible degree, which implies mechanization. This applies to both production and commerce, the outlays for preparing as well as moving goods.

The fourth characteristic is that of calculable law. The capitalistic form of industrial organization, if it is to operate rationally, must be able to depend upon calculable adjudication and administration. Neither in the age of the Greek city-state (polis) nor in the patrimonial state of Asia nor in western countries down to the Stuarts was this condition fulfilled. The royal "cheap justice" with its remissions by royal grace introduced continual disturbances into the calculations of economic life. The proposition that the Bank of England was suited only to a republic, not to a monarchy, was related in this way to the conditions of the time. The fifth feature is free labor. Persons must be present who are not only legally in the position, but are also economically compelled, to sell their labor on the market without restriction. It is in contradiction to the essence of capitalism, and the development of capitalism is impossible, if such a property-less stratum is absent, a class compelled to sell its labor services to live; and it is likewise impossible if only unfree labor is at hand. Rational capitalistic calculation is possible only on the basis of free labor; only where in consequence of the existence of workers who in the formal sense voluntarily, but actually under the compulsion of the whip of hunger, offer themselves, the costs of products may be unambiguously determined by agreement in advance. The sixth and final condition is the commercialization of economic life. By this we mean the general use of commercial instruments to represent share rights in enterprise, and also in property ownership.

To sum up, it must be possible to conduct the provision for needs exclusively on the basis of market opportunities and the calculation of net income. The addition of this commercialization to the other characteristics of capitalism involves intensification of the significance of another factor not yet mentioned, namely speculation. Speculation reaches its full significance only from the moment when property takes on the form of negotiable paper.

*General Economic History*, pp. 207–09

## The Development of Industrial Technique

It is not easy to define accurately the concept of the factory. We think at once of the steam engine and the mechanization of work, but the machine had its forerunner in what we call "apparatus"—labor appliances which had to be utilized in the same way as the machine but which as a rule were driven by water power. The distinction is that the apparatus works as the servant of the man while in modern machines the inverse relation holds. The real distinguishing characteristic of the modern factory is in general, however, not the implements of work applied, but the concentration of ownership of workplace, means of work, source of power and raw material in one and the same hand, that of the entrepreneur. This combination was only exceptionally met with before the 18th century.

Tracing the English development, which determined the character of the evolution of capitalism—although England followed the example of other countries such as Italy—we find the following stages. 1. The oldest real factory which can be identified (though it was still driven by water power) was a silk factory at Derwent, near Derby, in 1719. It was conducted on the basis of a patent, the owner of which had stolen the invention in Italy. In Italy there had long been silk manufacture with various property relations, but the product was destined for luxury requirements and belonged to an epoch which is not yet characteristic for modern capitalism, although it must be named here because the implements of work and all material and product belonged to an entrepreneur. 2. The establishment of wool manufacture (1738) on the basis of a patent after the invention of an apparatus for running a hundred bobbins at once by the aid of water power. 3. The development of half-linen production. 4. The systematic development of the pottery industry through experiments in Staffordshire. Earthen vessels were produced under a modern division of labor and the application of water power and with the ownership of work place and implements by an entrepreneur. 5. The manufacture of paper, beginning with the 18th century, its permanent basis being the development of the modern use of documents and of the newspaper.

The decisive factor, however, in the triumph of the mechanization and rationalization of work was the fate of cotton manufacture. This industry was transplanted from the continent to England in the 17th century and there immediately began a struggle against the old national industry established since the 15th century, namely, wool, a struggle as intense as that in which wool had previously been involved against linen. The power of the wool producers was so great that they secured restrictions and prohibitions on the production of half-linen, which was not restored until the Manchester Act of 1736. The factory production of cotton stuff was originally limited by the fact that, while the loom had been improved and enlarged, the spindle remained on the medieval level, so that the necessary quantity of spun material was not available. A succession of technical improvements in the spindle after 1769 reversed this relation and with the help of water power and mechanical aids great quantities of usable yarn could be provided while it was impossible to weave the same quantity with corresponding speed. The discrepancy was removed in 1785 through the construction of the power loom by Cartwright, one of the first inventors who combined technology with science and handled the problems of the former in terms of theoretical considerations.

But for all this revolution in the means of work the development might have stopped and modern capitalism in its most characteristic form never have appeared. Its victory was decided by coal and iron. We know that coal had been used in consumption, even in the middle ages, as in London, in Luttich and Zwickau. . . . But until the 18th century the technique was determined by the fact that smelting and all preparation of iron was done with charcoal. The deforestation of England resulted, while Germany was saved from this fate by the circumstance that in the 17th and 18th centuries it was untouched by the capitalistic development. Everywhere the destruction of the forests brought the industrial development to a standstill at a certain point. Smelting was only released from its attachment to organic materials of the plant world by the application of coal. It must be noted that the first blast furnaces appear as early as the 15th century, but they were fed with wood and were used not for private consumption but for war purposes, and in part also in connection with ocean shipping. In the 15th century, furthermore, was invented the iron drill for the preparation of cannon barrels. At the same time appeared the large heavy trip hammer, up to a thousand pounds weight, driven by water power, so that in addition to the handling of cast iron with the drill, mechanical forging was also possible. Finally, in the 17th century the rolling process was also applied in the modern sense of the word. . . .

The significance of the development just portrayed is to be found in three consequences. In the first place, coal and iron released technology and productive possibilities from the limitations of the qualities inherent in organic materials; from this time forward industry was no longer dependent upon animal power or plant growth. Through a process of exhaustive exploitation, fossil fuel, and by its aid iron ore, were brought up to the light of day, and by means of both men achieved the possibility of extending production to a degree which would have previously been beyond bounds of the conceivable. Thus iron became the most important factor in the development of capitalism; what would have happened to this system or to Europe in the absence of this development we do not know.[2]

The second point is that the mechanization of the production process through the steam engine liberated production from the organic limitations of human labor. Not altogether, it is true, for it goes without saying that labor was indispensable for the tending of machines. But the mechanizing process has always and everywhere been introduced to the definite end of releasing labor; every new invention signifies the extensive displacement of hand workers by a relatively small man power for machine supervision.

Finally, through the union with science, the production of goods was emancipated from all the bonds of inherited tradition, and came under the dominance of the freely roving intelligence. It is true that most of the inventions of the 18th century were not made in a scientific manner; when the coking process was discovered no one suspected what its chemical significance might be. The connection of industry with modern science, especially the systematic work of the laboratories, beginning with Justus von Liebig, enabled industry to become what it is today and so brought capitalism to its full development.

The recruiting of the labor force for the new form of production, as it developed in England in the 18th century, resting upon the concentration of all the means of production in the hands of the entrepreneur, was carried out by means of compulsion, though of an indirect sort. Under this head belong especially the Poor Law, and the Statute of Apprentices of Queen Elizabeth. These measures had become necessary in consequence of the large number of people wandering about the country who had been rendered destitute by the revolution in the agricultural system. Its displacement of the small dependent peasant by large renters and the transformation of arable land into sheep pastures—although the latter has occasionally been overestimated—worked together constantly to reduce the amount of labor force required on the land and to bring into being a surplus population, which was subjected to compulsory labor. Anyone who did not take a job voluntarily was thrust into the workhouse with its strict discipline; and anyone who left a position without a certificate from the master or entrepreneur was treated as a vagabond. No unemployed person was supported except under the compulsion of entering the workhouse.

In this way the first labor force for the factories was recruited. With difficulty the people adapted themselves to the discipline of the work. But the power of the possessing classes was too great; they secured the support of the political authority through the justices of the peace, who in the absence of binding law operated on the basis of a maze of instructions and largely according to their own dictates. Down into the second half of the 19th century they exercised an arbitrary control over the labor force and fed the workers into the newly arising industries. From the beginning of the 18th century, on the other hand, begins the regulation of relations between entrepreneur and laborer, presaging the modern control of labor conditions. . . .

Drawing together once more the distinguishing characteristics of western capitalism and its causes, we find the following factors. First, this institution alone produced a rational organization of labor, which nowhere previously existed. Everywhere and always there has been trade; it can be traced back into the stone age. Likewise we find in the most varied epochs and cultures war finance, state contributions, tax farming, farming of offices, etc., but not a rational organization of labor. Furthermore we find everywhere else a primitive, strictly integrated internal economy such that there is no question of any freedom of economic action between members of the same tribe or clan, associated with absolute freedom of trade externally. Internal and external ethics are distinguished, and in connection with the latter there is complete ruthlessness in financial procedure; nothing can be more rigidly prescribed than the clan economy of China or the caste economy of India, and on the other hand nothing so unscrupulous as the conduct of the Hindu foreign trader. In contrast with this, the second characteristic of western capitalism is a lifting of the barrier between the internal economy and external economy, between internal and external ethics, and the entry of the commercial principle into the internal economy, with the organization of labor on this basis. Finally, the disintegration of primitive economic fixity is also met with elsewhere, as for example in Babylon; but nowhere else do we find the entrepreneur organization of labor as it is known in the western world.

If this development took place only in the occident the reason is to be found in the special features of its general cultural evolution which are peculiar to it. Only the occident knows the state in the modern sense, with a professional administration, specialized officialdom, and law based on the concept of citizenship. Beginnings of this institution in antiquity and in the orient were never able to develop. Only the occident knows rational law, made by jurists and rationally interpreted and applied, and only in the occident is found the concept of citizen (*civis Romanus, citoyen, bourgeois*) because only in the occident again are there cities in the specific sense. Furthermore, only the occident possesses science in the present-day sense of the word. Theology, philosophy, reflection on the ultimate problems of life, were known to the Chinese and the Hindu, perhaps even of a depth unreached by the European; but a rational science and in connection with it a rational technology remained unknown to those civilizations. Finally, western civilization is further distinguished from every other by the presence of men with a rational ethic for the conduct of life. Magic and religion are found everywhere; but a religious basis for the ordering of life which consistently followed out must lead to explicit rationalism is again peculiar to western civilization alone.

*General Economic History*, pp. 224–33

## Sources

Max Weber, *Economy and Society,* ed. Guenther Roth and Claus Wittich (Berkeley: University of California Press, 1978), 2 vols.

———, *General Economic History* (New York: Collier Books, 1961).

# Selective Further Reading

## On Marx

Avineri, Shlomo, *The Social and Political Thought of Karl Marx* (Cambridge: Cambridge University Press, 1968).

Cohen, G. A., *Karl Marx's Theory of History: A Defence* (Oxford: Clarendon Press, 1978).

Lefort, Claude, 'Marx: From One Vision of History to Another', *Social Research* 45(4) (1978).

Maguire, John M., *Marx's Theory of Politics* (Cambridge: Cambridge University Press, 1978).

Mandel, Ernest, *Marxist Economic Theory* (New York: Monthly Review, 1972), 2 vols.

McLellan, David, *The Thought of Karl Marx* (London: Macmillan, 1971).

Mészáros, István, *Marx's Theory of Alienation* (London: Merlin, 1970).

Ollman, Bertell, *Alienation* (Cambridge: Cambridge University Press, 1971).

Sweezy, Paul, *The Theory of Capitalist Development* (New York: Monthly Review, 1942).

## On Lenin

Carlo, Antonio, 'Lenin on the Party', *Telos* 17 (1973).

Harding, Neil, *Lenin's Political Thought* (London: Macmillan, 1977–1981), 2 vols.

Hill, Christopher, *Lenin and the Russian Revolution* (Harmandsworth: Penguin, 1971).

Liebman, Marcel, *Leninism Under Lenin* (London: Merlin Press, 1980).

Lukács, Georg, *Lenin* (Cambridge, Mass.: M.I.T. Press, 1971).

Sweezy, Paul, and Harry Magdoff, eds., *Lenin Today* (New York: Monthly Review, 1970).

Weber, Gerda and Hermann, *Lenin: Life and Works* (London: Macmillan, 1980).

## On Weber

Beetham, David, *Max Weber and the Theory of Modern Politics* (London: Allen & Unwin, 1974).

Bendix, Reinhard, *Max Weber* (London: Methuen, 1966).

Gerth, Hans G., and C. Wright Mills, Introduction to *From Max Weber* (New York: Oxford University Press, 1946).

Giddens, Anthony, *Politics and Sociology in the Thought of Max Weber* (London: Macmillan, 1972).

Mommsen, Wolfgang, *The Age of Bureaucracy* (Oxford: Basil Blackwell, 1974).

Roth, Guenther, and Wolfgang Schluchter, *Max Weber's Vision of History* (Berkeley: University of California Press, 1979).

Stammer, Otto, ed., *Max Weber and Sociology Today* (Oxford: Basil Blackwell, 1971).

Wrong, Dennis, ed., *Max Weber* (Englewood Cliffs, N.J.: Prentice-Hall, 1970).

## General

Bendix, Reinhard, and Seymour Martin Lipset, eds., *Class, Status, and Power* (New York: Free Press, 1966).

Benson, Leslie, *Proletarians and Parties* (London: Methuen, 1978).

Bottomore, T. B., *Classes in Modern Society* (London: Allen & Unwin, 1965).

Giddens, Anthony, *The Class Structure of the Advanced Societies,* 2nd ed., (London: Hutchinson, 1980).

Habermas, Jürgen, *Towards a Rational Society* (London: Heinemann, 1971).

Mann, Michael, *Consciousness and Action Among the Western Working Class* (London: Macmillan, 1973).

Parkin, Frank, *Class Inequality and Political Order* (London: Paladin, 1972).

_____, 'Social Stratification', in *A History of Sociological Analysis,* ed. Tom Bottomore and Robert Nisbet (New York: Basic Books, 1978).

Westergaard, J. H., and H. Resler, *Class in a Capitalist Society* (London: Heinemann, 1975).

Wright, Erik Olin, *Class, Crisis, and the State* (London: New Left Books, 1978).

# · II ·

# Contemporary Theories
# of Class and Class Conflict

# Introduction

## Class Places and Class Boundaries

In this section, we offer a sample of current attempts to develop further the ideas established by the 'classical' thinkers. It will be evident how much current work in class theory remains strongly indebted to those thinkers. We have not attempted to provide a comprehensive survey of contemporary theoretical debates about classes and class conflict; this would hardly be possible within the relatively limited space available in a single volume that aims to cover a range of more empirical literature. Thus we have only included contributions that are relatively recent and have concentrated upon those that have stimulated the most discussion.

Nicos Poulantzas's analysis of classes, the first in this section, has to be understood against the general background of the style of contemporary Marxist thought initiated by Louis Althusser. Whatever views one may have of Althusser's version of Marxism, it has helped to stimulate an impressive array of work in a variety of disciplines. This includes a range of writings by Poulantzas on classes and the state. But to those one may add the revitalisation of urban studies led by Manuel Castells; the development of Marxist anthropology as furthered by such writers as Godelier, Meillassoux, and Terray; and the studies of precapitalist societies in Europe produced by Anderson.

It would be out of the question to attempt to provide a full sketch of Althusser's views here. But it is relevant to mention his critiques of two established traditions of Marxist interpretation. One of these concerns thinkers influenced by Hegel, such as Lukács in his early writings, whom Althusser sees as introducing an illegitimately teleological conception of classes. Classes are conceived of as 'subjects', as agents acting in a purposive way. Althusser rejects this type of approach; but he also rejects naïve forms of Marxism that see classes as purely economic phenomena. According to Althusser, every class society consists of three 'levels', combined differently in varying types of society. These levels are the economic, the political, and the ideological. It is wrong to suppose, Althusser claims, that the economic 'determines' what happens at the other levels of social organisation in any simple sense. The relation between the various institutional sectors of a society is a complex one, and this complexity is reflected in the nature of class formations. Capitalist societies, or 'social formations', are certainly primarily structured around the capital/wage labour relation; but this relation is refracted through the overall institutional form of the society. Moreover, class relations are influenced by what Althusser calls 'conjunctures'. 'Conjunctures' refer to specific circumstances of history, limited in time and place.

These notions form the basis of Poulantzas's conception of classes. Classes are defined 'primarily' by their role in the economic sphere; but they are also strongly infused with political and ideological elements. Poulantzas makes a distinction between the 'place' of a class in the structural relations between these three levels and its 'position' in a conjuncture (these notions are critically analysed in a subsequent article by R. W. Connell). The 'place' of a class refers to the way in which it is structured by particular configurations of the economic, political, and ideological. The 'position' of a class in a conjuncture connotes the specific class alliances, tactics, and so on adopted by the members of a class in a particular historical situation. The use of these ideas leads to complex and often abstruse analyses of class situations. But there is no doubt that they allow Poulantzas to acknowledge that class relationships in actual societies rarely if ever conform to wholesale confrontations between 'bourgeoisie' and 'proletariat'.

The economic aspects of class, Poulantzas holds, are defined above all by their place in the relations of production. A ruling class, he says, cannot be specified merely in terms of juridical relations, that is, who formally owns the means of production. What really matters is who *controls* the means of production, using that control as a mode of extracting surplus from the exploited classes. In capitalism (he agrees with Marx) the extraction of surplus value is the basis of exploitative class relationships and serves to characterise the main exploited class—the working class. The working class cannot be defined as 'wage earners' because although every worker is a wage earner, the reverse does not follow. The working class consists only of productive workers, that is, those who directly produce surplus value. Most 'white-collar' workers are wage earners, but they are not part of the working class because they are concerned with the circulation of commodities rather than with their production.

White-collar workers, in Poulantzas's conception, belong to what he calls the 'new petty bourgeoisie' (a term which he prefers to the commonly used 'new middle class'). Political and ideological criteria become of particular importance in specifying who belongs to the new petty bourgeoisie. According to Poulantzas, the 'new' and 'old petty bourgeoise' (owners of small firms or businesses) can be said to form a single class in terms of their class place. This is because they share similar political and ideological criteria: the outlook of both tends to involve individualism and 'career advancement', antipathy to unionisation, and 'aspirations to bourgeois status'. To say this, Poulantzas emphasises, is not to say that in particular conjunctures, the petty bourgeoise usually acts as a consolidated class. On the contrary, as with other classes, there are normally major divisions or 'fractions' which ally themselves with sections of other classes.

What applies to the working class and petty bourgeoisie—or 'middle class'—also applies to the dominant class and its relations to the state. The dominant class is typically split into various fractions, which in different conjunctures may enter into various differing alliances, or struggles, with segments of subordinate classes. This connects with the celebrated idea of the 'relative autonomy' of the state from the ruling class. Two conceptions of the state can be found in Marx's writings. One is that taken up by Lenin, according to which the state is the direct agency of the repressive power of the dominant class. Poulantzas claims adherence, however, to a second view which can be supported by appeal to certain of Marx's writings. This is that the state is not the immediate 'instrument' of the ruling class but has a degree of power independent of that class. According to this idea, which Poulantzas develops, the state (or sections of the state apparatus) protects the long-term framework of capitalist production; this may mean that the state enters into conflicts with fractions of capital whose short-term policies might not be adjudged compatible with these broader aims. Thus, the state may, for example, attempt to pass antitrust legislation which might be bitterly contested by the capital interests involved.

Poulantzas's writings rather strongly accentuate questions of what Erik Olin Wright calls 'class boundaries': where the dividing lines between classes lie and how these connect to the alliances formed between class fractions in definite economic or political struggles. In various of his writings, Wright has criticised aspects of Poulantzas's views; but he is also fairly strongly influenced by Poulantzas's approach, as the discussion included here indicates. Poulantzas admits the influence of political and ideological factors on class formation and also accepts that there may be complicated relations between class fractions. But, Wright says, he does not pursue the implications of his ideas fully enough. In his discussion of the petty bourgeoisie in particular, Poulantzas acknowledges that the class is involved in multiple affiliations. However, he does not take the further step of recognising that some classes occupy *objectively contradictory* places in the class structure.

All classes, Wright admits, are intrinsically antagonistic or contradictory; but some classes occupy 'doubly contradictory' class locations. He explicates this notion in terms of three basic processes involved in the formation of capitalism: loss of control over the labour process by workers, the separation between formal ownership of capital and actual directive power in firms, and the development of bureaucratic, managerial hierarchies in industrial organisations. These three processes are integral to the structuring of the primary class relation in capitalism, the capital/wage-labour relation. Each refers to intersecting dimensions of power: control over the labour task, control over labour power, and control over investments or the allocation of resources. The two major classes occupy unambiguous locations in respect of all of these dimensions. The capitalist class has three plus signs: the capitalist entrepreneur is the directive authority controlling investment, the organisation of labour power, and the nature of labour tasks in the firm. The working class has all minus signs: its members are excluded from all three forms of control. Other classes, however, have a mixture of pluses and minuses; they are in contradictory class locations. The 'new petty bourgeoisie' or new middle class are in the most contradictory class place of all. They have, Wright says, quoting Harry Braverman, 'one foot in the bourgeoisie and one in the proletariat'—a highly uncomfortable position indeed, one might say!

Since Wright diverges significantly from Poulantzas's more general views and explicitly rejects aspects of Althusser's 'structuralist Marxism', his ideas must in some considerable degree be exempted from the strictures that Connell directs against 'the Althusserian approach to class'. As Connell remarks, the importance of Poulantzas's writings is that they seek to depart from overly simple, deterministic accounts of classes and class conflict frequently associated with Marxism. But he finds major flaws in Poulantzas's arguments (as well as in those of another follower of Althusser, Carchedi). The distinction between class 'place' and 'position' is quite unsatisfactory since it is neither particularly clear nor employed in a consistent fashion. Rather than providing a coherent framework for analysing the ways in which structured class relations connect to actual conduct or 'practices', it specifically severs the one from the other. Thus, Poulantzas's writings, like those of his mentor Althusser, display an odd combination of a 'tight-laced conceptual system', on the one hand, and 'a promiscuous application of class categories' in conjunctural analyses, on the other. Such an approach cannot generate an adequate understanding of history, which becomes an abstract kaleidoscope of 'conjunctures'.

Poulantzas's concepts, Connell argues, are heavily dependent upon a rather vulgar version of functionalism. The functionalist cast of these, according to Connell, connects closely with the defects in the approach. Poulantzas's work moves back and forth between abstract structural classification (class 'places') and concrete happenings (class 'positions'). Since there is no coherent mode of connecting these, the gap is filled by functionalist assertions. Specific events are related to the abstract structural typologies of classes via the contributions they make to the 'whole', that is, by means of the functions they are presumed to fulfill. The 'relative autonomy' of the state, for example, is defined by Poulantzas in a directly functionalist vein: the state, he says, 'has the particular function of constituting the factor of cohesion between the levels of a social formation'.

There are political implications to these criticisms, in Connell's view. Analysing class relations in terms of 'places', 'positions', and 'functions' allows no conceptual space for the capabilities of social actors to understand the conditions of their activity and their interests. The outcome is likely to be a peculiarly uncompromising form of Leninism—even coming close to Stalinism—in which those who are supposed to benefit from socialism have to follow policies imposed by the 'vanguard party'. Such a standpoint, Connell avers, 'systematically discredits any strategy based on spontaneity, self-management, and popular mobilisation'.

## The Division of Labour, Class Structuration, and
## Strategies of Closure

The theory of the division of labour plays a very significant part in Marx's writings. From his earliest to his later works he insisted that the expansion of the division of labour is closely bound up with the alienating character of labour in capitalist production and that socialist society would be predicated upon a radical transformation, or 'abolition', of the division of labour. On the whole, however, subsequent Marxist authors have not added a great deal to Marx's own observations. Braverman's work *Labour and Monopoly Capital* is a notable exception to this and has deservedly attracted a large amount of discussion in the contemporary literature of class theory.

Braverman sets out to combat interpretations of the division of labour which see it as a unitary process of 'differentiation' occurring across societies of different types. Drawing upon a distinction made by Marx, he argues that capitalism initiates a type of division between labour tasks which contrasts fundamentally with what went before. The 'social division of labour' has existed in all societies prior to the advent of capitalism. It involves a differentiation between tasks devoted to the making of whole products—epitomised in craft skills. Capitalism introduces the 'detailed or technical division of labour', based upon the fragmentation of craft skills—expressed perhaps above all in the repetitive operations performed by a worker on a production line.

According to Braverman (these ideas are not detailed in the section reproduced below), the spread of the technical division of labour is a major phenomenon whereby capital via 'management' secures and consolidates its control over labour. For the growth of the detailed division of labour drains knowledge of, and control over, the labour process, away from the worker. Craft workers, even when employed as wage workers, still retain a substantial degree of control over the labour task because of the skilled nature of their work. But the development of capitalism increasingly promotes the dissolution of craft skills as work becomes broken down into separate, simple tasks carried out by workers who need little or no training.

In *Labour and Monopoly Capital,* Braverman argues that 'scientific management', as invented by Frederick Taylor around the turn of this century, provided a strong impetus to the process of 'de-skilling' in capitalism. Taylor set out 'scientifically' to decompose labour tasks with the aim of securing greater efficiency of production. By providing a theory which fitted with, and further extended, existing managerial strategies, scientific management accelerated the progression of the detailed division of labour. This progression Braverman labels 'the general law of the capitalist division of labour'. However, although he does not develop the case at any length, he believes that this 'general law' is not limited to countries ordinarily thought of as capitalist. For Lenin enthusiastically adopted Taylorist principles in the Soviet Union; thenceforth, according to Braverman, the detailed division of labour became as much a part of East European as of Western industry.

Braverman's ideas have been strongly criticised (see Section Four, below), and with justification. But they offer an important point of articulation between

Marxist conceptions of class and the kinds of problems raised by Weber. In some respects, as Anthony Giddens points out below, Braverman's work leads to as pessimistic conclusions as those reached by Weber; for the development of the technical division of labour, allowing less and less control by workers over the labour task, is presented as a unilateral and seemingly inevitable one. Giddens's formulation of class theory is based upon the supposition that a sympathetic reconstruction of Marx's concepts of class and class conflict must confront the Weberian challenge and should be prepared to draw selectively upon Weber's works. As he explains, he does not regard his views as thereby 'Weberian' in character—although some of the Marxist authors represented below have regarded these as such.

In contrast to Wright, Giddens does not see the question of class boundaries as fundamental to class theory; classes are not separated by dividing lines like the territorial boundaries on maps. The stress should be placed rather upon the main elements involved in class 'structuration'. Classes are not groups, but neither is it useful to treat classes as aggregates of life chances, as Weber does. By stressing class structuration, Giddens means to accentuate the modes in which structured social forms are founded upon class relationships. He distinguishes several sources of class structuration in capitalist societies, using the notion of 'market capacity' as a point of reference. A specific feature of capitalism is the asymmetrical involvement of employers and workers in commodity and labour markets, in which workers, as Marx specified, sell their labour power as a commodity. 'Market capacity' refers to the attributes which individuals bring to the bargaining counter in the formation of the capitalist labour contract. According to Giddens's emphasis, divergencies in market capacity are both actively utilised as resources by employers and workers and at the same time are features of institutionally reproduced characteristics of class relations.

The major sources of class structuration are as follows: first, the degree of closure of mobility chances, a phenomenon that influences the continuity of class relationships across the generations; second, the nature of the division of labour within organisations, which includes specific reference to the sorts of processes analysed by Braverman; and third, the authority system of the enterprise. In insisting that this has to be conceptually separated from the division of labour, Giddens wants to distinguish various possible connections that might exist between technology and control within productive organisations. Finally, in underlining the importance of 'distributive groupings' (especially those relating to urban patterns and neighbourhood segregation), Giddens seeks to recognise that class structuration is not only influenced by factors internal to the workplace.

A basic element of Giddens's discussion of class conflict is his distinction between 'class awareness' and two forms of class consciousness, 'conflict consciousness' and 'revolutionary consciousness'. Class awareness tends to be the characteristic cognitive style of the new middle class or 'new petty bourgeoisie' and refers to much the same features mentioned by Poulantzas: individualism and a competitive career orientation. But class awareness, paradoxically, may take the form of the very denial that classes exist. In distinguishing 'conflict consciousness' from 'revolutionary consciousness', Giddens acknowledges something of the force of Lenin's arguments—without accepting that a 'vanguard party' should be regarded as the means of bridging the two. Revolutionary consciousness is not, moreover, a phenomenon unique to middle-class intellectuals. It tends to develop where workers are able to form a perspective which 'relativises' existing alignments of industrial authority: when they grasp possibilities of radically transforming capitalist economic and political institutions. 'External' leadership may help in this regard but only in circumstances that already stimulate such a 'relativising' consciousness.

In approaching themes connecting Marx and Weber, Giddens argues that Marxists have tended to be insufficiently critical of Weber's analysis of bureaucracy. The critique of Weber here has direct implications for discerning the limitations of Braverman's approach. For, in spite of some very important differences between their ideas, both authors underestimate the capability of those in subordinate positions to sustain control over the context of their activities. Neither Braverman's 'general law' of capitalist production nor the 'iron law of oligarchy' formulated by Weber's follower and colleague Robert Michels, withstands scrutiny. There is not a 'one-way' movement of power upwards in capitalist firms or other organisations. Rather there is what Giddens calls a 'dialectic of control' in organisations: shifting alignments of resources, in which power often becomes significantly recovered by subordinates.

Unlike the other authors represented here, Frank Parkin writes as an explicit follower of Weber and critic of Marx. How far the concepts he develops are actually incompatible with a revised Marxist standpoint is disputable. In the book from which the selection below is excerpted, *Marxism and Class Theory*, Parkin sets out to provide a critique of 'Althusserian approaches to class' even more biting than that given by Connell. To replace what he (like Connell) sees as the excessive formalism of Althusser, Poulantzas, and others, he draws upon Weber's notion of 'social closure'.

By 'closure', Parkin refers to the capability of groups to exclude 'outsiders' and to monopolise resources denied to others. He intends the notion of closure to be central to class theory but regards it as relevant to the monopolisation of resources according to other criteria also, such as ethnic or sexual criteria. The selection included below mainly concerns his attempt to apply the idea of social closure to class analysis. Closure by means of what he calls 'exclusion' is the principal mode in which classes are formed. The formation of dominant classes in different types of society has been achieved via monopolistic control over resources which include those given primacy by Marx—land or capital—but also armed force or 'exoteric knowledge'.

In capitalist societies, according to Parkin, there are two predominant modes of exclusionary closure: control of property or, more specifically, capital; and control over professional qualifications and credentials. In Parkin's view, the former of these has to be interpreted in a broader sense than that involved in Marx's analysis, which accords centrality to the conception of surplus value. The important question in deciding whether a class system exists in a given society is not whether there is extraction of surplus value but whether exclusionary power is used to acquire and sustain special material privileges. In accentuating the importance of 'credentials' as modes of exclusionary closure (something which he discusses in more detail in parts of his book not included here), Parkin wants to emphasise class differentiation among the 'propertyless'. This is, in varying ways, a concern of each of the writers represented in this section. But whereas Poulantzas, Wright, and Braverman in their work do not give much attention to 'credentialism' in class formation, Giddens and Parkin accord it considerable importance.

# · 4 ·

# On Social Classes

## Nicos Poulantzas

What are social classes in Marxist theory? They are groups of social agents, of men defined *principally* but not exclusively by their place in the *production process,* i.e. by their place in the economic sphere. The economic place of the social agents has a *principal* role in determining social classes. But from that we cannot conclude that this economic place is sufficient to determine social classes. Marxism states that the economic does indeed have the determinant role in a mode of production or a social formation; but the political and the ideological (the superstructure) also have an important role. For whenever Marx, Engels, Lenin and Mao analyse social classes, far from limiting themselves to the economic criteria alone, they make explicit reference to political and ideological criteria. We can thus say that a social class is defined by its *place* in the ensemble of social practices, i.e. by its place in the ensemble of the division of labour which includes political and ideological relations. This place corresponds to *the structural determination* of classes, i.e. the manner in which determination by the structure (relations of production, politico-ideological domination/subordination) operates on class practices—for classes have existence only in the class struggle.[1] This takes the form of the effect of the structure on the social division

---

•Abridged from *New Left Review* 78 (1973): 27–35, 37–39, 47–50.

[1]This text was originally produced at the request of the trade-union federation CFDT (*Confédération Française Democratique de Travail*). It was circulated in roneoed form by the CFDT-BRAEC Centre (document no. 9) for use by CFDT cadres. It is therefore an attempt at a brief presentation for working-class militants of elements of theoretical analysis applied to the present conjuncture. These elements are drawn from my two works, *Political Power and Social Classes* and *Fascism and Dictatorship.*

of labour. But it should be pointed out here that this determination of classes, which has existence only in the class struggle, must be clearly distinguished from *class position* in the *conjuncture*. In stressing the importance of political and ideological relations in the determination of classes and the fact that social classes have existence only in the class struggle, we should not be led into the 'voluntarist' error of reducing class determination to class position. From that error flow extremely important political consequences, which will be mentioned in the sections dealing with technicians, engineers and the labour aristocracy. Yet the economic criterion remains determinant. But how are we to understand the terms 'economic' and 'economic criterion' in the Marxist conception?

## Social Classes and Relations of Production

The 'economic' sphere is determined by *the production process* and the place of the agents, i.e. by their distribution into social classes by *the relations of production:* in the unit consisting of production/consumption/division of the social product, it is production which has the determinant role. The distinction between the classes at this level is not, e.g. a distinction based on relative sizes of income (a distinction between 'rich' and 'poor'), as was believed by a long pre-Marxist tradition and as is still believed today by a whole series of sociologists. The undoubted distinction between relative levels of income is itself only a consequence of the relations of production.

What then are the production process and the relations of production which compose it? In the production process, we find first of all *the labour process:* it is that which in general designates man's relation to nature. But the labour process always appears in an historically determined social form. It exists only in its unity with relations of production. In a society divided into classes, the relations of production consist of a double relation which encompasses men's relations to nature in material production. These two relations are relations first between men and other men—class relations, and secondly between the agents of production and the object and means of labour—the productive forces. These two relations thus concern the relation of the non-worker (the owner) to the object and means of labour and the relation of the immediate producer (direct worker) to the object and means of labour. These relations involve two aspects: (a) Economic ownership: by this is meant the real economic control of the means of production, i.e. the power to assign the means of production to given uses and so to dispose of the products obtained. (b) Possession: by this is meant the capacity to put the means of production into operation.

### The Owners and the Means of Production

In every society divided into classes, the first relation (owners/means of production) always coincides with the first aspect: it is the owners who have real control of the means of production and thus exploit the direct workers by extorting surplus value from them in various forms. But this ownership is to be understood as real economic ownership, control of the means of production, to be distinguished from *juridical* ownership, which is sanctioned by the law and belongs to the superstructure. Certainly, the law generally ratifies economic ownership, but it is possible for the forms of juridical ownership not to coincide with real economic ownership.

We can illustrate this by two examples, beginning with the case of *the big farmers* in the division of classes in the countryside. According to Lenin, they belong to the rich peasantry, even though they do not have formal, juridical ownership of the land, which belongs to the rentier capitalist. These big farmers belong to the rich peasantry not because of their high incomes, but because they have real control of the land and the means of labour, of which they are thus the effective economic owners. I mention this case merely as an example. Space does not permit a detailed analysis of the class divisions of the peasantry, which does not in itself constitute a single class. It should, however, be pointed out that we can divide the countryside into big landowners, rich, medium and poor peasants, such that each class encompasses groups arising from different forms of ownership and exploitation, only if we make a rigorous distinction between formal, juridical ownership and real, economic ownership.

The case of the USSR and the 'socialist' countries is a second example. This is highly controversial, but it should not be omitted here. In these countries, formal, juridical ownership of the means of production belongs to the state, which is held to be 'the people's state'; but real control (economic ownership) certainly does not belong to the workers themselves—as we can see from the extinction of the Soviets and the workers' councils—but to the directors of enterprises and to the members of the party apparatus. It can therefore be argued that the form of collective juridical ownership conceals a new form of economic 'private' ownership; and hence that one should speak of a new 'bourgeoisie' in the USSR. In reality, the abolition of class exploitation cannot be equated simply with the abolition of juridical private ownership, but with the abolition of real economic ownership—i.e. control of the means of production by the workers themselves.

These considerations have a bearing on the question of the transition to socialism. By keeping in mind the all-important theoretical and real distinction between economic and formal, juridical, ownership, we can see that the mere *nationalization* of enterprises is not a solution. This is not only because nationalizations are adapted by the bourgeoisie to their own interests. It is because even when they are accompanied by a change in state power, a nationalization or a take-over of the economy by the state only changes the form of juridical ownership. In the last resort, the one thing which can fundamentally modify economic ownership and thus lead to the abolition of classes is the control of production by the workers themselves.

### The Exploited Class and the Means of Labour

Let us return to our second relation—that of the direct producers (the workers) to the means and object of labour. This relation defines *the exploited class*. It can take various forms, according to the various modes of production in which it occurs. In pre-capitalist modes of production, the direct producers (the workers) were not entirely separated from the object and means of labour. In the case of the feudal mode of production, for instance, even though the lord had both juridical and economic *ownership* of the land, the serf had *possession* of his parcel of land, which was protected by custom. He could not be purely and simply dispossessed by the lord. In that mode of production, exploitation was by *direct extraction of surplus labour,* in the form of *corvée* payable in labour or in kind. In other words, economic ownership and possession were distinct in that they did not both depend on the same relation between owners and means of production. By contrast, in the capitalist mode of production, the direct producers (the working class) are completely dispossessed of their means of work, of which the capitalists have the actual possession: Marx called this the phenomenon of the 'naked worker'. The worker possesses only his labour-power, which he sells as a *commodity,* and this fact determines the generalization of the commodity form. Thus the capitalist extracts surplus labour not in a direct way, but rather through the medium of labour embodied in the commodity—by amassing *surplus value.*

Important consequences follow from this. The *production process* is defined not by technological factors, but by relations between men and the means of production; it is defined therefore by the unity of the labour process and the relations of production. In societies divided into classes, there is no such thing as 'productive labour' as such, understood as a neutral term. In every mode of production divided into classes, productive labour is labour corresponding to the relations of production of that mode: it is that labour which gives rise to a specific form of *exploitation.* In such societies, production always stands for division, exploitation and struggle between classes. Thus in the capitalist mode of production, productive labour is that which (always on the basis of use-value) produces exchange value in the form *commodities,* and so *surplus value.* It is precisely in this way that the *working class* is economically defined in the capitalist mode of production: productive labour relates directly to the division between classes in the relations of production.

### Productive and Unproductive Labour

This formulation allows us to solve certain problems, while it also poses new ones. The working class is not defined by its *wages,* since wages are a juridical form in which the product is divided up according to the contract governing the buying and selling of labour-power. While every worker is a wage earner, not every wage earner is a worker, since not every wage earner is necessarily a productive worker, i.e. one who produces surplus value (commodities). Marx provides some explicit analyses on this point: he considers, for example, that transport workers (railwaymen, etc) are productive workers, belonging to the working class. This is because a commodity does not exist until it appears on the market: and in the definition of productive labour, the important factor is the commodity (surplus value); whereas wage earners in commerce, banks, advertising agencies, service industries, etc, are not included among productive workers. This is because some of them belong to the sphere of circulation, while the rest do not produce surplus value, but merely contribute to its realization.

The problem is yet more complicated with respect to the technicians and engineers working within and on the periphery of material production in enterprises: a group which includes those who are often (incorrectly) called 'bearers of science'. There is no coherent or explicit account of this problem to be found in Marx, who, in confining himself to the economic plane, in fact produces two more or less contradictory responses. In *Theories of Surplus Value* and the *Grundrisse,* Marx uses the notion of *collective worker.* In view of (a) the progressive socialization of the productive forces and the labour process, and (b) the increasing interpenetration of the various tasks contributing to commodity production, Marx argues that science tends to become part of the productive forces and that technicians, through the medium of the collective worker, should be considered part of the working class. This leads to the notion that they form a labour aristocracy—which Lenin considered to be a stratum of the working class itself. But in *Capital* Marx clearly considers that this category of agents is not part of the working class, since science is not a direct productive force, as only its applications enter into the production process. Moreover these applications contribute only to the increase and realization of surplus-value, not to its direct production. So technical agents do not form part of the working class. . . .

From this issue, we can move to an important problem. We stated above that the production process consists of the *unity* between the labour process and the relations of production. We can now put forward an additional proposition: within this unity it is not the labour process (including 'technology' and the 'technical process') which has the dominant role: *rather it is the relations of production which have primacy over the labour process and the 'productive forces'.* This has an important bearing on the question of social classes. The determination of classes depends on the relations of production, which relate directly to the social division of labour and the politico-ideological superstructure, not to the data of any 'technical process' as such. *The technical division of labour is dominated by the social division.* So we do not define productive labour as consisting of those who take part in production understood in a technical sense, but as consisting of those who produce surplus-value and who are thus exploited as a class in a determinate manner, i.e. those who occupy a determinate place in the social division of labour.

## Mode of Production and Social Formation

Before we go on to the political and ideological criteria necessary for delimiting social classes, we should pause to consider the classes in a concrete mode of production and social formation or 'society'. In talking of a *mode of production* or of a form of production, we are placing ourselves at a general and abstract level, e.g. the slave, feudal and capitalist modes of production. We are, as it were, 'isolating' these modes and forms of production in social reality, in order to examine them theoretically. But as Lenin demonstrated in *The Development of Capitalism in Russia,* a concrete society at a given moment of time *(a social formation)* is composed of several modes and forms of production which coexist in it in combination. For example, capitalist societies at the start of the 20th century were composed of (i) elements of the feudal mode of production, (ii) the form of simple commodity production and manufacture (the form of the transition from feudalism to capitalism) and (iii) the capitalist mode of production in its competitive and monopoly forms. Yet these societies were certainly capitalist societies: this means that the capitalist mode of production was *dominant* in them. In fact, in every social order, we find the dominance of one mode of production, which produces complex effects of *dissolution* or *conservation* on the other modes of production and which gives these societies their character (feudal, capitalist, etc). The one exception is the case of societies in transition, which are, on the contrary, characterized by an *equilibrium* between the various modes of production.

To return to social classes: if we confine ourselves to modes of production alone, examining them in a pure and abstract fashion, we find that each of them involves two classes—the exploiting class, which is politically and ideologically dominant, and the exploited class, which is politically and ideologically dominated: masters and slaves in the slave mode of production, lords and serfs in the feudal mode of production, bourgeois and workers in the capitalist mode of production. But a concrete society (a social formation) *involves more than two classes,* in so far as it is composed of various modes and forms of production. No social formation involves only two classes: but the two fundamental classes of any social formation are those of the dominant mode of production in that formation. Thus in contemporary France, for example, the two fundamental classes are the bourgeoisie and the proletariat. But we also find there the traditional petty bourgeoisie (craftsmen, small traders), dependent on the form of simple commodity production, the 'new' petty bourgeoisie composed of non-productive wage earners, dependent on the monopoly form of capitalism and several social classes in the countryside, where vestiges of feudalism are still to be found in a transformed state (e.g. forms of share-cropping).

These considerations have an important bearing on the question of *alliances* between the working class and the other popular classes. The petty bourgeoisie and the popular classes in the countryside (agricultural labourers, poor peasants, middle peasants) are in fact *classes* which differ from the working class. Now in so far as the two fundamental classes are the bourgeoisie and the working class, it is true that in the course of their expanded reproduction the other classes *tend to polarize* around the working class. But this does not mean that as classes they dissolve into an undifferentiated mass: they are still *classes* with their own specific interests. In other words, the concepts of 'class' and 'people' are not coextensive: *according to the conjuncture,* a class may or may not form part of the 'people', without this affecting its class nature.

It is here that the problem of alliances arises. On the one hand, the working class must accept responsibility in its alliances for the *specific interests of the classes* which make up the 'people' or the 'popular masses' along with it, as for instance in the worker–peasant alliance advocated by Lenin. On the other hand, it must not lose sight of the fact that—as in every alliance—contradictions do exist between the specific interests of the working class, *qua* class, and, the other popular classes. By recognizing these facts, we provide ourselves with the means of giving a just solution to the contradictions 'among the people'.

This is important since there are two other interpretations of the phenomenon, both equally mistaken. According to the first interpretation, upheld by many sociologists, the transformations which capitalist societies are currently undergoing are supposed to have given rise to a vast 'intermediate class' which comprises all social groups except the bourgeoisie and proletariat and which, by virtue of its numerical weight, provides the real pillar upholding modern societies. As has been noted, we are here faced with several classes: there is no justification at present for claiming that these intermediate classes are fused into a single class. . . .

## Political and Ideological Criteria

It is now time to develop the other side of the thesis, outlined in the introduction, that purely economic criteria are not sufficient to determine and locate social classes. This becomes particularly obvious when we consider a concrete social formation. Here it becomes absolutely necessary to refer to positions within the ideological and political relations of the social division of labour; and this becomes even clearer when we examine the question of the *reproduction* of social classes. . . .

The need to refer to political and ideological criteria in defining classes is particularly clear when we deal with the *petty bourgeoisie*, or the question of whether there is such a thing as a petty bourgeois *class*, and what ensembles of agents are part of it. In general it is thought that two large groups of agents with quite different positions in production are part of the petty bourgeoisie. The first is the 'traditional' petty bourgeoisie, which is tending to decline in size: these are the small-scale producers and small traders (small property). They include forms of artisanal work and small family businesses in which one and the same agent is both owner of the means of production and of labour and is the direct worker. Here there is no economic exploitation in the strict sense, inasmuch as these forms do not employ paid workers (or only very rarely do so). Labour is principally provided by the real owner or the members of his family, who are not remunerated in the form of wages. Small-scale producers derive profit from the sale of their goods and from participating in the total redistribution of surplus value, but they do not extort surplus value directly. Secondly there is the 'new' petty bourgeoisie, which tends to increase under monopoly capitalism. It consists of the *non-productive wage-earning workers* mentioned above; we should add to it civil servants employed by the state and its various apparatuses. These workers do not produce surplus value. Like others, they sell their labour-power and their wage is determined by the price of reproducing their labour-power, but they are exploited by the direct extortion of surplus labour, not by the production of surplus value.

Now these two large groups occupy different and utterly dissimilar positions in production. Can they then be considered to constitute a *class*, the petty bourgeoisie? To this there are two possible replies. The first admits the intervention of political and ideological criteria. It can be held that these different positions in production and the economic sphere do, in fact, have *the same effects* at the political and ideological level. Both small holders and those wage earners who live out their exploitation in the form of 'wages' and 'competition' far removed from production present the same political and ideological characteristics for different economic reasons: petty bourgeois individualism; attraction to the *status quo* and fear of revolution; the myth of 'social advancement' and aspirations to bourgeois status; belief in the 'neutral State' above classes; political instability and a tendency to support 'strong States' and bonapartist regimes; revolts taking the form of 'petty bourgeois' jacqueries. If this is correct, then these *common* ideologico-political characteristics provide sufficient ground for considering that these two ensembles with different places in the economy constitute a relatively unified class, the petty bourgeoisie.

Yet even in this case, nothing prevents us from distinguishing between *fractions of one and the same class.* As we shall see later in the case of the bourgeoisie, Marxism establishes distinctions *between fractions* of a class. Fractions are distinct from simple strata since they coincide with important economic differentiations and, as such, can even take on an important role as social forces, a role relatively distinct from that of the other fractions of their class. It might thus be possible to establish that the petty bourgeois fraction of non-productive wage earners is closer to the working class than the fraction comprising the traditional petty bourgeoisie. In talking of fractions, it should also be possible to introduce the element of *the conjuncture:* to establish that one or other of the fractions is nearer or further from the working class according to the conjuncture. (See especially the currently important process of the proletarianization of artisanal production.) It should also be possible to introduce differentiations between *strata* of the petty bourgeoisie, with particular reference to ideologico-political divergences over and beyond the ideologico-political position basically common to the petty bourgeoisie as a whole: these divergences depend on the particular situation of the various petty bourgeois ensembles, particularly with respect to their *reproduction.* But it should not be forgotten that we are still basically concerned with a single class and that our attitude towards these fractions and strata, whether we are discussing alliances with them or predicting their political behaviour (especially their instability), should be framed accordingly. This position seems to be the more correct.

A second position has two versions: (a) The term 'petty bourgeoisie' can be reserved for the traditional petty bourgeoisie and the nonproductive wage earners be described as a new social class. But this poses difficult problems in theory and practice. Unless we consider that the capitalist mode of production has been superseded and that we are now in some kind of 'post-industrial' or 'technocratic' society which produces this new class, how can we maintain that capitalism itself produces *a new class* in the course of its development? This thesis is possible for the ideologists of the 'managerial class' and the 'technostructure', but it is unthinkable for Marxist theory. (b) Following the Communist Party, the non-productive wage earners can be assigned not to the petty bourgeoisie but to the 'intermediate strata'. We have already considered one reason why this view is false. Another is that while Marxism uses the terms *strata, fractions and categories* to designate particular ensembles, it yet remains true that these strata, fractions and categories *always belong to a class.* The labour aristocracy is certainly a specific stratum, but a stratum *of* the working class. The 'intellectuals' or the 'bureaucracy' are, as we shall see, certainly particular *social* categories, but *they belong to the bourgeois or petty bourgeois class.* This is one of the features which distinguishes Marxism from various American conceptions of social stratification. By defining social groups in an entirely fanciful fashion, these conceptions dilute and eliminate social classes. Marxism on the other hand introduces differentiations in a rigorous fashion *within class divisions*. Fractions, strata and categories are not 'outside' or 'alongside' social classes: they form part of them. . . .

## The Ideological Apparatuses of the State

Some observations are necessary on the form in which the contradictions between dominant, hegemonic and reigning classes and fractions are expressed within the *state apparatus*. The important point to bear in mind is that the state is composed of *several apparatuses:* broadly, the *repressive apparatus* and the *ideological apparatuses,* the principal role of the former being repression, that of the latter being the elaboration and incubation of ideology. The ideological apparatuses include the churches, the educational system, the bourgeois and petty bourgeois political parties, the press, radio, television, publishing, etc. These apparatuses belong to the state system because of their objective function of elaborating and inculcating ideology, irrespective of their formal juridical status as nationalized (public) or private. The repressive apparatus contains several specialized branches—army, police, administration, judiciary, etc. It has already been stated that the terrain of political domination is not occupied by the hegemonic class or fraction alone but by an ensemble of dominant classes or fractions. Because of this, the contradictory relations between these classes and fractions is expressed in the form of *power relations* within the apparatuses and their branches. These latter therefore do not all crystallize the power of the hegemonic class or fraction, but may express the power and interests of other dominant classes or fractions. It is in this sense that we can talk of a relative autonomy (a) of the various apparatuses and branches *vis-á-vis* each other within the state system and (b) of the ensemble of the state *vis-á-vis* the hegemonic class or fraction.

In the case of an alliance or compromise between the bourgeoisie and landed aristocracy in early capitalism, the bourgeoisie had its seat of power in the central bureaucratic organization, while the landed aristocracy had its in the church (in particular the catholic church). Such dislocations can also appear between the actual branches of the repressive apparatus: for example, before the arrival of Nazism in Germany between the two World Wars, the big landowners had their seat of power in the army, big capital in the judiciary, while the administration was shared between big and medium capital. In the case of the transition towards the hegemony of big capital, the administration and the army often constitute the seat of power (the 'military-industrial complex'), while Parliament continues to constitute medium capital's seat of power: that is one of the reasons for the decline of Parliament under monopoly capitalism. Because of their function, the ideological apparatuses in particular possess a greater relative autonomy than the repressive apparatus and they can sometimes provide seats of power for classes other than the dominant classes. This is sometimes true of the *petty bourgeoisie,* because of the alliances and compromises made between it and the dominant bloc. In France especially, these compromises have taken on a great importance for historical reasons, and the *educational system* has for a long time constituted a state apparatus, as it were, 'made over' to the petty bourgeoisie. The petty bourgeoisie has thus for a long time been set up as a *class supporting the system.*

None of this means that the capitalist state is an ensemble of separate parts, expressing a 'share-out' of political power among the various classes and fractions. On the contrary, over and beyond the contradictions within the apparatuses, the capitalist state always expresses a *specific internal unity, the unity of the power of the hegemonic class or fraction.* But this happens in a complex fashion. The functioning of the state system is assured by the *dominance* of certain apparatuses or branches over others: and the branch or apparatus which is dominant is generally that one which constitutes the seat of power of the hegemonic class or fraction. Thus, when hegemony is modified, modifications and displacements also occur in the dominance of certain apparatuses and branches *vis-á-vis* others. It is moreover these displacements which determine the changes in forms of state and forms of regime.

Thus every concrete analysis of a concrete situation must evidently take into account both relations of class struggle and real power relations within the state apparatuses, the latter being generally concealed beneath formal institutional appearances. Precisely analysis of power relations within the apparatuses can help us to locate the hegemonic fraction with accuracy. For example, by noting the dominance of one apparatus or branch over others and by also noting the specific interests served by that apparatus in a dominant fashion, we can draw some conclusions concerning the hegemonic fraction. But this must be a *dialectical* method: it is possible to start from the other side, by locating the hegemonic fraction, with its privileged relations to an apparatus or branch, within the ensemble of relations of a society; and in this way to solve the question of which is the dominant apparatus in the state, i.e. the apparatus by means of which the hegemonic fraction holds *the real controlling levers* of the state. *But it is also clear that in the complex relation between class struggle and apparatuses,* it is the class struggle which has the principal role. Institutional modifications do not lead to social movements, as a whole series of institutionalist sociologists believe: it is the class struggle which determines how the apparatuses are modified.

## Expanded Reproduction of Social Classes

. . . The expanded reproduction of social classes (of social relations) involves *two aspects which cannot exist in isolation from one another.* First, there is the expanded reproduction of the positions occupied by the agents. These positions mark out the *structural determination* of classes, i.e. the manner in which determination by the structure (relations of production, politico-ideological domination/subordination) operates in class practices. The way in which classes are determined also governs the way in which they are reproduced: in other words, as Marx himself emphasized, the very existence of a mode of production involving bourgeoisie and proletariat entails the expanded reproduction of these classes. Secondly there is the reproduction and distribution of the *agents* themselves to these positions. This aspect of reproduction, which involves the questions of who occupies a given position, i.e. who is or becomes a bourgeois, proletarian, petty bourgeois, poor peasant, etc, and how and when he does, *is subordinate to the first aspect*—the reproduction of the actual positions occupied by the social classes: i.e. it is subordinate to the fact that in its expanded reproduction, capitalism is reproducing the bourgeoisie, proletariat and petty bourgeoisie in a new form in its current monopoly phase or to the fact that it is tending to eliminate certain classes and class fractions within the social formations where its expanded reproduction is taking place (e.g. the small-holding peasantry, petty bourgeoisie, etc). In other words, while it is true that the agents themselves must be reproduced—'trained' and 'subjected'—in order to occupy certain places, it is equally true that the distribution of agents does not depend on their choices or aspirations but on the very reproduction of these positions. It is important to emphasize that the distinction between the two *aspects* of reproduction (reproduction of positions and of agents) *does not coincide* with the distinction between reproduction of social relations and reproduction of labour power. These two aspects are features of the ensemble of reproduction, inside which the reproduction of the social relations under discussion is dominant. But in the ensemble of reproduction, including the reproduction of social relations, the reproduction of places constitutes the *principal aspect*.

# · 5 ·

# Class Boundaries and Contradictory Class Locations

## Erik Olin Wright

## An Alternative Conceptualization of Class Boundaries

Perhaps the most serious general criticism of Poulantzas's perspective[1] centres on his treatment of ambiguous positions within the class structure. In his analysis of the working class, *any* deviation at all from the pure working-class criteria . . . is sufficient for exclusion from the proletariat; in his analysis of the bourgeoisie, on the other hand, it is necessary to deviate on *all* criteria in order to be excluded from the capitalist class. In neither case is the possibility allowed that positions within the social division of labour can be objectively contradictory.[2]

### Contradictory Locations Within Class Relations

An alternative way of dealing with such ambiguities in the class structure is to regard some positions as occupying *objectively contradictory locations within class*

---

*From Erik Olin Wright, *Class, Crisis, and the State* (London: New Left Books, 1978), pp. 61–83.

1. Nicos Poulantzas, *Classes in Contemporary Capitalism* (London: New Left Books, 1975).

2. Poulantzas at one point does suggest the possibilities of ambiguous cases when he writes: "The mental/manual labour division is reproduced as a tendency, in the sense that it does not provide a typological classification into rigid compartments for this or that particular agent, and that what matters for us here is its social functioning in the existence and reproduction of social classes." (Ibid., p. 256.) This theme, however, is never developed or given any theoretical specificity in its own right. At most, Poulantzas suggests that there may be some ambiguity in the application of a particular criterion for class position, but not that there may be ambiguities created by contradictions among criteria.

*relations*. Rather than eradicating these contradictions by artificially classifying every position within the social division of labour unambiguously into one class or another, contradictory locations need to be studied in their own right. This will be the primary objective [in what follows (eds.)].[3] (In a sense, of course, all class positions are "contradictory locations", in that class relations are intrinsically antagonistic, contradictory social relations. The point is that certain positions in the class structure constitute doubly contradictory locations: they represent positions which are torn between the basic contradictory class relations of capitalist society. Rather than refer to these positions with a cumbersome expression such as "contradictory locations within the basic contradictory class relations", I will for convenience simply refer to them as "contradictory class locations".)

So far, our discussion of class structure has centered around the elaboration of various criteria for class. This has perhaps been somewhat misleading. When the word "criteria" is used, there is usually an implication that the purpose of the analysis is the construction of formal, abstract typologies. Ambiguities in the class structure then appear as classification problems in the typology, as failures of analytical imagination rather than as objective characteristics of the society itself. The concept of contradictory locations within class relations, however, does not refer to problems of pigeon-holing people within an abstract typology; rather it refers to objective contradictions among the real processes of class relations. To fully grasp the nature of the class structure of capitalist societies, therefore, we need first to understand the various processes which constitute class relations, analyse their historical transformation in the course of capitalist development, and then examine the ways in which the differentiation of these various processes has generated a number of contradictory locations within the class structures of advanced capitalist societies.

To anticipate the conclusion of the analysis, three clusters of positions within the social division of labour can be characterized as occupying contradictory locations within class relations . . . : 1. *managers and supervisors* occupy a contradictory location between the bourgeoisie and the proletariat; 2. certain categories of *semi-autonomous employees* who retain relatively high levels of control over their immediate labour process occupy a contradictory location between the working class and the petty bourgeoisie; 3. *small employers* occupy a contradictory location between the bourgeoisie and the petty bourgeoisie. Our first task is to analyse how these contradictory locations emerge out of the ·dynamics of class relations in advanced capitalist society.

---

3. Carchedi's analysis (see "On the Economic Identification of the New Middle Class", *Economy and Society*, Vol. 4, No. 4 [1975] and "Reproduction of Social Classes at the Level of Production Relations", *Economy and Society*, Vol. 4, No. 4, pp. 362–417) of the new middle classes bears a certain resemblance to the present discussion of contradictory locations within class relations. Carchedi defines the new middle classes as positions which perform both the "global function of capital" and the "function of the collective worker" and thus "are only identifiable in terms of contradiction". For a discussion and critique of Carchedi's analysis, see Wright, "Class Structure and Income Inequality", unpublished Ph.D. Dissertation, Dept. of Sociology, University of California, Berkeley.

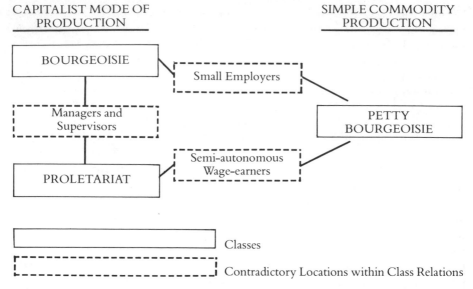

| CAPITALIST MODE OF PRODUCTION | SIMPLE COMMODITY PRODUCTION |

*Figure 1.*    The Relationship of Contradictory Class Positions to Class Forces in Capitalist Society

## The Processes of Class Relations

Three interconnected structural changes in the course of capitalist development can help us to unravel the social processes underlying class relations in advanced capitalism:[4] the progressive loss of control over the labour process on the part of the direct producers; the elaboration of complex authority hierarchies within capitalist enterprises and bureaucracies; and the differentiation of various functions originally embodied in the entrepreneurial capitalist.[5] Since each of these developments has been thoroughly studied elsewhere, I will only briefly review them here in order to give more substance to the social processes used in the rest of the analysis.

*Loss of control over the labour process by workers.*

The saga of the progressive dispossession of the direct producers in the course of capitalist development has been told many times. The point that needs stressing here is that the loss of control over the labour process is not an all-or-nothing phenomenon, but has occurred gradually over a long period of time and exists in varying degrees even today. In the earliest capitalist production process, the direct producers generally maintained considerable control over the

---

4. See Wright, Chapter 2, for a considerably more elaborate discussion of these processes of class relations.

5. The point of studying these three historical transformations is less to understand their historical origins as such, than to use structural re-orderings of the capitalist system as a way of gaining insights into the social processes underlying class relations in contemporary capitalism. The epistemological assumption is that a number of distinct social processes are congealed in the class relation between the proletariat and the bourgeoisie and that an analysis of the historical transformations of that class relation is a way of gaining knowledge about the underlying processes themselves.

labour process. Often, especially in cottage industries, they even owned all or part of their immediate means of production. Such a situation made it much easier for the direct producers to control the pace of their labour and the length of their working day, thus making it more difficult for capitalists to raise the rate of exploitation. The net result was that workers' control over their own labour acted as a serious constraint on the accumulation process in early capitalism.[6]

Much of the history of class struggle between capitalists and workers, especially in the 19th century, can be seen as a struggle over the terms of the control of the labour process.[7] As Stephen Marglin has argued, one of the major impulses for the creation of factories was the desire to undermine worker control.[8] At a minimum factory owners had much greater control over the length of the working day, and generally over other aspects of the labour process as well.

Once workers were gathered within factories, the assault on their remaining control of the labour process continued in the form of technical innovations which fragmented the production process and progressively "deskilled" the labour force.[9] Capitalists could force workers to work in the factory for ten hours by the clock, but as long as the worker maintained real autonomy in the labour process it was difficult for the capitalist to be sure of getting anywhere near ten hours of actual labour from the worker. The close supervision of the labour process is much easier when tasks are simple and routinized and their pace is determined by machinery rather than the worker. Thus, capitalists look for innovations which tend to reduce skill levels and reduce the autonomy of workers on the job. The culmination of this process was the mass production assembly line regulated by principles of Taylorism, in which the worker lost all autonomy and became virtually a human component of machinery itself.

The reverse tendency also exists within capitalism. As technology changes, new skills are needed and new categories of jobs are created in which the worker may have greater immediate control over the labour process. Furthermore, in recent decades the crude scientific management advocated by Taylor has been replaced at least partially in some corporations by "human relations" approaches to the problem of worker productivity. One part of such new approaches is, in principle, the "enrichment" of jobs and the enlargement of the sphere of decision-making under the control of the worker.

Both of these counter-tendencies to the general process of deskilling and the erosion of worker autonomy in the labour process, however, still reflect the salience of control over the labour process as a dimension of class relations. While new skills are continually being created, it is also true that there is constant pressure to reduce the skill levels needed to perform a given task. Thus, for example, when computers were first being developed, the actual operators of computer hardware tended to be engineers. Gradually over the past twenty years this job has been "deskilled" until, at present, computer operators are technicians with only one or two years of post-high school training.

---

6. See Wright, Chapter 3, p. 170.
7. See especially Katherine Stone, "The Origins of Job Structures in the Steel Industry", *Review of Radical Political Economics,* Vol. 6, No. 2, Summer 1974.
8. "What Do Bosses Do?", *Review of Radical Political Economics,* Vol. 6, No. 2, 1974.
9. See Harry Braverman, *Labour and Monopoly Capitalism,* New York 1974.

As for the various experiments with worker participation, such enlarged autonomy is almost always confined within very narrow limits and is always seen as a way of getting workers to work more productively. That is, control is relinquished—and generally peripheral control at that—only when it is more than compensated for by increasing production. Thus, in a report to the Conference Board[10] entitled "Job Design for Motivation", Harold Rush writes: "The current emphasis [in job design] is on gaining internal motivation from the employee so that he performs his tasks with more dedication and commitment, as contrasted with coercion, robot-style control, and machine-like pacing. . . . The design and redesign of jobs may be said to have a single purpose, though it is a purpose with a double edge: to increase both employee motivation and productivity."[11]

Greater worker control of the labour process, or what is often called "worker participation", is one important form of this redesigning of jobs to increase productivity. In a second Conference Board report entitled "Worker Participation: New Voices in Management", John Roach writes: "A Conference Board survey of top level executives in 50 countries indicates that participation concepts are winning increased acceptance as approaches to improving productivity, motivating job satisfaction, and resolving labour-management problems both within and outside traditional collective bargaining processes. Indeed, responses from the international panel suggest that a widening emphasis on participation is adding a broad new dimension to the operation of free enterprise in the Western World. That is not to say that management has decided it should share any of its board-room prerogatives with unions, works councils, or other worker representatives. On the contrary, the general mood of the 143 executives cooperating in the Board's survey is that management must resist attempts to usurp its ultimate authority to make the big decisions."[12]

Far from contradicting the importance of control of the labour process as a dimension of class relations, the sporadic trends towards increased worker participation reveal the underlying logic of this dimension. Capital tries to extract as much actual labour out of the worker during the work day as possible (this would hardly be denied by any capitalist). Control over the labour process is a basic means of accomplishing this. Under certain historical conditions, for example when a large proportion of the industrial work force are newly proletarianized petty bourgeois (artisans, peasants, etc.) with little experience of factory discipline and without proper work habits, strict and despotic control of the labour process may be the most effective structure of control from the

---

10. The Conference Board is a nonprofit business research organization which is, in its own words, "an institution for scientific research in the fields of business economics and business management. Its sole purpose is to promote prosperity and security by assisting in the effective operation and sound development of voluntary productive enterprise." Members of the Conference Board are drawn from the top executives of the largest corporations in the United States and generally the views of the Conference Board can be interpreted as reflecting the "vanguard" position of the American capitalist class.

11. Harold Rush, "Job Design for Motivation: Experiments in Job Enlargement and Job Enrichment", *Conference Board Report* No. 515, New York 1971.

12. John Roach, "Worker Participation: New Voices in Management" *Conference Board Report* No. 564, New York 1973.

capitalist point of view. Under contemporary conditions, a partial relaxation of direct control may accomplish the same end.[13] In any event, social relations of control over the labour process remain a basic dimension of class relations.

*The differentiation of the functions of capital.*

No development in capitalist social relations has been used more often as "proof" that Marx's image of class structure is outmoded than the so-called "separation of ownership and control" in the modern corporation. Of course, no one can deny the considerable growth of managerial hierarchies in the modern corporation and the general decline of the traditional family-owned firm in favour of the joint-stock company (although, as Zeitlin forcefully argues, there are considerable data to indicate that the proponents of the "managerial revolution" thesis have grossly exaggerated these changes).[14] The issue is not whether professional managers play a bigger role in running corporations today than 100 years ago, but how such positions should be structurally interpreted in terms of a theory of class relations.

The apparent separation of ownership and control in the large corporation hides a complex process involving a whole series of structural transformations and differentiations. Two such transformations are of particular importance for our discussion: the functional differentiation between economic ownership and possession, and the partial dissociation between legal ownership and economic ownership. In the 19th century, all three of these dimensions of ownership were embodied in the entrepreneurial capitalist. As part of the process of the concentration and centralization of capital, these three dimensions of ownership have tended to become at least partially differentiated.

The partial separation of economic ownership (control over the flow of investments into production, or more concretely, control over *what* is produced) from possession (control over the production process, or control over *how* things are produced) is a consequence of the concentration and centralization of capital within the accumulation process. Increasing concentration and centralization has encouraged the differentiation of economic ownership and possession for two reasons: first, and most obviously, as the scale of both ownership and production increases, it becomes less and less practical for the same individuals to be equally involved in both functions. Competitive pressures will tend to push capitalists to hire professional managers to deal with specific aspects of production and eventually to help coordinate the production process as a whole. Secondly, as Poulantzas has emphasized, there is a tendency in monopoly capitalism for the concentration and centralization of economic

---

13. This is not to suggest that the capitalist simply decides what structure of control of the labour process is most advantageous for increasing the rate of exploitation, and then proceeds to adopt that form of control. In the 19th century there was often considerable resistance on the part of craft labour to efforts at deepening capitalist control over the labour process, and at the present many of the experiments in enlarged worker participation, especially in Europe, have been the result of pressures from workers rather than initiatives from capitalists. Control of the labour process is a constant object of class struggle (or perhaps more precisely: it is a dimension of class struggle), and the actual patterns of control which emerge should be seen as the outcome of such struggle and not simply manipulative devices used by capitalists.

14. Maurice Zeitlin, "Corporate Ownership and Control: the Large Corporation and the Capitalist Class", *American Journal of Sociology,* Vol. 79, 1974.

ownership to develop more rapidly than the concentration and centralization of possession, i.e. for a diverse collection of production processes to be formally united under a single economic ownership. In such circumstances it becomes impossible for the two functions of capital—ownership and possession—to be completely united in a single position.

Capitalist development has also been characterized by a gradual dissociation between formal legal ownership and real economic ownership. This is the famous phenomenon of the dispersion of stock ownership in the large corporation. The fact of such dispersion has been the core datum used by supporters of the managerial revolution thesis to argue that the control of the corporation has moved from property owners to professional managers. Marxists have generally drawn quite different conclusions. Building on the arguments of Hilferding, De Vroey writes: "Concerning the second aspect of the separation of ownership and control, i.e., the dissociation between legal ownership and ownership as a relation of production, the Marxist interpretation is as follows: the dispersion of stock among a large number of small owners is accepted as a matter of fact, and explained as a means to mobilize the ever increasing amount of capital needed for accumulation. But rather than seeing the dispersion of stock as an obstacle to concentrated control, Marxism interprets it in exactly the opposite way: as a means for reinforcing the actual control of big stockholders, who thus succeed in commanding an amount of funds out of proportion to their actual ownership. Paradoxically, dispersion of stock thus favors the centralization of capital."[15] For the managerial revolution proponents to prove their case, therefore, it is not enough to show that stock is widely dispersed. They must show that real economic ownership is in the hands of managers, i.e., that they actually control the accumulation process as a whole. The emphasis on economic ownership as opposed to formal legal ownership should not be taken to imply that legal title to stocks and other forms of property is irrelevant to understanding class relations. On the contrary: as long as capitalist relations of production remain embedded in the legal superstructure of private property, formal legal ownership is in general a *necessary* condition for economic ownership. The point of the distinction between economic and legal ownership is that formal title is not a *sufficient* condition for actual participation in the control of the investment and accumulation process.[16]

*The development of complex hierarchies.*

The same process of concentration and centralization of capital that generates the basic differentiation of economic ownership and possession, also gener-

---

15. Michael DeVroey, "The Separation of Ownership and Control in Large Corporations", *The Review of Radical Political Economics,* Vol. 7, No. 2, 1975.

16. The debate on the relationship between legal ownership and real economic ownership becomes especially important in the analysis of class relations in societies where all property is legally owned by the State (such as the USSR or China). The most vigorous defenders of the thesis that legal ownership is of entirely secondary significance tend to be those who wish to demonstrate that such countries are essentially capitalist. I will not address the questions of class in such state-owned economies. In the West, legal ownership cannot be relegated to a purely epiphenomenal status. Legal title to property remains the essential vehicle for controlling resources in capitalist societies and thus shaping the entire accumulation process. Not all individuals who own stock are part of the bourgeoisie, but all occupants of bourgeois class locations own substantial quantities of stock (or other forms of property in the means of production).

ates various forms of internal differentiation within each of these dimensions of ownership. First let us look at relations of possession. Relations of possession concern the direction and control of the capitalist production process. Such direction involves two analytically separable aspects: first, control of the physical means of production; second, control of labour. Even in the earliest capitalist enterprise, there was some structural differentiation between these two aspects. Foremen were typically excluded from any real control of the physical means of production, yet played an important role in the supervision of workers. As the capitalist enterprise expanded, additional layers of supervision were added, leading eventually to the complex hierarchy of social control within the monopoly corporation. Capitalist development has also produced an elaborate hierarchy within the other aspect of possession, control over the physical means of production. At the highest levels of the hierarchy, top managers control the entire apparatus of production.[17] Below them, various middle levels of management participate in the control of segments of the production process. At the bottom, certain categories of workers maintain some real control over their immediate production process (i.e. over *how* they do their jobs). A similar line of reasoning can be developed for economic ownership. In the earliest capitalist enterprise, economic ownership was not organized hierarchically. A single figure was essentially responsible for the entire accumulation process. In the modern corporation, however, different levels of economic ownership can be distinguished. Full economic ownership refers to participation in the control of the overall investment and accumulation process. Typically, the highest executives in the corporation and certain members of the board of directors would occupy this position. Under most circumstances, full economic ownership implies a substantial level of formal legal ownership as well. Below this level there are executives and managers who participate in decisions concerning investments in either sub-units of the total production process (e.g. branches) or partial aspects of the entire investment process (e.g. marketing). Finally, minimal economic ownership involves control over *what* one produces in one's immediate labour process, even though one has no control over what is produced in the production process as a whole.[18] These various hierarchical levels within the relations of economic ownership and relations of possession are summarized in Table 1.

On the basis of this brief sketch of historical developments within capitalist

---

17. "Level" refers principally to the scope of control attached to a particular position, rather than the formal location within an organizational hierarchy (although the two would generally tend to coincide). The word "control" in this context should not be taken to imply that the *individual* who occupies a particular social position controls the means of production as an individual. Rather the word designates a social relationship between the position and the means of production. To say that top managers "control the entire apparatus of production" does not mean that any one individual by him/herself controls the entire apparatus, but rather that the individual occupies a position which participates in the control of the entire apparatus of production.

18. Such residual economic ownership constitutes genuine ownership to the extent that genuine control over the disposition of resources—what is produced—exists. Of course, in most corporate settings such minimal ownership is highly constrained by higher level ownership relations, both in the sense that the range of possible uses of resources is limited by higher up decisions and in the sense that the magnitude of resources available for use may be strictly determined from above. When such control over what is produced becomes so marginal as to be irrelevant to the overall accumulation process, then it ceases to make sense to talk about even residual forms of economic ownership.

*Table 1.* **Hierarchical Levels Within Ownership Relations**

| | RELATIONS OF ECONOMIC OWNERSHIP (CONTROL OVER WHAT IS PRODUCED) | RELATIONS OF POSSESSION (CONTROL OVER HOW THINGS ARE PRODUCED) | | LEGAL OWNERSHIP |
|---|---|---|---|---|
| | | CONTROL OF MEANS OF PRODUCTION | CONTROL OVER LABOUR POWER | |
| *Full control* | Control over the overall investment and accumulation process | Control over the entire apparatus of production | Control over the entire supervisory hierarchy | Sufficient stock to ensure influence on investments and accumulation |
| *Partial control* | Participation in decisions concerning either sub-units of the total production process or partial aspects of the entire investment process | Control over one segment of the total production process | Control over one segment of the supervisory hierarchy | Sufficient stock to ensure financial stake in profits of corporation (stock is a significant part of income) |
| *Minimal control* | Control over *what* one produces in one's immediate labour process | Control over one's immediate instruments of production; over *how* one does one's own job | Control over the direct producers, over immediate subordinates but not part of the hierarchy as such | Marginal stock ownership (stock is an insignificant part of income) |
| *No control* | Complete exclusion from participation in decisions about what to produce | Negligible control over any aspect of the means of production | No ability to invoke sanctions on other workers | No stock ownership |

relations of production, it is possible to isolate three central processes underlying the basic capital-labour relationship: control over the physical means of production; control over labour power; control over investments and resource allocation. The first two of these comprise what Poulantzas has called possession; the third is essentially the same as economic ownership. Again, it must be stressed that these three processes are the real stuff of class relations in capitalist society; they are not merely analytic dimensions derived from *a priori* reasoning.[19]

The fundamental class antagonism between workers and capitalists can be viewed as a polarization on each of these three underlying processes or dimensions: capitalists control the accumulation process, decide how the physical means of production are to be used, and control the authority structure within the labour process. Workers, in contrast, are excluded from the control over authority relations, the physical means of production, and the investment process. These two combinations of the three processes of class relations constitute the two basic antagonistic class locations within the capitalist mode of production.

When the capitalist system is analysed at the highest level of abstraction—the level of the pure capitalist mode of production—these are the only class positions defined by capitalist relations of production.[20] When we move to the next lower level of abstraction—what is generally called the level of the "social formation"—other class positions appear.

They appear, first of all, because real capitalist societies always contain subordinate modes of production other than the capitalist mode of production itself. In particular, simple commodity production (i.e., production organized for the market by independent self-employed producers who employ no workers) has always existed within capitalist societies. Within simple commodity production, the petty bourgeoisie is defined as having economic ownership and possession of the means of production, but having no control over labour power (since no labour power is employed). The relationship of the petty

---

19. The non-arbitrariness of the choice of these three dimensions of class relations is reflected in their correspondence to the three elements in the formal value equations of Marxist political economy (total value = C + V + S). The control over the physical means of production represents relations of control over constant capital; control over labour implies relations of control over variable capital; and control over investments and accumulation implies relations of control over surplus value. (This correspondence was suggested by Michael Soref).

20. There is a strong tradition within Marxism which limits the definition of classes to this most abstract level. Such simple polarization views of class insist that except for the residues of classes from pre-capitalist modes of production, all positions within capitalist society fall either within the capitalist class or the working class. Typically, in such analyses all wage-earners are considered workers. The basic weakness of simple polarization views of the class structure is that they assume that the simplicity of class relations at the level of abstraction of the mode of production can be directly translated into a corresponding simplicity at the level of concrete societies. The added complexities of concrete social structures are taken to be of purely secondary importance. They may contribute to divisions within classes, but they in principle can have no effects on the criteria for class boundaries. This is a fundamentally incorrect way of understanding the relationship between abstract and concrete levels of analysis. Abstract relations do not obliterate the importance of concrete complexities, but rather render them theoretically intelligible. As we will see below, contradictory class locations can be understood only with reference to the basic polarized class relations of the capitalist mode of production, and yet they cannot be reduced to those polarized class positions.

*Table 2.* **Unambiguous Locations Within Class Relations**

| | PROCESSES UNDERLYING CLASS RELATIONS | | |
|---|---|---|---|
| | *Economic Ownership* | *Possession* | |
| | Control over investments and the accumulation process | Control over physical means of production | Control over the labour power of others |
| Bourgeoisie | + | + | + |
| Proletariat | − | − | − |
| Petty bourgeoisie | + | + | − |

+ Full Control   − No Control   (See Table 1 for precise definitions.)

bourgeoisie to the polarized class positions of the capitalist mode of production is illustrated in Table 2.

A second way in which additional class positions appear when we leave the abstraction of the pure capitalist mode of production is that the three processes which constitute capitalist social relations of production do not always perfectly coincide. This non-coincidence of the dimensions of class relations defines the contradictory locations within class relations.

### The Analysis of Contradictory Locations Within Class Relations

We will explore two different kinds of contradictory locations: 1. contradictory locations between the bourgeoisie and the proletariat, i.e. locations defined by contradictory combinations of the three processes underlying class relations within the capitalist mode of production; 2. contradictory locations between the petty bourgeoisie and both the proletariat and the bourgeoisie, i.e. locations situated between the capitalist mode of production and simple commodity production.[21] Table 3 presents the basic relationship between the unambiguous locations illustrated in Table 2 and the contradictory locations. In addition to the three social processes discussed above, this chart also contains three juridical categories: legal ownership of property, legal status as the employer of labour power, and legal status as a seller of labour power. These three juridical processes have been included because they so often are treated as the determinants of class position. It must be kept in mind in referring to them that the juridical criteria are of strictly secondary importance; the fundamental issue remains the patterns of contradictory locations defined by the three substantive processes of class relations.

*Contradictory Locations Between the Proletariat and the Bourgeoisie.*
One thing is immediately obvious from Table 3. The contradictory quality of a particular location within class relations is a variable rather than all-or-

---

21. We will not discuss contradictory locations that occur because an individual simultaneously occupies two class positions within social relations of production. For example, a craftsman who works in a factory on weekdays may operate as a self-employed petty-bourgeois artisan on weekends and evenings. While such dual class membership may be important in certain historical circumstances, it does not pose the same kind of analytical problem as positions which are themselves located in a contradictory way within class relations.

**Table 3.  Contradictory Locations Within Class Relations**

| | SUBSTANTIVE SOCIAL PROCESSES COMPRISING CLASS RELATIONS | | | JURIDICAL CATEGORIES OF CLASS RELATIONS | | |
| --- | --- | --- | --- | --- | --- | --- |
| | *Economic Ownership* | *Possession* | | *Legal Ownership* | | *Wage Labour* |
| | Control over investments, resources | Control over the physical means of production | Control over the labour power of others | Legal ownership of property (capital, stocks, real estate etc.) | Legal status of being the employer of labour power | Sale of one's own labour power |
| *Bourgeoisie* | | | | | | |
| Traditional capitalist | Partial | + | + | + | + | – |
| Top corporate executive | + | + | + | Partial | – | Minimal |
| *Contradictory location between the proletariat and the bourgeoisie* | | | | | | |
| Top managers | Partial | + | + | Minimal | – | Partial |
| Middle managers | Minimal | Partial | Partial | – | – | + |
| Technocrats | Minimal/– | Minimal | Minimal | – | – | + |
| Foremen/line supervisors | – | – | Minimal | – | – | + |
| *Proletariat* | – | – | – | – | – | + |

**Table 3.** (*Continued*)

| | SUBSTANTIVE SOCIAL PROCESSES COMPRISING CLASS RELATIONS | | | JURIDICAL CATEGORIES OF CLASS RELATIONS | | |
| --- | --- | --- | --- | --- | --- | --- |
| | *Economic Ownership* | *Possession* | | *Legal Ownership* | | *Wage Labour* |
| | Control over investments, resources | Control over the physical means of production | Control over the labour power of others | Legal ownership of property (capital, stocks, real estate etc.) | Legal status of being the employer of labour power | Sale of one's own labour power |
| *Contradictory location between the proletariat and the petty bourgeoisie* | | | | | | |
| Semi-autonomous employees | Minimal | Minimal | – | – | – | + |
| *Petty bourgeoisie* | + | + | – | + | – | – |
| *Contradictory location between the petty bourgeoisie and the bourgeoisie* | | | | | | |
| Small employers | + | + | Minimal | + | Minimal | – |

+ Full control    Partial: Attenuated control    Minimal: Residual control    – No control
(See Table 1 for precise definitions.)

nothing characteristic. Certain positions can be thought of as occupying a contradictory location around the boundary of the proletariat; others as occupying a contradictory location around the boundary of the bourgeoisie.

The contradictory location closest to the working class is that of foremen and line supervisors. Foremen typically have little real control over the physical means of production, and while they do exercise control over labour power, this frequently does not extend much beyond being the formal transmission belt for orders from above. It is difficult to say whether during the course of capitalist development over the past century, the class location of foremen has moved closer to or further from the working class. On the one hand, the early foreman often participated directly in the production process alongside workers and even defended workers against arbitrary treatment by the boss. On the other hand, the foreman in the nineteenth-century factory often had much greater personal discretion and personal power than today. In the nineteenth century, authority within the capitalist factory was typically organized in much the same way as an army. There was a simple chain of command and the authority at each level was absolute with respect to the level below. Such a system Marx aptly termed "factory despotism", and foremen in such a factory had at least the potential of being petty despots. As the capitalist enterprise grew in scale and complexity, the authority structure gradually became more bureaucratized. As Weber would put it, foremen increasingly became the administrators of impersonal rules rather than the dispensers of personal fiats.

Richard Edwards, in a study of work norms in bureaucratically structured capitalist organizations, describes this shift in authority relations as follows: "What distinguishes modern enterprises from their earlier and cruder prototypes—and in particular, what distinguishes bureaucratic organization from simple hierarchy—is that in bureaucratically organized enterprises, the exercise of power becomes *institutionalized*. External, arbitrary, personal commands from the boss are replaced by established rules and procedures: 'rule of law' replaces 'rule of personal command'. Work activities become directed by rules. Supervisors at all levels, no longer directing the worker's activities by personal instruction, merely enforce the rules and evaluate (reward or penalize) their subordinates according to pre-established criteria for adequate work performance. More and more, the work structure is designed so that administrative control can replace executive control."[22] The development of the capitalist enterprise has thus pushed foremen in two opposing directions: they have moved further from workers by becoming less involved in direct production, and they have moved closer to workers by gradually having their personal power bureaucratized. Superficially at least, it would seem that the first of these tendencies probably dominated during the first part of this century, while the second tendency probably dominates today. In any event, when the control of supervisors over labour power becomes so attenuated that the supervisor lacks even the

---

22. *Alienation and Inequality: Capitalist Relations of Production in Business Enterprises,* Ph.D. Dissertation, Department of Economics, Harvard, p. 102.

capacity to invoke negative sanctions, then the position really merges with the working class proper and should no longer be thought of as a contradictory location. This would be the case, for example, of the chief of a work team who has certain special responsibilities for coordinating activities of others in the team, but lacks any real power over them.

At the other end of the contradictory location between workers and capitalists, top managers occupy a contradictory location at the boundary of the bourgeoisie. While top managers are generally characterized by limited participation in economic ownership, they differ little from the bourgeoisie in terms of relations of possession. Again, at the very top of the managerial hierarchy, corporate executives essentially merge with the capitalist class itself.

The most contradictory locations between the bourgeoisie and the proletariat are occupied by middle managers and what can loosely be termed "technocrats". Technocrat in this context refers to technicians and professionals of various sorts within the corporate hierarchy who tend to have a limited degree of autonomy over their own work (*minimal* control over what they produce and how they produce it) and a limited control over subordinates, but who are not in command of pieces of the productive apparatus. Middle managers, on the other hand, control various pieces of the labour process; they have control not only over immediate subordinates but over part of the authority hierarchy itself. Both middle managers and technocrats have, in Harry Braverman's words, one foot in the bourgeoisie and one foot in the proletariat. In discussing new technical occupations and middle management, Braverman writes: "If we are to call this a 'new middle class', however, as many have done, we must do so with certain reservations. The old middle class occupied that position by virtue of its place outside the polar class structure; it possessed the attributes of neither capitalist nor worker; it played no direct role in the capital accumulation process, whether on one side or the other. This 'new middle class', by contrast, occupies its intermediate position not because it is outside the process of increasing capital, but because, as part of this process, it takes its characteristics from *both sides.* Not only does it receive its petty share of the prerogatives and rewards of capital, but it also bears the mark of the proletarian condition."[23] Unlike line supervisors and foremen on the one hand, and top managers on the other, middle managers and technocrats do not have a clear class pole to which they are attached. The contradictory quality of their class location is much more intense than in the other cases we have discussed, and as a result it is much more difficult to assess the general stance they will take within class struggle.

*Contradictory Locations Between the Petty Bourgeoisie and Other Classes.*

The analysis of the contradictory locations between the petty bourgeoisie and other classes poses a somewhat different problem from the contradictory locations between the bourgeoisie and the proletariat, since it involves locations between different modes of production rather than within a single mode of production.

The contradictory location between the petty bourgeoisie and the bourgeoisie is conceptually simpler than between the petty bourgeoisie and the

---

23. Braverman, *Labor and Monopoly Capital,* p. 467.

proletariat. The distinctive feature of capitalist production is the appropriation of surplus-value through the exploitation of workers in the labour process. In simple commodity production, on the other hand, there is no exploitation; whatever surplus is produced is generated by the petty-bourgeois producer and his/her family. In general, of course, the surplus is likely to be very small and thus little if any accumulation is likely to occur. When a petty-bourgeois producer employs a single helper, there is an immediate change in the social relations of production, for the labour of a worker can now be exploited. Still, the surplus-value appropriated from a single employee is likely to be very small; most importantly, it is likely to be less than the surplus product generated by the petty-bourgeois producer him/herself. This is especially likely since frequently in petty-bourgeois production a considerable amount of labour is contributed by unpaid family members. As additional employees are added, the proportion of the total surplus product that is generated by the petty-bourgeois family declines. At some point it becomes less than half of the total surplus product, and eventually becomes a small fraction of the total surplus. At that point, the petty-bourgeois producer becomes firmly a small capitalist. There is no *a priori* basis for deciding how many employees are necessary to become a small capitalist. This number would vary considerably for different technologies employed in production and for different historical periods. In any event, between such a small capitalist and the pure petty-bourgeois producer lies the contradictory location between the capitalist class and the petty-bourgeoisie.

The contradictory location between the petty bourgeoisie and the proletariat can perhaps best be understood by returning to the historic process of proletarianization of the petty bourgeoisie. The central dynamic underlying this transformation was the need of capital to increase its control over the labour process. Each step of the transformation involved a deeper penetration of capitalist domination into the labouring activity of direct producers, until in the classic form of scientific management, the direct producer has no control whatsoever over his/her work. This process is constantly being re-enacted within capitalism; it is not a process which was somehow completed at the beginning of this century.

Today there are still categories of employees who have a certain degree of control over their own immediate conditions of work, over their immediate labour process. In such instances, the labour process has not been completely proletarianized. Thus, even though such employees work for the self-expansion of capital and even though they have lost the legal status of being self-employed, they can still be viewed as occupying residual islands of petty-bourgeois relations of production within the capitalist mode of production itself. In their immediate work environment, they maintain the work process of the independent artisan while still being employed by capital as wage labourers. They control *how* they do their work, and have at least some control over *what* they produce. A good example of this is a researcher in a laboratory or a professor in an elite university. Such positions may not really involve control over other people's labour power, yet have considerable immediate control over conditions of work (i.e. research). More generally, many white-collar technical employees and certain highly skilled craftsmen have at least a limited form of this autonomy in their immediate labour process. Such minimal control over the physical means of production by employees outside of the authority hierarchy constitutes the basic contradictory location between the petty bourgeoisie and the proletariat.

While there is some debate on the question, it seems likely that in the course of capitalist development over the past fifty years, this particular kind of contradictory location has been somewhat reduced. It is certainly true that white-collar employees have increased as a proportion of the labour force, but as Braverman has forcefully shown, this expansion of white-collar employment has been combined with a constant proletarianization of the working conditions of white-collar labour. It remains to be shown whether the net effect of these two tendencies—the expansion of white-collar employment and the proletarianization of white-collar work—has increased or decreased the contradictory locations between the working class and the petty bourgeoisie. At any rate, it seems almost certain that the large majority of white-collar employees, especially clerical and secretarial employees, have—at most—trivial autonomy on the job and thus should be placed within the working class itself.

How much autonomy is really necessary to define a position as occupying the contradictory location between the working class and the petty bourgeoisie? Surely the criterion of absolutely any autonomy whatsoever is too broad. While the historical data on the labour process are rather meagre, it is unlikely that more than a small fraction of the working class was ever characterized by the classic image of the fully proletarianized worker, totally under the control of the capitalist through a minutely subdivided labour process governed by principles of scientific management. Most workers, most of the time, have been able to maintain at least some residual control over their immediate labour process. Similarly, it would be inappropriate to restrict the concept of "semi-autonomy" to positions which, like university professors, have extremely high levels of control over the pace of work, the scheduling of work, the content of work, etc. Clearly, then, a certain amount of arbitrariness will inevitably enter into any attempt rigorously to define the semi-autonomous employee class location.[24]

Provisionally, the minimum criterion for semi-autonomy which I will adopt is that such positions must involve at least some control both over what is produced (minimal economic ownership) as well as how it is produced (minimal possession). This means that positions such as laboratory technicians would not be included in the semi-autonomous category since such positions would generally not involve any control over what kind of experiments were done in the lab, even though a technician might have very considerable control over other conditions of work (pace, breaks, techniques used, etc.). A research scientist, on the other hand, would often not simply have autonomy over how he/she

---

24. A similar problem exists with the other contradictory locations. How many employees are necessary to transform a small employer (the contradictory location between the petty bourgeoisie and the bourgeoisie) into a proper capitalist? How residual must the authority of a foreman be before he/she should be considered a worker? How much participation in investment decisions is necessary before a top manager should be thought of as part of the bourgeoisie itself? In every case, therefore, there will be ambiguous locations right at the boundaries of polarized classes, and a certain arbitrariness will occur whenever formal criteria are applied to such positions. The semi-autonomous employee category, however, poses additional problems because of the ambiguities in the very concept of "autonomy".

performed an experiment, but over what experiments were performed. Research scientists, therefore, would be firmly within the semi-autonomous employee category.[25]

Several other contradictory locations could be discussed. For example, the owners of fast food and gas station franchises could be seen as occupying a contradictory location between the petty bourgeoisie or small employers and managers. While they maintain some of the characteristics of self-employed independent producers, they also become much more like functionaries for large capitalist corporations. Professors with large research grants which enable them directly to hire research assistants, secretaries, etc., could be thought of as occupying a contradictory location between the semi-autonomous employees and small employers. Other special cases could be given, but the most important contradictory locations are the ones discussed above.

---

25. There is an important relationship between Poulantzas's discussion of mental labour and this discussion of semi-autonomous employees. Poulantzas defines mental labour as labour which involves "secret knowledge" of the production process, in the sense of having knowledge about the organization and coordination of the production process as a whole. Poulantzas also emphasizes that to be mental labour (in his sense of the term) it is not enough to simply have such knowledge; it is necessary to actually use it within the production process. . . . Semi-autonomous employees are, in these terms, employees with such knowledge of the production process as a whole, who have the capacity to use such knowledge on their jobs. This is what it means to have minimal control over what is produced and how it is produced.

# · 6 ·

# A Critique of the Althusserian Approach to Class

## R. W. Connell

Marxism in the late nineteenth and early twentieth century had a profound intellectual impact by asserting the importance of economic processes in the pattern of historical change. In the course of polemic and political conflict, this theme hardened into the "economism" which Lenin and others rejected, and which Althusser wished to oppose in theory. In order to do so, and to produce credible accounts of the flux of history and the complexity of conjunctures, while holding to the orthodox Marxist doctrine of determination-by-the-economic, Althusser produced the various translation devices . . . : the distinction between instances, the idea of their relative autonomy, overdetermination, and determination in the last instance by the economic; and the distinction between logical levels of analysis, between the level of the structures and the level of their effects, between the abstract analysis of the mode of production and the concrete analysis of conjunctures in history.

It is the last of these that is crucial in the application of the theory of class. To follow the way it works, and the way it solves the dilemma of historicity, it is necessary to go into a bit of detail. I will concentrate mainly on one crucial example, the treatment of the problem by Poulantzas in *Political Power and Social Classes*. Analogous distinctions are made by other authors, and in others of Poulantzas' writings; but it is worked out in greater detail and explicitness here than anywhere else.

Poulantzas accepts the general Althusserian distinction between three instances (or levels) within a mode of production or social formation; and he

•Abridged from *Theory and Society* 8(3) (1979): 321–45.

accepts the general distinction between an abstract level (the mode of production) and a more concrete level (social formation) in which several modes of production may be combined. In constructing the concept of class, as we have already seen, he introduces a third conceptual distinction, which, so to speak, operates at right angles to the others: the distinction between the field of the structures and the field of social relations.

This distinction is in fact built in to his definition of class . . . :

> In this sense, if class is indeed a concept, it does not designate a reality which can be placed in the structures; it designates the effect of an ensemble of given structures, an ensemble which determines social relations as class relations.[1]

(To translate roughly: there is a field of social relations, which gets organized along class lines by the combined influence of all the structures.) The field of social relations is "circumscribed by the limits set by structures"—i.e. structural determination operates on classes—and being so determined, it also has its three instances. Yet it is distinct, with its own characteristics and dynamics, and is capable of becoming "dislocated" from the structures. For this is the field in which the class struggle occurs. This struggle in fact *is* the opposition between the practices of the different classes, which come to a head in class politics ("political class struggle"), the "nodal point" of the process of transformation of the whole system. The analysis of this field of conflicting class practices requires new concepts (e.g. "interests" and "power") which do not appear in the analysis of the structures. This field is the site of the "conjuncture," the current situation in which classes and other groupings appear in the guise of "social forces," and which is the object of political practice—notably, attempts to revolutionize the lot.[2]

The field distinction at first led Poulantzas to deny that the concept of "class" was strictly applicable within the field of the structures. In *Classes in Contemporary Capitalism* he retreated from this austerity. But he retained the field distinction, in slightly altered terminology, as the distinction between the class "place" in the field of structural determination and the class "position" in the conjuncture, adding a little diagram (Table 1) to make it all clear.[3] Poulantzas is very clear that place and position need not coincide; in fact a great deal of his analysis, in both books, turns on the idea that they don't.

It is worth reflecting on what this theoretical evolution has given us. Starting from the general analysis of the mode of production, we have (within the field of the structures) the more concrete level of the social formation, which need not correspond with all its constituent modes of production in the classes it gives rise to. Within social formations (and within the field of social relations), we have three distinct and relatively autonomous instances which may be, in fact normally are, dislocated from each other, and on each of which a class may or may not have a distinct existence. We have, beside the field of the structures,

---

1. N. Poulantzas, *Political Power and Social Classes* (London: NLB and Sheen & Ward, 1973), 67–8.

2. This exposition is a summary of points from *ibid.*, 68–98, where the quoted phrases will be found.

3. N. Poulantzas, *Classes in Contemporary Capitalism* (London: NLB, 1975), 15.

## Table 1.

| PRACTICES/CLASS STRUGGLE | |
| --- | --- |
| **STRUCTURAL DETERMINATION/ CLASS PLACES** | **CONJUNCTURE/ CLASS POSITIONS** |

SOCIAL DIVISION OF LABOUR (Social classes, fractions, strata, categories)

*IDEOLOGY*
relations of ideological
domination/subordination
　　　　　　　　ideological struggle

*POLITICS*
relations of political
domination/subordination
　　　　　　　　political struggle

*ECONOMICS*
relations of production/
relations of exploitation
　　　　　　　　economic struggle

Concepts of strategy: social forces, power bloc, "people"

the field of social relations; the two may be, in fact normally are, dislocated from each other. Poulantzas rather breathlessly suggests that in a particular case we have "a set of relations of dislocation between two systems of relations of dislocation."[4]

To put it in another light, we have here a truly formidable engine for generating variations on the original Marxist themes, while still preserving the *language* of Marxist analysis and the *form* of ultimate determination by the economic. It is, nevertheless, a fairly rigorous development of the concepts of unevenness, condensation, displacement and mutations within the structure introduced in the later part of Althusser's essay "On the Materialist Dialectic," and of his interesting critique of homogeneous conceptions of historical time in *Reading Capital*. Poulantzas indeed applies it directly to the question of time in denying any necessary sequences in the history of capitalism and the capitalist state:

Because of the coexistence in a capitalist formation of several modes of production and of several forms of the CMP and because of the complex articulation of instances, each with its own time-sequence, the dominance in a capitalist formation of one form of the CMP over another is not expressed in a simple development. In a social formation we may find a stage dominated by monopoly capitalism and the interventionist state before a stage dominated by private capitalism and the liberal state. . . .[5]

The distance that has been travelled from the simple evolutionism and notions of ever-deepening class conflict in vulgar marxism is obvious.

With this historical license granted them, the classes in the field of the conjuncture become almost sportive. They form alliances and break them, follow each other in and out of power, appear and disappear as social forces. The

4. *Political Power and Social Classes*, 91.
5. *Ibid.*, 154.

extent of this flexibility is perhaps best seen in Poulantzas' account of the "power bloc," the set of dominant classes or fractions of classes in its relation to the state. He defines a hegemonic class or fraction, which is the one that dominates the others in the power bloc and holds state power in its unity. But it does not always have to be the same one that holds hegemony in the society at large; nor the one that is actually the ruling class; nor the one that is in charge of the state! All these "are sometimes identical and sometimes distinct."[6] Poulantzas in fact doubles his flexibility by introducing another, local, field distinction, between the field of political practices and the "political scene." By this device he is enabled to argue that the hegemonic class may actually be absent from the political scene; and in certain situations the ruling class need not even be part of the power bloc. Politics makes strange bedfellows.

What Poulantzas is trying to do in these arguments is plain enough. He wants to escape simple-minded theories of causality, avoid conspiracy theories of the state, and make his Marxism able to deal with the enormous complexities of history. But, we may ask, if the classes in the field of the conjuncture have such flexibility, what connection do they really retain with the firmament of the structures, whence their determination supposedly issues? Hirst, who has raised the question of the "place" *vs* "position" distinction in Poulantzas, calls it "incoherent and unstable."[7] This is a bit strong; the distinction is coherent enough, in its derivation from the general Althusserian position. But it is, I think, fair to call the result unstable. It sometimes stretches the link between structure and event to the verge of incredibility (cf. the example of the "ruling class" outside the "power bloc"). More generally, the argument gives no guide to any systematic pattern in the extent of the "dislocations"; it suggests on the contrary that these are always specific to the conjuncture; and consequently, the analyses always appear to be *ad hoc*. On the other hand, the distinction sometimes collapses wearily into an identity, where the class-in-history becomes simply a personification. Odd examples of this can be found scattered widely through Althusser and Poulantzas; a late but fairly extended and important one is the analysis of monopoly and non-monopoly capital in *Classes in Contemporary Capitalism,* where the structural category itself seems to have strategies and desires, form alliances, and experience successes and failures.

Let us consider why this should be so, how this instability in the analysis arises. Obviously it turns on the nature of the relationship between the two fields. This is, specifically, a relationship of determination between the structures and their effects in the field of social practices, where the classes, thus determined, interact. It is worth recalling Althusser on "structural causality" to get a grip on the relation between the structures and history:

the effects are not outside the structure, are not a pre-existing object, element, or space in which the structure arrives to *imprint its mark:* on the contrary . . . the structure is immanent in its effects, a cause immanent in its effects in the Spinozist sense of the term,

---

6. *Ibid.,* 240–250.

7. P. Q. Hirst, "Economic Classes and Politics", in Hunt, ed., *Class and Class Structure,* 125–154, at 133–142.

that *the whole existence of the structure consists of its effects,* in short that the structure, which is merely a specific combination of its peculiar elements, is nothing outside its effects.[8]

The structures are not entities, things-in-the-world which are separate from other entities called classes or events. Both structure and class are concepts, and the field distinction is merely a distinction in thought, part of the conceptual apparatus that we are offered to help get a grip on all these goings-on.

In one of the few discussions in this literature of the problems of analyzing this relationship, Poulantzas observes that classes recognized in the abstract analysis of a mode of production need not be present as an autonomous class in the social formation, or as a social force in the conjuncture.[9] A class is distinct there only when its economic existence is reflected in the other instances (of structure or practice) by a specific presence. How do we recognize this presence in the ideological and political instances? By "pertinent effects." What are these? The consequences of some "new element which cannot be inserted in the typical framework which these levels [instances] would present without this element," i.e. which change the pattern of class struggle on these levels. Pertinent effects only appear in specific conjunctures.

There are a number of difficulties in this notably obscure passage, but here I am concerned with only one: its circularity, and the light that throws on the field distinction. The object of the whole analysis is to move from the field of structural determination to the conjuncture in the field of social practices. But the relevance of the structural analysis—structures existing only in their effects—is entirely fixed by the analysis of the conjuncture itself, where "pertinent effects" are deciphered. One cannot rest the link with the structures on the notion of the "typical framework" found at various levels: Poulantzas has already explicitly rejected any identification of the structural with the temporally permanent (that suffers from historicism); and anyway, what is "typical" can only be known through the analysis of other conjunctures, which first have to be deciphered in the same way, whereupon we are trapped in an endless regress. (The first conjuncture, like the last instance, never comes.) On the other hand, one cannot characterize a conjuncture *a priori* in structural terms (even given a complete analysis of the conjunctures immediately before and after the one in question), because that would violate basic doctrines such as on time and relative autonomy.

In short, there is no way of establishing coherently the relationship between the fields. The analysis is unstable because it is based on an antinomy embedded in the field distinction itself, an antinomy that *has to be there* because the field distinction, in some form or other, is necessary to make the whole theoretical system work. The dilemma is solved, to the extent that it is, in an essentially *linguistic* way. A tacit covenant is made to speak about social formations and conjunctures in the same language. The link between the two fields is that the first provides the linguistic and logical framework for the definition of the

---

8. L. Althusser and E. Balibar, *Reading Capital* (London: NLB, 1970), 188–189.

9. This paragraph is based on the discussion in *Political Power and Social Classes,* 77–84. There seems to be an ambiguity in this text as to whether the social formation and the conjuncture are actually in separate fields, as implied by other passages. I have used a terminology that assumes a resolution of this.

concepts used in the second, and nothing more. "Structural determination" becomes a *logical meta-relation* among the concepts of the second field, where all that is actually being said about society is said. The abstract analysis of the first field (based on Marx on the capitalist mode of production) sharply limits the number and names of class concepts that can be deployed in the second field; but puts little other restraint on what can be done with them there.

If this argument is correct, I think it goes a good way towards explaining the peculiar style of Althusserian class analysis, that characteristic combination of a tight-laced conceptual system with a promiscuous application of class categories in practice. And it helps specify the underlying attitude to history. History becomes a kaleidoscope, whose pieces can be re-arranged by a twirl of the conceptual barrel. Historical events can legitimately be picked up if they are "relevant illustrations of the subject under investigation," and put down again if they are not, like Poulantzas' facts about fascism.[10] History can be schematized at will, like Carchedi's three stages of capitalism (which never concretely occurred like that). Indeed history becomes to a considerable extent redundant. It is much easier to work out class analysis on the basis of purely imaginary examples, which Carchedi proceeds to do in his central arguments on the definition of the new middle class and its proletarianization.[11] We begin to see why the categories of mobilization and class formation are absent from the theoretical apparatus. They are not needed: the class already exists, ahead of time, as a possibility within the theoretical system; it is simply *recognized* when needed in the analysis of a conjuncture.

Some of the early arguments about conjunctures, such as Althusser's remarks on the condensation of contradictions in a revolutionary situation, suggested that the historicity of class and class relations was to be taken very seriously. But the development of the conceptual apparatus systematically suppressed this. What is actually realized in the theory of class expounded in these texts is a radical ahistoricity. The categorical and functionalist alternatives in the definition of class discussed in the previous section, are simply typical forms of the ahistorical conceptualization of class, and completely consistent with the working of the theory. They can have no place in socialist theory.

## Making It Seem to Work: The Althusserian Two-step

Because it has no historical method of proof, this literature constantly falls back on sheer postulation. What appear to be important substantive conclusions about the world are often analytic truths, logical deductions from the definitions and postulates. Let us take a simple, though important case: Poulantzas' proposal that "the bureaucracy has no power of its own," which he argues both in *Political Power and Social Classes* and *Classes in Contemporary Capitalism*. This appears to be an important (and false) claim about the actual state of affairs in

---

10. N. Poulantzas, *Fascism and Dictatorship* (London: NLB, 1974), 13.

11. G. Carchedi, *On the Economic Identification of Social Classes* (London: Routledge & Kegan Paul, 1977), 90–91, 181–182.

capitalist societies. But on close examination it turns out not to be an exposé of hidden impotence beneath the striped trousers, but a purely analytic statement, which follows from his definition of bureaucracy (which he declines to admit as a class or fraction of a class) and his definition of power ("the capacity of a social class to realize its specific objective interests").[12] So when a follower of Poulantzas argues that the state bureaucracy has no power of its own, all she is really saying is that she speaks a conceptual language in which, *whatever* the state bureaucracy does, it will not count as "power."

Still on the subject of the state organizations, Carchedi provides another example of the solution of a serious problem by deft postulation. In trying to sort out the class position of state employees, he distinguishes capitalist state activities from non-capitalist state activities, and suggests that the former are really no different from privately owned enterprises, and therefore give rise to the same class categories among their employees. This would seem on the face of it to involve some difficulty: surely private companies are owned by capitalists who are trying to extract profits for themselves from the labor of their employees, and this process is the basis of class relations in the firm? And surely such ownership is *not* involved in the case of state enterprises—which is precisely why they can be concentrated in low-profit, infrastructural areas of the economy? But it *is,* in Carchedi's conceptual world:

> While in the individual enterprise the legal ownership belongs to the individual capitalist, and in the joint-stock company it belongs to the stockholders, in the state-owned enterprise the legal ownership belongs to the whole of the bourgeoisie, rather than to a very limited part of it. This can be seen from the fact that . . . in the state-owned company the revenue goes to the state, i.e. to the bourgeoisie as a whole. . . .[13]

The capitalist nature of the state enterprise, and thus the class identification of its employees, is established by postulation, in the form of a tacit definition of the state as the agent of ownership by the-bourgeoisie-as-a-whole.

Similarly Poulantzas' stand in *Political Power and Social Classes* against "reformist" and "revisionist" socialism's reliance on the state—a profoundly important and very difficult strategic issue for the labor movement—boils down to the *analytic* link he makes between the state (in its relative autonomy) and the power of the bourgeoisie. *By definition,* the state cannot go beyond the limit set by the interests of the bourgeoisie in the maintenance of its position; though where this limit (the "line of demarcation") falls may shift from conjuncture to conjuncture. Even if the state is stirring up the masses, encouraging dominated classes to work against dominant ones? *By definition,* this is to the advantage of the latter. And even when government and ruling class hate each other, the government still (by definition) functions as the political organizer of the dominant classes.[14] You can't win. In effect, the kinds of strategies now being explored by European socialist and communist parties, the "revolutionary reforms" proposed by Gorz and Holland, the traditional strategies of the

---

12. *Political Power and Social Classes,* 351 etc. (104 for the definition of power); *Classes in Contemporary Capitalism,* 169 etc.

13. *Economic Identification,* 129–130.

14. *Political Power and Social Classes,* 191, 272–273, 285, etc.

Anglo-Scandinavian labor parties, the strategies of local working class mobilizations to gain control of the regional state machinery, are all ruled out in advance—by definition.

It is instructive to watch the definitional two-step by which a key concept for the polemic against reformism, the unity of state power, is presented by Poulantzas:

that particular feature of the capitalist state which makes the institutions of state power . . . present a *specific* internal cohesion: this cohesion can be perceived in its effects.[15]

Following through Poulantzas' argument, we find that this cohesion is a condition of the relative autonomy of the capitalist state; and relative autonomy is needed for the state to function as a medium of bourgeois class power, which in turn is needed because the bourgeoisie, as we learn from Marx, is incapable of organizing itself politically. State power has unity only so far as it is the unity of the dominant classes; the hegemonic class or fraction among them holds power in its unity; which is equivalent to the unity of the power bloc, which depends on the dominance of the hegemonic class or fraction. But the bourgeoisie can't organize their own dominance (they can't organize their way out of a paper bag, it seems), nor, thus, the unity of the power bloc. Therefore they require the state to be "the factor of the political unity of the power bloc under the protection of the hegemonic class or fraction." Finally, "with regard to the dominant classes and fractions, the capitalist state *presents an intrinsic unity,* combined with its relative autonomy, not because it is the tool of an already politically unified class, but precisely because it is the *unifying factor* of the power bloc."

After plodding round this little circle for a while, we are not surprised to learn that even when the legislature and the executive reflect different classes, state power is still not divided, as one might think.

In this case, in fact, the unity of institutionalised power is maintained by being concentrated around the dominant place where the hegemonic class or fraction is reflected. The other powers function more especially as *resistances* to the dominant power: inserted into the unitary function of the state, they contribute to the organisation of the hegemony of the class or fraction which is reflected as a political force in the dominant power.[16]

So the "specific internal cohesion" of the state is still a "unity" even when there is resistance—or to put it more plainly, class conflict—*within* the state, because *all* state powers are "inserted" into the "function" of the state, which is *by postulation* unitary.

Poulantzas' treatment of the relation between the bourgeoisie and the state (the essential logic of which recurs in *Classes in Contemporary Capitalism*) is thus essentially a network of definitional arguments. These elaborate some scathing remarks of Marx on the political incompetence of the mid-Victorian bourgeoisie into a general rule ("everything happens as if the specific coordinates of the struggle of the dominant classes contribute to prevent their political organization"), which defines a function for the capitalist state to perform ("it takes charge, as it were, of the bourgeoisie's political interests and realizes the function

---

15. *Ibid.,* 255. The following points can be found on pp. 282–300.
16. *Ibid.,* 305.

of political hegemony which the bourgeoisie is unable to achieve").[17] A system of definitions, translation devices and transformation rules then allows anything and everything to be reinterpreted as consistent with these postulates.

When I first came across this kind of thing in Althusserian writing, I thought that it was simply a matter of arbitrary arguments being defended from the obvious criticisms by a certain amount of definitional shuffling. I no longer think so. The shuffling is there, but it isn't arbitrary. In the case just discussed, for instance, Poulantzas was not going round in that circle for nothing. He wanted people to believe that socialism requires smashing the capitalist state, and a Leninist party to do it, and a dictatorship of the proletariat to follow. And in one way or another the argument must yield a way of rejecting any other strategy. If the hegemonic class *always* holds state power in its unity, it is no use doing anything by way of trying to get a little bit of it to use for other purposes—that only helps them organize. The fact that this is a definitional trick rather than a serious argument takes quite a long time to discover, especially as the logic of the whole thing is buried in the appalling jargon in which most of this literature is written. At least Althusser is more transparent:

Marx thus proves irrefutably that the working class cannot hope to gain from the modern growth of productivity before it has overthrown capitalism and seized state power in a socialist revolution.[18]

I have never seen a clearer statement of the usefulness of theory for not seeing what is right in front of your nose.

We are now, I think, in a position to understand the much-debated "functionalism" of the Althusserian school, and the specific form this takes in their arguments about class. To say that their arguments are functionalist does not just mean that they use the term "function," as when Althusser says that the Ideological State Apparatuses "function by ideology" and the Repressive ones "function by violence" (one might as well say "work by ideology," etc.), or when Carchedi speaks of "functions" performed in the labor process (one might as well say "operations" or "tasks"). As Merton pointed out thirty years ago, the term "function" is often used for quite different meanings, while the essential idea of functionalism can be conveyed in other words.[19]

Though it is not the use of the term that makes them so, both Althusser's and Carchedi's arguments just referred to are parts of functionalist analyses, of ideology and production relations respectively. This follows from the rejection of "historicism" and the eschewal of historical analysis. To give *force* to the positions taken up by means of definition and postulation, to make it seem to work as an account of the constraints in social structure, and not just as a definitional grid for classifying things, they are repeatedly forced into a functionalist logic. In functionalism, things are analyzed in terms of the contribution they make to the well-being or continued existence of a larger system of a certain

17. *Ibid.*, 284.

18. L. Althusser, *Lenin and Philosophy* (London: NLB, 1971), 82.

19. R. K. Merton, *Social Theory and Social Structure,* revised ed., (Glencoe, Ill.: Free Press, 1957), 20–25. (This essay was first published in 1949.)

kind, and their explanation flows from the idea of their indispensability for that system (or more mildly, their usefulness for it).

That this kind of argument is common in the works being discussed is hardly open to doubt. It is even embedded in some of the definitions, for instance Poulantzas' view that

the state has the particular function of constituting the factor of cohesion between the levels of a social formation.[20]

As Laclau has noted, anything that can be analyzed as helping to perform the function thus becomes part of the concept of the state. Hence the otherwise extraordinary list of "Ideological State Apparatuses" offered by Althusser in his essay on that theme, which includes churches, schools, trade unions, mass media, the family, literature, the arts, sports, "etc." To the extent that these materialize ideology and help reproduce, however indirectly, capitalist relations of production, they must be included within a functional definition of the state.

The stress in contemporary Marxism on the analysis of the reproduction of capitalism, if it is not resolutely maintained as a historical category, almost inevitably leads to functionalism. This is true, for instance, of the new Marxist sociology of the city offered by Castells, Lojkine, and others, which is significantly influenced by Althusserian theory. There is quite a strong tendency here to construe the labor force as being called into existence, and maintained, by the functional requirements of capital—by the "necessity" inherent in the continued existence of the system—which thus provides the explanation of urban forms through the need to provide for the collective consumption needs of the labor force.[21] But a functionalist analysis can operate at a lower level than that of the whole society—for instance within Carchedi's analysis of production relations. Carchedi's economic definition of his three major classes rests on the function (or in the case of the "new middle class," the combination of functions) they perform in production. He starts out by defining one function—that of "the collective worker"—in a non-functionalist way, simply as the increasingly complex set of technical tasks involved in actually producing a commodity, in short, as the organization of work in a labor process. He then uses the same word, "function," to refer to the very different business of organizing matters so as to extract surplus value from the production of commodities. This is the function of the capitalist, or, as it is subdivided and delegated, the function of the "global capitalist" (Mr. Fat?), or, more felicitously, "the global function of capital."

The general, social content of a function under monopoly capitalism is determined by either performing the function of the collective worker or the global function of capital.[22]

The features of the second function, e.g. the element of control and surveillance, are deduced from general features of the system, e.g. "the fact that, under capitalism, the relations of production are antagonistic." From general features

---

20. *Political Power and Social Classes*, 44.

21. See the papers by Pickvance, Lojkine and Castells in G. C. Pickvance, *Urban Sociology* (London: Tavistock, 1976).

22. *Economic Identification*, 59.

of the system, also, it is deduced that there is a sharp separation between the two functions, such that while performing one you can't perform the other. On this idea rests Carchedi's characterization of the new middle class and his theories of the determination of its income and the process of its "proletarianization".

Now so far as real history goes, this is plainly wrong. There are many features of capitalist production which show the labor process as inextricably fused with processes of social control: among them, the decomposition of tasks in manufacturing and office work, the centralization of information and the use of automated production equipment, the production of new technologies and their repressive implementation. There is a socialist theoretical literature on this (*inter alia,* Marcuse and Habermas on technology as ideology), a recent body of research (notably from Braverman and his followers), and forms of struggle in the workplace that address it (such as "role contestation" in the movement for workers' control). But all this *cannot* register in Carchedi's analysis, because his model of the production process requires two distinct functions to be performed, in order that there should be both material commodities and surplus-value. The labor process must therefore be such that the functions can be exclusive.

Here the element of argument by postulation is hard to distinguish from the element of functionalism. They merge together in the context of a highly abstract model of capitalism which is simply assumed to represent the reality of the world. The general point in which all this issues, can be put this way: the economically-defined classes in Carchedi, the state in Poulantzas, the ideological apparatuses in Althusser, are all theorized in terms of the function they perform in a social order *whose class nature is known a priori,* as it is specified in the analysis of "the structures" at the most abstract level. The constraint in the Althusserian theory of society is the necessity to have those functions performed which will preserve or reproduce that known structure.

Since a pattern of causation usually cannot be demonstrated (in the absence of a historical method), the analysis constantly falls back on "as if" arguments. Thus Althusser, in his first essay on the subject, explaining the functional necessity of ideology:

It is as if human societies could not survive without these *specific formations,* these systems of representations (at various levels), their ideologies.[23]

Or Poulantzas, on a theme already discussed:

Everything happens precisely as if the state permanently played the role of political organiser of the power bloc.[24]

Or on the theme of education in mass schools:

Everything takes place as if, even when the petty-bourgeois agents [i.e. children] are educated in apparatuses [i.e. schools] that appear from formal considerations as over-whelmingly designed for the working class, their forms of education are still radically distinct from the forms of the latter.[25]

---

23. *For Marx,* 232.
24. *Political Power and Social Classes,* 299.
25. *Classes in Contemporary Capitalism,* 260–261.

In this last case, the "as if" argument allows Poulantzas to evade the facts to the extent of interpreting a statistical tendency in intra-school streaming as a class boundary, and to ignore the specific integrative importance of common schooling. (The latter is a curious omission, for him.) The converse is the "only-an-effect" argument. The centralization of decision-making in companies seems to be an important change in power structure, perhaps linked with computers, which might seem to need some reconsideration of orthodox marxist views (as observed above); but don't worry, Poulantzas explains, it is only an effect of changes in the relations of production. Classes themselves, in economic life, seem to take the form of gradations of income, not fundamental cleavages; but don't worry, the hierarchy of levels of income is only an effect of the relations of production.[26] In the "as if" argument, the missing but required facts are conjured up in mid-air; in the "only-an-effect" argument, the present but unpleasant facts are conjured away. How these "effects" are produced is never explained; here the systematic ambiguity of the relationship between fields, discussed in the last section, is decidedly convenient.

I have given only a few examples of these arguments, though literally scores could be produced. The question of forms of argument is far from being a verbal quibble, for it is in such dress that the Althusserian approach, normally developed at an extremely abstract level, touches ground; and here its fundamental character can be deciphered. To me, the most telling moment of all comes when Carchedi is expounding his theoretical framework, and explains that determined instances over-determine the determinant instance, but the determinant one sets the limits to its own overdetermination . . . One has heard this before. But then comes the illustration:

For example, the non-capitalist sector must always be subordinated to the capitalist one, or the capitalist system will cease to be such.[27]

*Or the capitalist system will cease to be such!* There it is, in a nutshell: the point that links functionalism, definitional argument, ahistoricity, top-down abstractions, and marxist orthodoxy all together. We know the system is capitalist; we have a model of it which, because it comes from Marx, must be right; therefore those things which the model tells us about must be there in reality, or the capitalist system will cease to be such. The non-capitalist sector must be subordinated to the capitalist, the labor process must be subordinated to the surplus-value producing process, the state must present an intrinsic unity, reformist parties must contribute to the organization of bourgeois hegemony, the ideological apparatuses must function to insert workers in their class places, and so on and so forth, or the capitalist system will cease to be such. It is, indeed, unarguable—given the definitions, and a completely closed conceptual system.

At a couple of points in his book Carchedi addresses the question of functionalism. At one, having specified that the capitalist is in fact involved in doing some of the world's work, he says that nevertheless the fundamental role (in the package defining the capitalist) reverts to the element of ownership, and that it was necessary to stress this "in order not to be accused of functionalism." A little further on

---

26. *Ibid.*, 130, 182, 18, 20.
27. *Economic Identification*, 48.

he suggests that in studying the income of the new middle class, we should avoid "a functionalist explanation" of the type that says that the more important functions get the higher incomes, *à la* Davis and Moore's theory of stratification. (Carchedi promptly suggests two functionalist explanations of his own, however, on the next page.)[28] It would seem that Carchedi's notion of "functionalism" equates it with consensus theory, and that he thinks if you stress issues of ownership and exploitation, you are adequately protected from functionalist ideology. Plainly, that is an adequate protection from the specific version of functionalism that we find in Parsons or Davis and Moore. But as Merton pointed out in the essay already mentioned, functionalism as such does not depend on postulates of social consensus, and is not *necessarily* aligned with political conservatism. There can be a Marxist functionalism. Where it differs from Parsonian functionalism is in its *a priori* assumption of class society, in its analysis of everything in terms of its functional relation to the reproduction of the postulated class structure, and its implicit relationship to the Revolution.

To coin a term, this is a bipolar functionalism. By this I don't mean anything to do with Carchedi's two "functions" in the production process, which is indeed a simpler conception and quite compatible with orthodox functionalism. It is rather the position implicit in his remark that:

In the case of the labour aristocracies, it is the economic which assigns the dominant role to the ideological because the capitalist economic structure, in order to reproduce itself, needs to introduce within the working class several types of bourgeois ideologies (e.g. reformism).[29]

What is implicit here is, shadowing the successful performing of this function, a kind of anti-function which negates it, whose functionaries are the bearers of the revolutionary line. Indeed this was mentioned only a few lines before, where Carchedi suggested that a complete definition of the proletariat must involve the ideological and political as well as the economic, and therefore would include only that part of the working class which had developed a proletarian class consciousness, and also had joined "the worker's party" and joined in proletarian political practice. (Incidentally, if Carchedi means by "the worker's party" what Marxists usually do, then in a country like Australia his definition of the proletariat would embrace one-fortieth of one per cent of the economically active population, approximately. On the loosest definition possible, it embraces a little over one per cent.) A more elaborate example is given when Poulantzas, running down his version of Althusser's list of ideological state apparatuses, comes to "the political parties, the unions," and adds, in parentheses,

(with the exception, of course, of the *revolutionary* party or trade union organisations).[30]

The naiveté of this, in a world where 57 different sects each proclaim themselves *the* revolutionary party, is charming; but the implications are not. The effect of Althusserian bipolar functionalism is to claim that every practice outside that of

---

28. *Ibid.*, 88, 95–96.

29. *Ibid.*, 145–146.

30. N. Poulantzas, "The Problem of the Capitalist State", *New Left Review*, 1969, no. 58, 67–78, at 77.

the revolutionary party *actually* subserves the reproduction of the capitalist system. I am not making a merely logical point here, but a very practical one, because this theoretical position comes through again and again in the statements that Althusserians, or other Marxists influenced by Althusserian notions, make about all kinds of practical issues. Examples that come immediately to mind are urban politics, where, as Pickvance notes, this approach refuses ever to see "the authorities" as a source of change or concession until they are forced, and hence systematically devalues any strategy of working-class mobilization to capture local state power; and welfare, where the effect is to make any achievable welfare measures appear only to stabilize and help reproduce capitalism.[31] The obverse of this is to claim scientific justification for one line and one line only; in short, to imply that anyone interested in moderate reform, let alone socialism, must join "the" revolutionary party. The specific form of Althusserian functionalism, then, has a definite political point. It is closely connected with a conventional, October-in-Petrograd, big-bang theory of the transition to socialism.

## The Politics of Theorizing

If class analysis is, as I suggested at the start, fundamentally the social theory produced by and for socialist politics, the ultimate significance of a line of class theory is political. This view would undoubtedly be accepted by Althusser, Poulantzas and Carchedi; so let us consider the political tendency of their theorizing about class. Althusser of course began with a political act in the realm of theory, the campaign to defend Marxism against humanism. It was in the course of this that he developed his critique of the "problematic of the subject," and his melancholy doctrine that the socialist theory of class society cannot be about people and their action on history, but that:

the structure of the relations of production determines the *places* and the *functions* occupied and adopted by the agents of production, who are never anything more than the occupants of these places, insofar as they are the "supports" (*Träger*) of these functions.[32]

What is the political significance of this apparently abstruse epistemological doctrine? It begins to be spelled out especially in Althusser's and Poulantzas's work on ideology. What ideology is about, is "inserting" people into a place already defined for them by the structures, a class place. Classes can *not* be understood properly as created by a process of mobilization, in which people struggle to take control of their own destiny. We have already noted Poulantzas's rejection of Marx's view on this: construing classes in terms of a process of class formation is historicist, empiricist, subjectivist, ultimately idealist, and not quite *comme il faut*. Being thus inserted, the working class cannot formulate correct theory on its own, because it is (by definition) permanently dominated by bourgeois and petty-bourgeois ideology. Marxist science must be imported

---

31. On the former point G. C. Pickvance, "On the Study of Urban Social Movements", in *Urban Sociology*, 198–218, at 204; on the latter, B. Trainor, "Epistemology, the State and Welfare", *Arena*, 1977, no. 47–48, 146–162.

32. *Reading Capital*, 180.

from outside to criticize what the working class itself thinks, set it straight, and rescue it from the "deformations" to which it is naturally heir. Guess who will do this? Why, folks, our old friend the revolutionary party, which will eventually lead us forward to "the socialist democracy of the dictatorship of the proletariat."[33]

The methodological position from which class theory is constructed thus leads, indirectly but inevitably, to an account of the working class that justifies the vanguard-party theory of socialist organization, and systematically discredits any strategy based on spontaneity, self-management, and popular mobilization. This trend of logic is strongly supported by an atmospheric effect in Althusserian writing which is quite important, though I have mostly ignored it in order to concentrate on explicit ideas about class. I refer to its convoluted methods of argument and its abominable literary style. It may be that the French texts suffer somewhat from bad translation into English, though I am informed that they are not regarded as examples of classically limpid French prose either. But no one can say it is an effect of translation (or writing in a foreign language) when Carchedi takes forty mortal pages of definitional waffle to introduce the banal observation that in advanced capitalism some people do the work, other people organize them in order to extract a profit, and other people do a bit of both. (No satire intended—this is, literally, the guts of his theory of the economic identification of classes.) The whole literature has almost totally corrupted the language of a good many English-speaking followers of the Althusserian School.

The political point of this is that there is no way that people who write class analysis like this can be intending to address the working class, or even the socialist movement at large. People who do wish to serve the mass movement, and be corrected by it, must constantly struggle to clarify, to speak in the plainest possible language. If someone doesn't, then there must be a different audience and role intended.

The cultural character of the putative vanguard is sufficiently indicated by the Althusserian attitude towards other intellectuals. I have already mentioned the re-reading of Marx to purge him of anything smacking of passion and humanity; and the purification of Marxism which purified it of most of Gramsci, Lukacs, Korsch, Sartre, Reich, the Frankfurt school, Trotsky, in short most of what was interesting and innovative in Marxism in the last sixty years. The attitude to Trotsky is particularly instructive. To Althusser he is practically a nonperson, not mentioned at all in *For Marx* or *Lenin and Philosophy,* and only once in his contribution to *Reading Capital,* in passing in a list of Marxist political leaders. In *Political Power and Social Classes* Poulantzas adopted the same attitude. Trotsky is mentioned only once in its text; and it is worth quoting the passage in its entirety:

Moreover, theoretical research [on the state apparatus] has been widely distorted because of the errors of Trotsky's analyses and in particular because of the ideological rubbish churned out by his successors. I shall therefore try to avoid the ideological terrain of this

---

33. *Political Power and Social Classes,* 183–184, 204–206, 356; cf. *For Marx,* 254.

discussion by staying close to the scientific analyses provided by Marx, Engels, Gramsci and Lenin on this subject.[34]

Keep close to mother! By 1970, when he wrote *Fascism and Dictatorship,* Poulantzas was adopting a much kindlier attitude to Trotsky. Partly he had to take him seriously because there is simply no way you can miss Trotsky in discussing communist views of fascism in the 1920s; but also, in the meantime, Poulantzas had moved politically towards a position which made criticism of the Soviet Union more acceptable.

In making these attitudes credible, some importance must be assigned to the ahistorical functionalist theory of class and the state. Having such a theory allows one to go back through the history of socialism with a kind of timeless mark-sheet, handing out awards for strategy and tactics: this person is right here, that one is wrong there, someone else is inevitably wrong. The reason for being wrong politically always has to do with having "deviated" in theory, failed to appreciate the relative autonomy of the state, or built too much on the spontaneity of the workers. Fighting over lost battles this way is a great pastime among Marxist theorists, which has the useful effect of bolstering the importance of theory in the present. Above all it confirms the impression of there being one and only one line which will bring about the overthrow of capitalism, which is awfully difficult to discover and hold to even within the revolutionary vanguard.

The political effect of the bipolar functionalism discussed in the last section is to reinforce a particular view of the transition to socialism, a big-bang theory of revolution. In Carchedi's words,

The characteristic element of the transition from capitalism to socialism is that the socialist production relations can be established only through a revolution which gives first of all the political and ideological power to the proletariat.[35]

Remembering that Carchedi's "proletariat" is a tiny politically-organized minority, this easily fits with an elitist view of how the revolutionary rupture is to be encouraged:

. . . it is impossible for the working class to achieve a developed class consciousness without an organisation which wages an economic, political, and ideological fight against the class enemy under the leadership of a vanguard.[36]

All of this is good grey Marxist-Leninist orthodoxy, and was there long before Althusser and his school. Their originality was not in producing any new political strategies (as they have produced few new ideas of any kind), but in building a massive theoretical system which made *this* strategy appear not the dubious choice it actually is, but a logical necessity stemming from the inner-most nature of capitalism.

To be generous, the functionalist tendency at least encourages a kind of militancy, a focus on changing the whole class system rather than getting

---

34. *Political Power and Social Classes,* 325.
35. *Economic Identification,* 148.
36. *Ibid.,* 41.

bogged down in the bits. The effect of the categorical tendency in the conception of class is to render this an abstract militancy. To the extent that classes are understood essentially as sets of people (or even "production agents") who meet a particular criterion (as in the whole debate over class boundaries), they are not seen as groups that in any sense constitute themselves by their actions and hence by a transforming practice. The necessity of militancy, in other words, is not generated from the lived experience of the class. (The categorical logic of theory here corresponds to the traditional bolshevik disdain for the limitations of the spontaneous consciousness of the working class.) Rather it hangs in the air, as a kind of categorical imperative deduced from the structures.

When we now take into account the distinction in the theory of class between the field of the structures (whence this militancy about social transformation arises) and the field of practice and conjunctures, a further political conclusion emerges: it is that no political conclusion can be deduced from the structural analysis, except the demand for militancy itself. The conjuncture is, as Althusser and Poulantzas make very clear, the site and object of political practice; and, as they also make clear, the characteristics of a conjuncture can never be deduced from an analysis of the structural determinations of the classes in it. In short, we have a militancy without substance, in the sense that it cannot ever, of itself, propose what is to be done. At least in the present. The game Poulantzas plays, of going back and correcting theoretically the strategy and tactics of the socialists who actually had to improvize a response to fascism in the heat of a complicated, violent, and unexpected struggle, can only be done retrospectively. And we cannot draw from it rules for the future. As Althusser said—and it is one of his most profound insights—"are we not always in exceptional situations?"

Let me draw these points together. The implicit politics of Althusserian class theory as theoretical practice, is an abstract militancy, without a political "line" of its own, providing a general justification for a revolutionary vanguard party led by an educated but fairly intolerant elite who are the bearers of Marxist science; and a general devaluation of strategies connected with spontaneity, mobilization from below, incremental change, or use of the existing state.

That sounds, on the whole, pretty familiar. It sounds not very different from what Althusser came out of, i.e. European Stalinism. The ear-marks of Stalinism are visible enough: the justification for a revolutionary elite within the labor movement; the denunciation of most of the creative (and therefore heterodox) work in twentieth-century Marxism; the bland assumption that there is one proper revolutionary party, and so on. At a deeper level, the theory works in the same direction: the priority of the structures, the bipolar functionalism, the abstract militancy that they produce; in the Althusserian world, the revolution itself—a transformation of the structures, scientifically speaking—seems to occur behind the backs of the workers. That terrible intervention of living, sweating, bleeding human beings in their own history, that is the basis of all radicalism, is methodologically ruled out of "Marxist science" by Althusserian Marxism. Here, I think, is its fundamental affinity with Stalinist politics, which is precisely characterized by the combination of a notional militancy with a practical suppression of grass-roots socialism.

I stress "fundamental affinity" rather than making a direct equation, for two reasons. First, it is plain enough that Althusser and the others do not mean deliberately to defend Stalinism. Althusser personally has had a complicated and ambiguous debate with the ghost of Stalin, in the course of which he has attempted to identify Stalinism as a deviation (basically economist) within authentic Marxism. Opinions may reasonably differ about this exercise; I am inclined to agree with Callinicos that the distancing hasn't gone very far, that the fundamental affinity is still there.[37] The second reason is more general. The political meaning of an intellectual position cannot be read directly from its content. To do that would be to adopt an ahistorical method, exactly the kind of essentialism into which the Althusserians fall in denouncing humanism, historicism, and the rest. Rather, its political significance must be judged also in terms of its context, the situation in which it is active, and the possibilities and intractabilities of that situation.

## Acknowledgment

I am indebted to a number of friends and colleagues who have commented on and argued with the ideas advanced here; above all to Teresa Brennan, whose critical intelligence and political perception have profoundly influenced the view of Marxism on which this argument is based.

---

37. A. Callinicos, *Althusser's Marxism* (London: Pluto, 1976), 89ff. This brief and witty book is, with Laclau, the best analysis of the Althusserian system I have seen, and I would like to acknowledge a general debt to its ideas.

· 7 ·

# Capitalism and the Division of Labour

## Harry Braverman

The earliest innovative principle of the capitalist mode of production was the manufacturing division of labor, and in one form or another the division of labor has remained the fundamental principle of industrial organization. The division of labor in capitalist industry is not at all identical with the phenomenon of the distribution of tasks, crafts, or specialties of production throughout society, for while all known societies have divided their work into productive specialties, no society before capitalism systematically subdivided the work of each productive specialty into limited operations. This form of the division of labor becomes generalized only with capitalism.

This distinction is made clear, for instance, in Herskovits' description of the division of labor in primitive societies:

Only rarely is any division of labor within an industry—or, as it might be termed, subdivision of labor—encountered among nonliterate folk. Such intra-industrial specialization would be encountered only in the production of such larger capital goods as houses, canoes, or fish-weirs.[1] Even here, it is the rule in such cultures that an arrangement of this sort is temporary; moreover, each worker devoting himself to a part of a specific task is most often competent to perform other phases of the work besides that on

---

•From Harry Braverman, *Labor and Monopoly Capital* (New York: Monthly Review Press, 1974), pp. 70–84.

1. Herskovits here performs the customary economic miracle of transforming "houses, canoes, or fish-weirs" into "capital goods," in accordance with the bourgeois-centric view which unself-consciously projects backward and forward throughout history the categories specific to capitalist production, and according to which houses become "capital" even when they were only structures people built as dwellings.

which he may at the moment be engaged. . . . Thus in groups where the primary division of labor is along sex lines, every man or woman not only will know how to do all those things that men or women habitually do among them, but must be able to do them efficiently. As we move to societies of somewhat greater economic complexity, we find that certain men may spend a larger proportion of their time than others doing wood-carving or iron-working, or certain women making pots or weaving cloth; but all the members of the groups will have some competence in the techniques controlled by those of a given sex. In still other nonliterate societies, certain men and women specialize not only in one technique, but in a certain type of product, as, for instance, where one woman will devote her time to the production of pots for everyday use and another make pottery exclusively for religious rites. It must again be stressed that, except under the most unusual circumstances, we do not find the kind of organization where one woman characteristically specializes in gathering the clay, another in fashioning it, and a third in firing the pots; or, where one man devotes himself to getting wood, a second to roughly blocking out the proportions of a stool or figure, and a third to finishing it.[2]

Herskovits gives us here a picture of a division of labor into crafts, a differentiation which in the beginning owes much to sex roles. By and large, however, there is no division of tasks within the crafts. While men or women may habitually be connected with the making of certain products, they do not as a rule divide up the separate operations involved in the making of each product.

This form of division of labor, characteristic of all societies, is, if we follow Marx's terminology, called the *social division of labor*. It is a derivative of the specific character of human work: "An animal forms things in accordance with the standard and the need of the species to which it belongs, whilst man knows how to produce in accordance with the standard of every species."[3] The spider weaves, the bear fishes, the beaver builds dams and houses, but the human is simultaneously weaver, fisherman, builder, and a thousand other things combined in a manner which, because this takes place in, and is possible only through, society, soon compels a social division according to craft. Each individual of the human species cannot alone "produce in accordance with the standard of every species" and invent standards unknown to any animal, but the species as a whole finds it possible to do this, in part through the social division of labor. Thus the social division of labor is apparently inherent in the species character of human labor as soon as it becomes social labor, that is, labor carried on in and through society.

As against this general or social division of labor, there stands the division of labor in detail, the manufacturing division of labor. This is the breakdown of the processes involved in the making of the product into manifold operations performed by different workers.

The practice of regarding the social and the detailed divisions of labor as a single continuum, a single abstract technical principle, is by far the greatest source of confusion in discussions of this subject.[4] The division of labor in

---

2. Melville J. Herskovits, *Economic Anthropology: A Study in Comparative Economics* (2nd ed.; New York, 1960), p. 126.

3. Karl Marx, *Economic and Philosophic Manuscripts of 1844,* edited and with an introduction by Dick J. Struik (New York, 1964), p. 113.

4. "But, in spite of the numerous analogies and links connecting them," Marx warned, "division of labour in the interior of a society, and that in the interior of a workshop, differ not only in degree, but also in kind" (Karl Marx, *Capital,* vol. I [Moscow, n.d., p. 334).

society is characteristic of all known societies; the division of labor in the workshop is the special product of capitalist society. The social division of labor divides society among occupations, each adequate to a branch of production; the detailed division of labor destroys occupations considered in this sense, and renders the worker inadequate to carry through any complete production process. In capitalism, the social division of labor is enforced chaotically and anarchically by the market, while the workshop division of labor is imposed by planning and control. Again in capitalism, the products of the social division of labor are exchanged as commodities, while the results of the operation of the detail worker are not exchanged within the factory as within a marketplace, but are all owned by the same capital. While the social division of labor subdivides *society,* the detailed division of labor subdivides *humans,* and while the subdivision of society may enhance the individual and the species, the subdivision of the individual, when carried on without regard to human capabilities and needs, is a crime against the person and against humanity.

The view which ignores the distinction between the social and detailed divisions of labor is given typical expression in the following comments: "Social differentiation and division of labor are universal attributes of human society. Contrary to the view persisting into the recent past that primitive man lives in completely homogeneous and amorphous groups, modern knowledge of primitive and peasant communities reveals much complexity and specialization. . . . Modern specialization cannot therefore be contrasted with an assumed society or period having no division of labor. The difference is one of degree and not of kind."[5] Wilbert Moore here forces us to assume that the division of society among trades, crafts, professions "cannot be contrasted" with the breakup of those occupations, that there is no difference "in kind" between the practice of farming, cabinetmaking, or blacksmithing, and the repeated tightening of a single set of bolts hundreds of times each day or the key punching of thousands of cards each week throughout a lifetime of labor, because *all* are expressions of the "division of labor." On this level of abstraction, obviously, nothing can be learned about the division of labor, except the banal and apologetic conclusion that being "universal," each of its manifestations is probably inevitable. Needless to say, this is precisely the conclusion that bourgeois society prefers.

It is for this reason that the popularity of Emile Durkheim's work, *The Division of Labor in Society,* has grown as its applicability to the modern world has dwindled. Durkheim adopts just such a level of abstraction in his approach: "The only way to succeed in objectively appreciating the division of labor is to study it first in itself, entirely speculatively, to look for its use, and upon what it depends, and finally, to form as adequate a notion as possible of it."[6] He proceeds in this fashion, determinedly avoiding the specific social conditions under which the division of labor develops in our epoch, celebrating throughout his proposition that "the ideal of human fraternity can be realized only in propor-

---

5. Wilbert E. Moore, "The Attributes of an Industrial Order," in S. Nosow and W. H. Form, eds., *Man, Work, and Society* (New York, 1962), pp. 92–93.

6. Emile Durkheim, *The Division of Labor in Society* (Glencoe, Ill., 1947), p. 45.

tion to the progress of the division of labor,"[7] until in the last tenth of his work he discovers the division of labor in the factories and offices of modern capitalism, and dubs them "abnormal forms." But, as has been noted by a recent critic, M. C. Kennedy, "when we inspect these abnormal forms throughout the world, it becomes difficult to find one clear-cut case of the normal division of labor." Kennedy is absolutely right when he calls Durkheim's "normal" form of the division of labor "the ideal of a moralistic sociologist and not a sociologist of morals."[8]

Our concern at this point, therefore, is not with the division of labor in society at large, but within the enterprise; not with the distribution of labor among various industries and occupations, but with the breakdown of occupations and industrial processes; not with the division of labor in "production in general," but within the capitalist mode of production in particular. It is not "pure technique" that concerns us, but rather the marriage of technique with the special needs of capital.

The division of labor in production begins with the *analysis of the labor process*—that is to say, the separation of the work of production into its constituent elements. But this, in itself, is not what brings into being the detail worker. Such an analysis or separation, in fact, is characteristic in every labor process organized by workers to suit their own needs.

For example, a tinsmith makes a funnel: he draws the elevation view on sheetmetal, and from this develops the outline of an unrolled funnel and its bottom spout. He then cuts out each piece with snips and shears, rolls it to its proper shape, and crimps or rivets the seams. He then rolls the top edge, solders the seams, solders on a hanging ring, washes away the acid used in soldering, and rounds the funnel to its final shape. But when he applies the same process to a quantity of identical funnels, his mode of operation changes. Instead of laying out the work directly on the material, he makes a pattern and uses it to mark off the total quantity of funnels needed; then he cuts them all out, one after the other, rolls them, etc. In this case, instead of making a single funnel in the course of an hour or two, he spends hours or even days on each step of the process, creating in each case fixtures, clamps, devices, etc. which would not be worth making for a single funnel but which, where a sufficiently large quantity of funnels is to be made, speed each step sufficiently so that the saving justifies the

---

7. Ibid., p. 406.

8. M. C. Kennedy, "The Division of Labor and the Culture of Capitalism: A Critique" (Ph.D. diss., State University of New York at Buffalo, 1968, pp. 185–86; available from University Microfilms, Ann Arbor, Mich.).

Georges Friedmann says that had Durkheim lived to see the further development of the division of labor, "he would have been obliged to consider 'abnormal' most of the forms taken by labour in modern society, both in industry and in administration, and even more recently in commerce (I am thinking of the American supermarkets)" (Georges Friedmann, *The Anatomy of Work* [London, 1961, and Glencoe, Ill., 1964], p. 75). The idea that anyone writing several generations after the Industrial Revolution, and after Adam Smith, Babbage, Ure, Marx, and countless others, needed to wait for the "American supermarkets" to learn about the division of labor in capitalism is not convincing. But, in general, Friedmann's gingerly handling of Durkheim, whom—despite the fact that in his succeeding pages he finds little of value in the book—he calls "the most vigorous mind that has ever worked on this great problem," testifies to the inflated reputation of Durkheim's contribution.

extra outlay of time. Quantities, he has discovered, will be produced with less trouble and greater economy of time in this way than by finishing each funnel individually before starting the next.

In the same way a bookkeeper whose job it is to make out bills and maintain office records against their future collection will, if he or she works for a lawyer who has only a few clients at a time, prepare a bill and post it at once to the proper accounts and the customer statement. But if there are hundreds of bills each month, the bookkeeper will accumulate them and spend a full day or two, from time to time, posting them to the proper accounts. Some of these postings will now be made by daily, weekly, or monthly totals instead of bill by bill, a practice which saves a great deal of labor when large quantities are involved; at the same time, the bookkeeper will now make use of other shortcuts or aids, which become practicable when operations are analyzed or broken up in this way, such as specially prepared ledger cards, or carbon forms which combine into a single operation the posting to the customer's account and the preparation of a monthly statement.

Such methods of analysis of the labor process and its division into constituent elements have always been and are to this day common in all trades and crafts, and represent the first form of the subdivision of labor in detail. It is clear that they satisfy, essentially if not fully, the three advantages of the division of labor given by Adam Smith in his famous discussion in the first chapter of *The Wealth of Nations:*

This great increase in the quantity of work, which, in consequence of the division of labour, the same number of people are capable of performing, is owing to three different circumstances; first, to the increase of dexterity in every particular workman; secondly, to the saving of the time which is commonly lost in passing from one species of work to another; and lastly, to the invention of a great number of machines which facilitate and abridge labour, and enable one man to do the work of many.[9]

The example which Smith gives is the making of pins, and his description is as follows:

One man draws out the wire, another straightens it, a third cuts it, a fourth points it, a fifth grinds it at the top for receiving the head; to make the head requires two or three distinct operations; to put it on, is a peculiar business, to whiten the pins is another; it is even a trade by itself to put them into the paper; and the important business of making a pin is, in this manner, divided into about eighteen distinct operations, which, in some manufactories, are all performed by distinct hands, though in others the same man will sometimes perform two or three of them.[10]

In this example, the division of labor is carried one step further than in the examples of the tinsmith and the bookkeeper. Not only are the operations separated from each other, but *they are assigned to different workers.* Here we have not just the analysis of the labor process but the creation of the detail worker. Both steps depend upon the scale of production: without sufficient quantities they are impracticable. Each step represents a saving in labor time. The greatest saving is embodied in the analysis of the process, and a further saving, the extent

---

9. Adam Smith, *The Wealth of Nations* (New York, 1937), p. 7.
10. Ibid., pp. 4–5.

varying with the nature of the process, is to be found in the separation of operations among different workers.[11]

The worker may break the process down, but he never voluntarily converts himself into a lifelong detail worker. This is the contribution of the capitalist, who sees no reason why, if so much is to be gained from the first step—analysis—and something more gained from the second—breakdown among workers—he should not take the second step as well as the first. That the first step breaks up only the process, while the second dismembers the worker as well, means nothing to the capitalist, and all the less since, in destroying the craft as a process under the control of the worker, he reconstitutes it as a process under his own control. He can now count his gains in a double sense, not only in productivity but in management control, since that which mortally injures the worker is in this case advantageous to him.[12]

The effect of these advantages is heightened by still another which, while it is given surprisingly little mention in economic literature, is certainly the most compelling reason of all for the immense popularity of the division of tasks among workers in the capitalist mode of production, and for its rapid spread. It was not formulated clearly nor emphasized strongly until a half-century after Smith, by Charles Babbage.

---

11. The distinction between the analysis of the labor process and the creation of the detail worker may be seen in these lines from a special report presented by George Wallis to the House of Commons about the American worker of the nineteenth century:

the American working boy develops rapidly into the skilled artizan, and having once mastered one part of his business, he is never content until he has mastered all. Doing *one* mechanical operation well, and only that one, does not satisfy him or his employer. He is ambitious to do something more than a set task, and, therefore, he must learn all. The second part of his trade he is allowed to learn as a reward for becoming master of the first, and so on to the end, if he may be said ever to arrive at *that*. The restless activity of mind and body—the anxiety to improve his own department of industry—the facts constantly before him of ingenious men who have solved economic and mechanical problems to their own profit and elevation, are all stimulative and encouraging; and it may be said that there is not a working boy of average ability in the New England States, at least, who has not an idea of some mechanical invention or improvement in manufactures. . . .

Nor does this knowledge of the two or three departments of one trade, or even the pursuit of several trades by one individual, interfere so much with the systematic division of labour as may be supposed. In most instances the change of employment is only made at convenient periods, or as a relief to the workman from the monotony of always doing one thing. . . . There is, however, one drawback to this otherwise successful violation of the economic law of sub-division. It is unfavourable to that perfect skill of hand, and marvellous accuracy, which is always to be found associated with the constant direction of attention and practice of the workman to one thing; and this is often very apparent in most of the manufactured articles of America. (New York Industrial Exhibition, Special Report of Mr. George Wallis, in Nathan Rosenberg, ed., *The American System of Manufactures* [Edinburgh, 1969], pp. 203–204).

12. We have much studied and perfected, of late, the great civilised invention of the division of labour; only we give it a false name. It is not, truly speaking, the labour that is divided; but the men: divided into mere segments of men—broken into small fragments and crumbs of life; so that all the little piece of intelligence that is left in a man is not enough to make a pin, or a nail, but exhausts itself in making the point of a pin, or the head of a nail. Now it is a good and desirable thing, truly, to make many pins in a day; but if we could only see with what crystal sand their points were polished—sand of human soul, much to be magnified before it can be discerned for what it is—we should think there might be some loss in it also. And the great cry that rises from all our manufacturing cities, louder than the furnace blast, is all in very deed for this—that we manufacture everything there except men. . . . (John Ruskin, *The Stones of Venice*, section II, chapter VI; quoted in Ken Coates, *Essays on Industrial Democracy* [London, 1971], pp. 44–45.)

In "On the Division of Labour," Chapter XIX of his *On the Economy of Machinery and Manufactures*, the first edition of which was published in 1832, Babbage noted that "the most important and influential cause [of savings from the division of labor] has been altogether unnoticed." He recapitulates the classic arguments of William Petty, Adam Smith, and the other political economists, quotes from Smith the passage reproduced above about the "three different circumstances" of the division of labor which add to the productivity of labor, and continues:

Now, although all these are important causes, and each has its influence on the result; yet it appears to me, that any explanation of the cheapness of manufactured articles, as consequent upon the division of labour, would be incomplete if the following principle were omitted to be stated.

*That the master manufacturer, by dividing the work to be executed into different processes, each requiring different degrees of skill or of force, can purchase exactly that precise quantity of both which is necessary for each process; whereas, if the whole work were executed by one workman, that person must possess sufficient skill to perform the most difficult, and sufficient strength to execute the most laborious, of the operations into which the art is divided.* [13]

To put this all-important principle another way, in a society based upon the purchase and sale of labor power, dividing the craft cheapens its individual parts. To clarify this point, Babbage gives us an example drawn, like Smith's, from pin manufacture. He presents a table for the labor employed, by type (that is, by age and sex) and by pay, in the English manufacture of those pins known in his day as "Elevens."[14]

| | | |
|---|---|---|
| Drawing wire | Man | 3s.3d. per day |
| Straightening wire | Woman | 1s.0d. |
| | Girl | 0s.6d. |
| Pointing | Man | 5s.3d. |
| Twisting and cutting | Boy | 0s.4½d. |
| heads | Man | 5s.4½d. |
| Heading | Woman | 1s.3d. |
| Tinning or whitening | Man | 6s.0d. |
| | Woman | 3s.0d. |
| Papering | Woman | 1s.6d. |

It is clear from this tabulation, as Babbage points out, that if the minimum pay for a craftsman capable of performing all operations is no more than the highest pay in the above listing, and if such craftsmen are employed exclusively, then the labor costs of manufacture would be more than doubled, *even if the very same division of labor were employed and even if the craftsmen produced pins at the very same speed as the detail workers.* [15]

---

13. Charles Babbage, *On the Economy of Machinery and Manufactures* (London, 1832; reprint ed., New York, 1963), pp. 175–76.

14. Ibid., p. 184.

15. Not all economists have missed this point. Alfred Marshall called it "Babbage's great principle of economical production" (Alfred Marshall, *Industry and Trade* [1919; reprint ed., London, 1932], p. 149). But Marshall, after all, wrote at a time when economists were still interested in the way things worked in the real world.

Let us add another and later example, taken from the first assembly line in American industry, the meatpacking conveyor (actually a *disassembly* line). J. R. Commons has realistically included in this description, along with the usual details, the rates of pay of the workers:

It would be difficult to find another industry where division of labor has been so ingeniously and microscopically worked out. The animal has been surveyed and laid off like a map; and the men have been classified in over thirty specialties and twenty rates of pay, from 16 cents to 50 cents an hour. The 50-cent man is restricted to using the knife on the most delicate parts of the hide (floorman) or to using the ax in splitting the backbone (splitter); and wherever a less-skilled man can be slipped in at 18 cents, 18½ cents, 20 cents, 21 cents, 22½ cents, 24 cents, 25 cents, and so on, a place is made for him, and an occupation mapped out. In working on the hide alone there are nine positions, at eight different rates of pay. A 20-cent man pulls off the tail, a 22½-cent man pounds off another part where good leather is not found, and the knife of the 40-cent man cuts a different texture and has a different "feel" from that of the 50-cent man.[16]

Babbage's principle is fundamental to the evolution of the division of labor in capitalist society. It gives expression not to a technical aspect of the division of labor, but to its social aspect. Insofar as the labor process may be dissociated, it may be separated into elements some of which are simpler than others and each of which is simpler than the whole. Translated into market terms, this means that the labor power capable of performing the process may be purchased more cheaply as dissociated elements than as a capacity integrated in a single worker. Applied first to the handicrafts and then to the mechanical crafts, Babbage's principle eventually becomes the underlying force governing all forms of work in capitalist society, no matter in what setting or at what hierarchical level.

In the mythology of capitalism, the Babbage principle is presented as an effort to "preserve scarce skills" by putting qualified workers to tasks which "only they can perform," and not wasting "social resources." It is presented as a response to "shortages" of skilled workers or technically trained people, whose time is best used "efficiently" for the advantage of "society." But however much this principle may manifest itself at times in the form of a response to the scarcity of skilled labor—for example, during wars or other periods of rapid expansion of production—this apology is on the whole false. The capitalist mode of production systematically destroys all-around skills where they exist, and brings into being skills and occupations that correspond to its needs. Technical capacities are henceforth distributed on a strict "need to know" basis. The generalized distribution of knowledge of the productive process among all its participants becomes, from this point on, not merely "unnecessary," but a positive barrier to the functioning of the capitalist mode of production.

Labor power has become a commodity. Its uses are no longer organized according to the needs and desires of those who sell it, but rather according to the needs of its purchasers, who are, primarily, employers seeking to expand the value of their capital. And it is the special and permanent interest of these purchasers to cheapen this commodity. The most common mode of cheapening

---

16. J. R. Commons, *Quarterly Journal of Economics,* vol. XIX, p. 3; quoted in F. W. Taussig, *Principles of Economics* (New York, 1921), p. 42.

labor power is exemplified by the Babbage principle: break it up into its simplest elements. And, as the capitalist mode of production creates a working population suitable to its needs, the Babbage principle is, by the very shape of this "labor market," enforced upon the capitalists themselves.

Every step in the labor process is divorced, so far as possible, from special knowledge and training and reduced to simple labor. Meanwhile, the relatively few persons for whom special knowledge and training are reserved are freed so far as possible from the obligations of simple labor. In this way, a structure is given to all labor processes that at its extremes polarizes those whose time is infinitely valuable and those whose time is worth almost nothing. This might even be called the general law of the capitalist division of labor. It is not the sole force acting upon the organization of work, but it is certainly the most powerful and general. Its results, more or less advanced in every industry and occupation, give massive testimony to its validity. It shapes not only work, but populations as well, because over the long run it creates that mass of simple labor which is the primary feature of populations in developed capitalist countries.

# · 8 ·

# Class Structuration and Class Consciousness

## Anthony Giddens

The major problems in the theory of class, I shall suggest, do not so much concern the nature and application of the class concept itself, as what, for want of a better word, I shall call the *structuration* of class relationships.[1] Most attempts to revise class theory since Marx have sought to accomplish such a revision primarily by refining, modifying, or substituting an altogether different notion for the Marxian concept of class. While it is useful to follow and develop certain of Weber's insights in this respect, the most important blank spots in the theory of class concern the processes whereby 'economic classes' become 'social classes', and whereby in turn the latter are related to other social forms. As Marx was anxious to stress in criticising the premises of political economy, all economic relationships, and any sort of 'economy', presuppose a set of social ties between producers. In arguing for the necessity of conceptualising the structuration of class relationships, I do not in any way wish to question the legitimacy of this insight, but rather to focus upon *the modes in which* 'economic' relationships become translated into 'non-economic' social structures.

One source of terminological ambiguity and conceptual confusion in the usage of the term 'class' is that it has often been employed to refer both to an

---

*From Anthony Giddens, *The Class Structure of the Advanced Societies,* 2nd ed. (London: Hutchinson, 1980), pp. 105–17, 296–311.

1. What I call class structuration, Gurvitch calls negatively 'résistance à la pénétration par la société globale'. Georges Gurvitch, *Le concept de classes sociales de Marx à nos jours* (Paris 1954), p. 116. . . .

economic *category* and to a specifiable cluster of social groupings. Thus Weber uses the term in both of these ways, although he seeks terminologically to indicate the difference between 'class' (as a series of 'class positions') and 'social class'. But in order to insist that the study of class and class conflict must concern itself with the interdependence of economy and society, it is not necessary to identify the term 'class' with the divisions and interests generated by the market as such. Consequently, in [this discussion (eds.)], I shall use the term in the sense of Weber's 'social class'—appropriately explicated. While there may be an indefinite multiplicity of cross-cutting interests created by differential market capacities, there are only, in any given society, a limited number of classes.

It will be useful at this juncture to state what class is *not*. First, a class is not a specific 'entity'—that is to say, a bounded social form in the way in which a business firm or a university is—and a class has no publicly sanctioned identity. It is extremely important to stress this, since established linguistic usage often encourages us to apply active verbs to the term 'class'; but the sense in which a class 'acts' in a certain way, or 'perceives' elements in its environment on a par with an individual actor, is highly elliptical, and this sort of verbal usage is to be avoided wherever possible. Similarly, it is perhaps misleading to speak of 'membership' of a class, since this might be held to imply participation in a definite 'group'. This form of expression, however, is difficult to avoid altogether, and I shall not attempt to do so in what follows. Secondly, class has to be distinguished from 'stratum', and class theory from the study of 'stratification' as such. The latter, comprising what Ossowski terms a gradation scheme, involves a criterion or set of criteria in terms of which individuals may be ranked descriptively along a scale. The distinction between class and stratum is again a matter of some significance, and bears directly upon the problem of class 'boundaries'. For the divisions between strata, for analytical purposes, may be drawn very precisely, since they may be set upon a measurement scale—as, for example, with 'income strata'. The divisions between classes are *never* of this sort; nor, moreover, do they lend themselves to easy visualisation, in terms of any ordinal scale of 'higher' and 'lower', as strata do—although, once more, this sort of imagery cannot be escaped altogether. Finally we must distinguish clearly between class and elite. Elite theory, as formulated by Pareto and Mosca, developed in part as a conscious and deliberate repudiation of class analysis. In place of the concept of class relationships, the elite theorists substituted the opposition of 'elite' and 'mass'; and in place of the Marxian juxtaposition of class society and classlessness they substituted the idea of the cyclical replacement of elites *in perpetuo*. Their use of terms such as 'governing class' and 'political class' is in fact confusing and illegitimate. . . .

## The Structuration of Class Relationships

It is useful, initially, to distinguish the *mediate* from the *proximate* structuration of class relationships. By the former term, I refer to the factors which intervene between the existence of certain given market capacities and the formation of classes as identifiable social groupings, that is to say which operate as 'overall' connecting links between the market on the one hand and structured systems of class relationships on the other. In using the latter phrase, I refer to 'localised' factors which condition or shape class formation. The mediate structuration of class relationships is governed above all by the distribution of mobility chances which pertain within a given society. Mobility has sometimes been treated as if it were in large part separable from the determination of class structure. According to Schumpeter's famous example, classes may be conceived of as like conveyances, which may be constantly carrying different 'passengers' without in any way changing their shape. But, compelling though the analogy is at first sight, it does not stand up to closer examination, especially within the framework I am suggesting here.[2] In general, the greater the degree of 'closure' of mobility chances—both intergenerationally and within the career of the individual—the more this facilitates the formation of identifiable classes. For the effect of closure in terms of intergenerational movement is to provide for the *reproduction* of common life experience over the generations; and this homogenisation of experience is reinforced to the degree to which the individual's movement within the labour market is confined to occupations which generate a similar range of material outcomes. In general we may state that the structuration of classes is facilitated *to the degree to which mobility closure exists in relation to any specified form of market capacity.* There are three sorts of market capacity which can be said to be normally of importance in this respect: ownership of property in the means of production; possession of educational or technical qualifications; and possession of manual labour-power. In so far as it is the case that these tend to be tied to closed patterns of inter- and intragenerational mobility, this yields the foundation of *a basic three-class system* in capitalist society: an 'upper', 'middle', and 'lower' or 'working' class. But as has been indicated previously, it is an intrinsic characteristic of the development of the capitalist market that there exist no legally sanctioned or formally prescribed limitations upon mobility, and hence it must be emphasised that there is certainly never anything even approaching complete closure. In order to account for the emergence of structured classes, we must look in addition at the proximate sources of structuration.

There are three, related, sources of proximate structuration of class relationships: the division of labour within the productive enterprise; the authority relationships within the enterprise; and the influence of what I shall call 'distributive groupings'. I have already suggested that Marx tended to use the notion of 'division of labour' very broadly, to refer both to market relationships and to the allocation of occupational tasks within the productive organisation. Here I shall use the term only in this second, more specific, sense. In capitalism, the division of labour in the enterprise is in principle governed by the promotion of productive efficiency in relation to the maximisation of profit; but while responding to the same exigencies as the capitalist market in general, the influence of the division of labour must be analytically separated as a distinctive source of structuration (and, as will be discussed later, as a significant influence upon class

---

2. We may, however, agree with Schumpeter that 'The family, not the physical person, is the true unit of class and class theory' (Joseph Schumpeter, *Imperialism, Social Classes,* Cleveland 1961). This is actually completely consistent with the idea that mobility is fundamental to class formation.

consciousness). The division of labour, it is clear, may be a basis of the fragmentation as well as the consolidation of class relationships. It furthers the formation of classes to the degree to which it creates homogeneous groupings which cluster along the same lines as those which are fostered by mediate structuration. Within the modern industrial order,[3] the most significant influence upon proximate structuration in the division of labour is undoubtedly that of technique. The effect of industrial technique (more recently, however, modified by the introduction of cybernetic systems of control) is to create a decisive separation between the conditions of labour of manual and non-manual workers. 'Machine-minding', in one form or another, regardless of whether it involves a high level of manual skill, tends to create a working environment quite distinct from that of the administrative employee, and one which normally enforces a high degree of physical separation between the two groupings.[4]

This effect of the division of labour thus overlaps closely with the influence of the mediate structuration of class relationships through the differential apportionment of mobility chances; but it is, in turn, potentially heavily reinforced by the typical authority system in the enterprise. In so far as administrative workers participate in the framing, or merely in the enforcement, of authoritative commands, they tend to be separated from manual workers, who are subject to those commands. But the influence of differential authority is also basic as a reinforcing agent of the structuration of class relationships at the 'upper' levels. Ownership of property, in other words, confers certain fundamental capacities of command, maximised within the 'entrepreneurial' enterprise in its classical form. To the extent to which this serves to underlie a division at 'the top', in the control of the organisation (something which is manifestly influenced, but not at all destroyed, if certain of the suppositions advanced by the advocates of the theory of the separation of 'ownership and control' are correct) it supports the differentiation of the 'upper' from the 'middle' class.

The third source of the proximate structuration of class relationships is that originating in the sphere of consumption rather than production. Now according to the traditional interpretations of class structure, including those of Marx and Weber, 'class' is a phenomenon of production: relationships established in consumption are therefore quite distinct from, and secondary to, those formed in the context of productive activity. There is no reason to deviate from this general emphasis. But without dropping the conception that classes are founded ultimately in the economic structure of the capitalist market, it is still possible to regard consumption patterns as a major influence upon class structuration. Weber's notions of 'status' and 'status group', as I previously pointed out, confuse two separable elements: the formation of groupings in consumption, on the one hand, and the formation of types of social differentiation based upon some sort of non-economic value providing a scale of 'honour' or 'prestige' on the other. While the two may often coincide, they do not necessarily do so, and it seems worthwhile to distinguish them terminologically. Thus I shall call 'distributive groupings' those relationships involving common patterns of the consump-

---

3. See below, pp. 264–9.
4. Lockwood, *The Blackcoated Worker* (London, 1958).

tion of economic goods, regardless of whether the individuals involved make any type of conscious evaluation of their honour or prestige relative to others; 'status' refers to the existence of such evaluations, and a 'status group' is, then, any set of social relationships which derives its coherence from their application.[5]

In terms of class structuration, distributive groupings are important in so far as they interrelate with the other sets of factors distinguished above in such a way as to reinforce the typical separations between forms of market capacity. The most significant distributive groupings in this respect are those formed through the tendency towards community or neighbourhood segregation. Such a tendency is not normally based only upon differentials in income, but also upon such factors as access to housing mortgages, etc. The creation of distinctive 'working-class neighbourhoods' and 'middle-class neighbourhoods', for example, is naturally promoted if those in manual labour are by and large denied mortgages for house buying, while those in non-manual occupations experience little difficulty in obtaining such loans. Where industry is located outside of the major urban areas, homogeneous 'working-class communities' frequently develop through the dependence of workers upon housing provided by the company.

In summary, to the extent to which the various bases of mediate and proximate class structuration overlap, classes will exist as distinguishable formations. I wish to say—as will emerge in detail in later chapters—that *the combination of the sources of mediate and proximate structuration distinguished here, creating a threefold class structure, is generic to capitalist society*. But the mode in which these elements are merged to form *a specific class system*, in any given society, differs significantly according to variations in economic and political development. It should be evident that structuration is never an all-or-nothing matter. The problem of the existence of distinct class 'boundaries', therefore, is not one which can be settled *in abstracto*: one of the specific aims of class analysis in relation to empirical societies must necessarily be that of determining how strongly, in any given case, the 'class principle' has become established as a mode of structuration. Moreover, the operation of the 'class principle' may also involve the creation of forms of structuration within the major class divisions. One case in point is that which Marx called the 'petty bourgeoisie'. In terms of the preceding analysis, it is quite easy to see why ownership of small property in the means of production might come to be differentiated both from the upper class and from the ('new') middle class. If it is the case that the chances of mobility, either inter- or intragenerationally, from small to large property ownership are slight, this is likely to isolate the small property-owner from membership of the upper class as such. But the fact that he enjoys directive control of an enterprise, however minute, acts to distinguish him from those who are part of a hierarchy of authority in a larger organisation. On the other hand, the income and other economic returns of the petty bourgeois are likely to be similar to the

---

5. It might be pointed out that it would easily be possible to break down the notion of status group further: according, for example, to whether the status evaluations in question are made primarily by others outside the group, and rejected by those inside it, etc.

white-collar worker, and hence they may belong to similar distributive group-ings. A second potentially important influence upon class formation is to be traced to the factor of skill differential within the general category of manual labour. The manual worker who has undergone apprenticeship, or a compara-ble period of training, possesses a market capacity which sets him apart from the unskilled or semi-skilled worker. This case will be discussed in more detail below; it is enough merely to indicate at this point that there are certain factors promoting structuration on the basis of this differentiation in market capacity (e.g., that the chances of intergenerational mobility from skilled manual to white-collar occupations are considerably higher than they are from unskilled and semi-skilled manual occupations).

So far I have spoken of structuration in a purely formal way, as though class could be defined in terms of relationships which have no 'content'. But this obviously will not do: if classes become social realities, this must be manifest in the formation of common patterns of behaviour and attitude. Since Weber's discussion of classes and status groups, the notion of 'style of life' has normally come to be identified as solely pertaining to the mode whereby a status group expresses its claim to distinctiveness. However, in so far as there is marked convergence of the sources of structuration mentioned above, classes will also tend to manifest common styles of life.

An initial distinction can be drawn here between 'class awareness' and 'class consciousness'.[6] We may say that, in so far as class is a structurated phenome-non, there will tend to exist a common awareness and acceptance of similar attitudes and beliefs, linked to a common style of life, among the members of the class. 'Class awareness', as I use the term here, does *not* involve a recognition that these attitudes and beliefs signify a particular class affiliation, or the recogni-tion that there exist other classes, characterised by different attitudes, beliefs, and styles of life; 'class consciousness', by contrast, as I shall use the notion, does imply both of these. The difference between class awareness and class con-sciousness is a fundamental one, because class awareness may take the form of *a denial of the existence or reality of classes.*[7] Thus the class awareness of the middle class, in so far as it involves beliefs which place a premium upon individual responsibility and achievement, is of this order.

Within ethnically and culturally homogeneous societies, the degree of class structuration will be determined by the interrelationship between the sources of structuration identified previously. But many, if not the majority, of capitalist societies are not homogeneous in these respects. Traditionally, in class theory, racial or religious divisions have been regarded as just so many 'obstacles' to the formation of classes as coherent unities. This may often be so, where these foster types of structuration which deviate from that established by the 'class principle'

6. This is not, of course, the same as Lukács' 'class-conditioned unconsciousness'; but I believe that Lukács is correct in distinguishing qualitatively different 'levels' of class consciousness. Lukács, op. cit., pp. 52ff.

7. cf. Poulantzas, *Political Power and Social Classes* (London, 1973). It is misleading, however, to speak of *classes sans conscience,* as Crozier does. See Michel Crozier, 'Classes sans conscience ou préfiguration de la société sans classes', *Archives européenes de sociologie* **1,** 1960; also 'L'ambiguité de la conscience de classe chez les employés et les petits fonctionnaires', *Cahiers internationaux de sociologie* **28,** 1955.

(as typically was the case in the battles fought by the rearguard of feudalism against the forces promoting the emergence of capitalism). The idea that ethnic or cultural divisions serve to dilute or hinder the formation of classes is also very explicitly built into Weber's separation of (economic) 'class' and 'status group'. But this, in part at least, gains its cogency from the contrast between estate, as a legally constituted category, and class, as an economic category. While it may be agreed, however, that the *bases* of the formation of classes and status groups (in the sense in which I have employed these concepts) are different, nonetheless the tendency to class structuration may receive a considerable impetus *where class coincides with the criteria of status group membership*—in other words, where structuration deriving from economic organisation 'overlaps' with, or, in Dahrendorf's terms, is 'superimposed' upon, that deriving from evaluative categorisations based upon ethnic or cultural differences. [8] Where this is so, status group membership itself becomes a form of market capacity. Such a situation frequently offers the strongest possible source of class structuration, whereby there develop clear-cut differences in attitudes, beliefs and style of life between the classes. Where ethnic differences serve as a 'disqualifying' market capacity, such that those in the category in question are heavily concentrated among the lowest-paid occupations, or are chronically unemployed or semi-employed, we may speak of the existence of an *underclass*. [9]

## Contradiction and the Genesis of Class Consciousness

In the previous section, a distinction has been made between 'class awareness' and 'class consciousness'. It can be said that, whereas class structuration presupposes the existence of class awareness, the existence of class consciousness is problematic. Class consciousness involves, first of all, the recognition, however vaguely defined, of another class or of other classes: perception of class identity implies cognisance of characteristics which separate the class of which one is a member from another or others. But it is possible to classify various 'levels' of class consciousness. [10] The most undeveloped form of class consciousness is that which simply involves *a conception of class identity and therefore of class differentiation*. This can be distinguished from a level of consciousness which involves a conception of class conflict: *where perception of class unity is linked to a recognition of opposition of interest with another class or classes*. The connection

---

8. Or, to use another terminology, where there is 'overdetermination' (Louis Althusser, *For Marx*, London 1969, pp. 89–128).

9. Marx's *Lumpenproletariat*, according to this usage, is only an underclass when the individuals in question tend to derive from distinctive ethnic backgrounds. Leggett has referred to the underclass as the 'marginal working class', defining this as 'a sub-community of workers who belong to a subordinate ethnic or racial group which is usually proletarianised and highly segregated' (John C. Leggett, *Class, Race, and Labor*, New York 1968, p. 14).

10. cf. Alain Touraine, *La conscience ouvrière* (Paris 1966), p. 17: 'il existe un grand nombre de combinaisons possibles entre les trois principes dont un assemblage très particulier constitue la conscience de classe: le *principe d'identité* qui est, plus encore que la définition d'un groupe d'appartenance, la définition d'une contribution, d'une fonction sociale et donc le fondement des revendications; le *principe d'opposition*, c'est-à-dire la définition du groupe antagoniste et plus précisément celle des obstacles au contrôle des travailleurs sur leurs œuvres; le *principe de totalité* qui definit le champ social dans lequel se situe la relation definie par les deux principes précédents'.

between this and the first level of class consciousness may be expressed, to borrow a Socratic term, as a *maieutic* one; in other words, it is mainly a process of developing and clarifying ideas which are latent in perceptions of class identity and differentiation. This distinction is not the same, however, as that made by Marx between a class 'in itself' and a class 'for itself'. In the first place, the Marxian distinction does not separate class structuration from class consciousness (as I have defined the latter term). But, more important in the context of the discussion here, Marx does not discriminate between class consciousness as perception of conflict of interest, and what I shall designate as the third level of consciousness—namely, *revolutionary class consciousness*. In contrast to conflict consciousness, this involves *a recognition of the possibility of an overall reorganisation in the institutional mediation of power and a belief that such a reorganisation can be brought about through class action.* In Marx's writings (although not in those of Lenin) the emergence of revolutionary class consciousness is assumed to be a direct outcome of, if not wholly indistinguishable from, consciousness of conflict of class interest. It will be a fundamental part of my argument here, however, that such is not the case; that the conditions underlying the genesis of revolutionary class consciousness are different from those involved in the formation of 'conflict consciousness'.

In the controversies which have surrounded Marxism since the late nineteenth century, the problem of the 'role of ideas', in relation to Marx's 'materialism', has occupied a prominent position. For, as it might seem, if the factors which govern social change are located in the infrastructure, and if ideas are in some sense merely a 'reflection' of the substratum, then the emergence of class consciousness is itself simply an epiphenomenon of the real process of movement which transforms one type of society into another. Such a position apparently removes man from his own history, and leads to the endemic difficulties faced by orthodox dialectical materialism in recognising the active or voluntaristic character of human conduct. The relatively recent publication of Marx's early writings, and the revitalisation of Marxist scholarship to which this has given rise, has effectively dispelled this interpretation.[11] The conception which is universalised in dialectical materialism is in fact treated by Marx as historically contingent—and, more specifically, as an expression of the reification characteristic of bourgeois thought. It is precisely a recovery of the capacity of the subject to separate reification from objectification which should be regarded (according to Marx) as the premise of the transformation of capitalism. In the Marxian view, then, consciousness is not the 'effect' of human activity in the material world, but constitutes the attribution of meaning which guides conduct, and is inseparable from that conduct.

In general terms, this may be regarded as an adequate theoretical background for the analysis of class consciousness. In accounting for the origins of diverse forms of class awareness and consciousness, there is thus no need to become embroiled in fruitless controversy over the relationship between the (so-called) 'material' and 'ideal', as if these were competing explanations of conduct. Class structuration necessarily expresses itself in terms of action ori-

---

11. See my *Capitalism and Modern Social Theory,* ch. 14 and *passim.*

ented to meanings; Marx's treatment of class consciousness is deficient not because it is 'mechanical', or considers ideas merely as 'epiphenomena', but for other reasons. Class structuration, therefore, always implies either class awareness or class consciousness. The problem, at least as regards the working class in capitalism, is to determine the conditions which facilitate the development of conflict or revolutionary consciousness. It should be made clear that, according to the argument outlined above, this is at the same time a problem of structuration—or rather of the specific *forms* of structuration whereby class consciousness is manifest; any level of class consciousness may be manifest in the conduct of all, or the majority, of the members of a class, or only in that of certain sectors or groups within it (trade unions, political parties, etc.).

In analysing the origins of class consciousness it is useful to make a distinction between *conflict* and *contradiction*. [12] Both terms appear in Marx's writings, but he does not make a clear differentiation between them. As a class society, capitalism is built upon a conflict of interest between capital and wage-labour; it is this class opposition, in Marxian theory, which is regarded as the ultimate source of the more particular social and economic 'contradictions' whereby the capitalist mode of production is undermined from within, by the growth of the set of productive forces which constitute incipient socialism. I shall use the term class 'conflict' to refer to an opposition of class interests: 'conflict consciousness' involves recognition of such an interest opposition. The term 'contradiction', however, I shall use to refer to a discrepancy between *an existing and an immanent mode of industrial control*. By 'industrial control', I mean the mediation of control within the enterprise, at any specific level of the authority structure. It will be a basic part of my argument in later chapters that the stability of capitalist society depends upon the maintenance of an insulation of economy and polity, such that questions of industrial organisation appear as 'non-political'. In fact, any threat to the system of industrial control has immediate implications of a political nature. I propose to advance the view in this book that conflict consciousness tends to become revolutionary consciousness only *where class conflict originates in contradiction;* and that, far from there being a necessary correspondence between these and the advancing maturity of capitalist society, as is assumed in Marxian theory, they only coincide under conditions which are distinct from those to which Marx gave most prominence.

We must first of all consider the factors which influence the development of conflict consciousness. In large part, these may be said to concern whatever promotes the *visibility* (transparency) of class structuration. This is the case, for example, with those characteristics of capitalism which Marx mentions as facilitating the emergence of a proletariat 'for itself', such as the 'homogenising' effects of mechanisation upon the labour task, or the significance of the large-scale factory in herding together a mass of workers in a single place. In each of these examples, the conditions of existence of individuals tend to make their common class characteristics readily visible. This is not so with the peasantry, whom Marx, speaking of nineteenth-century France, compares to a 'sack of

---

12. This may perhaps be regarded as a particular case of Lockwood's distinction of problems of 'social integration' and 'system integration'.

potatoes': the isolated nature of the working environment of the peasant tends to inhibit the perception that he shares common class interests with others. But other aspects of class structuration, to which Marx gives little attention, may influence, or even decisively effect, visibility.[13] Thus, as Weber pointed out, the manual worker may frequently feel more hostility towards the industrial manager, who issues commands to him and with whom he is in relatively direct contact, than towards the owner of the enterprise, or towards the even more remote banker or financier. Visibility is normally most strongly accentuated where there is a coincidence of class and status group criteria, especially where the latter involves an ethnic differentiation. Conflict consciousness, of course, need not be reciprocal, and indeed such normally is the case with the relationship between working class and middle class in capitalist society. The assertion of class interest on the part of the working class clashes with the typical class awareness of the middle class, whose members tend to perceive the social order in terms of individualistic notions of 'personal achievement' and 'initiative', etc.[14]

Perception of identity of class interests in opposition to another class or classes naturally fosters the development of organisations or agencies devoted to the advancement of those interests. It is to such agencies, of course, that Marx looked to supply the spearhead of the working-class movement. And it cannot be doubted that, in unions and political parties, conflict consciousness may be clarified and made more precise than is normally the case in the more diffuse class consciousness of the rank-and-file worker. These agencies are then in a position to react back upon, and to attempt to direct, the class consciousness of the mass. While the very institutionalisation of agencies, nominally set up to promote certain class interests, may provide a further factor intervening between the member of the class and the actual furthering of his interests, in general terms this is an acceptable interpretation of the processes involved in heightening conflict consciousness. What it does not adequately explain is why such consciousness should take a revolutionary form.

If the most important factor advancing conflict consciousness is *visibility* of class differentials, the most important factor influencing revolutionary consciousness is *relativity of experience* within a given system of production. Revolutionary consciousness, as I have defined it, involves a perception of the existing socio-economic order as 'illegitimate' and a recognition of modes of action which can be taken to reorganise it on a new basis. Such a perception is virtually always foreclosed for the members of chronically underprivileged groupings whose conditions of labour remain stable over time. Its creation implies a framework by reference to which individuals can distance their experience from the here-and-now, the 'given' social reality, and envisage the possibility of one which differs radically from it. The term 'relative deprivation' is inadequate as

---

13. cf., however, Engels' observation that 'poverty often dwells in hidden alleys close to the palaces of the rich; but, in general, a separate territory has been assigned to it, where removed from the sight of the happier classes, it may struggle along as it can' (Friedrich Engels, *The Condition of the Working Class in England in 1844,* London 1968, p. 26).

14. See below, pp. 185–6.

applied in this context. The experience of deprivation (which is necessarily 'relative', since an individual who feels himself to be deprived must in some sense orient himself to a standard of legitimacy) is simply one element in the picture; feelings of resentment of a diffuse nature only take on a revolutionary character when they are fused with a concrete project, however vaguely formulated, of an alternative order which can be brought into being.

Now in Marxian theory, as I have already indicated, conflict stemming from division of interest in class relationships is conflated with that deriving from contradiction. This helps to explain the origin of what is sometimes regarded as a blind-spot in Marx's conception of the development of the class consciousness of the proletariat in capitalism: that is, why the revolt of the working class should take the form of an orientation towards an *institutional* transcendence of the existing order. The answer, evidently enough, is that the working class are the bearers of a new 'principle' of social and economic organisation whose operation contradicts that regulating the capitalist mode of production. But it is not at all clear how the members of the working class come to perceive that this is so. Marx's analysis at this point tends to revert to referring to the results of the exploitative dependence of wage-labour upon capital and hence to the effects of 'emiseration' as manifest in the relative fixity of wages and the growth of the industrial reserve army. However, ... there is also a second Marxian theory of revolution, which looks instead to the clash between a 'backward', agrarian order, and the impact of 'advanced' technique. It is this sort of situation, I wish to say, which actually tends to underlie the formation of revolutionary class consciousness, rather than the former. In such circumstances, the emergence of contradiction is abrupt and marked, and has consequences which affect all aspects of the life of the worker, thus creating what may be regarded as the paradigm case for the (potential) development of revolutionary consciousness in the modern world.

Two things must be noted here. In the first place, the creation of revolutionary class consciousness does not necessarily occur, as Marx assumed, at least in his conception of the emergence of a revolutionary proletariat, out of the *maturity* of capitalism, as a simple heightening of conflict consciousness. Its sources are different, and there is no reason to hold that it is intrinsically linked with the sorts of social condition which act to produce or heighten conflict consciousness—a fact which has important implications, discussed further below. Second, it follows that the sources of revolutionary consciousness will tend to be linked either to those groupings on the fringes of 'incorporation' into a society based upon industrial technique (e.g., peasants whose traditional mode of production has been undermined), or conversely to those involved in the most progressive technical sectors of production.

Much of the literature on these matters, of course, has been primarily concerned with class consciousness as a source of impetus to political action, meaning here the formation of working-class parties with some kind of revolutionary programme. While I shall not in any way sidestep the issues raised in this regard, I do not propose to discuss the phenomena underlying party organisation in detail. I think that Lenin was essentially correct in asserting that 'the working class, solely by its own forces, is able to work out merely trade union consciousness',[15] but that it is mistaken to suppose that this can be transformed into revolutionary consciousness primarily through the medium of active party leadership. There are important elements of truth in Luxemburg's view of the origins of revolutionary consciousness, as compared to that of Lenin. For if we may agree with Lenin that revolutionary consciousness does not arise 'spontaneously' from the mature capitalist production, we may also accept that the factors generating such consciousness among the rank and file concern far more than the nature of political leadership, and have to be looked for in conditions of labour of the working class as such.

[The following section is taken from the "Postscript" (1979) to Anthony Giddens's *The Class Structure of the Advanced Societies.*]

## Marx and Weber: Class Society and Class Structuration

In this section I shall concentrate upon certain misunderstandings of my views that have quite often appeared in the critical literature: misunderstandings that certainly derive in some part from faults in my presentation. One of the most frequent interpretations that has been made of the book is that, since considerable space is devoted to discussion of Max Weber, and Weber's ideas are given serious consideration, its standpoint is a Weberian, or a 'neo-Weberian' one.[16] But I did not intend to defend a Weberian standpoint as against a Marxist one, nor did I intend to produce some sort of synthesis of Marx and Weber in respect of problems of class structure. In case this is not clear, I should emphasise that I do not think such a synthesis is either desirable or possible. Of course, the question of the intellectual connections between the writings of Marx and Weber is not at all easy to resolve, since there are interpretative problems on both sides.[17] But there can be no doubt at all that there are very deep-lying divergencies between both their overall methodological views and their more substantive writings, and that these are reflected directly in their respective analyses of capitalism, class and class conflict.[18]

The significance of Weber's work for class analysis, when juxtaposed to that of Marx, is that it identifies a number of important areas which are relatively undeveloped in Marx's writings. These include aspects of each of the four issues I have distinguished above. In all of these, as I tried to show in the book, Weber's work raises questions that must be directly confronted: 'the market' as a medium of class formation; the social and political significance of the 'new middle

15. V. I. Lenin, *What is to be Done?* (Oxford 1963), p. 63.

16. See, for instance, Rosemary Crompton and Jon Gubbay, *Economy and Class Structure* (London: Macmillan 1977), pp. 29–40 and *passim;* David Binns, *Beyond the Sociology of Conflict* (London: Macmillan 1977), pp. 47–54; Richard Ashcraft, 'Class and class conflict in contemporary capitalist societies', *Comparative Politics* **11,** 1979.

17. cf. 'Marx, Weber and the development of capitalism', in my *Studies in Social and Political Theory* (London: Hutchinson 1977).

18. For a brief discussion of these contrasts, see 'Marx and Weber: problems of class structure', in *Studies in Social and Political Theory,* op. cit.

class' in capitalism; the importance of bureaucracy as a form of domination; and the character of the state as a focus of political and military power. But in none of these instances did I adopt Weberian *solutions*.

A good deal of the criticism that has been levelled against *The Class Structure of the Advanced Societies (CSAS)* has focused upon my introduction of the concept of 'market capacity'. Critics have alleged that, in my analysis, 'the (Weberian) notion of "market capacity" replaces the (Marxist) relation to the means of production';[19] or again: 'it is apparent that Giddens' principal concern is the definition and analysis of class at the level of market encounter'.[20] But neither of these statements accurately describes my concerns; they really amount almost to gratuitous misreadings of the position I developed in the book. I placed a great deal of emphasis, in discussing the emergence of the modern class system, not upon markets as such,[21] but upon the nature of the *capitalist market*. My object in doing so was to seek to underline the distinctiveness of capitalist society in contrast to pre-existing types of social formation. Although I would no longer see the characterisation I offered of 'pre-class society' as either accurate or adequate, I still hold to the overall standpoint I established. Capitalism is a 'class society' in a more fundamental sense than feudalism or other types of society that have previously existed in history. For only with the advent of capitalism does an exploitative class relation become part of the very mechanism of the productive process itself—a phenomenon which has important implications for assessing the scope of Marx's 'historical materialism' and the base/superstructure problem.[22] In pre-capitalist societies, the exploitative process involves the appropriation of surplus production, but the relation of exploitation is not merged—as it is in capitalism—with the labour task itself. The formation of capitalism is not merely brought about by the expansion of commodity markets in what, following J. B. Macpherson, I called 'simple market society'. . . . The development of trade and commerce was a significant factor in the dissolution* of localised production/consumption relationships in postfeudal society, but in 'simple market society' the producer maintained a considerable amount of control over the labour process. The distinctive feature of capitalism, which constitutes it as a class society, is the intersection of commodity and labour markets within the process of production itself. As Marx emphasised so strongly in the first volume of *Capital,* the development of capitalism thus presupposes the creation of a mass of formally 'free' wage workers; labour-power becomes a commodity to be bought and sold. Without wishing to play the game of Marx-quotations, it might nevertheless be worthwhile repeating a passage from Marx. . . .

The historical conditions of its existence (i.e., the existence of capitalism) are by no means given by the mere circulation of money and commodities. It can spring into being *only when the owner of the means of production and subsistence meets in the market with the free*

---

19. Wini Breines and Margaret Cerullo, Review of *The Class Structure of the Advanced Societies, Telos* **28,** 1976, p. 235.

20. Binns, op. cit., p. 48.

21. cf. Karl Polanyi *et al., Trade and Market in the Early Empires* (New York: Free Press 1957).

22. cf. my *Central Problems in Social Theory* (London: Macmillan 1979), ch. 4.

*labourer selling his labour-power.* And this one historical condition comprises a world's history. Capital, therefore, announces from its first appearance a new epoch in the process of social production. [my italics]

Labour-power becomes 'a commodity like any other': at the same time, it *cannot* be a commodity like any other because it involves the activities of living beings. Property, as capital, confers a definite range of rights or capacities upon its owners or possessors, in the context of capitalist production. But the 'proper-tyless' are not merely inert objects to be disposed of at the will of the owners of capital. The possession of 'mere labour-power' also makes possible certain capacities of action for its possessors, .in relation to capital. In using the term 'market capacity', I did not intend to follow Weber's equation of 'class situation' with 'market situation'. I wanted rather to stress the centrality of the *labour contract* to the capitalist system. From the side of the capitalist, the labour con-tract involves the need to coordinate and control the activities of human beings over whom he has no prerogatives of the kind involved in feudal relations of fealty (nor a direct capability of physical coercion). From the side of the worker, the labour contract provides a basis for resisting the dominance of the employer, through attempting to operate sanctions upon the conditions under which labour-power is hired. The collective withdrawal of labour-power, or its threat, thus comes to constitute a major feature of capital-labour conflicts.

To suppose that, in capitalism, product and labour markets can be severed from the process of production is simply foolish or doctrinaire.[23] Moreover, it is useless to conjure up the ritual incantation that class relations are founded in the 'relations of production', if that phrase is left unexplained. Rather than substi-tuting the concept of 'market capacity' for 'relations of production', I wanted to identify what the main components of the relations of production are within the capitalist economic order: and to show how these are involved in the structura-tion of class relationships. The phrase, 'relations of production', is often used to run together three sorts of socio-economic relationships that I thought it impor-tant to distinguish. These are those involved in:

1. The division of labour within techniques of production (para-(technical relations).
2. The authority relations within the enterprise.
3. The connections between production and consumption, as involved in 'distributive groupings'.

Each of these has to be grasped in the overall context of the capital/wage-labour relation. Max Weber tended to separate each from the class structure of capital-ism, by regarding the first two as elements of a general process of 'rationalisa-

---

23. See, for instance, Crompton and Gubbay, op. cit.; Goran Therborn: *What Does the Ruling Class Do When it Rules?* (London: New Left Books 1978). pp. 138–43. The crude nature of the opposition which Therborn draws between a caricatured Weberian position and a dogmatically presented quasi-Althusserian interpretation of Marx is characteristic of this sort of standpoint. cf. Laclau's observation that 'The emergence of the free labour market is the decisive factor in the appearance of capitalism,' noted in critique of Althusser's and Balibar's formulation of the notion of mode of production (Ernesto Laclau, *Politics and Ideology in Marxist Theory,* London: New Left Books 1977, p. 75).

tion' of economic life, and relating the third to the sphere of 'status groups'. It is here precisely that Weber's view of 'class situation' as equivalent to 'market situation' is most consequential, as compared to Marx. In contrast to Weber's conception, my account of class structuration seeks to analyse these three sets of elements as integral to capitalism as a class society. I specifically set out to criticise (rather than merely to ignore, as many Marxists have been prone to do) the Weberian standpoint that 'starts from an assumption of the inherent rationality of technique which is viewed as the generator of a global process of rationalisation.'[24]. . .

One of my main aims in *CSAS* was to explore the relations between property and authority, or between what I would now call generically 'allocation' and 'authorisation', as structured resources constituting forms of domination.[25] The classical Marxian texts lack an adequate theory of bureaucratic domination, and Marxist authors have rarely given sufficient attention to integrating the critical analysis of class domination with the critical analysis of bureaucratic domination.[26] Weber's interpretation of the rise of modern capitalism as intrinsically promoting the spread of bureaucracy, and his linkage of bureaucratisation to a broader 'process of rationalisation' have to be directly confronted here. I did not pretend to offer an exhaustive analysis of Weber's notion of rationalisation,[27] but attempted to distinguish, as separable sources of class structuration, phenomena which Weber bound together along the dimension of rationalisation—bureaucratisation. Weber's analyses draw direct connections between paratechnical relations and the authority system of the productive enterprise; and between the authority system of the enterprise and the capitalist state. The rationality of technique is treated as integrally involved with the rationality of bureaucratic domination in the specification of these connections. Weber quite often compares bureaucracy directly to a machine: both are the most 'technically-rational' means of harnessing energies to the fulfilment of specific tasks. An individual within a bureaucratic organisation, Weber says, 'is only a single cog in an ever-moving mechanism which prescribes to him an essentially fixed rate of march'.[28]

Two basic questions suggest themselves. How far is the rationality of technique specifically an outcome of capitalist class domination? How valid is Weber's analysis of bureaucratic organisation, as implying the inevitable concentration of power within 'imperatively coordinated associations'? The connecting point between these questions is to be found in the concept of the division of

---

24. Terence Johnson, 'The professions in the class struggle', in Richard Scase, *Industrial Society: Class, Cleavage and Control* (London: Allen & Unwin 1977), p. 94. An accurate representation of my position in respect of the rationality of technique and authority is given in Louis Maheu, 'Rapports de classe et problèmes de transformation', in Louis Maheu and Gabriel Gagnon, *Changement social et rapports de classes* (Montreal: Presses de l'Université de Montréal 1978), pp. 21ff.

25. *Central Problems in Social Theory,* op. cit., pp. 100-1 and *passim.*

26. Marx himself dismissed as 'idiocy' Bakunin's suggestion that the controllers of 'collectively owned' property in a socialist society could create a new form of class domination.

27. cf., however my *Politics and Sociology in the Thought of Max Weber* (London: Macmillan 1972), pp. 44-9.

28. Max Weber, *Economy and Society* (New York: Bedmeister Press 1968), vol. 3, p. 998.

labour.[29] At the time when I wrote *CSAS* only a few general analyses of the division of labour in capitalist production, most notably that by Georges Friedmann,[30] were available. Since then, however, a major contribution dealing with this problem has appeared, Braverman's *Labour and Monopoly Capital*.[31]

Braverman's starting point is the sale of labour-power as a commodity: in selling their labour-power to the capitalist, workers cede control of the labour task. The consolidation and expansion of this control is the first imperative of 'management'.[32] The division of labour plays a crucial part in this process, but not the division of labour in general. Braverman insists upon the importance of distinguishing between the social and technical division of labour. The social division of labour, which involves the separation of tasks devoted to the making of whole products, is found in all societies; the technical division of labour, involving the detailed fragmentation of the labour task into repetitive operations carried out by different individuals, is specifically characteristic of capitalist production. The progression of the technical division of labour, Braverman argues, is central to management control of the labour process, since it enables knowledge of and command over the labour process to be taken more and more completely out of the hands of the worker. Taylorism, or 'scientific management', is the most developed and comprehensive form which this takes: the operations carried out by the worker are integrated into the technical design of production as a whole. The 'sieving off' of knowledge of and skill in work that is maximised by the application of Taylorism, according to Braverman, has today become intrinsic to the technological development of capitalism. Subsequent changes in management ideology which might seem to have replaced Taylorism, such as the emergence of the 'human relations approach', are in fact only of marginal significance. Taylorism has become the secular organising creed of capitalist production.

Braverman's analysis, as against that of Weber, allows us to show that the rationality of technique in modern industrial enterprise is not neutral in respect of class domination. The importance of this can scarcely be over-emphasised. Industrial technique embodies the capital/wage-labour relation within its very form. Class domination is shown to be the absent centre of the linkage Weber drew between the rationality of technique and the rationality of the most 'technically effective' form of authority: bureaucracy. Although Braverman's use of Marx's differentiation between 'the division of labour in society' and 'the division of labour in the workshop'—the social and technical division of labour— can be questioned,[33] his emphasis upon the integration of the capitalist division

---

29. cf. my *Capitalism and Modern Social Theory* (Cambridge: Cambridge University Press 1971), pp. 224–42.

30. Georges Friedmann, *Industrial Society* (Glencoe: Free Press 1955); cf. also *La travail en miettes*.

31. Harry Braverman, *Labor and Monopoly Capital* (New York: Monthly Review Press 1974).

32. A partly overlapping viewpoint is sketched in Stephen A. Marglin, 'What do bosses do?', in André Gorz, *The Division of Labour* (London: Harvester 1976).

33. The distinction between the social and technical division of labour is not as unambiguous as Braverman claims, nor is the technical division of labour peculiar to capitalism; Marx's critique of the division of labour (e.g., between the sexes, or town and country) is not confined to the technical division of labour.

of labour and management control is illuminating. Moreover, it offers the possibility of reconnecting the Marxian theme of 'alienated labour' directly with a socio-economic analysis of the nature of capitalist production.

This having been said, there are substantial limitations to, and objections that can be made against, Braverman's approach. I shall confine my discussion here to those which have some bearing upon issues raised by Weber's conception of bureaucracy.

First, although Braverman's discussion radically alters the nature of the connections Weber draws between technique and bureaucratic administration, Braverman has little to say about the 'internal' organisation of managerial authority in capitalistic enterprise.[34] Hence it is not clear what becomes of the knowledge and control of the labour process that is taken from the worker. To say merely that it is appropriated by 'capital' is as vague and unsatisfactory as talking of the 'global function' of capital as being that of the 'control and surveillance' of labour.

Second, Braverman describes the 'sieving off' of knowledge and skill from the worker as largely a one-way movement. The result, curiously, is an analysis which underestimates the consciousness and capabilities of workers as compared to management and which, notwithstanding its divergence from a Weberian model of progressive 'bureaucratic rationalisation', portrays a process seemingly as irreversible as that envisaged by Weber. In Braverman's work, this consequence derives in some part from his declared attempt to concern himself only with the '"objective" content of class', and not with the 'subjective will'.[35] But a great deal of his book is actually about the 'subjective will' of *management,* as manifest in Taylorism, etc. It is impossible to sever 'objective' and 'subjective' components of class in the manner in which Braverman tries to do, as if the first can be analysed separately and the second added in later[36]—here there is a definite similarity between the approaches of Braverman and Carchedi. Workers' knowledge of the labour process is not confined to the nature of the work task: the implications of technological change have been grasped by workers as well as management, and actively resisted by them. Historical studies of the American working class indicate not only that Taylorism had considerably less impact than Braverman suggests, in large degree because of worker resistance, but that the expansion of more 'humanistic' conceptions of industrial relations was also in some part an outcome of working class opposition to Taylorism.[37]

---

34. Braverman seems to consider that Sweezy's and Baran's *Monopoly Capital* has said more or less all there is to say about this. See his comments in Braverman, op. cit., pp. 251–6; Sweezy's preface to Braverman's book also appears to take the same view.

35. Braverman, op. cit., p. 27.

36. cf. Russell Jacoby's review of *Labor and Monopoly Capital, Telos* **29,** 1976; and Gavin Mackenzie, 'The political economy of the American working class', *British Journal of Sociology* **28,** 1977.

37. See Bryan Palmer, 'Class, conception and conflict; the thrust for efficiency, managerial views of labour and the working class rebellion, 1903–22', *Review of Radical Political Economy* **7,** 1975; H. G. J. Aitken, *Taylorism at Watertown Arsenal* (Cambridge, Mass.: Harvard University Press 1960); Stanley Aronowitz, *False Promises* (New York: McGraw-Hill 1973), and S. Aronowitz, 'Marx, Braverman, and the logic of capital', *Insurgent Sociologist,* Winter, 1978–9; Andrew L. Friedman, *Industry and Labour* (London: Macmillan 1977).

This point can be generalised, and focused back upon Weber's interpretation of bureaucracy. Most Marxist authors who have discussed Weber's treatment of bureaucracy have been insufficiently critical of the way in which Weber actually characterises bureaucratic hierarchies. That is to say, they have accepted that bureaucratic systems of administration do have the traits which Weber attributed to them, but treat these as an outcome of the class relations of capitalism. However, it is important to develop a more frontal attack upon Weber's thesis that the advance of bureaucratisation inevitably produces an increasingly rigid hierarchy of power within an organisation.[38] As Crozier has shown, the relations between offices in bureaucratic organisations offer spaces of potential control for subordinates that are not available in smaller, more traditional collectivities.[39] The generalised contrast which Weber tended to draw between the autonomy of action enjoyed by actors in traditional communities and the 'steelhard' nature of developed bureaucratic systems is not justifiable. In fact it is plausible to argue that the more tightly knit and inflexible the formal relations of authority in an organisation, the more they can be circumvented and manipulated by those in subordinate positions to their own advantage. Successful struggle for the maintenance of elements of control by subordinates is much more prevalent than Weber acknowledged.

The significance of struggle on the level of day to day practices is frequently left untheorised in Marxist analyses, both on the level of bureaucratic hierarchies and that of the shop-floor: Braverman's work is actually rather conventional in this respect. This tendency, especially pronounced among the more orthodox Marxist writers, is undoubtedly related to the 'failure' of workers in advanced capitalist countries to have produced a successful proletarian revolution. Less dramatic forms of worker resistance are thereby ignored or written off as insignificant. In *CSAS* I tried to sustain the claims that the successes of the labour movement have been very considerable, and that they have provided the major impetus transforming the 'liberal state' into the 'liberal–democratic state'. . . . Worker resistance is however important in regard of two other characteristics of the development of the working-class over the past century: the prominence of what I called 'conflict consciousness', as distinguished from 'revolutionary consciousness'; and the persistence of skill differentiations among manual workers. The prevalence of conflict consciousness is not surprising given the 'defensive' nature of the attempts of workers to maintain or recover aspects of control over circumstances of their labour that are excluded from the labour contract and materially eroded by technological development. Rejection of the routines of oppressive labour may take various forms, including absenteeism, sabotage, etc.[40] It would be quite mistaken to see the variety of day to day worker resistance as secondary and unimportant because it does not promise the imminent demolition of the capitalist mode of production.

---

38. Here I draw upon *Central Problems in Social Theory*, op. cit., pp. 147–50.
39. Michel Crozier, *The Bureaucratic Phenomenon* (London: Tavistock 1964).
40. cf. Aronowitz, *False Promises*, op. cit.

# · 9 ·

# Social Closure and Class Formation

## Frank Parkin

By social closure Weber means the process by which social collectivities seek to maximize rewards by restricting access to resources and opportunities to a limited circle of eligibles. This entails the singling out of certain social or physical attributes as the justificatory basis of exclusion. Weber suggests that virtually any group attribute—race, language, social origin, religion—may be seized upon provided it can be used for 'the monopolization of specific, usually economic opportunities'.[1] This monopolization is directed against competitors who share some positive or negative characteristic; its purpose is always the closure of social and economic opportunities to *outsiders*.'[2] The nature of these exclusionary practices, and the completeness of social closure, determine the general character of the distributive system.

Surprisingly, Weber's elaboration of the closure theme is not linked in any immediate way with his other main contributions to stratification theory, despite the fact that processes of exclusion can properly be conceived of as an aspect of the distribution of power, which for Weber is practically synonymous with stratification. As a result, the usefulness of the concept for the study of class and similar forms of structured inequality becomes conditional on the acceptance of certain refinements and enlargements upon the original usage.

An initial step in this direction is to extend the notion of closure to encom-

---

*From Frank Parkin, *The Marxist Theory of Class: A Bourgeois Critique* (London: Tavistock, 1979), pp. 44–54.

1. Weber (eds. Roth and Wittich) 1968: 342.
2. Weber (eds. Roth and Wittich) 1968: 342.

pass other forms of collective social action designed to maximize claims to rewards and opportunities. Closure strategies would thus include not only those of an exclusionary kind, but also those adopted by the excluded themselves as a direct response to their status as outsiders. It is in any case hardly possible to consider the effectiveness of exclusion practices without due reference to the countervailing actions of socially defined ineligibles. As Weber acknowledges: 'Such group action may provoke a corresponding reaction on the part of those against whom it is directed.'[3] In other words, collective efforts to resist a pattern of dominance governed by exclusion principles can properly be regarded as the other half of the social closure equation. This usage is in fact employed by Weber in his discussion of 'community closure' which, as Neuwirth has shown, bears directly upon those forms of collective action mounted by the excluded—i.e. 'negatively privileged status groups'.[4]

The distinguishing feature of exclusionary closure is the attempt by one group to secure for itself a privileged position at the expense of some other group through a process of subordination. That is to say, it is a form of collective social action which, intentionally or otherwise, gives rise to a social category of ineligibles or outsiders. Expressed metaphorically, exclusionary closure represents the use of power in a 'downward' direction because it necessarily entails the creation of a group, class, or stratum of legally defined inferiors. Countervailing action by the 'negatively privileged', on the other hand, represents the use of power in an upward direction in the sense that collective attempts by the excluded to win a greater share of resources always threaten to bite into the privileges of legally defined superiors. It is in other words a form of action having usurpation as its goal. *Exclusion* and *usurpation* may therefore be regarded as the two main generic types of social closure, the latter always being a consequence of, and collective response to, the former.[5]

Strategies of exclusion are the predominant mode of closure in all stratified systems. Where the excluded in their turn also succeed in closing off access to remaining rewards and opportunities, so multiplying the number of substrata, the stratification order approaches the furthest point of contrast to the Marxist model of class polarization. The traditional caste system and the stratification of ethnic communities in the United States provide the clearest illustrations of this closure pattern, though similar processes are easily detectable in societies in which class formation is paramount. Strategies of usurpation vary in scale from those designed to bring about marginal redistribution to those aimed at total expropriation. But whatever their intended scale they nearly always contain a

---

3. Weber (eds. Roth and Wittich) 1968: 342.

4. Neuwirth 1969.

5. These arguments were first tentatively sketched out in my 'Strategies of Social Closure in Class Formation' (Parkin 1974). In that publication the two types of closure were referred to as *exclusion* and *solidarism*. This latter term does not, however, satisfactorily describe a mode of collective action standing in direct opposition to exclusion, since solidaristic behaviour can itself be used for blatantly exclusionary ends. That is to say, solidarism does not properly refer to the purposes for which power is employed. The term *usurpation* more adequately captures the notion of collective action designed to improve the lot of a subordinate group at the expense of a dominant group. Solidarism is simply one means among others to this end. . . .

potential challenge to the prevailing system of allocation and to the authorized version of distributive justice.

All this indicates the ease with which the language of closure can be translated into the language of power. Modes of closure can be thought of as different means of mobilizing power for the purpose of engaging in distributive struggle. To conceive of power as a built-in attribute of closure is at the very least to dispense with those fruitless searches for its 'location' inspired by Weber's more familiar but completely unhelpful definition in terms of the ubiquitous struggle between contending wills. Moreover, to speak of power in the light of closure principles is quite consistent with the analysis of class relations. Thus, to anticipate the discussion, the familiar distinction between bourgeoisie and proletariat, in its classic as well as in its modern guise, may be conceived of as an expression of conflict between classes defined not specifically in relation to their place in the productive process but in relation to their prevalent modes of closure, exclusion and usurpation, respectively.

Moreover, stating the matter this way is equally consistent with that tradition that very properly places the concept of exploitation at the heart of class analysis. That is, in so far as exclusionary forms of closure result in the downward use of power, hence creating subordinate social formations, they can be regarded by definition as exploitative. Exploitation here defines the nexus between classes or other collectivities that stand in a relationship of dominance and subordination, on *whatever* social basis. There is no compelling reason why the term should be restricted to its conventional Marxist usage, referring to the appropriation of surplus value on the part of capital, since this is itself but one important case of the more general phenomenon of exclusionary closure. Collective efforts to restrict access to rewards and opportunities on the part of one social group against another, including one group of workers against another, can be regarded as inherently exploitative even though the relationship is not one of surplus extraction deriving from property ownership. Relations of dominance and subordination between bourgeoisie and proletariat, Protestants and Catholics, whites and blacks, men and women, etc., can all be considered as exploitative relationships in the neo-Weberian sense. The Marxist objection to such an expanded usage is that it violates the scientific status of the concept. According to Wolpe, for example,

'While the concept of exploitation can have a rigorous and explicit meaning in defining class relations, it becomes a vague, descriptive term in the characterization of relations between such entities as racial, national or cultural groups.'[6]

The reason for this is supplied by Bettelheim:

'Because the concept of *exploitation* expresses a *production relation*—production of surplus labour and expropriation of this by a social class—it necessarily relates to *class relations*. . . .'[7]

All that this really means, of course, is that Marxists choose to employ the concept in this narrower sense; such a meaning does not inhere in the term itself.

---

6. Wolpe 1975: 240.
7. Cited in Wolpe 1975: 240.

To broaden the meaning of the term to encompass relations of dominance and subjection other than those between capital and labour does not thereby signal a shift from a scientific or technical usage to a moral one; exploitation is a morally weighted concept *whichever* way it is used, and it is well to acknowledge this from the outset. This broader application of the concept has particular implications for the analysis of intra-class relations, shortly to be considered. First, though, it is necessary to flesh out these somewhat sketchy remarks with a more detailed exposition of the closure thesis.

As previously noted, exclusion is the predominant form of closure in all stratified societies. Historically, the rise and consolidation of ruling groups has been effected through monopolistic control over valued resources such as land, esoteric knowledge, or arms by a limited circle of eligibles marked out by certain social characteristics. Aristocratic domination and reproduction via the lineage system is the obvious example from European history of this type of closure. Bourgeois forms of exclusion, by contrast, do not typically rest upon the restrictions of descent of similar group membership criteria for their effectiveness, but more upon what Weber somewhat misleadingly calls the 'rational commitment to values'. Thus among non-hereditary examples of closure Weber mentions the use of '. . . qualifying tests, a period of probation . . . election of new members by ballot . . . or [admission] by virtue of achievements open to anyone'.[8] That is to say, the process of class formation and social reproduction of the bourgeoisie is significantly different from that of preceding classes in that the conditions of membership are, in principle at least, attainable by all. Exclusionary rules and institutions must always be justified by universal criteria that are indifferent to the pretensions or stigmata of birth. There is thus a permanent tension within this class resulting from the need to legitimate itself by preserving openness of access, and the desire to reproduce itself socially by resort to closure on the basis of descent.

In modern capitalist society the two main exclusionary devices by which the bourgeoisie constructs and maintains itself as a class are, first, those surrounding the institutions of property; and, second, academic or professional qualifications and credentials. Each represents a set of legal arrangements for restricting access to rewards and privileges: property ownership is a form of closure designed to prevent general access to the means of production and its fruits; credentialism is a form of closure designed to control and monitor entry to key positions in the division of labour. The two sets of beneficiaries of these state-enforced exclusionary practices may thus be thought of as the core components of the dominant class under modern capitalism. Before taking up the discussion of common class interests fostered by private property and credentials it may be useful to consider each of the two principal closure strategies separately.

It has already been remarked upon how the concept of property has been devalued in the modern sociology of class as a result of the heavy weighting accorded to the division of labour. This has not always been true of bourgeois sociology. Weber was in full accord with Marx in asserting that '"Property" and

---

8. Weber (ed. Parsons) 1964: 141.

"lack of property" are . . . the basic characteristics of all class situations'.[9] The post-Weberian tendency to analyse social relations as if the propertyless condition had painlessly arrived is perhaps a natural extension of the use of 'western' or 'industrial' to denote societies formerly referred to as capitalist. The post-war impact of functionalist theory certainly contributed to this tendency, since the proclamation of belief in the ultimate victory of achievement values and the merit system of reward naturally cast doubt on the importance of property as an institution. The inheritance of wealth after all requires notably little expenditure of those talents and efforts that are said to be the only keys to the gates of fortune.

The extent to which property has come to be regarded as something of an embarrassing theoretical anomaly is hinted at in the fact that it receives only the most cursory acknowledgment in Davis and Moore's functionalist manifesto, and even then in the shape of an assertion that 'strictly legal and functionless ownership . . . is open to attack' as capitalism develops.[10] To propose that the imposition of death duties and estate taxes constitutes evidence for an assault upon property rights is somewhat like suggesting that the introduction of divorce laws is evidence of state support for the dissolution of the family. Property in this scheme of things can only be understood as a case of cultural lag—one of those quaint institutional remnants from an earlier epoch which survives by the grace of social inertia.

Several generations earlier Durkheim had reasoned along similar lines in declaring that property inheritance was 'bound up with archaic concepts and practices that have no part in our present day ethics'.[11] And although he felt it was not bound to disappear on this account he was willing to predict that inherited wealth would 'lose its importance more and more', and if it survived at all it would only be 'in a weakened form'.[12] Durkheim was not of course opposed to private property as such, only its transmission through the family. 'It is obvious that inheritance, by creating inequalities amongst men from birth, that are unrelated to merit or services, invalidates the whole contractual system at its very roots.'[13] Durkheim wanted society made safe for property by removing those legal practices that could not be squared with conceptions of liberal individualism and which therefore threatened to cause as much moral and social disturbance as the 'forced' division of labour.

There was not much likelihood of property itself declining as an institution because it was part of the order of things invested with a sacred character, understood in that special Durkheimian sense of an awesome relationship rooted deeply in the *conscience collective*. Although the sacred character of property arose originally from its communal status, the source of all things holy, the marked evolutionary trend towards the individualization of property would not

9. Weber (eds. Gerth and Mills) 1948: 182.
10. Davis and Moore 1945: 247.
11. Durkheim 1957: 174.
12. Durkheim 1957: 175 and 217.
13. Durkheim 1957: 213.

be accompanied by any decline in its divinity. Personal rights to property were therefore seen by Durkheim as part of that general line of social development by which the individual emerges as a distinct and separate entity from the shadow of the group. The individual affirms himself as such by claiming exclusive rights to things over and above the rights of the collectivity. There is more than an echo here of Hegel's dictum that 'In his property a person exists for the first time as reason'.[14] As Plamenatz comments:

'It makes sense to argue, as Hegel does, that it is partly in the process of coming to own things, and to be recognized as their owners, that human beings learn to behave rationally and responsibly, to lead an ordered life. It is partly in the process of learning to distinguish mine from thine that a child comes to recognise itself as a person, as a bearer of rights and duties, as a member of a community with a place of its own inside it.'[15]

As Plamenatz goes on to say, however plausible as a defence of personal property this may be, as a defence of capitalist property relations it is 'lamentably inadequate'.[16]

The reason for this is that Hegel, like Durkheim, and many contemporary sociologists, never clearly distinguishes between property as rights to personal *possessions* and property as capital. Parsons is only one of many who reduces all forms of property to the status of a possession; this is understood as 'a right or a bundle of rights. In other words it is a set of expectations relative to social behaviour and attitudes.'[17] If property is simply a specific form of possession, or a certain bundle of rights, then everyone in society is a proprietor to some degree. On this reckoning there can be no clear social division between owners and non-owners, only a gradual, descending scale from those with very much to those with very little. This is well in line with Parsons' usual theoretical strategy of asserting the benign quality of any resource by reference to its widespread distribution. The possession of a toothbrush or an oilfield confers similar rights and obligations upon their owners, so that property laws cannot be interpreted as class laws. As Rose and his colleagues have suggested:

'the ideological significance of such a universalistic and disinterested legal interpretation of property in modern capitalist society is two-fold. First, as the law protects and recognises *all* private property, and as virtually all members of the society can claim title to *some* such property, it may be claimed that all members of society have some vested interest in the *status quo*. From such a perspective, therefore, it can be argued that, far from representing an irreconcilable conflict of interests, the distribution of property in modern capitalist society gives rise to a commensurability of interests, any differences being variations of degree rather than kind. The office developer, the shareholder, the factory-owner, the householder and even the second-hand car owner may thus be represented as sharing fundamentally common interests, if not identities.'[18]

What the sociological definition of property as possessions interestingly fails to ask is why only certain limited forms of possession are legally admissible.

---

14. Plamenatz 1975: 120.
15. Plamenatz 1975: 121.
16. Plamenatz 1975: 121.
17. Parsons 1951: 119. The entry in the index under 'Property' invites the reader to 'see Possessions'.
18. Rose et al. 1976: 703.

It is patently not the case, for example, that workers are permitted to claim legal possession of their jobs; nor can tenants claim rights of possession to their homes, nor welfare claimants enforceable rights to benefits. Possession in all these cases is pre-empted by the conflicting claims of employers, landlords, and the state respectively, which are accorded legal priority. Although the law may treat the rights of ownership in true universalistic fashion it is silent on the manner by which only some 'expectations' are successfully converted to the status of property rights and others not.

Even where property is understood in the narrower and politically more significant sense of ownership of the means of production, its importance for class analysis is not thereby affirmed. The reason for this is that the separation of ownership from the control of productive capital is felt to lead to its domestication, as it were, in the modern corporation. It is only when these two functions of ownership and control are fused, as in the case of landed property or the early capitalist enterprise, that property is believed to carry an explosive potential. The transition to the corporate firm apparently defuses capital not only by distributing it more widely but by placing it in the care of a managerial stratum that technically shares the same employee status as all other sellers of labour power. The social embodiments of capital thus merge indistinguishably into the category of labour, so transcending the old distinctions based on pure ownership. So much so that, in Parsons' view, we 'can clearly no longer speak of a "capitalistic" propertied class which has replaced the earlier "feudal" landed class'.[19] Parsons therefore recommends 'divorcing the concept of social class from its historic relation to both kinship and property as such'.[20]

However, it is Dahrendorf rather than Parsons who advances the most explicit and sustained case for making this divorce. By arguing that property is but one historically specific form of a more general phenomenon, authority, Dahrendorf is able to dampen any of those lingering hopes for the attainment of a classless society much in the way that Weber had earlier done, and on roughly similar grounds.[21] However, the effect of reconstituting property as authority is to wrench the analysis of class from its usual societal setting and to place it in a much narrower organizational one. Seen from this angle, a subordinate class exists within the confines of almost any bureaucratic locale, each one institutionally isolated from the rest. The appropriate class image would therefore seem to be 'a sack of potatoes' rather than anything suggestive of a social collectivity.

In Marx's schema, the propertyless are a class in the full sense in so far as the entire weight of the political and legal apparatus bears down upon them in whatever work situation or social setting they are found. In Dahrendorf's schema, the authority-less are a class only in a partial and limited sense in that they shed their subordinate status immediately upon leaving the physical location in which the rules of command and obedience operate. The moment an individual steps outside the 'imperatively co-ordinated association' he is at lib-

---

19. Parsons 1970: 24.
20. Parsons 1970: 24.
21. Dahrendorf 1959.

erty to assume other roles, including those invested with their own authority. Authority relations do not penetrate into the very pores of society in the way that property relations do, because there are a multitude of social spaces that are not and cannot be colonized by formal organizations. Marx's proletariat has no hiding place because the effects of property cannot be confined within restricted social zones any more than the effects of the market can. It is as a result of this that class is universalized. Redefining property as authority relations *particularizes* class by presenting it as a function of organizational forms that are themselves too fragmented and diverse to yield a general condition of subordination.

The question never seriously posed by Dahrendorf is: for what *purpose* is authority exercised and occasionally challenged? The command structure of a business enterprise is geared directly to the pursuit of profit, and those who staff the key posts are in effect the guardians of capital; they are not concerned with the enforcement of obedience as an end in itself. Similarly, any challenge to managerial authority by organized labour is usually for the specific purpose of redistributing the share between capital and labour. It does not arise from a romantic belief in the psychic benefits of insubordination. In other words, the authority exercised in an organization could be said to derive its meaning from the ends to which the organization is dedicated; authority is not something that is properly understood independently of its uses. That Dahrendorf should select the industrial firm as the paradigm case of his model is decidedly odd, because it is the one locus above all others where authority relations are inseparable from property rights. When workers occupy their factory and lock out management, the offence for which they are liable to be arraigned is not disobedience, which is a mere offence against authority, but unlawful trespass, which is an offence against property.

The fact that class conflict between managers and managed is not always containable or resolvable within the walls of the organization throws doubt on the status of authority as the ultimate cause of conflict. When the chips are down and conflict assumes a less benign character from its routinized version, authority is seen not to reside in the 'incumbency of positions' within the organization; it is seen to reside in the state—an external body charged with the duty of protecting the rights of property and appropriation. Managerial command over labour therefore takes place within a legal framework in which the inviolability of property is already guaranteed. Authority and its exercise may, in other words, be thought of more as an activity that is licensed by the state than as something that creates its own legitimacy from the logic of organization.

The background reality of the state is perhaps far more easily overlooked when the issue is posed as the exercise of authority rather than as rights over property. Clearly no-one would imagine otherwise than that the state would be the principal guardian of property, not the proprietors themselves. The images of the policeman, the courthouse, and the prison cell are almost inseparable from the idea of property. But these images tend to recede when authority displaces property as the leading idea because it does so often appear that industrial and other bureaucracies are self-regulating. It is only on those dramatic occasions that organizations themselves cannot handle that the wholly derivative nature of managerial authority is revealed through the intervention of external powers dedicated to the enforcement of property rights.

The case for restoring the notion of property into the centre of class analysis is that it is the most important single form of social closure common to industrial societies. That is to say, rights of ownership can be understood not as a special case of authority so much as a specific form of exclusion. As Durkheim expresses it, 'the right of property is the right of a given individual to exclude other individual and collective entities from the usage of a given thing'.[22] Property is defined negatively by 'the exclusion it involves rather than the prerogatives it confers'.[23] Durkheim's reference to *individual* rights of exclusion clearly indicates that once again he has possessions in mind, and that, characteristically, he sees no important distinction between objects of personal ownership, and the control of resources resulting in the exercise of power.

It is clearly necessary to distinguish property as possessions from property as capital, since only the latter is germane to the analysis of class systems. Property as capital is, to paraphrase Macpherson, that which 'confers the right to deny men access to the means of life and labour'.[24] This exclusionary right can obviously be vested in a variety of institutional forms, including the capitalist firm, a nationalized industry, or a Soviet enterprise. All these are examples of property that confers legal powers upon a limited few to grant or deny general access to the means of production and the distribution of its fruits. Although personal possessions and capital both entail rights of exclusion, it is only the exclusionary rights embedded in the latter that have important consequences for the life-chances and social condition of the excluded. To speak of property in the context of class analysis is then, to speak of capital only, and not possessions.

Once property is conceptualized as a form of exclusionary social closure there is no need to become entangled in semantic debates over whether or not workers in socialist states are 'really' exploited. The relevant question is not whether surplus extraction occurs, but whether the state confers rights upon a limited circle of eligibles to deny access to the 'means of life and labour' to the rest of the community. If such exclusionary powers are legally guaranteed and enforced, an exploitative relationship prevails as a matter of definition. It is not of overriding importance to know whether these exclusionary powers are exercised by the formal owners of property or by their appointed agents, since the social consequences of exclusion are not demonstrably different in the two cases. Carchedi and other neo-Marxists may therefore be quite correct in suggesting that 'the manager is capital personified'; but all that needs to be added is first, that this dictum holds good not only for monopoly capitalism, but for *all*, including socialism, systems in which access to property and its benefices is in the legal gift of a select few; and, second, that it squares far more comfortably with the assumptions of bourgeois, or at least Weberian, sociology than with classical Marxist theory.

---

22. Durkheim 1957: 142.
23. Durkheim 1957: 142.
24. Macpherson 1973.

# References

Dahrendorf, R., *Class and Class Conflict in Industrial Society* (London: Routledge, 1959).

Davis, K., and W. E. Moore, 'Some principles of stratification', *American Sociological Review* 10(2) (1945).

Durkheim, E., *Professional Ethics and Civic Morals* (London: Routledge, 1957).

Parkin, F., ed., *The Social Analysis of Class Structure* (London: Tavistock, 1974).

Parsons, T., *The Social System* (London: Routledge, 1951).

Plamenatz, J., *Karl Marx's Philosophy of Man* (Oxford: Clarendon, 1975).

MacPherson, C. B., 'A Political Theory of Property', in *Democratic Theory: Essays in Retrieval* (Oxford: Oxford University Press, 1973).

Neuwirth, G., 'A Weberian Outline of a Theory of Community: Its Application to the "Dark Ghetto"', *British Journal of Sociology* 20(2) (1969).

Weber, M., *From Max Weber,* ed. H.H. Gerth and C.W. Mills (London: Routledge, 1948).

———, *The Theory of Social and Economic Organization,* ed. T. Parsons (Glencoe: Free Press, 1964).

———, *Economy and Society,* ed. G. Roth and C. Wittich (New York: Bedminster Press, 1968).

Wolpe, H., 'The Theory of Internal Colonialism: The South African Case, in I. Oxaal et al., *Beyond the Sociology of Development* (London: Routledge, 1975).

# Selective Further Reading

Althusser, Louis, *For Marx* (London: New Left Books, 1977).

Althusser, Louis, and Etienne Balibar, *Reading Capital* (London: New Left Books, 1970).

Anderson, Perry, *Lineages of the Absolutist State* (London: New Left Books, 1974).

_____, 'The Antinomies of Antonio Gramsci', *New Left Review* 100 (1977).

Aronowitz, Stanley, *False Promises* (New York: McGraw-Hill, 1973).

Bertaux, Daniel, *Destins Pesonnels et Structure de Classe* (Paris: Presses Universitaires de France, 1977).

Braverman, Harry, *Labor and Monopoly Capitalism* (New York: Monthly Review Press, 1974).

Carchedi, G., 'On the Economic Identification of the New Middle Class', *Economy and Society* 4(1) (1975).

_____, *On the Economic Identification of Social Classes* (London: Routledge & Kegan Paul, 1977).

Castells, Manuel, *The Urban Question* (London: Edward Arnold, 1972).

Crompton, Rosemary, and Jon Gubbay, *Economy and Class Structure* (London: Macmillan, 1977).

Giddens, Anthony, *The Class Structure of the Advanced Societies,* 2nd ed. (London: Hutchinson, 1980).

Goldthorpe, John H., et al., *Social Mobility and Class Structure in Modern Britain* (Oxford: Clarendon Press, 1980).

Lockwood, David, *The Blackcoated Worker* (London: Allen & Unwin, 1958).

Lukács, Georg, *History and Class Consciousness* (Cambridge, Mass.: M.I.T. Press, 1971).

Offe, Claus, 'Political authority and the class structure', *International Journal of Sociology* 2(1) (1972).

Parkin, Frank, *Marxism and Class Theory: A Bourgeois Critique* (London: Tavistock, 1979).

Parsons, Talcott, *Essays in Sociological Theory* (Glencoe, Ill.: Free Press, 1954).

————, *Structure and Process in Modern Societies* (Glencoe, Ill.: Free Press, 1960).

Poulantzas, Nicos, *Political Power and Social Classes* (London: New Left Books, 1973).

————, *Classes in Contemporary Capitalism* (London: New Left Books, 1975).

Przeworski, Adam, 'The Process of Class Formation from Kautsky's *The Class Struggle* to Recent Debates', *Politics and Society* 7(4) (1978).

Wallerstein, Immanuel, *The Modern World-System* (New York: Academic Press, 1974).

Wright, Erik Olin, *Class, Crisis, and the State* (London: New Left Books, 1978).

# · III ·

# Classes, Elites, and the State

# Introduction

## Ownership and Control: The Upper Class

One of the most evident changes that has taken place in the capitalist economies since the nineteenth century is the increased 'concentration' of production. As we have seen, this phenomenon was predicted by Marx, and was in fact regarded by him as preparing the way for the eventual emergence of socialism. Since Marx's time, however, the increasing concentration of industry has been subject to a variety of interpretations, many of which have in fact been aimed at discrediting Marx's ideas. One such interpretation is that often referred to as 'managerialism'. According to this view, the concentration of industry has produced a split between the owners of capital in the large corporations and the managerial executives in those corporations. Since share-ownership in large firms tends to be diversified, the nominal 'owners' of the corporations no longer run them; control has passed into the hands of the top managers. Far from preparing the way for the development of socialism, so the argument runs, the separation of ownership and control has fragmented the capitalist class, dissolving the power of capital through a peaceful process of evolution rather than one of revolution. In this view, the managers have abandoned the search for profit maximisation characteristic of earlier entrepreneurial capitalism.

Marxists writing since Marx's own day have been divided in their assessments of the character and the significance of the separation of ownership and control. Some (and this includes Maurice Zeitlin, whose work is included below) hold that such separation has not proceeded nearly as far as has ordinarily been thought and hence that there remains a generic 'propertied class' who retain effective control of industrial production. Others have accepted that a major split between ownership and control has occurred in the advanced capitalist societies but have downplayed its implications. According to this second standpoint (taken by several of the authors in the preceding section), who formally 'owns' capital is not of great importance anyway. Whether or not capital-owners or 'propertyless' managers control the enterprise is not particularly significant since in each case the mechanisms of capitalist production remain the same.

Zeitlin's article is a useful contribution to these issues because it combines an insightful theoretical discussion with an analysis of a range of recent empirical material relevant to the debate. As he points out, by far the most common view of corporate power is the acceptance that, in the large corporations, ownership has more or less universally become separated from control: power has passed into the hands of the managers. Zeitlin recognizes that evaluation of this conventional wisdom raises both conceptual issues—especially that of what 'control' is taken to mean—and empirical questions. 'Control' is used vaguely in the sociological and economic literature (compare again some of the contributions in Section Two). We should distinguish responsibility for the day-to-day administration of corporations from the capability to influence or determine major issues of policy. It is quite possible—and indeed Zeitlin finds it to be generally the case—that control over basic policy decisions rests in the hands of owners rather than managers.

To study the operations of power in the higher echelons of the large corporations, Zeitlin says, means concretely examining 'constellations of intercorporate relationships'. It is not enough to pursue purely statistical analyses of the diversification of share-holding, as many students of the topic have done. Thus, Zeitlin provides materials concerning particular patterns of stock-holding and their involvement with the behaviour of the corporation in respect of profit maximisation, the connections between specific corporations and others in respect of policy formation concerning matters both internal and external to those corporations, the influence of interlocking directorships and patterns of family relationships, and the relations between industrial and financial organisations. Both the method of his analysis and the tentative conclusions he reaches, run counter to orthodox views of the uncomplicated nature of the separation of ownership and control.

The problems discussed by Zeitlin readily link to those which preoccupy Göran Therborn, who is also concerned to suggest that some conventionally established modes of conceptualising the power of dominant classes have to be placed in question. To decide what a 'ruling class' is in a capitalist society and what constitutes the nature of its 'rule', Therborn avows, we must give detailed attention to the question of how power should be conceptualised. He distinguishes three contrasting general approaches to the study of power. One he calls 'subjectivist'. This approach is above all absorbed with posing and answering the question 'who has power?' in a community or society. Power is seen here as a possession of individuals or networks of individuals. A second approach Therborn labels the 'economic': it is concerned less with who holds power than with how much power is generated in a society. It is about 'power to'—power to realise collective goals of some kind—rather than, as in the first type of approach, the power some individuals have 'over' others. The third standpoint, which Therborn calls 'dialectical-materialist', he says, is based upon the 'new [?] scientific study of history and society founded by Marx'.

This third approach does not wholly disavow the other two but synthesizes aspects of them. When we speak of 'power to', we have to confront the question 'power to *what*'? A Marxist analysis answers the question by connecting power to the class relations in a given society. To say merely that 'rulers rule' is tautological. Similarly, when we talk of 'power over', we have to ask what the consequences of such power are. This means that some of the issues with which studies of dominant classes have often been concerned—including a good deal of the ownership and control debate—are relatively unimportant. Questions about 'who holds power' are displaced by ones that enquire about the structure of the society which is sustained through the distribution and flow of power.

Therborn's analysis here meshes closely with the well-known debate between Ralph Miliband and Nicos Poulantzas over power and the state. In his book *The State in Capitalist Society,* Miliband offers an extensive discussion of the cohesiveness of capitalist classes in Western societies, seeking to analyse how far their members are drawn from similar backgrounds, whether they form cohesive elites, what relations exist between elite groups in various institutional sectors, and so on. Criticising this work, Poulantzas argues that the value of Miliband's book is limited because it confronts its opponents—'pluralist' theorists—on their own ground. Much more important than analysing what in Poulantzas's terms are not 'elites' but 'class fractions' is to analyse the structural components of the capitalist state. A capitalist state remains a capitalist state however divided its ruling class may be. Broadly speaking, Therborn sides with Poulantzas rather than with Miliband, although he acknowledges an indebtedness to both writers.

In studying 'what the ruling class does when it rules', Therborn concludes, the main objective should be to determine the influence of the state upon the continuance of a particular mode of production. The state in Marxist theory, he says, is a concentrated expression of power coordinated in class relationships; rather than typologies of elites, we need typologies of forms of state intervention in civil society, and of 'state structures'.

## The State and Marxist Theory

Therborn's reflections upon ruling classes and the state should be read in conjunction with the article by Claus Offe and Volker Ronge and that by Boris Frankel. Although Therborn claims that his analysis is but a development of a distinctive conception of the state to be found in Marx's writings, it is nowadays commonly admitted by Marxists and non-Marxists alike that Marx's comments on the state, even upon the capitalist state, are quite rudimentary and perhaps internally inconsistent. In recent years, however, a considerable amount of work has been devoted towards developing theories of the state which take their cue from Marx. The main focus of this book is upon class analysis, and therefore we have made no attempt to incorporate a full survey of contemporary

Marxist writings on state theory. However, discussion of the state certainly has to have a basic role in general considerations of class analysis.

Offe's writings have made a substantial impact upon current literature on the state and classes; we include contributions here both from Offe himself, and a more wide-ranging exposition by Frankel which contrasts Offe's ideas with other Marxist approaches to the theory of the state.

Offe's views have been developed in a variety of publications over the past decade and a half. His most general statement is to be found in his book *Structural Problems of the Capitalist State* (1972), which has yet to appear in full in English. The short article included here, however, summarises several of the main ideas developed at greater length in the book. Like Poulantzas and many other contemporary Marxists, Offe and Ronge reject an 'instrumentalist' conception of the state. The capitalist state is not simply the instrument of domination of the capitalist class. Offe's formulation of the nature of the state, however, differs from Poulantzas's version of its 'relative autonomy'. According to Offe, the principal concerns of the state are to do with sustaining an overall institutional order in which capitalistic mechanisms occupy a prime place but where the state mediates between class antagonisms rather than directly 'reproducing capital'.

Offe and Ronge identify four defining features of the capitalist state. First, privately owned capital, organised within the capital wage-labour relation, is the chief foundation of economic enterprise; economic ownership confers no direct political power. Second, the capital generated through private accumulation is the material basis upon which the finances of the state depend, these finances being derived from various modes of taxation upon wealth and income. Third, the state is therefore dependent upon a source of income which it does not itself directly organise, save in nationalised industries. The state thus has a general 'interest' in facilitating processes of capital accumulation. This interest does not derive from any alliance of the state with capital as such but from the generic concern of the state with sustaining the conditions of its own perpetuation. Fourth, in liberal democratic states of the 'Western' type, political power yielding access to state mechanisms has to be won by gaining mass electoral support. This political system, Offe and Ronge argue, helps mask the fact that state revenues are derived from privately accumulated wealth and not from the support of the electorate.

The consequence of these characteristics of the capitalist state is that it is in a structurally contradictory position; the state depends upon gaining some command over resources which are not regarded as 'political' and thus as falling within the scope of its organisational or administrative power. Apart from standard revenue raising mechanisms such as taxation, there is one major tactic the state officialdom can adopt in the face of this contradiction. This is that of 'extending the commodity form', which means trying to ensure that as many sectors of social life as possible can be organised through market transactions. An example which Offe has studied in some detail is education. Insofar, for instance, as the costs of higher education can be financed by a loan system to students organised by banks, the state is able to off-load financial commitments which it might otherwise have to shoulder directly. However, since the state is caught up in a contradictory role, such attempts constantly rebound: large areas of social life become 'decommodified' and have to be run by the state. This may occur simply because private enterprise is unable to operate them profitably— as, by way of illustration, the systems of rail transport and utilities in most countries—or for more complex reasons. All the various reasons for decommodification, however, relate back to one fundamental characteristic of capitalism, originally formulated by Marx, which Offe's characterisation of the activities of the state is meant to illuminate. This is that capitalism is a system founded upon private accumulation of capital, which however increasingly depends upon the provision of socialised services. The state finds itself chronically trapped within the contradictory pressures thus generated.

The capitalist state is basically a 'reactive mechanism', Offe argues. It does not possess the political legitimation (which a socialist state presumably would?) necessary to be able to approach the degree of fully developed socialisation that would enable it to cope with its increasingly complex involvements in various areas of social life. Offe's analysis is based upon the supposition that the root of the contradiction between private appropriation and socialised production (and consumption), the class conflict between capital and wage labour, has been more or less successfully controlled in capitalist societies by procedures of institutionalised wage bargaining and arbitration. But the conflicts thus suppressed spill out into other areas, into which the state is constantly drawn. 'Fiscal crises', a key expression of the state's inability to meet the financial burden of its commitments, are a particularly acute focus for such conflicts. Moreover, financial crises may arise at both national and local levels (the near-bankruptcy of New York is perhaps the most famous case in recent times).

Offe's standpoint, which has been developed in close association with Jürgen Habermas, is discussed at some length by Frankel, who claims that in certain respects it is superior to more orthodox Marxist interpretations of the state. Writers like Poulantzas and E. Mandel, Frankel says, however valuable their contributions may be in some ways, regard capitalist states only from a 'negative' perspective. That is to say, the state is treated only from the point of view of how far it stabilises capitalist economic enterprise or prevents the development of potentially revolutionary influences. Poulantzas, as has been indicated in a previous part of this book, even *defines* the capitalist state in such terms. Writers such as Offe, James O'Connor, and Habermas, by contrast, recognise that the role of the state is not—and cannot be—limited to 'reproducing' existing capitalist economic relations.

The activities of capitalist states can only be properly grasped, according to Frankel, if we resist the tendency to include too much under the notion of 'the state'. Recent Marxist literature, influenced by Althusser, and including Poulantzas, has included so much under the umbrella of the state that there is little left outside. The institutions or organisations which are included in the rubric of what Althusser calls the 'ideological state apparatuses' include the family, schools and colleges, churches, the media, and even unions and political parties. More or less everything, in other words, that is not an immediate part of material production, is lumped together as part of the state apparatus—and also, in a certain sense, as part of the 'superstructure'. This is probably closely associated with the functionalist stance of such authors as diagnosed by Connell: the state includes everything that 'functions' to keep the capitalist system going.

In Frankel's view, while we can hardly fail to recognise the increasing penetration of the state into numerous aspects of social life, we must retain a clear distinction between the state and civil society. If we do not, we cannot elucidate the connections or the interplay between them. The importance of the works of Offe and the others mentioned above is twofold: they adopt a more restricted definition of 'the state', and they recognise that the state is embroiled in the contradictions of capitalism, not merely a functional mechanism for its defence. Most orthodox Marxist writers recognise that besides the growth of the large corporations, an expansion of the activities of the state is basic to what is often called 'monopoly capitalism'. But they tend to assume that there has simply been an intensification of commodity production, rather than recognising concomitant processes of 'decommodification'.

Following this argument through, says Frankel, enables us to return with new insight to the debate between Miliband and Poulantzas (and hence to the discussion by Therborn referred to earlier). Rather than concentrating either upon 'elites' or upon 'class fractions', it is more important to analyse the institutional divisions which tend to underline them. A useful overall classification is between the state, monopoly and competitive sector implicated in industrial production. Sectors can easily cross-cut 'fractions'. Thus, for instance, a large corporation in the monopolistic sector can be simultaneously involved in a diverse range of capitalistic activities. According to Frankel, the monopoly sector is distinguished by strongly organised product markets, is capital intensive, merges national and international operations, and maintains relatively high wage levels. Both the competitive and state sectors are labour intensive, characterised by a low degree of technological sophistication; the competitive sector has relatively low levels of wages.

Each of the three principal sectors are themselves subdivided. Thus, while it is conventional to speak of 'the' state, we have to remember that states are composed of varying types of central, federal, and local forms of organisation. All contemporary states, national and local, directly employ large numbers of workers. Although the incomes of such workers are not directly dependent upon capital accumulation outside the state sector, they are related in an indirect way, as Offe's analysis suggests. For if capital accumulation in the private sector is not sustained, the state is unable to cope with its fiscal commitments.

The role of state as employer, Frankel emphasises, greatly influences the characteristics of class struggles in advanced capitalist societies. The monopoly sector has in most countries been able to 'make its peace' with the working class by means of allocating high wages in return for the support of organised union labour. This is the key sector in which capital/wage-labour conflict has become 'accommodated' to the system. 'Traditional' types of class conflict even in the competitive sector become substantially altered because of their relation to the state and monopoly sectors. Thus, the competitive sector may include 'underclasses'—members of minority ethnic groups—who are discriminated against by indigenous workers. Within the state sector, Frankel proposes, attention has to be given to the 'rationality' of state activities; Weber by no means had the last word to say on this matter. The rationalisation of the state, as it becomes more and more involved both directly in production and in providing a range of other services, is not part of an overall process of rationalisation of economic life and of culture. On the contrary, these processes exist in contradictory relation to one another, producing various continuing dislocations and tensions. Here Frankel's argument in some part complements Giddens's critique of Weber's association of capitalist development with unilateral processes of rationalisation and bureaucratisation.

# · 10 ·

# Corporate Ownership and Control: The Large Corporation and the Capitalist Class

## Maurice Zeitlin

The originating question of this article[1] is, how has the ascendance of the large corporation as the decisive unit of production affected the class structures and political economies of the United States, Great Britain, and other "highly concentrated capitalist" countries?[2] In particular, our concern is with the alleged "separation of ownership and control" of the large corporation and the presumed impact of this separation on the internal structures, if not actual social existence, of the "dominant" or "upper" classes in these countries. This article does not provide any answers to this difficult issue; rather it questions the evidence for the accepted ones, which underlie what Ralf Dahrendorf (1959), a leading proponent of the prevailing view, has called the "astonishing degree of consensus among sociologists on the implications of joint-stock companies . . . for the wider structure of society" (p. 42). This consensus extends, it should be emphasized, to other social science disciplines. E. S. Mason, though himself dissatisfied with economic theories derived from the prevalent view, wrote

• Abridged from *American Journal of Sociology* 79(5) (1974): 1073–80, 1089–1108.

1. I have benefited from the critical comments on an earlier draft of this article by many colleagues of diverse and often opposing theoretical persuasions, all of whom are absolved of any responsibilities for what follows. Thanks are due Michael Aiken, Robert Alford, Daniel Bell, G. W. Domhoff, Lynda Ewen, Robert Larner, Ferdinand Lundberg, Harry Magdoff, Robert K. Merton, Barrington Moore, Jr., Harvey Molotch, Willard F. Mueller, James O'Connor, Victor Perlo, and Paul M. Sweezy. The comments of the anonymous referees for the *AJS* were also useful. I am particularly grateful to the editors of the *Journal,* especially to Florence Levinsohn, for their careful reading and cogent criticisms.

2. Bain (1966, p. 102) refers here to the United States, England, Japan, Sweden, France, Italy, and Canada, which were included in his study.

recently (1967): "Almost everyone now agrees that in the large corporation, the owner is, in general, a passive recipient; that, typically, control is in the hands of management; and that management normally selects its own replacements" (p. 4). Peter Drucker (1971), himself an early managerial theorist, writes that ideas concerning the separation of ownership and control represent "the most conventional and most widely accepted theses regarding American economic structure" as expressed in "the prevailing and generally accepted doctrine of 'managerialism'" (pp. 50–51). . . .

The prevailing view is that the diffusion of ownership in the large corporation among numerous stock owners has resulted in the separation of ownership and control, and, by severing the connection between the family and private property in the means of production, has torn up the roots of the old class structure and political economy of capitalism. A new class of functionaries of capital, or a congeries of economic "elites," in control of the new forms of productive property, appear: nonowning corporate managers displace their capitalist predecessors. "The capitalist class," as Pitirim Sorokin (1953) put it, is "transformed into the managerial class" (p. 90). In Talcott Parsons's view (1953), "The *basic phenomenon* seems to have been the shift in control of enterprise from the property interests of founding families to managerial and technical personnel who as such have not had a comparable vested interest in ownership" (pp. 122–23; italics added).

In the view of these writers, a class theory of contemporary industrial society, based on the relationship between the owners of capital and formally free wage workers, "loses its analytical value as soon as legal ownership and factual control are separated" (Dahrendorf 1959, p. 136). This class theory is, therefore, inapplicable to the United States, England, and other countries in which ownership and control have been severed: it cannot explain, nor serve as a fruitful source of hypotheses concerning the division of the social product, class conflict, social domination, political processes, or historic change in these countries. Thus, Parsons and Smelser (1957) refer to the separation of ownership and control as "one particular change in the American economic structure which has been virtually completed within the last half century"—a "structural change in business organization [that] has been associated with changes in the stratification of the society." The families that once "controlled through ownership most of the big businesses . . . by and large failed to consolidate their positions as *the dominant class* in the society" (p. 254; italics added).

This "shift in *control* of enterprise from the property interests of founding families to managerial and technical personnel," according to Parsons (1953), is the "critical fact" underlying his interpretation that "the 'family elite' elements of the class structure (the Warnerian 'upper uppers') hold a secondary rather than a primary position in the overall stratification system" (p. 123). The shift in control, "high progressive taxation," and other "changes in the structure of the economy, have 'lopped off' the previous top stratum," leaving instead "a broad and diffuse one with several loosely integrated components. *Undoubtedly* its main focus is now on occupational status and occupational earnings. Seen in historical as well as comparative perspective this is a notable *fact,* for the entrepreneurial fortunes of the period of economic development of the nineteenth century, especially after the Civil War, notably failed to produce *a set of ruling families on a national scale* who as family entities on a Japanese or even a French pattern have tended to keep control of the basic corporate entities in the economy" (p. 123; italics added). Thus, in Parsons's view, a "'ruling class' does not have a paramount position in American society" (p. 119).

Similarly, Daniel Bell (1958) has argued that a "silent revolution" has subverted the former "relations between power and class position in modern society." In his view, "The *singular fact* is that in the last seventy-five years the established relations between the systems of property and family . . . have broken down," resulting in "the breakup of 'family capitalism,' which has been the social cement of the bourgeois class system" (italics added). If, in general, "property, sanctioned by law and reinforced by the coercive power of the State" means power, and if a class system is maintained by the "fusion" of the institutions of the family and private property, economic development in the United States has "effected a radical separation of property and family." Therefore, in his view, if "family capitalism meant social and political, as well as economic, dominance," that is no longer the situation in the United States. "The chief consequence, politically, is the breakup of the 'ruling class'"—"a power-holding group which has both an established *community* of interest and a *continuity* of interest" no longer exists in the United States (pp. 246–49).

The profound implications of the acceptance of the separation of ownership and control as a social fact are, according to Parsons, that the former relations between classes have been replaced by an occupational system based on individual achievement, in which "status groups" are ordered hierarchically in accordance with their functional importance. Further, as Dahrendorf has put it (1959), the basic social conflict is no longer between capital and labor because "in post-capitalist society the ruling and the subjected classes of industry and of the political society are no longer identical; . . . there are, in other words, in principle [*sic*], two independent conflict fronts. . . . This holds increasingly as within industry the separation of ownership and control increases and as the more universal capitalists are replaced by managers" (pp. 275–76). The political economy of capitalism and the class interests which it once served have been replaced by a sort of capitalism without capitalists (Berle 1954)—if not post-capitalist society—shorn of the contradictions and class conflicts that once rent the social fabric of "classical capitalism." The basis of social domination in such societies, as these theorists would have it, is no longer class ownership of the means of production, and such a class clearly does not "rule" in any sense, economically, socially, or politically. "The decisive power in modern industrial society," in Galbraith's (1971) representative formulation, "is exercised not by capital but by organization, not by the capitalist but by the industrial bureaucrat" (p. xix).

Assuredly, the answer to this "theory"—particularly the propositions concerning the separation of ownership and control—rests on empirical grounds (Bell 1958, p. 246). However, logic, concepts, and methodology are certainly intertwined and inseparable aspects of the same intellectual process of discovering the "facts."

One common source of conceptual and analytic confusion in the writings on the issue of ownership and control derives from a teleology of bureaucratic imperatives. Bureaucratization is implicitly assumed to be an inexorable historic process, so that even the propertied classes and their power have fallen before its advance. Parsons and Smelser (1957) have written, for example, that the "kinship-property combination typical of classical capitalism was *destined,* unless social differentiation stopped altogether, to proceed toward 'bureaucratization,' towards differentiation between economy and polity, and between ownership and control" (p. 289; italics added).

The tendency toward the bureaucratization of enterprise, and of management in particular, is taken as an index of the appropriation of the powers of the propertied class by the managers. This confuses the (*a*) existence of an extensive administrative apparatus in the large corporation, in which the proportion of management positions held by members of the proprietary family may be negligible; and (*b*) the locus of control over this apparatus. Dahrendorf (1959) for instance, noting that the managers of large enterprises generally have neither inherited nor founded them, concludes from this that these new managers, "utterly different than their capitalist predecessors," have taken control for themselves. In place of the "classical" or "full capitalist," there stands the bureaucratic manager and "organization man" (pp. 42, 46). From the observation that in the large corporation, functions that (allegedly) were fulfilled in the past by a single owner-manager are now institutionalized and split up among differing roles in the bureaucratic administrative organizations, it is concluded that bureaucratic management (if such it is) means bureaucratic control. However, there is nothing in bureaucratic management itself that indicates the bureaucracy's relationship to extrabureaucratic centers of control at the apex or outside of the bureaucracy proper, such as large shareowners or bankers, to whom it may be responsible.

Max Weber (1965) clearly conceptualized this relationship, referring to the "appropriation of control over the persons exercising managerial authority by the interests of ownership." If "the immediate appropriation of managerial functions" is no longer in the hands of the owners, this does not mean the separation of *control* from ownership, but rather "the separation of the managerial *function*" from ownership. "By virtue of their ownership," Weber saw, "control over managerial positions may rest in the hands of property interests *outside the organization as such*" (pp. 248–49; italics added).

It is precisely this relationship between propertied interests and the bureaucracy, and between "capitalists" and "managers," which has received at best inadequate and usually no attention among those who report that they have seen a "corporate revolution" silently abolish private ownership in the means of production. Thus, Daniel Bell (1961) can write that "private productive property, especially in the United States, is largely a fiction" (p. 44), and Dahrendorf (1959) can claim: "Capital—and thereby *capitalism*—has *dissolved* and given way in the economic sphere, to a plurality of partly agreed, partly competing, and partly simply different groups" (p. 47; italics added).

Two issues, then, have to be separated: (1) whether the large corporations continue to be controlled by ownership interests, despite their management by functionaries who may themselves be propertyless; (2) whether the undisputed rise of managerial functions means the rise of the functionaries themselves. Do they constitute a separate and cohesive stratum, with identifiable interests, ideas, and policies, which are opposed to those of the extant owning families? Are the consequences of their actions, whatever their intentions, to bring into being social relationships which undermine capitalism? How, with their "rise," is "the incidence of economic power" changed? (Bendix 1952, p. 119).

These are not merely analytically distinguishable issues. A number of social scientists, "plain marxists" preeminent among them,[3] concede the reality of the split between ownership and control in most large corporations. However, they reject the implication that this renders inapplicable to the United States and other developed capitalist countries a theory which roots classes in the concrete economic order and historically given system of property relations, and which focuses, in particular, on the relationship between the direct producers and the owners of the means of production. In their view, whatever the situation within the corporation as the predominant legal unit of ownership of large-scale productive property, the "owners" and "managers" of the large corporations, taken as a whole, constitute different strata or segments—when they are not merely agents—of the same more or less unified social class. They reject the notion, as Reinhard Bendix has observed (1952), "that people in the productive system constitute a separate social group because they serve similar functions and that they are powerful because they are indispensable" (p. 119). Rather, the corporations are units in a class-controlled apparatus of appropriation; and the whole gamut of functionaries and owners of capital participate in varying degrees, and as members of the same social class, in its direction (cf. Baran and Sweezy 1966, chap. 2; Miliband 1969, chap. 2; W. A. T. Nichols 1969, pp. 140–41; Playford 1972, pp. 116–18). This class theory, as we discuss below in detail, demands research concerning the ensemble of social relations, concrete interests, and overriding commitments of the officers, directors, and principal shareowners of the large corporations in general. Rather than limiting analysis to the relationship between the "management" and principal shareowners of a given corporation, the analysis must focus on the multiplicity of their interconnections with other "managements" and principal shareowners in other large corporations, as well as the owners of other forms of large-scale income-bearing property.[4] Were research to show that the putative separation of ownership and control within the large corporation is a "pseudofact" and that identifiable families and other cohesive ownership interests continue to control them, this might surprise certain "plain marxists," but it would, of course, be quite consistent with their

---

3. "Plain marxists" (uncapitalized) was C. Wright Mills's (1962) phrase to characterize thinkers to whom Marx's "general model and . . . ways of thinking are central to their own intellectual history and remain relevant to their attempts to grasp present-day social worlds" (p. 98). He listed such varied thinkers as Joan Robinson, Jean Paul Sartre, and Paul M. Sweezy, as well as himself, as plain marxists.

4. Domhoff (1967, pp. 47–62) and Kolko (1962, pp. 60–69), who may also be considered "plain marxists," reject as incorrect both the separation of ownership and control within the large corporation and argue that "managers" belong to the same social class as the "owners." Their books contain brief empirical studies of the ownership of stock (Kolko) and "upper-class membership" (Domhoff) of large corporate directors. This is also the view of Ferdinand Lundberg (1946, 1968), who, in particular, lays stress on the need to study the kinship relationships among the owners and executives—a point we discuss in some detail below.

general class theory.[5] Most important, were "managers" and "owners" to be found to occupy a common "class situation" (Weber 1968, p. 927), the theory that ownership and control of the large corporations reside in the same social class would be confirmed. In contrast, either set of findings would tend to invalidate the essential assumptions, propositions, and inferences of managerial theory. In any event, each alleged implication requires careful analysis and empirical testing on its own. . . .

[H]ow "control" is conceptualized is a critical question—apart from the problem of obtaining reliable and valid information. Following Berle and Means, "control" has generally been defined to refer to the "actual power to select the board of directors (or its majority)," although control may also "be exercised *not* through the *selection* of directors, but through *dictation* to the management, as where a bank determines the policy of a corporation seriously indebted to it" (Berle and Means 1967, p. 66; italics added). Thus control refers to the "*power* of determining the broad policies guiding a corporation and not to . . . the actual influence on the day to day affairs of an enterprise" (Goldsmith and Parmelee 1940, pp. 99–100; italics added). Control is not business management, or what Gordon (1966) has termed "business leadership" (p. 150). This would seem to be clear conceptually. However, in practice Berle and Means and their followers have simply assumed away the analytical issues by their operational definitions. They have merely assumed, rather than demonstrated, that once a cohesive ownership interest having at least a minimum specified proportion of the stock (whether 20% as in the original Berle and Means work or the current 10% criterion) disappears, the corporation slips imperceptibly and inevitably under "management control." At this point, presumably, the top officers, given the wide dispersion of stock among small shareowners and the officers' control of the proxy machinery, become capable of nominating and electing a compliant and subservient board of directors, of perpetuating themselves in office, and of abrogating, thereby, the control of proprietary interests (Gordon 1966, pp. 121–22; Larner 1970, p. 3; *Business Week,* May 22, 1971, p. 54). "In the

---

5. Though it might not accord with their "economic" theory. As we discuss briefly below, Baran and Sweezy (1966, chap. 2) discard the concept of "interest groups" or "communities of interest" binding together a number of corporations into a common system. They argue "that an appropriate model of the economy no longer needs to take account of them" (p. 18). Further, they also assert, without evidence, that they "abstract from whatever elements of outside control may still exist in the world of giant corporations because they are in *no sense essential* to the way it works" (p. 20; italics added). Unfortunately the issue is one which would require a new article, if not full-length monograph, to grapple with, and extended discussion here is impossible. However, I have not yet seen an explanation of why Baran and Sweezy have concluded that the question of "outside" or familial control is irrelevant to understanding the American political economy, nor why they should be so insistent on this point. They have not explained how the continuation of communities of interest and familial control groups would alter the ability of the system to face the problem of what they term "the tendency of surplus to rise," which is the central issue of their essay and cornerstone of their neo-marxian theory of "monopoly capitalism." If, as they argue, (*a*) the large corporations tend, in their interaction, to produce a "surplus" of investment funds in excess of private investment outlets; and (*b*) this disparity between a rising surplus and available investment outlets is a chronic threat of crisis in our political economy, how would this tendency be affected by the existence of controlling ownership interests in the "giant corporations"? How would this tendency be affected by "interest groups" able to coordinate the prices, production, sales, and investment policies of ostensibly independent corporations? Would not such groups, rather than the individual corporation, constitute the "basic unit of capital"? . . .

mature corporation," as Galbraith (1968) sums it up, "the stockholders are without power; the Board of Directors is normally the passive instrument of the management" (pp. 59, 90–95).

However, as I have emphasized repeatedly, it is necessary to study the concrete situation within the corporation and the constellation of intercorporate relationships in which it is involved before one can begin to understand where control is actually located. The Berle and Means method of investigation, the definitions and procedures utilized, do not, in fact, even begin to accord with the actual content of their own concept. For this reason, it seems advisable to conceptualize control in such a way as to link it inextricably with a method that is not reducible to a single criterion, such as a minimum percentage of stock held by a single minority bloc, but which requires instead a variety of interrelated yet independent indicators. The modalities of corporate control utilized by specific individuals and/or families and/or groups of associates differ considerably, vary in complexity, and are not easily categorized. Our concept of control must, therefore, compel attention to essential relationships. No less than the generic sociological concept of power, the concept of control, as Berle and Means (1967) themselves put it, is elusive, "for power can rarely be sharply segregated or clearly defined" (p. 66). The relationship between the actual locus of control, formal authority (bureaucratic executive posts), and legal rights (shareownership) is problematic. If control refers to the capacity to determine the broad policies of a corporation, then it refers to a social relationship, not an attribute. Control (or power) is essentially relative and relational: how much power, with respect to whom? (cf. Wrong 1968, p. 679; Etzioni 1968, pp. 314–15). Therefore, control is conceptualized here as follows: when the concrete structure of ownership and of intercorporate relationships makes it probable that an identifiable group of proprietary interests will be able to realize their corporate objectives over time, despite resistance, then we may say that they have "control" of the corporation (cf. Weber 1968, p. 926). To estimate the probability that a given individual or group controls a corporation, then, we must know who the rivals or potential rivals for control are and what assets they can bring to the struggle.

This has two obvious implications concerning the study of corporate control: it means that a specific minority percentage of ownership in itself can tell us little about the potential for control that it represents. We can discover this only by a case study of the pattern of ownership within the given corporation. However, it also means that confining our attention to the single corporation may, in fact, limit our ability to see the pattern of power relationships of which this corporation is merely one element; and it may restrict our understanding of the potential for control represented by a specific bloc of shares in a particular corporation. An individual or group's capacity for control increases correspondingly, depending upon how many other large corporations (including banks and other financial institutions) in which it has a dominant, if not controlling, position. The very same quantitative proportion of stock may have a qualitatively different significance, depending on the system of intercorporate relationships in which the corporation is implicated.

Of course, our reference here is to "structural" analysis rather than "behavioral" analysis of actual "struggles for control." Even such struggles, however, can rarely provide real insight concerning the question of control without the type of analysis emphasized here. Otherwise, one cannot know who the contending powers actually are—what may look like a "proxy fight" between "management" and certain shareowners, may, in fact, be a struggle between contending proprietary interests. The latter type of research, therefore, also requires the former, if it is to provide valid and reliable findings.

There remains the question as to what "broad corporate policies or objectives" are—over which control is to be exercised. I have found no usable definition in my studies of the writings on this question. Nor am I convinced it is amenable to definition apart from a specific theoretical framework in which it is conceptualized. We must have a theory of the objective necessities of corporate conduct and the imperatives of the political economy—and to attempt to outline such a theory here would take us rather far afield from the focus of this article. However, such questions as the following would be essential: what relationships must the corporations in an oligopolistic economy establish with each other? with the state? with foreign governments? with the workers? with sources of raw materials and markets? What common problems, which their very interaction creates, must they resolve? Then we may ask whether the individuals who actually decide among proposed long-range strategies and determine the "broad policies and objectives" of the corporations are merely members of "management."

We know, for instance, that the largest corporations in the United States are now typically "multinational" or "transnational" in the sense that the "sheer size of their foreign commitment," as *Fortune* puts it (Rose 1968, p. 101), and the "extent of their involvements is such that, to some degree, these companies now regard the world rather than the nation state as their natural and logical operating area." Is it the "managements" of these corporations that determine their broad policies? Or do the individuals, families, and other principal proprietary interests with the greatest material stake in these corporations impose their conceptions of the issues and demand that their objectives are pursued in order to maintain the "world . . . as their natural and logical operating area"? Here, clearly, we verge, once again, on the class questions raised at the outset of this article. To take a more limited issue, however: many of the multinational corporations face increasing risk of nationalization of their foreign properties. "Management" may plan for such contingencies, exercise their "discretion," and decide on the tactics to be adopted. When their planning goes awry or proves ineffective, however, must the management answer to their corporation's principal shareowners and other proprietary interests (such as banks) or not? Having left management in charge of the everyday operations of the corporations abroad, with little or no interference, do the principal proprietary interests have the power to interfere when deemed necessary? Without an analysis of concrete situations and the specific control structure of the corporations involved, we cannot answer such questions—though occasionally particular events momentarily illuminate the actual relationships involved (though they may still remain largely in the shadows). Thus, for example, the Chilean properties of Kennecott Copper Corporation and Anaconda Company were recently (1971) nationalized in Chile. These two corporations, which owned the major copper mines of

Chile, had adopted different long-range strategies to deal with the rising probability of nationalization. We cannot explore the details here, but suffice it to say that Kennecott's strategy was reportedly aimed at insuring, as Robert Haldeman, executive vice-president óf Kennecott's Chilean operations explained, "that nobody expropriates Kennecott without upsetting customers, creditors, and governments on three continents" (Moran 1973, pp. 279–80). Kennecott was able to "expand very profitably in the late 1960's with no new risk to itself and to leave, after the nationalization in 1971, with compensation greater than the net worth of its holdings had been in 1964. In contrast, Anaconda, which had not spread its risk or protected itself through a strategy of building transnational alliances, lost its old holdings, lost the new capital it committed during the Frei regime [preceding Allende's socialist administration], and was nationalized in 1971 without any hope of compensation" (Moran 1973, pp. 280–81).[6]

. Now, according to Berle and Means (1967, p. 104) and Larner (1970), pp. 74–79), both Kennecott and Anaconda have long been under "management control." In Kennecott's case, there is relatively persuasive evidence that it is, in fact, probably controlled by the Guggenheim family and associated interests rather than by "management."[7] Whether this is so or not, Kennecott's "success-

---

6. The destruction of the constitutional government and parliamentary democracy of Chile, and the death of her Marxist president, Dr. Salvador Allende, at the hands of the armed forces on September 11, 1973, has once again given Anaconda (and other foreign corporations) "hope of compensation." The military regime's foreign minister, Adm. Ismael Huerta, announced within a week of the coup, that the "'door was open' for resumption of negotiations on compensation for United States copper holdings nationalized by President Allende" (New York Times, September 30, 1973, p. 14).

7. Kennecott illustrates well our insistence on the importance of knowledge of a corporation's critical historic phases in disclosing the actual locus of control. The Guggenheim interests bought control of the El Teniente copper mine from the Braden Copper Company in 1908; in 1915 they sold it to the Kennecott Copper Corporation, in which Guggenheim Brothers was the controlling stockholder. In 1923, Utah Copper, in which the Guggenheims had a minority interest, also purchased a large bloc of Kennecott's shares (Hoyt 1967, p. 263). Yet for Berle and Means (1967) only six years later (their data were for 1929) Kennecott was "presumably under management control" (p. 104). When World War II began, as a historian close to the Guggenheim family has written, "the Guggenheims created a new Kennecott Copper Corporation, which would have three million shares. This corporation bought up the Guggenheim copper holdings," including 25% of Utah Copper Company's stock, and controlling interests in Copper River Railroad and other "Alaska syndicate holdings" (Hoyt 1967, p. 263). The Guggenheim Brothers also had (until purchased recently by the Allende government) the controlling interest in Chile's Anglo-Lautaro Nitrate Company, organized in 1931 out of previous nitrate holdings controlled by the Guggenheims (Lomask 1964, p. 281) and reorganized in 1951 by Harry Guggenheim (a senior partner of Guggenheim Brothers), to bring in two other smaller Guggenheim-controlled firms. Guggenheim presided as board chairman and chief executive officer of Anglo-Lautaro until his retirement in 1962. Previously, he had been "absent from the family business for a quarter of a century," until in 1949 his uncle enjoined him to reorganize Guggenheim Brothers (Lomask 1964, p. 65). In 1959 the Guggenheim Exploration Company, one of whose partners was a director of Kennecott Copper Corporation in which "the Guggenheim foundations" now also held large holdings, was also revived (Lomask 1964, p. 281). The son of one of the original Guggenheim brothers (Edmond A., son of Murry) "maintained an active interest in Kennecott Corporation" as a director (Lomask 1964, p. 295), while Peter Lawson-Johnston, a grandson of Solomon Guggenheim, was, as of 1966, a partner in Guggenheim Brothers, a director of the advisory board of Anglo-Lautaro, a director of Kennecott, a director of Minerec Corporation, the vice-president of Elgerbar Corporation, and the trustee of three Guggenheim foundations (Hoyt 1967, p. 348). In the period from roughly 1955 to 1965, Burch (1972, p. 48) found Kennecott had "significant family representation as outside members of the board of directors," and concluded it was under "possibly" Guggenheim family control. This is certainly a cautious understatement, given the historic evidence presented here, drawn from works by two writers close to the Guggenheim family.

ful tactics" in Chile did not test the reality of its alleged control by management. However, Anaconda's "management" was submitted to a rather clear test of the extent to which it had control. Within two months after the Chilean government "intervened" in Anaconda's properties and a month after it took over Anaconda Sales Corporation's control of copper sales, it was announced in the *New York Times* (May 14, 1971, p. 55) that Mr. John B. Place, a director of Anaconda, and a vice-chairman of the Chase Manhattan Bank (one of its four top officers, along with David Rockefeller, chairman, and the president and another vice-chairman) was to become the new chief executive officer of the Anaconda Company. (Other Anaconda directors who were bankers included James D. Farley, an executive vice-president of First National City Bank, and Robert V. Roosa, a partner in Brown Brothers, Harriman and Company.) As the *New York Times* reporter (Walker 1971) explained, Mr. Place had no mining expertise ("it is assumed he would not know a head frame from a drag line"), and though he had been an Anaconda director since 1969, he "lives in the East and has never attended the annual [stockholders] meeting held regularly in Butte, Montana," where Anaconda's most important American copper mines are located. In the wake of this Chase Manhattan officer's installation as Anaconda's chief executive officer, "at least 50% of the corporate staff," including John G. Hall, Anaconda's former president, "were fired. Chairman [C. Jay] Parkinson took early retirement" (*Business Week,* February 19, 1972, p. 55). The decimation of Anaconda's allegedly controlling management illustrates the general proposition that those who really have control can decide when, where, and with respect to what issues and corporate policies they will intervene to exercise their power.

## Profit Maximization?

Fortunately, some issues to which the question of control is relevant are somewhat more amenable to systematic, even quantitative, analysis than the ones just posed. Chief among these, which has occupied considerable theoretical, but little empirical, attention, is the proposition concerning "managerial discretion" (see and cf. Baumol 1959; Kaysen 1957, 1965; Marris 1963, 1964; Gordon 1966; Galbraith 1968; Simon 1957; Williamson 1963, 1970). It posits different motives and conduct for managers than owners, and, thereby, differences in the profit orientations of owner-controlled versus management-controlled corporations. "The development of the large corporation," as Gordon puts it (1966), "has obviously affected the goals of business decision-making. . . . It clearly leads to greater emphasis on the non-profit goals of interest groups other than the stockholders," such as the management. The executives "do not receive the profits which may result from taking a chance, while their position in the firm may be jeopardized in the event of serious loss" (pp. xii, 324). Dahrendorf has stated the proposition succinctly. In his view (1959), the separation of ownership and control "produces two sets of roles the incumbents of which *increasingly move apart* in their outlooks on and attitudes toward society in general and toward the enterprise in particular . . . Never has the imputation of a profit motive been further from the real motives of men than it is for modern bureaucratic managers. Economically, managers are interested in such things as rentability, efficiency and productivity" (p. 46; italics added). This is an oft-asserted but rarely investigated proposition, on which Larner has recently provided systematic negative evidence. Drawing on his study of the separation of ownership and control, he found the following: using multiple-regression analysis and taking into account assets, industrial concentration, Federal Reserve Board indices of economywide growth and fluctuation of profit rates, and equity-asset ratios, Larner found that the rate of profit earned by "management" and "owner"-controlled firms was about the same; both were equally profit oriented. Second, the evidence on fluctuations in profit rates suggested no support for the view that allegedly nonowning managements avoid risk taking more than owners do. Third, Larner found that the corporation's dollar profit and rate of return on equity were the major determinants of the level of "executive compensation." Compensation of executives, he concluded, has been "effectively harnessed" to the stockholders' interests in profits. In Larner's words, "Although control is separated from ownership in most of America's largest corporations, the effects on the profit orientations of firms, and on stockholders' welfare have been minor. The magnitude of the effects," he concluded (1970), "appears to be too small to justify the considerable attention they have received in the literature of the past thirty-eight years" (p. 66).[8]

---

8. Similar findings are reported in Kamerschen (1968, 1969), Hindley (1970), and Lewellen and Huntsman (1970). Contrary findings, which show small but statistically significant differences in profit rates between allegedly owner-controlled and allegedly management-controlled corporations, appear in Monsen, Chiu, and Cooley (1968). The study by Lewellen and Huntsman (1970) differed from the others cited here, since no attempt was made to contrast performance by owner versus management-controlled corporations. Their focus was on the specific question of whether a corporation's profitability or its sales revenue more strongly determined the rewards of its senior officers. By means of a multivariate analysis, they found that "both reported profits and equity market values are substantially more important in the determination of executive compensation than are sales—indeed, sales seem to be quite irrelevant—[and] the clear inference is that there is a greater incentive for management to shape its decision rules in a manner consonant with shareholder interests than to seek the alternative goal of revenue maximization" (pp. 718–19). The use of multiple-regression analysis (Larner) or analysis of variance (Monsen) does not resolve the problem of causation (time-order). It merely shows, at one point in time, how corporations classified under different types of control differ on selected variables. It might plausibly be argued that a control group, whether an individual, family, or coalition of business associates, might gradually dispose of its holdings in a corporation precisely because its profit performance was not satisfactory over a period of time—for reasons not connected to how it was managed. This might be particularly the case for small control groups, to whom not the corporation's profits as such but the dividend yield and price appreciation of their stockholdings ("combined return") is primary. Thus, a finding that owner-controlled corporations were more profitable than management-controlled corporations (assuming the latter exist) might simply mean that control groups do their best to retain control of the more profitable corporations and get out of those that are less profitable. A genuine causal study requires information on changes over time in types of control and in corporate performance. Unfortunately, the nature of the data available probably precludes such a study. Are the same corporations that were once owner controlled, more or less profitable once they come under management control? Take an extreme example. In 1923, Guggenheim Brothers sold control of Chile Copper Company, whose major asset was the Chuquicamata mine in Chile, to the Anaconda Copper Company, headed by John D. Ryan. The family was split over this issue: some of them thought that this would become an extraordinary profit-yielding asset—as it did; others were for accepting the immediate profits to be made by Ryan's offering price of $70 million for the controlling interest. The result was that, although they sold the controlling interest, the family retained a large block of stock as an investment (Hoyt 1967, pp. 258, 263). Did the loss of "family control" and its acquisition by Anaconda result in lessening effort at profit maximization in the Chile Copper Company? Posed in this way, the question appears (at least to me) to be rhetorical, though, of course, it is empirical.

Larner's findings contradict managerial theory, but are consistent both with neoclassical and neo-Marxian reasoning concerning corporate conduct: even where management is, in fact, in control, it is compelled to engage in a "systematic temporal search for highest practicable profits" (Earley 1957, p. 333). The conduct of the large corporation, in this view, whether under management control or ownership control, is largely determined by the market structure—the nature of competition, products produced, and the constraints of the capital markets (Peterson 1965, pp. 9–14; O'Connor 1971, p. 145). Growth, sales, technical efficiency, a strong competitive position are at once inseparable managerial goals and the determinants of high corporate profits—which, in turn, are the prerequisites of high managerial income and status (Earley 1956, 1957; Alchian 1968, p. 186; Sheehan 1967, p. 242; Baran and Sweezy 1966, pp. 33–34). Management need not spend "much of its time contemplating profits as such" (Peterson 1965, p. 9), so long as its decisions on pricing and sales and on the planning and organization of production must be measured against and not imperil corporate profitability. "This," argues Peterson, "is the essence of profit-seeking and of capitalist behavior in employing resources." Significant deviation from profit-maximizing behavior also would lead to the lowering of the market price of the corporation's stock and make it an attractive and vulnerable target for takeover—and the displacement of the incumbent management (Manne 1965; *Business Week,* May 22, 1971, p. 55). Furthermore, some economists have suggested that professional management, particularly the use of "scientific budgetary planning" and the emphasis on the "time-value of money" (Earley 1956; Earley and Carleton 1962; Tanzer 1969, pp. 32–34), strengthens, rather than weakens, the drive toward profit maximization. Whether or not managers are actuated by the "profit motive," as a subjective value commitment, "profit maximization" is an objective requirement, since profits constitute both the only unambiguous criterion of successful managerial performance and an irreducible necessity for corporate survival (Peterson 1965; Tanzer 1969, pp. 30–32). In the words of Robin Williams, Jr. (1959), "the separation of ownership and control shows that the 'profit motive' is not a *motive* at all . . . ; it is not a psychological state but a social condition" (p. 184).

This reasoning is persuasive and consistent with the findings that purportedly management-controlled and owner-controlled corporations are similarly profit oriented, and that profits and stock market values determine executive compensation. However, once again the difficulty is that since independent investigations concerning the control of the large corporations, including the two most recent and exhaustive studies by Larner and Burch, have come to very different conclusions, we cannot know if the "independent variable" has even been adequately measured. In reality, the allegedly management-controlled corporations may—appearances aside—continue to be subject to control by minority ownership interests and/or "outside" centers of control.

## Entangling Kinship Relations and Spheres of Influence

The problem is further complicated if, in fact, a number of seemingly independent corporations are under common control. Few today consider the concept of the "interest group" or "financial group" or "family sphere of influence" relevant to the workings of the large corporations. Indeed, Paul M. Sweezy (Baran and Sweezy 1966, pp. 17–20) has discarded the concept also, as noted earlier, although he was the principal author of the investigation for the NRC (1939) which provided one of the *two* most authoritative studies (the other by the TNEC) of the question to date (Goldsmith and Parmelee 1940, chap. 7). However, we know that the very object of such groups, as they were relatively well documented in the past, "is to combine the constituent companies into a system in such a way as to maximize the profits of the entire system irrespective of the profits of each separate unit," as Gardiner Means himself long ago pointed out (Bonbright and Means 1932, pp. 45–46). Much as in the multinational corporation's relations with its affiliates and subsidiaries, the constituent corporations in a group may adjust intercorporate dealings in such a way as to raise or diminish the profit rates of the different ostensibly independent corporations (cf. Rose 1968, p. 101; Tanzer 1969, pp. 14 ff.). Under such circumstances, studies attempting to compare the conduct of corporations, several of which may in fact be involved in different groups to which their policies are subordinated, cannot provide valid or reliable results. We cannot be certain what is being measured.

In the United States today, the Mellons and DuPonts are among the most publicized instances of enduring "family spheres of influence." The TNEC found the Mellon "family . . . to have considerable shareholdings in 17 of the 200 corporations, 7 of which they controlled directly or indirectly" (Goldsmith and Parmelee 1940, p. 123). Today, according to *Fortune* (Murphy 1967; see also Jensen 1971) the Mellons, utilizing "various connections, and through a complicated structure of family and charitable trusts and foundations" and other "eleemosynary arrangements," have known controlling interests in at least four of the 500 largest nonfinancial corporations (Gulf Oil, Alcoa, Koppers Company, and Carborundum Company), as well as the First Boston Corporation, the General Reinsurance Corporation, and the Mellon National Bank and Trust Company (the fifteenth largest United States bank by deposits [Patman Report 1968, p. 79]). In turn (according to the Patman Report [1968], p. 14), Mellon National Bank holds 6.9% of the common stock in Jones and Laughlin Steel, another of the top 500.[9] It seems as reasonable to hypothesize that the Mellons are only instances of a less visible but prevalent situation among principal proprietary families as to assume they are "deviant cases" or historical vestiges. Moreover, given such family "spheres of influence" which radiate out among several large corporations, it should be understood that the same small propor-

---

9. Jones and Laughlin Steel was classified under "management control" by Larner. Aside from the 6.9% Mellon National Bank holding, the Bank also has two directors on the Company's Board. Koppers Company, in which *Fortune* (Murphy 1967) claims the Mellons held at least 20%, was also classified as under "management control" by Larner, indicating the difficulty of locating "control" without access to "street knowledge" or insiders. This emphasizes again the secrecy in which holdings are shrouded and the fact that insufficient account of this is taken when considering "findings" about control centers. Larner himself notes, though without considering its possible general significance, that the Alcoa mandatory 10-K report filed with the SEC in 1963 states that no shareholder has more than 10% of the outstanding common shares, although from the proxy report and other sources he concluded that Alcoa was under Mellon control. *Fortune* (Murphy 1967) and the *New York Times* (Jensen 1971) estimate Mellon interests in Alcoa at 30%.

tion of the stock in the hands of such a family in a specific corporation carries different implications and potential for control than when held by a single individual with no other major resources and institutions to buttress his position. It is known that a great number of related individuals may participate in the ownership of a family bloc, utilizing a complex holding pattern to keep control concentrated, despite the diffusion of ownership. If control is exercised through entangling interests in several interrelated corporations, rather than limited to one, then such kinship information is vital to an understanding of the control structure. Indeed, the kinship relations between the top officers, directors, and principal shareholders of the large corporations (and banks) are the least studied but may be the most crucial aspect of the control structure.[10]

## Bank Control?

The banks are major institutional bases of economic power and corporate control which the managerialists, from Berle and Means to John Kenneth Galbraith, either have ignored or considered unimportant. Offering no substantial evidence to support his assertion, Gordon (1966) recently restated (in a new preface to his original study of the situation as of the 1930s) the accepted view that "large-scale industry is much less dependent on the banking community than it was a half-century ago, and such power as bankers have is less likely to be translated into corporate control than was true then" (p. ix). Noting the extensive interlocking between the largest banks and corporations, he simply claims that this is a "far cry from what was once meant by 'financial control'" (p. x). What implications such interlocking might have, Gordon fails to suggest. Galbraith's (1968) "commonplace observation" is that "the social magnetism of the banker" is "dwindling," and that the largest corporations are emancipated from reliance on bankers and outside sources of financing because they now have a source of their own capital, derived from their earnings, and "wholly under [their] own control" (pp. 68, 92).

Contrary to Galbraith's commonplace observations, however, uncommon but systematic research on the question does not seem to indicate decreased corporate dependence on external funds. For all U.S. firms whose assets exceed $5 million, John Lintner (1967) reports that "the dependence on outside liabilities for financing is about the same regardless of the size of the firm" and that the "relative shifts in the reliance on internal or external funds . . . have been re-

---

10. Larner's own statements in his notes on sources occasionally suggest how important, if not vital, is such kinship information if we are successfully to locate the actual centers of corporate control. Thus, for instance, Larner (1970) refers to *Moody's Industrials* as the source of his information that in the Dow Chemical Company, which he classified under "minority control," there were "78 dependents (plus spouses) of H. W. Dow [who] owned 12.6% of [the] outstanding common stock" (p. 75). Similar references were made to the Newberry Company, Cabot Corporation, and R. R. Donnelly & Sons Company, in which the descendants and kindred through marriage of the original founder are taken into account in establishing the share of these families in ownership. Clearly, systematic independent research of this type into the kinship interconnections of the principal shareowners, officers, and directors of the 500 largest corporations has not yet been done by anyone purporting to locate their centers of control. The outstanding recent unsystematic attempt to do this is, once again, the work of Ferdinand Lundberg (1968, chaps. 4–6).

markably stable over a full half century" (pp. 179, 184). The Federal Reserve Bank of San Francisco reports a sharp increase in the past decade in reliance on external funds for financing, and if the bank's data is reanalyzed to exclude depreciation allowances—on the premise that only profits can be used to finance net investments to increase the firm's capital stock—the reported trend is even more clearly toward dependence on external financing. Most important, the largest corporations are found to be least self-financing (cited in Fitch and Oppenheimer 1970, no. 1, pp. 68 ff.).

If, contrary to managerialist assumptions, the large corporations must continue to rely on the capital market no less than in the past, this is of critical importance: since the distribution of banking assets and deposits is highly skewed, this means that "reliance on external financing" is, in fact, dependence on a small number of very large financial corporations. As of 1964, the 100 largest commercial banks in the United States held 46% of all the deposits of the 13,775 commercial banks in the country. The 14 largest alone, representing one-tenth of 1% of all commercial banks, held 24% of all commercial bank deposits (Patman Report 1966, p. 804). Thus, the relationships between the large banks and corporations are essential to our understanding of the locus of corporate control. Where it might otherwise appear as if, lacking a visible controlling ownership interest, a corporation is under "management control," it may, on the contrary, be under the control of one or more banks and other financial institutions. Even in corporations in which a substantial minority of the stock (or even majority) is held by an identifiable ownership interest, this may not assure control: if the corporation has a long-term debt to a given bank or insurance company, has that institution's representatives on its board, and must receive prior approval of significant financial and investment decisions, then control of that corporation may be exerted from the "outside"; and this may be accentuated if several related financial institutions have a similar interest in that corporation. (The dismissal under the "prodding" of its bankers of Anaconda's chief executive officer and other top officers—discussed earlier—when their performance in Chile turned out to be inferior to Kennecott's and had led, in any case, to the company's deteriorating situation, seems to be a case in point [see *Business Week,* February 19, 1972, pp. 54–55]).

Whatever the dwindling "social magnetism" of the banker divined by Galbraith, this may be a questionable indicator of his economic power. Indeed, the Patman Committee, which gathered unprecedented information on the stockownership of large commercial banks, believes the power of the banks is growing. The committee found a ". . . pattern of control whereby large blocks of stock in the largest *non*financial corporations in the country are becoming controlled by some of the largest financial corporations in the country. "This," the Patman Committee concludes, "is shifting economic power back to a small group, repeating in somewhat different manner the pattern of the trusts of the late nineteenth and early twentieth centuries." This "emerging situation" appears to the committee to be one involving increasing "bank minority control." The committee found that the largest banks surveyed in 10 major cities, not including the West Coast, hold 5% or more of the common stock in 147 (29%) of the 500 largest industrial corporations. At least 5% of the common stock of 17 of the 50 largest merchandising companies and the same number of transportation companies is held by one or more of the 49 banks. These 49 banks are also represented on the boards of directors of 286 of the 500 largest industrial corporations. The same pattern appears among the 50 largest merchandising, utilities, transportation, and insurance companies (Patman Report 1968, p. 13). Whether or not, and to what extent, such fusion of financial and industrial capital indicates "financial" or "bank control" is an open question. However, it cannot be ignored if we want to understand its implications. Thus, Peter C. Dooley (1969) found that precisely those corporations—the largest ones—which the managerialists claim to be most independent of the banks, are in fact, most closely interlocked with large banks and other financial corporations. Among the 200 largest nonfinancial corporations, the greater the assets of the nonfinancial corporation, the greater the incidence of interlocks between them and the 50 largest financial corporations (32 banks and 18 insurance companies) (p. 318).

This may mean that the conceptualization of the largest corporations, banks, and insurance companies as independent institutions may obscure the actual coalescence of financial and industrial capital which has occurred. On the one hand, as noted above, large banks and insurance companies frequently are themselves principal shareholders in the large corporations. On the other, the very same individuals and families may be principal shareowners in large banks and large corporations, even when these do not have institutional holdings in one another. Aside from the Mellons, with controlling interests in at least four of the 500 largest nonfinancial corporations and in an investment bank, insurance company, and the fifteenth largest commercial bank, whom we noted above, other well-known industrialist families in the United States may be cited who also have dominant and/or controlling interests in the largest banks. For example, there are both branches of the Rockefeller families, as well as other principal families in the Standard Oil corporations. The Rockefellers and associates reportedly ( *Time,* September 7, 1962; Abels 1965, p. 358) held over 5% of the stock in the Chase Manhattan Bank (ranking second by deposits of all banks in 1963),[11] whose chairman of the board is David Rockefeller; the Stillman-Rockefeller families and associates are said to be dominant in the First National City Bank (ranking third in 1963) (*Fortune,* September 1965, p. 138). The Fisher and Mott families, among the principal shareowning families in General Motors, reportedly held over 5% of the stock of the National Bank of Detroit (U.S. Congress, 1963, pp. 227, 416), the country's sixteenth largest bank in 1963. The Henry Ford family owns 4% of the thirtieth ranking Manufacturer's National which, in turn, owns 7% of Ford Motor Company common stock (Patman Report 1968, p. 664). The M. A. Hanna family that controls at least two of the 500 largest corporations, National Steel and Consolidation Coal (Larner 1970, p. 120; Burch 1972, p. 58), has a dominant minority interest of at least 3% in the thirty-fourth ranking National City Bank of Cleveland (U.S. Congress 1963, p.

---

11. The 1963 rankings are given since this was the year of the House Select Committee's study. The source of the rankings is the *Fortune Directory for 1963.* The latest rankings by *Fortune* (July 1973) for 1972 are Mellon, 15; Chase, 3; First National City, 2; National Bank of Detroit, 18; National City Bank of Cleveland, 49.

165), which, in turn, holds 11% of the stock of Hanna Mining Company. These are, of course, merely instances, as I said, of prominent families whose interests overlap banking and industry. They illustrate the general theoretical issue, however, of the extent to which it is valid to speak at all of "bank control" of "industry"—as does the Patman Report, for instance, or other recent writers (Fitch and Oppenheimer 1970). Rather, these families' interests transcend the banks and corporations in which they have principal or controlling interests; and the banks may merely be units in, and instrumentalities of, the whole system of propertied interests controlled by these major capitalist families.

There appears, in fact, to be a special segment of the corporate world which represents the fusion of financial and industrial capital, to which Rudolf Hilferding (1910, chap. 23) long ago called attention, and whom he termed "finance capitalists" (cf. also Schumpeter 1955b, pp. 80–81; Lenin 1967, chap. 3; Sweezy 1942, pp. 261, 266). Hilferding was referring to "a circle of persons who, thanks to their own possession of capital or as representatives of concentrated power over other people's capital (bank directors), sit upon the governing boards of a large number of corporations. Thus, there arises a kind of personal union, on the one hand, between the different corporations themselves, [and,] on the other, between the latter and the banks, a circumstance which must be of the greatest importance for the policy of these institutions since a community of interests has arisen among them" (Hilferding [1910], as slightly reworded from the translation by Sweezy [1956], p. 261).

Do such "finance capitalists" or representatives of banks who sit on the boards of the large American corporations today, have a special role in coordinating the interests of these corporations? Do they differ, for example, from other outside directors that interlock the largest corporations between themselves, as well as with other firms? These are critical questions, which no single indicator can suffice to answer. We would need information concerning their own propertied interests, their relative wealth, their kinship relations, before being able to ascertain whether the "finance capitalist" represents a special social type in contrast to other officers and directors of the largest corporations and banks. One relevant issue, however, on which we do have some information, is the extent to which they are likely to sit on a number of large nonfinancial corporation boards, compared with "outside directors" (i.e., those who do not actually hold posts as officers in the corporate management) who are not bankers. I have analyzed raw data presented elsewhere (Smith and Desfosses 1972) on interlocking directorates among the 500 largest industrial corporations, ranked by sales, in 1968. What we find is that commercial and investment bankers are disproportionately over represented among the occupants of multiple corporate directorships (Table 1). Bankers constituted 21% of all outside directors in the 500 largest industrials, but well over twice that proportion among the outside directors with seats on three or more corporate boards. Indeed, the proportion of bankers who are outside directors rises directly with the number of corporate posts held. And among the select few ($N = 16$) outside directors having five or more posts, 56% were bankers; of the five outside directors with six or seven posts, four were bankers. Viewing the same relationship differently (Table 2), commercial and investment bankers stand out in

**Table 1. Principal Employer of Outside Directors of the 500 Largest Industrial Corporations in the United States in 1968 (%)**

| TYPE OF PRINCIPAL EMPLOYER | NUMBER OF SEATS OCCUPIED | | | | | | |
|---|---|---|---|---|---|---|---|
| | 1 | 2 | 3 | 4 | 5 | 6 plus | TOTAL |
| Other top 500 firm ......... | 13.9 | 25.9 | 15.7 | 12.9 | 18.2 | 0 | 15.4 |
| Law firm ........... | 14.1 | 10.3 | 3.4 | 3.2 | 9.1 | 0 | 13.0 |
| Bank........... | 18.5 | 25.8 | 41.6 | 45.1 | 45.5 | 80.0 | 20.9 |
| Commercial........ | 10.8 | 14.5 | 19.1 | 29.0 | 36.4 | 40.0 | 12.0 |
| Investment........ | 7.7 | 11.3 | 22.5 | 16.1 | 9.1 | 40.0 | 8.9 |
| Consulting firm........ | 6.3 | 6.0 | 1.1 | 6.5 | 0 | 0 | 6.0 |
| Other★ ........ | 47.3 | 32.0 | 38.2 | 32.3 | 27.2 | 20.0 | 44.7 |
| Total % ......... | 100 | 100 | 100 | 100 | 100 | 100 | 100 |
| Total N ......... | 1,932 | 282 | 89 | 31 | 11 | 5 | 2,350 |

Sources. Calculated from raw data given in Smith and Desfosses (1972, table 4, p. 65), on the composition of the outside directorships of the 500 largest industrials listed in *Fortune*, May 15, 1969, ranked by 1968 sales. Principal employer was obtained from information in the proxy statements of 460 corporations and from Standard and Poor's *Register of Corporations, Directors, and Executives*, 1970, for 35 corporations. Smith and Desfosses did not obtain information on five corporations.

★Types of employers which did not employ more than 5% of the total number of outside directors in the 500 largest industrials, including utilities; merchandising, insurance, real estate, railroad firms, as well as educational institutions, foundations, government agencies, plus "unlisted companies."

*Table 2.* **Number of the 500 Largest U.S. Industrial Corporations on Whose Boards Outside Directors Are Represented, by Type of Principal Employer, 1968**
(%)

| Type of Principal Employer | NUMBER OF SEATS OCCUPIED | | | | |
|---|---|---|---|---|---|
| | 1 | 2 | 3 | 4 plus | *(N)* |
| Other top 500 firm........ | 74 | 20 | 4 | 2 | (361) |
| Law firm............... | 89 | 9 | 1 | 1 | (306) |
| Bank | | | | | |
| Commercial.......... | 75 | 15 | 6 | 5 | (283) |
| Investment........... | 71 | 15 | 10 | 4 | (208) |
| Consulting firm.......... | 86 | 12 | 1 | 1 | (141) |
| •Other★ ................. | 87 | 9 | 3 | 11 | (1,051) |
| All outside directors ...... | 82 | 12 | 4 | 2 | (2,350) |

Sources.—See Table 1.
★See Table 1.

marked contrast to other outside directors in the top 500 corporations: a far higher proportion of them have multiple corporation posts than do outside directors from other top 500 corporations, law firms, consulting firms, or other types of companies and institutions. Outside directors from other top 500 corporations are second only to the bankers in the proportion with multiple directorships. But well over twice the proportion of bankers occupy multiple posts: 11% of the commercial bankers and 15% of the investment bankers have seats on three or more top 500 corporate boards compared with 6% of the directors from other top 500 firms.

## Who Controls the Banks?

Who the controlling interests are in the largest banks is not publicly known. The Select House Committee report on chain banking (1963) and the Patman Reports (1964, 1966, 1967) for the first time provided an authoritative glance—however limited—inside. The 1963 and 1964 reports listed the 20 largest shareholdings of record (and the percentage of stock held) in each of the 200 largest commercial bank members of the Federal Reserve System in recent years. The 1966 Patman Report focused on commercial banks' holdings of their own shares and also listed the total market values (though without calculating the percentages) of the outstanding stock held by all financial institutions in the 300 largest commercial banks in 1966; and the 1967 Patman Report also focused on holdings in the banks by other financial institutions, particularly the major commercial banks in 10 metropolitan areas. The lists of the reported "beneficial owners" of the banks' shares obtained by the Patman Committee have not been released to date. With only the shareholdings of record available so far, the same difficulties arise here as has already been discussed earlier in detail. Any attempt to locate the actual ownership interests by identifying recognizable surnames alone, without knowledge of kinship relations, nominees, etc., cannot provide reliable and valid information. A recent study of this type, based on the 1963 Select Committee report, and utilizing the 10% minimum to define an ownership-controlled bank, came to the predictable conclusion that "management control had become the dominant form of control among the large member banks by 1962," accounting for 75% of the banks (Vernon 1970, p. 654). In contrast, Burch (1972) utilized other business sources of information cited earlier, as well as the 1963 Select Committee report, investigated representation on boards of directors, and consulted several family histories. However, like Vernon, he did not attempt any systematic investigation of kinship ties, so, once again, his are absolutely minimum estimates of control of these banks by ownership interests. He studied only the 50 largest, and concluded that 30% were probably under family control, another 22% possibly under family control, and 48% probably under management control (pp. 89–96). Vernon (1970) broke down his analysis into categories by total bank assets, rather than ranks, so no direct comparison is possible from their published reports. However, of the 27 largest banks having $1 billion in assets or more, he classified only two under "owner control," with the possible addition of another three in which he identified an interest greater than 5% but less than 10% (p. 655). Of the 27 largest banks listed by Burch, however, he classified eight as probably family controlled and four more as possibly family controlled. Once again the disparities in results by two different methods are striking. Other close students of the banks (aside from the Patman investigators [1968, p. 91] already cited) object to the ownership level of 10% as "arbitrary." Thus, Eisenbeis and McCall (1972), financial economists at the Federal Deposit Insurance Corporation, state that "'minority control' can be achieved . . . through ownership of a much smaller proportion of stock than the arbitrary 10% levels" (p. 876).

In any event, the theoretical significance of such an alleged split between ownership and control in large banks was not suggested by Vernon, nor, to my knowledge, has any managerial theorist yet to suggest that the banks might somehow or other become non–profit–maximizing institutions, were they no longer under the control of specific ownership interests. Furthermore, neither Vernon nor Burch took account in their studies of the extent to which the banks themselves are interlocked and, most important, hold significant amounts of stock in each other. The Patman Committee (1966) did a survey, whose results have only been partially reported, which found that 57% of the 210 largest commercial banks hold more than 5% of their own shares and 29% hold more than 10% of their own shares. The banks (and other types of corporations) buy their own stock—sometimes termed "defensive buying" on Wall Street—to keep their shares out of the "unfriendly hands" of potential rivals for control.[12] If other financial institutions, including commercial banks, mutual savings banks, and insurance companies in which the same owning families appear

---

12. Corporations may purchase their own shares for other reasons: (1) to maintain the price of their stock, (2) to prepare for possible mergers and acquisitions, (3) to allow them to convert bonds to shares, etc. Whatever the reasons, such holdings are of use in control, when necessary.

among the principal shareholders, or which have long-standing business associations and common interests (including interlocks between banks and insurance companies), also hold the bank's stock, this further decreases the amount of stock which the principal individual and familial shareholders must own to maintain control. Nearly a third (30%) of the 275 large banks reported on by the Patman Committee had more than 10% of their shares which could be voted exclusively by other financial institutions. Nearly half (47%) had more than 5% of their shares similarly held (Patman Report 1966, p. 832). In addition, the extent and pattern of interlocking bank stockownership by the same principal shareowners is not known. Very preliminary data received by the Patman Committee found several "situations where the beneficial owners of large blocs of commercial bank stock are in fact holdings by a few families who have management connections with competitor banks in the same geographic area." Though banks may not legally interlock, officers and directors (and their families) of one bank may have principal shareholdings in other banks, and the preliminary data of the Patman Committee also revealed such situations (Patman Report 1966, pp. 878–79).

## Conclusion

Our review of discrepant findings on the alleged separation of ownership and control in the large corporation in the United States,[13] and of the problems entailed in obtaining reliable and valid evidence on the actual ownership interests involved in a given corporation, should make it clear that the absence of control by proprietary interests in the largest corporations is by no means an "unquestionable," "incontrovertible," "singular," or "critical" social "fact." Nor can one any longer have confidence in such assurances as the following by Robert A. Dahl (1970): "Every *literate* person now *rightly takes for granted* what Berle and Means *established* four decades ago in their famous study, *The Modern Corporation and Private Property*" (p. 125; italics added). On the contrary, I believe that the "separation of ownership and control" may well be one of those rather critical, widely accepted, pseudofacts with which all sciences occasionally have found themselves burdened and bedeviled.[14]

News of the demise of capitalist classes, particularly in the United States, is, I suspect, somewhat premature. In place of such generalizations, extrapolated

---

13. We have, of course, not reviewed empirical studies of the question in other countries. The principal study in England is by Florence (1961). The only other such systematic study of which I am aware is by Wheelwright (1957) on Australia, as well as my own forthcoming collaborative volume with Ewen and Ratcliff on Chile.

14. An example of a critical unwitting pseudofact appears in two articles by Daniel Bell (1958, 1961). In both articles, Bell refers to the "X" family of "Middletown" as an instance of the end of family control. "[B]y and large," Bell wrote (1958, p. 248; and similarly, 1961, p. 45), "the system of family control is finished. So much so that a classic study of American life like Robert Lynd's *Middletown in Transition,* with its picture of the 'X' family dominating the town, has in less than twenty years become history rather than contemporary life. (Interestingly enough, in 1957, the Ball family, Lynd's 'X' family, took in professional management of its enterprises, since the family lineage was becoming exhausted.)" Perhaps Bell really knows who now dominates Muncie, Indiana, and what role the Ball family plays there, but as an instance of "the breakup of family capital-

from an insufficiently examined American experience or deduced from abstract ahistorical theoretical premises, detailed empirical studies are necessary.

The methods and procedures, and the basic concepts and units of analysis, in such research will have to be quite different than those which have been most commonly employed in the past. Most important, such research must focus at the outset on the complex relationships in which the single corporation is itself involved: the particular pattern of holdings and their evolution within the corporation; and the relationships between it and other corporations; the forms of personal union or interlocking between corporate directorates and between the officers and directors and principal shareholding families; the connections with banks, both as "financial institutions" and the agents of specified propertied interests, including those who control the banks themselves; the network of intercorporate and principal common shareholdings. In a word, it will be necessary to explore in detail the institutional and class structure in which the individual large corporations are situated.

## References

Abels, Jules. 1965. *The Rockefeller Billions*. New York: Macmillan.

Adams, Bert. 1970. "Isolation, Function, and Beyond: American Kinship in the 1960's." *Journal of Marriage and the Family* 32 (November): 575–97.

Alchian, Armen. 1968. "Corporate Management and Property Rights." In *Economic Policy and the Regulation of Securities*. Washington, D.C.: American Enterprise Institute.

Bailyn, Bernard. 1955. *The New England Merchants in the Seventeenth Century*. Cambridge, Mass.: Harvard University Press.

Bain, Joe S. 1966. *International Differences in Industrial Structure: Eight Nations in the 1950's*. New Haven, Conn.: Yale University Press.

Baltzell, E. Digby. 1966a. "'Who's Who in America' and 'The Social Register': Elite and Upper Class Indexes in Metropolitan America." In *Class, Status, and Power*, edited by Reinhard Bendix and S. M. Lipset. 2d ed. New York: Collier-Macmillan.

————. 1966b. *Philadelphia Gentlemen: The Making of a National Upper Class*. New York: Macmillan.

Baran, Paul A., and Paul M. Sweezy. 1966. *Monopoly Capital*. New York: Monthly Review Press.

Barber, Eleanor G. 1955. *The Bourgeoisie in Eighteenth-Century France*. Princeton, N.J.: Princeton University Press.

---

ism" and the end of family control, this is a singularly poor choice. Given the context in which Bell refers to the "X" family, his statement is quite misleading, since Ball Brothers, Inc., which is, according to *Fortune,* probably among the 500 largest corporations, ranked by sales, in the country today, continues to be privately owned. "Edmund F. Ball, a founder's son, is chairman of the company, but he has employed plenty of non-family talent. . . . 'Ours is still,' says Edmund Ball, 'essentially a closely held, privately owned business'" (Sheehan 1966, p. 343).

Barber, Eleanor G., and Bernard Barber, eds. 1965. *European Social Class: Stability and Change*. New York: Macmillan.

Baumol, William J. 1959. *Business, Behavior, Value, and Growth*. New York: Macmillan.

Bell, Daniel. 1958. "The Power Elite—Reconsidered." *American Journal of Sociology* 64 (November): 238–50.

———. 1961. "The Breakup of Family Capitalism." In *The End of Ideology*. New York: Collier.

Bendix, Reinhard. 1952. "Bureaucracy and the Problem of Power." In *Reader in Bureaucracy*, edited by R. K. Merton, Ailsa P. Gray, Barbara Hockey, and Hanan C. Selvin. Glencoe, Ill.: Free Press.

Berle, Adolph, Jr. 1954. *The 20th Century Capitalist Revolution*. New York: Harcourt, Brace.

Berle, Adolph, Jr., and Gardiner C. Means. 1967. *The Modern Corporation and Private Property*. New York: Harcourt, Brace & World (originally published in 1932 by Macmillan).

Bernstein, Eduard. 1961. *Evolutionary Socialism*. New York: Schocken (originally published in Germany in 1899).

Bonbright, James C., and Gardiner C. Means. 1932. *The Holding Company*. New York: McGraw-Hill.

Burch, Philip H., Jr. 1972. *The Managerial Revolution Reassessed*. Lexington, Mass.: Heath.

*Business Week* (no author given). 1971. "The Board: It's Obsolete Unless Overhauled." May 22, pp. 50–58.

———. 1972. "An Ex-Banker Treats Copper's Sickest Giant." February 19, pp. 52–55.

Cavan, Ruth. 1963. *The American Family*. New York: Crowell.

Dahl, Robert A. 1970. *After the Revolution?* New Haven, Conn.: Yale University Press.

Dahrendorf, Ralf. 1959. *Class and Class Conflict in Industrial Society*. Stanford, Calif.: Stanford University Press.

Domhoff, G. William. 1967. *Who Rules America?* Englewood Cliffs, N.J.: Prentice-Hall.

———. 1970. *The Higher Circles: The Governing Class in America*. New York: Random House.

———. 1972. *Fat Cats and Democrats*. Englewood Cliffs, N.J.: Prentice-Hall.

Dooley, Peter C. 1969. "The Interlocking Directorate." *American Economic Review* 59 (June): 314–23.

Drucker, Peter F. 1971. "The New Markets and the New Capitalism." In *Capitalism Today*, edited by Daniel Bell and Irving Kristol. New York: Basic.

Earley, James S. 1956. "Marginal Policies of Excellently Managed Companies." *American Economic Review* 46 (March): 44–70.

———. 1957. "Comment." *American Economic Review. Papers and Proceedings* 47 (May): 333–35.

Earley, James S., and W. T. Carleton. 1962. "Budgeting and the Theory of the Firm." *Journal of Industrial Economics* 10 (July): 165–73.

Edwards Vives, Alberto. 1927. *La fronda aristocratica*. Santiago: Editorial del Pacifico.

Eisenbeis, Robert A., and Alan S. McCall. 1972. "Some Effects of Affiliations among Savings and Commercial Banks." *Journal of Finance* 27 (September): 865–77.

Etzioni, Amitai. 1968. *The Active Society*. New York: Free Press.

Fitch, Robert, and Mary Oppenheimer. 1970. "Who Rules the Corporations?" *Socialist Revolution* 1 (1): 73–107; also 1 (5): 61–114; 1 (6): 33–94.

Florence, P. Sargant. 1961. *Ownership, Control and Success of Large Companies: An Analysis of English Industrial Structure and Policy, 1936–1951*. London: Sweet & Maxwell.

Ford, Franklin L. 1953. *Robe and Sword: The Regrouping of the French Aristocracy after Louis XIV*. Cambridge, Mass.: Harvard University Press.

Forster, Robert. 1960. *The Nobility of Toulouse in the Eighteenth Century*. Baltimore: Johns Hopkins Press.

———. 1963. "The Provincial Noble: A Reappraisal." *American Historical Review* 68 (April): 681–91.

Galbraith, John K. 1968. *The New Industrial State*. New York: New American Library (also, "Introduction," 2d ed. 1971). New York: Houghton Mifflin.

Goldsmith, Raymond W., and Rexford C. Parmelee. 1940. *The Distribution of Ownership in the 200 Largest Nonfinancial Corporations*. In *Investigations of Concentration of Economic Power*. Monographs of the Temporary National Economic Committee, no. 29. Washington, D.C.: Government Printing Office.

Goode, William J. 1963. *The Family*. Englewood Cliffs, N.J.: Prentice-Hall.

Goode, William J., Elizabeth Hobbins, and Helen M. McClure, eds. 1971. *Social Systems and Family Patterns: A Propositional Inventory*. Indianapolis: Bobbs-Merrill.

Gordon, Robert A. 1966. *Business Leadership in the Large Corporation*. Berkeley: University of California Press (originally published in 1945 under the auspices of the Brookings Institution).

Heise, Gonzales, Julio. 1950. "La constitucion de 1925 y las nuevas tendencias politico-sociales." *Anales de la Universidad de Chile* 108 (80; 4th trimester): 95–234.

Hilferding, Rudolph. 1910. *Das Finanzkapital*. Munich: Literarische Agentur Willi Weisman.

Hindley, Brian V. 1970. "Separation of Ownership and Control in the Modern Corporation." *Journal of Law and Economics* 13 (April): 185–221.

Hoyt, Edwin P. 1967. *The Guggenheims and the American Dream.* New York: Funk & Wagnalls.

Hunter, Floyd. 1959. *Top Leadership, U.S.A.* Chapel Hill: University of North Carolina Press.

Jensen, Michael C. 1971. "A New Generation Comes of Age." *New York Times.* May 2, sec. 3, pp. 1, 5.

Kahl, Joseph. 1957. *The American Class Structure.* New York: Rinehart.

Kamerschen, David R. 1968. "The Influence of Ownership and Control on Profit Rates." *American Economic Review* 58 (June): 432–47.

————. 1969. "The Effect of Separation of Ownership and Control on the Performance of the Large Firm in the U.S. Economy." *Rivista internazaionale di schienze economiche e commerciali* 16 (5): 489–93.

Kaysen, Carl. 1957. "The Social Significance of the Modern Corporation." *American Economic Review* 47 (May): 311–19.

————. 1965. "Another View of Corporate Capitalism." *Quarterly Journal of Economics* 79 (February): 41–51.

Kolko, Gabriel. 1962. *Wealth and Power in America.* New York: Praeger.

Kornhauser, William. 1966. "'Power Elite' or 'Veto Groups'?" In *Class, Status, and Power,* edited by Reinhard Bendix and S. M. Lipset. 2d ed. New York: Collier-Macmillan.

Larner, Robert J. 1970. *Management Control and the Large Corporation.* Cambridge, Mass.: University Press, Dunellen.

Lenin, Nikolai. 1967. "Imperialism." In *Lenin: Selected Works.* New York: International Publishers (originally published in Petrograd in 1917).

Lewellen, Wilbur G., and Blaine Huntsman. 1970. "Managerial Pay and Corporate Performance." *American Economic Review* 60 (September): 710–20.

Lintner, John. 1967. "The Financing of Corporations." In *The Corporation and Modern Society,* edited by E. S. Mason. New York: Atheneum.

Lipset, S. M., and Reinhard Bendix. 1951. "Social Status and Social Structure: A Re-Examination of Data and Interpretations." Part 1. *British Journal of Sociology* 2 (September): 150–68.

Lomask, Milton. 1964. *Seed Money: The Guggenheim Story.* New York: Farrar, Straus.

Lundberg, Ferdinand. 1946. *America's Sixty Families.* New York: Citadel (originally published by Vanguard in 1937).

————. 1968. *The Rich and the Super-Rich.* New York: Bantam.

Luxemburg, Rosa. 1970. *Reform or Revolution.* New York: Pathfinder (originally published in Berlin in 1899).

Manne, Henry. 1965. "Mergers and the Market for Corporate Control." *Journal of Political Economy* 72 (April): 110–20.

Marris, Robin. 1963. "A Model of 'Managerial' Enterprise." *Quarterly Journal of Economics* 77 (May): 185–209.

———. 1964. *The Economic Theory of "Managerial" Capitalism.* London: Macmillan.

Marx, Karl. 1967. *Capital.* Vols. 1–3. New York: International (originally published in German in 1867, 1885, 1894).

Mason, E. S. 1967. "Introduction." In *The Corporation in Modern Society,* edited by E. S. Mason. New York: Atheneum.

Merton, Robert K. 1959. "Notes on Problem-Finding in Sociology." In *Sociology Today,* edited by R. K. Merton, Leonard Broom, and Leonard S. Cottrell, Jr. New York: Basic.

Metcalf, Lee. 1971. *Congressional Record* 117, pt. 17:22141.

Metcalf, Lee, and Vic Reinemer. 1971. "Unmasking Corporate Ownership." *Nation.* July 19, pp. 38–40.

Miliband, Ralph. 1969. *The State in Capitalist Society.* New York: Basic.

Mills, C. Wright. 1957. *The Power Elite.* New York: Oxford University Press.

———. 1962. *The Marxists.* New York: Dell.

Monsen, R. Joseph, Jr., J. S. Chiu, and D. E. Cooley. 1968. "The Effect of Separation of Ownership and Control on the Performance of the Large Firm." *Quarterly Journal of Economics* 8 (August): 435–51.

———. 1969. "Ownership and Management." *Business Horizons* 12 (August): 45–52.

Moore, Barrington. 1966. *Social Origins of Dictatorship and Democracy.* Boston: Beacon.

Moran, Theodore H. 1973. "Transnational Strategies of Protection and Defense by Multinational Corporations." *International Organization* 27 (Spring): 273–87.

Murphy, Charles J. V. 1967. "The Mellons of Pittsburgh." Part 1. *Fortune* 75 (October): 120 ff.

National Resources Committee (NRC). 1939. *The Structure of the American Economy.* Washington, D.C.: Government Printing Office. Reprinted in Paul M. Sweezy. 1953. *The Present as History.* New York: Monthly Review Press.

Nichols, W. A. T. 1969. *Ownership, Control, and Ideology.* London: Allen & Unwin.

O'Connor, James. 1971. "Who Rules the Corporation?" *Socialist Revolution* 2 (January/February): 117–50.

Parsons, Talcott. 1953. "A Revised Analytical Approach to the Theory of Social Stratification." In *Class, Status, and Power,* edited by Reinhard Bendix and S. M. Lipset. Glencoe, Ill.: Free Press.

Parsons, Talcott, and Neil Smelser. 1957. *Economy and Society.* London: Routledge & Kegan-Paul.

[Patman] Staff Report. 1964. *Twenty Largest Stockholders of Record in Member Banks of the Federal Reserve System.* 5 vols. U.S. Congress, House, Committee on Banking and Currency, Domestic Finance Committee. 88th Cong., 2d sess. Washington, D.C.: Government Printing Office (cited as Patman Report).

————. 1966. "Bank Stock Ownership and Control" (reprinted in Patman Report 1968, vol. 1).

————. 1967. "Control of Commercial Banks and Interlocks among Financial Institutions" (reprinted in Patman Report 1968, vol. 1).

————. 1968. *Commerical Banks and Their Trust Activities: Emerging Influence on the American Economy.* U.S. Congress, House, Committee on Banking and Currency, Domestic Finance Committee. 90th Cong., 2d sess. Washington, D.C.: Government Printing Office (cited as Patman Report).

Perlo, Victor. 1957. *The Empire of High Finance.* New York: International.

Peterson, Shorey. 1965. "Corporate Control and Capitalism." *Quarterly Journal of Economics* 79 (February): 1–23.

Playford, John. 1972. "Who Rules Australia?" In *Australian Capitalism,* edited by Playford and Douglas Kirsner. Harmondsworth: Penguin.

Rabb, Theodore K. 1967. *Enterprise and Empire: Merchant and Gentry Investment in the Expansion of England, 1575–1630.* Cambridge, Mass.: Harvard University Press.

Riesman, David, et al. 1953. *The Lonely Crowd.* Garden City, N.J.: Anchor.

Rochester, Anna. 1936. *Rulers of America.* New York: International.

Rose, Sanford. 1968. "The Rewarding Strategies of Multinationalism." *Fortune,* September 15, pp. 101–5, 180, 182.

Schumpeter, Joseph. 1955*a*. "Social Classes in an Ethnically Homogeneous Environment." In *Imperialism and Social Classes.* New York: Meridian (originally published in German in 1923).

————. 1955*b*. "The Sociology of Imperialism[s]." *Imperialism and Social Classes* (originally published in German in 1919).

Sheehan, Robert. 1966. "There's Plenty of Privacy Left in Private Enterprise." *Fortune,* July 15, pp. 224 ff.

————. 1967. "Proprietors in the World of Big Business." *Fortune,* June 15, pp. 178–83, 242.

Simon, Herbert A. 1957. *Administrative Behavior.* 2d ed. New York. Macmillan.

Smith, Ephraim P., and Louis R. Desfosses. 1972. "Interlocking Directorates: A Study of Influence." *Mississippi Valley Journal of Business and Economics* 7 (Spring): 57–69.

Soll, Ivan. 1969. *Introduction to Hegel's Metaphysics*. Chicago: University of Chicago Press.

Sorokin, Pitirim. 1953. "What Is a Social Class?" In *Class, Status, and Power*, edited by Reinhard Bendix and S. M. Lipset. Glencoe, Ill.: Free Press.

Sweezy, Paul M. 1953. "Interest Groups in the American Economy." In *The Present as History*. New York: Monthly Review Press.

———. 1956. *Theory of Capitalist Development*. New York: Monthly Review Press (originally published in 1942).

Tanzer, Michael. 1969. *The Political Economy of International Oil and the Underdeveloped Countries*. Boston: Beacon.

U.S., Congress, House, Select Committee on Small Business. 1963. *Chain Banking: Stockholder and Loan Links of 200 Largest Member Banks*. Washington, D.C.: Government Printing Office.

Vernon, Jack R. 1970. "Ownership and Control among Large Member Banks." *Journal of Finance* 25 (3): 651–57.

Villarejo, Don. 1961/62. *Stock Ownership and the Control of Corporations*. Radical Education Project. Ann Arbor, Mich. Reprint of articles in *New University Thought* (Autumn 1961 and Winter 1962).

Walker, Robert. 1971. "A Banker for Anaconda." *New York Times*, May 23, sec. 3, pp. 3, 11.

Weber, Max. 1965. *Theory of Social and Economic Organization*. Edited by Talcott Parsons. New York: Free Press (originally published in German in 1925).

———. 1968. *Economy and Society*. Edited by G. Roth and C. Wittich. New York: Bedminster (originally published in German in 1921).

Wheelwright, E. L. 1957. *Ownership and Control of Australian Companies*. Sydney: Law Book.

Williams, Robin, Jr. 1959. *American Society*. New York: Knopf.

Williamson, Oliver E. 1963. "Managerial Discretion and Business Behavior." *American Economic Review* 53 (December): 1032–57.

———. 1970. *Corporate Control and Business Behavior*. Englewood Cliffs, N.J.: Prentice-Hall.

Wrong, Dennis. 1968. "Some Problems in Defining Social Power." *American Journal of Sociology* 73 (May): 673–81.

Zeitlin, Maurice. 1967. *Revolutionary Politics and the Cuban Working Class*. Princeton, N.J.: Princeton University Press.

## · 11 ·

# What Does the Ruling Class Do When It Rules?

## Some Reflections on Different Approaches to the Study of Power in Society

### Göran Therborn

I

What is the place of power in society? What is the relationship between class and power? Answers differ, as is to be expected, given the obvious significance of class and power to the evaluation of a given society. The question itself, however, appears simple and straightforward enough. Ideological biases apart, what seems to be at issue is the famous question of scientific method, of what is the most adequate method to answer the question.[1] But is the question really so clear and simple? From what we know about "paradigms" (Kuhn) and "problematics" (Althusser) of science is it very likely that, for example, a proletarian revolutionary and critic of political economy (Marx), a German academic historian and sociological follower of Austrian marginalism (Weber), a descendant of Jeffersonian democracy (Mills), an admirer of contemporary liberal economics (Buchanan-Tullock, Parsons), or an adherent of some of the ruling political

• From *Insurgent Sociologist* 6(3) (1970): 3–16.

    1. See, e.g., R. Dahl, "A Critique of the Ruling Elite Model", *American Political Science Review (APSR)* 52 (1958), pp. 463–69; N. Polsby, "How to Study Community Power: The Pluralist Alternative", *Journal of Politics* 22 (1960), pp. 474–84; P. Bachrach-M. Baratz, "The Two Faces of Power", *APSR* 56 (1962), pp. 947–52; P. Bachrach-M. Baratz, "Decisions and Nondecisions: An Analytical Framework", *APSR* 57 (1963), pp. 641–51; R. Merelman, "On the Neo-Elitist Critique of Community Power", *APSR* 62 (1968), pp. 451–60; *APSR* 65 (1971), pp. 1063–80; F. Frey, "Comment: On Issues and Nonissues in the Study of Power", *APSR* 65 (1971), pp. 1081–1101; R. Wolfinger, "Rejoinder to Frey's 'Comment'", *APSR* 65 (1971), pp. 1102–04. An overview can be gained from the reader edited by R. Bell, D. Edwards, and H. Wagner, *Political Power* (New York: Free Press, 1969).

ideas of present-day USA (Dahl, Giddens[2]), would be concerned with the same problem and ask the same question—even when they use the same words?

Leaving subtler points and distinctions aside we can distinguish at least three different major approaches to the study of power in society. The first and most common one we might call the *subjectivist approach*. With Robert Dahl it asks: Who governs?[3] or with William Domhoff: Who rules America?[4] or in the words of a British theorist of stratification, W. G. Runciman: "who rules and who is ruled?"[5]or in the militant pluralist variant of Nelson Polsby: "Does anyone at all run this community?"[6]

This is a subjectivist approach to the problem of power in society not in the same sense as "subjective" in the so-called subjective conceptions of stratification, which refer to stratification in terms of subjective evaluation and esteem, in contrast to stratification in terms of, say, income or education. It is a subjectivist approach in the sense that it is looking for the *subject of power*. It is looking, above all, for an answer to the question, *Who* has power? A few, many, a unified class of families, an institutional elite of top decision-makers, competing groups, everyone, or no one really? The focus of the subjectivists is on the power-holding and power-exercising subject.[7]

The common subjectivist question can then be studied and answered in various ways. This has in fact given rise to a very lively methodological as well as substantial debate in the United States in the fifties and sixties, which still has not been superseded, between the "pluralists" and the elite and the ruling class theorists.[8] Essentially, it has been a debate within the framework of liberal political ideology and liberal political theory, accepting the liberal conception of democracy as a starting-point and then investigating whether the contemporary manifestations of liberal democracy, in the present-day United States or in other

---

2. According to Giddens the USA is the most democratic advanced society in the world: A. Giddens, *The Class Structure of the Advanced Societies* (London: Hutchinson, 1973), p. 175. For a comment on the issue, see below Dahl's conception of the prevailing regime in USA is expounded in, among other places, R. Dahl, *Pluralist Democracy in the United States: Conflict and Consent* (Chicago: Rand McNally, 1967).

3. R. Dahl, *Who Governs? Democracy and Power in an American City* (New Haven: Yale Univ. Press, 1961).

4. W. Domhoff, *Who Rules America?* (Englewood Cliffs, N.J.: Prentice-Hall, 1967).

5. W. G. Runciman, "Towards a Theory of Social Stratification", in F. Parkin, ed., *The Social Analysis of Class Structure* (London: Tavistock, 1974), p. 58.

6. Polsby, op. cit., p. 476.

7. In the egalitarian orientation of Bachrach-Baratz this focus is coupled with a look-out for who, if any, gain and who, if any, are handicapped by the existing "mobilization of bias". Besides their above-mentioned articles see their *Power and Poverty* (New York: Oxford University Press, 1970).

8. The substantial debate includes, from the elitist side, F. Hunter, *Community Power Structure* (Chapel Hill: Univ. of North Carolina Press, 1953); C. W. Mills, *The Power Elite* (New York: Oxford Univ. Press, 1956); W. Domhoff, op. cit; Bachrach-Baratz, op. cit.: M. Parenti, "Power and Pluralism: A View From the Bottom", in M. Surkin-A. Wolfe, eds., *An End to Political Science* (New York: Basic Books, 1970), pp. 111–43; M. Crenson, *The Un-Politics of Air Pollution* (Baltimore: The John Hopkins Press, 1971). Among the contributions of the pluralists are S. D. Riesman, et al., *The Lonely Crowd* (New York: Doubleday Anchor, 1953); R. Dahl, *Who Governs?;* E. Banfield, *Political Influence* (New York: Free Press, 1961). For references to the methodological discussion see above note 1.

Western countries, correspond or not to that conception. But it has also included important contributions from Marxist authors, who have basically confined themselves within this framework, accepting battle on the terrain chosen by the enemy.[9] The latter case, by the way, highlights the far-reaching effects of prevailing ideology, shaping even the form of opposition to itself.

Outside the subjectivist fold and its internal polemics about different methods and answers, another type of question is raised by some authors who base themselves on liberal economic ideology and liberal economic theory. We might label it the *economic approach*. In the businessman's manner, the question here is not who, but *how much*. Power is regarded above all as a capacity to get things done. The primary emphasis is on "power to" rather than "power over" and the crucial question is not the distribution but the accumulation of power. As a theory of power the economic approach features two main variants, a sociological and a utilitarian. The main proponent of the former is Talcott Parsons. Parsons conceives power "as a circulating medium, analogous to money"[10] and defines it as "generalized capacity to secure the performance of binding obligations by units in a system of collective organization when the obligations are legitimized with reference to their bearing on collective goals and where in case of recalcitrance there is a presumption of enforcement by negative situational sanctions—whatever the actual agency of that enforcement."[11]

In the utilitarian "economic theories of democracy," little attention and consideration is allotted the phenomenon of power and its conceptualization. Politics is seen from the perspective of an "individualist theory of collective choice" and the meaning of power is then derived from the assumed blessings of market exchange. "This approach", write Buchanan and Tullock, "incorporates political activity as a particular form of *exchange;* and, as in the market relation, mutual gains to all parties are ideally expected to result from the collective relation. In a very real sense, therefore, political action is viewed essentially as a means through which the power of all the participants may be increased, if we define power as the ability to command things that are desired by men."[12]

Although they can be said to share a common approach to power, inspired by liberal economics, concentrating as they do on non-conflictual "power to",

---

9. The most important example is R. Miliband, *The State in Capitalist Society* (London: Weidenfeld & Nicolson, 1969). The polar opposite kind of Marxist stance is exemplified by N. Poulantzas, *Political Power and Social Class* (London: NLB, 1973). In a well-argued article the latter has been criticized for not coming to grips with, and thus not really revealing the weaknesses of, the problematic of his opponents: E. Laclau, "The Specificity of the Political: The Poulantzas-Miliband Debate", *Economy and Society* (1975), pp. 87–110. Although mainly restricted to a distinction between different approaches to the problem of power, the present article tries to take account of the criticisms of both Poulantzas and Miliband. At the same time I am indebted to them both for their very valuable contributions.

10. T. Parsons, "On the Concept of Political Power", in idem, *Sociological Theory and Modern Society* (New York: Free Press, 1967), p. 306.

11. Ibid., p. 308.

12. J. Buchanan-G. Tullock, *The Calculus of Consent* (Ann Arbor: Univ. of Michigan Press, 1962), p. 23. Anthony Downs' somewhat less sanguine view of power does not refer to "power over" either, but to unequal "power to", because of inequalities of information and income. A. Downs, *An Economic Theory of Democracy* (New York: Harper & Row, 1957), pp. 257–58.

the two main variants of the economic approach also show differences that are by no means insignificant. In the sociological variant, power is generated and operates in social relationships, whereas in the utilitarian conception it is basically a non-relational asset. In both the problem of class and power by and large disappears.

With little of the elaborate theoretical imagination of the above-mentioned authors, the economic approach to power has also been applied to the problems of political development and "modernization", above all by Samuel P. Huntington. Huntington starkly emphasizes the importance of the "accumulation of power" over the question of its distribution. He opens his book *Political Order in Changing Societies* by proclaiming, "The most important political distinction among countries concerns not their form of government but their degree of government. The differences between democracy and dictatorship are less than the differences between those countries whose politics embodies consensus, community, legitimacy, organization, effectiveness, stability, and those countries whose politics is deficient in these qualities."[13] "Modern political systems differ in the amount of power in the system, not in its distribution."[14] To Huntington it is the general liberal ideas about economic development, rather than liberal economic theory, which provides the model.

The third approach might be named a structural-processual approach. But with its focus on society as an objective structured totality and on contradiction, motion, and change, we had perhaps better call it the *dialectical-materialist approach,* embodied in the new scientific study of history and society founded by Marx, historical materialism. Here the primary focus is on the historical social contexts and modalities of power, and the first question is: *What kind of society is it?* Then: *What are the effects of the state upon this society,* upon its reproduction and change?

The central task of *Capital* was not to identify those who have the wealth and those who are poor, nor those who rule and those who are ruled, but, as the author pointed out in his preface, to lay bare "the economic law of motion of modern society." That is, Marx was above all interested in how wealth and poverty, domination and subjugation are being (re)produced and how this can be changed. The basic focus of study is on neither property nor the property owners but on capital, that is, on (particular historical) relations of production and their relationship to the productive forces and to the state and the system of ideas.

## II

This third approach to the problem of power in society owes its more roundabout character to the fact that it seriously and systematically tries to tackle two fundamental problems largely neglected by the other approaches. One concerns "power to", the other relates to "power over".

13. S. Huntington, *Political Order in Changing Societies* (New Haven: Yale Univ. Press, 1968), p. 1.

14. Ibid., p. 144.

One question which should be seriously faced is: Power to do what? What is a particular amount of power used for? The utilitarian answer—to maximize one's utility—is hardly very satisfactory in view of the enormous variety of historical social forms, and thereby systems, of power. For the same reason we do not learn very much from Parsons' discussion of power in terms of realization of "collective goals."[15] Nor should it be assumed *a priori,* or made a part of the definition, that, as Parsons contends, power is exercised "in the interest of the effectiveness of the collective operation as a whole",[16] rather than in the interest of the exploitation of one class by another.

What "power to" means depends on the kind of society in which it operates. A Marxist analysis of a given society first of all focuses on its mode(s) of production, its system(s) of relations and forces of production.

By determining the relations of production the Marxist analyst at the same time determines *if* there are classes in the given society and *what* classes there are, because classes in the Marxist sense are people who occupy certain positions in society as basically defined by the relations of production. If immediate production—in husbandry, agriculture, industry, transport, etc.—and the appropriation and control of the surplus produced are separated among different role incumbents, and are not united in an individual or in a collective, there are classes. And the different modes of separation (slavery, feudalism, capitalism, etc.) mean different classes.[17]

Determining the relations of production does not pertain only to the *context* of political power. It is also directly related to the question of power, since the separation between the immediate producers and the appropriators of the surplus product entails specific relations of domination and subordination.[18] Exploitative relations of production directly involve relations of domination, and in what may be called *the* key passage of Marx's materialist interpretation of history he says, "The specific economic form in which unpaid surplus labour is pumped out of the direct producers, determines the relation of domination and servitude, as it emerges directly out of production itself and in turn reacts upon production." Marx then continues and makes his basic proposition about the relationship between the economy and the polity (the meaning, truth and fruitfulness of which proposition is under debate): "Upon this basis, however, is founded the entire structure of the economic community, which grows up out

---

15. Parsons, op. cit., p. 308.

16. Ibid., p. 318.

17. I have developed an analysis of the Marxist concept of class in my *Klasser och ekonomiska system* (Staffanstorp: Cavefors, 1971). Cf. the first part of my 'Classes in Sweden 1930–70', in R. Scase, ed., *Readings in the Swedish Class Structure* (London: Hutchinson, forthcoming).

18. Power in a society should of course be studied not only in terms of the non-specific, extra-organizational power of organizational elites, but also in terms of the mode of organization itself, particularly the mode of organization of people's working lives, which differ both in the kind and the amount of domination and independence. However, the Marxist focus on exploitation and class is related to the discussion of power only in the broad sense of the latter, in the sense of A significantly affecting B in a situation of possible negative sanctions against B's non-compliance. The specification of power in terms of responsibility, choice, and agreement, and distinctions between fate, coercion, authority, manipulation, and power, are internal to a subjectivist discourse and as such are outside the Marxist analysis proper. The latter does not start from "the point of view of the actor" but from ongoing social processes.

of the conditions of production itself, and consequently its specific political form. It is always the direct relation between the masters of the conditions of production and the direct producers which reveals the innermost secret, the hidden foundation of the entire social edifice and therefore also of the political form of the relation between sovereignty and dependence, in short of the particular form of the state." [19]

For the adherents of the subjectivist approach, in both its pluralist and elitist variants, to raise the problem of "power to do what?" means to ask: *What do rulers do when they rule? Where do the leaders lead the led?* To say or imply that what rulers do when they rule is to maintain their ruling position is at best trivial— and not infrequently wrong. Intentionally and unintentionally what rulers do and do not do affects the ruled, and the same sort of power subjects—in terms of personal background and present interpersonal relations—may affect the ruled in very different ways. There are different effects under pluralism or elitism, different effects under, say, military governments and centralized "oligarchical" organizations. [20] And there are many ways for a ruling class to exercise and maintain its rule, other than by supplying, from its own ranks, the political personnel. It may therefore be argued that rulers and ruling classes would be better identified not by their names and numbers, their social background and power career—although all this is of course not without importance—but by their actions, that is by the objective effects of their actions. From this perspective, the Marxist interjects into the subjectivist discussion, polarized around democracy and dictatorship or, in its contemporary, somewhat lower-pitched versions, pluralism and elitism: democracy of what class, dictatorship of what class?

There is a second aspect to what rulers do when they rule. Talcott Parsons once made a famous critique of utilitarianism for its inability to account for social order. [21] What all kinds of subjectivist elite and ruling class theorists are unable to do is to account for *social change*. Characteristically enough, the classical elite theorists, who really thought out the consequences of their theories, all basically held that society did not change. Instead they drew a picture of an eternal cycle of rising, ruling, degenerating, and falling elites. This goes for all of them, Gumplowicz, Mosca, Pareto, and Michels. [22] Ultimately they tended to reduce people and human society to biology. [23] Now, though men certainly are biological organisms, it is an obvious fact that human society has changed over

19. K. Marx, *Das Kapital* (Otto Meissner, 1921), III:2, p. 324; T. Bottomore-M. Rubel, eds., *Karl Marx, Selected Writings in Sociology & Social Philosophy* (London: Watts & Co., 1956), p. 99.

20. Consider, for instance, the sterility of the Michels type of organizational theory when faced with the completely different behavior of Social Democratic and Communist parties in August 1914 and September 1939, respectively.

21. T. Parsons, *The Structure of Social Action* (New York: McGraw-Hill, 1937).

22. See G. Therborn, *Class, Science and Society* (Goteborg: Revopress, 1974), ch. 4.2; English edition, London: NLB, 1976 forthcoming (American distributor: Humanities Press).

23. Pareto "extended" the theory of class struggle into the thesis that "The struggle for life and welfare is a general phenomenon for living beings." V. Pareto, *Les Systemes Socialistes* (Paris, 1902–03), II, p. 455. Michels referred to the struggle between organized workers and strikebreakers in terms of "struggle for feeding-ground." R. Michels, *Political Parties* (Glencoe: Free Press, 1958), p. 307.

the ages of its existence and has taken a number of forms. The task of a social science must necessarily be to analyse these different historical forms and their change. This cannot be done by taking the subjects of power, their psyche, their will, as the starting point, but only by taking the social context in which they rule.

The society in which the rulers rule contains certain possibilities and tendencies of change. The rulers rule in a certain stage of development of a certain social structure, and their rule both affects and is affected by the tendencies and contradictions inherent therein. The subjectivists stop before analysing these tendencies and contradictions and typically conclude: Look, only a few have power, that is bad! Or: Look many have power, that is good! It should be noted that the important thing in this context of power and change is the effect of the rule—not directly upon individuals, nor upon the gains and handicaps it means for persons and groups[24]—but upon the social structure and social relationships in which the individuals live, because it is the latter, rather than the sheer fact of being handicapped or exploited, which determine the possibilities of change and revolt.

Besides the problem of "power to", there is also a very important neglected problem involved in "power over". Are the different moments of the exercise of somebody's power over somebody else related to each other? If we assume neither that social life is completely random and unpatterned, nor that it is a unified, consensual, collective operation, then how should the relationships be studied and how can they be grasped?

At first sight it might appear gratuitous to call this a neglected problem, as it is precisely what the substantial polemics between pluralists and elitists have been about. True to their common subjectivist core, however, the pluralists and the elitists have concentrated on a secondary aspect of the problem. What they have been debating is whether there is an *interpersonal* relation between the different moments of power in society: Is there a cohesive elite which unites the different exercises of power by making the decisions in different areas? Or is there a fragmentation of decision-making between different little or not-connected groups? What this formulation of the issue does not take into serious account is that an interpersonal fragmentation of decision-making does not necessarily mean that the different power events are random and unpatterned. On the contrary, it is a basic, and it seems, warranted, assumption of social science that the events in human society are in some ways always patterned, and therefore possible to grasp by scientific analysis. What the elitism-pluralism theorists have been doing, then, is to concentrate on the existence or non-existence of one possible form of the patterning of power in society—and, it should be added, on a form which hardly seems to be the most important one in modern complex societies.

Little is gained in answering this kind of objection by referring to another kind of interpersonal identity than that ensured by overlapping membership in cohesive power groups—by referring, that is, to a common identity of ideas, to

---

24. This is in contrast to the approach of Bachrach-Baratz, op. cit.

a consensus of values.[25] How is a particular kind of consensus and its maintenance to be explained[26], and how does it actually operate, so general and abstract as it tends to be in modern societies? What objective social structures and social relationships are brought about and/or maintained, how are people's lives patterned by the different exercises of supposedly consensual power?

Important methodological critiques of pluralism have been developed by Bachrach and Baratz[27], and most recently by Lukes[28], with their inclusion of institutional "mobilization of bias" and of "non-decisionmaking"[29], and in the case of Lukes, of latent conflicts and of the effects of inaction.[30] But they do not deal with the present problem, of "power over." In fact, the subjectivist orientation of these authors seems to preclude a way out for the elitists in this respect. What their refined methods can do is to detect more hidden manifestations of elite rule, but they can hardly find social patternings of exercise of power other than those of a unified power subject. With Bachrach-Baratz this is strongly implied by their conception of power, and its related concepts, as an interpersonal relation between A and B.[31] With Lukes it follows from the author's moralistic concern with responsibility. For this reason Lukes is uninterested in impersonal forms of domination and wants to concentrate on cases where it can be assumed that the exerciser(s) of power could have acted differently from how they did. And in this context he throws in a distinction between power and fate![32] To Lukes too, then, power should be analysed primarily with a view to

---

25. Dahl has written, " . . . democratic politics is merely the chaff. It is the surface manifestation, representing superficial conflicts. Prior to politics, beneath it, enveloping it, restricting it, conditioning it, is the underlying consensus . . . among a predominant portion of the politically active members." R. Dahl, *A Preface to Democratic Theory* (Chicago: Univ. of Chicago Press, 1956), p. 132. But what if "consensus" is the surface manifestation of something else, "enveloping, restricting and conditioning" electoral politics?

26. This is a weak spot in the otherwise well-substantiated critique of pluralist theses by Miliband (op. cit.). Miliband basically shrinks from really analysing governments whose personnel is not recruited from the economic elite, and where the higher echelons of the administration may also be recruited otherwise. In such cases he merely refers to the ideology of the political leaders as part of a bourgeois consensus (see ch. 4, part IV). He does provide some empirical material and suggestions for a study of the problem, but it is fundamentally outside his model of control. For the analysis of advanced bourgeois democracies, of reformism, fascism, and military governments, a more complex model seems crucial. Similarly, the important works of William Domhoff, on the haute-bourgeois backgrounds and connections of American politicians and administrators, and on the cohesiveness of the top-most stratum of the US bourgeoisie, would benefit from being located in a much more elaborate conceptualization and analysis of the US power structure and of the contradictory development of US society.

27. Bachrach-Baratz, op. cit. (1962, 1963, 1970).

28. S. Lukes, *Power: A Radical View* (London: Macmillan, 1974).

29. A nondecision means "a decision that results in suppression or thwarting of a latent or manifest challenge to the values or interests of the decision-maker," Bachrach-Baratz, op. cit. (1970), p. 44.

30. Lukes, op cit., chs. 4, 7. Lukes draws upon the work of Crenson, op. cit.

31. Bachrach-Baratz, op. cit. (1970), ch. 2.

32. Lukes, op. cit., pp. 55–56. Cf. Marx: "I paint the capitalist and the landlord in no sense couleur de rose. But here individuals are dealt with only in so far as they are the personifications of economic categories, embodiments of particular class-relations and class interests. My standpoint, from which the evolution of the economic formation is viewed as a process of natural history, can less than any other make the individual responsible for relations whose creature he socially remains,

finding subjects of power, identifiable, free, and responsible originators of acts (and nonacts). He seems to remain stuck within the pluralist-elitist framework, of either a unified elite or various elites or leadership groups (whose interrelationship as a relation of power over others remains obscure, unless they themselves are aware of their relationship).

Marx opened up a path out of the pluralist-elitist impasse, one which seems to have remained almost completely unnoticed among sociologists and political scientists, including writers who have explicitly referred to Marx, more or less critically. The radical novelty and dissimilarity to others of the Marxian approach seems to have been drowned in subjectivist receptions and reinterpretations. The way out indicated by Marx is that the study of a given society should be not just a study of its subjects nor of its structure only, but also and at the same time should be an inquiry into its process of *reproduction*. Significantly, it is in the study of the process of reproduction that Marx analyses the class relationships of exploitation and domination.

Capitalist production, therefore, under its aspect of a continuous connected process, of a process of reproduction, produces not only commodities, not only surplus-value, but it also produces and reproduces the capital relation; on the one side the capitalist, on the other the wage-labourer.[33] In a critique of the subjectivist conceptions of market exchange in 18th- and 19th-century economics Marx provided a critique in advance of 20th-century sociologists as well: "To be sure, the matter looks quite different if we consider capitalist production in the uninterrupted flow of its renewal, and if, in place of the individual capitalist and the individual worker, we view them in their totality, the capitalist class and the working-class confronting each other. But in so doing we should be applying standards entirely foreign to commodity production."[34]

For the study of power in society the perspective of reproduction means that the commanding question of all the variants of the subjectivist approach—Who rules, a unified elite or competing leadership groups? Is the economic elite identical with or in control of the political elite?—is displaced by the question: What kind of society, what fundamental relations of production, are being reproduced? By what mechanisms? What role do the structure and actions and nonactions of the state (or of local government) play in this process of reproduction, furthering it, merely allowing it, or opposing it?

The analysis of reproduction makes possible an answer to the question of how the different moments of the exercise of power in society are interrelated, even if there is no conscious, interpersonal interrelation. They are interrelated by their reproductive effects. A given kind of relations of production may be reproduced without the exploiting (dominant) class defined by them being in

---

however much he may subjectively raise himself above them." *Das Kapital,* I, p. viii; *Capital* (London: Lawrence & Wishart, 1970), vol. 1, p. 10. Marx's view certainly did not mean that the power of the capitalist was a fate to submit to, but something that could be combatted and abolished. It does mean, however, that it is rather pointless to accuse the capitalists of not behaving like non-capitalists. The Marxian standpoint implies, of course, that the arm of criticism is replaced by the criticism of arms (i.e., the class struggle in all its forms).

33. Marx, op. cit., I, p. 541; Lawrence & Wishart editions, I, p. 578.

34. Ibid., p. 549 and p. 586, respectively.

"control" of the government in any usual and reasonable sense of the word, even though the interventions of the state further and/or allow these relations of production to be reproduced. And yet the fact that a specific form of exploitation and domination is being reproduced, *is* an example of class rule and is an important aspect of power in society.

### III

In order to bring forth and make comparable, in a sociological context, the distinctive character of the Marxian departure it may be useful at this point to go back and take a fresh look at the classical source of sociological anti-Marxist inspiration in the fields of class, power, and stratification, a source still very important, that is, Max Weber's treatment of class, status, and power in *Economy and Society.* No comprehensive analysis is intended here; rather the intention is only to spell out the relationship between the Marxist problematic and what Weber was preoccupied with in these texts.[35] "Texts" in the plural, because Weber deals with class, status, and power twice in *Economy and Society,* both in the first (and latest written) part presenting his conceptual system, and in the second, elaborating part.[36] As concepts they are introduced separately: parties in the third chapter on *Herrschaft,* estates or "status groups" *(Stände)* and classes in a fourth chapter of their own. Later, however, they are treated together, in the same section of the chapter on political communities.

In one of the best available introductions to Weber, Gerth and Mills write about Weber's concept of class: "In locating the class problem in the market and in the streams of income and property, Weber points towards production and its modern unit, the capitalist enterprise." Herein, the authors imply, Weber concurred with Marx, whereupon they point to the additional contribution of Weber: "By making this sharp distinction between *class* and *status,* and by differentiating between types of classes and types of status groups, Weber is able to refine the problems of stratification to an extent which thus far has not been surpassed."[37] Basically the same view of Marx and Weber is presented by Giddens, although he has his own criticisms of Weber and Weber's theories about class. Giddens also thinks that Weber and Marx had the same conception of the market: "In clarifying some of these matters we may start from the premise, which is fundamental for both Marx and Weber: that, in capitalism, the market is intrinsically a structure of power, in which the possession of certain attributes advantages some groupings of individuals relative to others."[38] According to

---

35. For an attempt to grasp the core of Weber's sociology, and its historical context, see, e.g., my *Class, Science and Society,* ch. 5.3.3.

36. M. Weber, *Wirtschaft und Gesellschaft* (Koln and Berlin: Kiepenheuer & Witsch, 1964), vol. I, pp. 211–14, 223–27, and vol. II, pp. 678–89 (hereinafter WG). The former is included in T. Parsons, ed., *Max Weber, The Theory of Economic and Social Organization* (New York: Free Press, 1964), pp. 407–12, 424–29, and the latter in H. Gerth-C. W. Mills, eds., *From Max Weber* (New York: Oxford Univ. Press, 1958), pp. 180–95.

37. Gerth-Mills, op. cit., p. 69.

38. Giddens, op. cit., pp. 101–02. See the similar view of Frank Parkin in his *Class, Inequality and the Political Order* (London: MacGibbon & Kee, 1971), p. 31.

Giddens: "There are two principal respects in which this [Weber's] analysis differs from Marx's 'abstract model' of classes. One is . . . the differentiation of 'class' from 'status' and 'party'. The second . . . equally important . . . is that, although Weber employs for some purposes a dichotomous model which in certain general respects resembles that of Marx, his viewpoint strongly emphasizes a pluralistic conception of classes."[39]

However, a primary precondition for any understanding of Weber's view of stratification and power and for any comparison of Weber and Marx in this respect is the realization of the fact that Weber's notion of capitalism was a product coming out of very dissimilar sources: Austrian marginalist economics, German historicism and some Marxian elements, and above all the attention paid to a historical economic system called capitalism.[40] One of the effects of this interesting combination of influences is that latterday readers of Weber tend to take Weber's use of Marxian-ringing words, like class or capitalism, as Marxian concepts.

As Gerth-Mills and Giddens quite rightly point out, Weber defines class in terms of position in the market. Weber emphasized: "But always this is the generic connotation of the concept of class: that the kind of change in the *market* is the decisive moment which presents a common condition for the individual's fate. 'Class situation' is, in this sense, ultimately 'market situation'."[41] Now, it is sufficient only to read the first four chapters of *Capital* to see—if one's sight has been sharpened enough, and that is a difficult social process—that Marx's analysis struck quite another path. Towards the end of the fourth chapter Marx wrote, "The consumption of labour power is completed, as in the case of every commodity, outside the limits of the market of the sphere of circulation. Accompanied by Mr. Moneybags and by the possessor of labour-power, we therefore take leave for a time of this noisy sphere, where everything takes place on the surface and in view of all men, on whose threshold there stares us in the face 'No admittance except on business'. Here we shall see, not only how capital produces, but how capital is produced."[42]

The focus of the Marxian analysis is not the market and the relations of circulation but the relations of production. Marx does not conceptualize classes in terms of their bargaining power on the market but as the agents or "supports" of the relations of production in the process of social reproduction and change. To grasp the two principal classes of capitalist society, one has in Marx's view to grasp the "law of motion" of capital and wage-labour.[43] Only after fifty-one chapters of work hereupon did Marx embark upon an exposition of the concept of class, and, as is well known, there remains only an unfinished draft.

To Weber, on the other hand, classes are not agents of specific socio-economic mechanisms, but market subjects—though they are only potentially

---

39. Giddens, op. cit., p. 42. Emphasis omitted.

40. For substantiation of this assertion the reader is referred to *Class, Science and Society*.

41. Weber, *WG,* vol. II, p. 680; Gerth-Mills, op. cit., p. 183.

42. Marx, op. cit., I, p. 138, and I, pp. 176–76, respectively.

43. "The classes are an empty phrase if I am not familiar with the elements on which they rest, e.g. wage labour, capital, etc.", Marx wrote in his methodological Introduction in *Gundrisse* (Berlin: Dietz, 1953), p. 21; English edition, Hammondsworth: Penguin, 1973), p. 100.

aware of their common identity—endowed with, or with the lack of, certain properties or acquisitions, which give them certain chances in the market bargaining. The Weberian question for determining what class A belongs to is: *How much does he have* (i.e., of market resources)? Whereas Marx asks: *What does he do?* What is his position in the process of production? Weber's question of definition is in turn an answer to Weber's primary problem of class: *How much is he likely to get* (of "provision with goods", "external conditions of life", and "subjective satisfaction or frustration")?[44] But what Marx answers is: *What is he likely to do* (basically, to maintain the present society, or to change it)?[45]

It is against this strict definition of class in market terms that Weber's concept of status groups has to be understood. Weber does not really think of class and status as two different dimensions of stratification, of economic position and social status, but rather as opposites. The existence of status groups derives from non-capitalist societies, is contrary to market rationality, and its modern survival interferes with the free development of capitalism. "Those men whose fate is not determined by the chance of using goods or services for themselves on the market, e.g., slaves, are not, however, a 'class' in the technical sense of the term. They are, rather, a 'status group'."[46] "Acquisition classes are favoured by an economic system oriented to market situation, whereas social strata develop and subsist more readily where economic organization is of a monopolistic and liturgical character and where the economic needs of corporate groups are met on a feudal or patrimonial basis." A certain group may be both a class and a stratum, and Weber points out that "Property classes often constitute the nucleus of a stratum." But he continues, and his point is: "Every society where strata play a prominent part is controlled to a large extent by conventional rules of conduct. It thus creates economically irrational conditions of consumption and hinders the development of free markets by monopolistic appropriation and by restricting free disposal of the individual's own economic ability."[47] In the section on class, status, and party in the second part of *Economy and Society* Weber tells us: "Now 'status groups' hinder the strict carrying through of the sheer market principle. In the present context they are of interest to us only from this point of view."[48]

In Marxist terms the distribution of status honor is an aspect of the functioning of ideology in society. From this perspective the most important point in the context appears to be not as, for instance, Frank Parkin has seen it, that the distribution of status honor does not rest on "the moral evaluations of the population at large . . . but mainly [on] the evaluations of dominant class members"[49], although this is correct. Rather, the point is that the Weberian dichot-

---

44. Weber, *WG*, vol I, p. 223; Parsons, ed., op. cit., p. 424.

45. The Marxist conception of class and class struggle developed, from German Ideology and *The Communist Manifesto*, out of a confrontation with German Idealism and Utopian Socialism. It was a means of discovering agents and mechanisms of social change other than well-meaning intellectuals or secret conspirers and education and coups-d'état: namely the oppressed classes themselves and their struggle against the exploiting classes.

46. Weber, *WG*, vol. II, p. 680; Gerth-Mills, op. cit., p. 183.

47. Weber, *WG*, vol. I, p. 227; Parsons, ed., op. cit., p. 429.

48. Weber, *WG*, vol. II, p. 682; Gerth-Mills, op. cit., p. 185.

49. Parkin, op. cit. (1971), p. 42.

omy of market class and status honor, deriving from the dichotomy of feudalism and capitalism as neoclassical economic ideal types, hinders an analysis of the functioning of ideology in capitalist class societies. On the one hand, the role of ideology in the reproduction and the class struggles of capitalist societies is inherent and central rather than external and dysfunctional (as suggested by Weber's marginalism-inspired conception of capitalist rationality). On the other hand, there seems to be little basis for assuming *a priori* that the role that ideology actually plays is reducible to prestige stratification, or even that this would be a more important function than, say, structuring the visibility of performances and rewards, forming individual and collective self-confidence and aspirations, and channelling discontent. It could be argued from a Marxist point of view, then, that Weber's distinction between class and status attributes not too much but too little importance to the role of social values in the analysis of class.

"Now: 'classes', 'status groups', and 'parties' are phenomena of the distribution of power within the community."[50] Weber's famous section on class, status, and party is about a typology of different subjects of power. So we should expect Weber to illustrate the fatal flaw of the subjectivist approach to power identified above. Such is the case. At first, Weber might seem to present an appealing, circumspect, common-sensical view of parties in the "sphere of power": "In any individual case, parties may represent interests determined through 'class situation' or 'status situation', and they may recruit their following respectively from one or the other. But they need be neither purely 'class' nor purely 'status' parties. In most cases they are partly class parties and partly status parties, but sometimes they are neither."[51] While conceiving of politics as a "play of interests", Weber adds that it should be noted that "in this context 'interest' is by no means necessarily primarily an economic category. In the first instance, it is a matter of political interests which rest either on the ideological basis or on an interest in power as such."[52]

What this conception of parties and power amounts to is best exemplified by Weber's examinations of different kinds of parties, i.e., of power-seeking and powerholding subjects. "The classic example of pure patronage parties in the *modern* state are the two great American parties of the last generation. Examples of parties oriented to objective policies and systems of value were given, e.g., by the older type of conservatism, nineteenth century liberalism, and the old middle class democratic parties, later Social Democracy—in all there has been a very prominent element of class interest—and the Centre party. Since the Centre has attained the principal points of its original programme it has become very largely a pure patronage party."[53]

This view of political parties follows rather directly from Weber's conception of sociology: trying to understand the subjective meaning individuals at-

---

50. Weber, *WG,* vol. II, p. 679; Gerth-Mills, op. cit., p. 181.

51. Weber, *WG,* vol. II, p. 689; Gerth-Mills, op. cit., p. 194.

52. Weber, *WG,* vol. I, p. 212; Parsons, ed., op. cit., p. 408.

53. Weber, *WG,* vol. I, p. 213; Parsons, ed., op. cit., p. 410. Parsons' translation has been corrected, since the changed word order in this translation makes it possible to interpret Weber, wrongly, as referring to the prominence of class interest in the American parties as well.

tach to their actions.[54] As a contribution to an understanding of power in society it does not take us very far. To know that the American parties are pure patronage parties does not tell us anything of what kind of society it is that the politicians—brought into government through parties "solely concerned with the attainment of power for their leaders and with securing positions in the administrative staff for their own members (patronage parties)"[55]—contribute to maintaining and developing. The Weberian approach completely avoids an analysis of what the patronage parties effectively do with their patronage. Therefore it is not very illuminating as an approach to the distribution of power, neither in the USA after the Civil War (age of the "robber barons", the rise of populism, and the beginning of US imperialism), nor in Weimar Germany, as a contribution to an understanding of the role the Centre party was going to play in the Weimar coalition.

Largely out of the Weberian tradition there have developed two recent conceptualizations of class and power, one by W. G. Runciman and the other by Anthony Giddens.[56]

Runciman treats "systems of stratification" basically in terms of political power and of different answers to the question, Who rules? He points out that he does not "imply that the chicken-and-egg debate on the primacy of economic class and political power is to be settled in favour of the latter, for the question in this form does not admit this sort of answer." "But", he continues, "in a different sense, political power has necessarily to have precedence since all actual property relations are subject to the tacit consent of those whose access to the means of physical coercion would enable them to disturb such relations if they choose."[57] That is a misleading way of formulating the problem and a sterile way of handling it. From a social-scientific point of view the people who have access to the means of physical coercion should also be seen as part of and determined by an ongoing structured social process. What would they do if and when they happened to choose to disturb the property relations or the relations of production? Unless they ultimately failed to do anything there would be new relations of production. But where would the latter come from? Would it be a convincing social-scientific explanation to say that they would be chosen by the controllers of the means of repression? Or should they rather be explained—and the effects of possible disturbances be predicted—by the historical social context, fundamentally defined by the systems of relations and forces of production, in which the power subjects are placed? Of course, no mechanical effect is to be expected from this determination, but rather a specific range of options, which it seems that the analyst of class and power should systematically take into account.[58]

---

54. See Weber, WG, vol. I, pp. 4, 7; Parsons, ed., op. cit., pp. 88, 96.

55. Weber, WG, vol. I, p. 210; Parsons, ed., op. cit., p. 407.

56. Runciman, op. cit.; Giddens, op. cit.

57. Runciman, op. cit., pp. 62–63.

58. Marx's comment on the possible effects of conquest are relevant here. "In all cases of conquest three things are possible. The conquering people subjugates the conquered under its own mode of production (e.g., the English in Ireland in this century and partly in India); or it leaves the old mode intact and contents itself with a tribute (Turks and Romans); or reciprocal interaction takes

Runciman distinguishes six stratification systems, primarily on the grounds of the basis of power of the governing elite: property ownership, force and/or guile, ethnic group membership, technical expertise, position with bureaucracy, and role among leadership cadres.[59] How does he, then, deal with the problem of what the governing elite does when it governs? Very simply and straightforwardly, by brushing all difficult cases away, by assuming no international interaction among the remaining cases, and by predicting these remaining cases will carry on basically along the same lines as before. (Runciman illustrates his theory with five countries manifesting different combinations of his ideal types: "neocapitalist" Britain, "social-democratic" Sweden, "state socialist" Soviet Union, "revolutionary socialist" China, and "ethnocratic" South Africa. No particular logic is, correctly, attached to this five-country classification.) This is an appealing scientific modesty. Unfortunately, however, many people concerned with questions of power and class are confronted with somewhat less modest and less easily resolved problems.

For example: What will be the likely effects upon the systems of power in different capitalist countries, developed and underdeveloped, of foreseeable tendencies in the development of capitalism as an international system, i.e., in the development of the international system of capitalist relations and forces of production? Where will the military governments of Peru, Chile, Syria, Portugal, and Indonesia—all likely to be classified in Runciman's ideal types as based on force, although not any one of them necessarily on guile—lead their countries? Is it likely that they will all go in the same direction? How do we account for the rather different effects of the governing elites of China and Algeria, both of which seem to have to be classified as based on "role among leadership cadres" and "position with bureaucracy"?

Runciman does not just modestly leave important and difficult problems aside, but glosses over them with a quip: " . . . in capitalist society, the market functions as a state police, just as the party (or under certain conditions the army) functions as the capitalist class of socialist society."[60] Glossed over in this way are such real problems as: What will and can the forces of repression do if a leftwing government comes into power, e.g., in France, and tries to push through a program leading to socialism? Is it true or not that the Soviet Union is a state capitalist society? Is it true or not that the army in Egypt plays the role of capitalist class in the Egyptian economy? Modesty is seldom innocent.

As a broad, ambitious, and theoretically articulate contribution to the study of class, Giddens' work deserves a full-scale critical appraisal. Such an appraisal is beyond the scope of this paper, and I shall limit myself to some remarks about Giddens' conceptualization of the problem of class and power.

---

place, whereby something new, a synthesis arises (the Germanic conquest in part)." Grundrisse, p. 18; English edition, p. 97. Marx in this context deals with the relationship between production and distribution and his point is that the mode of production determines the mode of distribution even in the case of conquest: In the present context the point is that Marx also emphasizes that victorious violence takes place in a social context, which determines the effects of the violence and the control of the means of repression.

59. Runciman, loc. cit.

60. Runciman, op. cit., p. 64.

Giddens, who is here in large and respectable company, finds it hard to accept—in view of the complex market processes in a money economy—that exploitation is not just a distributive effect of capitalism but that capitalist production *is* (one historical form of) exploitation.[61] Significantly enough, Giddens' criticisms of Marx on this point are particularly crude and have nothing of the considered reflection of several of his other critical assessments of Marx.[62] Instead of exploitative relations of production Giddens takes, as his starting point for an analysis of classes, differences in market capacity of different individuals and groups, and he then focuses on the structuration of these differences into distinguishable classes.[63]

This has important consequences. Above all it means that classes are no longer analyzed as the supports of particular social structures and processes. They consist of individuals with different bargaining power on the market, and therefore with different life-chances. Thus Giddens formulates the problem of class and political power in an outrightly subjectivist way. To grasp the problem he locates it with the help of a typology of "elite formations and power in the class structure". The typology combines four dimensions: open/closed recruitment, high/low elite integration, broad/restricted range of issues over which power is exercised, consolidation/diffuseness in the sense of small/great control from below.[64] The reader will recognize the framework in which the pluralist-elitist debate has been taking place.

Giddens himself makes a stand in that debate, rallying, with some qualifications, to the side of the pluralists and against elitists such as Mills.[65] In Giddens' view, the United States is of all the Western countries the one which most closely approximates the case of an open, low-integrated elite, one whose power holds only over a restricted range of issues and is highly controlled from

---

61. Giddens, op. cit., pp. 95–96.

62. Giddens says, for instance, "For if the 'exploitative' character of capitalism is given in the extraction of surplus value from productive labour, then the abolition of exploitation in the classless society would apparently imply a return to a situation in which labour reaps the full reward of the value which it has created. But this is manifestly impossible, given the multiplicity of administrative functions . . ." (p. 96). Now, as Marx explicitly pointed out, surplus labour will always remain, being the basis of "civilization", but it does not need to take an antagonistic form, as a separation of the roles of producing and of appropriating the surplus product. They can be united in a collective social organization controlled by what Marx called "the associated producers". See, e.g., *Das Kapital*, III:2, pp. 354–5. Giddens then goes on to contend (p. 97): "Nothing in Marx's work indicates which mechanisms will control the 'rate' of extraction of surplus value in socialist society, and how accumulated value will be distributed." Apart from the confusion of surplus labour and surplus value in the quotation (the former will remain in a socialist society, the latter not), this statement just brushes aside the whole discussion and practice of the dictatorship of the proletariat in the Marxist tradition, from Marx's comments on the Paris Commune to the Cultural Revolution. Another crudity is the dismissal of Marx's observation on "the constantly growing number of middle classes"—that is, non-productive employees, not the petite bourgeoisie of independent shopkeepers and artisans—as "not (in) accord with the main weight of Marx's theoretical thinking" (p. 177). In fact, the observation on what had perhaps better be called the middle strata rather than middle classes, as they are not the supports of a particular relation of production, follows from the very theory of exploitation, for which Giddens has criticized Marx: the growth of the middle strata is directly related to the growth of the surplus product.

63. Giddens, op. cit., ch. 6.

64. Ibid., pp. 120ff.

65. Ibid., pp. 171, 175.

below.[66] Since there are other, equally subjectivist, answers to the question of power in the USA, it is hard to say what has been the effect of subjectivism and what has been the effect of liberal political ideology on Giddens, if one finds his thesis empirically completely unwarranted. To hold that the *only* advanced capitalist country which has never had a labor government, however reformist, which has never had a government elite even partially and temporarily drawn from the labor movement, and which has the lowest normal rate of voting at that, is the country with the *most* pluralistic and controlled elite, is hardly tenable. Nevertheless, certain effects of Giddens' neo-Weberian reconceptualization of class and power are clearly visible.

What appears to have caught and kept Giddens' attention is the relatively high rate of individual mobility into, and the possibly less intensive interpersonal relations among, the American *haute bourgeoisie,* in contrast to the aristocratic exclusiveness and stylized intercourse of the British.[67] Domhoff's research, however, makes this assumption about the American bourgeoisie rather dubious, or at least in need of careful qualification. What he does not pay attention to is the position in society of the bourgeois class, which individuals may move into and out of and in which the members may intermingle with each other or not. Position in society is defined (as above) not only by the economic strength and solidity of American capitalism, of which the bourgeoisie is the bearer, but also by the structural arrangements of the political system and the character of the dominant system of ideology in society. Since all this significantly affects the way people have to live their lives, and the relations of domination and subordination in society, Giddens' way of conceiving the problems of state and society and of class and power seems rather sterile, and at worst positively misleading.

## IV

The limited aim of this paper is to distinguish between different approaches to the problem of class and power, particularly between the dialectical-materialist (Marxist) approach and the variants of the subjectivist approach. Such a distinction seems important in order to open up possibilities for the application of the specific Marxist approach, given the fatal flaws of the prevailing subjectivist one. The distinction is particularly important at the present juncture in the social sciences, where, in spite of a renewed interest in and acknowledgement of Marx, an evaluation of the truth and fertility of Marxist theory tends to be made impossible by the amalgams currently fashionable in post-1968 sociology. In such eclectic constructions—which appear to be made according to a recipe like, one part Marx, two parts Weber, and two parts more recent sociology (including ingredients supplied by the cook himself), seasoned with differing amounts

---

66. Giddens thinks, however, that the USA "is probably more accurately classified" as possessing an elite closed rather than open in recruitment, although she "approximates much more closely than any European society" an openly recruited elite as well. Op. cit., pp. 171 and 120.

67. Ibid., pp. 166–67.

of hot (radical) and mild (liberal) spices—the distinctly Marxist analysis is drowned.

With such an aim, the present paper is not a direct contribution to the study of class and power. But within this limitation I will finally try to indicate a few guiding threads for a Marxist type of empirical investigation of the problem of class and power. That only rather general and tentative guiding threads will be offered reflects, I think, not only the limitations of the present paper and of its author, but also the fact that Marx opened up a radically new scientific path, to be constantly cleared of the lush vegetation of dominant ideologies, and on which only the very first steps in the direction of systematic theory have been taken.

The primary object of empirical study, for a grasp of the relations of class, state, and power, should be neither interpersonal relations between different elites (for instance, the government and the business elites), nor their social backgrounds, nor issues and decisions and non-decisions—although all this is important. The primary object should be the effects of the state on the (re)production of a given (whether found or hypothesized) mode (or modes) of production. The relations of domination entailed by the relations of production are concentrated in the state. Through the state the rule of the ruling class is exercised. The character of this rule has to be grasped from the effects of the state. There are two aspects to these effects: *what* is done (and not done) through the state, and *how* things are done that are done through the state. Therefore to direct our investigations and to locate and evaluate our findings we need a quite different typology of power systems than that supplied by, for instance, the elitists and the pluralists, or by Giddens and Runciman. We need a *typology of state interventions* and a *typology of state structures*.

The typology of state structures should distinguish among the differential effects (of legislative, administrative, and judiciary arrangements and procedures, of mechanisms of governmental designation, of organization of army and police, etc.) upon the extent to which the state can be used by different classes—that is, their effects on whether and to what extent the rule of a given class of people (with certain characteristics and qualifications as defined by their position in society) can operate through the state structure under investigation.[68] In this way broad types of state structures can be identified and distinguished in terms of their class character, for example feudal states, bourgeois states (in which Weberian bureaucracy is a prominent feature), and proletarian states (in which the principle of "politics in command", as realized in soviets, workers' parties, mass movements of cultural revolution, etc., seems to be a central characteristic). Various specific state apparatuses, such as legislative

---

68. This seems to indicate a way out of the dilemma posed by Claus Offe in his very penetrating essay, 'Klassenherrschaft und politisches System. Zur Selektivität politischer Institutionen', in his *Strukturprobleme des kapitalistischen Staates* (Frankfurt: Suhrkamp, 1972). This is an "objectivist" approach to the problem of the selectivity of the state, but it is not based on any definitions of the objective interests of the revolutionary class, which Offe rejects (p. 86). Neither does it mean that an empirical inquiry into the class character of the state only can be made post festum, as Offe concludes (p. 90), when the class struggle has developed to the point where the limits of a given state appear.

bodies, the judiciary, or the army, could also be studied from this point of view. It should of course not be assumed that a concrete state at a specific point in time necessarily has a homogeneous class character in all its institutions—which raises the problem then of how to establish its dominant class character.

To study the process by which the state actually operates we also have to have a typology of state interventions (including non-interventions significant to the (re)production of given relations of production). Such a typology could be almost endlessly refined. Basically, however, it should comprise two dimensions. One concerns what is done, and the other how it is done. In other words, one refers to the external effects of state intervention on other structures of society, above all on the relations of production, (but also on the ideological system), and the other refers to the internal effects upon the state itself. State intervention can either further, merely allow, or go against, and at the limit break, given relations of production.

And they can either increase, maintain, or go against, and at the limit break, given relations of political domination as embodied in the character of apparatuses of administration (and government) and repression. (The possibilities of successfully breaking given relations of production are fundamentally determined by the particular stage of the relations and forces of production, and the stage of the relations of force between classes which this implies.) The following table illustrates the types of state intervention possible along these two dimensions.

| Effect upon given relations of political domination (Structure of administration and repression) | Effect upon given relations of production | | |
|---|---|---|---|
| | Further | Allow | Go against/ Break |
| Increase | 1 | 2 | 3 |
| Maintain | 4 | 5 | 6 |
| Go against/ Break | 7 | 8 | 9 |

This typology can be applied both to a given political measure, such as a social security program, nationalization, a land reform, a school reform, etc., and to the sum of actions undertaken by a given government over a given period. It is in this way that the class character, in the Marxist sense, of a regime or a policy is to be ascertained. For example, a nationalization act or a land reform can allow and even further capitalist relations of production if it is carried out through the rules of the capitalist game, involving compensation more or less at market value, implementation through the established legislative and administrative procedure, and the creation of enterprises run by new owners using wage labor for profit (or for subsidizing other enterprises run for profit). But such measures can also be put into effect in the opposite manner, without necessarily meaning the complete abolition of capitalism in the society. A regional policy can be carried out with the help of various kinds of subsidies, such as tax rebates, to capitalist enterprises, thus following the logic of capitalist relations of production but making a certain localization of plants more profitable. But the same measure can also go against that logic, through mandatory planning. The class character is determined on the basis of the identity of the dominant (exploiting) class (i.e., the dominant class of the particular relations of production furthered or allowed by the interventions). If there is a discrepancy in the effects upon the relations of production and the structure of the state, this indicates a contradictory and unstable situation. For instance, in the case of the last period of Czarist Russia, the state furthered the developing capitalist relations of production while at the same time basically maintaining a largely pre-capitalist form of state; Soviet Russia in the 1920's allowed capitalist relations of production to develop while maintaining a proletarian dictatorship; and the Allende regime in Chile partly allowed, partly went against, capitalist relations of production while maintaining the existing state structure (its administration, judiciary, and army).

It should be underlined that, as a rule, there are a number of ways in which given relations of production can be furthered in a given situation. Opinions therefore usually differ over which is the best one. Consequently, a given state intervention may very well go against the current opinion of business organizations, but still further capitalist relations of production. The bourgeoisie as a class, and its interests, are not identical with the identity or ideas of a particular group of business leaders at a particular point in time. From this perspective we can understand the pattern that frequently appears in capitalist politics, wherein policies, when first introduced, are opposed by business groups and conservative parties, but once carried out, are accepted by them, with longer or shorter delay (e.g. collective bargaining, social security programs, Keynesian economics). This phenomenon is hidden by the issues-and-decisions approach of the pluralist methodologists.

*The ruling class* of a given society is the exploiting class of that exploitative system of relations of production furthered (above others, if there are other relations of production in the society) by the content and form of the totality of state interventions during a given period. The ruling class need not necessarily be the economically dominant class, in the sense of the exploiting class of the dominant mode of production in a society where there are several modes of production (e.g., self-subsistence farming, feudalism, petty commodity production, capitalism).

One possible refinement of the typology is to distinguish among their effects on the two different classes (exploiting and exploited) that bear the exploitative relations of production that the interventions in question further, allow, or go against. For instance reformist governments usually are to be found in squares 4 and 5 in the table above—although certain of their measures will be found in 1 and 2, as for example anti-strike measures—but a more refined typology would direct the study to their possible effects on the *relations of distribution within the given relations of production*. Another refinement, as regards the effects on the state, would be to differentiate between the class effects on the *administrative* and on the *repressive* apparatuses of the state. Fascist regimes, analyzed in terms of their effect on capitalist relations of production, belong in square 1, but they are more closely characterized within that type by their increase in the repressive apparatus of the bourgeois state.[69] A third elaboration would be to distinguish between effects of the state on different fractions of capital, e.g., industrial versus banking (or commercial or agrarian) capital, domestic versus foreign capital, big (monopoly) versus small capital. In this way different hegemonic fractions of the bourgeoisie can be identified.

What the ruling class does when it rules, in the Marxist sense, then, is not to make, as a compact unit, all important decisions in society. The rule of the ruling class is exercised by a set of objectively interrelated but not necessarily interpersonally unified mechanisms of reproduction, through which the given mode of exploitation is reproduced. The ruling class, in this sense, is not a unified power subject. The rule of the ruling class is not necessarily, and is usually not, expressed in conscious collective decisions and actions by the class as a whole. What the ruling class does when it rules is not primarily a matter of subjective intentions and actions. Its rule is embodied in an objective social process, through which a certain mode of production is maintained and expanded, guaranteed and furthered by the state. This means that the pluralist–elitist debate does not pertain to the existence of a ruling class in the radically different Marxist sense. What that debate is concerned with are certain aspects of the mode of organization of the ruling class, such as its cohesion.

It should be noticed that neither the existence of a ruling class, nor what class is the ruling class, nor the amount of its power, are defined here a priori. What classes there are has to be uncovered by an analysis of the relations of production in a given society. The ruling class has to be identified and the amount of its political power, the range of its rule, has to be ascertained by a study of the structure and the interventions of the state. The dialectical-materialist approach to power in society is an empirical approach, although of a quite different kind. Having located the ruling class, another task is then to lay bare the mechanisms of its rule, which includes finding an answer to why the actual interventions of the state function as such mechanisms.

The state power of the ruling class is part of the total reproduction process of society. As Poulantzas[70] has pointed out, there are two aspects of reproduction (and it should be added of revolution as well): the reproduction of the positions of the given social structure, and the reproduction of individuals who can occupy them. For example, capital, wage labor, and capitalist enterprise have to be reproduced, as does the state apparatus. The reproduction of position also involves, at least in the long run, the production and reproduction of a compatibility between the different levels of the social structure. The reproduction of capitalism requires not only the reproduction of capitalist enterprise but in the long run the reproduction of a compatible capitalist state as well.

But also, new generations of individuals—and the given individuals year in

---

69. Fascism is also distinguished by its furthering of monopoly capitalist relations of production, which points to still another distinction in terms of fractions of classes furthered or disadvantaged by the state interventions. Cf. N. Poulantzas, *Fascism and Dictatorship* (London: NLB, 1974).

70. N. Poulantzas, 'On Social Classes', *New Left Review* 78 (1973), p. 49.

and year out—have to be trained to occupy the given positions, to be qualified or subjected to fulfill adequately the tasks provided by the social structure. Out of the new-born infants a given proportion have to be reared to become owners and managers of capital, other portions to become workers, white collar employees, and administrative and repressive personnel, or petty-bourgeois farmers, shop-keepers, and artisans.

What broad types of mechanisms of reproduction—within which we can seek and find the concrete mechanisms in concrete societies—can be identified? One of primary importance is, of course, economic constraint. Economic constraint functions, in ways laid bare by specific economic analysis, in and through the stage of the productive forces, the inherent dynamics of the relations of production, and the interdependence of the forces and relations of production. It operates on various levels and decisively affects both the reproduction of positions and of the agents to occupy them. A given level of the development of the productive forces excludes certain relations of production, makes them untenable or obsolete and non-competitive; and the necessity for some kind of material reproduction then favors certain other relations of production, and determines the range of political options, such as for the Bolshevik government after the civil war. On a lower level, economic constraint imposes certain limits upon what a capitalist corporation or a feudal manor can do to stay in business, limits for instance on the extent to which one corporation or manor can tamper with the capitalist and feudal relations of production governing other corporations or manors. Economic constraint operates in a constant process to reproduce a certain structure of economic positions, by sanctions of bankruptcies, unemployment, poverty, and sometimes outright starvation. Economic constraint is an important mechanism for keeping even revolutionarily-conscious peasants and workers in line and harnessing them for the reproduction of the society they would like to overthrow.

Another important type of mechanism of reproduction is political, and includes two basic subtypes, administration and repression, which in modern societies are both regularly concentrated in a distinct state apparatus (or, rather, system of state apparatuses). Through administrative interventions—taxation, regulations, subsidies, countercyclical policies, etc.—the reproduction of a certain mode (or modes) of production is favored or hindered. Administration also functions in the reproduction of agents for the positions of the given modes of production, through such things as manpower policies (from binding peasants to their landlords to stimulating labor market mobility) and social security policies (from providing dreaded workhouses to supplying social security benefits, which function both to alleviate dangerous discontent and to stimulate business). Administrative interventions operate to ensure the overall compatibility of the substructures of society. The mechanism of administration also includes mechanisms for the reproduction of the state apparatus itself, embodied in constitutional provisions, procedures for the due handling of issues, or legal conceptions. These can hinder a government which may intend on far-reaching social change, or can restrict the accessibility to the state of certain classes or sections of classes.

Repression is the other important political mechanism of reproduction. The development or maintenance of certain modes of production can be repressed by the army, the police, prisons, or the executioner. Movements of opposition can be repressed in various ways and degrees. (One interesting and neglected object of study in this respect concerns to what extent the development of the labor movement in the United States has been stopped by repression, especially after World War I and World War II.) Individuals who refuse to accept any of the given positions can be taken care of, for instance in prisons or in mental hospitals.

Mechanisms of reproduction, then, are not only, nor even mainly, ideological, as sociologists are prone to assume.[71] But ideological mechanisms are of course important too. Their primary role is not in legitimating the prevailing system,[72] but rather in a differential shaping of aspirations and self-confidence and in a differential provision of skills and knowledge. This process of qualification and subjection, in which little human animals are formed into members of different classes, takes place in a number of ideological apparatuses: the family, the educational system, the church, the mass media, on-the-job training, and the workplace (where so much of the inculcation of hierarchy and

---

71. Parsons treats the problem of reproduction or "pattern-maintenance" solely in terms of transmission of values. For a relatively recent formulation see T. Parsons, *The System of Modern Societies* (Englewood Cliffs, N.J.: Prentice-Hall, 1971), pp. 10–15. Similarly all "social sources of stability" singled out by Parkin (op. cit., 1971, ch. 2) refer to ideological mechanisms: mobility, the educational system, religion, gambling, and the fostering of beliefs in luck. A noteworthy exception is H. F. Moorhouse's interesting account of the political and economic constraints imposed upon the British working class up to 1918 and their role in shaping later working class "deference", in his "The Political Incorporation of the British Working Class: An Interpretation," *Sociology* 7 (1973), pp. 341–59. See also the discussion by R. Gray, "The Political Incorporation of the Working Class," *Sociology* 9 (1975), pp. 101–04; H. F. Moorhouse, "On the Political Incorporation of the Working Class: Reply to Gray," ibid., pp. 105–10. See footnote 72, on the concentration (in the discussion of social reproduction) on legitimation, a preoccupation coming out of the Weberian tradition.

72. To identify the ideological mechanisms of reproduction with the processes of legitimation would imply that people do not revolt against the given rule under which they live because they regard it as legitimate. This seems hardly warranted. People may not revolt, political and economic constraints aside, because they do not know the kind of domination they are subjected to. That is, they may be held ignorant not only of its negative features but of its positive claims and achievements as well. They may be ignorant of alternatives, or they may feel themselves incapable of doing anything about it, even if they know of other possible types of societies. But this ignorance, disinterest, and lack of confidence are not simply there, as characteristics of certain individuals and groups, they are produced by definite social processes. See the important distinction between pragmatic and normative acceptance made by Michael Mann, "The Social Cohesion of Liberal Democracy," *American Sociological Review* 35 (1970), pp. 423–39. The one-eyed concentration on legitimation is often related to a normative conception: that every rule should be based on the true and knowing consensus of the ruled, thereby holding it legitimate. See, for instance, J. Habermas, *Legitimationsprobleme im Spatkapitalismus* (Frankfurt: Suhrkamp, 1973), esp. pp. 162 ff. But that is another question. Interestingly enough, Habermas and Offe both accept Weber's ideal type of competitive capitalism, against which they contrast modern capitalism with its enormously increased amount of state interventions, supposedly making more ideological legitimation necessary (Habermas, op. cit., Ch. II.; Offe, "Tauschverhaltnis und politische Steuerung. Zur Aktualitat des Legitimationsproblems," in Offe, op. cit., pp. 27–63). This view tends to veil the important role of ideology in the era of competitive capitalism—the era of human rights declarations, of the ascendance of bourgeois nationalism, and of still-strong established and dissenting religions—and to veil as well the economic and political mechanisms of crisis and revolution in the present period, a period which has witnessed the shattering of the economic foundations of the British Empire and is witnessing the shaking of the supremacy of the United States.

discipline takes place).[73] These apparatuses and the dominant ideological formation which takes place in them, are not necessarily congruent with each other. One particularly problematic relationship is that between the family and other apparatuses, such as the church and (above all in modern capitalism) the educational system. On the one hand, the family is an important mechanism of reproduction; but on the other, a certain amount of individual mobility is crucial to the reproduction of the system. For individual mobility implies that the commanding positions are occupied by more competent persons, as well as offering an obvious channel of discontent. As Marx pointed out, referring both to capitalist enterprise and to the Catholic Church of the Middle Ages: "The more a ruling class is able to assimilate the most prominent men of the dominated classes the more stable and dangerous is its rule."[74] Whereas Giddens, for instance, holds that, "Differential access to the educational system . . . is thus a central (and typical) mode of class exploitation,"[75] the Marxist perspective notes rather that rigidly differentiated access to the educational system tends to make exploitation *less* stable. In the Marxist perspective, what is most important to the reproduction of exploitation is not differential access to the educational system, but the differential educational system itself. Mobility, then, is essentially an ideological mechanism of reproduction. So also is another phenomenon dear to all subjectivists, interpersonal intercourse, which contributes to a common outlook among the representatives of different constituencies.

Through these mechanisms of reproduction the ruling class can exercise its rule and keep state power without necessarily having to supply the political and administrative personnel. The economic laws of motion of a given society set a very high threshold for their possible trespass by politicians. The structural arrangements of the state (its class character) circumscribe the state interventions decided upon by the government. The ideological mechanisms of reproduction shape both the politicians—even labor politicians with no personal intercourse with the bourgeois cream—and the population at large, including the exploited classes.

All these mechanisms operate in and through the conflict and struggle of classes. Class struggle then does not mean, even mainly, battles between unified, self-conscious entities. It means conflict and struggles between people who occupy different positions in exploitative modes of production.

Reproduction and revolution, consequently, are not to be understood in terms of mechanisms of reproduction versus class struggle. The reproductive mechanisms also produce, at the same time, mechanisms of revolution. To realize this is, of course, a basic feature of a dialectical approach. Marx analyzed, for instance, how the expanded reproduction of capital also meant the develop-

---

73. See the very important essay by Louis Althusser, "Ideology and Ideological State Apparatuses (Notes towards an Investigation)," in his *Lenin and Philosophy and Other Essays* (London: NLB, 1971), pp. 121–273. For unconvincing reasons, however, Althusser talks of ideological state apparatuses.

74. Marx, *Das Kapital*, III:2, p. 140; Bottomore-Rubel, op. cit., p. 190.

75. Giddens, op. cit., p. 131.

ment of contradictions between the relations and the forces of production. That analysis might be extended to the political and ideological processes of reproduction. For example, the strengthening of the state—and with it the strengthening of administrative and repressive operations of the state—which characterizes the modern, imperialistic state of capitalism, has been accompanied by more devastating contradictions among capitalist states. The two world wars of the 20th century gave rise to non-capitalist regimes among a third of humanity. Similarly, at the ideological level, the role of the intelligentsia, both in old Russia and China and recently in the advanced capitalist societies, testifies to the fact that the mechanism of qualification and subjection might also take on the character of a revolutionary mechanism, developing a contradiction between qualification and subjection. There are also mechanisms of revolution which operate in and through the class struggle. And, looked at from the other side of the same coin, the class struggle is fought in and through mechanisms of reproduction and revolution. But all that is another part of the story, and, maybe, part of another paper.

# · 12 ·

# Theses on the Theory of the State

## Claus Offe and Volker Ronge

The following notes give a brief outline of some of the theoretically relevant findings which the authors have made in two empirical studies of reformist state policies in West Germany.[1] These studies were concerned with the reform of vocational training and with a new programmatic approach to research and development policies. We believe that such case studies of certain state policies in specific policy areas are necessary to gain both theoretical understanding and political perspectives which cannot be gained either through deductive reasoning or immediate experience. For the sake of convenience, the organization of the argument is divided into eight points. These remarks are intended to provoke discussion and debate and are, of course, tentative in nature.

1. In Marxist theories of the state, there is a cleavage between two approaches. One approach suggests that there is a particular *instrumental* relationship between the *ruling class* (capital as a whole) on the one side and the state apparatus on the other side. The state thus becomes an instrument for promoting the common interests of the ruling class. We believe that this view is gravely misleading—including the version that is offered in the doctrine of "state monopoly capitalism" with its stereotyped proposition of a "merger of the monopolies and the state apparatus." The alternative view is that the state does not patronize certain interests, and is not allied with cer-

---

· From *New German Critique* 6 (1975): 139–47.

[1See Claus Offe, *Berufsbildungsreform* (Frankfurt: Schukamp, 1975)—eds.]

tain classes. Rather, what the state protects and sanctions is a set of *rules* and *social relationships* which are presupposed by the class rule of the capitalist class. The state does not defend the interests of one class, but the *common* interest of all members of a *capitalist class society.*

2. The concept of the *capitalist state* describes an institutional form of political power which contains the following four major elements:

   (a) Political power is prohibited from organizing production according to its own political criteria; property is *private* (be it property in labor power or property in means of production). Hence, it is not from political power, but from private freedom that decisions over the use of the means of production emerge.

   (b) Political power depends indirectly—through the mechanisms of taxation and dependence on the capital market—on the volume of private accumulation. The occupant of a power position in a capitalist state is in fact powerless *unless* the volume of the accumulation process allows that individual to derive the material resources (through taxation) necessary to promote any political ends.

   (c) Since the state *depends* on a process of accumulation which is beyond its power to *organize,* every occupant of state power is basically interested in promoting those conditions most conducive to accumulation. This interest does not result from alliance of a particular government with particular classes also interested in accumulation, nor does it result from any political power of the capitalist class which "puts pressure" on the incumbents of state power to pursue its class interest. Rather, it does result from an *institutional self-interest* of the state which is conditioned by the fact that the state is *denied* the power to control the flow of those resources which are indispensable for the *use* of state power. The agents of accumulation are not interested in "using" the power of the state, but the state must be interested—for the sake of its own power—in guaranteeing and safeguarding a "healthy" accumulation process upon which it depends.

   (d) In democratic political regimes, any political group or party can win control over institutional state power only to the extent that it wins sufficient electoral support in general elections. This mechanism plays a key role in disguising the fact that the material resources of state power, and the ways in which these are used, depends upon the revenues derived from the accumulation process, and not upon the preferences of the general electorate. There is a dual determination of political power in the capitalist state: by its institutional *form* access to political power is determined through the rules of democratic and representative government, by its material *content,* the use of political power is controlled by the course and the further requirements of the accumulation process.

3. Is there any method by which these divergent constitutional requirements of the capitalist state can be reconciled through the policies of a particular government? Yes, there is *one*. If the conditions can be created through which *every* citizen becomes a participant in *commodity relationships,* all of the four structural elements of the capitalist state are taken into account. As long as every owner of a unit of value can successfully exchange his/her value as a commodity, there is no need for the state to intervene in economic decision making; there is no lack of material resources needed by the state; there is no problem in maintaining a steady process of accumulation (which is only the net result of equivalent exchange between the owners of capital and the owners of labor power); and there is no problem in maintaining political support for a political party which manages to create this universe of commodities. It is only to the extent that values fail to operate in the commodity form that the structure of the capitalist state becomes problematic. The commodity form is the general point of equilibrium of the capitalist state. At the same time, accumulation takes place as long as every value appears in the form of a commodity. The link between the political and the economic structure of capitalist society is the commodity form. Both substructures depend upon the universalization of this form for their viability.

4. The key problem, however, lies in the fact that the dynamics of capitalist development seem to exhibit a constant tendency to *paralyze* the commodity form of value. Values cease to exist in the commodity form as soon as they cease seeking exchange for money or other values. To be sure, in an economic world consisting of commodities one can never be certain that one particular item offered on the market for sale will actually find a buyer. But in this simple case the failure of a value offered for exchange is supposed to be *self-corrective:* the owner of the exchange-seeking value will either be forced to lower the price or to offer an alternative good the use value of which does have higher chances of being bought. At least in the world of Jean Baptiste Say, an economy consisting of commodities is self-perpetuating: the failure of a good as a commodity leads to other goods less likely to fail. Similarly, parts of labor and parts of capital which are, as it were, temporarily thrown out of the commodity form in the course of an economic depression, create, through the very fact of their idleness, the preconditions for a new boom (at least if there is downward flexibility of prices). The functioning of this "healthy" self-corrective mechanism, however, does not seem to be the regular case, particularly in advanced capitalist societies. Marxist economic theory has developed various, though controversial, theorems which could explain such failure of self-corrective mechanisms. For example, it is assumed that monopolization of the economy leads to downward inflexibility of prices on the one side, and, to a constant flow of what Baran and Sweezy have called "surplus profit" on the other, i.e., monopolistic profits unsuc-

cessfully in search of investment outlets. Another explanation is based on the increasingly social character of production in capitalism. This means increasing division of labor within and among capitalist enterprises, hence increased specialization of every single unit of capital and labor, and hence diminished flexibility and adaptivity to alternative uses. Thirdly it has been argued that the periodic destruction of large parts of value through unfettered economic crises is by itself a healthy economic mechanism which will improve chances for the remaining values to "perform" as commodities, but that the conflict associated with such "cleansing off" of superfluous values tend to become explosive to the extent that they have to be prevented by state intervention and Keynesian policies.

Whatever may be the correct and complete explanation, there is plenty of everyday evidence to the effect that both labor and capital are thrown out of the commodity form, and that there is little basis for any confidence that they will be reintegrated into exchange relationships automatically.

5. It is equally evident that the most abstract and inclusive common denominator of state activities and state intervention in advanced capitalist societies is to *guard the commodity form of individual economic actors*. This, again, does not directly mean guarding the general interests of a particular class, but guarding the general interest of all classes on the basis of capitalist exchange relationships (*"Tausch als universale Verkehrsform"*). For instance, it would be mistaken to argue that state policies of education and training are designed to provide the necessary manpower for certain industries, since no one, least of all the state bureaucracy, has any reliable information as to what industry will need what type of skills at what time, or in what numbers. Such policies are instead designed to provide a *maximum of exchange opportunities* to both labor and capital, so that individuals of both classes can enter into capitalist relationships of production with each other. Likewise, research and development policies designed and funded by the state are by no means directed towards concrete beneficiaries (e.g., industries which can use the resulting technologies, or users of specific "civilian" technologies). These policies are designed to open up new markets, to shield the domestic economy against the intrusion of foreign competitors—briefly, to create and maintain the commodity form of value, in whose absence values become non-existent in a capitalist society.

6. The overwhelming concern of all state policies with the problem of guarding the commodity form of value is a relatively *new strategy* which in some capitalist states, like the U.S., is still subject to substantial political and ideological controversies. What are the alternative strategies open to the state in order to deal with the structural problem of failure of values to perform as commodities? The most "ancient" method seems to be *inaction*, i.e., hoping for the self-corrective mechanism in the course of which those units of value that

have dropped out of the commodity form are supposed to return to the market. The assumption is that the more unpleasant unemployment (of labor or capital) is, the sooner the owners of those values will return to the marketplace. The flaw in this logic lies, however, in trusting that owners of values do *not* have another option than to return to the commodity form. They do in fact have such options, of which emigration, delinquency and political revolt are only a few historical examples.

The second method is *subsidies and alimentation*. In this case, those owners of labor power and owners of capital who have lost their chance to participate in exchange relationships are allowed to survive under conditions artificially created by the state. Their economic existence is protected although they have dropped out of the commodity form, or they are prevented from dropping out because they are granted a claim for income derived from sources other than the sale of value. The problem with this "welfare state" type of dealing with "decommodified" values is that it becomes too costly in fiscal terms, thus sharpening the fiscal crisis of the state. Subsidizing the owners of values that have become obsolete as commodities is particularly costly for the state because it implies a category of expenditures which are by no means self-financing. They do not increase, but rather diminish the basis of future state revenues.

On the basis of these considerations, we wish to argue that the more and more dominant, more and more exclusive strategy of the capitalist state is to solve the problem of the obsolescence of the commodity form by *creating* conditions under which values can function as commodities. More specifically, these attempts develop in three directions: first, the saleability of *labor power* is enhanced through measures and programs directed towards education, training, regional mobility and general adaptivity of labor power. Second, the saleability of *capital* and manufactured goods is enhanced through transnational integration of capital and product markets, research and development policies, regional development policies, etc. Third, those *sectors of the economy* (which can be specified by industry, by region, by labor market segments) which are unable to survive within the commodity form on their own strength are allowed by plan to fall victim to market pressures and at the same time they are urged to modernize, i.e., to transform themselves into "marketable" goods. We suggest that the term *"administrative recommodification"* might be an appropriate label for this most advanced strategy of the capitalist state; it is basically different from both the "laissez faire" and "welfare state-protective" types of strategy sketched out above.

7. Policies which pursue the goal of reorganizing, maintaining and generalizing exchange relationships make use of a specific sequence of *instruments*. These instruments can be categorized in the following way. First we find *regulations and incentives* applied which are

designed to control "destructive" competition and to make competitors subject to rules which allow for the economic survival of their respective market partners. Usually these regulations consist in measures and laws which try to protect the "weaker" party in an exchange relationship, or which support this party through various incentives. Second, we find the large category of *public infrastructure investment* which is designed to help broad categories of commodity owners (again: both labor and capital) to engage in exchange relationships. Typical examples are schools of all kinds, transportation facilities, energy plants, and measures for urban and regional development. Third, we find attempts to introduce *compulsory schemes of joint decision making* and joint financing which are designed to force market partners to agree upon conditions of mutually acceptable exchange in an organized way, *outside* the exchange process itself, so that the outcome is reliable for both sides. Such compulsory schemes of mutual accommodation are to be found not only in the area of wage bargaining, but equally in areas like housing, education, and environmental protection.

8. Such attempts to stabilize and universalize the commodity form and exchange process by political and administrative means leads to a number of specific structural contradictions of state capitalist societies which in turn can become the focus of social conflict and political struggle. Such contradictions can be found on the economic, political and ideological levels of society. On the *economic* level, the very state policies which are designed to maintain and promote universal exchange relationships have the effect of *threatening the continuity* of those relationships. For all three of the above-mentioned instruments of economic policy making (regulations, infrastructure and compulsive accommodation) deprive the owners of capital of value to varying degrees, either in the form of *capital* that is just "taxed away," or in the form of *labor,* or in form of their *freedom* to utilize both of these in the way they deem most profitable. To the extent such state policies of "administrative recommodification" are "effective," they are bound to put a burden upon the owners of capital which has the paradoxical effect of making them *ineffective.* Since, in a capitalist society, all exchange relationships depend upon the willingness of owners of money capital to invest, i.e., to exchange money capital for constant capital and variable capital; since this willingness depends upon the expected profitability of investment; and since all observable state policies of recommodification do have the side-effect of depriving capital of either capital or labor power or the freedom to use both in profitable ways, the cure turns out to be worse than the illness. That is to say, reformist policies of the capitalist state by no means unequivocally "serve" the interests of the capitalist class: very often they are met by the most vigorous resistance and opposition of this class. Social conflicts and political struggles do not, of course, emerge automatically from this contra-

diction. They are waged by political forces which are willing and able to defend the reformist policies of the capitalist state against the obstructive resistance of the capitalist class itself.

A second structural contradiction is related to the organizational *power structures* created by such state strategies. It has often been observed by both liberal and Marxist social scientists that those sectors of the economy which are not immediately controlled by market mechanisms tend to expand (both in terms of labor power employed and value absorbed) in advanced capitalist social structures. The most obvious example is public administration and all the agencies that are created and controlled by it (like schools, transportation facilities, post offices, hospitals, public service institutions, welfare bureaucracies, the military, etc.). What is the explanation for the growth of the share of these organizations? In the most simplified form, the state's attempts to maintain and universalize the commodity form do require organizations which cease to be subject to the commodity form in their own mode of operation.

This can be demonstrated in the case of teachers. Although it is true that their labor power is *hired* for wage, it is not true that the *purpose* of their labor is to produce commodities for sale (which is the case in commercial enterprises). The purpose of their labor is, rather, to produce such use-values (skills, etc.) which put commodity owners (e.g., workers) in a position to actually sell their commodities. Therefore, schools do not *sell* their "products" (which hence do not assume the form of commodities), although they help to maintain and to *improve the saleability* of the commodities of the *recipients* of their products. But to the recipients the products of educational activities (i.e., the work of teachers) are distributed through channels different from exchange. The same is true in such organizations as public housing authorities, hospitals, transportation systems, prisons and other parts of the administrative apparatus. Although we often find nominal *fees* (as opposed to equivalent *prices*) as a mechanism playing a role in the distribution of their products and services, the prevailing mechanisms is by no means *sale* but such things as legal claims, legal compulsion, acknowledged need or simply free use.

One of the most debated and most controversial issues in the fields of liberal public economics and political science is just what mechanism of production and distribution of "public goods" could be substituted for the exchange mechanism that is inapplicable in the area of public production—an increasing part of production designed to maintain and to universalize the commodity form of property.

This strategy of *maintaining* the commodity form presupposes the growth of state-organized production facilities *exempt* from the commodity form. This, again, is a contradiction only in the structural sense,—a source of possible conflicts and destabilizing developments which in turn remain contingent upon political action. This contradiction can give rise to social conflicts and political struggles which try to gain popular control over exactly those "weakest links" in the world of commodities. Although it is a puzzle to many Marxists who consider themselves "orthodox," it still is hardly deniable that the major social conflicts and political struggles that have taken place during the decade of the sixties did *not* take place within exchange relationships between labor and capital, but took place as conflicts over the control over the service organizations that *serve* the commodity form without themselves being *part* of the commodity nexus. Conflicts in schools, universities, prisons, military organizations, housing authorities and hospitals are cases in point. We suggest that an explanation of this fact can be based on the consideration that such organizations represent the most advanced forms of erosion of the commodity form within capitalist exchange relationships themselves.

A third contradiction can be located on the ideological level, or in the normative and moral infrastructure of capitalist society. The commodity form does presuppose two related norms with which individual actors must comply. First, they must be willing to utilize the opportunities open to them, and they must constantly strive to improve their exchange position *(possessiveness);* and second, they must be willing to accept whatever material outcome emerges from their particular exchange relationship—particularly if this outcome is unfavorable to them. Such outcomes must, in other words, be attributed to either natural events or to the virtues and failures of the individual *(individualism).*

For a capitalist commodity economy to function, the normative syndrome of possessive individualism must be the basis both of the behavior of the actor as well as of his interpretations of the actual and future behavior of others. Our point is now that the contradiction of state capitalism on the ideological level results in the *subversion* of this normative syndrome of possessive individualism. To the extent that exchange relationships are prepared and maintained through visible political and administrative acts of the state, the actual exchange value any unit of property (be it in labor or capital) achieves on the market can be seen at least as much determined through *political* measures as through the *individual* way of managing one's property and resources. These resources themselves thus come to be seen as something resulting from, and contingent upon, political measures. Whether or not one receives exchange value for one's labor power, and how much of it, becomes—on the level of normative orientation—less a matter of adequate state policies in such areas as education, training, and regional development. Similarly, for the owner of capital, his market success does not depend upon his preparedness to take risks, his inventiveness and his ability to anticipate changes in demand, but instead upon state policies in such areas as tariffs, research and development, infrastructure supply and regional development. The structural weakening of the moral fiber of a capitalist commodity society—which is caused by the very attempts to stabilize and universalize the commodity form through policy measures—again does not imply any automatic tendency toward crises or the "breakdown" of capitalism. It can, however, become the focus of social conflict and political struggle which is oriented towards overcoming the obsolete commodity relationships as the organizing principle of social reproduction.

## · 13 ·

# On the State of the State: Marxist Theories of the State After Leninism

## Boris Frankel

### I

According to Mandel,[1] the state is a capitalist state because 1) the apparatus of the state is organized in a manner which corresponds to the general organization of capitalist society, e.g. hierarchy; 2) the state is the "ideal total capitalist" (Engels); 3) the state depends on the health of monopoly capital for its finances; 4) only a very small minority of state officials have decision-making powers; 5) promotion is based on adherence to bourgeois norms; 6) the state draws upon and co-opts cadres from trade unions and businesses to serve on its committees; 7) public officials are confined to "rational" solutions within the system; 8) anti-monopoly agencies which are supposed to protect the public's interest are powerless and depend on the very industries they are supposed to regulate; 9) the separation of powers means that there is no direct democracy by the working class. The parliamentary electoral process atomizes each worker to the confines of the ballot box and thereby enables the state to prevent collective anti-capitalist action; 10) the early bourgeois states witnessed parliament as the integration of varied class interests but the growth of monopoly capital coincided with the growth of working class parties, hence the state apparatus rather than parliament now serves as the principal medium for maintaining the rule of capital; 11) the state dramatically increases its role to socialize the costs of production through state planning; 12) the passing of reform legislation creates the

---

* Abridged from *Theory and Society* 7 (1979): 205–16, 220–27.

1. See E. Mandel, *Late Capitalism* (London, New Left Books, 1975), chapters 15, 16, 18.

social democratic illusion that the state could redistribute wealth; 13) the state has actually become a crisis manager and is forced to intervene on a massive scale at the economic, political, ideological and repressive level; 14) as it is a permanent crisis manager, the crisis in capitalism now becomes a permanent crisis of the state; 15) but as the forces of production outgrow the national state, they likewise outgrow the state's role and ability to control the supra-national industrial cycle. The state is thus subject to both domestic and foreign crises which it has to manage for the benefit of the capitalist class.

Looking at most of these major points, it is hard to deny the substantial truth and appeal of this analysis. Yet there is something seriously deficient in this whole perspective. Like many other Marxists, Mandel evaluates capitalist states only in terms of what these states do on behalf of the capitalist class, or how the very organizational structure and function of the apparatuses objectively prevent a socialist revolution from being implemented. Because the state is evaluated in terms of the classical polarization between reformism or revolution, Mandel, Poulantzas,[2] and others can only analyze the *negative* aspects of capitalist states. Short of winning state power, they have a major blind spot when it comes to evaluating all these structures and roles which states carry out, but which are all non-revolutionary. If one constantly sees all state services and functions as a consequence of the state's role as crisis manager, this does not at all mean that capitalist states are structurally confined to only *reproducing* capitalist social relations. The analyses made by Mandel and Poulantzas make it almost a logical impossibility for capitalist states to function in a manner which is not complimentary to the dominant classes. They represent two exaggerated positions (despite their important contributions) which are in turn based on their unrepentant adherence to "orthodoxy"—a heavy burden to carry for the sake of guaranteeing one's "revolutionary" credentials.

Unless Marxists undertake a thorough political economy of *internal* state apparatuses, there will be little prospect of overcoming the deficiencies already mentioned. But in order to undertake an internal anatomy of particular states, there first has to be agreement on the boundaries of state apparatuses. All Marxists agree that various institutions play a vital role in maintaining bourgeois hegemony, legitimacy, consensus, domination, but there is no agreement as to whether these institutions are part of the Ideological State Apparatus or not. The meteoric rise to popularity of Poulantzas' and Althusser's concept of the Ideological State Apparatus provides a useful focal point on the whole question of state and civil society and base and superstructure.

The endless interpretations of the importance of the "economic" flow back to the nature of early capitalist societies and their overt de-politicization of pre-capitalist social forms of production. In various pre-capitalist modes of production based on slaves and serfs, the labor process was inseparably and openly related to hierarchical, theocratic, blood, estate, or other social divisions. But in capitalist social formations there was a "defusion" and thus confusion as to the absolute forms of authority exercised by capitalists within their labor

---

2. N. Poulantzas, "The Capitalist State: A Reply to Miliband and Laclau", *New Left Review,* No. 95, 1976.

processes, and the general forms of authority and definition of citizenship in the society (outside of the factory). It was therefore perfectly correct for Marx to undertake an analysis of the mode of production in order to demystify bourgeois ideology and thus expose the interest and workings of the new bourgeois political and legal institutions. Marx was analyzing capitalist development which proceeded to accumulate with relatively little state involvement in planning or other complex market-supplementing activities which present capitalist states undertake. Part of the reason for the subsequent emergence of the notion of the state as a mere superstructure was due to the idealized notion of the "liberal state" (where the Market was responsible for most of the organizing of the productive processes), a situation which may have been closer to the truth in nineteenth century Britain rather than in other developing capitalist modes of production, e.g. Germany or Russia, where the state was heavily involved in capitalist industrialization. Another reason is that Marxism has only recently developed insights into the importance of indirectly productive institutions such as the family and school, which have all been hitherto lumped under the concept of "superstructure."

Althusser and Poulantzas attempt to systematize Gramsci's recognition that the boundaries between state and civil society overlap in capitalist social formations. They want to get away from the historicist notion of the states as the representative of general interests in contrast to the divergent interests embodied in civil society. Both Althusser and Poulantzas reject the vulgar mechanical notion of "base" and "superstructure," yet persist in sticking with these terms even though they attack the dichotomy of state and civil society. By allocating the media, schools, family, church, trade unions, political parties to the status of Ideological State Apparatuses, Poulantzas and Althusser create more problems than they solve. For example, they cannot differentiate between a) the logic of capital accumulation and the logic of state production and service; and b) the nature of bourgeois ideology and what prevents its reproduction.[3] Miliband, Laclau and Anderson have already pointed to the principal political and methodological errors associated with this approach.[4]

---

3. Laclau has summed up the absurd position that the concept of Ideological State Apparatus can lead to. If the state is the factor that maintains the cohesion of the social formation, then *everything* that contributes to this cohesion is part of the Ideological State Apparatus. According to Laclau, Poulantzas' list would be a short one: "the reformism of trade unions and social-democratic leaders constitutes a factor of cohesion, and consequently parties would be divided between a State wing and revolutionary wing and also, reductio ad absurdum, the mind of every individual would be schizophrenically divided between a state half, tending to the cohesion of the social formation and an anti-State half tending to its disruption. Is this not an extreme example of over-politicization of the various levels of a structure, historicist deviation against which Poulantzas warns us?" It is not surprising that Poulantzas has remained silent on the issue of Ideological State Apparatuses! See E. Laclau, "The Specificity of the Political." Also see G. Therborn, *What Does The Ruling Class Do when It Rules?* (London, 1978), p. 172, and P. Hirst, "Economic Classes and Politics" in A. Hunt, ed., *Class and Class Structure,* (London, 1977), pp. 125–154.

4. See R. Miliband, "Marxist Theory and the Modern State", *Arena,* No. 39, pp. 67–73; R. Miliband, "Poulantzas and the Capitalist State", *New Left Review,* No. 82, 1973, pp. 83–93; and P. Anderson, "The Antinomies of Antonio Gramsci", *New Left Review,* No. 100, pp. 34–38; E. Laclau, "The Specificity of the Political: the Poulantzas-Miliband Debate," *Economy and Society,* No. 1, 1975, pp. 87–110. The division of the state into Repressive Apparatus and Ideological State Apparatus has also produced a rift between Poulantzas and Althusser. In his more recent writings,

Lurking behind the difficulties associated with the notion of Ideological State Apparatuses is the old problem of base and superstructure. There is a tendency to see all those institutions which are outside the mode of production (a concept often seen in narrow terms as being no more than the factory, office and sales department), as being part of the superstructure. This is implicitly evident in the Althusserian argument concerning "the economic as being determinant in the last instance." What Althusser, Poulantzas and company continue to adhere to is a notion of institutions such as the family, school, and media as outside the production process, which are vital to the reproduction of "relations of production" *in the factory* and which are not part of the "base." For if the Repressive Apparatus and Ideological State Apparatus are part of the mode of production, then what is the point of talking about the capitalist state and its relative autonomy? Either there *are* distinctions between state and society or we speak of *everything* as being part of the State, or conversely, everything as being mode of production.[5] In short, what do the Althusserians mean by the "economic"; where is it located, and are the media, family and school determined in the last instance by the "economic," or do they determine it (because today they are also part of the "economic")? There is such a confusion of definitions as to what is "economic" and "extra-economic" that Althusser and Poulantzas hide more than they disclose. Let me therefore point to those writers who provide a more illuminating analysis of state power/class power and state apparatus/private apparatus relations.

## II

It should be made clear from the outset that the recent work of German and American political economists has taken place under quite different conditions compared to those in France, Italy or Britain. Both the United States and the

---

Poulantzas has criticized Althusser for ignoring the economic apparatuses of the state (see N. Poulantzas, *Fascism and Dictatorship*, London, New Left Books, 1974, p. 304); yet his own continued adherence to the division of the state into the "R.As" and "I.S.As" makes it difficult to see how he fits in the economic role of the state. Poulantzas argues that one cannot say the state intervenes economically; rather the state intervenes ideologically and repressively which are all connected to the reproduction of the general conditions of capitalist production. It is true that economic intervention can be simultaneously ideological and repressive, but this does not resolve the whole problem of what is *peculiar* to the state apparatuses or public sectors which are either benefiting capitalists by their form of intervention or endangering accumulation and legitimacy by the very quantitative and qualitative form of this intervention. For if one argues that the distinction between private and public apparatuses is basically a juridical distinction, then it is extremely difficult to comprehend what the difference is between private forms of intervention, e.g. the capitalist media, compared to public intervention which is not formally organized on the principle of profit, e.g. public broadcasting or schools.

5. Althusser and Poulantzas do not seem to be able to see that the media is no mere ideological apparatus, but rather a massive billion dollar capitalist production unit; they do not seem to see the family as the site of consumption and the indirect production of labor power, but *only* as the reproducer of ideology; they do not see the billion dollar educational industry which affects more than the reproduction of capitalist values, but also the accumulation prospects of building contractors, publishing houses and other capitalist units of production; moreover, even some trade unions, churches and political parties are large property owners, producers, shareholders, etc., and not merely superstructural agents uninvolved in the possesion or management of the mode of production; finally, they do not seem to comprehend the millions of state sector workers as more than mere

Federal Republic of Germany 1) are complex *federal* systems of government compared to the *unitary* state systems of France, Britain and Italy; 2) are the largest capitalist modes of production; 3) have weak or virtually non-existent revolutionary movements; 4) have never had social-democratic governments (in Germany the S.P.D. has never been in power on its own since 1945 while the U.S.A. doesn't even have a "Labor type" party); and 5) are the leading forces behind supra-state intervention and crisis management in the capitalist world. Given this context, the work of people such as Habermas, Offe, and O'Connor is much more realistic and contemporaneous as it is relatively distant from the tradition and rhetoric of the Communist and Trotskyist movements in France, Britain and Italy. However, in Germany the dispute between "revisionists" such as Habermas and Offe, and "orthodox" people such as Muller and Neususs is couched in the traditional language of Marx, Luxemburg and Bernstein.

It is quite common for both Marxists and non-Marxists to argue that the distinction between state and society is now inapplicable because of either the general bureaucratization of life, or the rejection of historicist divisions between private and public. Drawing freely from the works of Habermas, Offe, and O'Connor,[6] I would argue that it is vital to retain a clear distinction between state and civil society and between public and private sectors, despite the massive interrelation and interdependence of the latter. Only by recognizing these different spheres and the different logic of their functions can we get a real sense of the level and nature of specific forms of class struggle. One of the reasons why Habermas, Offe, and O'Connor are invaluable to a clarification of present forms of class struggle is that they focus most of their attention on the immanently contradictory role which present states have to sustain—that of maintaining both capitalist accumulation and the legitimation of this process. In other words, they are precisely concerned with the nature of crisis management which involves the forms of crises which states have to cope with (or instigate themselves), as well as the organizational logic of the public and private sectors which indicate why the avoidance or control of one form of crisis only serves to exacerbate another crisis elsewhere.

While these writers are "revisionist" in that they no longer accept Marx's law or value as comprehensive enough to explain state/capitalist relations in contemporary capitalist societies, they *are* fundamentally committed to the proposition that *class struggle,* and the analysis of classes, is a central key to

---

administrators and reproducers of capitalist relations—that is, they do *not* fully acknowledge the transformation of the *material* conditions of existence of millions of people who do not themselves produce surplus value, but whose economic relations would dramatically affect the private capitalist units of production should their numbers increase dramatically, or be reduced by half.

6. In particular see J. Habermas, *Legitimation Crisis,* Boston, Beacon Press, 1975; J. O'Connor *The Fiscal Crisis of the State,* New York, St. Martins Press, 1973; C. Offe, "The Theory of the Capitalist State and the Problem of Policy Formation" and "Introduction to Legitimacy Versus Efficiency," both in Lindberg, Alford, Crouch and Offe (eds.), *Stress and Contradiction in Modern Capitalism,* New York, Health & Co., 1975; C. Offe, "Crises and Crisis Management: Elements of a Political Crisis Theory", *International Journal of Politics,* Fall 1976, pp. 29–67; C. Offe and V. Ronge, "Theses on the Theory of the State", *New German Critique,* No. 6, 1975, pp. 137–147; C. Offe, "Political Authority and Class Structures (1972)" reprinted in P. Connerton (ed.), *Critical Sociology,* London, Penguin Books, 1976, pp. 388–421; and C. Offe, "The Abolition of Market Control and the Problem of Legitimacy" in *Kapitalistate,* Nos. 1 and 2, 1973/74.

illuminating not only the structures of state apparatuses, but especially the role of states in the modern transformation of exchange relationships which have created new material conditions for the reproduction of life in capitalist societies.[7] In explaining these "new material conditions," Marxists often refer to the prevalence of commodity production associated with the extraction of surplus value which in turn defines class relations. The focus is on why labor is reduced to the level of a commodity or the "exchange of equivalents." There have been hardly any analyses of modern capitalist societies which have investigated the extent and nature of commodified life, examining whether this exchange relation is the *sole* form of social organization. Actually, nearly all Marxian analyses emphasize the *reproduction* of commodity exchange relations and have not paid enough attention to the so-called contradictions of capitalism. This is where Habermas and Offe have very important insights to offer.

By undertaking substantial investigations of state activity in the accumulation of private capital, Habermas, Offe, Ronge, and Funke are able to point to those social forces which are subject to market, neo-market and non-market relations. There are no shortage of works depicting the passage of capitalism from laissez-faire to monopoly capitalism; nonetheless most of these writings assume that there has been a general *intensification* of commodity production rather than also examining the development of nonexchange value commodities and the concomitant weakening of the dominance of commodity fetishism. The conditions of production which have made possible an intensification of commodity fetishism (e.g. in the areas of art, food and capital intensive industries) have not developed without the parallel growth of weakened and/or non-exchange social relations. One can determine the extent of these tendencies by looking at the specific nature of particular state apparatuses and the level of involvement which these play in specific accumulation and legitimation processes. The extent to which the capitalist mode of production has been *re-politicized* is also an indication of the problems facing particular classes in their struggle to maintain control over *state power,* or to gain state power, or to limit certain state powers. Let me suggest an explanation.

In the *German Ideology* there is a famous passage where Marx and Engels make the distinction between the mental (i.e. thinkers and ideologists such as politicians, priests, journalists, etc.) and manual (those who run the factories) fractions of the ruling class. This division between the thinkers and the doers of the bourgeois class has been largely accepted without question by contemporary Marxists. Yet it is quite clear that the capitalist media and modern capitalist states are hardly just the thinkers of the capitalist class but rather massive productive forces of accumulation. The transformation of ideological production is a crucial problem which requires substantial modification of Marx's classical formulation despite its enduring richness. Rather than analyze the implications of this division for an understanding of capitalist forms of rule, Marxists such as Poulantzas have tended to concentrate on the mental and manual divisions within the proletariat rather than within the bourgeoisie. Even then the discus-

---

7. See B. Frankel, "Habermas Talking: An Interview", *Theory and Society,* Vol. 1, No. 1, 1974, p. 50, where Habermas states that "we have to go back, so to say, to the level of that analysis which Marx called historical materialism—this is the level of class struggle. . . ."

sion has generally been concerned with who are the new petty bourgeoisie or the new working class, i.e., attempts at classifying who is a worker or a non-worker by their relation to the productive process and ideological roles in situations of domination or subordination. Much of this discussion has involved disputes over what is productive or unproductive labor *without* locating or designating any difference between *state* sector employees and those working in *private* units of capital. That is, differences have been made between technicians, white collar and blue collar workers, or between service sector and industrial sector, rather than between workers subject to market relations and non-market forces, let alone those who are not even in the labor process. Both O'Connor and Offe go outside this search for the "real proletariat" by differentiating between labor processes in the state and private sectors rather than between merely *technical* divisions of labor, i.e. mental or manual work. Furthermore, they also investigate the nature of state apparatuses in terms of planning capacities, logic of operations and the question of whether capitalist states can possibly act as a collective capitalist, that is, overcoming the mental/manual divisions within the bourgeoisie and thus insuring that they don't tear one another to pieces. The study of particular capitalist states reveals the relative degree of *social cohesion* which *must* be maintained between the *bourgeoisie,* while the structure and role of states also illuminates the degree of social *division* in the *working class.*

O'Connor and Offe both argue that it is necessary to comprehend capitalist production and social relations according to the diverse forms of organizational logic which govern such *uneven* social formations. O'Connor subdivides the social production of the USA into the monopoly and competitive sectors plus the state or public sector. Offe and Habermas roughly concur with this division except that they also see a fourth sector in advanced capitalist societies which Offe calls the Residual Labor Power sector (and which O'Connor would probably identify as State Clients). Although Habermas, Offe and O'Connor do not make explicit reference to Poulantzas' critique of Miliband's use of elites, one can view their division of social formations into sectors as a further systemization of the Miliband/Poulantzas debate. It will be recalled that Poulantzas attacks the use of the term "elite" (as a non-Marxian category) because it fails to show that the bourgeoisie, far from being a homogenous social class, are rather divided between industrial, finance and other fractions of capital. Hence, the point was to analyze the different *logics* of capital accumulation of these fractions (and their conflicting relations with the state), rather than the social background and interpersonal relations of state and business elites. By concentrating on state, monopoly and competitive sectors, I believe that one can uncover the logic of accumulation processes in a more substantive manner than those analysts who adhere to the notion of fractions. This is because a sector analysis enables one to determine which forms of social production and relations of production are subject to the logic of market, neo-market and non-market forces. The use of sectors does not mean that fractions do not exist, but it enables one to distinguish why competitive sector units of production may be possibly more divided by their industrial or merchant (fraction) nature, than large diversified corporate units in the monopoly sector. In short, the use of sectors rather than fractions has its merits for the following reasons: a) It enables one to examine the important quantitative and qualitative scale of operations and relations of production which differentiate state sector from private sector production—whether it be agricultural, manufacturing or circulation processes. b) The notion of fractions of capital is not sufficiently rigorous and can also be misleading because modern capitalist units of production (e.g. General Motors or large banks) are simultaneously involved directly or indirectly in finance, industrial and merchant capital operations and investments. A false debate can develop over who rules the corporations, that is, does finance capital dominate or not. c) By giving attention to the private fractions of capital the state sector is either substantially ignored or *reduced* to the logic of operation of the private fractions, i.e. which fractions dominate the state. d) Without a notion of sectors it is difficult to comprehend why a capitalist industrial unit employing fifty workers has a substantially different economic and political relationship to a state apparatus compared to the relationship held by General Electric and other giant units.

Very briefly, the sectors can be distinguished from one another by the following. The monopoly sector is characterized by highly organized sales markets, capital intensive production, national and international operations and a relatively high wage level which is generally passed on in the form of price increases. On the other hand, the competitive and state sectors are *labor intensive* with low level mechanization. However, working conditions are substantially different. Capitalist units within the competitive sector are not "price makers" but are subject (depending on their size) to varying degrees of *dependence* upon, and *political* administrative *exclusion* from, capitalist accumulation in the monopoly sector. They are subject to price competition, and are unable to penetrate or expand beyond local or regional operations because of technical *and* administrative blocs imposed by monopoly capital and state "protection" (even though many states have anti-monopoly legislation). Thus many capitalist units in the competitive sector are either subject to the "laws of the market," or are determined by *direct* political and economic relations rather than by exchange relations as supposedly free and equal co-partners of monopoly capital on the market. All these conditions and limitations manifest themselves in the labor process where general wage levels, conditions of work, worker organizations and the like are relatively depressed.

Just as the private sector is subdivided, so too, are state sectors. Depending on the constitutional structure, level of historical development (both of capital labor movement), state apparatuses are subdivided according to varying degrees of central, federal, local or regional units of organization and statutory bodies. Various states may even run units of commodity production (e.g. Renault cars in France), which are wholly or partially nationalized. Workers may be employed in industries which are privately owned but produce only for the public sector, such as military contractors. The crucial distinction involves the *type* of labor within the state sector, the conditions of work, whether the worker is employed *directly* by the *state* or by private units, and in what way the production process is determined by either market forces, neo-market forces (e.g. limited private tendering for guaranteed profit-making state contracts), or by political/administrative decree (e.g. guaranteeing production or sales in state run, or state protected enterprises such as airlines). Most state sector workers are *not* governed by market conditions, although they are *indirectly* related to the accumulation process, depending on revenue for wages as well as their many (but not all) occupation roles which are carried out on capital's behalf. It is absolutely vital to distinguish between the role of labor as part of the organic composition of capital in the private sector, as opposed to the payment of state workers from *public funds* rather than directly from *private capital*. Additionally, the "residual labor power" sector is even further removed from exchange relations in that material conditions of pensioners, students, unemployed workers, prisoners, mental patients, and drafted soldiers are maintained predominantly by financial allocation of payments from the state, and to some extent from private pension and superannuation funds.

The significance of these sectors can be seen in the substantial political, ideological and economic divisions between state sector workers, state clients, and monopoly and competitive sector workers. Of course social divisions are not neatly and clearly cut in the sense that many workers and non-workers are related to, or socially mix with people who either work in one or more of the three sectors (e.g. workers who have a second or part-time job) or who are recipients of pensions, scholarships, or welfare checks. Nevertheless, it is possible to indicate the principal factors which have a major bearing on the possible reproduction of capitalist social relations as well as the level of political organization opposed to the capitalist class. *The degree of class organization decreases as one moves from the monopoly sector through to the "residual labor power" sector.* Many state sector workers, especially police and military personnel, were prevented from becoming unionized or affiliating with national union organizations. But even workers in repressive apparatuses are attempting to protect their wage structure by unionizing. These large scale movements to unionize all state sector workers in recent years have been consequential in particular struggles over cut-backs in public expenditure. Competitive sector workers and state clients are less organized and are more subject to the developments in the monopoly and state sector as to general social conditions of production and material existence. However, many state sector jobs were created in response to anti-"exchange relation" struggles that have taken place in recent years among those people, for example, among students, blacks, women, or poor tenants who are excluded from, or marginally related to, commodity production.

Any theory of capitalist states which does not take into account the employment of about one-quarter to more than one third of the labor force is useless. Offe, O'Connor and Habermas have attempted to explain the implications of this new constellation of class forces for the possibility and scope of present and future class struggles. What does the growth of so many millions of state workers mean to the continued functioning of the capitalist mode of production? O'Connor and Offe argue that the degree of growth in any of the four sectors has crucial repercussions on the level of commodity production. If the state sector or residual labor power sector grow disproportionally to the monopoly and competitive sectors, or if the level of conflict in any or all of the sectors intensifies, then particular capitalist social formations will be endangered. In most advanced capitalist societies the monopoly sector has only been able to grow either by reaching a class compromise and buying peace with large unions, by importing migrant labor, or both. However, the historical price (since 1945) of monopoly sector growth has been the winning by the working class of improved conditions for the reproduction of their own labor power, for instance, better education, housing, and health services. Habermas sums up the consequences of *immunizing* the monopoly sector from revolutionary upheavals as:

a) disparate wage developments and/or sharpening of wage disputes in the public service sector; b) permanent inflation, with corresponding temporary redistribution of income to the disadvantage of unorganized workers and other marginal groups; c) permanent crisis in government finances, together with public poverty (that is, impoverishment of public transportation, education, housing and health care); and d) an inadequate adjustment of disproportional economic developments, sectoral (agriculture) as well as regional (marginal areas).[8]

Because the state sector is largely *labor* intensive, the general conditions of wage levels in the monopoly and competitive sectors have greatly influenced the working conditions of state workers. This has differed from one capitalist social formation to another, depending on the period of rapid recruitment, level of unemployed, and national level of class organizations. In turn, the possibility of American, French or Australian state apparatuses to sack state workers is largely determined by the strength of the union movements, levels of resistance and conditions of employment.[9] The presence of millions of state workers also involves reconsideration of the concept of the "reserve army of the unemployed." While not being completely immune to general exchange relation conditions, state workers are, by and large, structurally outside those relations determined by the relative and absolute extraction of surplus value (except those workers in nationalized commodity producing plants). Here, then, is one of the reasons why wage policies have to be *administratively* imposed, given the failure of market mechanism to have *overall* depreciation effects on state sector workers.[10] Thus, while most capitalist societies are witnessing concerted efforts by the capitalist class to impose efficiency rationalizations (e.g. cut-backs, automation), this is a very precarious process because of the danger of class conflict, economic recession due to cuts in public works and services, and new forms of fiscal burdens on a diminishing percentage of wage earners and businesses who are reluctant to approve those very tax increases upon which the continued growth of capitalist accumulation and social harmony depends (given the ever increasing level of state intervention).

The paramount importance of maintaining the distinction between state and society is also tied to the dispute concerning current bourgeois policies involving cuts in state expenditure. Ian Gough has argued that it is quite wrong

---

8. J. Habermas, *Legitimation Crisis,* p. 38.

9. The mass sackings of public sector workers in New York would not be politically possible in Western Europe or Australia without major conflict—given the greater strength at the national level of union movements compared to those in the U.S.A.

10. Moreover, in particular countries such as Australia, state sector workers managed to obtain conditions equal to, or better than private sector workers (especially after 1972). It is no surprise to see the conservative Fraser Government (in Australia) attempting to remove conditions won by state workers, e.g. shorter hours, super-annuation, maternity leave and other conditions of labor which set costly precedents for private sector workers to imitate.

to regard the growth of the state "as an unproductive 'burden' upon the capitalist sector; more and more it is a necessary precondition for private capital accumulation."[11] He concludes that social services have to be cut because they constitute the social wage of the working class. Cutting this social wage would reduce living standards and "raise the rate of exploitation," thus, for example, enabling British capital to survive its crisis.[12] While Gough is partially correct in that much state expenditure does set the pre-conditions for capital accumulation, it is *both* indirectly productive *as well as* constituting a burden on private capital. This *contradictory* role of capitalist states can only be ascertained by going beyond the productive/unproductive labor debates. Gough, Yaffe, Fine, and Harris[13] are arguing in terms of commodity production according to the law of value. This approach, however is too narrow. We want to know why the capitalist class is clamoring for a restructuring of their public sectors, why ideological organs such as *The Economist* are advocating a reprivatization of the public sector (meaning to make it subject to market forces). The answer to this lies in the relations of production or rationality governing the state sector, that is, the internal logic of operation which *simultaneously* reproduces and yet *decreases* or negates exchange commodification.

The deficiency of notions such as state capitalism or naive prognoses concerning the bureaucratization or unlimited planning capacities of capitalist states can now be made clearer. There is a great deal of misunderstanding related to Habermas' argument that Marx's critique of political economy is insufficient for a modern critique of ideology and class power. Claims were made that Habermas threw class analysis out and rejected political economy in favor of epistemological, linguistic and other idealist perversions. Nothing could be further from the truth. Rather than rejecting Marx, Habermas, Offe, and O'Connor are trying to historicize and modify the law of value according to the new and changing historical conditions. This is why they are all concerned with the repoliticization of the mode of production which has destabilized capitalist societies. According to Offe and Ronge,[14] capitalist states are: (1) Not permitted to organize profitable production according to *political* criteria because property is private. (2) However, political power depends indirectly on the volume of taxation of the capitalist accumulation process. (3) Since the state is dependant upon the flow of resources which it cannot produce itself, there is a *self-interest* of occupiers of state power to promote the health of the accumulation process. (4) Thus political power is determined in a *dual* form, (a) by *formal* rules of the democratic electoral process, and also (b) by the *material content* of the accumulation process which sets the parameters of successful political administration. (5) As the capitalist class struggles to prevent the state sector from operating the production process, this characteristic of *exclusion* is contradicted by the growing need of private capital for capitalist states to "crisis manage." (6) Therefore

---

11. I. Gough, "State Expenditure in Advanced Capitalism", *New Left Review,* No. 92, 1975, p. 80.

12. *Ibid,* p. 91.

13. B. Fine and L. Harris, "The Debate on State Expenditure", *New Left Review* No. 98, 1976, p. 111.

14. See C. Offe and V. Ronge, "Theses on the Theory of the State".

the political administrative systems must increasingly regulate the accumulation process but without *materially* politicizing it—that is, without altering the very *logic* of private accumulation, which can only continue so long as the working class accept the prevailing forms of legitimation designed to conceal or deny this state intervention. . . .[15]

## III

If capitalist states are greatly involved in *market replacing* activities, then an adequate critique and comprehension of the nature of state administration and services has to be undertaken. This is only possible if we have some idea of the *rationality* which governs state sector activities. For too long this area has mainly been left to bourgeois theorists from Max Weber to the new public policy technocrats. But in recent years there has been a major dispute in Germany involving non-Marxists and Marxists such as Luhmann, Naschold, Mayntz, Funke, Hisch, Scharf, Offe and Habermas. The issues involve the capacity of modern capitalist states to plan, given the internal structure of administrative apparatuses, and the social bases of state planning, such as mass loyalty or co-operation from private capital. Of course, the reasons of the above people for looking at the nature of planning are quite opposed to one another. System theorists such as Luhmann are greatly perturbed at the inability of capitalist state administrations to avoid complexity (or breakdowns in efficiency) if the decision processes become more democratized. On the other hand, Habermas and Offe are concerned to dramatically *increase* mass participation and thereby also comprehend the crises in planning on behalf of capital, as well as to ultimately mobilize people in the task of destroying the power of capital. The results of this dispute over planning have been 1) the first analyses filling the void left by other Marxists who have concentrated mainly on capital/labor relations; 2) the first substantial critique of Weberian and modern bourgeois concepts of the state, especially the notion of bureaucracy; 3) the possibility of exposing the role of technology as ideology; and 4) the uncovering of the limits of state sector growth, that is, when a capitalist state ceases to function as a capitalist state because of its internal structure and external roles. For those of us who want to know and do more than just be resigned to take the road of parliamentary legalism or prepare for final violent confrontation, these analyses of the logic of state sectors are indeed welcome. Let me briefly outline the main contributions and then show how they are relevant to political action.

It must be stressed that all the following observations are related to the continued functioning of free elections, a free trade union movement, and are

---

15. While Offe has been influenced greatly by Habermas, they do not share common views on action and strategy. *Legitimation Crisis* incorporates the work of several projects that were undertaken at the Max Plank Institute in 1972/73. Offe and O'Connor have had close theoretical relations and Offe has taught seminars in the USA which were attended by *Kapitalistate* writers such as Erik Wright, Clarence Lo, and others. Both O'Connor and Offe are relatively weak in the areas of cultural and philosophical analysis, whereas Habermas makes up this deficit while maintaining his strength in the analysis of accumulation and administration problems.

*not* applicable to those capitalist states, (e.g., post-1973 Chile) where capitalist accumulation is made possible by outright violent repression. The distinction between *class* power and *state* power is illustrated by the fact that the capitalist class can only obtain what it needs so long as parliamentary democracy is not blatantly and consistently violated. It is within this context of a fluctuating class compromise that capitalist states gain a *limited* planning capacity. But before looking at the *limits* placed upon state planning by the *organized* strength of the working class, it is important to realize the inhibitions and opposition to state planning that come from private capitalist units of production and the various organizational units of the state sector.

Habermas and Offe *reject* the argument that capitalist states function either as the agent of the united monopoly capitalists, or as the spontaneous ("invisible hand") executive committee of the law of value. Given the ironic task of rational planning (sufficient taxes from wages and profits must be raised in order to rationally use these resources for programs designed to prevent crisis disturbances in the accumulation process), capitalist states are immediately burdened by incompatible priorities. Then there are the organizational limits: a) the state is limited by lack of information from private capitalists—hence insufficient co-ordination; b) a "collective capitalist'will" cannot emerge so long as freedom of investment enables capitalists to compete with one another; c) where there is close collusion between particular branches of state apparatuses and particular capitalist units of production, then the state is not able to maintain sufficient distance from these private interests in order to plan for them without objections based on short term interest; and d) the state vacillates between expected intervention and being forced to renounce this intervention—that is, between becoming *autonomous* of its capitalist clients (and thereby threatening them) or becoming *subordinate* to them and thereby damaging its legitimacy with the masses who still see it as neutral.

While these objections to the possibility of collective planning are important, there is still a more basic reason which involves the clear distinction between the rationality of capitalist production processes and the social inputs which govern limited state planning. Here the critique of Weber's concept of bureaucracy as well as the deficiency of the Althusserian position that capitalist commodity production and planning *are* compatible (and that it is only humanists who see this incompatibility and argue that there is not a capitalist mode of production in Eastern Europe) becomes relevant. It is interesting to note that Marxists and neu-Marxists, whether Althusserians or humanists such as Gouldner, Lefort, and Adorno, share a common blind spot when it comes to bureaucracy. Althusser and Bettleheim, both through their admiration of the Chinese experience as well as their failure to analyze the internal structure of state apparatuses, cannot see the substantial difference between state planning in Eastern Europe and the limited planning capacities of capitalist states. On the other hand, many Left people such as Gouldner, Adorno, and others have uncritically accepted the Weberian concepts of bureaucracy as further evidence of the general intensification, rationalization, or commodification of capitalist life. This perspective is not tenable because it fails to account for the different roles of technical rationality in private and public sectors—something which

Weber couldn't distinguish; hence it cannot explain why the expansion of the state—or the continued bureaucratization of the world—is *not* at all compatible with the needs or logic of private capitalist production if this expansion of the state sector adversely affects the accumulation of capital (witness all the recent cut-backs and restrictions on public sector growth); and finally, the recent synthesis of Marx and Weber is based on a wholly negative view of the state as being the epitome of domination. This obscures the contradictory nature of modern states which, I believe, have been major emancipatory forces and not *merely* repressive vehicles.

Whereas Weber could only point to the intrusion of the state into all spheres of life, this intervention has not been wholly or consistently repressive. In order to see why Weber's notion of bureaucratic rationality is inadequate, one must also recognize the major limits to his concept of legitimation as well as the weaknesses in his conception of economic action and political power, all of which make his understanding of the modern state—despite his reputation in this area—very shaky indeed. Space does not permit a full critique of Weber's concept of the state but the following points are important insofar as state planning capacities are concerned.

Weber saw the technical advantages of bureaucracy in its precision, speed, unambiguity, continuity, strict subordination to an impartial, impersonal, and generally calculative logic which maximized efficiency and hence technical attainment of goals. The modern state accumulated a monopoly of indispensable organizational power under the theorem: accumulated purposive rationality equals efficiency; the state is based on technical rationality hence the state subordinates all inefficient organization and power and becomes monolithic. In a penetrating analysis of policy formation, Offe knocks giant holes in the Weberian thesis.[16] He shows that the Weberian notion of bureaucracy has only limited relevance to the functioning of contemporary state apparatuses. Where state officials are merely concerned with allocating state resources in a routinized manner, for example, payment of welfare money, policing regulations as to eligibility, or any other activity which involves clearly fixed rules and sanctions, then a purposive rationality governs impartial bureaucratic forms of state action. But this technical rationality becomes *inapplicable* and *inefficient* when we examine the numerous forms of *productive* state activity. That is, productive not in the sense of producing surplus value, but rather in the sense that goods and services such as housing, education, health care, and transportation are not reducible to the mere repetition of impartial rules and sanctions. While there is plenty of bureaucratic administration tied to the running of hospitals, schools and other welfare agencies, there is nevertheless a substantial body of labor and functions which are intrinsically *use value* services and hence not determinable by calculation and neutrality:

The administration of "productive" state activities requires more than routinized allocation of state resources like money and justice. Additional questions have to be answered in order for "productive" state activity to begin, e.g.: what is the final product, or

---

16. See C. Offe, "The Theory of the Capitalist State and the Problem of Policy Formation"; for a critique of Weber's concept of legitimacy see J. Habermas, *Legitimation Crisis,* pp. 97–102; and *Toward a Rational Society,* Ch. 5.

purpose of state production? How much of it is needed in a particular situation? What is the most efficient way of producing it? Who should receive it? At what point in time and for what length of time? How should it be financed, and what priorities should be followed in case of cost increases and/or revenue decreases?[17]

Offe argues that productive functions are beyond the capacity of Weberian bureaucracy in the strict sense. The importance of recognizing the difference between "allocative" and "productive" state activity is crucial. It illuminates those state activities which *are* protecting and reproducing capitalist social relations, but it also enables us to see the difference between the *logic* underlying *exchange value* commodities and all those *use value* goods and services which are *not* reproducing dominant capitalist social relations.

According to Offe and Habermas, the capitalist mode of production is largely determined by a technical rationality of strict means–ends. In the private sector, there is an unambiguous application of resources which is directed by the logic of maximizing profit. Calculation and efficiency govern the organic composition of capital. The contradictions between capital and labor "are expressed directly in relations between quantities of values and indirectly in the social consequences of capital loss (bankruptcy) and deprivation of the means of subsistence (unemployment)."[18] These *strict* and *finite* parameters determine the logic of *commodity* production which *no* capitalist or worker can afford to ignore. The same is *not* true of *state sector policy making* or conditions of work on five counts:

First while capitalists are governed by the ultimate threat of bankruptcy or loss of profit, no such threshold governs state activity. That is, irrational or inefficient decisions by state administrations may result in social disorganization or deprivation but these consequences are not strictly quantifiable. In other words, it depends on the population as to what are regarded as *tolerable* disruptions to social life.

Second, no capitalist unit of production can avoid crises or contradictions by displacing the principle of profit maximization. State sectors, however, *can* displace crises via processes of bargaining which depend on the level of demands made by the classes in struggle. Rather than acting in an efficient, purposive manner, the reality of state administrations is their propensity for *avoiding* responsibility and crisis management. This reactive avoidance of crisis is particularly crucial when considering the capacity of bureaucracies to plan efficiently. All analyses which emphasize the interconnection of personal contacts between state administrators and business leaders *overestimate* the planning capacity of the post-industrial society technocrats. Bureaucracy is *inefficient* and a far from ideal instrument for planning.

Third, no capitalist state can increase its planning to the extent that freedom of investment ceases and private units of production become subordinate to *political* decisions rather than to the logic of private accumulation. This is because state production is very much involved with the need to maintain legitimacy and hence the bargaining process; in other words, the need to avoid crises has resulted in a major increase in non-exchange value goods and services. The

17. C. Offe, *ibid,* p. 136.
18. J. Habermas, *Legitimation Crisis,* p. 63.

state *cannot* plan on behalf of capital in a spontaneous manner. Planning involves discussion, articulation of priorities, and the need to *constantly justify* these policies to a democratic electoral process fragmented by class struggle. The *limited* planning capacity of re-politicized production is the *constant* attempt by bourgeois political parties to *guarantee* state assistance in capitalist accumulation *without* exacerbating mass demands that state policies should be oriented away from private needs and more to public use values. On the other hand, if capitalist states become openly responsible for poor administrative planning (resulting in loss of profits), then state administrators would become liable to pay compensation. At the moment, states relieve capitalists by paying for social costs created by accumulation, costs such as pollution and workers' injuries. However, greater state planning would open the doors to greater public scrutiny of private capitalist production decisions (i.e. politicize decisions of production), a situation greatly resisted by the capitalist class at the moment.

Fourth, given the limiting conditions of the democratic parliamentary process, capitalist states are *unable* to dispense with massive forms of *social use value* expenditure which many private units of production look upon with horror. In recent years the capitalist class has been fighting a battle to limit, exclude or prevent those forms of *use value* goods and services, such as public housing and health, which are extraterritorial structures—that is, forms of organization which are *foreign* to the logic of capitalist social relations. Insofar as capitalist states are massively involved in market-replacing activities, accumulation of capital is only possible if the social formation (through state administration) *increases* the amount of state production and state clients who are not irrelevant to commodity exchange, but who also *disrupt* and threaten the creation of profitable production. As Offe puts it,

In late capitalist societies the processes of exchange-regulated accumulation or capitalist growth are simultaneously dominant *and* "recessive"; in other words, although they are decisive for the stability of the system as a whole, they have at the same time been reduced in their potential to organize the vital activity of society to a small core area and have become increasingly obsolete. This leads to the creation of a new problem for the system of *late* capitalist societies: namely, the problem of preventing the regulatory processes of *administrative power*—which are *"foreign* to capital" and upon whose permanent expansion the central, monopolistic sphere of the economy is of course dependent—from becoming autonomous and overshadowing the dominance of privatized exchange relationships, whether through parasitic dysfunctionalization or through their revolutionary suspension.[19]

Fifth, the recognition by Habermas, Offe, O'Connor, Ronge, and Funke that modern capitalist states *both* reproduce and negate exchange commodity production has important implications both for Marxists and for defenders of the capitalist system. For Marxists, it involves abandoning the entrenched notion that capitalist states are only instruments for the defense and reproduction of capitalism. Moreover, they are forced to recognize that categories such as the capitalist state or state capitalism are not applicable to communist countries in Eastern Europe and China. This is because state production in Communist countries is not dependent on the logic of private capital accumulation. Economic policy is solely administratively and politically determined. *The relation*

---

19. C. Offe, "Crisis and Crisis Management", pp. 46–47.

*between size of use-value and exchange value commodities is irrelevant; whereas every increase in use-value production by capitalist states threatens the basis of exchange-value production.* While in Western capitalist societies the "foreign" element is *state organized non-exchange value* goods and services, the "foreign" element in Communist countries is the penetration of *capitalist production* and the operation of capitalist enterprises (by Communist societies) in foreign countries. The very political and material base of state power are completely different. Marxists who fall for general theories of bureaucracy are no better equipped to understand the dynamics of social change in different modes of production (e.g. in the USSR or Australia) than are the bourgeois ideological defenders of the mixed economy.

For bourgeois politicians and economists, the recognition of the contradictory role of capitalist states has resulted in a crisis of confidence and a search for alternative strategies. The faith that bourgeois political economy (whether Keynesian or Monetarist) is inherently capable of solving current crises is only believed by capitalists with an eye to past glories, and by Leftists who uncritically believe that capitalist states have an infinite capacity for technocratic solutions. It is little wonder that the recent historical growth of large state sectors has thrown capitalist classes into confusion. They are divided between working out new *limited* planning strategies (or major attempts at tax restructuring and efficiency drives) *within* the parliamentary process, or resorting to outright coercion and repressive discipline of the working classes. Both strategies are fraught with great danger. Moreover, even fascist solutions to defeat workers are themselves circumscribed by the precarious balance of international conflict (especially the possibility of nuclear war) which render rearmament and expansionary capitalist strategies (along the lines of Japan, Germany and Italy in the 1930s) no longer possible, short of suicidal conflict with the USSR. Similarly, the continuation of parliamentary processes or repressive alternatives will not necessarily guarantee accumulation processes if the as yet unknown ecological resources are depleted regardless of the organizational strength of the working class. All these factors are significant in that planning strategies are only possible if the monopoly and competitive sector units of production can resist nullifying one another and produce that fictitious collective will. It is for this reason that Offe asks:

What entitles us to talk about the "capitalist" state as if it were a part of social reality?[20]

No state in any capitalist society has been able to successfully and consistently reconcile the contradictory roles of maintaining accumulation and legitimation processes simultaneously without producing further crises:

The "reality" of the capitalist state can thus best be described as the reality (and dominance) of an unrealistic attempt. There is no method of policy formation available that could make this attempt more realistic. . . .[21]

In short, capitalist states can neither run on the basis of only technocratic rationality as Weber believed, nor are they able to supply this rationality in such an efficient manner as to not alter the very logic of private capitalist production.

---

20. C. Offe, "The Theory of the Capitalist State and the Problem of Policy Formation", p. 144.
21. *Ibid.*

# Selective Further Reading

Bachrach, P., and M. S. Baratz, 'The Two Faces of Power', *American Political Science Review* 56 (1962).

Block, Fred, 'The Ruling Class Does Not Rule: Notes on the Marxist Theory of the State', *Socialist Revolution* 7(3) (1977).

Boddy, R., and J. Crotty, 'Class Conflict, Keynesian Policies, and the Business Cycle', *Monthly Review* 26 (1974).

Dahl, Robert A., *Polyarchy: Participation and Opposition* (New Haven: Yale University Press, 1971).

———, *Who Governs? Democracy and Power in an American City* (New Haven and London: Yale University Press, 1975).

Giddens, Anthony, *A Contemporary Critique of Historical Materialism* (Berkeley: University of California Press, 1981).

Gold, D. A., et al., 'Recent Developments in Marxist Theories of the Capitalist State', *Monthly Review* 27(5–6) (1975).

Habermas, Jürgen, *Legitimation Crisis,* trans. T. McCarthy (London: Heinemann, 1976).

Held, D., and J. Krieger, 'Theories of the State', in *The State in Capitalist Europe,* ed. S. Bornstein et al. (London: Allen & Unwin, 1982).

Holloway, J., and S. Picciotto, eds., *State and Capital: A Marxist Debate* (London: Edward Arnold, 1978).

Jessop, B., 'Recent Theories of the Capitalist State', *Cambridge Journal of Economics* 1(4) (1977).

Lukes, Steven, *Power: A Radical Perspective* (London: Macmillan, 1974).

Mandel, E., *Late Capitalism* (London: New Left Books, 1975).

Miliband, Ralph, *The State in Capitalist Society* (London: Weidenfeld & Nicolson, 1969).

————, 'The Capitalist State—Reply to Nicos Poulantzas', in *Ideology in Social Science,* ed. R. Blackburn (London: Fontana, 1972).

————, *Marxism and Politics* (Oxford: Oxford University Press, 1977).

Miller, S. M., 'Notes on Neo-Capitalism', *Theory and Society* 2(1) (1975).

O'Connor, James, 'Who Rules the Corporations? The Ruling Class', *Socialist Revolution* 7(1971).

————, *The Fiscal Crisis of the State* (New York: St. Martins Press, 1973).

Offe, Claus, *Strukturprobleme des kapitalistischen Staates* (Frankfurt: Suhrkamp, 1972).

————, 'Structural Problems of the Capitalist State', *German Political Studies* 1 (1974).

————, *Berufsbildungsreform* (Frankfurt: Suhrkamp, 1975).

————, 'The Theory of the Capitalist State and the Problem of Policy Formation', in *Stress and Contradiction in Modern Capitalism,* ed. L. Lindberg et al. (Lexington, Mass.: Lexington Books, 1975).

————, *Industry and Inequality* (London: Edward Arnold, 1976).

Panitch, L., 'The Development of Corporatism in Liberal Democracies', *Comparative Political Studies* 10(1) (1977).

Parsons, T., and N.J. Smelser, *Economy and Society* (London: Routledge & Kegan Paul, 1957).

Poulantzas, Nicos, *Political Power and Social Classes* (London: New Left Books, 1973).

————, 'The Problem of the Capitalist State', in *Ideology in Social Science,* ed. R. Blackburn (London: Fontana, 1972).

————, *State, Power, Socialism* (London: Verso & New Left Books, 1980).

Rubinstein, W. D., 'Wealth, Elites, and the Class Structure of Modern Britain', *Past and Present* 76 (1977).

Schattschneider, E. E., *The Semi-Sovereign People: A Realist's View of Democracy in America* (New York: Rhinehart and Winston, 1960).

Schmitter, P. C., 'Still the Century of Corporatism?' *Review of Politics* 36(1) (1974).

————, 'Modes of Interest Intermediation and Models of Societal Change in Western Europe', *Comparative Political Studies* 10(1) (1977).

Scott, John, *Corporations, Classes and Capitalism* (London: Hutchinson, 1979).

Stanworth, Philip, and Anthony Giddens, *Elites and Power in British Society* (Cambridge: Cambridge University Press, 1974).

Therborn, Göran, *What Does the Ruling Class Do When It Rules?* (London: New Left Books, 1978).

Useem, M., 'The Inner Group of the American Capitalist Class', *Social Problems* 25 (1978).

Winkler, J. T., 'Corporatism', *Archives européennes de sociologie* 17(1) (1976).

Zeitlin, Maurice, 'On Class Theory of the Large Corporation', *American Journal of Sociology* 81(4) (1976).

Zeitlin, Maurice, ed., *American Society Inc.* (Chicago: Markham, 1970).

# ·IV·

# Technology, Conflict, and the Labour Market

# Introduction

## Factory Production and Labour Discipline

One of the foremost transitions that has accompanied the rise of capitalism, especially since the nineteenth century, the age of the spread of machine production, is the emergence of a 'workplace', distinct from the 'home'. The factory and the office have become a familiar part of the work experience of the mass of the population. Hence today it is hard to grasp the profound nature of the transformations which the consolidation of industrial capitalism has brought – about in our lives. Prior to the 'industrial revolution' in late eighteenth-century Britain, the majority of people lived in rural areas, and whether or not they were engaged in agricultural labour, their place of work was also their place of residence. Most forms of labour contrasted dramatically with those that became prevalent in the capitalist economic enterprise. We have already encountered aspects of such contrasts in Marx's discussion of alienated labour. The growing dominance of industrial production in the nineteenth century, however, involved something of a complete transformation in modes of life. In early nineteenth-century Britain, most of the population still lived in small communities, which had strongly established traditions of communal activity and mutual dependence. 'Work' was not clearly separated from the range of other activities which connected the individual to other members of the local community.

These traditions of agrarian life were shattered by the spread of industrialism. A people unaccustomed to the disciplines of regularised labour, governed by the clock, were required to adapt to a quite different style of daily life. What occurred in Britain in the nineteenth century, the moulding of an initially recalcitrant labour force to the demands of industrial discipline, has since been repeated in varying forms across the face of the contemporary industrialized world. But what accounts for the spread of factory production initially? And what kinds of changes in forms of life did the consolidation of industrial capitalism bring about in the daily life of the worker? There is a vast historical literature on these issues, and in this section we include two of the most significant discussions of recent years, from Stephen Marglin and E. P. Thompson.

As Marglin points out, the origin of the hierarchical discipline characteristic of the capitalistic workplace is a matter of quite fundamental importance to social theory. If, as Weber tended to presume and as is also held in orthodox economic theory, hierarchy is a price that has to be paid for the efficiency of industrial production, then Marx's hopes of transforming the division of labour appear as almost whimsically utopian. Even from within Marxist thought itself, in a famous article by Engels on 'authority', there seems to be an acceptance of the inevitability of strict hierarchical discipline in industrial production. Thus Engels, whom Marglin quotes in the opening pages of his article, says that 'large-scale industry' involves a 'veritable despotism' by its very nature; wanting to abolish this 'despotism', he continues, 'is tantamount to wanting to abolish industry itself, to destroy the power loom in order to return to the spinning wheel'. Isolation of these few passages perhaps makes Engels's views sound more crude than they actually were; and there seem to be considerable divergencies between Marx and Engels in respect of the potential reorganisation of industrial production in the context of a socialist society. But one cannot doubt the far-reaching implications of the issues involved. They relate closely to the matters raised by Braverman previously (and discussed in detail by David Stark below).

If the social sciences were able to utilise experimental method, Marglin says, it would be relatively easy to resolve the problem of whether 'despotic' or bureaucratic hierarchy is the necessary price of technological progress. We could design 'egalitarian technologies' and see what the results might be. In lieu of such possibilities, however, we have to adopt the more cumbersome method of trying to sort out the various influences historically. By examining the early spread of factory production in the nineteenth century, Marglin tries to examine how far the triumph of hierarchical authority in the workplace can be accounted for in terms of its superior efficiency.

Marglin admits, of course, that hierarchical organisations are not peculiar to capitalism but have existed in a variety of other contexts previously. In earlier forms of craft production, for instance, there was a strict hierarchical differentiation between masters, journeymen, and apprentices. However, the hierarchies of authority associated with capitalism are distinct from this more traditional form. Unlike in large-scale capitalist organisations, in the feudal guilds the master worked alongside his subordinates; apprentices could become journeymen and perhaps masters themselves in the eventuality of time; and the worker in the medieval guild sold his products not his labour power.

Following Marx and many later economic historians, Marglin distinguishes two main steps in the process whereby workers were expropriated from control of their means of production. The first is the so-called 'putting-out system', in which workers in cottage industries were employed by entrepreneurs who supplied their raw materials and sold their products. The putting-out system marked a major advance in the detailed division of labour; but workers still had considerable command over the labour process itself since they worked in their homes away from any direct or continuous supervision. The second phase is the spread of factory production, in which workers are assembled in a single work-place, or cluster of workplaces, and in which power machinery is characteristically prominent. The main thread of Marglin's argument is that neither stage in the development of industry can be explained in terms of advances in technical efficiency which they might have made possible.

Rather, they are to be explained in terms of the consolidation of the power of employers over a workforce consisting increasingly of wage labourers. In the phase of development dominated by the putting-out system, by expanding the division of labour, entrepreneurs were able to stabilise their ascendency over the overall process of production. Workers engaged in a relatively restricted labour task became dependent upon 'bosses' who could integrate their various contributions to the final product and dispose of that product on the market. But under the putting-out system, the authority of employer over the labour force was limited by the elements of control the workers maintained over the work task. Their work was often irregular, variable in quality and in quantity. The shepherding of the labour force into factories, Marglin argues, enabled employers to subject workers to direct supervision and by this means, as well as by further fragmenting the labour task via mechanisation, was able to achieve much higher levels of labour discipline than were previously possible.

Some of the key elements involved in the creation of a compliant industrial labour force are examined in Thompson's elegant discussion of time and work discipline. Picking up a clue from Mumford, who has claimed that the clock rather than the power machine is the distinguishing feature of the industrial age, Thompson studies the connections between changing perceptions of time and capitalistic domestic and factory labour. The practices of having a defined 'working day' and of organising one's daily habits according to clock time are very recent developments. In pointing up their significance, Thompson draws upon Evans-Pritchard's celebrated portrayal of time-reckoning among the Nuer—a portrayal that seems to hold good for a vast range of human cultures prior to eighteenth-century Europe. The temporal ordering of Nuer life is directly integrated with the cycle of activities in which the community is involved; 'time' is not the separable, abstract dimension that it has become in the industrialised societies today. 'Succession in time' is experienced in the succession of activities of daily life and the passing of the seasons.

It would not be accurate to call this a 'disregard for time'; but it certainly implies attitudes and modes of behavior that do not accord with the regularised clock time with which we have become familiar. Time experience in such communities is described by Thompson as 'task-oriented'. 'Task-oriented' labour is 'more humanly comprehensible than timed labour' because what the worker does is bound to felt necessities or needs rather than imposed from without; social life and labour intermingle with one another rather than 'work' being a separate sphere from other aspects of daily activity; and a sense of urgency is rarely present, in contrast to the pressurised nature of much modern industrial labour.

It is apparent how close this description comes to Marx's analysis of alienated labour, but Thompson indicates that it also connects very directly to Marx's mature writings on capitalism. For in the capitalist economy, according to Marx, the value of labour power and other commodities is measured in terms of units of labour time. Time which is sold to the employer is experienced as separate from 'free time', which is whatever is left over after work and at the disposal of the individual. Time becomes both a measure of scarce resources and itself a scarce resource, to employer and worker alike, although in different ways according to the asymmetrical character of their relationship. Time is no longer passed, as Thompson says, but spent.

Thompson's work lends support to Marglin's standpoint. As long as manufacturing industry remained within the putting-out system, Thompson shows, the coordination of a detailed division of labour remained difficult and the development of the division of labour retarded. Prior to the concentration of activities in the factory, work retained that irregularity characteristic of peasant labour. Moreover, many workers were involved in more than one occupation either on a continuous basis or in periodic cycles during the year. The eradication of irregular habits of labour, and the synchronising of workers in a complex division of labour, was in the early period of industrial capitalism a protracted process. As Thompson adds, it has never been one that has been wholly successful. Many workers today continue to honour 'Saint Monday'; absenteeism and high rates of labour mobility remain characteristics of the more numbing forms of industrial labour.

## The Labour Process and Labour Markets

That workers have, in various ways, actively resisted the imposition of forms of labour discipline thought desirable by employers or by management and continue to do so today is a leading theme of Stark's article. His work can be read as a critical appreciation of Braverman's *Labour and Monopoly Capital*. Stark recognises the enduring nature of Braverman's contribution to class theory but also shows it to have some serious shortcomings. Some of what Stark has to say, however, is also relevant to the critique of the approach of other authors discussed earlier (most particularly, Poulantzas and Wright).

Braverman's work is found by Stark first of all to be open to question in respect of historical accuracy. Braverman writes of 'scientific management' as though it enjoyed an immediate and lasting success in industry in the United States and elsewhere. However, many employers distrusted Taylor's schemes— as Taylor himself often resentfully complained. Taylor was an active propagandist for his ideas, but they did not at all always find a favourable audience among industrialists. More important perhaps, since it is possible to claim that weaker or partial versions of Taylorism were eventually incorporated into management strategies in numerous industries, is Braverman's surprising disinclination to analyse worker resistance as a major obstacle to the implementation of Taylorist policies.

The relative absence of discussion by Braverman of worker resistance to the imposition of disliked forms of labour organisation has been noted by many commentators. Stark shows that it is in some part the result of a misleading use that Braverman makes of Marx's distinction between class 'in itself' and class 'for itself'. Braverman equates the first of these with 'objective' factors in class relations, the second with 'subjective' factors. He then says that in his book he is going to confine his analysis to 'objective' aspects of class. But this leads to a curious imbalance in the book because much of it—being concerned with the importation of Taylorism into managerial strategy—is necessarily about the 'subjectivity' of industrialists and managers. Thus, what one might have imagined would have been at the forefront of a self-declaredly 'Marxist' work, class struggle as an integral feature of industrial relations, barely gets a look in at all.

Stark tries to correct this imbalance, tracing the fate of Taylorism, as he puts it, 'through the prism of class struggle'. There has not been as inexorable a process of 'de-skilling' over the past century as Braverman contends. Craft workers have found various ways of defending their position—against other sectors of the working class as well as against employers. In part by methods of labour market 'closure', limiting recruitment to an occupation demanding special aptitudes and lengthy training, craft workers have quite consistently been able to protect established privileges. The implications of this are clear and important: class struggle, at least at the 'site' of production, over control of the labour process, may be directly involved in the chronic fragmentation of the working class rather than producing its unification.

Jill Rubery's study helps flesh out this conclusion by focussing upon conflicts in different sectors of labour markets. The influence of the labour market upon class formation and consciousness has, at least until quite recently, been poorly analysed by many class theorists. Indeed, because of a supposed association with 'Weberianism', Marxists have quite often neglected it altogether. It is evident that this was a serious mistake, as contemporary work on labour market segmentation demonstrates. Rubery distinguishes two sorts of theoretical approach associated with this contemporary work: 'dual labour market' theories and what she calls 'radical' theories. The former explain the segmentation of labour markets primarily by reference to technological change, the latter more by reference to the strategies used by employers or management in dealing with the labour force. Radical theories were in some part developments out of dual labour market theories; Rubery's argument is that more attention to the activities of workers themselves is required to pursue these developments still further.

The pioneering work of Doeringer and Priore was particularly important in the emergence of dual labour market theory. Their work is based upon the idea that in advanced capitalism, 'protected' or sheltered segments of labour markets become dislocated from other sectors in which workers lack such security. Thus, firms tend to have a strong commitment to their skilled workers and, in the interests of maintaining a stable skilled labour force, will pay them wages of a high enough level to inhibit their movement to other firms in the external labour market. According to Doeringer and Priore, the labour market thus becomes divided into primary and secondary sectors. Technology and, consequently, workers' skills have become increasingly firm-specific in advanced capitalism; these factors explain why corporations need a stable 'core' labour force. The primary sector, in this view, is the main locus of significant technological innovation. In the secondary sector of labour markets, security of employment is low, as are wages, and a range of other economic conditions compare unfavourably with those prevalent in the primary sector.

Radical labour market theories admit the influence of technological change in market segmentation but inject a more direct class component. The segmentation of labour markets is a phenomenon sustaining employer control by dividing the labour force against itself. According to this approach, there are typically more than two axes of fragmentation in labour markets. Besides the separation of primary and secondary sectors, there is also differentiation in internal labour markets. Those workers in the most peripheral sectors of labour markets, with the weakest conditions of labour, tend to be subject to general social discrimination: female or ethnic minority workers (or both). Since workers in the more sheltered sectors of labour markets are unlikely to identify their interests with such groups, employers are able to pay low wages to those in peripheral sectors without much fear of organised worker opposition.

Braverman's work, Rubery argues, has some considerable relevance to the elaboration of radical theories of labour markets. In common with Stark, however, Rubery points out that because Braverman sought to exclude 'subjective' factors of working-class consciousness, he provides no analysis of bargaining or of wage determination. In order to combat de-skilling, the more established sectors of the labour force mobilise to control entry to occupations and protect their privileged position even if the actual technological content of the labour task becomes altered. Rubery thus reaches conclusions similar to those of Stark. Class struggle carried on in an organised way by certain sectors of the labour force conjoins with managerial strategies to generate labour market segmentation. Employers are inclined to acquiesce in recognising sheltered labour market positions, especially in internal labour markets; or they are in some part forced to acquiesce by the power of certain sectors of the labour force.

## · 14 ·

# What Do the Bosses Do? The Origins and Functions of Hierarchy in Capitalist Production

### Stephen A. Marglin

### Introduction: Does Technology Shape Social and Economic Organization or Does Social and Economic Organization Shape Technology?

Is it possible for work to contribute positively to individual development in a complex industrial society, or is alienating work the price that must be paid for material prosperity? Discussions of the possibilities for meaningful revolution generally come down, sooner or later, to this question. If hierarchical authority is essential to high productivity, then self-expression in work must at best be a luxury reserved for the very few regardless of social and economic organization. And even the satisfactions of society's elite must be perverted by their dependence, with rare exception, on the denial of self-expression to others. But is work organization determined by technology or by society? Is hierarchical authority really necessary to high levels of production, or is material prosperity compatible with nonhierarchical organization of production?

Defenders of the capitalist faith are quite sure that hierarchy is inescapable. Indeed their ultimate line of defense is that the plurality of capitalist hierarchies is preferable to a single socialist hierarchy. To seal the argument the apologist may call on as unlikely a source of support as Friedrich Engels. Perhaps it was a

•Abridged from *Review of Radical Political Economics* 6(2) (1974): 60–70, 81–86, 89–92.
    NOTE: The research on which this paper reports is still in progress. It is published in its present form to stimulate discussion and comment. This paper represents my initial and in parts preliminary thinking on this subject, and no attempt has been made to reflect the many helpful criticisms and suggestions I have received.

momentary aberration, but at one point in his career at least Engels saw authority as technologically rather than socially determined:

If man, by dint of his knowledge and inventive genius, has subdued the forces of nature, the latter avenge themselves upon him by subjecting him, in so far as he employs them, to a veritable despotism, *independent of all social organization.* Wanting to abolish authority in large-scale industry is tantamount to wanting to abolish industry itself, to destroy the power loom in order to return to the spinning wheel.[1]

Going back to the spinning wheel is obviously absurd, and if the producer must typically take orders, it is difficult to see how work could in the main be anything but alienating.

Were the social sciences experimental, the methodology for deciding whether or not hierarchical work organization is inseparable from high material productivity would be obvious. One would design technologies appropriate to an egalitarian work organization, and test the designs in actual operation. Experience would tell whether or not egalitarian work organization is utopian. But social science is not experimental. None of us has the requisite knowledge of steel-making or cloth-making to design a new technology, much less to design one so radically different from the present norm as a serious attempt to change work organization would dictate. Besides in a society whose basic institutions—from schools to factories—are geared to hierarchy, the attempt to change one small component is probably doomed to failure. For all its shortcomings, neoclassical economics is undoubtedly right in emphasising *general* equilibrium over *partial* equilibrium.

Instead of seeking alternative designs, we must take a more roundabout tack. In this paper it is asked why, in the course of capitalist development, the actual producer lost control of production. What circumstances gave rise to the boss-worker pyramid that characterizes capitalist production? And what social function does the capitalist hierarchy serve? If it turns out that the origin and function of capitalist hierarchy has relatively little to do with efficiency, then it becomes at least an open question whether or not hierarchical production is essential to a high material standard of living. And workers—manual, technical, and intellectual—may take the possibility of egalitarian work organization sufficiently seriously to examine their environment with a view to changing the economic, social, and political institutions that relegate all but a fortunate few to an existence in which work is the means to life, not part of life itself.

It is the contention of this paper that neither of the two decisive steps in depriving the workers of control of product and process—(1) the development of the minute division of labor that characterized the putting-out system and (2) the development of the centralized organization that characterizes the factory system—took place primarily for reasons of technical superiority. Rather than providing more output for the same inputs, these innovations in work organization were introduced so that the capitalist got himself a larger share of the pie at the expense of the worker, and it is only the *subsequent* growth in the size of the

---

1. F. Engels, "On Authority," first published in *Almenacco Republicano,* 1894; English translation in Marx and Engels, *Basic Writings in Politics and Philosophy,* L. Feuer (ed.), Doubleday and Co., Garden City, New York, 1959, p. 483. Emphasis added.

pie that has obscured the class interest which was at the root of these innovations. The social function of hierarchical work organization is not technical
efficiency, but accumulation. By mediating between producer and consumer,
the capitalist organization sets aside much more for expanding and improving
plant and equipment than individuals would if they could control the pace of
capital accumulation. These ideas, which are developed in the body of this
paper, can be conveniently divided into four specific propositions.

1. The capitalist division of labor, typified by Adam Smith's famous
   example of pin manufacture, was the result of a search not for a
   technologically superior organization of work, but for an organization which guaranteed to the entrepreneur an essential role in the
   production process, as integrator of the separate efforts of his
   workers into a marketable product.

2. Likewise, the origin and success of the factory lay not in technological superiority, but in the substitution of the capitalist's for the
   worker's control of the work process and the quantity of output, in
   the change in the workman's choice from one of how much to work
   and produce, based on his relative preferences for leisure and goods,
   to one of whether or not to work at all, which of course is hardly
   much of a choice.

3. The social function of hierarchical control of production is to provide for the accumulation of capital. The individual, by and large
   and on the average, does not save by a conscious and deliberate
   choice. The pressures to spend are simply too great. Such individual
   (household) savings as do occur are the consequence of a lag in
   adjusting spending to a rise in income, for spending, like any other
   activity, must be learned, and learning takes time. Thus individual
   savings is the consequence of growth, and not an independent cause.
   Acquisitive societies—precapitalist, capitalist or socialist—develop
   institutions whereby collectivities determine the rate of accumulation. In modern capitalist society the pre-eminent collectivity for
   accumulation is the corporation. It is an essential social function of
   the corporation that its hierarchy mediate between the individual
   producer (and shareholder) and the market proceeds of the corporation's product, assigning a portion of these proceeds to enlarging the
   means of production. In the absence of hierarchical control of production, society would either have to fashion egalitarian institutions
   for accumulating capital or content itself with the level of capital
   already accumulated.

4. The emphasis on accumulation accounts in large part for the failure
   of Soviet-style socialism to "overtake and surpass" the capitalist
   world in developing egalitarian forms of work organization. In according first priority to the accumulation of capital, the Soviet Union repeated the history of capitalism, at least as regards the relationship of men and women to their work. Theirs has not been the

failure described by Santayana of those who, not knowing history, unwittingly repeat it. The Soviets consciously and deliberately embraced the capitalist mode of production. And defenders of the Soviet path to economic development would offer no apology: after all, they would probably argue, egalitarian institutions and an egalitarian (and community oriented) man could not have been created over night, and the Soviet Union rightly felt itself too poor to contemplate an indefinite end to accumulation. Now, alas, the Soviets have the "catch-up-with-and-surpass-the-U.S.A." tiger by the tail, for it would probably take as much of a revolution to transform work organization in that society as in ours.

The following sections of this paper take these propositions one by one, in the hope of filling in sufficient detail to give them credibility.

## Divide and Conquer

Hierarchy was of course not invented by capitalists. More to the point, neither was hierarchical production. In precapitalist societies, industrial production was organized according to a rigid master-journeyman-apprentice hierarchy, which survives today in anything like its pure form only in the graduate departments of our universities. What distinguished precapitalist from capitalist hierarchy was first that the man at the top was, like the man at the bottom, a producer. The master worked along with his apprentice rather than simply telling him what to do. Second, the hierarchy was linear rather than pyramidal. The apprentice would one day become a journeyman and likely a master. Under capitalism it is a rare worker who becomes even a foreman, not to mention independent entrepreneur or corporate president. Third, and perhaps most important, the guild workman had no intermediary between himself and the market. He generally sold a product, not his labor, and therefore controlled both product and work process.

Just as hierarchy did not originate with capitalism, neither did the division of labor. The *social* division of labor, the specialization of occupation and function, *is* a characteristic of all complex societies, rather than a peculiar feature of industrialized or economically advanced ones. Nothing, after all, could be more elaborate than the caste division of labor and its accompanying hierarchy in traditional Hindu society. Nor is the *technical* division of labor peculiar to capitalism or modern industry. Cloth production, for example, even under the guild system was divided into separate tasks, each controlled by specialists. But, as we have said, the guild workman controlled product and process. What we have to account for is why the guild division of labor evolved into the capitalist division of labor, in which the workman's task typically became so specialized and minute that he had no product to sell, or at least none for which there was a wide market, and had therefore to make use of the capitalist as intermediary to integrate his labor with the labor of others and transform the whole into a marketable product.

Adam Smith argues that the capitalist division of labor came about because of its technological superiority; in his view, the superiority of dividing work into ever more minutely specialized tasks was limited only by the size of the market.[2] To understand the limitations of this explanation requires clarity and precision on the meaning of "technological superiority," and the related ideas of technological efficiency and inefficiency; indeed, these ideas are central to the whole story told in this paper. We shall say, in accordance with accepted usage, that a method of production is technologically superior to another if it produces more output with the same inputs. It is not enough that a new method of production yield more output per day to be technologically superior. Even if labor is the only input, a new method of production might require more hours of labor, or more intensive effort, or more unpleasant working conditions, in which case it would be providing more output for more input, not for the same amount. It will be argued here that—contrary to neoclassical logic—a new method of production does not have to be technologically superior to be adopted; innovation depends as much on economic and social institutions—on who is in control of production and under what constraints control is exercised.

The terms "technological efficiency" and "technological inefficiency," as used by economists, have meanings that are slightly at variance with the ordinary, every-day ideas of better and worse that they evoke. A method of production is technologically efficient if no technologically superior alternative exists. It is inefficient if a superior alternative does exist. Thus more than one method of production may be—and generally is—technologically efficient if one looks only at a single product. Wheat, for example, can be efficiently produced with a lot of land and relatively little fertilizer, as in Kansas, or with a lot of fertilizer and relatively little land, as in Holland.

But if one views technological superiority and efficiency from the point of view of the whole economy, these concepts reduce, under certain circumstances, to *economic* superiority and efficiency. Under text-book assumptions of perfect and universal competition, the technologically efficient method of production is the one that costs least, and cost reduction is an index of technological superiority.[3] The relationship between minimum cost and technological efficiency is a purely logical one and does not depend at all on whether or not the world exhibits the assumptions of the model. On the other hand, the relevance of the identification of technological with economic efficiency depends absolutely on the applicability of the assumptions of the competitive model to the development of capitalism. In critical respects the development of capitalism necessarily required denial, not fulfillment, of the assumptions of perfect competition.

In a way it is surprising that the development of capitalist methods of work

---

2. The attribution of the division of labor to efficiency antedates Adam Smith by at least two millenia. Plato, indeed, argued for the political institutions of the Republic on the basis of an analogy with the virtue of specialization in the economic sphere. Smith's specific arguments were anticipated by Henry Martyn three quarters of a century before the publication of the *Wealth of Nations*. See *Considerations Upon the East-India Trade* (London, 1701).

3. For a concise and elegant discussion of the relationship between technological efficiency and least-cost methods of production, see Tjalling Koopmans, *Three Essays on the State of Economic Science,* McGraw-Hill, New York, 1957, essay 1, especially pp. 66–126.

organization contradicts essential assumptions of perfect competition, since perfect competition has virtually nothing to say about the organization of production! Indeed, even the firm itself, a central economic institution under capitalism, plays no essential role in models of the competitive economy;[4] it is merely a convenient abstraction for the household in its role as producer and does nothing that households could not equally well do for themselves. Defenders of the faith from Wicksell to Samuelson have grandly proclaimed the perfect neutrality of perfect competition—as far as the model goes, workers could as well hire capital as capitalist workers![5] Alas, the failure of the competitive model to account for one of the most distinctive features of capitalism (and of socialism imitating capitalism)—the pyramidal work order—is for neoclassical economists a great virtue rather than a shortcoming; it is supposed to show the great generality of the theory. Generality indeed: neoclassical theory says only that hierarchy must be technologically efficient to persist, but denies the superiority of capitalist hierarchy (workers can just as well hire capital, remember!). This is to say very little, and that little, it will be argued, quite wrong.

To return to Adam Smith. *The Wealth of Nations* advances three arguments for the technological superiority of dividing labor as finely as the market will allow.

(This) great increase of the quantity of work, which, in consequence of the division of labor, the same number of people are capable of performing, is owing to three different circumstances; first, to the increase of dexterity in every particular workman; secondly, to the saving of the time which is commonly lost in passing from one species of work to another; and lastly, to the invention of a great number of machines which facilitate labor and abridge labor, and enable one man to do the work of many.[6]

Of the three arguments, one—the saving of time—is undoubtedly important. But this argument has little or nothing to do with the minute specialization that characterizes the capitalist division of labor. A peasant, for example, will generally plow a whole field before harrowing it rather than alternating plow and harrow, furrow by furrow—in order to economize on the set-up time. But peasant agriculture is the antithesis of capitalist specialization; the individual peasant normally undertakes all the activities necessary to bring a crop from seed to marketable product. In respect of set-up time, there is nothing to differentiate agriculture from industry. To save "the time that is commonly lost in passing from one species of work to another" it is necessary only to continue in a single activity long enough that the set-up time becomes an insignificant proportion of total work time. The saving of time would require at most only that each

---

4. At least in the constant-returns-to-scale version of the competitive economy. Any other version implies the existence of a factor of production (like "entrepreneurial effort") that is not traded on the market, and with respect to which the model is therefore noncompetitive.

5. "We may, therefore, assume either that the landowner will hire laborers for a wage . . . or that the laborers will hire the land for rent." Knut Wicksell, *Lectures on Political Economy* (translated by E. Classen), Routledge & Kegan Paul, London, 1934, Volume I, p. 109.

"Remember that in a perfectly competitive market it really doesn't matter who hires whom; so have labor hire 'capital'" . . . , Paul Samuelson, "Wage and Interest: A Modern Dissection of Marxian Economic Models," *American Economic Review*, December, 1957.

6. A. Smith, *The Wealth of Nations* (Cannan edition), Random House, New York, 1937, p. 7.

worker continue in a single activity for days at a time, not for a whole life time. Saving of time implies *separation* of tasks and *duration* of activity, not *specialization*.

Smith's third argument—the propensity to invention—is not terribly persuasive. Indeed, the most devastating criticism was voiced by Smith himself in a later chapter of *The Wealth of Nations:*

> In the progress of the division of labor, the employment of the far greater part of those who have by labor, that is, of the great body of the people, come to be confined to a few very simple operations, frequently to one or two. But the understandings of the greater part of men are formed by their ordinary employments. The man whose life is spent in performing a few simple operations, of which the effects too are, perhaps, always the same, or very nearly the same, has no occasion to exert his understanding, or to exercise his invention in finding out expedients for difficulties which never occur. He naturally loses, therefore, the habit of such exertion and generally becomes as stupid and ignorant as it is possible for a human creature to become. . . .
>
> It is otherwise in the barbarous societies, as they are commonly called, of hunters, of shepherds, and even of husbandmen in that crude state of husbandry which preceeds the improvement of manufactures. In such societies the varied occupations of every man oblige every man to exert his capacity, and to invent expedients for removing difficulties which are continually occurring. Invention is kept alive, and the mind is not suffered to fall into that drowsy stupidity, which, in a civilized society, seems to benumb the understanding of almost all the inferior ranks of people.[7]

The choice does not, however, seem really to lie between stupidity and barbarity, but between the workman whose span of control is wide enough that he sees how each operation fits into the whole and the workman confined to a small number of repetitive tasks. It would be surprising indeed if the workman's propensity to invent has not been diminished by the extreme specialization that characterizes the capitalist division of labor.

This leaves "the increase of dexterity in every particular workman" as the basis of carrying specialization to the limits permitted by the size of the market. Now if Adam Smith were talking about musicians or dancers or surgeons, or even if he were speaking of the division of labor between pin-making and cloth-making, his argument would be difficult to counter. But he is speaking not of esoteric specializations nor of the social division of labor, but of the minute division of ordinary, run-of-the-mill, industrial activities into separate skills. Take his favorite example of pin manufacture:

> in the way in which this business is now carried on, not only the whole work is a peculiar trade, but it is divided into a number of branches, of which the greater part are likewise peculiar trades. One man draws out the wire, another straights it, a third cuts it, a fourth points it, a fifth grinds it at the top for receiving the head; to make the head requires two or three distinct operations; to put it on, is a peculiar business, to whiten the pins is another; it is even a trade by itself to put them into the paper; and the important business of making a pin is, in this manner, divided into about eighteen distinct operations, which in some manufactories, are all performed by distinct hands, though in others the same man will sometimes perform two or three of them. I have seen a small manufactory of this kind where ten men only were employed, and where some of them consequently performed two or three distinct operations. But though they were very poor, and there-

---

7. Smith, *op. cit.*, pp. 734–35.

fore but indifferently accommodated with the necessary equipment, they could, when they exerted themselves, make among them about twelve pounds of pins in a day. There are in a pound upwards of four thousand pins of a middling size. Those ten persons, therefore could make among them upwards of forty-eight thousand pins in a day. Each person, therefore, making a tenth part of forty-eight thousand pins, might be considered as making four thousand eight hundred pins in a day. But if they had all wrought separately and independently, and without any of them having been educated to this peculiar business, they certainly could not each of them have made twenty, perhaps not one pin in a day. . . .[8]

To the extent that the skills at issue are difficult to acquire, specialization is essential to the division of production into separate operations. But, judging from the earnings of the various specialists engaged in pin-making, these were no special skills. At least there were none that commanded premium wages. In a pin manufactory for which fairly detailed records survive from the early part of the nineteenth century, T. S. Ashton reported wages for adult males of approximately 20 shillings per week, irrespective of the particular branch in which they were engaged.[9] Women and children, as was customary, earned less, but again there appear to be no great discrepancies among the various branches of pin production. It would appear to be the case that the mysteries of pin-making were relatively quickly learned, and that the potential increase in dexterity afforded by minute division of tasks was quickly exhausted. Certainly it is hard to make a case for specialization of workmen to particular tasks on the basis of the pin industry.[10]

The dichotomy between specialization and the separate crafting of each individual pin seems to be a false one. It appears to have been technologically possible to obtain the economics of reducing set-up time *without* specialization. A workman, and his wife and children, could have proceeded from task to task, first drawing out enough wire for hundreds or thousands of pins, then straightening it, then cutting it, and so on with each successive operation, thus realizing the advantages of dividing the overall production process into separate tasks.

Why, then, did the division of labor under the putting-out system entail specialization as well as separation of tasks? In my view the reason lies in the fact

---

8. Smith, *op. cit.*, pp. 4–5.

9. T. S. Ashton, "The Records of a Pin Manufactory—1814–21," *Economica,* November, 1925, pp. 281–292.

10. For another example, cotton handloom weaving, though described by J. L. and Barbara Hammond in a volume entitled *The Skilled Laborer* (Longmans Green, London, 1919), was apparently a skill quickly learned (p. 70). A British manufacturer testified before a parliamentary committee that "a lad of fourteen may acquire a sufficient knowledge of it in six weeks." Duncan Bythell's *The Handloom Weavers,* (Cambridge University Press, Cambridge, England, 1969), which is my immediate source for the manufacturer's testimony, is quite explicit: "Cotton handloom weaving, from its earliest days, was an unskilled, casual occupation which provided a domestic by-trade for thousands of women and children . . ." (p. 270).

The apparent ease with which, according to the Hammonds, women replaced male woolen weavers gone off to fight Napoleon suggests that woolen weaving too was not such a difficult skill to acquire (*op. cit.*, pp. 60–162). Indeed the competition of women in some branches of the woolen trade was such that in at least one place the men felt obliged to bind themselves collectively "not to allow any women to learn the trade" (*ibid.*, p. 162), an action that would hardly have been necessary if the requisite strength or skill had been beyond the power of women to acquire. The role of war-induced labor shortages in breaking down artificial sex barriers, and the subsequent difficulties in re-establishing these barriers is reminiscent of American experience in World War II.

that without specialization, the capitalist had no essential role to play in the production process. If each producer could himself integrate the component tasks of pin manufacture into a marketable product, he would soon discover that he had no need to deal with the market for pins through the intermediation of the putter-outer. He could sell directly and appropriate to himself the profit that the capitalist derived from mediating between the producer and the market. Separating the tasks assigned to each workman was the sole means by which the capitalist could, in the days preceding costly machinery, ensure that he would remain essential to the production process as integrator of these separate operations into a product for which a wide market existed; and specialization of men to tasks at the sub-product level was the hallmark of the putting-out system.

The capitalist division of labor, as developed under the putting-out system, embodied the same principle that "successful" imperial powers have utilized to rule their colonies: divide and conquer. Exploiting differences between Hindu and Muslim in India—if not actually creating them—the British could claim to be essential to the stability of the sub-continent. And they could, sometimes with ill-concealed satisfaction, point to the millions of deaths that followed Partition as proof of their necessity to stability. But this tragedy proved only that the British had *made* themselves essential as mediators, not that there was any inherent need for British mediation of communal differences.

Similarly, the development of an industrial system dependent on capitalist integration does not prove that the capitalist division of labor was technologically superior to integration by the producer himself. The putter-outer's peculiar contribution to production was handsomely rewarded not because of any genuine scarcity of the ability to integrate separate functions; rather the scarcity was artificially created to preserve the capitalist's role. . . .

## The Emergence of the Factory

The minute specialization that was the hallmark of the putting-out system only wiped out one of two aspects of workers' control of production: control over the product. Control of the work process, when and how much the worker would exert himself, remained with the worker—until the coming of the factory.

Economic historians customarily ascribe the growth of the factory to the technological superiority of large-scale machinery, which required concentration of productive effort around newly harnessed sources of energy—water and steam. The first factories, according to T. S. Ashton, arose in the beginning of the eighteenth century when *"for technical reasons,* small groups of men were brought together into workshops and little water-driven mills."[11] But the beginnings of the modern factory system are usually associated with Richard Arkwright, whose spinning mills displaced the domestic manufacture of cotton yarn. Arkwright's "water frame," it is said, dictated the factory organization of spinning: "Unlike the jenny, the frame required, for its working, power greater

---

11. T. S. Ashton, *The Industrial Revolution 1760–1830,* Oxford University Press, London, 1948, p. 33. Emphasis added.

than that of human muscles, and hence from the beginning the process was carried on in mills or factories."[12] Other authorities agree. Thus Paul Mantoux: ". . . the use of machines distinguishes the factory from (the putting-out system), and gives its special character to the new system as against all preceeding ones. . ."[13] And, more recently, David Landes has written

The Industrial Revolution . . . required machines which not only replaced hand labor but compelled the concentration of production in factories—in other words machines whose appetite for energy was too large for domestic sources of power and whose mechanical superiority was sufficient to break down the resistance of the older forms of hand production.[14]

These authorities, it should be said, recognize the other advantages the factory afforded, particularly a system of discipline and supervision that was impossible under the putting-out system. "It was", as Ashton says, "the need for supervision of work that led Peter Stubbs to gather the scattered filemakers into his works at Warrington."[15] Mantoux also notes the "obvious advantages from the point of view of organization and supervision"[16] of bringing together many workers into a single workshop. According to Landes the need for discipline and supervision turned "the thoughts of employers . . . to workshops where the men would be brought together to labor under watchful overseers."[17] And elsewhere Landes is even more explicit. "The essence of the factory," he writes in an introduction to a volume of essays on the development of capitalism, "is discipline—the opportunity it affords for the direction of and coordination of labor."[18]

Nevertheless, the advantages of discipline and supervision remain, in the conventional view, secondary considerations in accounting for the success of the factory system, if not for the motivation behind it. In the same breath as Mantoux notes the organizational advantages of the factory, he concludes that "the factory system . . . was the necessary outcome of the use of machinery."[19] Similarly, while identifying discipline as the essence of the factory, Landes attributes its success to technological factors: "the triumph of concentrated over dispersed manufacture was indeed made possible by the economic advantages of power-driven equipment. The factory had to beat cottage industry in the marketplace, and it was not an easy victory."[20]

---

12. *Ibid.*, p. 72.

13. P. Mantoux, *The Industrial Revolution in the Eighteenth Century*, Harper and Row, New York, 1962, p. 39 (first English edition published in 1928).

14. D. S. Landes, *The Unbound Prometheus*, Cambridge University Press, Cambridge, England, 1969, p. 81.

15. *The Industrial Revolution, op. cit.*, p. 109. See also Ashton, *An Eighteenth Century Industrialist*, p. 26.

16. *The Industrial Revolution in the Eighteenth Century, op. cit.*, p. 246.

17. Landes, *op. cit.*, p. 60.

18. D. S. Landes, (ed.), *The Rise of Capitalism*, Macmillan, New York, 1966, p. 14.

19. Mantoux, *op. cit.*, p. 246.

20. *Ibid.*, p. 14. Cf. Herbert Heaton, *The Yorkshire Woolen and Worsted Industries*, Oxford University Press, Oxford, 1920: "the major part of the economic advantage of the factory springs from the use of machinery capable of performing work quickly, and the use of power which can make the machinery go at high speed." p. 352.

The model underlying this reasoning is easy to identify: the factory survived, therefore it must have been a less costly method of production than alternatives. And in the competitive market economy, only least-cost methods are technologically efficient, provided efficiency is defined in an economy-wide sense. Hence the factory must have been technologically superior to alternatives.

However, the very mention of supervision and discipline as motivations for the factory ought to put one on guard against a too-easy identification of cost-minimization with technological efficiency. In the competitive model, there is no scope for supervision and discipline except for that imposed by the market mechanism.[21] Any recognition of the importance of supervision and discipline as motivating forces behind the establishment of factories is tantamount to admission of important violations of the assumptions of perfect competition, and it follows that cost minimization cannot be identified with technological efficiency. Thus, technological superiority becomes neither necessary nor sufficient for the rise and success of the factory.

It will be argued presently that the agglomeration of workers into factories was a natural outgrowth of the putting-out system (a result, if you will, of its internal contradictions) whose success had little or nothing to do with the technological superiority of large-scale machinery. The key to the success of the factory, as well as its inspiration, was the substitution of capitalists' for workers' control of the production process; discipline and supervision could and did reduce costs *without* being technologically superior.

That the triumph of the factory, as well as the motivation behind it, lay in discipline and supervision, was clear to at least one contemporary observer. The leading nineteenth century apologist for the factory system, Andrew Ure, quite explicitly attributed Arkwright's success to his administrative prowess:

The main difficulty (faced by Arkwright) did not, to my apprehension, lie so much in the invention of a proper self-acting mechanism for drawing out and twisting cotton into a continuous thread, as in . . . training human beings to renounce their desultory habits of work, and to identify themselves with the unvarying regularity of the complex automation. *To devise and administer a successful code of factory discipline, suited to the necessities of factory diligence, was the Herculean enterprise, the noble achievement of Arkwright.* Even at the present day, when the system is perfectly organized, and its labor lightened to the utmost, it is found nearly impossible to convert persons past the age of puberty, whether drawn from rural or from handicraft occupations, into useful factory hands. After struggling for a while to conquer their listless or restive habits, they either renounce the employment spontaneously, or are dismissed by the overlookers on account of inattention.

---

21. Ronald Coase appears to be unique in recognizing that the very existence of capitalist enterprise is incompatible with the reliance of perfect competition on the market mechanism for coordinating economic activity. Coase, however, sees the capitalist firm as the means not for subordinating workers but for saving the costs of the market transactions:

a firm will tend to expand until the costs of organizing an extra transaction within the firm become equal to the costs on the open market or the costs of organizing in another firm.

See "The Nature of the Firm," *Economica* vol. IV, 1937, pp. 386–405, reprinted in Stigler and Boulding (eds.), *Readings in Price Theory,* Irwin, Chicago, Illinois, 1952, pp. 331–351. The quotation is from p. 341 of Boulding and Stigler.

If the factory Briareus could have been created by mechanical genius alone, it should have come into being thirty years sooner; for upwards of ninety years have now elapsed since John Wyatt, of Birmingham, not only invented the series of fluted rollers, (the spinning fingers usually ascribed to Arkwright), but obtained a patent for the invention, and erected "a spinning engine without hands" in his native town . . . Wyatt was a man of good education, in a respectable walk of life, much esteemed by his superiors, and therefore favorably placed, in a mechanical point of view, for maturing his admirable scheme. But he was of a gentle and passive spirit, little qualified to cope with the hardships of a new manufacturing enterprise. *It required, in fact, a man of a Napoleon nerve and ambition, to subdue the refractory tempers of work-people accustomed to irregular paroxysms of diligence.* . . . Such was Arkwright.[22] (Emphasis added.)

Wyatt's efforts, and his ultimate failure, are shrouded in mystery. Indeed, it is impossible to sort out his contribution from the contribution of his collaborator, Lewis Paul. No model of the Wyatt-Paul machine survives, but Mantoux supports Ure's judgment that Wyatt and Paul anticipated Arkwright in all technical essentials. Arkwright's machine, according to Mantoux, "differs from that of Wyatt only in its details. These trifling differences cannot explain Arkwright's triumphal success."[23]

Contemporary evidence suggests that the problems of organizing the work force played a substantial part in the failure of the Wyatt-Paul enterprises. The correspondence between the principals and their officers suggest a continuing preoccupation with discipline. Edward Cave, a financial backer as well as a licensee, set up shop with hand-powered equipment in anticipation of finding a suitable water mill. Early on he wrote to Paul: "I have not half my people come to work today, and I have no great fascination in the prospect I have to put myself in the power of such people."[24] Discipline did not improve once the Cave factory became mechanized. When Wyatt visited the new spinning mill at Northampton in 1743 he found that "only four frames were regularly at work, since there were seldom hands enough for five."[25] The search for new methods of discipline continued. A month later, Cave's lieutenant wrote Wyatt:

I think they (the workers) have done as much in four days this week as they did in a week when you were here . . . There were not hands enough to work all five engines but four is worked complete which did about 100 skeins a day one with another, nay some did 130. One reason for this extra advance is Mr. Harrison (the mill manager) bought 4 handkerchers one for each machine value about 1/2d p. each and hung them over the engine as prizes for the girls that do most. . . .[26]

These crude attempts to "subdue the refractory tempers of work-people" by judicious use of the carrot apparently came to nought. One of the few indisputable facts about the Wyatt-Paul attempts is that they failed. And between Wyatt

---

22. A. Ure, *The Philosophy of Manufacturers,* Charles Knight, London, 1835, pp. 15–16. Military analogies abound in contemporary observations of the early factory. Boswell described Mathew Boulton, Watt's partner in the manufacture of steam engines, as "an iron captain in the midst of his troops" after a visit to the works in 1776 (quoted in Mantoux, *op. cit.,* p. 376).

23. Mantoux, *op. cit.,* p. 223. Wadsworth and Mann differ. See Alfred P. Wadsworth and Julia DeLacy Mann, *The Cotton Trade and Industrial Lancashire,* Manchester University Press, Manchester, England, 1931, pp. 482–483.

24. Quoted in Julia DeLacy Mann, "The Transition to Machine-Spinning" in Wadsworth and Mann, *op. cit.,* p. 433.

25. *Ibid.,* p. 436.

26. *Ibid.,* p. 437.

and Arkwright no one managed to bring Wyatt's invention to a successful conclusion, a remarkable failure indeed if the defects of machine spinning were primarily technological in nature. . . .

None of this is to deny the importance of the technological changes that have taken place since the eighteenth century. But these changes were not independent causes of the factory. On the contrary, the particular forms that technological change took were shaped and determined by factory organization. It is not accidental that technological change atrophied within the putting-out system after Hargreaves's jenny but flourished within the factory. On the demand side, the capitalist provided the market for inventions and improvements, and his interest lay—for reasons of supervision and discipline—with the factory. The supply side was only slightly more complex. In principle, an inventor might obtain a patent and license the use of his inventions to putter-outers or, indeed, to independent producers. In practice, as long as production took place in scattered cottages, it was difficult if not impossible to detect and punish piracy of patent rights. It was much easier to enforce patent rights with production concentrated into factories, and this naturally channeled inventive activity into the more remunerative market. And of course many improvements were by their very nature nonpatentable, and their benefits were under capitalist economic organization capturable only by entrepreneurs.

This argument may be thought to imply a *dynamic* technological superiority for the factory system, for it may fairly be interpreted as suggesting that the factory provided a more congenial climate for technological change. A more congenial climate for innovation does not, however, imply technological superiority, dynamic or static. For the factory's superiority in this domain rested in turn on a particular set of institutional arrangements, in particular the arrangements for rewarding inventors by legal monopolies vested in patents. An invention, like knowledge generally, is a "public good": the use of an idea by one person does not reduce the stock of knowledge in the way that consumption of a loaf of bread reduces the stock of wheat. It is well understood that public goods cannot be efficiently distributed through the market mechanism; so patents cannot be defended on efficiency grounds. . . .

There remains one loose end in this account of the rise of the factory: why did the market mechanism, which has been supposed by its defenders from Adam Smith onwards to harness the self-interest of the producer to the public interest, fail to provide adequate supervision and discipline under the putting out system? Discipline and supervision, it must be understood, were inadequate only from the point of view of the capitalist, not from the point of view of the worker. And though it is true that in a sufficiently abstract model of perfect competition, profits are an index of the well-being of society as a whole as well as capitalists' well-being, this identity of interests does not characterize any real capitalist economy, no more the "competitive" capitalism of Adam Smith's day than the monopoly capitalism of our own. In the perfectly competitive model, there are no capitalists and no workers, there are only households that dispose of different bundles of resources, all of which—labor included—are traded on markets in which no one possesses any economic power. For this reason, laborers can equally well be thought to hire capital as capitalists labor, and the firm plays no significant role in the analysis. By contrast, the hallmark of the putting-out system was a specialization so minute that it denied to the worker the relatively wide (competitive!) market that existed for products, replacing the product market with a narrow market for a subproduct that, in a limited geographical area, a few putter-outers could dominate.[27] This perversion of the competitive principle, which lies at the heart of the capitalist division of labor, made discipline and supervision a class issue rather than an issue of technological efficiency; a lack of discipline and supervision could be disastrous for profits without being inefficient.

The indiscipline of the laboring classes, or more bluntly, their laziness, was widely noted by eighteenth century observers.

It is a fact well known (wrote a mid-century commentator) . . . that scarcity, to a certain degree, promoted industry, and that the manufacturer (worker) who can subsist on three days work will be idle and drunken the remainder of the week. . . . The poor in the manufacturing counties will never work any more time in general than is necessary just to live and support their weekly debauches. . . . We can fairly aver that a reduction of wages in the woolen manufacture would be a national blessing and advantage, and no real injury to the poor. By this means we might keep our trade, uphold our rents, and reform the people into the bargain.[28]

Indiscipline, in other words, meant that as wages rose, workers chose to work less. In more neutral language, laziness was simply a preference for leisure! Far from being an "unreasonable inversion of the laws of sensible economic behavior,"[29] a backward bending labor-supply curve is a most natural phenomenon as long as the individual worker controls the supply of labor. . . .

As Britain's internal commerce and its export trade expanded, wages rose and workers insisted in taking out a portion of their gains in the form of greater leisure. However sensible this response may have been from their own point of view, it was no way for an enterprising capitalist to get ahead. Nor did the capitalist meekly accept the workings of the invisible hand.

His first recourse was to the law. In the eighteenth century, Parliament twice enacted laws requiring domestic woolen workers to complete and return work within specified periods of time. In 1749 the period was fixed at twenty-one days, and in 1777 the period was reduced to eight days.[30] But more direct action proved necessary. The capitalist's salvation lay in taking immediate control of the proportions of work and leisure. Capitalists' interests required that the worker's choice become one of whether or not to work at all—the only choice he was to have within the factory system.

---

27. On the power of bosses over workers see, among others, Landes, *op. cit.*, p. 56; E. P. Thompson, *The Making of the English Working Class,* Random House, New York, 1963, Chapter 9, especially the quotations on pp. 280, 297. Adam Smith was quite explicit: "Masters are always and everywhere in a sort of tacit, but constant and uniform combination, not to raise the wages of labor above their actual rate. To violate this combination is everywhere a most unpopular action, and a sort of reproach to a master among his neighbors and equals. We seldom, indeed hear of this combination, because it is the usual, and one may say, the natural state of things which nobody hears of." *The Wealth of Nations,* op. cit., Book I, Chapter 8, pp. 66–67.

28. J. Smith, *Memoirs of Wool* (1747); quoted in E. P. Thompson, *op. cit.,* p. 277.

29. The characterization is Landes's, *Unbound Prometheus,* p. 59.

30. Heaton, *op. cit.,* p. 422. These laws had historic precedents. Unwin reports a municipal order dating from 1570 in Bury St. Edmunds requiring spinsters to work up six pounds of wool per week. Employers were to give notice to the constable in the event any one failed to obey the order (*op. cit.,* p. 94).

# · 15 ·

# Time, Work-Discipline, and Industrial Capitalism

## E. P. Thompson

Tess . . . started on her way up the dark and crooked lane or street not made for
hasty progress; a street laid out before inches of land had value, and when one-
handed clocks sufficiently subdivided the day. *(Thomas Hardy)*

## I

It is commonplace that the years between 1300 and 1650 saw within the intellectual culture of Western Europe important changes in the apprehension of time.[1] In
the *Canterbury Tales* the cock still figures in his immemorial role as nature's time-
piece: Chauntecleer—

> Caste up his eyen to the brighte sonne,
> That in the signe of Taurus hadde yronne
> Twenty degrees and oon, and somwhat moore,
> He knew by kynde, and by noon oother loore
> That it was pryme, and crew with blisful stevene. . . .

But although "By nature knew he ech ascensioun/Of the equynoxial in thilke
toun", the contrast between "nature's" time and clock time is pointed in the image—

> Wel sikerer was his crowyng in his logge
> Than is a clokke, or an abbey orlogge.

This is a very early clock: Chaucer (unlike Chauntecleer) was a Londoner, and was
aware of the times of Court, of urban organization, and of that "merchant's time"

---

*Abridged from *Past and Present* 38 (1967): 56–61, 70–71, 73, 90–96.

1. Lewis Mumford makes suggestive claims in *Technics and Civilization* (London, 1934), esp.
pp. 12–18, 196–9: see also S. de Grazia, *Of Time, Work, and Leisure* (New York, 1962), Carlo M.
Cipolla, *Clocks and Culture 1300–1700* (London, 1967), and Edward T. Hall, *The Silent Language*
(New York, 1959).

which Jacques Le Goff, in a suggestive article in *Annales,* has opposed to the time of the medieval church.[2]

I do not wish to argue how far the change was due to the spread of clocks from the fourteenth century onwards, how far this was itself a symptom of a new Puritan discipline and bourgeois exactitude. However we see it, the change is certainly there. The clock steps on to the Elizabethan stage, turning Faustus's last soliloquy into a dialogue with time: "the stars move still, time runs, the clock will strike". Sidereal time, which has been present since literature began, has now moved at one step from the heavens into the home. Mortality and love are both felt to be more poignant as the "Snayly motion of the mooving hand"[3] crosses the dial. When the watch is worn about the neck it lies in proximity to the less regular beating of the heart. The conventional Elizabethan images of time as a devourer, a defacer, a bloody tyrant, a scytheman, are old enough, but there is a new immediacy and insistence.[4]

As the seventeenth century moves on the image of clock-work extends, until, with Newton, it has engrossed the universe. And by the middle of the eighteenth century (if we are to trust Sterne) the clock had penetrated to more intimate levels. For Tristram Shandy's father—"one of the most regular men in everything he did . . . that ever lived"—"had made it a rule for many years of his life,—on the first Sunday night of every month . . . to wind up a large houseclock, which we had standing on the back-stairs head". "He had likewise gradually brought some other little family concernments to the same period", and this enabled Tristram to date his conception very exactly. It also provoked *The Clockmaker's Outcry against the Author:*

The directions I had for making several clocks for the country are countermanded; because no modest lady now dares to mention a word about winding-up a clock, without exposing herself to the sly leers and jokes of the family . . . Nay, the common expression of street-walkers is, "Sir, will you have your clock wound up?"

Virtuous matrons (the "clockmaker" complained) are consigning their clocks to lumber rooms as "exciting to acts of carnality".[5]

However, this gross impressionism is unlikely to advance the present enquiry: how far, and in what ways, did this shift in time-sense affect labour discipline, and how far did it influence the inward apprehension of time of working people? If the transition to mature industrial society entailed a severe restructuring of working habits—new disciplines, new incentives, and a new human nature upon which these incentives could bite effectively—how far is this related to changes in the inward notation of time?

---

2. J. le Goff, "Au Moyen Age: Temps de L'Eglise et temps du marchand", *Annales, E. S. C.,* xv (1960); and the same author's "Le temps du travail dans le 'crise' du XIVe Siècle: du temps médiéval au temps moderne", *Le Moyen Age,* lxix (1963).

3. M. Drayton, "Of his Ladies not Comming to London", *Works,* ed. J. W. Hebel (Oxford, 1932), iii, p. 204.

4. The change is discussed Cipolla, *op. cit.*; Erwin Sturzl, *Der Zeitbegriff in der Elisabethanischen Literatur* (Wiener Beiträge zur Englischen Philologie, lxix, Wien-Stuttgart, 1965); Alberto Teninti, *Il Senso della Morte e l'amore della vita nel rinanscimento* (Milan, 1957).

5. Anon., *The Clockmaker's Outcry against the Author of . . . Tristram Shandy* (London, 1760), pp. 42–3.

## II

It is well known that among primitive peoples the measurement of time is commonly related to familiar processes in the cycle of work or of domestic chores. Evans-Pritchard has analysed the time-sense of the Nuer:

The daily timepiece is the cattle clock, the round of pastoral tasks, and the time of day and the passage of time through a day are to a Nuer primarily the succession of these tasks and their relation to one another.

Among the Nandi an occupational definition of time evolved covering not only each hour, but half hours of the day—at 5-30 in the morning the oxen have gone to the grazing-ground, at 6 the sheep have been unfastened, at 6-30 the sun has grown, at 7 it has become warm, at 7-30 the goats have gone to the grazing-ground, etc.—an uncommonly well-regulated economy. In a similar way terms evolve for the measurement of time intervals. In Madagascar time might be measured by "a rice-cooking" (about half an hour) or "the frying of a locust" (a moment). The Cross River natives were reported as saying "the man died in less than the time in which maize is not yet completely roasted" (less than fifteen minutes).[6]

It is not difficult to find examples of this nearer to us in cultural time. Thus in seventeenth-century Chile time was often measured in "credos": an earthquake was described in 1647 as lasting for the period of two credos; while the cooking-time of an egg could be judged by an Ave Maria said aloud. In Burma in recent times monks rose at daybreak "when there is light enough to see the veins in the hand".[7] The Oxford English Dictionary gives us English examples— "pater noster wyle", "miserere whyle" (1450), and (in the New English Dictionary but not the Oxford English Dictionary) "pissing while"—a somewhat arbitrary measurement.

Pierre Bourdieu has explored more closely the attitudes towards time of the Kabyle peasant (in Algeria) in recent years: "An attitude of submission and of nonchalant indifference to the passage of time which no one dreams of mastering, using up, or saving. . . . Haste is seen as a lack of decorum combined with diabolical ambition". The clock is sometimes known as "the devil's mill"; there are no precise meal-times; "the notion of an exact appointment is unknown; they agree only to meet 'at the next market'". A popular song runs:

It is useless to pursue the world, No one will ever overtake it.[8]

---

6. E. E. Evans-Pritchard, *The Nuer* (Oxford, 1940), pp. 100–4; M. P. Nilsson, *Primitive Time Reckoning* (Lund, 1920), pp. 32–3, 42; P. A. Sorokin and R. K. Merton, "Social Time: a Methodological and Functional Analysis", *Amer. Jl. Sociol.*, xlii (1937); A. I. Hallowell, "Temporal Orientation in Western Civilization and in a Pre-Literate Society", *Amer. Anthrop.*, new ser. xxxix (1937). Other sources for primitive time reckoning are cited in H. G. Alexander, *Time as Dimension and History* (Albuquerque, 1945), p. 26, and Beate R. Salz, "The Human Element in Industrialization", *Econ. Devel. and Cult. Change*, iv (1955), esp. pp. 94–114.

7. E. P. Salas, "L'Evolution de la notion du temps et les horlogers à l'époque coloniale au Chili", *Annales E. S. C.*, xxi (1966), p. 146; *Cultural Patterns and Technical Change*, ed. M. Mead (New York, UNESCO, 1953), p. 75.

8. P. Bourdieu, "The attitude of the Algerian peasant toward time", in *Mediterranean Countrymen*, ed. J. Pitt-Rivers (Paris, 1963), pp. 55–72.

Synge, in his well-observed account of the Aran Islands, gives us a classic example:

While I am walking with Michael someone often comes to me to ask the time of day. Few of the people, however, are sufficiently used to modern time to understand in more than a vague way the convention of the hours and when I tell them what o'clock it is by my watch they are not satisfied, and ask how long is left them before the twilight.[9]

The general knowledge of time on the island depends, curiously enough, upon the direction of the wind. Nearly all the cottages are built . . . with two doors opposite each other, the more sheltered of which lies open all day to give light to the interior. If the wind is northerly the south door is opened, and the shadow of the door-post moving across the kitchen floor indicates the hour; as soon, however, as the wind changes to the south the other door is opened, and the people, who never think of putting up a primitive dial, are at a loss. . . .

When the wind is from the north the old woman manages my meals with fair regularity; but on the other days she often makes my tea at three o'clock instead of six. . . .[10]

Such a disregard for clock time could of course only be possible in a crofting and fishing community whose framework of marketing and administration is minimal, and in which the day's tasks (which might vary from fishing to farming, building, mending of nets, thatching, making a cradle or a coffin) seem to disclose themselves, by the logic of need, before the crofter's eyes.[11] But his account will serve to emphasize the essential conditioning in differing notations of time provided by different work-situations and their relation to "natural" rhythms. Clearly hunters must employ certain hours of the night to set their snares. Fishing and seafaring people must integrate their lives with the tides. A petition from Sunderland in 1800 includes the words "considering that this is a seaport in which many people are obliged to be up at all hours of the night to attend the tides and their affairs upon the river".[12] The operative phrase is "attend the tides": the patterning of social time in the seaport follows *upon* the rhythms of the sea; and this appears to be natural and comprehensible to fishermen or seamen: the compulsion is nature's own.

In a similar way labour from dawn to dusk can appear to be "natural" in a farming community, especially in the harvest months: nature demands that the grain be harvested before the thunderstorms set in. And we may note similar "natural" work-rhythms which attend other rural or industrial occupations: sheep must be attended at lambing time and guarded from predators; cows must

---

9. Cf. *ibid.*, p. 179: "Spanish Americans do not regulate their lives by the clock as Anglos do. Both rural and urban people, when asked when they plan to do something, gives answers like: 'Right now, about two or four o'clock' ".

10. J. M. Synge, *Plays, Poems, and Prose* (Everyman edn., London, 1941), p. 257.

11. The most important event in the relation of the islands to an external economy in Synge's time was the arrival of the steamer whose times might be greatly affected by tide and weather. See Synge, *The Aran Islands* (Dublin, 1907), pp. 115–6.

12. Public Rec. Off., W. O. 40/17. It is of interest to note other examples of the recognition that seafaring time conflicted with urban routines: the Court of Admiralty was held to be always open, "for strangers and merchants, and seafaring men, must take the opportunity of tides and winds, and cannot, without ruin and great prejudice attend the solemnity of courts and dilatory pleadings" (see E. Vansittart Neale, *Feasts and Fasts* [London, 1845], p. 249), while in some Sabbatarian legislation an exception was made for fishermen who sighted a shoal off-shore on the Sabbath day.

be milked; the charcoal fire must be attended and not burn away through the turfs (and the charcoal burners must sleep beside it); once iron is in the making, the furnaces must not be allowed to fail.

The notation of time which arises in such contexts has been described as task-orientation. It is perhaps the most effective orientation in peasant societies, and it remains important in village and domestic industries. It has by no means lost all relevance in rural parts of Britain today. Three points may be proposed about task-orientation. First, there is a sense in which it is more humanly comprehensible than timed labour. The peasant or labourer appears to attend upon what is an observed necessity. Second, a community in which task-orientation is common appears to show least demarcation between "work" and "life". Social intercourse and labour are intermingled—the working-day lengthens or contracts according to the task—and there is no great sense of conflict between labour and "passing the time of day". Third, to men accustomed to labour timed by the clock, this attitude to labour appears to be wasteful and lacking in urgency.[13]

Such a clear distinction supposes, of course, the independent peasant or craftsman as referent. But the question of task-orientation becomes greatly more complex at the point where labour is employed. The entire family economy of the small farmer may be task-orientated; but within it there may be a division of labour, and allocation of roles, and the discipline of an employer-employed relationship between the farmer and his children. Even here time is beginning to become money, the employer's money. As soon as actual hands are employed the shift from task-orientation to timed labour is marked. It is true that the timing of work can be done independently of any time-piece—and indeed precedes the diffusion of the clock. Still, in the mid-seventeenth century substantial farmers calculated their expectations of employed labour (as did Henry Best) in "dayworkes"—"the Cunnigarth, with its bottomes, is 4 large dayworkes for a good mower", "the Spellowe is 4 indifferent dayworkes", etc.;[14] and what Best did for his own farm, Markham attempted to present in general form:

A man . . . may mow of Corn, as Barley and Oats, if it be thick, loggy and beaten down to the earth, making fair work, and not cutting off the heads of the ears, and leaving the straw still growing one acre and a half in a day: but if it be good thick and fair standing corn, then he may mow two acres, or two acres and a half in a day; but if the corn be short and thin, then he may mow three, and sometimes four Acres in a day, and not be overlaboured. . . .[15]

---

13. Henri Lefebvre, *Critique de la Vie Quotidienne* (Paris, 1958), ii, pp. 52–6, prefers a distinction between "cyclical time"—arising from changing seasonal occupations in agriculture—and the "linear time" of urban, industrial organization. More suggestive is Lucien Febvre's distinction between "Le temps vécu et le temps-mesure", *La Problème de L'Incroyance au XVIe Siècle* (Paris, 1947), p. 431. A somewhat schematic examination of the organization of tasks in primitive economies is in Stanley H. Udy, *Organisation of Work* (New Haven, 1959), ch. 2.

14. *Rural Economy in Yorkshire in 1641 . . . Farming and Account Books of Henry Best,* ed. C. B. Robinson (Surtees Society, xxxiii, 1857), pp. 38–9.

15. G. M., *The Inrichment of the Weald of Kent,* 10th edn. (London, 1660), ch. xii: "A generall computation of men, and cattel's labours: what each may do without hurt daily", pp. 112–8.

The computation is difficult, and dependent upon many variables. Clearly, a straightforward time-measurement was more convenient.[16]

This measurement embodies a simple relationship. Those who are employed experience a distinction between their employer's time and their "own" time. And the employer must *use* the time of his labour, and see it is not wasted: not the task but the value of time when reduced to money is dominant. Time is now currency: it is not passed but spent. . . .

Attention to time in labor depends in large degree upon the need for the synchronization of labour. But in so far as manufacturing industry remained conducted upon a domestic or small workshop scale, without intricate subdivision of processes, the degree of synchronization demanded was slight, and task-orientation was still prevalent.[17] The putting-out system demanded much fetching, carrying, waiting for materials. Bad weather could disrupt not only agriculture, building and transport, but also weaving, where the finished pieces had to be stretched on the tenters to dry. As we get closer to each task, we are surprised to find the multiplicity of subsidiary tasks which the same worker or family group must do in one cottage or workshop. Even in larger workshops men sometimes continued to work at distinct tasks at their own benches or looms, and—except where the fear of the embezzlement of materials imposed stricter supervision—could show some flexibility in coming and going.

Hence we get the characteristic irregularity of labour patterns before the coming of large-scale machine-powered industry. Within the general demands of the week's or fortnight's tasks—the piece of cloth, so many nails or pairs of shoes—the working day might be lengthened or shortened. Moreover, in the early development of manufacturing industry, and of mining, many mixed occupations survived: Cornish tinners who also took a hand in the pilchard fishing; Northern lead-miners who were also smallholders; the village craftsmen who turned their hands to various jobs, in building, carting, joining; the domestic workers who left their work for the harvest; the Pennine small-farmer/weaver. . . .

The work pattern was one of alternate bouts of intense labour and of idleness; wherever men were in control of their own working lives. (The pattern persists among some self-employed—artists, writers, small famers, and perhaps also with students—today, and provokes the question whether it is not a

---

16. Wage-assessments still, of course, assumed the statute dawn-to-dusk day, defined, as late as 1725, in a Lancashire assessment: "They shall work from five in the morning till betwixt seven and eight at the night, from the midst of March to the middle of September"—and thereafter "from the spring of day till night", with two half hours for drinking, and one hour for dinner and (in summer only) half hour for sleep: "else, for every hour's absence to defaulk a penny": *Annals of Agriculture*, xxv (London, 1796).

17. For some of the problems discussed in this and the following section, see especially Keith Thomas, "Work and Leisure in Pre-Industrial Societies", *Past and Present*, no. 29 (Dec. 1964). Also C. Hill, "The Uses of Sabbatarianism", in *Society and Puritanism in Pre-Revolutionary England* (London, 1964); E. S. Furniss, *The Position of the Laborer in a System of Nationalism* (Boston, 1920: repr. New York, 1965); D. C. Coleman, "Labour in the English Economy of the Seventeenth Century", *Econ. Hist. Rev.*, 2nd ser., viii (1955–6); S. Pollard, "Factory Discipline in the Industrial Revolution", *Econ. Hist. Rev.*, 2nd ser., xvi (1963–4); T. S. Ashton, *An Economic History of England in the Eighteenth Century* (London, 1955), ch. vii; W. E. Moore, *Industrialization and Labor* (New York, 1951); and B. F. Hoselitz and W. E. Moore, *Industrialization and Society* (UNESCO, 1963).

"natural" human work-rhythm.) On Monday or Tuesday, according to tradition, the hand-loom went to the slow chant of *Plen-ty of Time, Plen-ty of Time:* on Thursday and Friday, *A day t'lat, A day t'lat.*[18] The temptation to lie in an extra hour in the morning pushed work into the evening, candle-lit hours.[19] There are few trades which are not described as honouring Saint Monday: shoemakers, tailors, colliers, printing workers, potters, weavers, hosiery workers, cutlers, all Cockneys. Despite the full employment of many London trades during the Napoleonic Wars, a witness complained that "we see Saint Monday so religiously kept in this great city . . . in general followed by a Saint Tuesday also". . . .[20]

In all these ways—by the division of labour; the supervision of labour; fines; bells and clocks; money incentives; preachings and schoolings; the suppression of fairs and sports—new labour habits were formed, and a new time-discipline was imposed. It sometimes took several generations (as in the Potteries), and we may doubt how far it was ever fully accomplished: irregular labour rhythms were perpetuated (and even institutionalized) into the present century, notably in London and in the great ports.[21]

Throughout the nineteenth century the propaganda of time-thrift continued to be directed at the working people, the rhetoric becoming more debased, the apostrophes to eternity becoming more shop-soiled, the homilies more mean and banal. In early Victorian tracts and reading-matter aimed at the masses one is choked by the quantity of the stuff. But eternity has become those never-ending accounts of pious death-beds (or sinners struck by lightning), while the homilies have become little Smilesian snippets about humble men who by early rising and diligence made good. The leisured classes began to discover the "problem" (about which we hear a good deal today) of the leisure of the masses. A considerable proportion of manual workers (one moralist was alarmed to discover) after concluding their work were left with

several hours in the day to be spent nearly as they please. And in what manner . . . is this precious time expended by those of no mental cultivation? . . . We shall often see them just simply annihilating those portions of time. They will for an hour, or for hours together . . . sit on a bench, or lie down on a bank or hillock . . . yielded up to utter vacancy and torpor . . . or collected in groups by the road side, in readiness to find in whatever passes there occasions for gross jocularity; practising some impertinence, or uttering some jeering scurrility, at the expense of persons going by. . . .[22]

---

18. T. W. Hanson, 'The Diary of a Grandfather', *Trans. Halifax Antiq. Soc.,* 1916, p. 234.

19. J. Clayton, *Friendly Advice to the Poor* (Manchester, 1755), p. 36.

20. *Report of the Trial of Alexander Wadsworth against Peter Laurie* (London, 1811), p. 21. The complaint is particularly directed against the Saddlers.

21. There is an abundant literature of nineteenth-century dockland which illustrates this. However, in recent years the casual labourer in the ports has ceased to be a "casualty" of the labour market (as Mayhew saw him) and is marked by his preference for high earnings over security: see K. J. W. Alexander, "Casual Labour and Labour Casualties", *Trans. Inst. of Engineers and Shipbuilders in Scotland* (Glasgow, 1964). I have not touched in this paper on the new occupational time-tables introduced in industrial society—notably night-shift workers (pits, railways, etc.): see the observations by "Journeyman Engineer" [T. Wright], *The Great Unwashed* (London, 1868), pp. 188–200; M. A. Pollock (ed.), *Working Days* (London, 1926), pp. 17–28; Tom Nairn, *New Left Review,* no. 34 (1965), p. 38.

22. John Foster, *An Essay on the Evils of Popular Ignorance* (London, 1821), pp. 180–5.

But how far did this propaganda really succeed? How far are we entitled to speak of any radical restructuring of man's social nature and working habits? I have given elsewhere some reasons for supposing that this discipline was indeed internalized, and that we may see in the Methodist sects of the early nineteenth century a figuration of the psychic crisis entailed.[23] Just as the new time-sense of the merchants and gentry in the Renaissance appears to find one expression in the heightened awareness of mortality, so, one might argue, the extension of this sense to the working people during the industrial revolution (together with the hazard and high mortality of the time) helps to explain the obsessive emphasis upon death in sermons and tracts whose consumers were among the working-class. Or (from a positive stand-point) one may note that as the industrial revolution proceeds, wage incentives and expanding consumer drives—the palpable rewards for the productive consumption of time and the evidence of new "predictive" attitudes to the future[24]—are evidently effective. By the 1830s and 1840s it was commonly observed that the English industrial worker was marked off from his fellow Irish worker, not by a greater capacity for hard work, but by his regularity, his methodical paying-out of energy, and perhaps also by a repression, not of enjoyments, but of the capacity to relax in the old, uninhibited ways.

There is no way in which we can quantify the time-sense of one, or of a million workers. But if it is possible to offer one check of a comparative kind. For what was said by the mercantilist moralists as to the failures of the eighteenth-century English poor to respond to incentives and disciplines is often repeated, by observers and by theorists of economic growth, of the peoples of developing countries today. Thus Mexican paeons in the early years of this century were regarded as an "indolent and child-like people". The Mexican mineworker had the custom of returning to his village for corn planting and harvest:

His lack of initiative, inability to save, absences while celebrating too many holidays, willingness to work only three or four days a week if that paid for necessities, insatiable desire for alcohol—all were pointed out as proof of a natural inferiority.

He failed to respond to direct day-wage incentives, and (like the eighteenth-century English collier or tinner) responded better to contract and sub-contract systems:

Given a contract and the assurance that he will get so much money for each ton he mines, and that it doesn't matter how long he takes doing it, or how often he sits down to contemplate life, he will work with a vigour which is remarkable.[25]

In generalizations supported by another study of Mexican labour conditions, Wilbert Moore remarks: "Work is almost always task-orientated in non-indus-

---

23. Thompson, *The Making of the English Working Class,* chaps. xi and xii.

24. See the important discussion of forecasting and predictive attitudes and their influence upon social and economic behaviour, in P. Bourdieu, *op. cit.*

25. Cited in M. D. Bernstein, *The Mexican Mining Industry, 1890–1950* (New York, 1964), ch. vii; see also M. Mead, *op. cit.,* pp. 179–82.

trial societies . . . and . . . it may be appropriate to tie wages to tasks and not directly to time in newly developing areas".[26]

The problem recurs in a dozen forms in the literature of "industrialization". For the engineer of economic growth, it may appear as the problem of absentee-ism—how is the Company to deal with the unrepentant labourer on the Came-roons plantation who declares: "How man fit work so, any day, any day, weh'e no take absen'? No be 'e go die?" ("How could a man work like that, day after day, without being absent? Would he not die?")[27]

. . . the whole mores of African life, make a high and sustained level of effort in a given length of working day a greater burden both physically and psychologically than in Europe.[28]

Time commitments in the Middle East or in Latin America are often treated somewhat casually by European standards; new industrial workers only gradually become accus-tomed to regular hours, regular attendance, and a regular pace of work; transportation schedules or the delivery of materials are not always reliable. . . .[29]

The problem may appear as one of adapting the seasonal rhythms of the coun-tryside, with its festivals and religious holidays, to the needs of industrial pro-duction:

The work year of the factory is necessarily in accord with the workers' demands, rather than an ideal one from the point of view of most efficient production. Several attempts by the managers to alter the work pattern have come to nil. The factory comes back to a schedule acceptable to the Cantelano.[30]

Or it may appear as it did in the early years of the Bombay cottonmills, as one of maintaining a labour force at the cost of perpetuating inefficient methods of production—elastic time-schedules, irregular breaks and meal-times, etc. Most commonly, in countries where the link between the new factory proletariat and their relatives (and perhaps land-holdings or rights to land) in the villages are much closer—and are maintained for much longer—than in the English experi-ence, it appears as one of disciplining a labour force which is only partially and temporarily "committed" to the industrial way-of-life.[31]

---

26. W. E. Moore, *Industrialization and Labor* (Ithaca, 1951), p. 310, and pp. 44–7, 114–22.

27. F. A. Wells and W. A. Warmington, *Studies in Industrialization: Nigeria and the Cameroons* (London, 1962), p. 128.

28. *Ibid.*, p. 170. See also pp. 183, 198, 214.

29. Edwin J. Cohn, "Social and Cultural Factors affecting the Emergence of Innovations", in *Social Aspects of Economic Development* (Economic and Social Studies Conference Board, Istanbul, 1964), pp. 105–6.

30. Manning Nash, "The Recruitment of Wage Labor and the Development of New Skills", *Annals of the American Academy*, cccv (1956), pp. 27–8. See also Manning Nash, "The Reaction of a Civil-Religious Hierarchy to a Factory in Guatemala", *Human Organization*, xiii (1955), pp. 26–8, and B. Salz, *op. cit.* (note 6 above), pp. 94–114.

31. W. E. Moore and A. S. Feldman (eds.) *Labor Commitment and Social Change in Developing Areas* (New York, 1960). Useful studies of adaptation and of absenteeism include W. Elkan, *An African Labour Force* (Kampala, 1956), esp. chaps. ii and iii; and F. H. Harbison and I. A. Ibrahim, "Some Labor Problems of Industrialization in Egypt", *Annals of the American Academy*, cccv (1956), pp. 114–29. M. D. Morris, *The Emergence of an Industrial Labor Force in India* (Berkeley, 1965) discounts the seriousness of the problems of discipline, absenteeism, seasonal fluctuations in em-

The evidence is plentiful, and, by the method of contrast, it reminds us how far we have become habituated to different disciplines. Mature industrial societies of all varieties are marked by time-thrift and by a clear demarcation between "work" and "life."[32] But, having taken the problem so far, we may be permitted to moralize a little, in the eighteenth-century manner, ourselves. The point at issue is not that of the "standard-of-living". If the theorists of growth wish us to say so, then we may agree that the older popular culture was in many ways otiose, intellectually vacant, devoid of quickening, and plain bloody poor. Without time-discipline we could not have the insistent energies of industrial man; and whether this discipline comes in the forms of Methodism, or of Stalinism, or of nationalism, it will come to the developing world.

What needs to be said is not that one way of life is beter than the other, but that this is a place of the most far-reaching conflict; that the historical record is not a simple one of neutral and inevitable technological change, but is also one of exploitation and of resistance to exploitation; and that values stand to be lost as well as gained. . . .

It is a problem which the peoples of the developing world must live through and grow through. One hopes that they will be wary of pat, manipulative models, which present the working masses only as an inert labour force. And there is a sense, also, within the advanced industrial countries, in which this has ceased to be a problem placed in the past. For we are now at a point where sociologists are discussing the "problem" of leisure. And a part of the problem is: how did it come to be a problem? Puritanism, in its marriage of convenience with industrial capitalism, was the agent which converted men to new valuations of time; which taught children even in their infancy to improve each shining hour; and which saturated men's minds with the equation, time is money.[33] One recurrent form of revolt within Western industrial capitalism, whether bohemian or beatnik, has often taken the form of flouting the urgency of respectable time-values. And the interesting question arises: if Puritanism was a necessary part of the work-ethos which enabled the industrialized world to break out of the poverty-stricken economies of the past, will the Puritan valuation of time begin to decompose as the pressures of poverty relax? Is it decomposing already? Will men begin to lose that restless urgency, that desire to consume time purposively, which most people carry just as they carry a watch on their wrists?

---

ployment, etc. in the Bombay cotton mills in the late nineteenth century, but at many points his arguments appear to be at odds with his own evidence: see pp. 85, 97, 102; see also C. A. Myers, *Labour Problems in the Industrialization of India* (Cambridge, Mass., 1958), ch. iii, and S. D. Mehta, "Professor Morris on Textile Labour Supply", *Indian Economic Journal*, i, no. 3 (1954), pp. 333–40. Professor Morris's "The Recruitment of an Industrial Labor Force in India, with British and American Comparisons", *Comparative Studies in Society and History*, ii (1960) flattens and misunderstands the British evidence. Useful studies of an only partially "committed" labour force are G. V. Rimlinger, "Autocracy and the early Russian Factory System", *Jour. Econ. Hist.*, xx (1960) and T. V. Von Laue, "Russian Peasants in the Factory", *ibid.*, xxi (1961).

32. See G. Friedmann, "Leisure and Technological Civilization", *Int. Soc. Science Jour.,* xii (1960), pp. 509–21.

33. Suggestive comments on this equation are in Lewis Mumford and S. de Grazia, cited note I above; Paul Diesing, *Reason in Society* (Urbana, 1962), pp. 24–8; Hans Meyerhoff, *Time in Literature* (Univ. of California, 1955), pp. 106–19.

If we are to have enlarged leisure, in an automated future, the problem is not "how are men going to be able to *consume* all these additional time-units of leisure?" but "what will be the capacity for experience of the men who have this undirected time to live?" If we maintain a Puritan time-valuation, a commodity-valuation, then it is a question of how this time is put to *use,* or how it is exploited by the leisure industries. But if the purposive notation of time-use becomes less compulsive, then men might have to re-learn some of the arts of living lost in the industrial revolution: how to fill the interstices of their days with enriched, more leisurely, personal and social relations; how to break down once more the barriers between work and life. And hence would stem a novel dialectic in which some of the old aggressive energies and disciplines migrate to the newly-industrializing nations, while the old industrialized nations seek to rediscover modes of experience forgotten before written history begins:

the Nuer have no expression equivalent to "time" in our language, and they cannot, therefore, as we can, speak of time as though it were something actual, which passes, can be wasted, can be saved, and so forth. I do not think that they ever experience the same feeling of fighting against time or of having to co-ordinate activities with an abstract passage of time because their points of reference are mainly the activities themselves, which are generally of a leisurely character. Events follow a logical order, but they are not controlled by an abstract system, there being no autonomous points of reference to which activities have to conform with precision. Nuer are fortunate.[34]

Of course, no culture re-appears in the same form. If men are to meet both the demands of a highly-synchronized automated industry, and of greatly enlarged areas of "free time", they must somehow combine in a new synthesis elements of the old and of the new, finding an imagery based neither upon the seasons nor upon the market but upon human occasions.

---

34. E. Evans-Pritchard, *op. cit.,* p. 103.

# · 16 ·

# Class Struggle and the Transformation of the Labour Process: A Relational Approach

## David Stark

Harry Braverman's *Labor and Monopoly Capital: The Degradation of Work in the 20th Century* stands as a necessary point of departure for the study of the relationship between class structure and class struggle in American society. Charting a new direction for historical and sociological investigation, Braverman's work involves a dual object of study: the transformation of the labor process in capitalist society and the changes in the structure of the American working class during this century. In its persuasive account of the debasement of work in capitalist society, *Labor and Monopoly Capital* commands our attention as a powerful moral document. Yet Braverman's work is more than merely descriptive. Since reference is increasingly made to *Labor and Monopoly Capital* both as an authoritative history and as a theoretical guide for further research, this essay critically examines Braverman's presentation of the reorganization of work in the early decades of this century and the theoretical assumptions which underlie it.[1] The limitations of Braverman's historical account are traced to his adoption of the traditional Marxist problematic of class-in-itself and class-for-itself. Situated within the same problematic, neither the preoccupation with abstract classification schemes for identifying class boundaries nor the ascertainment of the presence or absence of class consciousness places class struggle at the center

*Abridged from *Theory and Society* 9 (1980): 89–103, 116–30.

1. A previous version of this paper was presented at the conference on "New Directions in the Labor Process," SUNY-Binghamton, April, 1978. I would like to thank Jeremy Brecher, Monique Djokic, Geoff Fougere, Jerry Karabel, David Karen, and Theda Skocpol for their very helpful criticisms and suggestions.

of analysis. The alternative analytic strategy which is proposed in this essay focuses on relations of conflict and alliance between and within the historically determined organizations which are constitutive of class formation across the various levels of social structure.

In his analysis of the ways in which the labor process is shaped by capitalist property relations, Braverman argues that the developmental logic of the capitalist mode of production results in an increasing loss of control of the production process by the direct producers. Using the distinction between juridical ownership and actual control of the labor process,[2] he develops a periodization of the capitalist mode of production based on his observation that capitalists' legal ownership of the tools, materials, and products of production historically preceded capitalists' real control of the methods and process of production. With this periodization Braverman follows a line of analysis developed in *Capital* where Marx made a distinction between the "formal" subordination and the "real" subordination of labor to capital.[3]

For Marx, this real subordination occurred during the industrial revolution when capitalists transformed the organizational and technological basis of production.[4] Braverman, a century later, shows that the industrial revolution left significant areas of production in which workers still maintained real control over aspects of the labor process. The protracted transition from "formal" to "real" capitalist control of production thus found a new phase in the "rationalization" movement at the turn of this century.

Braverman sees the control exercised by a predominantly skilled labor force displaced by two developments: the reorganization of production and supervision according to the principles of "scientific management" and the revolution in science and technology which produced (and continues to transform) modern machinery. Broad knowledge of the production process was taken from the working class and embodied in a management organization dedicated to capitalist efficiency, in an institutionalized science subordinated to capital, and in a system of machinery animated only to the extent that human beings were inserted between other, mechanical parts. Braverman rightly frames the chang-

---

2. The issue of "ownership versus control" is familiar to social scientists from the debate over "managerialism" which opened in the 1930s and developed into a lively controversy during the 1960s. See Adolph Berle, Jr. and Gardiner C. Means, *The Modern Corporation and Private Property* (New York, 1932); James Burnham, *The Managerial Revolution* (New York, 1941); Robert Fitch and Mary Oppenheimer, "Who Rules the Corporations?" *Socialist Revolution* 4–6 (1970); and Maurice Zeitlin, "Corporate Ownership and Control: The Large Corporations and the Capitalist Class," *American Journal of Sociology* (March, 1974), pp. 1073–1119. Braverman's contribution has been to move from the analysis of decision-making in corporate board rooms to an analysis of processes taking place on the shop floor and in the clerical office. Not "who rules the corporation?" but "who controls the labor process and how?" becomes the fundamental question the answer to which indicates the shape of the dominant property relations of capitalist society. The focus on control of the labor process becomes the theoretical first (and perhaps exclusive) principle in Braverman's scheme for characterizing a mode of production and for analyzing its dynamics.

3. Karl Marx, *Capital Vol. I* (New York, 1967), especially pp. 184, 314–315. For an interesting use of this distinction, see Gareth Stedman Jones, "Class Struggle and the Industrial Revolution," *New Left Review* #90, (March–April, 1975).

4. Prior to this time, capitalists' "formal" control (the appropriation of the products of labor) rested on a pre-existing process which had been developed within a different mode of production— simple commodity production.

ing configurations of the labor process and class structure as a broad historical problem and correctly focusses on the period around the turn of the century when the labor process was significantly reorganized. But it is precisely in Braverman's historical account of the reorganization of work that several problems of the analysis and interpretation emerge.

## Anomalies in Braverman's Account

The first source of difficulty lies in Braverman's conception of Frederick Taylor's program of scientific management as the embodiment of capital's farsightedness. Braverman presents Taylorism as enjoying almost immediately favorable reception by management on both sides of the Atlantic eager to adopt the new practices proposed by the "father of scientific management." In fact, however, American and European[5] industrialists exhibited considerable hesitancy in introducing the work reorganization schemes advocated by Taylor and his close followers. Management resistance to the scientific managers erected obstacles to their entry into firms and thwarted the introduction of their suggestions or prematurely halted their work even when they had gained access to the shop floor. In testimony given at a Congressional hearing Taylor indicted the severity of management reluctance to follow the directions of the "efficiency engineers":

Nine-tenths of the trouble with those of us who have been engaged in helping people to change from the older types of management to the new management—that is, to scientific management—nine-tenths of our trouble has been to "bring" those on the management's side to do their fair share of the work and only one-tenth of our trouble has come on the workman's side. Invariably we find very great opposition on the part of those on the management's side to do their new duties.[6]

Taylor's claims (in attempts to improve his public relations) that his schemes met with little worker opposition were, as we shall see, completely unfounded. But, although also exaggerated for the same purposes, his complaints about management recalcitrance contained an important element of truth. For example, Taylor's infamous experiments with the laborer, Schmidt, in the yards at Bethlehem Steel led him to devise procedures whereby only 140 men would be needed to do the work which previously required more than 400. Yet Bethlehem's owners were not pleased with Taylor's new system and in April, 1901, Taylor's employment at Bethlehem was abruptly terminated.[7] Taylor later wrote of this experience:

They did not wish me, as they said, to depopulate South Bethlehem. They owned all the

---

5. Paul Devinat, *Scientific Management in Europe*, International Labor Organization Studies and Reports, Series B, #17 (Geneva, 1927) and Lyndall Urwick, *Scientific Management in Britain* (London, 1938) discuss the slowness with which European industrialists responded to Taylor and his followers.

6. Frederick Taylor, *Testimony Before the Special House Committee* (New York, 1912), p. 43.

7. Robert Hessen, "The Transformation of Bethlehem Steel, 1904–1909," *Business History Review*, Vol. 46 #3 (1972); and Wilton J. Nadworny, *Scientific Managers and the Unions 1900–1932* (Cambridge, Mass., 1955), pp. 10–12.

houses in South Bethlehem and the company stores, and when they saw we were cutting the labor force down to about one-fourth, they did not want it.[8]

An examination of historical materials indicates that the imagery which Braverman attempts to create of eager industrialists beating a path to Taylor's door is far less accurate than that of Taylor's proselytizing zeal, his active courting of cautious employers, and his cajolery and persuasion when confronting his more reluctant clients.[9] This conclusion seems especially valid if we adopt a narrow definition of "scientific management". According to historian Brian Palmer, Taylorism, as a total system of management, was far too rigorous to be implemented in most establishments.

While Taylor's works—*Shop Management* and *The Principles of Scientific Management*— were widely read, and while it is possible to maintain that Taylor's conception of "scientific management" was the cutting edge of the efficiency movement, there is little to indicate that Taylorism was adopted by large numbers of industrial concerns . . . . Thus, "scientific management" secured a foothold only in certain, small-scale precision production industries—gunsmithing, typewriter production, button manufacturing— of the industrial northeastern states.[10]

Another historian, Milton Nadworny, estimates that approximately 63,000 workers were employed under various scientific management schemes at the time of Taylor's death in 1915.[11] Robert Hoxie's famous report for the U.S. Commission on Industrial Relations in 1914 concluded that "no single shop was found which could be said to represent fully and faithfully the Taylor system as presented in the treatise on 'Shop Management'"[12]

The second major problem with Braverman's historical account is that he presents the reorganization of the labor process as the outcome of a conscious design rather than as the product of the struggle of contending groups. Not only does he ignore the conflicts between capitalists and the "scientific managers," but he also fails to integrate into his analysis the shopfloor and political struggles of workers against rationalization. It is not unfair to argue that Braverman portrays the capitalist class as veritably omniscient and the working class as infinitely malleable. The consequence of this line of analysis is that Braverman sees the outcome of the reorganization of work—that is, the labor process today—as the fulfillment of capitalist farsightedness, the successfully completed

---

8. Quoted in Hessen, *ibid*. Soon after Taylor's dismissal from Bethlehem, his assistant, Henry Gantt, was also dismissed. Gantt then attempted to introduce bonus systems and new production methods in numerous firms but encountered difficulties with management in every case. In fact, it was not until 1910 that Gantt found a cooperative management environment. See Nadworny, *op. cit.*, pp. 14–15. A detailed discussion by Daniel Nelson and Richard Campbell, "Taylorism vs. Welfare Work: H. L. Gantt and the Bancrofts," *Business History Review* (Spring, 1972) of one of Gantt's unsuccessful ventures during this decade indicates that his scientific management practices came into conflict with the firm's established paternalistic policies.

9. Nadworny, *op. cit.*, pp. 1–34.

10. Brian Palmer, "Class, Conception and Conflict: The Thrust for Efficiency, Managerial View of Labor and the Working Class Rebellion, 1903–1922," *Review of Radical Political Economics*, vol. 7 #2 (Summer, 1975), p. 32.

11. Nadworny, *op. cit.*, p. 85.

12. Hoxie, quoted in Daniel Nelson, *Managers and Workers: Origins of the New Factory System in the United States, 1880–1920* (Madison, 1972), p. 69.

imposition of conscious design onto social reality. The transition from "formal" to "real" subordination of labor to capital becomes, in Braverman's work, the transition from formal subordination to total domination. [13]

Braverman's account must thus be confronted with studies by several generations of industrial sociologists (and a growing literature by social historians) which document the perennial resistance of workers to rationalization and the real limitations to any managerial strategy for complete control of the labor process. [14] By neglecting the minor skirmishes over the pace of work, the persistence of informal work groups which attempt to regulate output, and the organized struggles over the hours, conditions, and supervision of work, Braverman obscures the important ways in which the labor process is a "frontier of control," [15] the scope and depth of which is determined, in large part, by the degree of militancy and the forms of organization of the working class. But there is perhaps an even more significant problem than Braverman's omission of working class resistance in his one-dimensional account of the reorganization of work: the analysis seems to preclude the possibilities that the "rationalization" of the labor process could produce new "control" problems. Assembly line production, for example, decreases the degree of direct cooperation among workers, but the objective interdependence of workers also increases their ability to disrupt production either through individual acts of sabotage, collective activity, or the more passive form of simply not showing up for work. [16]

---

13. This development occurs even though Braverman amplifies, in his introductory theoretical discussion, the qualitative aspect of the labor theory of value which rests on the distinction between labor and labor power. But he does so only to account for why capital intervened in the labor process—most particularly to account for why capitalists introduced certain kinds of machinery and reorganized production according to the principles of scientific management. But from this point on, the broad theoretical thrust of Braverman's book would indicate that capitalists no longer face the "problem" (from their perspective) of labor-power as the "variable" component of capital. For Marx, this "variable" aspect of labor-power was manifested at many levels—in the day-to-day recalcitrance of workers; in the minor skirmishes over the pace of work; in the organized struggles over the hours, conditions, and supervision of work; and in the larger conflicts between workers and employers over the relative shares of the total social surplus and the broader reproduction of society. In Braverman's scheme, the timing and patterns of changes in the labor process are not shaped by conflict between classes but by the one-dimensional unfolding (or perfecting) of extremely centralized and bureaucratically administered organizations. As an organizational theorist, Braverman's object of study is the firm itself as opposed to the relations between firms and the contradictory processes of societal development. *Labor and Monopoly Capital* begins with Marx's labor theory of value but ends with Weber's "iron cage".

14. From a broad range of different theoretical approaches see Stanley B. Mathewson, *Restriction of Output Among Unorganized Workers* (Southern Illinois University, 1931); Orvis Collins, Melville Dalton, and Donald Roy, "Restriction of Output and Social Cleavage in Industry," *Applied Anthropology* (Summer, 1946); William F. Whyte, *Money and Motivation* (New York, 1955); Michel Crozier, *The Bureaucratic Phenomenon* (Chicago, 1964); Philippe Bernoux, "Les U.S. face à l'organisation industrielle," *Sociologie du Travail* (1972); Ken Kusterer, "Knowledge on the Job: Workers' Know-How and Everyday Survival in the Workplace," Ph.D. Dissertation, Washington University (St. Louis, 1976); and Andrew Friedman, "Responsible Autonomy versus Direct Control over the Labour Process," *Capital and Class*, #1 (Spring, 1977).

15. The phrase is from Carter Goodrich, *The Frontier of Control* (London, 1976), originally published in 1920.

16. It is clear that capitalists are increasingly alarmed at the magnitude of absenteeism. See Special Task Force to the Secretary of HEW, *Work in America* (Cambridge, Mass., 1973). For interesting quotations on the problem from management's perspective see James O'Connor, "Productive and Unproductive Labor," *Politics and Society*, vol. 5 #2 (1975). Within marxist categories,

In Italy, for example, workers in auto assembly, metals, and other industries have turned the complex interdependence of the factory against management by using tactics such as systematic sabotage, "go slows," and "rolling strikes" (brief stoppages scattered in plants from shop to shop, line to line, according to an agreed timetable such that while some people are working, others are striking in different parts of the factory). By disorganizing production without leaving the place of work (and forfeiting earnings), such internal conflicts "increase the damage to the firm without increasing the cost to workers and thereby avoid some of the problems of the traditional strike."[17] In this strategy, some tactics have been facilitated by the capitalist organization of production itself. Even the time-punch card—one of the symbols of the tyranny of the factory—has been used by workers as a means of co-ordinating their actions. Some "rolling strikes" in Italian firms have been articulated on an "individual by individual basis in such a way that every worker strikes according to a different timetable which varies according to the last digit of the accounting number or the color of the card taken out by each worker at the beginning of the shift."[18] Braverman's perspective from inside the Weberian iron cage would certainly not have predicted that extreme forms of rationalization could themselves have made possible new strategies and tactics of working class militancy.

The third source of problems in Braverman's analysis is located in his account of changes in class structure. Braverman's description and explanation of the major changes in the skill and occupational composition of the American working class during the twentieth century contains a serious deficiency, since the starting point of this process is painted in blurred tones. A detailed profile of the skill and occupational composition of the working class in the late nineteenth century is not presented. But throughout *Labor and Monopoly Capital,* a suggestive picture of the nineteenth century worker emerges nonetheless, as Braverman evokes an image of the nineteenth century world as a society populated by skilled craftsmen. As numerous studies of nineteenth century labor reveal, the high visibility of skilled craftsmen in Braverman's depiction may be an accurate representation of their *centrality* in the production process but it distorts their numerical importance since skilled workers did not constitute even a majority of the labor force.[19] Around the turn of the century when the various systems of

---

the growing rates of absenteeism are one example of how the struggle over "absolute surplus value" continues even after the production of "relative surplus value" is the dominant development within the society. Absolute surplus value has traditionally been discussed in terms of the length of the working day, but the concept is analytically generalizable to refer to the *duration* (as opposed to the productivity or intensity) of labor. The struggle between workers and employers over *how long* workers will be subject to the constraints of the organization (how many hours per day, or days per week, or years in a lifetime) thus encompasses a broad range of activities from absenteeism to collective struggles over retirement.

17. Ida Regalia, Marino Regini, and Emilio Reyneri, "Labour Conflicts and Industrial Relations in Italy," in Alessandro Pizzorno and Colin Crouch, eds., *The Resurgence of Class Conflict in Western Europe since 1968* (London, 1978), pp. 111–117.

18. *Ibid.,* p. 113.

19. Data on skill levels taken from census sources from 1870 to 1920 are presented in Peter J. Hill, "Relative Skills and Income Levels of Native and Foreign-born Workers," *Explorations in Economic History,* vol. 12, #1 (Jan., 1975).

scientific management or other rationalization schemes were introduced, skilled craftsmen held positions in manufacturing at the apex of a stratified labor force with a mass of semi-skilled and unskilled workers (often in positions of direct subordination) below them.[20] Thus, the scenario of a unilinear decline from the homogeneously skilled working class of the nineteenth century to the homogeneously unskilled working class of the twentieth lacks an accurate point of departure.

Although Braverman is attempting to explain the transition from craft to bureaucratic administration of production, he never presents a detailed examination of the craft tradition. While the individual craftsman's broad knowledge of the production process is made a cornerstone of the analysis, the social relations in which he is embedded (his connections to other craftsmen and his relationship to workers outside the craft) are not discussed. In this sense, the nineteenth century craftsman occupies an elusive position in the shadows of Braverman's framework—always present but never fully illuminated. This obscurity has several important consequences. Since the craft tradition is never given careful scrutiny, it can exist within Braverman's argument both as an ideal referent to a golden age in the past and as an illustrative model for socialist organization of the labor process in the future. Moreover, the active role of craft organizations in combatting—and later facilitating—rationalization is not examined.

## Class-in-Itself and Class-for-Itself

The empirical failings of Braverman's historical account outlined above cannot be corrected through simple amendments to his argument since they arise from the basic theoretical assumptions with which he approached his task. The most important of these is his conceptualization of class relations—particularly, his assumption that the concepts of class-in-itself and class-for-itself are adequate tools for analyzing the shape and dynamics of class relations in capitalist society. Within this traditional Marxist problematic the first term refers to a set of "objective" conditions while the second refers to a range of "subjective" factors. The historical effectivity of a class is viewed as the process whereby an objectively determined class-in-itself becomes a subjectively mature class-for-itself, conscious of its historical mission and organized for solidary action. Analysis proceeds from the first moment of classification (identifying classes on the basis of economic relations) to evaluation (ascertaining the extent to which subjective sentiments, "consciousness," and collective action correspond to the identified class lines). Analysts who write within the problematic usually posit a relationship between the two terms which is either wholly deterministic or completely voluntaristic. The inevitability of the working class' transition to the status of a class-for-itself is seen, in the first case, as the product of time (the "ripening of

---

20. See David Brody, *Steelworkers in America, The Nonunion Era* (New York, 1960); David Montgomery, "Workers' Control of Machine Production in the Nineteenth Century," *Labor History* (Fall, 1976); Nelson, *op. cit.;* and Robert Ozanne, *A Century of Labor-Management Relations at McCormick and International Harvester* (New York, 1967).

objective conditions") and, in the second, as the product of historical intervention by an organized party.[21] But in both cases, the actual collectivities-in-struggle which will emerge as historical actors along class lines are viewed as uniquely determined by objective economic positions.[22]

Braverman's adoption of this problematic can be clearly seen in his analysis of the capitalist class and its activities. His presentation of rationalization as the product of a conscious design, for example, springs directly from this conceptualization since, in his scheme, the capitalist class is not only a class-in-itself but a class-for-itself, fully conscious of its historical interests and organized to achieve them. Within the type of analysis which Braverman conducts, a class is dominant by virtue of its superior subjectivity—its consciousness of itself and its interests. Moreover, the shape of an historical epoch is given by this subjectivity. The essence of a society is the particular rationality of its dominant class and this essence can be found in each instance or realm of social life. In capitalist society every part of the whole participates in (and is the expression of) capitalist rationality and all parts function smoothly to reproduce the totality. Thus, for Braverman, the organization of work, the social sciences which "habituate the worker to the job," the institutions of science, the development of technology, and the commodification of everyday life are all expressions of capitalist rationality.

As the dominated class in capitalist society, on the other hand, the working class is analyzed along a different dimension of the adopted problematic:

No attempt will be made to deal with the modern working class on the level of its consciousness, organization, or activities. This is a book about the working class as a class *in itself,* not as a class *for itself.*[23]

Braverman has chosen such an approach, he tells us, because

what is needed first of all is a picture of the working class as it exists, as the shape given to the working population by the capital accumulation process.[24]

Can the shortcomings of Braverman's historical analysis—his inadequate portrayal of the relationship between capitalists and scientific managers, his failure to see that rationalization gives rise to new contradictions, and his neglect of the role of craft and other working class organizations in shaping the occupational structure—be remedied within the problematic of class in- and for-itself? It might be argued that the problems of *Labor and Monopoly Capital* arise not from the problematic but from Braverman's selective application of the traditional formula. A ready alternative would fill in the missing ingredient; preserving the distinction between class-in-itself and class-for-itself, it would complete Braverman's account by examining the development of working class consciousness.

21. See Adam Przeworski, "Proletariat into Class: The Process of Class Formation from Karl Kautsky's *The Class Struggle* to Recent Controversies," *Politics and Society* vol. 7, #4 (1974), pp. 348–349.

22. *Ibid.,* pp. 366–367.

23. Harry Braverman, *Labor and Monopoly Capital: The Degradation of Work in the 20th Century* (New York, 1974), pp. 26–27.

24. *Ibid.,* p. 27.

Given the ways in which the terms "class for itself" and "class consciousness" are currently defined and used, such additions do not seem advisable. When not seeing class consciousness as a simple reflection of some "objective" conditions, all too often analysis is conducted in a binary manner—class consciousness becomes something present or absent, true or false, trade union or revolutionary. Such work usually proceeds by imputing certain interests to a group or class and then assessing the extent to which their actions or ideology correspond to the theoretically proper course. Additional barriers to sociological and historical analysis are also found in the identification of the social location of "class consciousness". In many cases, class consciousness is seen to reside either at some metaphysical level as the consciousness of an Historical Actor or at a socio-psychological level as the aggregate of the individual "consciousnesses" of the members who make up a class. Both of these tendencies arise from the ways in which class analysis is traditionally conducted. Rather than focusing on class as a relationship, this type of class analysis proceeds by identifying the members who "make up" the class; this aggregate is then given the properties of a purposive actor.

To speak polemically: a class is not "composed of" individuals; it is not a collection or aggregation of individuals. *Classes,* like the social relations from which they arise, exist in an antagonistic and dependent relation to each other. Classes are constituted by these mutually antagonistic relations. In this sense, class analysis has an important structuralist component since the object of study is not the elements themselves but the relations between them.

Likewise, the capacity for class organization is a property of the relations within classes. Here our attention is directed to the degree and forms of connectedness within a class. The capacity for working class organizations to disseminate information, to evaluate strategies, and to coordinate activity is shaped by the internal structure of these organizations and by such connections as ethnic, craft, skill, and community ties.[25] In some cases these ties reach across skill

25. To repeat the above points in somewhat different terms; I am arguing that we turn our attention from the problem of "class composition" to that of "class formation". In many cases class analysis has been conducted as a marxist demography which identifies the skill, ethnic, racial, or gender characteristics of the individuals who compose a class. Although this basic information is not unimportant, more significant questions concern the extent to which intra- or inter-ethnic, racial, etc. relations facilitate or inhibit the communication of ideas and the co-ordination of activity within particular historical settings (from community struggles to national politics). On the shift from demographic characteristics to social structural relations in the study of urban protest movements see C. G. Pickvance, "From 'Social Base' to 'Social Force': Some Analytical Issues in the Study of Urban Protest," in *Captive Cities: Studies in the Political Economy of Cities and Regions,* edited by Michael Harloe (London, 1977), pp. 175–186. See also J. C. Mitchell, "The concept and use of social networks," in *Social Networks in Urban Situations,* edited by J. C. Mitchell (Manchester, 1969); and especially Mark Granovetter, "The Strength of Weak Ties," *American Journal of Sociology,* vol. 78 (1973), pp. 1360–1380. John Foster develops an interesting social network approach (using patterns of marriage, and in one case, even attendance at funerals) in his study of social cohesion among both the working class and the bourgeoisie of two cities in industrializing England. Foster's order of causality seems curiously reversed, however, in arguing that a higher degree of "class consciousness" led to a higher rate of inter-marriage across working class trades in one of his communities. *Class Struggle and the Industrial Revolution* (New York, 1974). On the importance of kinship, autonomous village political organization, and other social relations as forms of class organization in peasant societies see Eric R. Wolf, *Peasant Wars of the Twentieth Century* (New York, 1969); Theda Skocpol, *States and Social Revolutions* (Cambridge, 1979); and Hamza Alavi, "Peasant Classes and Primordial Loyalties," *Journal of Peasant Studies,* vol. 1, #1 (1973).

levels, communities, or industries. In all cases these ties are not merely formed by shared attributes since, for example, ethnicity[26] (or craft organization) is not an aggregation of the characteristics of individual "members" but is a relationship in which cognitive categories and the degree and forms of connectedness must be actively maintained.[27] Additionally, the capacity for organization (its extensiveness, intensiveness, and the "targets" of its activity) are shaped by its embeddedness in the larger social structure.[28] We shall not understand this activity (its processes or its effects) by simply placing it on a scale of "class consciousness".

The shift from an aggregational analysis to a relational one must also be accompanied by a shift in the level of abstraction at which analysis is conducted. In many cases, class analysis is carried out at the level of a mode of production,[29] especially by theorists who see their task as the rigorous formulation of more

---

26. For an interesting argument that ethnicity is not simply an attribute but a social category which is actively created through social relations see William L. Yancey, Eugene P. Ericksen, and Richard N. Juliani, "Emergent Ethnicity: A Review and Reformulation," *American Sociological Review*, vol. 41 #3 (1976), pp. 391–403.

27. In arguing that cognitive categories are an important factor contributing to the emergence or maintenance of formal and informal connections, analysis necessarily leads to the important role of tradition or culture (the two terms not being synonymous). But the role of tradition or culture is never completely independent of social structural relations. Without entirely reducing culture to its organizational embodiments, it could be argued that culture never exists apart from its reproduction. Culture, as communication (both as form and content) carried through language and everyday ritual, requires repeated transmission in face-to-face encounters or relations; and perhaps even more than others, *class specific* cultural forms such as song, dance, and play require organizational forms for their maintenance. E. P. Thompson's fascinating study of plebian culture in 18th century England points to the importance of rituals, songs, and street performances as the subordinate class' mocking counterpoint to the "theatre of class hegemony and control." See his "Eighteenth-century English society: class struggle without class?" *Social History*, vol. 3 #2 (May, 1978), pp. 133–165. But with the undermining of organizational forms, however informal, "working class culture" can lose its cohesive and oppositional character. Gareth Stedman Jones, for example, shows that important aspects of nineteenth century London working class culture were transformed as the organizations in which people spent their non-working time changed from those of politicized recreation of "entertainment". Gareth Stedman Jones, "Working Class Culture and Working Class Politics in London, 1870 to 1900: Notes on the Remaking of a Working Class," *Journal of Social History*, vol. 7 (1973–73). John Alt, likewise, presents an interesting account of the de-formation of the American working class focussing on changing patterns of community and recreation in "Beyond Class: The Decline of Labor and Leisure," *Telos* #28 (1976).

28. Cf. Michael Schwartz, *Radical Protest and Social Structure* (New York, 1977).

29. The concept *of mode of production* is contrasted here with that of *social formation* (viz, a society). The concepts have neither the same referent nor the same analytic status. A social formation may contain *more than one mode of production* as well as political structures, such as the state, which are not reducible to the various modes of production found within the boundaries of the society. An analysis written at the level of a mode of production is conducted at a high level of abstraction since it attempts to identify and explain the most important structural relations and tendencies of a mode of production. These tendencies will be found in a modified form (they will not exist in their "pure" form) when one examines that mode of production within a particular social formation since here it will exist in a competing and coexisting relationship with other modes of production and states structures also present in that society. For example, the United States prior to the civil war was a social formation with (at least) three modes of production: industrial capitalism of the northeast, the slave mode of production of the South, and the petty commodity mode of production of the agrarian midwest. The state was the arena of the struggle of classes within and between these modes of production but its logic could not be reduced to this struggle. For a more thorough discussion of these concepts see Samir Amin, "Modes of Production and Social Formations," in *Ufahamu* (Winter, 1974).

sophisticated schemes of classification.[30] The project of identifying, at a high level of abstraction, the most general tendencies of the class structure of a mode of production often has several unfortunate consequences.[31] First, it tends to see classes as constituted solely by economic (production) relations and to sidestep the problem that classes do not exist apart from their relation to the state. In order to understand class struggle and to analyze its role in the development of a mode of production, however, we must take into account the political struggle between classes within the state as well as the relationship between the state and the mode of production. Secondly, the project tends to be conducted through a static, unhistorical, analysis. The debate about class becomes a battle of classification—in many cases a survey of the social topography of class boundaries rather than a study of the processes of class formation and the real historical battles which produce the evershifting lines of demarcation.

Rather than seeing interests either solely at the level of the individual (and aggregating the individual interests defined by the distribution of particular attributes such as opinions or attitudes) or solely at the level of a mode of production (as, for example, by identifying the members of a class on the basis of their "shared interest in socialism"), the analysis below proceeds from the historically defined interests produced by the tensions and contradictions within and between organizations. These organizations may be informal (based, for example, on interactions within the work situation or on the networks of kinship or residence) or formal (craft organizations, trade unions, professional associations, firms, state agencies, political parties, etc.). But in both cases their interests, capacities, and resources are not posited a priori by the analyst but emerge historically, subject to changes in direction and magnitude based on the shifting patterns of relations (of conflict and alliance) within and between organizations. A relational analysis which focusses on the interaction of organizations (rather than on the attributes of individuals or the global properties of

---

30. For example, G. Carchedi, "On the Economic Identification of the New Middle Class," Economy and Society, vol. IV, #1, (1975) and Erik Wright, "Class Boundaries in Advanced Capitalist Societies," New Left Review 98 (1976).

31. Braverman for example has written his analysis at the level of a mode of production. In this sense, it is useful to contrast the method with that of Capital, its apparent model. Both books seem to be written at the level of a mode of production with each drawing its historical examples from a single society—Marx from England, and Braverman from the United States. But Marx deals quite differently with the methodological problems posed by his analysis. In very important ways, Marx's analysis is successful to the extent that he abandoned the rigid distinction between mode of production and social formation. England is not simply a case from which Marx draws examples to illustrate his structural argument. Rather we find the English working class interwoven within the fabric of Marx's categories. To make an even stronger statement: the English working class and its struggles push forward the development of Marx's categories within Capital. Capital is not a history of the English working class; and it is not simply an analysis of capitalism in England. But Marx draws on the struggle of the English working class since he believed that class political struggles and certain forms of state intervention effected by these struggles become constitutive of the capitalist mode of production. In Capital, Marx's categories do not "unfold" from some pre-established logic. Nor are they a set of static structural relations which (to the extent that they take history into account) are merely read backwards to reveal a "structural dynamic." Rather, the method of Capital indicates that Marx's categories are propelled by historical development. This reading of Marx makes the Factory Acts the pivotal "event" in Capital since the shift from analysis of the production of absolute surplus value to relative surplus value hinges on class struggle and factory legislation.

modes of production) is not incompatible with a class analysis, but, in fact, is inseparable from it.[32] Once the problematic of class-in- and for-itself is set aside, it becomes apparent that a class never exists as a single collectivity-in-struggle but as a multiplicity of collectivities-in-struggle. The study of the forms and dynamics of these groups is the task of class analysis.

My alternative interpretation of the reorganization of work, then, places neither classification nor class consciousness at the center of the analysis but gives priority to the analysis of class struggle. The argument sketched below is not a fully developed alternative explanation of the introduction of "scientific management," but an outline of a different strategy for investigating the problem. The examination of the reorganization of work around the turn of the century through the prism of class struggle does not yield a pattern of social relations characterized merely by capitalist thrust and working class resistance, but rather a complex configuration of the constitutive organizations of the state, the capitalist class, the working class, and an emerging new middle class. The activities of any participating group cannot be understood in isolation, but only in their relation to the total field of competing and coexisting organizations.

## The Craft Tradition

My re-examination of the introduction of scientific management begins with a brief discussion of the practices of the craft tradition. David Montgomery has identified three levels of organization through which the craftsmen of the nineteenth century achieved significant control of the labor process.[33] The first level of control was achieved through informal organization at the local level and involved the process whereby craftsmen enforced what Montgomery calls a "mutualistic ethical code". This code included regulations on the stint (quotas for production) and rules and norms regarding manly behavior towards one's boss and fellows. At the same time that the worker learned a craft, he acquired a view of the world, and his knowledge was inseparable from the moral code and the set of connections to other workers which he acquired in the process. The functional autonomy of the craft and the dignified, respectable, and patriarchal behavior which was its prescribed accompaniment were enforced externally by

---

32. The perspective developed here has been strongly influenced by Schwartz, op. cit,; Theda Skocpol, "France, Russia, China: A Structural Analysis of Social Revolutions," *Comparative Studies in Society and History,* vol. 18, #2 (April, 1976); and Robert Brenner, "Agrarian Class Structure and Economic Development in Pre-Industrial Europe," *Past and Present* (Feb., 1976). Anton Blok's study of mafia within a Sicilian village and Geoff Fougere's analysis of the organization of urban politics have also shaped my ideas. See Blok, *The Mafia of a Sicilian Village* (New York, 1974) and Fougere, "The Structure of Government and the Organization of Politics," Harvard University, Department of Sociology, unpublished manuscript (1978).

33. David Montgomery, "Workers' Control of Machine Production in the Nineteenth Century," *Labor History* (Fall, 1976), pp. 485–509. Montgomery's article is important because it challenges any interpretation of labor history which present workers' control of the labor process as suffering a completely linear decline from some golden age of guild production to the present. Montgomery presents evidence which suggests that, although craftsmen lost significant control in their first confrontation with industrial production, during the last third of the nineteenth century craft autonomy within the labor process actually increased.

strikes and slowdowns and "internally" by expulsion from the union or by ritual castigation imposed by disdainful craftsmen.[34]

In the last decades of the century, the provision of the craftsmen's moral code developed a higher form of craft control in the enactment and enforcement of union work rules which the craft unionists termed "legislation". These work rules indicate the establishment of a second level of control forged through connections between groups of workers within the same craft in different locales. The third level of control struggles emerged when sympathy strikes involving members of different trade unions were conducted to support attempts to enforce these work rules or to win union recognition. Skilled craftsmen were thus forging important connections across locales and industries.

In short, Montgomery's account makes it clear that the development and maintenance of the functional autonomy of the craftsmen were only possible given collective action.[35] What Montgomery chooses not to emphasize is the extent to which the same collective action which enforced the principles of craft control and local autonomy were also used to uphold a third principle of the craft tradition: exclusivity. The craftsmen's moral code defined not only relations among craftsmen and relations between employers and workers (or, at least attempted to do so), but also the relations of the collectivity of craftsmen within a trade against those unskilled who stood outside the craftsmen's web. But this protective mesh of moral code and kin and ethnic ties produced by the craftsmen of the nineteenth century became their own entanglement as they faced the rationalizing efforts of capitalists and their consultants at the century's turn. It is the entire configuration of craft tradition and practices which must be examined if we are to understand the process of rationalization in all of its complexity.

Craft organization of production rested on a core of craftsmen who controlled not only their own labor but often directly supervised and controlled the labor of unskilled workmen who were beneath them. The crafts' relation of competition with their employers had produced peculiar relations of coexistence with them as well. In several important industries where the "internal contract" system prevailed (such as coal, steel, machining, and arms assembly) craftsmen stood, in a sense, as middlemen within the production process contracting to their employers through a set of market relations internal to the firm and subcontracting to their subordinates through various piece work or other sweating schemes which often involved relations of petty exploitation.[36] In

---

34. See James Hinton, *The First Shop Steward's Movement* (London, 1973) for details of the moral codes and rituals of British craftsmen.

35. In contrast to Braverman, who locates the craftsmen's autonomy in their technical skills, Montgomery argues that "a simple technological explanation for the control exercised by nineteenth-century craftsmen will not suffice. Technical knowledge acquired on the job was embedded in a mutualistic ethical code also acquired on the job, and together these attributes provided workers with considerable autonomy at their work and powers of resistance to the wishes of their employers." *op. cit.*, p. 492.

36. On the internal contract system see Nelson, *op. cit.*, pp. 36–37; for subcontracting in carpentry and in the needle trades, Montgomery, *op. cit.*, p. 492; for the "helper" system in iron and steel, Brody, *op. cit.*, and Kathy Stone, "The Origins of Job Structures in the Steel Industry," *Review of Radical Political Economics* vol. 6 no. 4 (Summer, 1974); in coal, Victor Greene, *The Slavic Community on Strike* (Notre Dame, 1968).

other industries (such as pottery, glass, and foundry) without actual "inside contracting," manufacturers

who relied on skilled craftsmen to perform some part of the production process often used the helper system, which bore many similarities [to subcontracting]. The craftsman hired his assistants or "helpers" and paid their wages from his earnings. In most cases the company paid the skilled worker for his output, and he in turn paid the helper a fixed rate.[37]

In the helper system the craftsman's managerial (if not to say entrepreneurial) functions were more circumscribed, but responsibility for supervision of the work of others was still a regular part of his tasks. Although (as Montgomery points out) many of the work rules in the craft union "legislation" were intended to curb tendencies toward upwardly mobile individualism and to discourage craftsmen from identifying their interests with that of the owners,[38] the self-regulation of various subcontracting practices could not alter the basic structural arrangement which cast many craftsmen in the role of middlemen inside the firm. Moreover, craftsmen protected their positions of relatively higher status and earnings by erecting stringent barriers to entry into the trade.

## The Industrial Engineers

Scientific management was an attempt to smash craft control of the labor process and to replace the craft forms of supervision with a bureaucratic administration of production. More than the simple replacement of one middleman (the craftsman–subcontractor) with another (the scientific manager), the project involved a fundamental transformation of the relations between all the relevant actors within the organization of the firm. As capitalists around the turn of the century sought to increase their output (and profits) in response to growing markets, they moved to abandon the subcontracting and helper systems. But the particular forms which this reorganization of work and supervision assumed were not solely the result of capitalists' initiative, since the persons who came to occupy the new positions of bureaucratized supervision had some ideas of their own about the shape, responsibilities, and autonomy of these positions. In this sense, the occupants of the new positions did not simply "fill in" a set of "empty places" created by forces completely divorced from their own activity, but actually participated, within a constellation of struggling classes, in the creation of these positions themselves.

Scientific management, thus, emerged alongside, and as a response to, the transformation of the occupational position of the industrial engineer. From 1880 to 1920, the engineering profession in the United States increased by over 2,000 percent from 7,000 to 136,000 members.[39] This growth occurred within the emerging modern corporation and transformed the character of the occupation. No longer the independent small businessman who worked in and directly

---

37. Nelson, *op. cit.,* p. 38.

38. Montgomery, *op. cit.,* pp. 492 and 495.

39. Edwin Layton, *The Revolt of the Engineers* (Cleveland, 1971), p. 3.

oversaw the operations of his own machine shop, the industrial engineer became an *employee* in a large capitalist firm.[40]

The ranks of these engineers were filled neither by the sons of the working class nor of the bourgeoisie. In 1924, the Society for the Promotion of Engineering Education administered a questionnaire to 4,079 freshmen in engineering schools. Edwin Layton's report of the findings of this study permits no better summary:

A very large proportion of the parents of these students were members of the old middle class: 42.5 percent were owners or proprietors of business. Of the remainder, more than one-quarter were members of the new middle class: 28.2 percent were employed in executive or supervisory positions and 5.6 percent of the total were skilled workers, but only 2.7 percent were unskilled workmen and 3.5 percent were clerks.

The engineering students surveyed by the 1924 study were drawn from the poorer and less well-educated segments of the middle class. Almost all of the parents who were owners or proprietors were engaged in small mercantile enterprises or farming.[41]

The structural position of the industrial engineer had shifted from one *outside* (or alongside) the capitalist mode of production (the old engineer had been an artisan or petty commodity producer who directly controlled both investment decisions and the use of his own labor power) to one squarely *inside* a reorganized capitalist mode of production. The patterns of recruitment into the occupation echoed these changes as its new ranks were formed from the dissolution of the occupations of artisan, shopkeeper, and farmer which had constituted the old middle class. But it was the new positions which more accurately deserve the appellation "middle" since they stood mid-way between workers and capitalists within the emerging corporate and state bureaucracies.[42]

In this light Frederick Taylor's efforts can be seen as a strategic attempt to further the interests of this growing occupation. His promise to eliminate, or at least to mediate, class conflict within the firm demonstrated an acute awareness of the structural position of the industrial engineer. Although Taylor's program for accomplishing this "mediation" could only be realized through a frontal attack on craft practices, his work was interpreted by the scientific management community as the articulation of an *engineer's ideology* rather than as simply a development of capitalist managerial thought.[43] If Taylor hoped to displace the skilled craftsman, he proposed to do so in a way which increased the industrial engineer's room to maneuver within the capitalist firm.

At the same time that scientific management dismantled the old forms of craft autonomy, it seemed to promise (to a large segment of the expanding engineering occupations) new forms of professional autonomy within the emerging bureaucratic organizations. The basis for the defense of this professional autonomy, Taylor and his followers believed, would rest in the esoteric knowledge and set of practices generated internally within the industrial engi-

---

40. *Ibid.,* p. 135.

41. *Ibid.,* p. 9.

42. On the location of the old middle class outside the capitalist mode of production and the location of new managerial, technical, and supervisory positions in a "contradictory class location" within a reorganized capitalist mode of production see Wright.

43. Layton, *op. cit.,* p. 140.

neering community. Appeals to science and the objective laws of nature would provide the basic ideological underpinnings for this autonomy; and time study and the other technical operations of their schemes would provide the necessary material practices for displaying their expertise. The scientific managers' systematization of the knowledge and experience of the skilled craftsman would be codified in a universal language (governed by the rules of scientific discourse), but the encoding and decoding of this translation would be a monopoly of the engineer. The ideology of the "One Best Way" had a dual target:

> Both sides must recognize as essential the substitution of exact scientific investigation and knowledge for the old individual judgement or opinion, either of the workman or the boss.[44]

This philosophy had a programmatic edge as well. In Taylor's proposed form of industrial organization, engineers would direct the day-to-day operations of the plant and the organizing principle of the firm would be a hierarchy of expertise. Given this challenge to the authority of traditional management, it is not surprising that the scientific managers should have encountered significant opposition from their capitalist employers.[45] But capitalists' resistance to the scientific managers' attempts to exert their professional autonomy was not the only factor accounting for their reluctance to introduce the efficiency schemes. More troublesome than the engineers' threats to their authority were the real disruptions of production caused by workers hostile to the introduction of the new forms of management. The risk of strikes and other forms of industrial disruption entered into the calculations of every capitalist who contemplated reorganizing work and supervision. . . .[46]

## Conclusion

In contrast to Braverman, my discussion of the craft practices of the nineteenth century emphasized not technical skills but forms of organization as the basis for craft control. This approach—focussing not on skills as individual attributes but on relations within the context of particular organizational and inter-organizational arrangements—should be useful in analyzing the project of the scientific

---

44. Frederick Taylor, *Scientific Management* (New York, 1947), p. 31.

45. Cf. Nelson's study of 29 firms under scientific management from 1901–1917, *op. cit.*, pp. 68–79. Layton gives us some understanding of why owners may have been reluctant to adopt scientific management in its entirety: "Installing scientific management was a lengthy process, requiring from two to four years. During this period Taylor insisted it was absolutely necessary that the engineer responsible be given complete authority or the attempts would fail. This demand constituted one of the chief impediments to the acceptance of scientific management by business, but Taylor stubbornly refused to budge. Taylor had opened the possibility of an independent role for engineers in an area in which their position had been that of bureaucratic subordinates. He was not willing to compromise this newly found autonomy." Edwin Layton, *op. cit.*, p. 139.

46. Management fear of worker disruptions of production upon the introduction of efficiency schemes is a repeated theme in the European writings on scientific management. See, for example Urwick, *op. cit.*, p. 9. Devinat writes that European industrialists' hesitancy to adopt the new schemes was related to their perceptions of working class opposition to scientific management in the United States and their anticipation of a similar response from their own workers: "Side by side with Taylor's ideas, the hostile attitude of the American workers crossed the Atlantic." *op. cit.*, p. 23.

managers (and their occupational base, the industrial engineers).[47] Taylor's emphasis on exact, "scientific," knowledge, I argued, was an attempt to bolster the position of experts within the emerging new form of corporate organization. But technical skill and knowledge was not the sole basis of power within the reorganized capitalist firm.[48] Certainly the newly acquired (and newly produced) knowledge of the engineers did not confer control of the production process to them. Rather, this knowledge (or more accurately, the way in which it was collectively organized, protected, and maintained), gave the industrial engineers a resource with which they could attempt to increase their autonomy.

During the first period of scientific management from roughly 1890 to World War I, capitalists and their paid consultants struggled over the forms in which scientific management would be introduced. The outcome of this conflict was that the scientific managers were forced to compromise their autonomy, first, because there were a variety of competing schemes from which capitalists could choose and second, because "manufacturers began to employ Taylor's system piecemeal, dropping its more ambitious claims and using college-trained management engineers as part of the regular staff."[49]

The second period, from World War I to the Depression, thus saw members of the scientific management community in the forefront of efforts to organize the various engineering occupations *as a profession*. While the struggle for expanded autonomy continued within the individual firm, it also moved to a wider institutional sphere. Morris Cooke, who figured prominently in the attempts of the scientific managers to cooperate with the trade union leadership (and thus both to mitigate the attack on scientific management from one flank and to carve out a role for the management engineer in the growing field of "labor relations"), spearheaded these efforts to organize the diverse engineering occupations into a profession. Cooke's campaign involved: attempts to align civil engineering with the movement for municipal reform (which carried him into an attack on the utility companies); attempts to alter decision-making structures of various engineering societies by eliminating the secrecy and censorship which allowed a powerful business minority to control these organizations; and, above all, attempts to create a single professional organization for

---

47. It also serves as a basis for questioning Braverman's extraordinary pessimism concerning the possibilities both of worker militance and of new forms of workers' control of the production process not based on the craft model. The reorganization of the labor process gives rise to new forms of struggle as every system of domination at the same time yields new forms of social knowledge and organization which can undermine it. Or in Gramsci's words: "Every relationship of hegemony is necessarily an educational one . . ." *Selections from the Prison Notebooks,* trans. by Quintin Hoare and Geoffrey Smith (New York, 1971), p. 350.

48. This issue poses one final problem in Braverman's analysis. Braverman places overwhelming emphasis on technical knowledge of the production process. When workers possess it, it affords them control of their own labor power within the labor process. The reorganization of work is presented in terms of dichotomous marxist categories as the process whereby knowledge is taken away from the working class by capital. But the use of the structural (logical) categories obscures the importance of organizational (sociological) factors since specialized knowledge is now located within a "new middle class"—among scientists, technicians, middle-level supervisors, and certain professionals. This knowledge does not confer control of the production process to them but it does provide a resource with which they can exert some control over their own labor power within the labor process.

49. Layton, *op. cit.,* p. 213.

engineers thereby breaking the grip of business interests who were capable of controlling the engineering societies linked to specific industries.[50] Several such federations or profession-wide organizations were established, yet none proved viable. Magali Sarfatti-Larson presents a persuasive argument that engineering's failure to organize as a profession is attributable to a combination of factors: the particular character of the engineer's product (as a concrete piece of hardware or blueprint or structure—rather than a service—which made collegial review difficult); the structure of the "profession" distributed across numerous industries; the evolving career patterns which (in the United States) gave many engineers at least the hope of moving into management positions; and the source and rapidity of technical innovation all posed insurmountable obstacles to the engineers' professional project.[51]

Scientific management ultimately failed to gain complete autonomy for the industrial engineer either within the firm or within a larger institutional sphere. But this attempt was not without important effects on the social relations of production not only within the internal organizational sphere of the modern corporation but also within the broader processes of societal reproduction. For although scientific management failed as a total program for industrial management, many of its themes became part of an ideology of other occupations which were emerging during this same period.[52] The ideology of technical expertise was developed by engineers, the first and most rapidly growing occupation of a "new middle class"[53]; this ideology came to serve other occupations as they systematized their cognitive categories and developed new organiza-

---

50. *Ibid.*, pp. 154–200, and Edwin Layton, "Science, Business and the American Engineer," in Robert Perrucci and Joel Gerstl, eds., *The Engineers and the Social System* (New York, 1969).

51. See Magali Sarfatti Larson, *The Rise of Professionalism: A Sociological Analysis* (Berkeley, 1977), p. 28. It may be interesting to contrast the failures of the industrial engineers to organize as a profession with the strategy adopted by the managerial groups analyzed by Alfred Chandler in *The Visible Hand* (Cambridge, Mass., 1977). David Nobel, in *America By Design,* (New York, 1977), argues that the engineers in fact became managers rather than a group with separate interests and identifications.

52. Cf. Samuel Haber, *Efficiency and Uplift: Scientific Management in the Progressive Era. 1890–1920* (Chicago, 1964); Raymond Callahan, *Education and the Cult of Efficiency* (Chicago, 1962); and especially, Magali Larson, *op. cit.*

53. Cf. Barbara and John Frenreich, "The Professional-Managerial Class," *Radical America* (March–April, 1977); Nicos Poulantzas, *Classes in Contemporary Capitalism* (London, 1976); Alvin W. Gouldner, *The Future of Intellectuals and the Rise of the New Class* (New York: Seabury Press, 1979); and George Ross, "Marxism and the New Middle Classes: French Critiques," *Theory and Society*, 5/2 (1978). Wright's *(op. cit.)* "contradictory class position" between the working class and the capitalist class describes positions which are very similar to those defined in the "new middle class" approaches. I am concerned less about the label with which we identify certain positions and more that we see these positions as the outcome of struggles in which this class, stratum, group (however labelled) actively participates. Val Burris presents a strong case that there is a new middle class. His excellent use of census data from 1900 to the present documents the expansion of this class as well as identifies its major segments. Although his categories are much more discrete than this summary, his data suggest that the new middle class expanded in two major waves of a qualitatively different character: the first from the turn of the century to World War II among managerial and supervisory personnel within industry, and the second from World War II to the present among "reproductive" personnel (social services, education, etc.) within the state. Burris' finding of stagnation in growth (and actual absolute decline among some segments) of this class in recent years have important implications for class realignments in American politics. See "Towards an Historical Understanding of the New Middle Class," unpublished manuscript, Department of Sociology, University of Oregon (1978).

tional forms (the "professional project") in their attempts to define and maintain their privileged position over and against the working class and struggled to increase their autonomy from the capitalist class in the schools, the universities, and the state.

The reorganization of work in the early decades of this century was not the simple product of a group of far-sighted industrial engineers any more than it was the direct result of an omniscient capitalist class. The basic need for this reorganization (as well as the limits of its development) was set by a broad process which can best be termed capital accumulation. But, as I have argued in this paper, the particular forms, timing, and ideological effects of this reorganization in the United States were conditioned by the patterns of interacting organizations including the state and emergent occupational groups as well as the constitutive formal and informal organizations of the capitalist class and the working class. Relegating these patterns to the status of only epiphenomenal effects of an underlying and determinant process of capital accumulation obscures important political consequences which arise from these patterns themselves. To identify only a few: the contemporary system of American "industrial relations" finds its origins in the forms and timing of the reorganization of work examined in this essay. Although they did not spring into existence in their fully developed forms (and although their patterns did not evidence an uninterrupted unilinear development), many of the elements—and the relations between them—of contemporary American labor relations were prefigured during the period studied here. For we find, especially during the crucial period of World War I, the American labor movement in a situation of double jeopardy—heavily dependent on the state to provide the basic legal conditions for organizing, but without a party of its own to struggle politically to maintain these conditions in periods when state managers find it less expedient to continue or extend these arrangements. With a significant part of the organized labor force concentrated in war-related industry, with collective bargaining defined as a set of technical operations in which legal and engineering experts from both sides engage in processes of productivity bargaining, and with the routinization of tasks and erosion of traditional work rules conducted under the aegis of conservative trade unions, we observe, in that period, a pattern of labor relations closely corresponding to that of our own.

The period of the transformation of the labor process during the early decades of this century was also an important period of class formation with significant consequences for the contemporary constellation of class relations. The reorganization of work, as Braverman correctly argued, led to a dramatic disjuncture between design and execution. But despite Frederick Taylor's prescription that "all possible brainwork should be removed from the shop floor and centered in the planning or laying-out department of the firm" (a scheme which capitalists could endorse if that planning department remained firmly in their control), the separation between hand and brain could never be so radical as to remove all discretion and subjectivity from the labor process. What the reorganization of work did accomplish was to provide the basic conditions for the ideologically sharp division between "mental" and "manual" labor. But this dichotomous ideological division located within the social relations of production[54] did not produce or correspond to a simple, dichotomous class structure, since new occupational groups were emerging between capitalists and workers both within industrial organizations and within the expanding bureaucracies of education and state social services. The project of scientific management gave a particular ideological charge to the "mental" labor of these new occupations. The creed of specialized knowledge and technical expertise became the formative basis of a new and more complex ideology around which a class could cohere. This ideology would not have an unmediated relationship to the occupants of the new class positions since its reproduction would be bound up with new organizational forms with which the new occupational groups struggle for their political and economic interests. In attempting to defend their claims to technical expertise or to maintain the currency value of their certified degrees, the members of these new occupations stand not with one foot in the working class and one foot in the capitalist class but with one foot in a professional association and one foot in a bureaucratic (corporate or state) organization. The constellation of relations of conflict and alliance between these associations and other organizations arising from work, community, and political life must be the object of study in the analysis of class relations in the current period.

---

54. Cf. Poulantzas, *op. cit.*

# · 17 ·

# Structured Labour Markets, Worker Organisation, and Low Pay

## Jill Rubery

The persistence of low paid sectors in an affluent, advanced capitalist society has been attributed in recent American literature to the emergence of noncompetitive, or structured labour markets. Firms operate *internal* labour markets providing high wages and secure employment. This limits the mobility of workers both within the internal or *primary* labour market sector, and between the primary and the residual, competitive *secondary* sector. No competitive equalisation of wages takes place, and differences in wage levels may be maintained over the long term if the system of segmentation reduces class consciousness, or if there is divergent development in the economic structure.

Segmentation of the labour market has long been considered a cause of inequality and low wages in the labour market (Mill, 1849; Cairnes, 1874). Recent work in this area, however, effectively divides into two types. The first builds upon the 19th-century notion of non-competing groups in the labour market, where social and political inequality is inherited and children are confined to the same segment of the labour market as their parents. Added to this model is the effect of discrimination in setting up further barriers to mobility, barriers which become more resilient in a world of imperfect information, where prejudiced beliefs can become self-justifying (Myrdal, 1944; Akerlof, 1970; Spence, 1973). These theories, often called theories of 'low level equilib-

* Abridged from *Cambridge Journal of Economics* 2(1) (1978): 17–21, 23–25, 27–36.
NOTE: I am grateful to Frank Wilkinson for his invaluable help and encouragement from the start of my work in this area. I would also like to thank the editors of the *Cambridge Journal of Economics* and Diane Flaherty for their advice during the final stages of preparation of this paper.

rium traps', continue the methodology of orthodox theory, where the origins of inequality are exogenous to the economic system, but add to the analysis a process of reinforcement of existing social and political inequality through the operation of the labour market.

The second approach, with which we shall be primarily concerned in this paper, adopts a different methodology and looks at the relationship between the development of the economic structure and the emergence of segmented labour markets. In these models inequality originates within the economic system. Two main sets of theories have been produced using this methodology: dual labour market theories (Doeringer and Piore, 1971) and radical theories (Gordon, 1972; Edwards, Reich and Gordon, 1975). Dual labour market theories look primarily to technological developments under capitalism or to the divergent development of the industrial structure to explain the emergence of labour market segmentation. Radical theories attribute the origins of stratification in the labour market to the capitalists' need to divide and rule the labour force.

Many of the specific elements of the dual labour market and radical approaches can be found in orthodox economics. It has been recognised for some time that labour is often more properly considered as a quasi-fixed factor to the firm rather than variable (Oi, 1962), particularly if there are costs of hiring and firing, and investment in job-specific skills (Marshall, 1920; Becker, 1964). These considerations have led to the development of theories of internal labour markets similar to dual labour market theories. Further, discrimination theories have been used under both approaches to explain the concentration of certain groups in different segments of the labour market. Under the second approach, discrimination only reinforces and does not create inequality. The development of non-competing groups and internal labour markets has seriously reduced the explanatory power of the orthodox theory of wage determination. Dual labour market and radical theories attempt to offer some explanation of the extent of the development of internal labour markets, and its effects on those workers left outside, by relating the analysis to the economic structure.

This important new approach has so far progressed in an *ad hoc* fashion. Dual labour market theory built on theories of internal labour markets, theories of discrimination, and general theories of dualism or divergent development in the economy. The radical approach attempted to place the dual labour market theory in an historical and ideological framework. Each new contribution adopted parts of the previous theories, with no one theory developing its arguments from first principles. The result, we shall argue, is that the analysis as it now stands is more a rationalisation of the present structure of the American labour market than an explanation of how this was arrived at from the range of development paths open to it. It is this particular aspect of the American theories which has made them so far so difficult to apply to the analysis of labour market structures outside the US. There is evidence that there is some degree of segmentation in the British external labour market, and non-competitive organisation of the internal industry or firm labour forces, but the form and nature of this labour market segmentation differs from that found in the US (Mackay *et al.*, 1971).

We shall argue in this paper that the main reason for the lack of general applicability of the American theories arises from the almost exclusive attention paid to the actions and motivations of the capitalists in developing a structured labour market, and the consequent neglect of the role of worker organisation in the process. Further inadequacies appear in the theory because the consideration of major change in the economic structure is limited to one historical epoch: the end of the 19th and the beginning of the 20th centuries, which saw the development of widespread factory and machine production and the emergence of monopoly capitalism. Change in the economic structure at this time may indeed have been more intensive and extensive than in other eras, but the almost total concentration on this period results in a rather static analysis of present-day labour market structure. Recent work by Braverman (1974) has pointed to the importance of continuing the analysis of the evolution of the employment structure into the period of monopoly capitalism. Significant changes in occupational structure, skills and labour force participation have taken place, changes which may particularly affect the structure and importance of low paid occupations.

If a more general approach to the analysis of labour market segmentation is to be developed which could explain differences between, for instance, the UK and US labour market structures, as well as developments within a given labour market, two major changes must be made. First, workers and worker organisation must be assigned an active role in the development of labour market structure. Second, changes in the employment structure under monopoly capitalism must be taken into account, and their effects on labour market segmentation examined. This analysis must, we shall argue, be carried out within the context of a continuous struggle between capitalists and workers on the industrial front, over wages and over control of production. . . .

## Dual Labour Market and Radical Theories

### Dual Labour Market Theory

The development of an analysis of low pay, emphasising the importance of the economic structure, began with dual labour market theory. This built upon the work of Slichter (1950), Lester (1952), Kerr (1954) and others in the 1950s, which pointed to the development of internal, or balkanised, labour markets under modern capitalism. The contribution of dual labour market theory was to consider the effects of the development of internal labour markets not only on those included within them, but also on those excluded from this sheltered sector, and confined to the residual competitive secondary sector.

Internal labour markets develop, according to the theory, because skills are becoming more firm-specific and a worker's productivity is becoming more and more a function of his on-the-job training and experience, and hence of his length of service within a firm. In order to encourage the development of a stable labour force, an employer will pay his workers more than their opportunity wage in the external labour market, thus reducing the incentive to mobility among the workers. With mobility restricted or eliminated, there will be little market influence on the shape of the internal wage structure of the firm, which will come to be determined by custom and by rules. The labour market will thus be divided up into relatively independent sections.

Doeringer and Piore (1971) took up this theory and looked at its implications for the labour market as a whole.[1] In their model the market is divided into primary and secondary sectors. Technology and workers' skills have become less general and more firm-specific and a stable labour force has become more necessary. To induce stability, high wages and prospects of advancement are offered by restricting the number of 'ports of entry', to each of which a promotion ladder is attached, with progress up the ladder determined by seniority. The provision of such employment conditions, however, is costly. The need for a stable labour force applies only to certain types of jobs; where incentives to stability are not necessary, wages remain low, security of employment is not assured, and promotion prospects are few. This type of job forms the secondary sector; the former constitutes the primary sector.

An important aspect of dual labour market analysis is the emphasis on the interaction between developments in the economic structure, developments in technology and the pattern of labour market behaviour. Technological developments required a reduction in labour mobility, but only the development of oligopolistic markets, which allow firms much greater control and certainty in their product and factor markets, permitted the formation of stable, high paid labour forces. The secondary sector, in turn, provides that degree of flexibility still required by the system. Expansion of the primary sector over the trade cycle can be achieved by subcontracting to the secondary sector, or by employing secondary sector workers on a temporary basis. Likewise, the technologically determined division of the labour market is reinforced by the reactions of workers to their position in the market. Workers confined to the secondary sector develop attitudes and modes of behaviour which turn them into inherently unstable workers, unsuitable for employment in the primary sector.[2]

In this theory, all positive developments take place in the primary sector. It is here that technology is changing, that new labour market structures are developed. Changes in the secondary sector serve only to reinforce its already dominant characteristics; that is, its lack of structure, stagnant technology and absence of differentiation between workers.

---

1. We are confining our discussion of dual labour market theory to the Doeringer-Piore model. Many other variants of the dualism hypothesis have been presented; for instance, Bluestone (1971) has stressed the importance of industrial structure in determining dualism, and Vietorisz and Harrison (1973) have looked at the problem of divergent technological development in the economy. Many of these other theories are more fruitful than the Doeringer-Piore model, but they are still only partial approaches and not as well known or as often cited.

2. Doeringer and Piore and some radical theorists (Gordon, 1972) argue that secondary workers may become objectively unsuitable for the primary sector. Their proposition of restricted mobility between the two sectors could be maintained under the weaker assumption that secondary sector workers become labelled as unsuitable for the primary sector, a reformulation which would make their analysis more generally applicable. The emphasis in these theories on the development of a subculture in the labour force is probably one example of how this approach has been particularly influenced by the characteristics of the American labour market, where the blacks could be considered to form a lower class (Piore, 1975, p. 114), distinct in attitudes and orientation from the working class.

## The Development of the Radical Approach

Doeringer and Piore emphasised the importance of technology in the development of dualism in the labour market. Control of the labour force enters into the model only in so far as employers cannot expect workers to form a stable labour force unless they are offered advantages over and above the external market wage. Control plays a much more central part in radical theories. These theories developed out of the dual labour market approach in an attempt to incorporate this theory 'into a more general radical framework, convinced that the dual labour market hypotheses can be generated by radical theory and that radical theory provides some important historical foundations for the specific conclusions of dual market analysis' (Gordon, 1972, p. 52). At the outset, the requirement of a stable labour force for the efficient functioning of complex technology was retained, but added to it was another, and complementary, determinant of stratification: the need for capitalists to control the labour force, which, with the development of factory production, was becoming more homogeneous and thus more likely to unite against them. Stratification would allow the capitalists to 'divide and rule' the labour force. Jobs were divided up into grades, or clusters, but within each grade promotion ladders were established. This stratification served to reduce the likelihood of the development of class consciousness between grades in the labour force, but within each grade the promotion ladders provided the incentive necessary to motivate the workers. According to Gordon (1972, p. 77):

employers will seek to develop in the labor force a kind of 'hierarchy fetishism'—a continual craving for more and better job titles and status, the satisfaction of which leads eventually to intensified hunger for still more and better job titles and job status . . . And in order to create hierarchical incentives without providing too many mobility opportunities, in order to satisfy 'hierarchy fetishism' without simultaneously establishing a continuum of relationships among workers along which they can develop common class consciousness—employers may find it useful to forge hierarchical ladders within clearly differentiated job clusters.

The capitalists were apparently remarkably successful in their strategy, in as much as they developed 'hierarchy fetishism' among their workers at the same time as they were restricting opportunities for mobility and, indeed, as real skill differences were declining.

Radical theory extends the analysis of stratification to emphasise differentiation between workers within internal labour markets as well as between the secondary and primary sectors. The lowest stratum of workers may either be attached to the bottom of the job hierarchy within a particular firm or industry, or be employed in secondary sector industries or occupations located outside the internal labour market sector. Those groups most subject to discrimination and prejudice would be concentrated in these low paid, menial occupations. This segmentation serves two purposes. First, the existence of a lower stratum increases the status and status orientation of those in the higher strata. Second, workers in the upper strata are unlikely to identify with the interests of the blacks and women concentrated in the menial occupations, and thus low wages can be paid to these workers without risk of class opposition.

Over time, the need to control the labour force has come to be considered the major determinant of stratification in the labour market, and indeed a conflict has been identified between the system of work organisation which may be efficient for technology and that which affords capitalists the most 'control' over the labour force (Bowles and Gintis, 1975; Gordon, 1976). Gordon has called these two aspects of efficiency the technological, or quantitative, aspect and the control, or qualitative, aspect, where 'a production process is qualitatively [most] efficient if it maximises the ability of the ruling class to reproduce its domination of the social process of production and minimises producers' resistance to ruling class domination of the production process' (1976, p. 22). Gordon further argues that, as workers' organisation becomes stronger, qualitative considerations will become dominant and employers will increasingly make their choice of technique and method of work organisation on the basis of the opportunity to control. . . .

## Monopoly Capitalism and the Employment Structure

In radical theory, major change in the structure of labour markets was brought about by major change in the economic structure. The late 19th and early 20th centuries saw not only the development of monopoly capitalism and the spread of factory and machine production, but also the destruction of old craft skills and the progressive homogenisation of the labour force, a process which was reversed by the introduction of systems of job ladders to provide artificial divisions within it. Braverman has shown the importance of moving on from the changes that took place in the early stages of monopoly capitalism and large-scale factory production to the evolution of employment structure with the spread and development of monopoly capitalism. He suggests that the period of monopoly capitalism has been characterised by a progressive reduction in skills for the mass of workers, a redistribution of employment to those occupations where productivity increases have been lowest, and a growth in the supply of wage labour as capitalism has moved into domestic production and displaced domestic labour. His thesis suggests a progressive reduction in divisions within the mass of the labour force, based on a levelling down of the skilled workers, rather than, as in human capital theorists' analysis, a levelling up as the standards of education and the general productivity level of workers increase.

The implications of Braverman's thesis for the development of stratification have yet to be fully considered. Radical theorists have used the analysis to justify their claim that divisions in the labour market are artificial, imposed by capitalists to counter the homogenisation of the labour force and thus prevent the development of class opposition. Braverman himself suggests there may be progressive polarisation in the distribution of earnings, with labour piling up in low paid, low productivity occupations (1974, pp. 392–395). These hypotheses may be better considered after a more detailed examination of changes in employment structure, starting with the distribution of employment and moving on to changes in the nature of skills and the composition of the labour force. This discussion will also lead us on from a consideration of specific criticisms of dual labour market and radical theory to the development of a more general approach to the analysis of labour market structure, in which the role of worker organisation may be integrated.

## Distribution of Employment

The process of capitalist development creates new industries, new markets, new technologies, new institutional systems and new concentrations of capital; at the same time it destroys or forces adaptation in existing industries, markets, technologies and institutions. The process of development, therefore, necessarily involves changes in the employment distribution across occupations, industries and sectors.

Within each occupation, industry or sector, the nature and structure of jobs will depend on the scale and technique of production, and the method of work organisation. Yet developments in these three directions do not take place at the same rate throughout the economy. Braverman has argued that there will be a tendency for labour to be displaced from those occupations where technological progress is fastest. Displacement through technological progress may or may not be offset by increases in the demand for high productivity industries but, at least within each industry, employment will increase relatively in those occupations least affected by technological change:

labour tends to pile up in the industries and occupations which are less susceptible to engineered improvements in labour productivity . . . we see in capitalist industry a secular trend to accumulate labour in those portions of industry and trade which are least affected by the scientific-technical revolution; service work, sales and other forms of marketing, clerical work insofar as it has not yet been mechanised, etc. The paradox that the most rapidly growing mass occupations in an era of scientific-technical revolution are those which have least to do with science and technology need not surprise us. The purpose of machinery is not to increase but to decrease the numbers of workers attached to it (Braverman, 1974, pp. 383–384).

Similarly, capitalist production does not develop in all sectors and industries at the same time, not at the same rate or on the same scale. Thus, Braverman argues, it is into the service and retail sectors that capitalism has recently expanded fastest, bringing about a change in mode of production, scale of production and method of work organisation, as a result of the widespread introduction of scientific management techniques. Likewise, clerical employment has undergone a significant change in technique and method of work organisation, associated with an increase in the scale of clerical operations. This can in turn be attributed to changes in techniques in the production process, where mental labour is progressively separated from manual labour, and to the need under monopoly capitalism to devote a growing share of resources to the realisation of surplus value, through marketing, sales and accountancy.

Uneven development takes place as much within as between industries and sectors. The existence of relatively obsolete techniques of production, even in industries characterised by rapid rates of technical progress, adds yet another dimension to the complex employment pattern that capitalist development creates. The firms operating on the margin, on the smallest scale, using the oldest techniques, which paradoxically may require the highest skills, may be operating also in the secondary sector, or the lowest part of the labour market. In some sense this employment can be considered 'marginal' or 'peripheral' to the economy. Yet this is only one kind of 'typical' secondary sector employment, which is usually argued to include, for instance, workers in services and retail trade and the lower grades of clerical employment. These occupations do not readily fit the classification 'marginal' or 'peripheral'. Demand for service sector and clerical employment has been generated, at least in part, by the development of the monopoly capitalist sector, the 'core'. At the same time, technological progress in the 'core' may have displaced labour, providing the sources of labour supply for these occupations. Further, some of these occupations have provided new areas for the spread of the capitalist mode of production.

Not all secondary–sector-type employment can thus be said to be characterised by stagnant technology and methods of work organisation. Further, the relationship between developments in the two sectors must be carefully analysed. If Braverman's hypothesis is correct, the future development of monopoly capitalism will lead to a relative increase in secondary sector employment. In that case, the interesting question is, of course, how far these currently low paid occupations could be transformed into primary-type occupations; this transformation, we shall argue, must depend on the potential for, and the effect of trade union development. . . .

The bargaining position of workers did not enter directly into Braverman's study. . . . [Moreover] because he has no analysis of bargaining he fails to develop a theory of wage determination. Competitive theory, and perhaps an orthodox Marxist approach, would predict a tendency towards equalisation of wage levels with the progressive homogenisation of labour. Braverman points instead to a progressive polarisation of earnings in the US, for 'industrial sectors in the United States in which employment is relatively stagnant are the sectors with wage rates above the average, while the sectors in which employment is growing most rapidly are those with lower than average wage rates' (p. 393). Yet it is, in Braverman's analysis, precisely in those industrial sectors [the highly mechanised sectors—eds.] that the division of labour and homogenisation of the labour force have progressed furthest. In these sectors, too, labour is being displaced and demand for labour is falling, factors which under competitive theory also depress wages. Implicit in Braverman's theory seems to be a belief that workers' wages are determined not by the skill of the worker, but by the productivity of the organisation. However, to justify this theory of wage determination it would be necessary to put worker organization back into the centre of the discussion. . . .

The aspect of Braverman's analysis of skill which is important to an understanding of the development of worker organisation is the 'relative homogeneity of the workforce' and 'the interchangeability of person and function'. Even if, at present, workers possess special skills that cannot be easily acquired by other workers, these skills may still become obsolete with the progress of technology and work organisation. Indeed Braverman argues that management will design their techniques of production in order to deskill these workers. Thus all workers are threatened by the obsolescence of skills, or by replacement by other equally skilled workers who are in plentiful supply. This threat may induce defensive actions on the part of the workers to stratify the labour force, control entry to occupations and maintain skill status long after these skill divisions have become irrelevant.

Thus the progress of capitalism both destroys old skills and creates new ones, providing new opportunities for organisation and control and provoking defensive attempts to maintain old skill divisions in the labour force, with varying degrees of success. The counterpart of this development for capitalists is that new technologies and work organisations provide new opportunities to impose control and also confront capitalists with new problems in obtaining their desired output.

### Composition of the Labour Force

As capitalism has developed, new groups of labour have been drawn into the wage labour force. When capitalism expands into new sectors, labour is displaced, and forms new supplies of wage labour. Recently, the most important area where labour has been displaced has been domestic production. The spread of capitalist production and state services into this area has 'released' female labour onto the market. Immigration has provided further sources of supply for the labour market in certain periods.

The introduction of new supplies of wage labour in different historical periods may lead to segmentation of the labour market. Those workers previously at the bottom of the structure take advantage of these new supplies to move up their hierarchy, but at the same time protect themselves against the increased competition in the labour market (Baran and Sweezy, 1966, ch. 9). Female workers are still largely confined to certain segments of the labour market, as are Commonwealth immigrants in the UK, and blacks in the US. Their wages tend to be low, and they may be available for work at lower reserve wage levels than the white male majority group. Substitution of women for men may lead to a real decline in relative wages in an occupation, and reduce employment opportunities for men; hence the incentive for males to try to confine women to a different segment of the labour force. It is not our intention here to develop a theory of racism or sexism, only to indicate how the changes in composition of the labour force provide some kind of 'natural' segmentation of the labour force, and further, how the ability of capitalism continuously to generate new supplies of labour forces the existing labour force to organise and protect itself against new competition.

### The Struggle for Control Under Monopoly Capitalism

. . . [T]he development and spread of monopoly capitalism have had a much more complex impact on the employment structure than that identified in radical theory. Recognition of this complex development raises the possibility that the analysis of the struggle between capitalists and workers has so far been too simple and too static.

For example, on the one hand it is clear that the development of factory production did reduce the importance of general skills, and thus made it possible for a homogeneous labour force to develop. On the other hand, viewing this development from the Braverman perspective, it is also clear that this process increased the control of capitalists over the speed and method of production; this indicates that the homogenisation of the labour force is not the overriding problem for management which radical theory suggests. The establishment of a system of high wages, secure employment and promotion ladders may, from this viewpoint, be thought to indicate workers' success in regaining some of the control lost through the destruction of the craft system, rather than a further increase in capitalists' control.

The development of the employment structure clearly does present capitalists with problems, but of a more complex nature than radical theory has suggested. The problem of control for capitalists is not just one of preventing the development of class consciousness, but of organising the social relations of production. Introduction of new technology disrupts existing social relations and may meet trade union opposition. This resistance may be more than a bargaining tactic to gain a share in productivity increases, for the new technology may undermine the existing system of worker organisation, whose strength is based on workers' knowledge and control of the existing technique. The introduction of new technology may, on the one hand, present management with the opportunity to break down worker organisation, yet the very resistance that this induces may limit management's ability to introduce best practice techniques quickly and cheaply. Further regrouping and restructuring of worker organisation round new technologies and work organisation may present management with similar problems the next time the system of production has to be adapted.

In order to understand the problems for management we must examine further the actions and motivations of workers. Our discussion of the development of monopoly capitalism has pointed to major problems for workers and for workers' organisation. Braverman's thesis suggests that there is a continuous threat of displacement of labour, and redundancy of skills. Full employment is in some sense only relative: each new phase of capitalist expansion creates new supplies of labour by displacing labour from production outside the capitalist mode, by displacing labour through the extension and intensification of mechanisation, or by drawing in new workers from the international pool of surplus labour. Workers' defence against competition in the labour market is to organise to control the supply of labour. Attempts may be made at the macro level to limit the supply of new types of labour, such as females or immigrants. More importantly, workers will organise to control entry into an occupation, firm or industry. Such control must be to the detriment of groups excluded from the organised sectors, as it reduces their mobility and may even increase competition in the external labour market. The development of worker organisation may thus create segmentation in the external labour market.

The establishment and maintenance of bargaining positions within the organised sector may further depend on stratification of the labour force. Insofar as workers are acting defensively against the threat of substitution and competition, their most effective tactic is to differentiate themselves from potential competitors. Such protection through differentiation may be provided by various systems, from union organised apprenticeship schemes to promotion lines based on strict seniority provisions. Both types of system provide shelter from labour market competition for the incumbent workforce, although the former offers protection only for one group of workers, whilst the second extends protection down through the whole range of jobs by restricting entry to the bottom of the hierarchy. Clearly both systems also offer various degrees and methods of control for management; this is the point on which the radical theories have focused. On the other hand, in both cases, the existence of a structured labour force, where jobs are strictly defined, and workers are not interchangeable, provides a bargaining base for labour against management's attempts to increase productivity and introduce new technology. Changes in job ladders, skill demarcations and the pace of work become areas for bargaining, whereas a homogeneous labour force, interchangeable in function, would lay itself open not only to competition from the external market but also to further declines in workers' control of production and a continuous undermining of bargaining power. Divisions by custom, rule and status are essential parts of any union's bargaining strategy. Reducing the differentiation between workers and developing job rotation may decrease the monotony of work, increase class cohesiveness, and create opportunities for workers to control the pace and method of work. However, unless they organise to seize these opportunities and to create a bargaining position based on this new organisation of work, the development of a more homogeneous labour force may undermine the basis of workers' industrial organisation.

The development of capitalism not only presents problems for worker control and organisation, inducing defensive tactics on the part of existing trade union organisations, but it also offers new opportunities for organisation. Thus the development of machine technology may to some extent have undermined the skilled union's basis for organisation and control but, by transforming much unskilled labour into semi-skilled labour or, rather, by increasing the proportion of the labour force directly involved in the mechanised production process, it increased the bargaining power of a large section of the labour force. Semi-skilled workers were now in control of a greater volume of production, and further represented a threat to skilled workers as the real skill differential declined, thus forcing some skilled unions to recruit semi-skilled workers, whilst in other industries organisation of semi-skilled workers proceeded independently.

The strategy of worker organisation and its effects on the structure of the labour market have so far been discussed only at the general level, and no evidence has yet been presented to back up our line of argument. Full supporting evidence would require detailed study of the development of labour market structures across industries, and preferably across countries. At this stage, it is possible only to cite some examples of how worker organisation in the UK has been involved in the development of structured labour markets, briefly comparing the UK experience with that of the US, but also calling into question the radical theorists' contention that even in the US the development of structured labour markets has been both to the disadvantage of workers and independent of worker organisation.

## Worker Organisation and the Development of Structured Labour Markets in the United Kingdom

Worker organisation operates to control the supply of labour both at the macro and at the micro level. In the UK control of aggregate labour supplies has been attempted at various times by means of a number of different strategies. Recently, the role of the working class family in the 19th century in limiting the supply of female labour, and thereby improving the bargaining power of the working class, has been documented (Humphries, 1977). The unlimited participation of family labour, according to Marx, would not only depress the general wage level by increasing the relative surplus population, but would also reduce the limit below which the wage level could not fall, i.e. the labour-time necessary to maintain the worker and his dependents.

Efforts to control the length of the working day, in particular the campaign to introduce the 10-hour day, were aimed at preventing workers from being forced to work long hours to protect their jobs in the face of competition from the surplus population, and thereby inadvertently increasing competition in the labour market (Marx, 1954, ch. 10). Similarly, the movement to establish legal minimum wages through the trade board system was aimed, in part, at squeezing out the sweater operating with cheap labour, often subsidised family labour, in an attempt to reduce undercutting and competitive pressure on wages, at the possible expense of employment, particularly secondary family employment (Bayliss, 1962, pp. 7–8). A more recent example of control, though one considered less respectable and honourable than the above mentioned campaigns, is provided by the rigid conditions placed on the use of immigrant labour, particularly Polish labour, after the Second World War (Castles and Kosack, 1973, pp. 29–30).

Most effective efforts to control the labour supply take place at the level of occupation, firm or industry. The technical conditions of production provide the basis for the development of worker organisation, but, in the UK, the system of worker organisation has often been strong enough to withstand the obsolescence of the skills on which it has been based. Thus Hinton (1973, pp. 61–62) argues that the engineers in the UK successfully maintained their craft demarcations until 1914 despite the fact that 'a substantial proportion of the work performed by craftsmen, at the craft rate, required little of their skill'. Only the 'vast expansion of engineering production required by the war effort revealed the degree to which the genuine skill content of the craftsmen's work had declined'. Indeed, Turner (1962, p. 114) has gone so far as to argue that: 'From the viewpoint of trade union development, at least, workers are thus "skilled" and "unskilled" according to whether or not entry to their organisation is deliberately restricted, and not in the first place according to the nature of the occupation itself.'

However, as in the case of the engineering workers, the ability to maintain skill differentials after they have become technologically redundant is limited. Various defensive tactics were available to the skilled unions. In the case of shipbuilding, the craft unions forestalled the threat of dilution (the substitution of unskilled and semi-skilled for skilled workers) by amalgamations with other unions representing 'lesser but possibly competing skills' and later insisted on apprenticeships as the only means of entry into each organised trade. Thus, 'few new operations were free to be taken up by semi-skilled' (Wilkinson, 1975, pt. 2, p. 5). Some cotton craft unions or closed unions, presented with the threat of dilution, opened up their recruitment to those groups of less skilled workers from which the 'skilled' workers were recruited (Turner, 1962). In engineering, Hinton (1973) describes how the shop stewards' movement realised the seriousness of the dilution threat, and attempted not only to preserve craft control, but also to develop organisation in all grades, along with an industrial, rather than a craft, policy on wages and labour supply. In the UK iron and steel industry, Wilkinson (1977, p. 103) shows how 'successive groups of less skilled workers established themselves in the formalised industrial relations system and how this modified collective bargaining and redistributed the industry's wage fund in favour of the newly organised groups'. The skilled workers gave way, partly out of altruism, but also because of the increasing importance of ancillary grades in the production process.

Deskilling of the labour force in the UK thus often led to an extension of organisation to semi-skilled and unskilled workers and some reduction in differentials, whilst a structured, sheltered labour market, based on control of entry was still maintained. Deskilling of skilled workers was often matched by an increase in the bargaining position and sometimes the skill of previously unskilled workers. Child (1967, p. 162) documented the technological developments in the printing industry in the late 19th and early 20th centuries which led to a decline in the proportion, though not in numbers, of skilled craftsmen. Technical progress also created a new class of semi-skilled men and 'in many cases the "semi-skilled" machine operators required greater manual dexterity and occupied posts of greater responsibility than many of the "craftsmen"'. The effects of technical progress over the same period on skilled workers in the steel industry may have balanced each other out, increasing responsibility whilst decreasing the need for specialist knowledge, but it certainly transformed 'the largely unskilled force of "underhands" into one of semi-skilled operatives', thus improving their bargaining position relative to the skilled workers (Wilkinson, 1974, p. 7).

The introduction of new technology in the UK has often required compromise by management with the unions. Management have conceded shares in the productivity gains from the new technology in order to allow the smooth and rapid introduction of the new techniques. In the case of printing, management agreed to the first formal collective bargaining agreements to obtain this end (Child, 1967, p. 203). Bargaining over changing the method of work organisation, and thus the system of worker control, to suit the new technology, now commonly called 'productivity bargaining', often has not come until later (McKersie and Hunter, 1973, p. 349). Even when the structure of labour force organisation has become technologically irrelevant, worker organisation has often been sufficiently strong to extract large rewards for relaxing outmoded restrictive practices and skill demarcations. Such has been the case in the shipbuilding industry, where rigid demarcation and expensive demarcation disputes between the numerous skilled unions had clearly damaged the competitive position of the industry. Indeed it was this desperate economic position that forced the skilled unions into conceding some relaxation of demarcation; but in return they have been rewarded with rapidly rising wages (Wilkinson, 1975, pt. 6, p. 17).

Trade unions have probably played a more active role in the formation of structured labour markets in the UK than in the US.[3] The explanation may lie in the different level of maturity of the two economies at the time of the development of large-scale factory production and mechanisation. Trade unions were better organised and more established in the UK than in the US, and capitalists may have been forced to introduce their new technologies through a process of compromise with the unions, rather than through outright suppression.[4] The effect of this different heritage could be that new technologies and scientific management techniques have not been introduced as extensively or intensively in the UK as in the US, owing to much more effective resistance by the trade union movement (McKersie and Hunter, 1973, p. 372). The reasons for the different historical developments of trade unions and labour market structures in the two countries would no doubt be a fruitful area for research.

Nevertheless, there is evidence that the role of unions, or worker resistance, in developing structured labour markets in the US has been underestimated, for instance in the work of Kahn on longshoring in San Francisco. Craft systems of organisation have been maintained in some industries in the US or have only recently been broken down (McKersie and Hunter, 1973, p. 370–371). More importantly, there is evidence that the bureaucratic system of control set up in the steel industry, usually taken as the exemplar for radical theory, has not solved all the problems of control for capitalists. Proposed changes to the system of work organisation have been successfully resisted by unions over a long period of time (McKersie and Hunter, 1973, pp. 372–373). Clauses in the employment contract resulted in 'unnecessary manpower and prevented flexibility in job assignments'; but the unions succeeded in preventing changes through strike action. Further, there is evidence that the job evaluation scheme introduced into the steel mills has provided almost automatic increases for some workers with changes in technology and increases in productivity (Stieber, 1959, p. 312). These increases result from the weighting given to responsibility for machinery and materials in the job evaluation scheme, a weighting which Katherine Stone (1975) uses as evidence that real skill is not involved in the different job specifications, indicating that the technology would allow the development of systems of job rotation with no differentiation by skill. The high weight for factors likely to lead to wage increases for workers in line with productivity increases at least raises the possibility of direct union or worker

---

3. McKersie and Hunter (1973, p. 370) estimate that 25% of total employment in the UK is involved in industries based on the craft system, compared with 10% in the US.

4. Hinton (1973, p. 13) argues that the development of working class consciousness between 1910 and the early 1920s in the UK was contained because a 'combination of ruling class flexibility, reformist initiative within the labour movement, and an economic recession which weakened the power and undermined the ambition of ordinary workers, made possible a new and lasting accommodation of organised labour within the capitalist system'. The suppression of unions and the establishment of a bureaucratic system of control were thus not the only tactics open to capitalists.

involvement in the development of job structures in the industry. Certainly Katherine Stone seems to have played down too far the role of unions in the maintenance and adaptation of the system of job structures, when she identifies the change from promotion on the basis of favouritism to promotion on the basis of seniority as being a change in 'form' but not in 'content' of the system of control. The development of a system of promotion by seniority resolves the problem of competition within the plant for the limited number of high paid jobs, and by doing so may even increase the cohesiveness of workers in their struggle over such issues as general pay increases. . . .

## Structured Labour Markets and the Persistence of Low Pay

It is now time to draw together our discussion, and consider its implications for the analysis of low pay. Stratification of the labour force, in dual labour market and radical theories, and in many orthodox theories (Bergmann, 1971), is identified as an explanation of the development and persistence of low paid sectors in the economy. The major difference between these new approaches and orthodox theory is that now the development of stratification is rooted in the development of the capitalist system. A necessary development of this analysis, we have argued, is to include more fully the effect of worker organisation in the development of structured markets. However, trade union development is not to be regarded as an exogenous influence on labour market structure. Rather worker organisation attempts to control the competition in the labour market that the capitalist system generates, and, further, adapts and restructures itself in response to developments in the economic structure.

The development of monopoly capitalism continually disrupts industrial organisation. Labour is displaced as skills become redundant and as capitalism moves from old into new areas. This process, which destroys both jobs and skills, creates real problems for workers as competition for jobs necessarily reduces their bargaining power. This emphasis on the effects of competition is in direct contrast to the orthodox approach, where workers use a competitive labour market to equalise net benefits between different occupations. Instead, in our analysis, a worker's main concern under competition is to obtain and keep a job.[5] Workers act defensively to protect themselves from the competition of the external labour market, to obtain job security and higher wages, to the exclusion and possible detriment of those remaining in the unorganised sector.

Our discussion has also indicated how, over time, trade union structure has altered, and how previously unorganised sectors have been drawn in, to the greater or lesser detriment of existing organized groups, and of those left out-

---

5. A comparison of Marshall's and Marx's treatment of the length of the working day illustrates this different approach to the effects of competition. Marshall (1920, p. 527) argued that the marginal principle would ensure that labourers must be 'paid for every hour at a rate sufficient to compensate them for the last, and most distressing hour'. Marx (1954, p. 595) argued that competition would force workers to work longer and expend more effort, not for more money but to secure their jobs. 'The overwork of the employed part of the working-class swells the ranks of the reserve, whilst conversely the greater pressure the latter by its competition exerts on the former, forces these to submit to over-work and to subjugation under the dictates of capital.'

side. Expansion of trade union organisation tends to extend primary-sector-type employment, improving job security and wages. However the effect of this development on the overall shape of the distribution of earnings is not clear. It is possible that the expansion of trade union organisation may increase the difficulties of developing organisation for those still excluded (Kahn, 1975, p. 13). The barriers to the extension of primary sector employment throughout the job structure may be strong, both for the reasons suggested by radical and dual labour market theorists, and because of the resilient barriers to mobility, or competition, set up by trade union organisation. They may be exacerbated if, as Braverman suggests, the share of typically low paying, low productivity occupations is increasing, together with the share in employment of typically low paid labour, such as women, immigrants and part-time labour.

This is no place to predict developments in the shape and composition of the earnings structure, or in the mobility pattern. What is clear, however, is that in contrast to the presumption in orthodox theory, the development of the economic structure cannot be relied upon to extend the share of 'good' jobs requiring high skill and associated with high productivity industries.[6] Monopoly capitalism may create job structures increasingly dominated by low skilled, low productivity occupations, and where the share of labour directly involved in the production process of high productivity industries is likely to decline. The effect of these trends on the position of workers in the labour market will depend on their ability to maintain, develop, extend and reshape their organization and bargaining power. For instance, Braverman suggests that the pattern of development of the employment structure under monopoly capitalism may result in a polarisation of the earnings distribution. This argument is based on an implicit assumption that workers are strong enough to obtain shares in the productivity increase of their own enterprises, but are not strong enough outside the high productivity sectors to ensure a sharing out of the increases in national income across the whole range of occupations. This belief may or may not be correct, but his analysis points to the importance both of the employment structure and of trade union organisation in determining the distribution of earnings.

A fuller integration of the effect of worker organisation into the study of labour market structure should clearly not be at the expense of an analysis of the relationship between economic structure and labour market inequality. Indeed, we are suggesting that the effects of the dynamics of the economic structure on the labour market are much more important and complex than those that dual labour market and radical theories describe. The development of stratification is clearly a complex process and any analysis must include those determinants already identified in dual labour market and radical theory. The tendency to uneven development in the economy, the development of non-competing

---

6. One orthodox economist, Perlman (1976, pp. 149–150) has recently admitted that 'there will always be bad jobs'. Indeed he argues: 'The dual labour market is here to stay; competitive efficiency in industrial manpower development requires it. Steps to randomise the probability of membership in the secondary sector call for more equality of opportunity. But the pessimistic result of the dual labour market would remain; secondary workers would be poverty prone. The social gain would lie in reducing the disproportionate share of particular demographic groups in dead-end, low-level jobs.'

groups in the labour force, and the attempts by capitalists to re-establish control over their labour forces will all influence the nature and degree of stratification in the labour market. So far, however, we have argued that the analysis of the development of the employment structure has both been too partial and too static. The spread and development of monopoly capitalism involves much more continuous change in employment structure than that allowed for in dual labour market and radical theory. Trade union organisation adds to the complexity of the picture. Worker organisation has been shown to have played an important part in developing and shaping structured labour markets, but its own development has been determined, in its turn, by changes in the employment structure. A more evolutionary, dynamic analysis of the development of the labour market structure is thus necessary. Such an analysis would admit the possibility of a whole continuum of shades of segmentation across industries, occupations and sectors, in line with the complex pattern of development of the economic structure and of trade union structure.

## References

Akerlof, G. A. 1970. Qualitative uncertainty and the market for lemons. *Quarterly Journal of Economics,* August.

Baran, P. and Sweezy, P. 1966. *Monopoly Capitalism,* New York, Monthly Review Press.

Bayliss, F. 1962. *British Wages Councils,* Oxford, Basil Blackwell.

Becker, G. 1964. *Human Capital,* New York, NBER.

Bergmann, B. 1971. The effect on white incomes of discrimination in employment, *Chicago Journal of Political Economy,* March/April.

Bluestone, B. 1971. The characteristics of marginal industries, in Gordon, D. M. (ed.), *Problems in Political Economy: an Urban Perspective,* Lexington, Mass., D. C. Heath.

Bowles, S. and Gintis, H. 1975. Class power and alienated labour, *Monthly Review,* March.

Braverman, H. 1974. *Labor and Monopoly Capital,* New York, Monthly Review Press.

Cairnes, J. E. 1874. *Some Leading Principles of Political Economy,* London, Macmillan.

Castles, S. and Kosack, G. 1973. *Immigrant Workers and Class Structure in Western Europe,* Oxford, OUP.

Child, J. 1967. *Industrial Relations in the British Printing Industry,* London, Allen and Unwin.

Doeringer, P. and Piore, M. 1971. *Internal Labor Markets and Manpower Analysis,* Lexington, Mass., D. C. Heath.

Edwards, R. C., Reich, M. and Gordon, D. M. (eds.), 1975. *Labor Market Segmentation,* Lexington, Mass., D. C. Heath.

Gordon, D. M. 1972. *Theories of Poverty and Underdevelopment*, Lexington, Mass., D.C. Heath.

Gordon, D. M. 1976. Capitalist efficiency and socialist efficiency, *Monthly Review*, July–August.

Hinton, J. 1973. *The First Shop Stewards' Movement*, London, Allen and Unwin.

Humphries, J. 1977. Class struggle and the persistence of the working-class family, *Cambridge Journal of Economics*, September.

Kahn, L. 1975. *Unions and Labor Market Segmentation*, Ph.D. thesis, University of California, Berkeley.

Kerr, C. 1954. The balkanisation of labor markets, in Bakke, E. W. and Hauser, P.M. (eds.), *Labour Mobility and Economic Opportunity*, New York, MIT Press.

Lester, R. A. 1952. A range theory of wage differentials, *Industrial and Labour Relations Review*, July.

Mackay, D. I., Boddy, D., Brack, J., Diack, J. A. and Jones, N. 1971. *Labour Markets under Different Employment Conditions*, London, Allen and Unwin.

Marx, K. 1954. *Capital*, vol. 1 (1887 translation), London, Lawrence and Wishart.

Marshall, A. 1920. *Principles of Economics*, 8th ed., London, Macmillan.

McKersie, R. B. and Hunter, L. C. 1973. *Pay, Productivity and Collective Bargaining*, London, Macmillan.

Mill, J. S. 1849. *Principles of Political Economy*, 2nd ed., London, John W. Parker.

Oi, W. 1962. Labor as a quasi-fixed factor, *Chicago Journal of Political Economy*, December.

Perlman, R. 1976. *The Economics of Poverty*, New York, McGraw-Hill.

Piore, M. 1975. Notes for a theory of labor market stratification, in Edwards, *et al.* (1975).

Slichter, S. 1950. Note on the structure of wages, *Review of Economics and Statistics*, February.

Spence, M. 1973. Job market signalling. *Quarterly Journal of Economics*, August.

Stieber, J. 1959. *The Steel Industry Wage Structure*, Cambridge, Mass., Harvard UP.

Stone, K. 1975. The origins of job structures in the steel industry, in Edwards *et al.* (1975).

Turner, H. A. 1962. *Trade Union Growth, Structure and Policy*, London, Allen and Unwin.

Vietorisz, T. and Harrison, B. 1973. Labor market segmentation: positive feedback and divergent development, *American Economic Review*, May.

Wilkinson, F. 1974. *The British Iron and Steel Industry in Historical Perspective,* mimeo, Cambridge, Department of Applied Economics.

Wilkinson, F. 1975. *Demarcation in Shipbuilding,* mimeo, Cambridge, Department of Applied Economics.

Wilkinson, F. 1977. Collective bargaining in the steel industry in the 1920s, in Saville, J. (ed.), *Essays in Labour History 1918–39,* London, Croom Helm.

# Selective Further Reading

Aranowitz, Stanley, 'Marx, Braverman, and the Logic of Capital', *Insurgent Sociologist* (Winter 1978–1979).

Beynon, H., *Working for Ford* (Harmondsworth: Penguin, 1974).

Blackburn, R. M., and Michael Mann, *The Working Class in the Labour Market* (London: Macmillan, 1979).

Burawoy, Michael, 'Toward a Marxist Theory of the Labour Process: Braverman and Beyond', *Politics and Society* 8(3–4) (1978).

Castles, S., and G. Kosak, *Immigrant Workers and Class Structure in Western Europe* (Oxford: Oxford University Press, 1973).

Corrigan, Philip, 'Feudal Relics or Capitalist Monuments?', *Sociology* 11(3) (1977).

Doeringer, P., and M. Priore, *Internal Labour Markets and Man-power Analysis* (Lexington, Mass.: D. C. Heath, 1971).

Edwards, R. C., M. Reich, and D. M. Gordon, eds., *Labour Market Segmentation* (Lexington, Mass.: D. C. Heath, 1975).

Engels, F., 'On Authority', in Marx and Engels, *Basic Writings in Politics and Philosophy,* ed. L. Fever (Garden City, N.Y.: Doubleday, 1959).

Goldthorpe, J., and G. Llewellyn, 'Class Mobility in Modern Britain: Three Theses Examined', *Sociology* 11 (1977).

Gorz, André, 'Workers' Control', *Socialist Revolution* (November–December 1970).

Gorz, André, ed., *The Division of Labour* (London: Harvester, 1976).

Hibbs, D. A., 'Industrial Conflict in Advanced Industrial Societies', *American Political Science Review* 70(4) (1976).

Hobsbawn, E. J., *Labouring Men: Studies in the History of Labour* (London: Weidenfeld & Nicolson, 1964).

Jacoby, Russell, Review of *Labor and Monopoly Capital, Telos* 29 (1976).

Johnson, Terence, 'The Professions in the Class Struggle', in *Industrial Society: Class, Cleavage, and Control,* ed. Richard Scase (London: Allen & Unwin, 1977).

Mayer, Charles, 'Between Taylorism and Technocracy', *Journal of Contemporary History* 25 (1975).

Montgomery, David, 'Workers' Control of Machine Production in the Nineteenth Century', *Labor History* (Fall 1976).

Mumford, Lewis, *Technics and Civilization* (London, 1934).

———, *The Myth of the Machine* (London, 1967).

Nichols, Theo, ed., *Capital and Labour* (London: Fontana, 1980).

Noble, David, 'Technological Change and the Class Struggle: The Case of the Machine Tool Industry', *Politics and Society* 8(3–4) (1978).

O'Connor, James, 'Productive and Unproductive Labor', *Politics and Society* 5(3) (1975).

Rowthorn, Bob, 'Skilled Labor in the Marxist System', *Bulletin of the Conference of Socialist Economists* (September 1974).

Salaman, Graeme, *Class and the Corporation* (London: Fontana, 1981).

Saville, J., ed., *Essays in Labour History: 1918–39* (London: Croom Helm, 1977).

Stone, Katherine, 'The Origins of Job Structures in the Steel Industry', *Review of Radical Political Economics* (Summer 1974).

Thompson, E. P., *The Making of the English Working Class* (Harmondsworth: Penguin, 1968).

Wright, Erik Olin, and Perrone, Luca, 'Marxist Class Categories and Income Inequality', *American Sociological Review* 42 (1977).

Zimbalist, Andrew, 'The Limits of Work Humanization', *Review of Radical Political Economics* (Summer 1975).

# · V ·

# Class Consciousness
and Ideology

# Introduction

It should be clear from discussions in the preceding section, developed particularly in respect of the critique of Braverman, that it is an error to identify Marx's distinction between class 'in itself' and class 'for itself' with a differentiation between class and class consciousness. The concept of 'class consciousness', as it has come down to us from Marx, is potentially ambiguous. All class relations involve 'consciousness' because they are composed of the activity of human individuals. The forms of consciousness embedded in the social practices which express class relations have to be distinguished from *consciousness of common class interests*. The connections between these, as the contributions included below indicate, may be complex.

David Lockwood's typology of 'working class images of society' has provoked an extended debate in the literature of class theory. According to Lockwood, the attitudes and views which workers hold about the class system, and their part in it, are heavily influenced by their experiences in their local environment. Their conceptions of the larger society are in some substantial degree the outcome of generalisation from inequalities or deprivations they experience directly in their own lives. Since the work settings and communities in which workers live are diverse, we should expect to find divergences in characteristic forms of 'social imagery'. Research indicates, Lockwood says, that there are three basic types of work and community relationships that can be distinguished in a developed capitalist society, associated with three types of class outlook on the part of workers. First, there is that type of standpoint associated with what Lockwood calls the traditional or 'proletarian' worker. Second, there is another traditional set of attitudes, which he refers to as 'deferential'. Third, there is a relatively novel form of class consciousness, characteristic of what Lockwood labels the 'privatised' worker.

'Proletarian traditionalism' is the type which appears to come closest to the development of class consciousness envisaged by Marx as likely to be of central importance to capitalism. Here the two levels of class consciousness mentioned above coalesce in a way which emphasises collective class interest in the context of overall class struggle. Proletarian traditionalism is however most common in the more isolated forms of working-class community, in which most workers are involved in the same or similar industries. In these 'solidary' and rather homogeneous communities, workers share a strong sense of pride in the jobs they do and a commitment to each other. There is usually a distinctive 'occupational culture' expressing feelings of comradeship. Labour in such communities has not become as completely dissociated from other aspects of social life as it has in larger and more heterogeneous urban environments.

Class consciousness in such communities is 'proletarian' in the sense that there are deep sentiments of division between 'us' (the workers) and 'them' (bosses and management and the 'authorities' outside the local area). The division between 'us' and 'them' is experienced as one of antagonism and of power; workers feel their lives to be determined by forces over which they have little command. Their image of society as a whole conforms, broadly speaking, to a Marxist one insofar as it is dichotomous. Society is divided into dominant and oppressed classes. Nonetheless, these workers do not appear in Lockwood's account to be revolutionary in their outlook. In the terms of Giddens's distinction mentioned in Section Two, their attitudes comprise a distinctive form of 'conflict consciousness'.

While the proletarian worker sees society in terms of a dichotomy of power, the deferential worker conceptualises the social order as a prestige hierarchy. Various gradations may be recognized on this hierarchy, and the relations between these are not perceived as antagonistic. The deferential worker recognises his or her lowly position in the hierarchy as legitimate and in social relations with superiors defers to their attitudes and ideas of how things should be. The individual accepts that he or she is merely 'working class' and should not have aspirations either to rise to a higher station in life or to challenge those in authority. Deferential workers are most likely to be found in those settings in which they are in direct relation with employers or other local 'notables'. These are usually small-scale enterprises rather than large firms, particularly those in rural areas, where patterns of deference are more strongly sanctified by tradition. Relationships in these contexts tend to be paternalistic and personal.

While their attitudes and behaviour are in some respects very distinct from one another, proletarian and deferential workers do share certain things in common. Both are to be found in what are, according to Lockwood, 'backwaters of national industrial and urban development'. In other words, they work and live in settings that are in the course of dissolution. They are both also traditionalist in outlook, likely to defend stubbornly their existing beliefs and modes of life because these represent what is familiar. Such traditionalism, Lockwood suggests, is another facet of living in relatively isolated communities. Most significant of all, in Lockwood's eyes, is that their participation in tightly knit communal relationships reinforces their sentiments of solidarity—the one with fellow workers, the other with an overall hierarchy of status group relationships.

The third type of class consciousness hence differs in important ways from each of the others, and the strong inference of Lockwood's analysis is that it is coming more and more into prominence with the further development of contemporary capitalism. The 'privatised' worker is oriented primarily to securing economic prosperity, measured in terms of income and material possessions. Such is the typical outlook of a worker living and working in settings in which the older types of community relations have been largely destroyed. It is 'an ideological reflection of work attachments that are instrumental and of community relationships that are privatised'. The privatised worker is characteristically employed in large corporations to which he or she feels no particular moral commitment, or antagonism either. (Here there may be some connection with the literature discussed in the preceding section. Privatised workers would presumably for Lockwood be mainly concentrated in the more protected segments of labour markets. They will 'trade off' loyalty to the firm for appropriate monetary rewards. However, Lockwood sees such workers as basically individualistic rather than as developing strong modes of collective action and labour market closure that will help sustain a high level of material reward.)

Privatised workers are likely to be more mobile residentially than their traditionalist counterparts. For the most part, they tend to be concentrated in low-cost public housing, where there is little of the communal solidarity associated with the other types of class consciousness. Privatised workers live an isolated, home-centred existence. Such workers may continue to belong to unions and even actively support militant union activity. But they do not value union membership in the way characteristic of proletarian workers; unions are valuable only for the economic pressure they may apply to secure better material rewards.

The general applicability of Lockwood's typology, which is largely derived from British research, has been doubted by many critics. Both 'proletarian' and 'deferential' workers seem less common historically among the American labour force, which nonetheless has often been very strongly militant. Lockwood makes no mention of ethnic underclasses or of the influence of sexual divisions in the workforce. If we cast the net more broadly, looking at countries such as France and Italy, something like the reverse of Lockwood's general inferences seems to be the case. 'Proletarian' and 'deferential' workers appear very prominently, but not quite as Lockwood describes them. The prominence of Communist parties politically and mixed affiliations to Marxist doctrines and to Catholicism in various sectors of the labour force seem to fit only uneasily within Lockwood's typology.

Michael Mann's article has a more comparative bent, although he confines his attention to a discussion of British and American research materials. His objective is not so much to categorise forms of class consciousness as to work out a critique of theories of advanced capitalism which stress its consensual character. Many Marxist and non-Marxist social scientists alike have presumed that the apparent relative stability of contemporary capitalist societies—and their seeming immunity to the revolutionary transformation Marx anticipated—is the result of ideological consensus. The working class, it is reasoned, accepts the same broad overall values as do other classes. Talcott Parsons's belief in the 'common value-system' that integrates the various collectivities within a single order in societies such as the United States or Britain here shares a good deal in common with Althusser's description of the 'ideological state apparatus'. For Althusser also emphasises the cohesive effect that schools, universities, and the media have in sustaining the hegemony of capitalism.

Mann sets out to question such a viewpoint on a combination of theoretical and empirical grounds. He details several conceptual difficulties with the idea that common values cohere social systems. Because values are 'shared', it does not necessarily mean that they are interpreted in the same way by different groups or classes. Some of the most divisive conflicts in history, in fact, have been associated with opposing interpretations of the 'same' set of symbols— such as wars between Protestants and Catholics in postmedieval Europe. Moreover, the values incorporated within the institutional order of a society may be inconsistent with one another, again tending to produce schism rather than consensus. Finally, in the complex societies of advanced capitalism, values and norms which are confined to specific institutional sectors, rather than shared by everyone, may be the most important sources of stability.

These difficulties have in some respects been acknowledged by the 'consensus theorists', who admit that acceptance of a common value system in any actual society tends to be far from complete. We have to be careful however, Mann says, to define carefully what 'acceptance' means. A person can 'accept' a certain order of things pragmatically, without feeling any normative commitment to it; we must distinguish such pragmatic acceptance from 'normative acceptance' of a given social order. Which of these in fact tends to predominate?

Mann brings together a variety of empirical research materials in order to formulate an answer. His conclusions run counter to the thesis that there is a general consensus of values in either the United States or Britain. Middle-class people, on the whole, tend to exhibit greater consistency of belief and agreement over values than do the working class. Insofar as there are common values held by the working class, they tend to be hostile to the system rather than supportive of it. There is more 'dissensus' between classes than there is 'consensus'. If this is so, however—if consensus theories are wrong—what accounts for the relatively stable character of capitalist societies? Mann suggests that what really matters in 'holding a society together' is that the dominant class or classes share consensual beliefs, not that all classes in society do so. Thus, the continued imperviousness of Western capitalism to radical social change does not imply that workers have become normatively 'integrated' into the system. 'There is a fair amount of consensus among the rulers', in Mann's words, but it 'does not extend very far down the stratification hierarchy'. According to Mann's analysis, attitudes that conform roughly to those Lockwood calls 'proletarian' do exist fairly widely among the working class but are only diffusely and vaguely expressed. However, these *coexist* with pragmatic attitudes towards labour on an everyday level that seem to have some affinities with Lockwood's 'privatised' type.

If Mann's results do not seem to accord all that closely with Lockwood's discussion, they dovetail rather neatly with the ideas developed by Nicolas Abercrombie and Bryan Turner. Their discussion proceeds on a more general level of the analysis of ideology. In Marx's writings, they claim, two divergent conceptions of ideology can be discerned. One conception suggests what Mann would call a consensus theory of society—the sort of view that is conveyed by the famous assertion by Marx (see Section One) that 'the ideas of the ruling class are in every epoch the ruling ideas'. The dominant class, in other words, is able to ensure that its values are shared by those in subordinate classes. Alongside this view, however, is something of a contrary thesis. For Marx seems to suggest that, in a class society, each class is capable of forging its own particular perspective. The working class, after all, is supposed to be the carrier of an idea system—socialism—which is counter to the ideology of the dominant class.

There are various ways, Abercrombie and Turner accept, in which these seemingly divergent conceptions might be reconciled. Most Marxists however, they suggest, have opted for a 'consensus-type' theory. The basis of such views is that the ruling class, because of its monopoly of economic and political power, is able to determine the 'production of ideas', thereby ensuring the preeminence of values and beliefs which legitimate ruling class domination. This still leaves open the possibility which Mann notes, that oppositional movements may be generated through the reinterpretation of ruling values so as to give them a radical twist. In fact, the authors argue, 'consensus theories' of ideology are historically inaccurate, and they proceed to show that this is the case in feudalism and capitalism alike. The medieval period is often regarded as an 'age of faith', in which the Catholic Church maintained an ideological stranglehold over all levels of society. However, recent historical research indicates that the peasantry followed local cults that were quite distant from the ideas proclaimed by the official Church. The rural clergy were influential in peasant communities, but the practices they sanctioned often deviated from central orthodoxy.

Much the same, the authors continue, applies to the early formation of commercial and industrial capitalism. 'Bourgeois individualism', the secular ideology of a rising entrepreneurial class in the seventeenth and eighteenth centuries, did not diffuse downwards to the emergent class of wage workers. Their compliance in the series of changes that led to the ascendancy of capitalistic enterprise was secured, first of all, by their forcible expropriation from the land and then by the economic necessity of having to find paid employment. As has been discussed in an earlier section, the formation of a compliant labour force with the rise of large-scale industry in the nineteenth century was a process fraught with serious difficulties for employers. Some historians, including Thompson, have argued that, in Britain at least, Methodism played an important ideological role in calming working-class rebelliousness. According to Abercrombie and Turner, however, the influence of Methodism among the working class was in fact quite restricted. Moreover, the 'official' Victorian morality of prudish respectability and sexual inhibition made little impact on the more hedonistic style of life of those in the lower orders of society. So far as contemporary capitalism is concerned, the authors accept the view of Mann and others that the bulk of the working class holds beliefs less coherent in character and, in some respects, substantially divergent from those of their rulers. 'The dominant ideology', they argue, reiterating Mann's view, 'is best seen as securing the coherence of the dominant class.' It is as well to remember, however, in the light of previous sections of this book, that even this can easily be exaggerated; members of dominant classes may tend to hold similar overall beliefs and values, but all such classes are themselves typically 'fractionalised'. The concluding comments of Abercrombie and Turner are of some interest here. In the relatively early stages of capitalist development, capitalism involved the transmission of property on a family basis, thus being associated with moral norms emphasising paternal authority and family loyalty. In an era in which there are fewer family-owned firms as such, such norms lose their hold, and the mechanisms of class domination at the same time become more complex.

# · 18 ·

# Sources of Variation in Working-Class Images of Society

## David Lockwood

For the most part men visualise the class structure of their society from the vantage points of their own particular *milieux*, and their perceptions of the larger society will vary according to their experiences of social inequality in the smaller societies in which they live out their daily lives. This assumption that the individual's social consciousness is to a large extent influenced by his immediate social context has already proved its usefulness in the study of 'images of society' and it has been stated most clearly by Bott, who writes: 'People do have direct experience of distinctions of power and prestige in their places of work, among their colleagues, in schools, and in their relationships with friends, neighbours, and relatives. In other words, the ingredients, the raw materials, of class ideology are located in the individual's various primary social experiences, rather than in his position in a socio-economic category. The hypothesis advanced here is that when an individual talks about class he is trying to say something, in a symbolic form, about his experiences of power and prestige in his actual membership groups and social relationships both past and present.'[1] Working from very similar premises, several quite independent investigations have suggested that there seem to be two broad ways in which individuals conceptualise class structure: 'power' or 'conflict' or 'dichotomous' models on the one hand; and 'prestige' or 'status' or 'hierarchical' models on the other. Further it has been proposed that the social ideology of the working class tends to take the form of a power model whereas that of the middle class approximates the hierarchical

---

· From *Sociological Review* 14(2) (1966): 249–67.
1. Elizabeth Bott: *Family and Social Network*, London, 1957, p. 163.

model. Although some of these studies have noted variations in social imagery within the working class, they have concentrated chiefly on explaining the variations between the classes. Thus the power or dichotomous ideology of the working class and the hierarchical ideology of the middle class have been accounted for primarily in terms of differences in the industrial life chances and life experiences of manual and non-manual employees.[2]

While the similarity of the findings of these various investigations is very striking, it is also quite clear from other studies that the industrial and community *milieux* of manual workers exhibit a very considerable diversity and it would be strange if there were no correspondingly marked variations in the images of society held by different sections of the working class. Indeed, on the basis of existing research, it is possible to delineate at least three different types of workers and to infer that the work and community relationships by which they are differentiated from one another may also generate very different forms of social consciousness. The three types are as follows: first, the traditional worker of the 'proletarian' variety whose image of society will take the form of a power model; secondly, the other variety of traditional worker, the 'deferential', whose perception of social inequality will be one of status hierarchy; and, thirdly, the 'privatised' worker, whose social consciousness will most nearly approximate what may be called a 'pecuniary' model of society.[3]

The 'traditional worker' is, of course, a sociological rather than an historical concept; a concept relating to workers who are located in particular kinds of work situations and community structures rather than one purporting to give a description of the working class as a whole at some particular point of time. Moreover, the concept encompasses not only the most radical and class conscious segment of the working class (the proletarian worker) but also its most socially acquiescent and conservative elements (the deferential worker). Yet, distinct as the two traditionalists are from one another in social and political outlook, they do share several characteristics which make them traditionalists and thus distinguish them from the privatised worker. It would seem best, then, to begin with an account of the work and community structures underlying proletarian and deferential traditionalism.[4]

---

2. See E. Bott, *op. cit.*; O. A. Oeser and S. B. Hammond: *Social Structure and Personality in a City*, London, 1954; H. Popitz, H. P. Bahrdt, E. A. Jueres, and H. Kesting: *Das Gesellschaftsbild des Arbeiters*, Tuebingen, 1961; A. Willener: *Images de la société et classes sociales*, Berne, 1957; R. Hoggart: *The Uses of Literacy*, London, 1957; A. Kornhauser, H. J. Sheppard and A. J. Mayer: *When Labor Votes*, New York, 1956; A. Andrieux and J. Lignon: *L'ouvrier d'aujourd'hui*, Paris, 1960. Ralf Dahrendorf was the first to draw attention to the similarity of the conclusions of Popitz, Willener, and Hoggart, in his book, *Class and Class Conflict in Industrial Society*, Stanford, 1959, pp. 280–289.

3. On the traditional and privatised working class see David Lockwood: 'The "New" Working Class', *European Journal of Sociology*, Vol. I, No. 2, 1960; and John H. Goldthorpe and David Lockwood: 'Affluence and the British Class Structure,' *Sociological Review*, Vol. II, No. 2, 1963. The present paper may be regarded as an extension of these earlier statements and in particular as an elaboration of one major element in the normative dimension of 'class'. John Goldthorpe and I have worked together so closely on the wider problem of which this paper is a part that I find it difficult to say where my thoughts end and his begin. Although he may not fully agree with my interpretation, the present essay draws much from a paper of his entitled 'Attitudes and Behaviour of Car Assembly Workers', which will be published shortly in the *British Journal of Sociology*.

4. Work and community relations do not, of course, exhaust the range of variables which may affect the formation of models of society. In particular, the experience of social mobility (in the

The most highly developed forms of proletarian traditionalism seem to be associated with industries such as mining, docking, and ship-building; industries which tend to concentrate workers together in solidary communities and to isolate them from the influences of the wider society.[5] Workers in such industries usually have a high degree of job involvement and strong attachments to primary work groups that possess a considerable autonomy from technical and supervisory constraints.[6] Pride in doing 'men's work' and a strong sense of shared occupational experiences make for feelings of fraternity and comradeship which are expressed through a distinctive occupational culture. These primary groups of workmates not only provide the elementary units of more extensive class loyalties but work associations also carry over into leisure activities, so that workers in these industries usually participate in what are called 'occupational communities'.[7] Workmates are normally leisure-time companions, often neighbours, and not infrequently kinsmen. The existence of such closely-knit cliques of friends, workmates, neighbours and relatives is the hallmark of the traditional working class community. The values expressed through these social networks emphasize mutual aid in everyday life and the obligation to join in the gregarious pattern of leisure, which itself demands the expenditure of time, money and energy in a public and present-oriented conviviality and eschews individual striving 'to be different'. As a form of social life, this communal sociability has a ritualistic quality, creating a high moral density and reinforcing sentiments of belongingness to a work-dominated collectivity. The isolated and endogamous nature of the community, its predominantly one-class population, and low rates of geographical and social mobility all tend to make it an inward-looking society and to accentuate the sense of cohesion that springs from shared work experiences.[8]

---

present context, downward mobility) is most likely to have the effect of predisposing a worker towards a hierarchical, rather than a class, model. This is so for two reasons: first, because the experience of social mobility makes a person more sensitive to the fact of hierarchical social distance; and secondly because the downwardly mobile worker is likely to have been socialised into a set of values ordered around a concept of status hierarchy. However, the number of socially mobile persons in any particular section of the working class will be determined to a large extent by the self-same factors that shape their work and community relationships, i.e., by the industrial and occupational structure of a particular locale.

5. The first to draw attention to this phenomenon in a systematic way were C. Kerr and A. Siegel: 'The Inter-industry Propensity to Strike: An International Comparison', in A, Kornhauser, R. Dubin, and A. M. Ross: Industrial Conflict, London, 1954. See also, for example, The Dock Worker, University of Liverpool Department of Social Science, Liverpool, 1954; and N. Dennis, F. Henriques, and C. Slaughter: Coal is Our Life, London, 1956.

6. R. Blauner: 'Work Satisfaction and Industrial Trends in Modern Society', in W. Galenson and S. M. Lipset: Labor and Trade Unionism, New York, 1960, p. 343, et seq.

7. The defining characteristics of an occupational community are: (1) Workers in their off-hours socialize more with persons in their own line of work than with a cross-section of occupational types; (2) Workers 'talk shop' in their off-hours; (3) The occupation is the reference group; its standards of behaviour, its system of status and rank, guide conduct. Ibid, p. 351.

8. The one-industry town with its dominant occupational community would seem to produce the most distinctive form of proletarian traditionalism. But, given a relatively isolated community with a stable and pre-ponderantly working class population, a quite high degree of proletarian traditionalism is perfectly compatible with industrial diversification. Indeed, industrial diversification may promote the stability of the population by allowing a man to change his work without leaving the locality.

Shaped by occupational solidarities and communal sociability the proletarian social consciousness is centred on an awareness of 'us' in contradistinction to 'them' who are not a part of 'us'. 'Them' are bosses, managers, white collar workers and, ultimately, the public authorities of the larger society. Yet even though these outsiders are remote from the community, their power to influence it is well understood; and those within the community are more conscious of this power because it comes from the outside. Hence the dominant model of society held by the proletarian traditionalist is most likely to be a dichotomous or two-valued power model. Thinking in terms of two classes standing in a relationship of opposition is a natural consequence of being a member of a closely integrated industrial community with well-defined boundaries and a distinctive style of life. It may well be, as Popitz has argued, that the propensity to hold a dichotomous social imagery is a general one among industrial workers in large establishments: certainly the social divisions of the workplace, the feeling of being subject to a distant and incomprehensible authority, and the inconsiderable chances of escaping from manual wage earning employment are all conducive to the formation of such an ideology.[9] But is it probable that this image of society is fully developed only among those workers whose sense of the industrial hiatus is strengthened by their awareness of forming a quite separate community. Moreover, to anticipate the subsequent discussion, it would seem that the tendency to adopt a power model of society is most evident among workers who have a high degree of job involvement and strong ties with their fellow workers. In other kinds of work situations, where these factors are absent, or nearly so, the whole significance of the workplace as a determinant of a dichotomous class ideology is correspondingly reduced.

Our knowledge of the second variety of traditional worker is rather skimpy and results mainly from the efforts that have been made to track down that elusive political animal, the 'deferential voter'.[10] It may be assumed, however, that the model of society held by the deferential worker is a prestige or hierarchical, rather than a power or dichotomous model. In fact, given that people who think of social divisions in terms of status or prestige usually distinguish higher and lower strata as well as status equals, his model is likely to be at least a trichotomous one.[11] Further, the deferential worker does not identify himself with his superiors or strive to reach their status; he defers to them socially as well as politically. His recognition of authentic leadership is based on his belief in the intrinsic qualities of an ascriptive elite who exercise leadership paternalistically

---

9. Popitz, *et al.*, *op. cit.*, pp. 237 *et. seq.*

10. For an exposition of the political philosophy to which he is held to respond, see S. M. Beer: *Modern British Politics,* London, 1965, pp. 91–102. For a preliminary report on the investigation by R. T. McKenzie and A. Silver, see: 'Conservatism, Industrialism, and the Working Class Tory in England', *Transactions of the Fifth World Congress of Sociology,* Louvain, 1964, Vol. *III,* pp. 191–202. See also R. Samuel: 'The Deference Voter', *New Left Review,* January–February 1960; Mark Abrams: 'Class and Politics', *Encounter,* October 1961; W. G. Runciman: *Relative Deprivation and Social Justice,* London, 1966, Chapter IX. Probably the best description of the deferential traditionalist and his social context is by Margaret Stacey: *Tradition and Change,* Oxford, 1960. See also the highly instructive paper by D. E. G. Plowman, *et. al.:* 'Local Social Status in England and Wales', *Sociological Review,* Vol. *10,* No. 2, 1962.

11. E. Bott, *op. cit.,* p. 176.

in the pursuit of 'national' as opposed to 'sectional' or 'class' interests. But how refined his image of the status hierarchy really is, or how exactly he perceives his own position in it, is not known. It is merely suggested that he has a conception of a higher and unapproachable status group of leaders, his 'betters', the people who 'know how to run things', those whose performance is guaranteed by 'breeding'; and that he himself claims to be nothing grander than 'working class'. However, given these elements, it is possible to go a little further and to draw the not unreasonable, but wholly speculative, conclusion that the deferential worker thinks in terms of at least a four-fold division of society. Since he thinks in terms of 'genuine' or 'natural' leaders in both a local and a national context, it is likely that he thinks also of 'spurious' leaders and, by implication, of 'misguided' followers. Spurious leaders are those who aspire to leadership, and indeed from time to time acquire it, without possessing the requisite qualities. They may have achieved wealth, power and position, but they lack the hereditary or quasi-hereditary credentials which the deferential worker recognises as the true marks of legitimacy.[12] Misguided followers are those, broadly in the same layer of society as himself, who refuse to acknowledge the objects of his deference, and who aid and abet the spurious leaders in usurping authority.[13] If the deferential worker has an image of society as a status hierarchy, then the existence of 'undeferential' workers is almost a necessary condition for the protection of his own sense of self-esteem. There are few instances of lower status groups who both accept the legitimacy of the status hierarchy and fail to discover groups with an even lower status than their own.

Whatever niceties of status differentiation enter into the ideology of the deferential traditionalist, it would seem that he does hold a hierarchical model of some kind, and it would seem worthwhile exploring the hypothesis that such a model of society will be the product of very special work and community relationships. Here, studies of the deferential voter do not take us very far. The findings that these voters are more likely than non-deferentials to be elderly, to be women, to have low incomes and to come from rural areas are demographic facts relating to the properties of individuals rather than facts relating to the properties of the social systems in which these individuals are located.[14] Nor is it to be assumed that all deferential voters will be deferential traditionalists. The latter, like proletarian traditionalists, must be thought of as an extreme type, characterised by a combination of social roles which, taken together, are most likely to lead to a hierarchical social imagery.

The typical work rôle of the deferential traditionalist will be one that brings him into direct association with his employer or other middle class influentials and hinders him from forming strong attachments to workers in a similar

12. See M. Stacey, *op. cit.,* pp. 159–160, on the tensions between the traditional and non-traditional segments of Banbury.

13. 'They support the parties of their 'social betters' while insisting on their own position at the bottom of the social ladder. Compared with their neighbours, they are not interested in a party which stands for the ordinary working class and which aims to raise the standard of living of *ordinary* people.' M. Abrams, *op. cit.,* p. 42.

14. M. Abrams, *op. cit.,* p. 42; R. Samuel, *op. cit.,* p. 11; R. T. McKenzie and A. Silver, *op. cit.,* p. 199.

market situation to his own. These work conditions are most clearly present in the sorts of occupations that are to be found in small towns and rural areas, although they are by no means entirely absent in larger urban centres. Workers in various kinds of service occupations, in non- (or rather pre-) industrial craft jobs, those working in small scale 'family enterprises', and in agricultural employment, are workers who are most exposed to paternalistic forms of industrial authority.[15] The essence of this work situation is that relationship between employer and worker is personal and particularistic. The worker has an unique position in a functional job hierarchy and he is tied to his employer by a 'special relationship' between them and not only by considerations of economic gain.

In the making of the deferential traditionalist certain features of community life will also play an important part in fixing and sharpening the sense of hierarchy that he acquires in his rôle as worker. Small, relatively isolated and economically autonomous communities, particularly those with well-differentiated occupational structures and stable populations, provide the most favourable settings for the existence of 'local status systems'. The key characteristic of such systems is that the allocation of status takes place through 'interactional' rather than through 'attributional' mechanisms.[16] The boundaries of the several status groups making up the local system are maintained by various means of social acceptance and rejection in both formal and informal association. People do not judge one another from a distance and attribute status on the basis of a few, readily observable criteria, such as the amount of an individual's material possessions. Status groups (or rather the cliques of which they are constituted) are membership as well as reference groups. Through close acquaintance, people have a detailed knowledge of each other's personal qualities and can apply relatively complex criteria in deciding who is worthy of membership of a particular status group. There is also widespread consensus about the rank order of status groups in the community, so that lower strata regard their lowly position less as an injustice than as a necessary, acceptable, and even desirable part in a natural system of inequality. Local status systems, therefore, operate to give the individual a very definite sense of position in a hierarchy of prestige, in which each 'knows his place' and recognises the status prerogatives of those above and below him. For the deferential traditionalist, such a system of status has the function of placing his work orientations in a wider social context. The persons

---

15. See the account of 'traditional' firms in M. Stacey, *op. cit.*, pp. 27–28; and the discussion of paternalism in D. Lockwood, *The Black-coated Worker*, London, 1958, pp. 78–81 and 141–149. A more fully developed system—'patriarchalism'—is portrayed by Solomon B. Levine: *Industrial Relations in Postwar Japan*, Urbana, 1958, pp. 36–38.

16. On the concepts of 'local status systems' and 'interactional' status systems, see D. E. G. Plowman, *et. al., op. cit.*, especially pp. 186–195. The distinction between interactional and attributional status systems is also made by M. Young and P. Willmott when they contrast the 'face-to-face' relationships of Bethnal Green with the 'window-to-window' relationships of Greenleigh. See M. Young and P. Willmott: *Family and Kinship in East London*, London, 1957, especially pp. 134–135. The perception of status groups as interactional groups is basic to the fully developed status or hierarchical model of society as E. Bott makes clear when she writes that: 'status was not conceived in relative terms as a continuum. Each class was given a specific subculture' and 'each category differed from others in sub-culture and prestige' so that 'individuals in one class, if they happened to meet, might associate with one another as equals in informal interaction.' E. Bott, *op. cit.*, pp. 176–177.

who exercise authority over him at his place of work may not be the same persons who stand at the apex of the local status system, but the structural principles of the two social orders are homological; and from neither set of relationships does he learn to question the appropriateness of his exchange of deference for paternalism.

Although in terms of social imagery and political outlook the proletarian and deferential traditionalists are far removed from one another, they nevertheless do have some characteristics in common. They are first of all traditionalists in the sense that both types are to be found in industries and communities which, to an ever increasing extent, are backwaters of national industrial and urban development. The sorts of industries which employ deferential and proletarian workers are declining relatively to more modern industries in which large batch or mass production techniques are more and more the major modes of production. Again, the small isolated country town, or the mining village, or the working class enclave, such as is represented by the dockworkers' community, are gradually becoming linked with, or absorbed into, larger urban concentrations and with an increased amount of voluntary and involuntary residential mobility of the labour force the close link between place of work and community is being broken down.

They are also traditionalists in the sense that their horizons of expectations do not extend much beyond the boundaries of the communities in which they live and of which they are, so to speak, 'founding members'. This again is largely a product of the social isolation and social stability of both the deferential and proletarian communities. Workers in such environments are as unlikely to change their patterns of consumption as they are their political loyalties, because in both cases they are encapsulated in social systems which provide them with few alternative conceptions of what is possible, desirable, and legitimate.

Finally, and perhaps most significantly, the work and community relationships of traditional workers involve them in mutually reinforcing systems of interpersonal influence. The effect of group membership on class ideology will, of course, vary depending on the type of traditional worker under consideration. In the case of the deferential worker, his rôle in a paternalistic authority structure at work and his position in a local status system in the community both predispose him to think of society in terms of hierarchy. In the case of the proletarian traditionalist, his membership of the work gang and his participation in the system of communal sociability lead to a conception of a 'class-divided' society. But although the effects of group membership are very different in the two cases, both the deferential and the proletarian traditionalists are highly integrated into their respective local societies; and this means that their attitudes and behaviour are to a large extent influenced and controlled by means of direct face-to-face encounters. In this way, they experience a sense of belonging to actual social groups which are marked off from other groups by boundaries that are maintained through social interaction. This consciousness of definite social placement in turn affects their perception of the class structure. Whether their models of society are basically hierarchical or basically dichotomous, the fact that traditional workers have a strong sense of group membership means that they will tend to see 'strata' or 'classes' as active social formations and not merely as amorphous aggregrates of individuals. In this respect, the social consciousness of the traditional worker differs markedly from that of the privatised worker, whose model of society is shaped by work and community relationships which do not convey, to the same extent, an awareness of group affiliation.

The social environment of the privatised worker is conducive.to the development of what may be called a 'pecuniary' model of society. The essential feature of this ideology is that class divisions are seen mainly in terms of differences in income and material possessions. Naturally, there will be few individuals who think of class divisions in purely pecuniary terms. But the social consciousness of many individuals in the 'new working class' may be closer to this pecuniary model of society than to either of the two types of social imagery previously discussed.[17] Basically, the pecuniary model of society is an ideological reflection of work attachments that are instrumental and of community relationships that are privatised.[18] It is a model which is only possible when social relationships that might provide prototypical experiences for the construction of ideas of conflicting power classes, or of hierarchically interdependent status groups, are either absent or devoid of their significance.

The work situation of the privatised worker is such that his involvement in the job and his attachments to the enterprise and to his fellow workers are slight. Numerous studies have provided us with the generalisation that workers employed in large factories with mass-production technologies and doing jobs which are highly specialised, repetitive, and lacking in autonomy, are workers for whom, in Dubin's words, 'work and the workplace are not central life interests' and for whom work is viewed 'as a means to an end—a way of acquiring income for life in the community'.[19] Under these conditions, work is a deprivation which is performed mainly for extrinsic rewards; and 'money-mindedness', the calculative exchange of labour power for maximum pay, is the predominant motive for remaining in the job. Frequently isolated from their workmates by the constraints of technology, and seeking no close relationships in a work situation that is viewed in purely instrumental terms, such 'alienated' workers do not form cohesive groups inside the factory and they are not prone to form occupational communities outside the factory. Their main attitude to work is that of its being a necessary evil: and given this orientation they have no desire to carry over into their leisure time the atmosphere and associations of work.[20] In all these respects—the low involvement in the job itself, the lack of cohesive work groups, the absence of occupational communities—privatised

17. See J. H. Goldthorpe and D. Lockwood, *op. cit.*, pp. 149–154, for a discussion of these two terms.

18. R. Dubin: 'Industrial Workers' Worlds', *Social Problems*, Vol. 3, January 1956, p. 135. Also see C. Argyris: *Personality and Organization*, New York, 1957, especially Chapter IV; R. Blauner, *op. cit.*

19. The general theme is quite old. See, for example, Karl Marx on 'The Power of Money in Bourgeois Society', *Economic and Philosophical Manuscripts of 1844*, London, 1959. A more recent Marxist interpretation which concentrates on the work situation is that by Andre Gorz: 'Work and Consumption', *Towards Socialism*, edited by Perry Anderson and Robin Blackburn, London, 1965, especially pp. 348–349.

20. R. Blauner, *op. cit.*, p. 351.

workers differ significantly from the traditional worker, and more especially from the proletarian traditionalist. Relative to the latter, the privatised worker finds himself in a work situation that is socially isolating and, to a large extent, socially meaningless; a situation in which the dominant relationship is the cash-nexus. But, although he is 'alienated' labour, he is unlikely to possess a strongly developed class consciousness because his involvement in work is too low to allow for strong feelings of any kind, except perhaps the desire to escape from it altogether. He is neither deeply involved with his work–mates nor deeply antag-onistic to his employer; on the whole his attitude to both more nearly approxi-mates one of indifference.[21]

These tendencies of the work life are reinforced and accentuated by a certain form of community life which is increasingly representative of the new working class: namely, the social structure of the council, or the private, low-cost hous-ing estate.[22] From the present point of view, the most salient feature of these estates is that they bring together a population of strangers, who have little in common, save that they have all experienced residential mobility and that most of them gain their livelihood from some kind of manual labour. In such com-munities, social life is very different from the communal sociability of the traditional working-class community. Unrelated by the ascriptive ties of kin-ship, long-standing neighbourliness and shared work experiences, and lacking also the facility for readily creating middle-class patterns of sociability, workers on the estates tend to live a socially isolated, home-centred existence. Such conditions favour the emergence of attributional rather than interactional status systems. Whereas in the traditional proletarian community status is allocated (or more precisely made indeterminate) through the individual's participation in several overlapping cliques, the status order of the housing estate is based on conspicuous consumption, by means of which people judge their social stand-ing relative to others without usually associating with them in formal or infor-mal leisure-time activities. The low housing density of the estate, its lack of recreational amenities, the uprootedness of its inhabitants and their limited capacities for creating new styles of sociability produce a society in which residents are only superficially acquainted and associated with those who live around them. The attributional nature of the status ranking that arises from this situation in turn induces an acquisitiveness and a sensitivity to competitive consumption that are quite alien to the communal sociability of proletarian traditionalism.

The work and community settings just described are the breeding grounds of the privatised worker, and his socially isolated existence not only predisposes, but also enables, him to adopt a pecuniary model of class structure. In the first place, he is strongly motivated to view social relationships in pecuniary terms. Lacking close primary group ties inside and outside the work situation, at work he is wage-oriented and in the community consumption-oriented. Just as

---

21. On the significance of intensity, as opposed to direction, of involvement, see A. Etzioni: *A Comparative Analysis of Complex Organizations*, New York, 1961, p. 9.

22. Some of the abundant literature on this topic is summarised in J. Klein: *Samples from English Culture*, London, 1965, Vol. II, Chapter 5.

money wages become of salient importance in attaching him to his work rôle, so, too, consumer durables are of primary significance in mediating his status with his neighbours. This pattern of motivation is neither natural nor accidental. If the privatised worker is more of an economic man than the proletarian or the deferential traditionalist, it is because his environment conspires to make him so.[23] Secondly, however, the work and community relationships that foster this pecuniary outlook are unlikely to give the individual a feeling of definite social location through membership of either a status group or a class fraternity. The privatised worker may be a trade unionist and he may live in a community where status is reckoned by material possessions; but from neither of these sources will he derive more than a rudimentary awareness of belonging to a cohesive group and hence of the social distance between such groups.

By contrast with the proletarian traditionalist, the privatised worker will tend to join and support his trade union for instrumental rather than class solidaristic reasons. Given his materialistic, home-centred aspirations, the trade union for him is less the symbolic expression of an affective attachment to a working class community than a utilitarian association for achieving his private goal of a rising standard of living. Lacking the class consciousness which the proletarian traditionalist acquires from his involvement in solidary work groups and communal sociability, the privatised worker expects his union to devote itself exclusively to bettering the economic position of his own job category rather than to dissipate any of its resources in pursuing the more distant political objective of changing the wider society. As far as he is concerned, the trade union is a 'service organisation', not part of a social movement; and, far from his union membership providing him with a consciousness of class, his orientation to trade unionism reflects precisely his lack of such a sentiment.

By contrast with the deferential traditionalist, the privatised worker is unlikely to be made aware of a system of status groups arranged in a stable hierarchy of prestige. His neighbours on the estate are mostly manual wage-earners like himself, socially undistinguished from one another save by marginal differences in their ownership of consumer durables. This means that whatever status distinction arises from the competition to possess these goods is inherently unstable and too superficial to be the source of a sense of unbridgeable social distance. Moreover, in so far as status groups fail to coalesce, the pattern of sociability in the community will remain privatised and there will be small opportunity for the individual to experience personal acceptance by his status equals or personal rejection by his status superiors. Hence, in the typically attributional status system of the housing estate, the worker will not learn to perceive status as a phenomenon that manifests itself in group relationships.

The daily social encounters of the privatised worker do not, therefore, lead him to think of a society divided up into either a hierarchy of status groups or an opposition of class. His model of society is one in which individuals are associ-

---

23. It is of course possible that, in addition, a process of 'self-selection' occurs, so that those workers who are more instrumental in their work orientations and less well integrated into their local communities than other workers are more likely to enter and remain in the jobs and communities of the kind described.

## WORK SITUATION

| | Involvement in Job: | Interaction and Identification with Workmates: | Interaction and Identification with Employers: |
|---|---|---|---|
| Middle Class[24] | + | + | + |
| Deferential | + | – | + |
| Proletarian | + | + | – |
| Privatised | – | – | – |

## COMMUNITY STRUCTURE

| | Interactional Status System: | Occupational Community: | Occupational Differentiation: |
|---|---|---|---|
| Middle Class | + | + | + |
| Deferential | + | – | + |
| Proletarian | + | + | – |
| Privatised | – | – | – |

ated with, and dissociated from one another less by any type of social exchange than by the magnitude of their incomes and possessions.

Before going on to outline the elements of this pecuniary model of society, it may be useful to summarise the argument thus far by a table which differentiates proletarian, deferential, and privatised workers in terms of work and com-

24. Since this paper concentrates on manual workers, only the briefest comments on the position of the middle class employee are called for. Here 'middle class' refers to the administrative, managerial, technical and professional white collar group (i.e., excluding lower grade clerical employees, who in many respects are similar to the privatised worker, as well as entrepreneurs). This group is included in the paradigm partly because their presence gives it a certain pleasing symmetry; but also because the same variables that are used to differentiate the three types of manual worker would also appear to be relevant in analyzing the social situation of non-manual employees. From the paradigm, it can be seen why the white collar employee is predisposed to hold a hierarchical model of society. What cannot be seen is why his hierarchical ideology differs from that of the deferential worker. This is because a variable relating to chances and expectations of upward mobility is not included in the table, which, since it was designed to show differences within the manual group, implicitly assigns a low and constant value to this variable. It is also quite obvious from the work of Prandy that there is much more variation in the work situation of the white collar employee than is suggested by the above scheme (see K. Prandy: *Professional Employees*, London, 1965). The characterisation of the middle class employee in terms of community variables is likewise undoubtedly something of an oversimplification. However, even as it stands, the following points can be made in defence of the present scheme. First, there is ample evidence that middle class employees of the kind in question do find their work intrinsically more rewarding and are more highly involved in their jobs than most industrial workers. Secondly, because their working relationships usually bring them into close contact with higher management and administration as well as with small groups of workers of their own rank, they are likely to identify themselves with both 'the firm' and their colleagues. Thirdly, because of their high job involvement, they are likely to form occupational communities; and this tendency should be more pronounced the more they are geographically mobile and thus the more they are dependent on friendships acquired through their occupational rôles. Fourthly, middle class employees are likely to live in occupationally mixed communities. Simply because there are relatively so few men in the middle ranges of white collar employment, it is almost inevitable that their neighbours will include small-scale entrepreneurs, independent professionals, lower grade clerical and sales employees, and perhaps even highly paid manual workers. Finally, white collar employees are likely to be involved in interactional status systems. Whether social visiting, or membership of and participation in voluntary associations is taken as a measure of communal (and hence status) interaction, the middle classes rank so much higher than the privatised working class that the difference is qualitative.

munity variables. The meanings of the terms used to describe these variables, should now be evident from the foregoing discussion.

The social isolation of the privatised worker reflects itself in his ideology of a 'de-socialised' class structure.[25] The single, overwhelmingly important, and the most spontaneously conceived criterion of class division is money, and the possessions, both material and immaterial, that money can buy. From this point of view, for example, education is not thought of as a status-conferring characteristic, but rather simply as a good that money can buy and as a possession that enables one to earn more money. In general, power and status are not regarded as significant sources of class division or social hierarchy. Power is not understood as the power of one man over another, but rather as the power of a man to acquire things: as purchasing power. Status is not seen in terms of the association of status equals sharing a similar style of life. If status is thought of at all it is in terms of a standard of living, which all who have the means can readily acquire. It may not be easy to acquire the income requisite to a certain standard of living and hence qualify for membership in a more affluent class; but given the income there are no other barriers to mobility.

Within this pecuniary universe, the privatised worker tends to see himself as a member of a vast income class which contains virtually the great mass of the population. This class may be called 'the working class' or 'the middle class'. Whatever it is called, it is a collection of 'ordinary people' who 'work for a living' and those who belong to it include the majority of manual and non-manual employees. They are united with one another, not by having exactly the same incomes, but by not having so much or so little income that their standard of living places them completely beyond the upper or lower horizons. A minority of persons in the society have either so much wealth or such an impoverished existence that they lie outside the central class. They are the very rich and the very poor. Since the main criterion of class membership is money, the lower and, especially, the upper limits of the central class are hard to define, and are consequently defined arbitrarily or regarded as indeterminate.[26] In general the 'upper' or 'higher' or 'rich' class is not perceived as wielding power or deserving of respect. It is simply a vague category of 'all those up there' who have incomes

---

25. In singling out the basic features of this model of society I have been influenced by my reading of the responses to an open-ended question on class which was part of the interview schedule used in a study of a sample of affluent workers. I should stress, however, that the responses to this particular question have not yet been systematically analyzed, and that the present paper can in no way be regarded as a description of the findings of this part of the study. For an account of the study, see John H. Goldthorpe, David Lockwood, Frank Bechhofer, and Jennifer Platt: 'The Affluent Worker and the Thesis of *Embourgeoisement:* Some Preliminary Research Findings', *Sociology,* Vol. *I,* No. 1, 1967.

26. To take two examples from our own study: First, a man who has a conception of a two-fold class system: the 'rich' and the 'middle class'. 'Q—What is the main thing that decides which class someone's in? A—Money. Q—Just money? A—If you've got an income coming in, say £5,000 a year, that brings you a rich person; if you've got an income of £1–2,000 or just under, you're middle class.' (034) Secondly, a man who holds a two-class model, and calls his classes the 'higher class' and the 'working class'. 'Q—What's the one main thing that decides which class a person's in? A— Money. The more money a person has the better he can live. Q—Where does the working class end and the higher class begin? A—The more money you have, the higher you get—but there *isn't* an end to the working class. Q—Are there any other differences between classes? A—No, it's just the money.' (035)

and possessions and a standard of life that are completely beyond the bounds of possibility as far as the ordinary worker is concerned.[27] The rich, however, are different from the rest only in the sense of Hemingway's rejoinder to Scott Fitzgerald: that they have much more money.[28]

Finally, the central class with which the privatised worker identifies himself is seen as a relatively new phenomenon, brought about by the incorporation of the old middle class into the new 'working class', or, alternatively, by the incorporation of the old working class into the new 'middle class'. Whether the end result of the change is seen as a 'working class' or a 'middle class', its identity is basically an economic one; people are assigned to this central class because they have roughly similar levels of income and possessions. Because the convergence of the 'old' working and middle classes is seen in essentially economic terms, the designation of the new central class as 'middle' or 'working' would seem to be largely a matter of how the change is perceived as having taken place rather than an expression of status- or class-consciousness.[29] Indeed, the logic of a purely pecuniary model of society leads to neither class consciousness nor status consciousness but to commodity consciousness. Class and status models entail a perception of social groups whose boundaries are identifiable by acts of power and deference. But the pecuniary universe is one in which inequalities are not expressed through social relationships at all. Income and possessions may be the marks of persons, but unlike power and status they do not involve persons in relationships of inequality with one another. Inequalities take on an extrinsic and quantitative, rather than an intrinsic and qualitative form. In fact, compared with power and prestige, money is not inherently a divider of persons at all; it is a common denominator, of which one may have more or less without its thereby necessarily making a difference to the kind of person one is.

---

27. This tendency of persons in socially ambiguous positions to enlarge their own class and to relegate the remainder of the population indiscriminately to the periphery is well known. 'Some people who placed themselves in the 'working class' made differences within it but lumped together everyone else as 'the rich'. The more remote the people of another class, the less opportunity there is for checking fantasy against fact, so that the individual can see in such people what he wants to see.' E. Bott, *op. cit.*, p. 165. 'The earnings of these suburbanites permit some of them to call themselves 'middle class' but the framework of hierarchy of class that is meaningful to these workers is not a conceptual framework that applies to society as a whole, but one that is limited to what is possible for them . . . there is a tendency to lump together as 'way up there' everyone whose income is greater than the upper limit of what is possible for them . . . to be 'middle class', then, probably means to them, not what sociologists mean by middle class, but rather the *middle of the working class* . . . the 'upper' middle class, white collar worlds of engineers, junior executives, professionals and would be professionals are completely beyond their ken; this latter milieu is alien to them, beyond their limits of possibility.' B. M. Berger: *Working Class Suburb*, Berkeley, 1960, pp. 85 and 89.

28. This is, of course, an extreme position. In fact, deviations from a purely materialistic interpretation of class structure are likely to occur in both an ascriptive and moralistic direction. Thus, the 'rich' class may be seen as containing persons whose wealth is inherited and/or undeserved ('The idle rich'). Similarly, the 'very poor' may be seen as containing persons who are lacking in ability and/or lacking in motivation to raise themselves ('poor character').

29. If the pecuniary model of society appears to resemble the 'sociology' of class that is frequently purveyed via mass media ('We're all middle class nowadays' or 'We're all workers nowadays'), the reason for this may very well be that the privatised worker is more likely to be reached by mass communication and more readily influenced by its message. Because of his relative social isolation, he may be more exposed to impersonal influence; and, given his affluence and privatisation, the view that class differences are on the wane is a plausible one for him to maintain.

In so far as the privatised worker thinks in terms of the pecuniary model, he has, of course, a somewhat distorted view of the class structure. All available evidence indicates that the amount of informal social interaction between the lower middle and upper working classes is very small and that, in this sense at least, class boundaries are still quite distinct. The privatised worker's idea of a vast central class, differentiated only by marginal differences in income and possessions, is not, therefore, an accurate sociological picture. At the same time, it must be noted that the boundary between the middle and working classes is probably maintained as much by work and residential segregation as by personal exclusion. Thus, from this point of view, the mechanisms of class dissociation operate in a way which is not entirely incompatible with an image of a 'de-socialized' class structure.

There is, finally, no suggestion that the pecuniary model of society is to be thought of as a direct product of working class affluence.[30] The pecuniary model is an outcome of the social rather than the economic situation of the privatised worker; and he is only able to hold such a theory of society in so far as his social environment supports such an interpretation. His relative privatisation, his lack of a sense of class cohesion and his isolation from any system of hierarchical social status are the conditions under which he can view his society simply in pecuniary terms.

A purely pecuniary ideology is, of course, just as much of a limiting case as a purely class or purely status model of society. But it may be that it is at least as relevant as the other two in understanding the social and political outlook of the increasingly large section of the working class that is emerging from traditionalism.[31]

---

30. Renate Mayntz, in her study of social class in Euskirchen, notes the contrary tendency: for income models to increase in importance, the lower the income of the respondent, and suggests that this is so because at the lower levels 'diese materielle Frage ein wichtiges, oft sorgenvolles Problem des taeglichen Lebens ist.' *Soziale Schichtung und Sozialer Wandel in einer Industriegemeinde,* Stuttgart, 1958, p. 99. This essentially *ad hoc* explanation is not very convincing. In the absence of privatisation there is no sociological reason why privation any more than affluence should lead to a pecuniary model of society.

31. The related concepts of *privatisation, instrumentalism,* and *pecuniary ideology* are merely intended to serve as points of reference for the study of the new working class. As such, they help to specify the conditions affecting the direction of working class politics, and yield the conclusion that this will take the form of 'instrumental collectivism'. Recently, Perry Anderson has argued that instrumental collectivism could be the basis for the development of a new 'ideological collectivism' (a sort of Hegelian synthesis in which the rational elements of an otherwise apolitical instrumental collectivism combine with the radical elements of an otherwise parochial solidaristic collectivism). The major activating force of this new radicalism could in turn be a sense of relative deprivation arising from new aspirations for power and status. Thus, John Westergaard has suggested that working class radicalism could have its sources in workers' aspirations for middle class status in the community; and others, including Gorz and Mallet, see the work situation as the potential locus of a new radicalism stemming from workers' demands for 'control' over production. However, in so far as the work and community *milieux* of the new working class generate 'privatisation' and 'instrumentalism', neither of these radicalizing aspirations is likely to emerge and to lead to ideological collectivism. On the contrary, since a privatised style of life is likely to create aspirations for higher consumption rather than for higher status, and since instrumentalism devalues work save as a means to higher consumption, the most probable form of radicalism is that which centres on immediate 'shop-floor' demands for maximizing earnings; a form of radicalism in its way just as parochial, if not more so, than the solidaristic collectivism of the traditional worker. See *Towards Socialism, op. cit.,* pp. 108, 265, 317, *et seq.*

# · 19 ·

# The Social Cohesion of Liberal Democracy

## Michael Mann

It is now some years since Dahrendorf and others made their attacks on consensus theory and their pleas for a "mixed theory" of social cohesion. But, despite all the complexities of individual sociologists' arguments, there is still agreement between almost all theorists that *some* minimal degree of value consensus exists in liberal democratic societies, permitting them to handle conflict and remain stable. What is especially surprising is that this belief is at its strongest among latter-day conflict theorists, who admit that value consensus exists but deny its "validity" by their use of "false consciousness." In this paper I will attempt empirical testing of the theories of both "consensus" and "false consciousness" sociologists.

The theoretical orthodoxy of those I loosely term "consensus theorists" is to be found in this quotation from an editorial introduction to an American symposium on political socialization:

Political socialization refers to the learning process by which the political norms and behaviors acceptable to an ongoing political system are transmitted from generation to generation ... A well-functioning citizen is one who accepts (internalizes) society's political norms ... Without a body politic so in harmony with the ongoing political values, a political system would have trouble functioning smoothly. ... (Sigel, 1965:1; for a similar statement see Rose, 1965:29)

Using such an approach, several well-known studies have argued that the stability and "success" of democratic societies depend on the sharing of general political and prepolitical values. In these studies, Great Britain and the United

---

· From *American Sociological Review* 35 (1970): 423–39.

States are taken as examples of successful liberal democracies and often contrasted explicitly or implicitly with "less successful" democracies (e.g. Almond and Verba, 1963; Lipset, 1964; Easton and Dennis, 1967). Thus, Dahl (1967:329–330), reviewing previous studies, concludes that "Americans ordinarily agree on a great many questions that in some countries have polarized the citizenry into antagonistic camps. One consequence of this massive convergence of attitudes is that political contests do not usually involve serious threats to the way of life of significant strata in the community," while Rose has stated ". . . enduring consensus is one of the most distinctive features of politics in England" (1969:3; see also his 1965 work).

We now might ask "what is this consensus about?" And here different writers would produce different answers. Firstly, there are those who stress the commitment of social members to *ultimate values,* of which examples might be generalized beliefs in equality and achievement (Lipset, 1964). Others, however, stress commitment to social *norms,* of which well-known examples are an adherence to the "rules of the democratic game" and opposition to those who introduce strong conflictual elements (such as class ideology) into politics (Dahl, 1967; McKenzie and Silver, 1968). Finally, there are writers who stress commitment to *beliefs* about how society is actually organized, of which there are two main varieties. The first stresses the harmonistic structure of society and political elites (against, say, a belief in class conflict), while the second stresses the essential benevolence of other individuals within the society, for example, the trustworthiness of others (see respectively Easton and Dennis, 1967, and Almond and Verba, 1963). According to these writers, widespread commitment to any or all of these values, norms and beliefs confers legitimacy and stability on present social structure. The "false consciousness" writers agree that this widespread commitment exists, but deny that it thus confers legitimacy on society. Before turning to their arguments, however, let us examine the conceptual problems arising from the asserted link between consensus and social cohesion. There are in fact four main objections to the statement that shared values integrate and legitimate social structures.

(1) Most general values, norms and social beliefs usually mentioned as integrating societies are extremely vague, and can be used to legitimate any social structure, existing or not. As Parsons (1951:293) notes, conservatives and revolutionaries alike appeal to common values of "social justice," "democracy," and "peace." Even the most monolithic of societies is vulnerable to radical appeals to its core values. For example, medieval rebels were often clerics appealing to common Christian values, as did John Ball in the 1381 Peasants' Revolt in England:

> When Adam delved and Eve span,
> Who was then a gentleman?

But at the same time respectable, established clerics unwittingly primed their congregations by emphasizing these "leveling" aspects of Christianity in their sermons (Owst, 1961: Chaps. 5 and 6). Most "consensus theorists" accept the force of this argument. Dahl, for example, though concluding that the stability of American democracy rests on consensus about fundamentals, admits that these are often vague and of doubtful influence on actual behavior (see also Rose, 1965:30).

(2) Even if a value is stated precisely, it may lead to conflict, not cohesion. For while some values unite men, others necessarily divide them. An extreme example of this fact is the consensus among the Dobu people on the values of suspiciousness and treachery (quoted by van der Berghe, 1963). The more consensus there is about such values, the greater the ensuing conflict. Clearly it is only some values which lead to integration, and we had better stick to safe statements like "the more widely interpersonal trust is valued, the greater the social integration" (cf. Almond and Verba, 1963). In short, we have to specify the content of a value if we are to predict its consequences.

(3) The standards embodied in values are absolute ones, and it is difficult for such absolutes to co-exist without conflict. For example, the modern Western values of "achievement" and "equality"—emphasized by Lipset—each limit the scope of the other. Turner (1953–54) has noted that such value-conflict is ubiquitous in societies, which develop ways of "insulating" values from each other. Cohesion is therefore affected by the relative success of society's insulation processes as well as by the nature of the values themselves.

(4) The final objection is related to the third: where insulation processes operate, cohesion results precisely because there is no common commitment to core values. For example, in a society which values achievement, a lower class is more likely to acquiesce in its inequality if it places less stress on achievement aspirations than on other values. Moreover, the cohesion of any functionally differentiated society must partly depend on the learning of role-specific values. In a business firm, for example, though all managers may need some degree of commitment to common organizational goals, they also need differential commitment to role values—the engineer to product quality, the accountant to cost, the personnel manager to industrial peace—for the survival and efficiency of the firm. Thus either role- or class-specific values may contribute more to social cohesion than general core values.

As I have indicated, these problems have been perceived by consensus theorists. Their modifications of a naive, traditional view of consensus (such as Kingsley Davis, 1948, posited) have been paralleled by recent modifications to "conflict theory" which in the modern context means Marxist theory.

Just as no consensus theorist would posit the existence of complete harmony, no Marxist would claim that complete disharmony characterized society. He would admit, firstly, that some form of social cooperation is necessary in the pursuit of scarcity, and, secondly, that subordinate classes within society always appear to "accept" their position at least to some extent (Giddens, 1968: 269). Yet the precise meaning of this word "accept" has greatly troubled Marxists. We must distinguish two types of acceptance: *pragmatic* acceptance, where the individual complies because he perceives no realistic alternative, and *normative* acceptance, where the individual internalizes the moral expectations of the ruling class and views his own inferior position as legitimate. Though pragmatic acceptance is easy to accommodate to Marxism, normative acceptance is not, and the unfortunate popularity of the latter concept has contributed to the inadequacies of much modern Marxist theory.

Writers like Marcuse (1964) and Hacker (1957) have agreed with the consensus theorists that value consensus does exist, and that normative acceptance characterizes the working class in present-day liberal democracies. Such a position can be only reconciled with a Marxist approach by utilizing the concept of "false consciousness" and asserting that normative acceptance is "false" in the sense that it leads workers to ignore their true interests. Yet false consciousness is a dangerous concept, for if we define interests totally independently of the orientations of those concerned, "religious mania alone speaks here" (Geiger, quoted by Dahrendorf, 1959:175). Nevertheless, the concept of false consciousness is tenable if we can demonstrate two of three things: that an indoctrination process has occurred, palpably changing working-class values, or that the indoctrination process is incomplete, leaving indoctrinated values in conflict with "deviant" ones in the mind of the worker; and thirdly, in *both* cases we still have to be able to rank the rival sets of values in order of their "authenticity" to the worker if we are to decide which is more "true." This is a formidable task, barely begun by Marxists. On the first point they are in conflict with the many research findings which show that it is comparatively difficult for the mass media and other indoctrination agencies to change existing values (to which they might justifiably reply that as ruling-class values are in essence traditional, they do not have to be taught afresh). The second point they have obscured by general denunciations of total indoctrination. The third problem of "authenticity" has always been faced by Marxists, but has been too often solved by assertion rather than by evidence.

We are now in a position to derive testable propositions from each of the broad theoretical positions described above. The crucial questions are empirical: *to what extent do the various classes in society internalize norms, values and beliefs which legitimate the social order?* And, *do such norms, values and beliefs constitute true or false consciousness,* as defined above? Present sociological writings offer no coherent answer to these questions. One distinguished group of writers has argued that a "minimum" legitimating consensus does exist in certain liberal democracies, thereby contributing to the stability of their regimes (e.g. Almond and Verba, 1963; Dahl, 1967; Easton and Dennis, 1967). But other empirical investigations of the extent of political value consensus in one of those liberal democracies, the United States, provide opposite conclusions and, moreover, provide hints that the individual's own internal belief system may not be consistent (Agger et al., 1961; McClosky, 1964, Prothro and Grigg, 1960, Converse, 1964). An impasse has been reached. As Easton has remarked (1965:197): ". . . the actual specification of the degree of consensus . . . is an empirical rather than a theoretical matter and is one that has never been fully faced up to, much less resolved through testing whole systems." Such is the intention of the main part of this paper.

## The Data

The data consist of a variety of findings from other writers' empirical investigations into value-commitment in Britain and the United States. The values, norms, and beliefs analyzed here are all ones supporting, or destructive of, the present social structure of those countries. Most concentrate on issues regarding the legitimacy of the social stratification system. Following Parkin (1967), I have labeled supporting values *dominant,* and destructive values *deviant.* Dominant values are generally promulgated by ruling groups to legitimate their rule; deviant values, by groups contesting that legitimacy.

Nearly all the results used here consist of responses to agree–disagree questions. They are presented in Tables 1 to 4. The first column of these tables contains the investigator's name and reference, together with references to other studies which produced similar findings. The second column gives brief details of the sample used, and the third column gives the gist of the question asked. The fourth column gives details of subsamples where available. This paper gives only the subsamples corresponding to the broad occupational stratification hierarchy in liberal democracies, with the groups presented in descending order.[1] The term "class" will be loosely used in the text to describe the main groups, though the authors of the studies themselves use a variety of terms. The fifth column shows the percentage agreement among the sample to the question. The final column presents a classification system designed to show briefly which, if any, theory the finding tends to support. If 75% or more of respondents·agree with a dominant value, the final column contains "Dominant Consensus." If 75% agree with a deviant value, this is labeled "Deviant Consensus." Obviously, 75% is an arbitrary cutoff point between consensus and dissensus, but its general level seems not unreasonable. Where a clear majority of a sample endorses a value, this may still be a significant finding, and thus any agreement of between 60% and 75% has been labeled either "Dominant" or "Deviant Dissensus," according to the direction of the majority. Where there is almost complete, i.e. between 40% and 60%, disagreement, this has been labeled simply "Dissensus." One further classification has been made: where class differences emerge, in that upper classes endorse dominant values significantly more, and deviant values significantly less, than lower classes, this is labeled "Dissensus between Classes."[2]

One important reservation must be made before we turn to the actual results: this type of secondary analysis of published material suffers from important methodological disadvantages. One major problem is that the questions actually used in different studies are rarely identical, and—as all sociologists well know—very slight changes of cue in a question can produce markedly differing results. This difficulty will not be shirked—for example, the effect on respondents of the single word "class" will be discussed—but as we are looking for consistency between findings from different surveys, question bias will usually be randomized. The same should also apply to the difficulties of comparing responses of samples of differing compositions at different points of time and place. However, it must be emphasized that conclusions drawn from such secondary analysis can be only tentative until confirmed by primary research.

---

1. There is no analysis in this paper of racial aspects of stratification, though these are obviously extremely important in the United States, and increasingly so in Britain.

2. The reverse trend does not in fact occur. Note that no tests of *statistical* significance are used here—the populations sampled by the studies are too diverse and ill-reported for this. "Significant" differences indicates merely "clear" differences in this paper.

# Results

In this section we analyze respondents' views on the legitimacy of social structure, and particularly class structure, in Britain and the United States. As the principal function of a social stratification system is to regulate the distribution of scarce resources, we will start by observing how much people, particularly working-class people, want those scarce resources.

Sociological studies of "achievement motivation" are our first pieces of evidence. Several have shown that almost all persons, of whatever class, will agree with statements like "It is important to get ahead" (Scanzoni, 1967:456; Mizruchi, 1964:95; Veness, 1962:153), and some useful pointers to what respondents mean by this are now emerging. Most important, working-class people are more likely than middle-class people to think of success as achieved solely in the occupational sphere, and are more likely to conceive of it as materialistic, economic success (Mizruchi, 1964:77–90). The crucial question then is "Can their economic aspirations be met, given the constraints of the stratified occupational system?" There is evidence that the answer to this is "No." In a comparative analysis of British and American schoolboys, Stephenson demonstrated that the lower the social class of the boy, the more his occupational aspirations outran his occupational expectations. Thus, later on it is the working class pupils ". . . who lower most their aspirations when it comes to considering plans or expectations" in the occupational sphere (Stephenson 1958:49; for supporting evidence see Caro and Pihlblad, 1965). This process seems to continue in the world of work itself. It has been a frequent research finding in industrial sociology that, in identical jobs, older workers are more satisfied than younger ones. The most probable explanation of this is Kornhauser's, applied to his own findings: ". . . men in the routine types of work come over the years to accept and make the most of their situation" (1967:77). From a very early age the lower class person begins to realize that he is at the bottom of a stratification hierarchy (Bettelheim and Sylvester, 1950; Himmelweit et al., 1952). Probably starting with universalistic achievement values, he gradually redefines his aspirations in a more and more role-specific way, so that his lot can become acceptable.

The nature of this "acceptance" is, of course, crucial as I argued earlier. Does this redefinition of goals lead to normative or to pragmatic acceptance? One test of this is the extent to which lower classes regard as legitimate the opportunity structure which has disadvantaged them. In this respect, dominant values are clear: success comes to those whose energies and abilities deserve it, failures have only themselves to blame. Is this argument accepted by lower class persons? Table 1 provides an answer.

We can see that, by and large, the samples hold dominant beliefs about the opportunity structure. Though these results show clearly the biasing effects of leading questions, almost all respondents endorse the key cues of "ability" and "hard work" while much smaller numbers endorse "luck," "pull" and "too hard for a man." Yet there are slight indications here that these beliefs might not be of great significance for the respondents. Thus the Blauner and the Mercer and Weir studies show that respondents are more likely to be cynical about the opportunity structure that confronts them in their actual working lives. This

**Table 1. The Legitimacy of the Opportunity Structure**

| AUTHOR | SAMPLE | STATEMENT | SUBSAMPLE | % AGREEMENT | CLASSIFICATION |
|---|---|---|---|---|---|
| Mizruchi (1964:82) (cf. Berelson et al., 1954:58; Lenski, 1963:165) | U.S. small town adults | Ability determines who gets ahead | a) Social Classes I–III<br>b) Social Classes IV, V | 97<br>92 | Dominant Consensus |
| Veness (1962:144) | a) English boys and girls aged 13–17, representative national sample<br>b) Boys only | Hard work (and not luck or influence) is how to get on | a) Grammar School<br>b) Technical School<br>c) Modern School | 88<br>93<br>88 | Dominant Consensus |
| | | Status achieved by effort in children's essays | a) Grammar School<br>b) Technical School<br>c) Modern School | 79<br>63<br>30 | Dissensus between classes |
| Kornhauser (1965:210) | U.S. male workers | Luck and "pull" determines who gets ahead | a) White collar<br>b) Nonfactory workers<br>c) All factory workers (including d and e)<br>d) Small town factory workers<br>e) Routine production workers | 13<br>26<br>36<br>32<br>50 | Dissensus between classes<br><br>Dominant consensus in middle class |
| Blauner (1964:206) | U.S. factory workers national sample | "cynical" factors determine promotion in own organization | .. | 39 | Dominant Dissensus |
| Mercer & Weir (1969:122) | English male clerical and technical workers, large town | Ditto | .. | 28 | Dominant Dissensus |
| McKenzie & Silver (1968:140) | English urban working class. Labour and Conservative voters only | Too hard for a man with ambition to get ahead | .. | 51 | Dissensus |

**Table 2. Harmonistic and Conflictual Images of Society**

| AUTHOR | SAMPLE | STATEMENT | SUBSAMPLE | % AGREEMENT | CLASSIFICATION |
|---|---|---|---|---|---|
| Form & Rytina (1969:23) | U.S. adults, medium• town (the "analytic sample") | Holding pluralist models of society rather than class or power elite models | a) Rich<br>b) Middle<br>c) Poor | 65<br>59<br>57 | Borderline<br>Dissensus<br>Class differences not significant |
| Lewis (1964–65:176) | U.S. white males, medium town | Rating U.S. citizenship more important than class membership | ‥ | "Almost" 90 | Dominant Consensus |
| Manis & Meltzer (1954:33–35) | U.S. male textile workers, medium town with history of labour disputes | a) Social classes are inevitable and desirable<br><br>b) Social classes are *either* enemies or in conflict, *or* partners or in paternalistic relationship | ‥<br><br>‥ | 56<br><br>33 }<br>46 | Dissensus<br><br>Dissensus |
| Leggett (1964:230) | U.S. male manual workers, metropolis | The rich get the profits | a) Employed<br>b) Unemployed | 62<br>76 | Deviant<br>Dissensus |
| McClosky (1964:370) | U.S. national ("general electorate") sample | a) The laws are rich man's laws<br>b) Poor man doesn't have a chance in the law courts | ‥ | 33<br><br>43 | Dominant<br>Dissensus<br>Dissensus |
| Kornhauser (1965:220) (cf. Haer, 1956–57:140; Lipsitz, 1964:957) | U.S. male workers | Big business has too much power | a) White collar workers<br>b) All factory workers | 54<br>79 | Dissensus between classes<br>Deviant consensus within lower class |

| Source | Sample | Statement | Subgroup | % | Classification |
|---|---|---|---|---|---|
| Nordlinger (1967:178) | English male urban manual workers* | Class conflict is important in England | .. | 55 | Dissensus |
| McKenzie & Silver (1968:135) (cf. Cannon, 1967:168) | English urban workers. Labour and Conservative voters only | Upper class has always tried to exploit working class | .. | 51 | Dissensus |
| Goldthorpe et al. (1968b:26) | English affluent workers, medium town | The laws favour the rich | a) White collar<br>b) Manual workers | 59<br>72 | Virtual deviant<br>Dissensus |
| Mercer & Weir (1969:121) | English male clerical and technical workers, large town | Management and workers are a team, and not on opposite sides | .. | 54 | Dissensus |
| Goldthorpe et al. (1968a:73, 85) | As above | a) Ditto<br>b) Work study engineers are antiworker | a) White collar<br>b) Manual workers<br>Manual workers only | 76<br>67<br>55 | Dominant<br>Dissensus<br>Dissensus |
| Goldthorpe et al. (1968b:26) (cf. Cannon, 1967:168; McKenzie & Silver, 1968:127) | As above | a) Big business has too much power<br>b) Trade unions have too much power | a) White collar<br>b) Manual workers<br>a) White collar<br>b) Manual workers | 63<br>60<br>72<br>43 | Deviant<br>Dissensus<br>Dissensus<br>Dissensus between classes |

*As only one-third of manual workers vote Conservative, the Conservative bias of this sample has been removed by weighting double the % of Labour voters in all cases.

kind of interpretation is strengthened by the Veness (1962) findings. These are based on schoolchildren's essays describing imaginary "successes" in future life. Very large class differences emerge in the essays. In the essays of the grammar and technical school boys (destined for the most part for occupational success), success and status are seen as coming from steady achievements in the occupational sphere. In those of the secondary modern boys (the future manual workers), however, the idea of cumulative status is usually absent, and, instead, success comes from either a quiet, happy life or sudden fame in sport and entertainment. From this, it seems probable that, though lower class children may endorse general platitudes about the importance of ambition, these have little actual relevance for their own life-projects. Turner (1964), in his study of American high-school seniors, also comes to this conclusion, stressing that we can only assess the importance of values in society by considering their *relevance* to peoples' lives.

For further tests of our theories we can turn to respondents' images of the entire social structure to see whether *they* hold to theories of harmony or conflict. Table 2 presents the relevant findings.

This mass of conflicting results permits no easy generalizations. It is true that significant class differences in the direction predicted by Marxist theory emerge in several parts of this table. But not even the statement "Big business has too much power" evokes deviant consensus among the working class of both countries. In only two other cases is there even a clear majority for a deviant value among the working class: for "The rich get all the profits" and (probably) for "The laws favour the rich."[3] And when we examine these most favoured statements we see that none mentions "class" and all are couched in what might be termed simplistic "common man" language. By contrast in Table 2, all the more abstract and sophisticated models of society evoke less support, whether they be basically dominant or deviant in content. We may note, for example, in the studies of Form and Rytina (1969) and of Manis and Meltzer (1954) that dissensus results from presenting alternative abstract theories of society to working class respondents. Moreover, the single word "class" produces dissensus among them whenever it occurs, except significantly when in the Lewis study it is decisively rejected in favour of nationality. This, then, is another problem to be faced later: why is the working class able and willing to produce deviant simplistic views of society but not deviant abstract ones?

Another type of study which enables us to perceive men's images of ongoing social structure is analyzing "political efficacy," that is a man's estimate of his own ability to affect the political government. A belief in high efficacy is certainly consonant with what we have termed dominant values, though a belief in low efficacy is not necessarily deviant to the extent of supporting the redistribution of political power. The relevant research findings are set out in Table 3.

All but one of the questions produce dissensus among respondents. Again, however, significant class differences appear, with at least half the working-class

---

3. Taking note of McClosky's statement that more of the lower occupational groups in his sample have significantly deviant beliefs than higher groups (1964:371). He does not, however, present these differences statistically.

**Table 3. Images of Political Efficacy**

| AUTHOR | SAMPLE | STATEMENT | SUBSAMPLE | % AGREEMENT | CLASSIFICATION |
|---|---|---|---|---|---|
| Thompson & Horton (1960:191–4) (cf. for white collar, Haer, 1956–7:140) | U.S. adults, small town | Neither exercising nor believing in possibility of exercising political control ("politically alienated") | a) Managers and Officials<br>b) Professionals<br>c) White collar<br>d) Labour | 33<br>38<br>47<br>68 | Dissensus between classes |
| McClosky (1964:371) | U.S. national "general electorate" sample | a) Nothing I do has any effect on politics<br><br>b) No use being interested in politics | ...<br><br>... | 62<br><br>21 | Deviant Dissensus<br>Dominant Consensus |
| Nordlinger (1967:97) (cf. McKenzie & Silver, 1968:124) | English male urban manual workers | People like me have no ability to influence government | ... | 43 | Dissensus |
| Agger et al. (1961:479) (for b cf. Berelson et al. 1954:58; Kornhauser et al., 1956:190) | U.S. adults in metropolitan area | a) People are very frequently manipulated by politicians<br><br>b) Politicians usually represent the general interest | ...<br><br>... | 60<br><br>58 | Deviant Dissensus<br><br>Dissensus |
| Nordlinger (1967:105, 109) | As above | Selfish minority groups control government Which groups?<br>a) big business, rich, upper classes<br>b) trade unions | ...<br><br>...<br><br>... | 63<br><br>65 }<br>17 } | Deviant Dissensus<br><br>N.B. Total = c 110%<br>Deviant Dissensus |

**Table 4. Norms Relating to Class Action and Equality**

| AUTHOR | SAMPLE | STATEMENT | SUBSAMPLE | % AGREEMENT | CLASSIFICATION |
|---|---|---|---|---|---|
| Kornhauser (1965: 213–220) | U.S. male workers | a) Workers should have more control of industry | a) White collar<br>b) All factory workers | 37<br>60 | Dissensus between classes |
| | | b) Always side with union against company | All factory workers | 60 | Deviant dissensus |
| Leggett (1964:230) | U.S. male manual workers, metropolis | a) Supporting working-class action in rent protest | a) Employed<br>b) Unemployed | 31<br>46 | Dissensus |
| | | b) Wanting wealth equally divided | a) Employed<br>b) Unemployed | 9<br>16 | Dominant Consensus |
| Nordlinger (1967:178) | English male urban, manual workers | a) In favour of reducing class differentials | .. | 79 | Deviant Consensus |
| Benney et al. (1956:140–141) (for b cf. Goldthorpe et al. 1968a:109) | English adults, medium town | a) Large inequalities are wrong<br>b) Workers should have more control in industry | .. | 48*<br>47 | Dissensus<br>Dissensus |
| Nordlinger (1967:181) | As above | b) Working class should stick together to get ahead | .. | 41 | Dissensus |
| Sykes (1965:303) | Scottish males, nationalized steelworks | Preferring to bargain with employer collectively | a) Clerks<br>b) Workers | 4<br>100 | Consensus within, dissensus between classes |
| McClosky (1964:369) | U.S. national "general electorate" sample | a) Government should give work to unemployed | .. | 47 | Dissensus |

| | | | | |
|---|---|---|---|---|
| | | b) Government should give everyone good standard of living | .. | 55 | Dissensus |
| Lenski (1963:152) (cf. Kornhauser, 1965:218) Key (1965:124) | U.S. adults, metropolis | Government should do more for housing, unemployment, education, etc. | a) Middle Class | 40 | Dissensus |
| | | | b) Working Class | 57 | Dissensus |
| | U.S. national sample | Ditto | a) Nonmanual | 28 | Dominant |
| | | | b) Manual | 31 | Dissensus |

*This figure was arrived at by averaging the percentages among Labour and Conservative voters, who are equally represented in the country as a whole but not in Benney's sample.

respondents choosing the mildly deviant alternative. Clearly then we must consider the possibility, argued by Thompson and Horton (1960), that there is considerable political alienation among the working class. And at the very least, the numerous inconsistencies in political beliefs emerging in the McClosky study indicate that a person's attitudes to political authority may have little significance for him. Again, we have to consider not only a person's stated attitude but also its importance for him.

From the confused images of society revealed in Tables 2 and 3, we might predict that confusion would also be evident in working-class norms regarding political action, and this is indeed revealed in Table 4.

Here, the two statements supporting class action (Leggett a and Nordlinger b) produce dissensus. The statement "Workers should have more control in industry" produces no consistent majority. Very few of one working-class sample want wealth equally divided, only about half of another mixed-class sample think that large inequalities are wrong, but in a third, working class, sample there is consensus in favour of reducing class differentials (one possible explanation of the last finding is that "class" is such an unpopular term that almost everyone is in favour of reducing it). Clearly, if most social groups had consistent and meaningful normative systems, the results would be less affected by the exact wording of questions, the composition of samples, etc.

A further trend emerges from Table 4 which we also noticed in Table 1: that deviant values are more likely to be endorsed if they are presented as relevant to respondents' everyday lives. Thus 60% of Kornhauser's (1965) samples say that in disputes they always side with the union and only 5% with the company, while all of Sykes' (1965) manual workers, in marked contrast to his clerks, support collective rather than individual bargaining. Note also that in Table 2, 55% of Goldthorpe et al's (1968a) manual sample saw work study engineers as opposed to worker interests, though 67% had in general seen worker-management relations in harmonistic terms. Again there seems to be a disjunction between general abstract values and concrete experience.

Such a disjunction is the main theme of Free and Cantril's (1967) study of American political attitudes, and their evidence can advance our argument considerably. They asked respondents two series of questions to test their liberalism/conservatism, the first on specific issues of government intervention in favour of redistribution (which they term the "operational" spectrum), the second on general issues of individualist versus interventionist philosophies (the "ideological" spectrum). Typical examples are, in the first spectrum, "Do you approve of Medicare?" and in the second "We should rely more on individual initiative . . . and not so much on governmental welfare programs." Table 5 presents their main results.

As the authors comment, the results are positively schizophrenic, with a large proportion of the electorate operationally liberal but ideologically conservative. Significantly, white manual workers are among the most schizoid groups (though Negroes are consistently liberal). Similar findings have also been reported by Selznick and Steinberg (1969:220). Such findings have obvious bearing on the problem of false consciousness discussed earlier in this paper: it is interesting that writers as obviously non-Marxist as Free and Cantril (1967)

*Table 5.* **Ideological and Operational Spectrums in American Political Attitudes**

| | IDEOLOGICAL SPECTRUM | | OPERATIONAL SPECTRUM | |
|---|---|---|---|---|
| Completely Liberal* | 4% | ⎱ 16% | 44% | ⎱ 65% |
| Predominantly Liberal | 12 | ⎰ | 21 | ⎰ |
| Middle of the Road | 34 | | 21 | |
| Predominantly Conservative | 20 | ⎱ 50% | 7 | ⎱ 14% |
| Completely Conservative | 30 | ⎰ | 7 | ⎰ |
| | 100% | | 100% | |

Source: Free and Cantril, 1967: 320.

*The scoring system is quite complicated and the reader is referred to Free and Cantril, p. 220-221.

should conclude their study by remarking that present American ideology is out of touch with American realities (i.e. false) and should therefore be reformulated.

Finally, we can examine the suggestion that political and social stability is in part a function of consensus on pre-political values. Many writers have argued this, asserting in particular that liberal democracy "works" because its members trust each other. The most satisfactory evidence for this comes from Almond and Verba's (1963) influential study, but even their findings seem rather suspect on closer examination. It is indisputable that their results show a greater degree of consensus on values such as interpersonal trust among British and American respondents than among respondents in the "less successful" democracies of Italy, Mexico, and West Germany. However, there are equally significant differences in value-commitment according to the only (and indirect) measure of social class used, the formal education of the respondent. The least educated groups are consistently the least politically confident and trusting. Moreover, when Almond and Verba produce their results on the extent of commitment to the norm of interpersonal trust, they tend to obscure one very significant finding, which is difficult to fit into their general theoretical position. It is that the *degree* of value commitment, even in Britain and the United States, is still minimal. In Table 4 (on p. 267) Almond and Verba demonstrate that more respondents in Britain and the States than in the other countries agree with five similar statements whose tenor is that "people can be trusted." But additionally, on two of the five items in the U.S. and on three of them in Britain, only a minority of respondents show themselves as "trustful." Also, in Table 5 (on p. 269), a majority of those with only primary education in these countries agree with the deviant statement "No one is going to care much what happens to you, when you get right down to it," which statement Almond and Verba think "reflects the most extreme feeling of distrust and alienation" (p. 268). Unfortunately, the authors do not present the results of the other questions according to educational level, but it would not be unreasonable to assume that the majority of lower class respondents would emerge as distrustful on the less extreme questions. Clearly, Almond and Verba's analysis of the stability of liberal democracy is at best partial, neglecting as it does the lack of value consensus between classes.

From all these findings four trends, which are in need of explanation, clearly emerge:

1. value consensus does not exist to any significant extent;

2. there is a greater degree of consensus among the middle class than among the working class:

3. the working class is more likely to support deviant values if those values relate either to concrete every day life or to vague populist concepts than if they relate to an abstract political philosophy;

4. working class individuals also exhibit less internal *consistency* in their values than middle-class people

We can now return to our general theories with these trends in mind.

## Discussion

If there is not value consensus, what remains of value consensus theory? Obviously the more extreme and generally stated versions of the theory are untenable, but many others have been rather more cautious, asserting merely that some "minimum" level of consensus about certain "critical" values is necessary to social cohesion. As this level is never precisely specified, we cannot very easily come to grips with the argument. Let us approach the problem by asking *why* some measure of consensus is considered necessary for social cohesion. The answer lies in one of sociology's most sacred tenets: that values are by definition beliefs governing action. As action itself must be considered nonrandom, and as men do actually cooperate with one another, then it would seem to follow that there is some degree of congruence between their values. This seems plausible, for if men cooperate they must come to some form of agreement, explicit or implicit, to share power. There is, of course, no such social contract which does not rest on shared normative understandings (Durkheim, 1964: 206–19).

But when we consider whole complex societies, it is not clear that all social members can be considered as parties to the social contract. The ordinary participant's social relations are usually confined to a fairly narrow segment of society, and his relations with society as a whole are mostly indirect, through a series of overlapping primary and secondary groups. We may characterize his meaningful life as being largely on an everyday level. Thus his normative connections with the vast majority of fellow citizens may be extremely tenuous, and his commitment to general dominant and deviant values may be irrelevant to his compliance with the expectations of others. As long as he conforms to the very specific role behavior expected of him, the political authorities may not trouble themselves with his system of beliefs.

If this is so, we might develop the following hypothesis: *only those actually sharing in societal power need develop consistent societal values.* There are two available tests of this hypothesis and both support it. Firstly, McClosky (1964) has shown that there is a far greater internal consistency in the political values of political activists in the United States than in the population at large.[4] Clearly it is the former who daily face the problems of power-sharing. Secondly, there are the various class differences demonstrated earlier in this paper, and obviously, the middle class is closer to centers of power than is the working class. Etzioni (1964) has argued persuasively that the normative orientations of lower participants in "utilitarian" organizations like the industrial firm are largely irrelevant to the quality of their role-performance. Might this be also true of the lower classes in liberal democracy? Their compliance might be more convincingly explained by their pragmatic acceptance of specific roles than by any positive normative commitment to society. There is even evidence that lower class parents and children are in a similar relationship: Rosen (1967) shows that the working-class parent disciplines his children by "eliciting specific behavioral conformities" from them, whereas the middle-class parent attempts more to persuade his children to internalize norms and to generalize them to a variety of situations. The attachment of the lower classes to the distant state may be expected to be far less normative and more pragmatic than their attachment to the primary familial group.

While rejecting more extreme versions of harmonistic theories, we must also do the same with Marxist ones. There is little truth in the claims of some Marxists that the working class is systematically and successfully indoctrinated with the values of the ruling class. Though there is a fair amount of consensus among the rulers, this does not extend very far down the stratification hierarchy. Among the working-class there is almost complete dissensus on most of the general dominant-deviant political issues we have investigated. We have seen that two types of deviant values are widely endorsed by working class people: firstly, values which are expressed in concrete terms corresponding to everyday reality, and, secondly, vague simplistic divisions of the social world into "rich" and "poor." Everyday social conflict is experienced, and to some extent is referred to what Ossowski has described as the eternal struggle between "rich" and "poor," "rulers" and "ruled," "idle drones" and "worker bees" (Ossowski, 1963: 19–30). But the one is concrete and the other is vague; there is no real political philosophy uniting the two in the working-class consciousness. Instead, at the political level are rather confused values with surprisingly conservative biases. How these political values come to be is of crucial theoretical importance, for it is their presence which keeps the working-class from noncompliance in the political order. It is not value-consensus which keeps the working-class compliant, but rather a *lack* of consensus in the crucial area where concrete experiences and vague populism might be translated into radical politics. Whether a harmonistic or a conflictual theory can best account for their compliance now turns on whether this lack of consensus is "free" or "manipulated," on how it is produced. Though we need more studies of the operation of

---

4. See also Converse's (1964) excellent argument on this point: he maintains that it is a tiny minority consisting of highly educated, political activists which has an internally consistent, considered, and stable set of political beliefs.

socialization processes, at least one of them, the school system, has been extensively studied.

Studies of the school systems of Britain and the United States have generally concluded that the school is a transmitter of political conservatism, particularly to the working-class. Hess and Torney (1967) find that the school is the most important political socialization agency for the young child, and that its efforts are directed toward the cultivation of nationalism and a benevolent image of established political authority. Greenstein stresses benevolence, too, noting that the child's view of the world is deliberately "sugarcoated" by adults: "Books such as *Our Friend the Farmer* and *How the Policeman Helps Us* are couched in language which closely resembles some of the preadolescent descriptions of the political leaders reported in this survey" (1965:46). Both Zeigler (1967) and Litt (1963) stress how teachers strive to keep the conflictual elements of politics out of the classroom unless, paradoxically, they are dealing with upper class children. As Litt puts it, politics is presented as a ". . . formal mechanistic set of government institutions with the emphasis on its harmonious legitimate nature rather than as a vehicle for group struggle and change" (1963:73). Abrams (1963) comes to a similar conclusion from his review of textbooks used in British schools: he notes that they often try to avoid mentioning nonbenevolent occurrences such as economic slumps or industrial conflict, and where they cannot avoid them, the events are presented as "just happening" with no real attempt at explanation. Other studies have shown that schools also attempt to inculcate individualism and competitiveness in pupils; e.g., the child is taught that any form of achievement is gained at the expense of others (e.g. Henry, 1965; Friedenberg, 1963). It is of especial interest that the dominant values thus taught in schools are precisely the ones we have already noted as being present in adult working-class consciousness. Individualism we saw expressed strongly in Table 1, while a strong preference for ties of nationality over class, was also evident in Table 2. Furthermore, Litt and Zeigler's observations about teaching on the American political system enable us to trace back the origin of another supposed American core-value, belief in the legitimacy of the Constitution (see Dahl, 1967, for an assertion of the importance of this value to American democracy).[5]

We must be careful to specify the limits of this indoctrination. It is rarely direct, though the daily oath to the U.S. flag, or the granting of holidays to children in Britain if they will cheer visiting royalty, clearly come into this category. More usually, dominant-deviant issues are not presented at all to children. The essential point is that "the realities of the political process" (to use Litt's phrase) and the populist deviant tradition of the lower class are ignored in the classroom. Presumably the working class child learns the latter from his family and peers;[6] certainly he experiences something of the former when he enters the world of work, so his manipulated socialization is only partial. We

---

5. Respondents' attitudes on this issue have not been analyzed here, as there is no comparable British issue.

6. Though the evidence here is conflicting. Hess and Torney (1967) state that the families they investigated also transmit nationalism and political benevolence, but Carter (1962) finds that British working class families transmit a cynical populism.

may aptly describe these socialization processes as the mobilization of bias (the phrase of Bachrach and Baratz, 1962). As the child gets older, he becomes increasingly cynical in his political and social attitudes (Hess and Easton, 1960; Hess, 1963; Greenstein, 1965), but he has difficulty in putting them into abstract terms. What has been ignored in childhood is unlikely to be grasped in adulthood, given working class difficulties with abstract concepts (cf. Bernstein, 1961; findings replicated by Hess and Shipman, 1965). Hence we can see agencies of political radicalism, like the trade unions and the British Labour Party, struggling against their opponents' ability to mobilize the national and feudal symbols to which the population has been taught to respond loyally in schools and in much of the mass media (McKenzie and Silver, 1968:245). Thus the most common form of manipulative socialization by the liberal democratic state does not seek to change values, but rather to perpetuate values that do not aid the working class to interpret the reality it actually experiences. These values merely deny the existence of group and class conflict within the nation-state society and therefore, are demonstrably false.

Thus there are strong suggestions that the necessary mixed model of social cohesion in liberal democracy should be based more on Marxist conflict theory than sociologists have usually thought. A significant measure of consensus and normative harmony may be necessary among ruling groups, but it is the absence of consensus among lower classes which keeps them compliant. And if we wish to explain this lack of consensus, we must rely to some extent on the Marxist theories of *pragmatic role acceptance* and *manipulative socialization*. Of course, the existence of contrary harmonistic processes is feasible. Alongside coercive processes there may exist elements of voluntary deference, nationalism, and other components of normative integration in liberal democracy. It is often difficult to distinguish the two. Yet sociologists can no longer assert that these elements produce value consensus between social members and value consistency within them. Thus whatever "legitimacy" liberal democracy possesses is not conferred upon it by value consensus, for this does not exist.

However, these results do not contradict all such affirmations of the legitimacy of social structure. Though I have demonstrated the existence of present-day false consciousness, this is insufficient as a total explanation of pragmatic role acceptance. For the reason why most working-class people do "accept" (in whatever sense) their lot and do not have consistent deviant ideologies, we must look back to the historical incorporation of working-class political and industrial movements in the 19th and 20th centuries within existing structures. Dahl's historical analysis would lead to the same conclusion as that of Marcuse, that the institutionalization of class conflict has resulted in a closing of the "political universe." But, of course, whereas Marcuse stresses that this process was itself dominated by the manipulative practices of the ruling class,[7] Dahl has stressed its elements of genuine and voluntary compromise. Clearly, the historical as well as the present-day theory must be a "mixed" one. Yet one obstacle to the development of a more precise mixed theory in the past has been the failure of most sociologists to take the Marxist tradition in social theory seriously. In

---

7. For a rather more detailed and better argued statement of this, see R. Miliband, 1961.

particular, they have dismissed the crucial concept of "false consciousness" as being nonscientific. Yet in this paper we have seen fulfilled two of the preconditions for an empirically-grounded theory of false consciousness. Firstly, we saw quite clearly a conflict between dominant and deviant values taking place within the individual. Secondly, we found some evidence of the alternative precondition, the actual indoctrination of dominant values. Thus the third precondition, the ranking of conflicting values by an analysis of "who gains and who loses" can be investigated, and some relevant suggestions have been made here. The central argument of this paper is that the debate between harmonistic theories and Marxist theories must be an empirical one. The way is open to further empirical investigations.

## References

Abrams, P. 1963. "Notes on the Uses of Ignorance." Twentieth Century (Autumn):67–77.

Agger, R. E., M. N. Goldstein, and S. A. Pearl. 1961. "Political cynicism: Measurement and meaning." Journal of Politics 23:477–506.

Almond, G. and S. Verba. 1963. The Civic Culture. N.J.: Princeton University Press.

Bachrach, P. and M. S. Baratz. 1962. "Two faces of power." American Political Science Review 56:947–952.

Benney, M., A. P. Gray and R. H. Pear. 1956. How People Vote: A Study of Electoral Behaviour in Greenwich. London: Routledge and Kegan Paul.

Berelson, B. R., P. F. Lazarsfeld, and W. N. McPhee. 1954. Voting. University of Chicago Press.

Bernstein, B. 1961. "Social class and linguistic development: A theory of social learning." Pp. 288–314 in A. H. Halsey et al. (eds.), Education, Economy and Society. Glencoe: The Free Press.

Bettelheim, B. and E. Sylvester. 1950. "Notes on the impact of parental occupations." American Journal of Orthopsychiatry 20:785–795.

Blauner, R. 1964. Alienation and Freedom. Chicago University Press.

Cannon, I. C. 1967. "Ideology and occupational community: A study of compositors." Sociology, 1:165–185.

Caro, F. G. and C. T. Pihlblad. 1965. "Aspirations and expectations." Sociology and Social Research 49:465–475.

Carter, M. P. 1962. Home, School and Work. Oxford: Pergamon Press.

Converse, P. E. 1964. "The Nature of belief systems in mass publics." Pp. 206–261 in D. E. Apter (ed.), Ideology and Discontent. Glencoe: The Free Press.

Dahl, R. A. 1967. Pluralist Democracy in the United States: Conflict and Consent. Chicago: Rand McNally.

Dahrendorf, R. 1959. Class and Class Conflict in an Industrial Society. London: Routledge and Kegan Paul.

Davis, K. 1948. Human Society. New York: Macmillan.

Durkheim, E. 1964. The Division of Labor in Society. New York: The Free Press.

Easton, D. 1965. A Systems Analysis of Political Life. New York: John Wiley.

Easton, D., and J. Dennis. 1967. "The child's acquisition of régime norms: Political Efficacy." American Political Science Review 61:25–38.

Easton, D., and R. D. Hess. 1962. "The child's political world." Midwest Journal of Political Science 6:229–246.

Etzioni, A. 1964. A Comparative Analysis of Complex Organization. New York. The Free Press.

Form, W.H. and J. Rytina. 1969. "Ideological beliefs on the distribution of power in the United States." American Sociological Review 34:19–31.

Free, L. A. and H. Cantril. 1967. The Political Beliefs of Americans. New Brunswick: Rutgers University Press.

Friedenberg, E. 1963. Coming of Age in America. New York: Random House.

Giddens, A. 1968. "'Power' in the recent writings of Talcott Parsons." Sociology 2 (September):257–272.

Goldthorpe, J.H., D. Lockwood, F. Bechhofer, and S. Platt. 1968a. The Affluent Worker: Industrial Attitudes and Behaviour. Cambridge University Press.

_____. 1968b. The Affluent Worker: Political Attitudes and Behaviour. Cambridge University Press.

Greenstein, F.I. 1965. Children and Politics. New Haven: Yale University Press.

Hacker, A. 1957. "Liberal democracy and social control." American Political Science Review 51: 1009–1026.

Hacr, J. L. 1956–57. "Social stratification in relation to attitude toward sources of power in a community." Social Forces, 35:137–142.

Henry, J. 1965. "Attitude organization in elementary school classrooms," Pp. 215–233 in G. D. Spindler (ed.), Education and Culture. New York: Holt, Rinehart and Winston.

Hess, R. D. 1963. "The socialization of attitudes toward political authority: Some cross national comparisons." International Social Science Journal 15:542–559.

Hess, R. D. and D. Easton. 1960. "The child's image of the president." Public Opinion Quarterly 24:632–644.

Hess, R. D. and V. C. Shipman. 1965. "Early experience and the socialization of cognitive modes in children." Child Development 36:869–886.

Hess, R. D. and J. V. Torney. 1967. The Development of Political Attitudes in Children. Chicago: Aldine.

Himmelweit, H., A. H. Halsey, and A. N. Oppenheim. 1952. "The views of adolescents on some aspects of the Social class structure." British Journal of Sociology, 3:148–172.

Key, V. O. Jr. 1965. Public Opinion and American Democracy. New York: Knopf.

Kornhauser, A. W., A. L. Sheppard, and A. J. Mayer. 1956. When Labor Votes. New York: University Books.

Kornhauser, W. 1965. The Mental Health of the Industrial Worker. New York: John Wiley.

Leggett, J.C. 1964. "Economic insecurity and working-class consciousness." American Sociological Review 29:226–234.

Lenski, G. 1963. The Religious Factor. New York: Anchor Books.

Lewis, L. S. 1964–65. "Class consciousness and the salience of class." Sociology and Social Research, 49:173–182.

Lipset, S. M. 1964. First New Nation. London: Heinemann.

Lipsitz, L. 1964. "Work life and political attitudes: A study of manual workers." American Political Science Review 58:951–962.

Litt, E. 1963. "Civic education, community norms and political indoctrination." American Sociological Review 28:69–75.

Manis, J.G. and B.N. Meltzer 1954. "Attitudes of textile workers to class structure." American Journal of Sociology 60:30–35.

Marcuse, H. 1964. One-Dimensional Man. London: Routledge and Kegan Paul.

McClosky, H. 1964. "Consensus and ideology in American politics." American Political Science Review 58:361–382.

McKenzie, R. and A. Silver. 1968. Angels in Marble: Working-class Conservatives in Urban England. London: Heinemann.

Mercer, D. E. and D. T. H. Weir. 1969. "Orientations to work among white collar workers." Pp. 112–145 in Social Science Research Council (eds.), Social Stratification and Industrial Relations. Cambridge: Social Science Research Council. Revised version of paper forthcoming in John H. Goldthorpe and Michael Mann (eds.), Social Stratification and Industrial Relations. Cambridge University Press.

Miliband, R. 1961. Parliamentary Socialism. London: Allen and Unwin.

Mizruchi, E. H. 1964. Success and Opportunity. New York: The Free Press.

Nordlinger, E. A. 1967. The Working Class Tories. London: MacGibbon and Kee.

Ossowski, S. 1963. Class Structure in the Social Consciousness. London: Routledge and Kegan Paul.

Owst, G. R. 1961. Literature and Pulpit in Medieval England. Oxford: Blackwell.

Parkin, F. 1967. "Working class conservatives: A theory of political deviance." British Journal of Sociology, 18:278–290.

Parsons, T. 1951. The Social System. London: Routledge and Kegan Paul.

Prothro, J. W. and C. W. Grigg. 1960. "Fundamental principles of democracy: Bases of Agreement and Disagreement." Journal of Politics 22:276–294.

Rose, R. 1965. Politics in England. London: Faber. 1969 Studies in British Politics. London: Macmillan, 2nd Edition.

Rosen, B. C. 1967. "Family structure and value transmission." Pp. 86–96 in R. J. Havighurst et al. (eds.), Society and Education. Boston: Allyn and Bacon.

Scanzoni, J. 1967. "Socialization, n achievement and achievement values." American Sociological Review 32:449–456.

Selznick, G. J. and S. Steinberg. 1969. "Social class, ideology, and voting preference." Pp. 216–226 in C. S. Heller (ed.), Structured Social Inequality. New York: Macmillan.

Sigel, R. 1965. "Assumptions about the learning of political values." Annals of the American Academy of Political and Social Science 361:1–9.

Stephenson, R. M. 1958. "Stratification, education and occupational orientation." British Journal of Sociology 5:42–52.

Sykes, A. J. M. 1965. "Some differences in the attitudes of clerical and of manual workers." Sociological Review 13:297–310.

Thompson, W. E. and J. E. Horton. 1960. "Political alienation as a force in political action," Social Forces, 38:190–195.

Turner, R. 1953–54. "Value conflict in social disorganization." Sociology and Social Research, 38:301–308.

———. 1964. The Social Context of Ambition. San Francisco: Chandler.

Van den Berghe, P. L. 1963. "Dialectic and functionalism: Toward a theoretical synthesis." American Sociological Review 28:695–705.

Veness, T. 1962. School Leavers: Their Aspirations and Expectations. London: Methuen.

Zeigler, H. 1967. The Political Life of American Teachers. Englewood Cliffs, New Jersey: Prentice-Hall.

# · 20 ·

# The Dominant Ideology Thesis

## Nicholas Abercrombie and Bryan S. Turner

The view that religion, or more generally common culture, can be manipulated to the political advantage of the dominant class can be traced back through the rational criticism of the Enlightenment *philosophes* to Plato's 'golden lie'. However, the main impetus for contemporary analysis of dominant ideologies comes from Marx and Engels' *The German Ideology* and, partly through the influence of Marxism on the sociology of knowledge, the thesis occurs in many areas of sociological research, particularly in studies of politics and culture. Its argument is, very basically, that there is in most class societies a pervasive set of beliefs that broadly serves the interests of the dominant class. This dominant ideology is then adopted by subordinate classes which are thereby prevented from formulating any effective opposition. A number of assumptions and implications in this conventional position require further examination, in particular the notion that capitalist societies *require* a dominant ideology to ensure the continuing political superiority of the dominant class.

In criticizing the dominant ideology thesis here we examine the position of subordinate classes in feudalism, early and late capitalism, in order to show that these classes rarely, or never, shared the ideology of the dominant class. The role of ideology in feudalism and early capitalism was to ensure the accumulation and inheritance of property which had the effect of creating some political

• From *British Journal of Sociology* 29(2) (1978): 149–70.

NOTE: This paper was first presented at a seminar in the Department of Sociology at the University of Lancaster. We are grateful to the participants of that seminar, especially John Urry, for their helpful comments.

coherence within the dominant class. The limitations on the spread of dominant ideologies throughout class society were to some extent a consequence of the fact that these societies did not possess an institutional machinery for disseminating the beliefs of dominant classes. In late capitalism[1] there are important changes in the development of institutions which can carry dominant values (such as the centralization of compulsory education), but we suggest that there is still no *requirement* for a clearly defined dominant ideology because of changes in the nature of dominant classes. Given the historical scope of this examination, evidence for certain sections of the argument is necessarily schematic. Our aim is primarily to suggest various ways of reinterpreting existing studies of ideology in relation to class structure. In the course of this reinterpretation, we wish to focus on a question which has been rarely or inadequately posed, namely, what is the function of the dominant ideology for the dominant class? The stages in our argument (the ideological conditions of various forms of social organization, the presence of institutional means of dissemination, the place of ideology in late capitalism) are not intended to be logically dependent on each other. Each section of the paper is thus a relatively autonomous contribution to the debate about dominant ideologies.

## Marx's Two Theories of Ideology

Marx and Engels can be said to have developed, at least implicitly, two theories of ideology. The first is based on the formula from the *Preface* that 'social being determines consciousness' which is usually interpreted as 'social class determines consciousness'. Each class by virtue of its particular relationship to the means of production and out of its general conditions of existence generates for itself (typically through the medium of class intellectuals) a culture which gives expression to its material conditions. Since social classes have different economic circumstances, they also have different interests, so that ideas grasp, represent and promote separate interests. In short, each class forms its own system of beliefs, the character of which is determined by the particular interests of the class. As Marx says in *The Eighteenth Brumaire of Louis Bonaparte*,

Upon the different forms of property, upon the social conditions of existence, rises an entire superstructure of distinct and peculiarly formed sentiments, illusions, modes of thought and views of life. The entire class creates and forms them through tradition and upbringing.[2]

---

1. In this paper we wish to avoid confronting the specific theoretical difficulties which are associated with the technical distinction between 'competitive capitalism' and 'monopoly capitalism'. For an account of the competitive/monopoly distinction, cf. Nicos Poulantzas, *Classes in Contemporary Capitalism*, London: NLB, 1975, pp. 134 ff. The terms 'early' and 'late capitalism' are descriptive categories which refer to changes in the organization of capitalism in Great Britain such as the separation of ownership and control, the concentration of capitalist production and the crucial role of the state in economic organization. We also deliberately ignore the set of issues which are raised in Marx's treatment of ideology by the distinction between reality/appearance in the analysis of alienation. This issue is separate from the class analysis of ideology. For a discussion of the appearance/reality issue cf. Norman Geras 'Essence and Appearance: Aspects of Fetishism in Marx's *Capital*' *New Left Review*, no. 65, January–February 1971, pp. 69–85.

2. K. Marx, *The Eighteenth Brumaire of Louis Bonaparte*, in Marx, K. and Engels, F., *Selected Works*, London, Lawrence and Wishart, 1968, pp. 117–18.

The second theory, again from the *Preface,* claims that 'the economic structure of society, the real foundation' determines 'a legal and political superstructure'. The theory that the base determines the superstructure can be rendered in terms of class relations by noting that the base (relations and forces of production) is associated with dominant and subordinate classes which exercise functions of (in capitalism) labour and capital. The base determines the superstructure in the sense that each mode of production has a dominant class which generates a dominant ideology; the effect of the dominant ideology is to facilitate the subordination of the working class. The classical version of this theory is to be found in *The German Ideology* where Marx and Engels assert that the ideas of

the ruling class are in every epoch the ruling ideas, i.e. the class which is the ruling *material* force of society, is at the same time its ruling *intellectual* force.[3]

Since each mode of production has a dominant class which controls both material and mental production, each mode of production has a dominant ideology. The dominant class is able to impose its system of beliefs on all other classes. The adoption of the ideology of the ruling class by dominated classes helps to inhibit the development of a revolutionary consciousness and thereby contributes to the reproduction of existing conditions of the appropriation of surplus labour.

The two theories are potentially in conflict with one another. The first suggests that each class forms its own system of belief in accordance with its own particular interests which will be basically at variance with those of other classes. The second suggests that all classes share in the system of belief imposed by the dominant class. For example, according to the theory of 'ruling ideas', the British working class in the nineteenth century should have shared the same beliefs as the bourgeoisie. However, when Engels wrote about the working class, his commentary illustrates the 'social being' theory of beliefs, namely that each class has its own beliefs:

The bourgeoisie has more in common with every other nation of the earth than with the workers in whose midst it lives. The workers speak other dialects, have other thoughts and ideals, other customs and moral principles, a different religion and other politics than those of the bourgeoisie.[4]

The separate interests and material conditions of the two classes produce two cultures rather than a dominant ideology imposed by a class which owns the means of mental production.

It would be possible to suggest various arguments whereby these apparently contradictory theories could be reconciled. In the case of the British working class, one might argue that, for example, their reformist consciousness was overdetermined by both the dominant ideology of the capitalist class and their own class-based beliefs. Our argument in later sections of this paper will be that this type of solution is not entirely satisfactory. Most conventional Marxist

---

3. K. Marx and F. Engels, *The German Ideology,* London, Lawrence and Wishart, 1974, p. 64.

4. F. Engels, *The Condition of the Working Class in England in 1844,* London, Allen and Unwin, 1968, p. 124.

theories, and more generally sociological theories dependent on them, eventually come down to an implicit imagery of class/ideological relations in which one class (the ruling class) *does* something to another class which is underneath it. The result has been that Marxist theories often obscure the relationship of dominant class to dominant ideology. There is sometimes an admission that dominant classes do believe in their own ideology but we still need to ask what are the consequences of this for the organization of class relations. By raising this type of question, it is possible to pinpoint the analytical weaknesses of conventional interpretations which rely too heavily on convenient slogans like 'religion is the opium of the masses'.

The force of the potential conflict between the two theories of ideology can be underlined by observing that this issue in Marxism is endemic to contemporary sociology in general. For example, there is a similar analytic problem in Parsons' theory of socialization in dominant values through the cultural mechanisms of the family, church and school. The centrality of values as a theoretical solution for 'the problem of order' has made it difficult to produce a theory of the emergence and maintenance of deviant, sub-cultural value systems in relation to deviant behaviour. In *The Social System*,[5] Parsons simply treats deviant role behaviour as a product of inadequate socialization; more typically, sociologists[6] rely on Durkheimian assumptions about the effects of deviance on boundary maintenance. The problem for functionalists, however, arises most critically in the case of modern, differentiated social systems which are characterized by cultural pluralism. Differentiation produces social systems which are highly adapted to their societal environment, but it also creates a legitimation crisis,[7] which arises from competing and diverse sets of beliefs. Berger and Luckmann's answer appears to be that, while pluralism does indeed generate crises, there exists a bed-rock ('sedimentation') of taken-for-granted beliefs which are sufficient to make everyday worlds manageable.[8] The point of these observations is not to assess the adequacy of functionalist theories of knowledge but merely to point out the similarity of analytic difficulties in functionalist sociology and Marxism. Functionalists are committed both to the notion that a common value system is a necessary condition for the existence of a social system, and to the theory of structural differentiation which creates pluralistic value systems. Marxists are committed to a theory of 'ruling ideas' and to the theory that each class, because of its own interests, has its own unique culture.

These two Marxist theories of ideology also raise problems of a more methodological character; both have to provide some specification of what will count as 'the dominant ideology' or 'the ideology of a class'. For example, many Marxist theories of culture tend to render the doctrine as being one about those systems of belief that are particularly obvious. Thus in studying a particular society's culture the dominant ideology is taken to be that which is 'obvious' or

---

5. Talcott Parsons, *The Social System,* London, Routledge & Kegan Paul, 1951, pp. 251 ff.

6. For example, K. T. Erikson, *Wayward Puritans,* New York, Wiley, 1966.

7. For a recent analysis, cf. Jürgen Habermas, *Legitimation Crisis,* London, Heinemann, 1976.

8. Peter L. Berger and Thomas Luckmann, *The Social Construction of Reality,* London, Allen Lane, 1967, pp. 85 ff.

most widely available in written texts; it is simply that set of beliefs which occurs statistically most frequently in a sample of cultural products. The problem, however, is not merely one of content analysis; it is that the obvious ideology *may* be that appropriate to the dominant class but it may also not be. The nature of this ideology will depend on the constitution and class relationships of the intellectual stratum. That is, the most pervasive system of belief may be that appropriate to a rising but not yet dominant class. In the sixteenth and seventeenth centuries, for example, individualist doctrines of all kinds were prominent, although they are beliefs that are often said to be appropriate to a capitalist class that was not then economically or politically dominant. Everything in cases of this kind depends on the character of the apparatus that creates and distributes knowledge and opinion, and, in particular, on the constitution and class affiliation of the intellectual stratum. Intellectuals are not always closely bound to the dominant class and, when they are not, it is not unlikely that the most pervasive beliefs will not be those of the dominant class. In sum, conventional interpretations of the dominant ideology thesis often do not indicate how such ideologies are to be identified, and are equally unspecific about their actual content.

## The Dominant Ideology and Social Classes

The basic assumption of the 'ruling ideas' model is that the dominant class, because it controls the means of mental production, is able to force, or at least ensure, that the dominated classes think their thoughts within the concepts provided by the belief systems of the dominant class. It may even be that the rebellions and protests of the subordinate classes are expressed through the medium of the dominant ideology since articulate, oppositional forms of thought are not available. At the very least, the theory must assume that there is a common culture in which all classes share and that the content and themes of that common culture are dictated by the dominant class. In fact it is typically the case that subordinate classes do *not* believe (share, accept) the dominant ideology which has far more significance for the integration and control of the dominant class itself.

In *Capital,* Marx states that

the mode of production of material life dominates the development of social, political and intellectual life generally . . . is very true for our own times, in which material interests preponderate, but not for the middle ages, in which Catholicism, nor for Athens and Rome, where politics, reigned supreme.[9]

This observation by Marx has been elaborated by Marxists like Althusser and Poulantzas[10] to mean that the economic base determines which structure (politics, ideology or the economic) in any given mode of production is domi-

---

9. K. Marx, *Capital,* London, Lawrence and Wishart, 1970, vol. i, pp. 85–6n.

10. Louis Althusser and Etienne Balibar, *Reading Capital,* London, NLB, 1970, pp. 216 ff. Nicos Poulantzas, *Political Power and Social Classes,* London, NLB and Sheed and Ward, 1973, pp. 11–33.

nant. Briefly, this view of political and ideological structures means that certain modes of production may require functional support from 'non-economic factors'. In feudalism, for example, where peasants by customary right have certain privileges over the use of land, extra-economic means (political/ideological structures) are required in order to extract labour-service from the peasantry. Hence, Poulantzas wants to argue that religion was a dominant region of the ideological structure in societies characterized by the feudal mode of production. This theory would imply, in terms of the 'ruling ideas' model, that the peasantry shared the religion of feudal lords or, to employ a term favoured by Poulantzas, the peasantry were 'contaminated' by the ideology of the landlords with the effect that their revolutionary interests were impeded.

In general, there are good grounds for believing that the European peasantry existed outside the ambit of the dominant Christian orthodoxy of the Church as a ruling institution. The peasantry were symbolically separated from the official mysteries of the Church by the liturgical rituals; whereas in the early Church the priest had celebrated Mass facing the people, in the medieval period he turned his back on them and retreated to the fastnesses of the sanctuary, separated from the people's part of the Church by a forbidding screen. Finally, the Mass was read in a tongue the people could not understand.[11]

On the face of it, the development of the confessional in the thirteenth century as a public, compulsory obligation on all believers under the monopoly of the Church which distributed grace from the Treasury of Merit, would look like strong evidence for 'the ruling ideas' model. The problem is that, while the peasantry probably only attended a short shrift on major and minor festivals and while absenteeism was rife, the nobility had spiritual directors in constant attendance. It would seem odd that the dominant class should be more plagued by problems of guilt and conformity than the dominated classes. Some doctrines in secular as well as religious use, might also be seen as candidates for the function of the dominant ideology. The 'Great Chain of Being',[12] for instance, was a theory of the ranking of all beings in the universe, starting with God and the angels, working through the various conditions of men, and ending with the animals. Although such a doctrine appeared to give religious and even natural sanction to the feudal social order, it was simply not generally available to the peasantry since it was so often couched in an intellectualized form.

Religion is often cited as *the* dominant ideology of the feudal period. However, another example would be the role of theocratic theories of kingship in medieval society. Kingship was legitimated on one of two principles. The popular (ascending) theory suggested that the king was a landlord who, like other landlords, had responsibilities to society and was answerable to the community for the exercise of his privileges. The sacramental (descending) theory stated that the king was above society and responsible to God not men. A dominant ideology of this sort should presumably serve to legitimate kingship to the

---

11. Friedrich Heer, *The Medieval World,* New York, Mentor, 1963, p. 199. For further critical comment, cf. David Martin, *The Religious and the Secular,* London, Routledge & Kegan Paul, 1969, ch. 2.

12. Arthur O. Lovejoy, *The Great Chain of Being,* Cambridge, Mass., 1936.

subordinate class, but in practice the main significance of the debate over the nature of kingship was to establish a relationship between barons and the king. The doctrine of theocratic kingship was utilized to justify the king to his barons, not to the peasantry.

These issues concerning the religiosity of the peasantry and the institutional dominance of the Church bear directly on the problem of secularization. While many sociologists of religion have been committed to the historical myth that the feudal period was an 'age of faith', Martin Goodridge[13] has recently re-examined comprehensively the contemporary evidence on religion among the peasantry in France, Italy and England to show that the peasantry was generally alienated from the orthodox beliefs and institutions of the official Church. While the rural clergy were symbolically influential, they were often an unreliable channel for Christian belief; they were, even in nineteenth-century France, too badly educated to provide sermons.[14] Throughout the medieval period, the Church appears to have experienced great difficulty in ensuring that some of its minimal requirements, such as the Easter communion, were adhered to by the poorer sections of the laity.[15] Our argument here is probably most aptly summarized by the religious sociologist, Gabriel Le Bras:

Catholicism was the ruler's religion. Civil registers were kept by the priests. Basic acts of Christian life were imposed by canon law. Orthodoxy was strictly enforced to discourage heresy and schism. Christianity came to be the religion of the French by virtue of the monarchical constitution.[16]

Official Christianity appears to have been relatively unsuccessful in securing the rural peasantry within the precise confines of orthodox belief and practice.

A similar kind of argument applies to early capitalist societies. Again the conventional view is that there was a dominant ideology which infected the working class. It is suggested, for example, that individualism, especially as expressed in the doctrines of the British utilitarians, was the key component of the dominant ideology of the bourgeoisie and penetrated all features of bourgeois political economy, morality and religion. Bourgeois political economy *(laissez faire,* the night-watchman state, the individual conscience) is usually regarded as the dominant ideology of a social class which was economically and

---

13. Martin Goodridge, 'The ages of faith: romance or reality?', *The Sociological Review,* vol. 23, 1975, pp. 381–96.

14. C. Marcilhacy, *Le diocèse d'Orléans au milieu du XIXème siècle,* Paris, Sirey 1964. For a general criticism of the myth of pre-industrial religiosity, cf. David Martin, *The Religious and the Secular: studies in secularization,* London, Routledge & Kegan Paul, 1969.

15. On the enforcement of confession, cf. Bryan S. Turner, 'Confession and social structure', *The Annual Review of the Social Sciences of Religion,* vol. 1, 1977, pp. 29–58. The low level of institutional commitment and participation in fifteenth-century Flanders is discussed in Jacques Toussaert, *Le sentiment religieux en Flandre à la fin du Moyen-Age,* Paris, 1963. In a later period, the general features of religious adherence in Britain are analysed by Keith Thomas, *Religion and the Decline of Magic,* London, 1971. The significance of the research of Toussaert and Thomas for the study of secularization is considered in David Martin, 'The secularization question', *Theology,* vol. 76, 1973, pp. 81–7. Further evidence on lay/clerical differences can be found in Renè Luneau, 'Monde rural et Christianisation: prêtrex et paysans français du siècle dernier', *Archives Sciences Sociales des Religions,* vol. 43, 1977, pp. 39–52.

16. Gabriel Le Bras, 'Déchristianisation: mot fallacieux', *Social Compass,* vol. 10, 1963, pp. 445–52 and quoted in Goodridge, op. cit., p. 385.

politically triumphant after 1850.[17] There are a number of problems with this interpretation. The syndrome of beliefs associated with individualism has a very ancient ancestry and this makes it difficult to connect individualism in any specific way with *modern* bourgeois capitalism. For example, Goldmann's *The Philosophy of the Enlightenment*[18] connects the beliefs concerned with contract, individualism, free will, universalism and equality with the rise of commercial markets as early as the thirteenth century. Similarly, Chenu[19] traces the rise of the individual, subjective conscience and the transformation of morality from objective laws to subjective intention from the growth of urban markets in the thirteenth century. In Britain, clear indications of 'bourgeois culture' (individualism, conscience, rights, contract) can plainly be found in the seventeenth century. The implication of these analyses of the early origins of 'bourgeois culture' is that the so-called dominant ideology of early capitalism was in fact the ideology, not of a dominant class, but of an ascendant class. The doctrines of the autonomous, subjective individual were used by the commercial, ascending bourgeoisie to criticize and challenge the ideological *status quo*. Further, this oppositional and pristine individualism becomes very much altered as the capitalist mode of production becomes established. This development can be most clearly seen in the evolution of British utilitarianism. Bentham's studies of the British legal system were an attack on conventional jurisprudence which he regarded as serving the interests of the landed aristocracy rather than the bourgeoisie. Benthamite philosophy was an attack on the 'sinister interests' which prevailed in parliament (that is, the over-representation of aristocratic families). By contrast, the later philosophy of J. S. Mill had much more conservative implications. Mill, frightened by the prospect of an uneducated working class controlling parliament and influenced by de Toqueville's study of American democracy, wrote to defend parliamentary institutions for the benefit of the middle class which was being undermined by a proletarian mass.[20] Towards the end of classical utilitarian individualism, Spencer attempted to provide an evolutionist defence of the individual against state intervention in a period when the state was becoming increasingly important for British capitalism (in education, sanitation, town planning, economic protection, overseas expansion). Even if we did assume that individualism was the dominant ideology of capitalism, it would be difficult to show that the working class in British capitalism actually adhered to these beliefs. At best, it might be possible to show that the labour aristocracy was utilitarian and that as the labour aristocracy became increasingly

---

17. Cf. Perry Anderson 'Origins of the present crisis', *New Left Review*, vol. 23, January/February, 1964, pp. 26–53.

18. Lucien Goldmann, *The Philosophy of the Enlightenment*, London, Routledge & Kegan Paul, 1973, pp. 18 ff.

19. M. D. Chenu, *L'éveil de la conscience dans la civilisation médiévale*, Paris, 1969. Further research into this area is presented in Thomas N. Tentler, 'The Summa for confessors as an instrument of social control', in Charles Trinkaus and Heiko A. Oberman (eds), *The Pursuit of Holiness in Late Medieval and Renaissance Religion*, Leiden, E. J. Brill, 1974 and Barbara H. Rosenwein and Lester K. Little, 'Social Meaning in the Monastic and Mendicant Spiritualities', *Past and Present*, no. 63, May 1974, pp. 4–32.

20. Cf. Sheldon S. Wolin, *Politics and Vision*, London, George Allen and Unwin, 1961, ch. 9; J. H. Burns, 'J. S. Mill and Democracy 1829–61', *Political Studies*, 5, 1957, reprinted in J. B. Schneewind (ed.) *Mill*, London, Macmillan, 1969, pp. 280–328.

influential in the leadership of the trade unions after the 1880s, working class beliefs were 'contaminated' by the dominant ideology.

There are, of course, a number of other candidates for the role of 'the dominant ideology' in early capitalism. One such is Methodism. Thompson has argued that

Methodism obtained its greatest success in serving *simultaneously* as the religion of the industrial bourgeoisie . . . and of wide sections of the proletariat.[21]

In the debate over Methodism from Halévy to Simmel, Thompson's argument does, of course, have some support, but the strength of his position is weakened when one considers that, after the great boom in Methodism (in terms of membership/population ratios) between 1800 and 1850, all branches of Methodism never amounted to more than 3½ per cent of the total population.[22] Radical working-class Methodists tended to leave their predominantly petty bourgeois chapels because of the 'no politics rule' which successfully divorced religion from political struggle.[23] The problem of any argument which would regard religion in general as an aspect of the dominant ideology of capitalism is that the working class was largely 'unchurched' by 1851.[24] It is difficult to see how the churches could efficiently and effectively dispense the 'opium of the masses' when the working class were absent from the churches.

The counter-argument would be that, while the *organized* churches had failed to secure the allegiance of the working class to the dominant ideology, the working class were still dominated by 'Victorian morality' and religion through other, sometimes unofficial, means. The dominant Victorian moral norms of respectability, sexual puritanism, aspiration and asceticism were in fact the norms of the working class. Unfortunately, this secondary argument is also totally unconvincing. Engels' view that the two classes of Victorian Britain were two races apart with different religions, moralities and politics is much closer to the mark. Primary and secondary evidence all point to the fact that, in terms of religion and morality, the working class and the capitalist class occupied separate cultures.[25] It is worth recalling that Weber's extensive research in the comparative sociology of religion led him to the view that the modern working class is 'characterized by indifference to or rejection of religion' because in capitalist conditions

21. E. P. Thompson, *The Making of the English Working Class*, Harmondsworth, Penguin, 1968, p. 391.

22. For an overview of the Halévy thesis, cf. Michael Hill, *A Sociology of Religion*, London, Heinemann, 1973, ch. 9. The national statistics of Methodist development are examined in Robert Currie, *Methodism Divided*, London, Faber and Faber, 1968, ch. 3.

23. On the political characteristics of Methodist chapels, cf. John Kent, *The Age of Disunity*, London, Epworth, 1966. The classical rejection of the thesis that Methodism played a crucial role in protecting England from revolution is presented in E. J. Hobsbawm, 'Methodism and the Threat of Revolution in Britain', in *Labouring Men*, London, Weidenfeld and Nicolson, 1972, ch. 2.

24. H. Mann, *Census of Great Britain 1851, Religious Worship in England and Wales*, London, Routledge, 1854. The major documents on religion and the working class are edited in Edward Royle, *Radical Politics 1790–1900*, 'Religion and Unbelief', London, Longman, 1971.

25. A. MacIntyre, *Secularization and Moral Change*, London, O.U.P., 1976. Ronald Pearsall, *The Worm in the Bud*, London, Weidenfeld and Nicolson, 1969; Kellow Chesney, *The Victorian Underworld*, London, Pelican, 1972.

the sense of dependence on one's own achievements is supplanted by a consciousness of dependence on purely social factors, market conditions, and power relationships guaranteed by law . . . the rationalism of the proletariat, like that of the bourgeoisie of developed capitalism . . . cannot in the nature of the case easily possess a religious character and certainly cannot easily generate a religion.[26]

Attempts by English capitalists like William Ibbotson, the owner of a Sheffield steel works, to use Christianity to discipline factory workers were, as a consequence, repeatedly unsuccessful.[27]

So far we have argued that in feudalism and early capitalism, there is little convincing evidence to suggest that the subordinate classes accepted the dominant ideology. In late capitalism the position is more complicated. Thus, it is often argued that there is a dominant ideology which is a major factor in inhibiting the development of a revolutionary consciousness in the working class. Miliband, for example, draws on Gramsci's concept of hegemony to suggest that there is, in Western capitalist societies, 'a process of massive indoctrination'.[28] This is achieved as 'the result of a permanent and pervasive effort, conducted through a multitude of agencies' and specifically by the effort of members of the dominant classes who 'are able, by virtue of their position, for instance as employers, to dissuade members of the subordinate classes, if not from holding, at least from voicing unorthodox views'.[29] However, most contemporary sociological research rejects the 'dominant ideology' view in favour of an account of British working class culture which stresses its dualistic character. There has recently been a great deal of work on this issue and, although there are clearly differences of emphasis between various authors, the overall conclusion is that working class consciousness is characterized by a fluctuating relationship between 'dominant' and 'subordinate' conceptions. For example, Hill in a recent study of dockworkers[30] concluded that workers would adopt more 'militant' postures in concrete situations, like the issue of trade unionism at the workplace, than they would towards more abstract questions, like the significance of trade union power at the national level. Again, Mann concludes that 'at every turn we have been confronted by a profound dualism in the worker's situation and his consciousness. . . . Surges of class consciousness are continually undercut by economism and capitalism survives'.[31] Parkin sees the normative order as being made up of three competing meaning systems—a dominant value system, a subordinate value system which promotes accommodative responses to inequality, and a radical value system which promotes opposition. Thus, in 'most Western societies all three meaning-systems tend to

26. Max Weber, *Economy and Society*, Totowa, Bedminster Press, 1968, p. 486.

27. E. R. Wickham, *Church and People in an Industrial City*, London, Lutterworth Press, 1957, p. 106.

28. R. Miliband, *The State in Capitalist Society*, London, Weidenfeld and Nicolson, 1969, p. 182.

29. Ibid., p. 181.

30. Stephen Hill, *The Dockers: Class and Tradition in London*, London, Heinemann, 1976. Further commentary on ideology and inconsistency is presented in Theo Nichols and Peter Armstrong, *Workers Divided*, London, Fontana, 1976.

31. Michael Mann, *Consciousness and Action among the Western Working Class*, London, Macmillan, 1973, p. 68.

influence the social and political perceptions of the sub-ordinate class'[32] al-though it is still the case that different groups will have differential access to each of the three. Other writers[33] suggest that two forms of consciousness, the dominant ideology and a form of oppositional belief, coexist in the working class and are in tension with one another. Each system of belief comes to the surface at different times. The latter is mobilized in periods of conflict, particularly in strikes, while the former is adopted as a set of beliefs appropriate to more peaceable times. In sum, we suggest that, at least, the literature demonstrates the minimum conclusion necessary for our argument, namely that subordinate classes in contemporary capitalism do not *straightforwardly* adopt the dominant ideology.

The conclusion that dominant ideologies are not held, or are held in a moderated way, by subordinate classes, clearly conflicts with the conventional 'ruling ideas' model. Further, this model has little to say about the manner in which the dominant classes do or do not hold the dominant ideology. This problem is thought to be of little significance and the only relevant point seems to be that the dominant classes should not be seen as cynically manipulating the dominated classes; they do believe what they say. We wish to argue that just as the dominated classes do *not* hold the dominant ideology, the dominant classes *do*. This implies a redirection of sociological interests, for the chief impact of dominant beliefs is on the dominant not the dominated classes. To use another vocabulary, the prime function of the dominant ideology is towards the dominant class. To some extent we have already made this point in the earlier discussion. The dominant classes have been both the bearers and the recipients of orthodox religiosity, of conventional morality and conformist politics. While the shrift of the peasant was short and infrequent, the confessions of nobles under the guidance of spiritual directors was long and permanent. Attempts to enforce regular confessions on the poor usually drove the laity from the Church.[34] Again the doctrines of individualism and utilitarianism were not formulated or appreciated by the working class; they were abstract theories produced by intellectuals. Even to the extent that individualism moulded religious beliefs, the dominated classes remained relatively untouched. Again the 'true' believers in the personal morality of the Victorian period were the bourgeoisie.

## The Apparatus of Transmission

The effect of our argument so far is to turn the conventional ruling ideas model on its head for we have suggested that, in terms of what people believe, the dominant ideology has a greater impact on the dominant classes than on the

---

32. Frank Parkin, *Class Inequality and Political Order,* London, Paladin, 1972, p. 82.

33. See, for example, R. Blackburn, 'The Unequal Society', in R. Blackburn and A. Cockburn (eds), *The Incompatibles,* Harmondsworth, Penguin Books, 1967.

34. This effect of the confessional was a major aspect of the conflict between Jesuits and Jansenists. A detailed analysis is presented in Theodore Zeldin (ed.), *Conflicts in French Society,* London, George Allen and Unwin, 1970, ch. 1.

dominated. This conclusion is supported by some consideration of the apparatus by which beliefs are created and transmitted. This is an area in which the classical Marxist theory is comparatively weak. In that theory the ruling class has to 'persuade' subordinate classes of the truth and moral relevance of a set of beliefs which are contrary to the interests of the subordinate class. This would seem to imply the existence of an extremely powerful set of agencies which transmit beliefs downwards from the dominant classes and it has often seemed difficult to show that the agencies available are that powerful. We now attempt to argue that the apparatuses of transmission of belief are not very efficient in reaching the subordinate classes, and moreover, are more likely to affect the dominant class. For example, in feudal societies, the Church, in the form of preachers, mendicant monks and priests, constituted the main agent of transmission of the ideological structure. However, the actual practice of the Church was to erect both language and ritual barriers between peasant laity and priesthood. In addition the medieval Church was characterized by massive regional, national and cultural diversities. In these respects the teachings of the Church were likely to be impenetrable to the peasantry but less so to the rather more literate dominant class who in any case would have had close personal contact with the priesthood.[35] In early capitalism, as we have already indicated, the Church was even less open to the subordinate classes, and at this time the apparatus of transmission was probably at its weakest. However, the development of mass education and a system of mass communication do seem to promise a more effective apparatus. Nonetheless it could be argued that the education available to the elite, particularly in the nineteenth and the first half of the twentieth century, is a great deal more intensive and more likely to be formative of a coherent set of beliefs than that provided for the subordinate classes.[36] We conclude that, until fairly recently, the dominant classes were greatly more exposed to the apparatus of ideological distribution than were the subordinate classes and that they still are exposed to at least the same degree. One can suggest that the fact that the apparatus has become potentially more efficient is one of the reasons that subordinate classes in contemporary society have been drawn more closely into the dominant ideology. Therefore, we do not wish to argue that the dominant ideology is *never* believed by the subordinate classes, only that it is more pertinent for the dominant classes. It could be argued that any ideological incorporation is a *secondary* effect of the development of the educational system.

These arguments prompt the suggestion that the dominant ideology does not function to secure compliance from the dominated classes. Indeed it might be said that *compliance* of this kind (or even pragmatic acceptance) is irrelevant as long as there are other mechanisms of coercion. In British feudalism, the struggle for control of the means of production was settled eventually by enclosures,

---

35. For a brief discussion of the levels of literacy of various sectors of society in medieval Europe, cf. J. Curran, 'Mass Communication as a social force in history', being Unit 2 of The Open University 'Mass Communications and Society Course', Milton Keynes, The Open University Press, 1977.

36. John Wakeford, *The Cloistered Elite*, London, Macmillan, 1969. N. Abercrombie, et al., *The University in the Urban Environment*, London, Heinemann Educational Books, 1974.

not religion. The alternative to ideological compliance is, however, not inevitably to resort to force. The conventional Marxist 'ruling ideas' model is, at least covertly, tinged with Weberianism; it rests partly on the assumption that without continuous legitimation social actors will not accept a social system which relies on the frequent employment of naked force. For conventional Marxism, the dominant ideology has the effect of making power appear legitimate in the eyes of the dominated class. While the ruling class may well desire a situation in which subordinate classes accept existing class relations as legitimate or God given, there is a sense in which this form of compliance may be unnecessary. In modes of production where the subordinate classes have been alienated from the means of production (for example, competitive capitalism), the fact that workers have to labour to live will itself constitute a permanent pressure towards their co-optation (Marx's 'the dull compulsion of economic relations'). One illustration of this pressure can be found in the fact that peasant opposition to feudal authority was typically seasonal since, particularly at harvest time, the conditions of everyday life in peasant agriculture systematically inhibited active, sustained opposition.[37] Similarly, banditry was a seasonal occupation of unattached men.[38] In capitalism, the 'coercion of everyday life' is reinforced by the fact that urban workers during economic crises cannot return to self-sufficiency off the land; the same also holds for agricultural wage labourers. In capitalism, especially before unionization, the working class is effectively controlled by everyday exigencies in that capitalists decompose labour by employing migrant, women or child labourers, extend the working day or ensure that necessary labour time is at the bare minimum. We do not of course wish to exaggerate our argument with the claim that the coercion of the workplace or the routine of everyday life is a complete explanation of working class quiescence and that ideology is completely irrelevant. However, we *do* wish to suggest that the importance of ideological compliance is exaggerated and that the real significance of the dominant ideology lies in the organization of the dominant class rather than in the subordination of dominated classes.

### The Ideological Structure of Late Capitalism

In earlier parts of this paper we argued that the working class in late capitalism does not in any straightforward sense adopt the dominant ideology. The best interpretation of working class consciousness is that it is dualistic, involving some accommodation with the dominant ideology. Connected with this feature is the greater efficiency of the apparatus of transmission of dominant beliefs. In sum, our argument that dominant ideology functions for the dominant rather than subordinate class has to be expressed less forcefully for the contemporary phase of capitalism than for either feudalism or competitive capitalism, although the general drift of the argument can still be sustained.

---

37. Cf. Teodor Shanin, 'The peasantry as a political factor', *Sociological Review,* vol. 14, 1966, pp. 5–27; on the conditions of peasant involvement in radical political protest, Eric Wolf, *Peasant Wars of the Twentieth Century,* London, Faber and Faber, 1971.

38. E. J. Hobsbawm, *Bandits,* Harmondsworth, Pelican, 1972.

We now have to re-examine these arguments by considering the ideological structure of monopoly capitalism. This is a large subject, and our comments are necessarily brief and schematic. Again, our main intention is to cast doubt on the conventional interpretation.

Sociological interpretations of the ideological structure of late capitalism are notable for their lack of specificity, but, more importantly, for their bewildering variety. The reader is offered an enormous range of characterizations of belief ranging from the advocacy of the rights of private property to doctrines of utilitarianism. We will argue in the last section of this paper that many of these characterizations are anachronistic in the sense that they are more appropriate to early capitalist societies. However, the diversity of dominant ideologies on offer may indicate more than a simple failure to agree since it may suggest that there are good grounds for supposing that there is no strongly marked dominant ideology in modern capitalist societies. Whereas moral beliefs played an important function in the ideology of early capitalism, the moral region of ideology is more or less irrelevant in late capitalism for supporting the economic and political place of the dominant class. More precisely we would like to argue that there is only a very weakly defined dominant ideology and there is considerable 'pluralization of life-worlds'.[39] The net effect is that there is a lesser degree of ideological coherence in late capitalist societies than in the others that we have discussed. That there are paradoxes in this position will be plain, since it involves taking seriously the conclusions, though not the reasoning, of two arguments often thought to be discredited, namely the 'End of Ideology' thesis, and the view that the diversity of opinion and belief in the modern world is sociologically significant.

In the 1950s political sociology claimed that advanced capitalism was characterized by the end of ideology.[40] The liberal ideologies of the West had solved the major institutional problems of political participation with the result that the ideologies of the Left, which presupposed class conflict, were now irrelevant. A typical response to this thesis was to provide evidence of continuing class struggle, social inequality and ideological confrontation. Thus, Miliband in *The State in Capitalist Society* pointed to the crucial role of legitimating institutions (family, church, school, mass media) in maintaining and justifying the capitalist system of class inequality. More recently, Westergaard and Resler have argued that the ideology of private property, individualism and achievement is closely connected with continued existence of social inequalities. The oddity of this reply to the end of ideology thesis is that it regards the supposed dominant ideology of early capitalism (such as *laissez-faire* liberalism) to be also the dominant ideology of *late* capitalism. This type of theoretical response consequently ignores major changes in the institutional forms of capitalism (such as changes in forms of ownership, control and possession) and changes in the nature of the capitalist class. In fact, the ideology of owners of small capitalist firms in the

---

39. On the concept of 'life-world', cf. Alfred Schutz and Thomas Luckmann, *The Structures of the Life-World,* London, Heinemann, 1974.

40. For a discussion of the end of ideology thesis in the works of Edward Shils, Seymour Martin Lipset and Daniel Bell, cf. Alasdair MacIntyre, *Against the Self-Images of the Age,* London, Duckworth, 1971, ch. 1.

private sector is frequently in opposition to the beliefs and interests of large capitalist enterprises, multinational firms and the state industries. These conflicts between different sectors of capital find part of their ideological expression in Britain in policy struggles within the Conservative Party between different groups who represent conflicting interests within capital. Since early and late capitalism in Britain are still based on a form of socio-economic organization where profit is privately appropriated, it is to be expected that beliefs and institutions connected with the support of private property would continue to play an important part in the ideological system of capitalism, but it is difficult to claim that this feature of the ideology of capitalism is dominant.

The end of ideology thesis focused on the issue of whether the subordinate classes were no longer committed to radical alternative politics. We would suggest a reinterpretation of this issue by looking at the commitment of the dominant class to various ideologies. It could be claimed that the dominant class was characterized by an end of ideology in the 1950s and early 1960s in Britain in the limited sense that the various components of the dominant class converged on a common political platform, namely the 'welfare consensus'.[41] For example, in the post-war era there was at least minimal agreement over the mixed economy, industrial efficiency, the importance of welfare provision, the need for formal equality of opportunity in education and so on. Identification with this form of consensual politics represented a balance between the interests of various sections of society, although its net effect was to favour the interests of one particular fraction of capital. The so-called 'dominant ideology' of late capitalism is thus at best an uneven and uneasy amalgam of assumptions about private property and about the importance of state intervention in economic life.

Our reinterpretation of the end of ideology thesis involves the claim that there is no decisive, clearly articulated and uniform set of beliefs which provides comprehensive coherence for the dominant class. Another manner of expressing this position would be to suggest that there has been a proliferation or pluralization of beliefs, world-views and ideologies, an argument very familiar to sociologists.[42] We would argue that the proliferation of world-views, though confined mostly to the moral sphere, is significant. One index of the end of a central ideology in the region of morality is the development of certain doctrines in moral philosophy where it is no longer possible to specify in any coherent, authoritative fashion what will count as 'duty' or 'responsibility'. The changes in moral philosophy from Moore to Ayer presents an ethical map of the transitions within the capitalist mode of production.[43] Of course, the fact that pluralism and secularization appear to attend the differentiation and specialization of

---

41. Andrew Gamble, *The Conservative Nation,* London, Routledge & Kegan Paul, 1974.

42. On the general issue of pluralism and plausibility of beliefs, cf. Berger and Luckmann, op. cit. The proliferation of religious views is discussed in Bryan Wilson, *Contemporary Transformations of Religion,* London, OUP, 1976. Further consideration of the notion of 'pluralism' is to be found in M. Haug, 'Social and Cultural pluralism as a concept in social system analysis', *American Journal of Sociology,* vol. 73, 1967, pp. 294–304.

43. These fundamental transitions in moral philosophy are discussed within a sociological framework by Alisdair MacIntyre, *A Short History of Ethics,* London, Routledge & Kegan Paul, 1967, ch. 18 and in Ernest Gellner *Words and Things,* Harmondsworth, Penguin, 1968.

social systems has been specifically commented on by sociologists. For example, Berger and Luckmann claim that in a pluralistic society there exists

a shared core universe taken for granted as such, and different partial universes coexisting in a state of mutual accommodation . . . outright conflict between ideologies has been replaced by varying degrees of tolerance or even cooperation.[44]

## An Alternative Explanation?

In the earlier parts of this paper we have argued, as against the conventional 'ruling-ideas model', that (1) subordinate classes in general do not hold the dominant ideology (2) ruling classes generally do hold it (3) consideration of the apparatus of transmission of belief lends plausibility to (1) and (2), and (4) in modern capitalism there is not such a well-defined dominant ideology. Completeness would require a well constructed alternative theory of the dominant ideology which would account for these phenomena. We do not attempt such a theory. Rather we offer some comments which might form its outline, an outline which is still consistent with Marx's other postulates.

We suggest that the dominant ideology is best seen as securing the coherence of the dominant class. This is clearly not an argument about the requirements of a mode of production at a general, abstract level as is provided, for example, by Hindess and Hirst.[45] In fact we believe that it is impossible to produce a concept of ideology as a requirement at the level of mode of production, and that there are in any case important difficulties associated with the distinction between pure modes of production and concrete social formations.[46] It could be argued, therefore, that our discussion is pitched at an intermediate level in the sense that it makes claims about the necessary requirements of capitalism as that mode of production developed in a particular *kind* of society.

In feudalism and early capitalism, the conservation of private property—its inheritance, distribution, accumulation and investment—was of crucial significance for the continuity and reproduction of relations of production. In concrete terms, secure channels for the conservation and accumulation of property were necessary conditions of existence for the maintenance and expansion of the feudal manor and the family firm. Re-formulating Marx, we might express this significance by saying that, from this requirement of property, there arose a superstructure of political, legal and moral beliefs which grasped at the level of ideas, this functional requirement. Private property in land and capital required a relatively stable marriage system, clear laws of inheritance, principles of legitimacy, adoption and re-marriage. The dominant ideology provided this complex of legal, moral and religious values which have the function of conserving property. In addition, the dominant ideology provided a psychology of

---

44. Berger and Luckmann, op. cit., p. 142.

45. Barry Hindess and Paul Q. Hirst, *Pre-Capitalist Modes of Production,* London, Routledge & Kegan Paul, 1975, pp. 1–20.

46. Some features of the epistemological problems relating to the notion of concrete social formations and theory in sociology and Marxism are discussed in Bryan S. Turner, 'The structuralist critique of Weber's sociology', *British Journal of Sociology,* vol. 28, 1977, pp. 1–15.

guilt which inhibited illicit sexuality, disregard of parents' wishes for suitable mates, respect for the (economic) needs of the family. In short, the dominant ideology was aimed at preventing 'marrying out'—an act which threatens the continuity and concentration of family wealth. In feudalism, it was Catholicism, on the one hand, and the system of honour, on the other, which provided the ideological mechanisms for insuring the loyalty of sons and daughters to family property. The confessional system of family spiritual directors was ideally suited to achieving this aim since it provided constant supervision of orthodox (conformist) patterns of sexuality, duty and marriage. The dominant ideology was only in a very secondary fashion concerned with the sexual life of peasants and workers. The stability of peasant families was of little interest to landlords concerned with the selection of suitable mates and dowries for their sons, the constancy of their spouses and the good behaviour and honour of daughters. One might say that feudal lords were as worried by romantic love as they were by the prospect of peasant rebellions.

The religious and moral core of the dominant ideology thus attempted to guarantee the family as a mechanism for the conservation of property; it functioned to provide a degree of normative coherence in the dominant class. Other aspects—legal and political—were also significant in providing this coherence. The dominant ideology had to minimize the possibility of fractions within the dominant class which would challenge its coherence. The long struggle in medieval societies over the theocratic and feudal character of the king represented such an attempt to establish a common basis between barons and the king. The dominant ideology was a cultural mechanism which had the role of protecting the dominant class from the threats of intra-and inter-class struggles. It effectively unified the dominant class by imposing a code of morality upon it, by ensuring that members of the class more or less believed the same thing. These dominant moralities in feudalism and early capitalism were also markedly inegalitarian, a feature whose effect was to separate the dominant class (in its own eyes) from other classes. In feudalism, honour was a personal status inherited by noble birth which eliminated the peasantry from the circle of cultural value. In early capitalism, the ethic of achievement served to define the wealthy as the religiously saved. While most commentaries by conventional Marxism on the dominant ideology of competitive capitalism have focused on political ideology (such as individual political rights), morality was probably more significant for the system.[47] Furthermore, the accumulation of capital in early capitalism in Britain was heavily dependent on privately generated investment funds, an additional indication of the importance of the coherence of the property owning class.

The existence of a dominant moral ideology does not, of course, imply that it will be uniformly imposed on the dominant class without opposition from certain strata or fractions within that dominant class. The tradition of Courtly Love, for example, was at one level an obvious threat to the moral code of the noble family. However, the main themes of Courtly Love poetry (humility,

---

47. For a recent discussion of the relationship between the family and capitalist relations of production, cf. E. Zaretsky, *Capitalism, The Family, and Personal Life,* London, Pluto Press, 1976.

courtesy, adultery and romantic sexuality), recognized that, since marriage was in fact a contract for the security of property, romantic love could only exist outside marriage. Courtly Love, while appearing to be a form of deviance within the dominant feudal class, in fact gave explicit recognition to the contractual significance of marriage for property. This tradition of poetry also recognized that romantic love was necessarily ephemeral and insignificant when contrasted with the sacred values for which the Church stood.[48] Romantic poetry gave expression to a form of aristocratic truancy rather than open rebellion. Similarly, the existence of systematic prostitution in Victorian London gave tacit support to the idea that marriage was a contract rather than a romantic/sexual relationship.

Our argument is that 'Victorian morality' with its emphasis on sexual control, paternal authority and family loyalty was important for the control of family property. We are, of course, aware of contemporary reappraisals of the traditional view that all Victorians were sexually inhibited. It is in fact quite clear that there were many 'Other Victorians' with secret lives involving pornography, prostitution, homosexuality and perversion. Our argument for the economic role of Victorian moral beliefs does not require that there should be no deviance within the dominant classes or their middle class agents. The notion that marriage was a contract rather than a sexual union carried with it the implication that sexual entertainments had to be sought outside the home. Two comments on *My Secret Life*–a book representative of Victorian pornography—are important in this connection.[49] Firstly, the existence of organized prostitution was very much an 'open secret' especially in London and the large seaports. Secondly, this sexual autobiography is in many respects an anthropological exploration of the sordid underworld associated with certain working class occupations. It serves to demonstrate the gulf which separated the working and upper classes in terms of moral expectations in Victorian England. The deviance of a number of eminent Victorians and the availability of organized prostitution and commercialized pornography thus provide paradoxical support for the view that there was widespread commitment in the dominant class for preserving marriage as a viable economic contract. On the basis of his comprehensive study of Victorian sexuality, Pearsall comes to the conclusion that the exotic pornographic interests of Victorians like Richard Burton, Frederick Hankey and Henry Ashbee were the product of a society which was based on a

conspicuous to keep sex where it belonged—in silence and between sheets. . . . There was hardly room at all for prosaic sex; where sex was mentioned it was in nutty, esoteric, exotic . . . ultra-romantic contexts.[50]

---

48. The complex secular and religious dimensions of Courtly Love poetry are discussed in C. S. Lewis, *The Allegory of Love,* London, OUP, 1938, ch. 1 Further commentaries on this problem are presented in Edward Wagenknect (ed.), *Chaucer: Modern Essays in Criticism,* New York, Galaxy Books, 1959.

49. For a discussion of *My Secret Life* and other aspects of Victorian pornography, cf. Steven Marcus, *The Other Victorians,* London, Weidenfeld and Nicolson, 1966.

50. Pearsall, op. cit., p. 507.

The peculiarities of Victorian pornography and sexual deviance points, there-fore, to the coherence of 'family morality' as the dominant moral code of the Victorian capitalist class.

By contrast the coherence of the dominant class in late capitalism is *relatively* unimportant since the economic functioning of this form is not dependent on the existence of a dominant class which retains capital within the family struc-ture. For example, monopoly firms (especially multinational corporations) are not family firms, they are not privately owned, and they do not generally depend on inherited or family capital for finance. Instead they have recourse to financial institutions (banks, the state, pension funds, stock market). This indi-cates the real significance of the divorce between ownership and control. It is not that the divorce weakens the concept of a dominant class; rather it is that this class no longer represents the private ownership and control of capital. The implication of this argument is that, as compared with early capitalism, there is *relatively* less need for a dominant ideology in monopoly capitalism.

Finally, we should add two points of clarification. Firstly, one should not exaggerate the difference between forms or stages of capitalism. For example, we have distinguished between early and late capitalism. However these are still forms of *capitalism* and we suggest that associated with any form of capitalism there must be certain doctrines or beliefs, in particular those stressing the rights of private property. Thus in late capitalism there is still a residue of such beliefs though a dominant ideology greatly more extensive than this is not present. Secondly, we do not deny the existence of a propertied class in late capitalism. We suggest that this is rather an effect of the continued private appropriation of profit rather than one of its conditions of existence.

# Selective Further Reading

Abercrombie, N., et al., *The Dominant Ideology Thesis* (London: Allen & Unwin, 1980).

Adorno, Theodor, 'Culture Industry Reconsidered', *New German Critique* 6 (Fall 1975).

Barthes, R., *Mythologies* (London: Cape, 1972).

Bell, Daniel, *The Cultural Contradictions of Capitalism* (London: Heinemann, 1976).

Bernstein, B., 'Social Class and Linguistic Development: A Theory of Social Learning', in *Education, Economy and Society,* ed. A. H. Halsey et al. (Glencoe, Ill.: Free Press, 1961).

Birnbaum, Norman, 'The Sociological Study of Ideology (1940–1960)', *Current Sociology* 9 (1960).

Bisseret, N., *Education, Class Language, and Ideology* (London: Routledge & Kegan Paul, 1979).

Bulmer, M., ed., *Working Class Images of Society* (London: Routledge, 1975).

Centre for Contemporary Cultural Studies, *On Ideology* (London: Hutchinson, 1978).

Clark, John, et al., eds., *Working Class Culture* (London: Hutchinson, 1979).

Foucault, Michel, *Power/Knowledge* (New York: Pantheon, 1980).

Gallie, Duncan, *In Search of the New Working Class* (Cambridge: Cambridge University Press, 1978).

Giddens, Anthony, *Central Problems in Social Theory* (Berkeley: University of California Press, 1979).

Goldthorpe, J. H., D. Lockwood, F. Beckhofer and S. Platt *The Affluent Worker* (Cambridge: Cambridge University Press, 1968), 3 vols.

Habermas, Jürgen, 'Science and Technology as Ideology', in *Towards a Rational Society* (Boston: Beacon, 1970).

———, *Legitimation Crisis* (Boston: Beacon, 1975).

Hamilton, R., *Class and Politics in the United States* (New York, 1972).

Held, David, 'Crisis Tendencies, Legitimation, and the State', in *Habermas: Critical Debates,* ed. J. Thompson and D. Held (Cambridge, Mass.: M.I.T. Press, 1982).

Horkheimer, Max, and Theodor Adorno, *Dialectic of Enlightenment* (New York: Herder & Herder, 1972).

Huaco, George A., 'On Ideology', *Acta Sociologica* 14 (1971).

Hunt, Pauline, *Gender and Class Consciousness* (London: Macmillan, 1980).

Larrain, Jorge, *The Concept of Ideology,* (London: Hutchinson, 1979).

Leiss, William, *The Domination of Nature* (Boston: Beacon, 1974).

Lipset, S. M., *Political Man* (London, 1963).

Lukács, George, *History and Class Consciousness* (Cambridge, Mass.: M.I.T. Press, 1971).

MacIntyre, Alasdair, *Against the Self-Images of the Age* (London: Duckworth, 1971).

Mann, Michael, *Consciousness and Action Among the Western Working Class* (London: Macmillan, 1973).

Marcuse, Herbert, *One-Dimensional Man* (Boston: Beacon, 1964).

Martin, David E., and David Rubinstein, eds., *Ideology and the Labour Movement* (London: Croom Helm, 1979).

Newby, Howard, *The Deferential Worker* (Harmondsworth: Penguin, 1979).

Parkin, Frank, 'Working Class Conservatives', *British Journal of Sociology* 18(3) (1967).

Waxman, Chaim I., *The End of Ideology Debate* (New York: Funk and Wagnall, 1968).

Willis, Paul, *Learning to Labour* (Westmead: Saxon House, 1977).

Zaretsky, Eli, *Capitalism, the Family, and Personal Life* (London: Pluto, 1976).

# ·VI·
# Capitalism, Gender, and Patriarchy

# Introduction

The attentive reader may have noticed that in many of the preceding articles reprinted in this book, however radical the pretensions of some of the authors, the pronoun 'he' is habitually used as a generic indicator for both sexes. Whether or not this is important in itself, it is symptomatic of the fact that most class theory and analysis has been centred upon males; and it has rarely been closely associated with the study of the family. Marx wrote virtually nothing about possible intersections between class exploitation and the exploitation of women. Engels did attempt such a task however, in *The Origins of the Family, Private Property, and the State*. In this book he tried essentially to tie the origins of sexual domination to the emergence of private property, which in turn was regarded as the condition of the development of the state. The earliest forms of society, according to Engels, were matriarchal: women were more powerful than men. But this relation between the sexes became reversed with the formation of private property. Although Engels's view of how this process occurred is not especially clear, it was supposedly associated directly with the advent of private property (and therefore class) since men assumed supremacy to protect inheritance. Accordingly, sexual exploitation in Engels's analysis is explained as an offshoot of class exploitation. Engels was not reluctant to draw the implications of this standpoint either: with the transcendence of capitalism, and thus of class divisions, sexual exploitation will also disappear. The development of capitalism, he believed, paves the way for the overcoming of sexual exploitation because the main form of deprivation to which women are subject in capitalist society is exclusion from equal participation in the labour force. In a socialist society, such equality of participation will be the basis of achieving equality in other spheres.

Although opinion is somewhat divided on the matter, most are agreed that there is little in Engels's account that can be defended today. The sources which Engels drew upon for evidence of the existence of a matriarchal stage of society have been substantially discredited. Contemporary anthropology seems to have been unable to come up with a single authenticated instance of a society in which women are dominant over men although there are considerable variations in relations of power between the sexes in different societies. The connection Engels drew between private property and male domination also appears invalid; no direct relation of this kind seems to exist. Finally, Engels's proposals for the emancipation of women are of limited interest today, to say the least.

For these reasons, the classical Marxist texts do not have a great deal to offer directly to those who would wish to relate class analysis more systematically to gender and to the family. In recent years, there has developed a fiercely argued debate about how far Marxist ideas can be modified so as to help illuminate the origins of patriarchy (male domination). Some authors believe that Marxism should have analytical and political preeminence over feminism, that is, that Marxism *can* be developed so as to yield plausible explanations of the origin and nature of patriarchy. Others hold that feminism has priority over Marxism: Marx's class theory, they say, simply is not an adequate vehicle for either understanding patriarchy or for developing practical programmes of social change that would alter existing imbalances of power between the sexes.

Since these problems have now become the focus of lively discussion, it is not surprising to find a burgeoning of literature concerned with exploring the interlacing of class and gender divisions. Elizabeth Garnsey offers a general survey of the issue, concentrating her attention upon a critique of existing approaches to class analysis in respect of the industrialised countries but seeking at the same time to make some positive suggestions about how some of their shortcomings might be remedied. She argues that examining the effects of inequalities in the sexual division of labour on the class system entails revising in a fundamental way some of the established concerns of class theory.

Established approaches to class analysis, according to Garnsey, have taken one of two views upon the relevance of sexual exploitation or inequality to class systems. One standpoint simply asserts that sexual inequality is of no direct interest for the analysis of class systems because it derives from quite different factors—the opposite view, as it were, to that expressed by Engels. A second standpoint accepts that inequalities between the sexes may strongly influence class relationships but holds that class theory cannot explain the existence of these inequalities. Those authors taking the second standpoint have the virtue of recognising that the labour force is sexually heterogeneous and that the effects of this heterogeneity upon class structure must be studied. But most such writers still see the impact of women's work as of secondary importance in the structuration of class systems.

Neither viewpoint is satisfactory, in Garnsey's view, but before attempting to suggest how a superior mode of analysis might be developed, she offers a concise documentation of some of the major imbalances in the distribution of males and females in the labour force. One argument that has frequently been used to support both positions referred to above is that the family, not the individual, is the proper unit for class analysis. This depends upon the assumption that the class position of families is above all determined by the occupational position of the male head of the household. Garnsey produces various arguments to rebut such an assumption. In capitalist societies, most families are not engaged in production as a unit but as individual wage earners or employers. A high proportion of household units are made up of single adults, of one-parent families, or of families where the adult male is unemployed or retired. Moreover, the assumption indicated above does not allow for analysis of the contribution of women's work, inside the household as domestic labour and outside the household as paid wage labour, to the resources of the family. Surveying the existing literature, Garnsey says that it is simply not justifiable to write as though the activities and attitudes of women are just a pale reflection of those of the males in families. The relation between the sexes is conditioned by the division of labour in the family itself and by a variety of connections between the 'internal' division of labour and the broader economic system.

Garnsey concludes by identifying two arenas in which these connections should be studied. One is the labour market, in respect of which she draws upon theories of segmented labour markets such as have been referred to in Section Four above. Women tend to cluster in secondary sectors of labour markets. The reasons for this no doubt include direct male prejudices against women workers but derive also from a range of other factors that restrict female participation in the labour force. The involvement of women in unpaid domestic labour, caring for the house, and child-rearing loom large in such factors and is the second area of analysis which Garnsey discusses. Domestic labour, she says, may not be 'productive labour' in the Marxist sense (although this is an issue which has been much debated) but it is still 'socially necessary labour' which acts as a major prop to capitalistic class systems—and to persisting inequalities in Eastern European societies also.

Heidi Hartmann's article elaborates upon similar issues but places the problem of the sexual division of labour in a broader anthropological perspective. Patriarchy, she accepts, certainly does not originate with capitalism, but the emergence of capitalist production systematically alters preexisting patterns of sexual exploitation. The process of expropriation of workers from control of their means of production in the early development of capitalism, Hartmann argues, had more disastrous effects upon women than upon men. This can be grasped if we examine the work of women in the sixteenth and seventeenth centuries in England. In agrarian production during this period, the men normally worked in the fields while women looked after small vegetable gardens or orchards, tended livestock, and also spun and wove cloth. A proportion of their products was usually sold in local markets, and in this way women contributed in a significant fashion to the household economy, although family structure was strongly patriarchal. As smaller farmers were displaced by enlarged farming estates, a certain proportion of men were able to stay on as agricultural wage labourers; but women experienced relatively higher unemployment.

With the growth of domestic industries organised under the putting-out system, women recovered a significant role in production, on the basis of utilising traditional skills, especially in the production of textiles. But the levels of payment were normally very low for female labour. With the spread of the factory, women (and children) were frequently forced into noxious conditions, which male workers resisted for a longer period. It has been suggested, Hartmann notes, that employers regarded woman as more docile and less independent than the more recalcitrant male labour force; and perhaps, given their general subordination in the family, their presumption was correct. Women also seem from the early years of industrial capitalism to have been less well organised collectively than men; and men used the labour unions in some part deliberately to further undermine the position of women in the labour market. The capacity of men to organise in order to attain a degree of power vis-à-vis employers was thus reinforced by the habit of command within the family, as well as by the superior privileges men held in the state.

The development of capitalist industry, therefore, served to intensify the subordination of women by increasing male dominance of the economic and political spheres, now separated from the 'home'. Even though, among manual workers, a high proportion of women continued to participate in the labour force—and their families required their income to survive even at a modest level—women as a whole became more dependent economically upon men. The pattern of development in the United States was rather different from that in England. There seems early on to have been a more inflexible division of labour in the colonial farming families, with women confined to domestic manufacture. However labour shortages at a later period seem to have opened to women a wider range of job opportunities than were available on the other side of the Atlantic. Unions, however, frequently restricted female membership and actively tried to promote the exclusion of women from large sectors of the labour market. In some degree, this was stimulated by benevolent motives— preventing women from having to do physically exhausting jobs in industry— and in some degree by the belief that 'the woman's place is in the home'. But the role of employers in all this was also of course important; here Hartmann's analysis looks again to the conception of segmented labour markets.

Jane Humphries's work provides further material on the connections between capitalism and the working-class family. The writings of Marx and Engels, she claims, do not explain why the family persists through the development and maturity of capitalism. She refers to a much-quoted paragraph in Marx's relatively early writings, in which he states that among the capitalist class the family only survives as a mechanism for the transmission of property whereas among the working class the family has already substantially ceased to exist. Marx can take such a view only because the family is regarded as a property relation, as 'reducible' to private property. Such was effectively the basis of the views elaborated in Engels's *Origins of the Family, Private Property, and the State*. The existence of the family and of the sexual division of labour is not seen to pose any problems of analysis that cannot be handled through the theory of class relations. Hence the family becomes 'invisible' in Marx's discussion in *Capital* and his other major writings, an institution, which, like the state, will wither away with the arrival of socialism. The family in Marx, Humphries says, 'is like the firm in neo–classical economics—a black box whose inner workings are simultaneously neglected and mystified'. In *Capital*, Marx bases his analysis upon the individual wage worker, having nothing to say about domestic labour in the household.

Recent Marxist literature, on the other hand, has given considerable attention to domestic labour and its contribution to the overall reproduction of capital. There is some variation in approaches which have been developed, but a general measure of agreement exists. The wages which wage workers derive from capital, it is held, presume a definite input of domestic labour; surplus labour is indirectly extracted from the work of the housewife and fed into the process of surplus value creation in the economy at large. However, this type of approach is defective, Humphries argues, because it approaches the matter solely from the point of view of the power of capital. Echoing what Stark and Rubery have to say in a rather different context, she claims that the missing factor is class struggle; the power of capital has never gone unchallenged. The persistence of the working-class family cannot be explained if we do not see such a perspective as central.

Humphries sees the working-class family essentially as a source of support, sustaining personal ties in a social world increasingly penetrated by the dislocating effects of capitalistic expansion. She invokes historical evidence from the period of the industrial revolution to demonstrate that family relationships were perpetuated, even strengthened, at a time when the working-class family was ceasing to be itself a productive unit. Such relationships had a material base. Kinship relations, within the nuclear family, and in more extended kin networks, provided material support in the face of unemployment, illness, and other circumstances of deprivation. In making such provision, the family received the indirect support of the state. Families were legally expected to care for those regarded as their dependents; since they were often unable to do so, a range of state-provided services came to complement what they could provide. But these involved harsh penalties for those forced to rely upon them and hardly served to replace family ties. The workhouse was hated and feared.

Humphries's thesis, then, is that attempts of the working class to defend family relationships were an integral element of the class struggles in early industrial capitalism. 'Kinship ties', in her words, 'were strengthened because they provided the only framework controllable by the working class'. But there is a second dimension to her argument also. Most Marxist discussions of the Acts preventing the use of child labour and of the factors that limited female participation in the labour force as wage labour have again concentrated largely upon the perspective of capital. But it is plausible to claim that working-class people recognised that these restrictions served to defend against the cheapening of labour power. Humphries's views should at this point be compared with those of Hartmann, who places more emphasis upon patriarchal attitudes in limiting women's involvement in the labour force. Humphries admits the importance of such attitudes but maintains that there was also a definite communality of interest on the part of the working-class family as a whole in securing legislation of such a sort. A consequence of struggles to defend these common interests, because they thereby helped both confine women to the home and weaken their bargaining power in the industrial sphere, was the accentuation of the sexual division of labour.

In concluding her analysis, Humphries reiterates her plea that the family should neither be conceptually eradicated from class analysis (as in the writings of Marx and Engels), nor be regarded negatively, as supposedly undermining class cohesion (which she says is the view taken in many more recent Marxist accounts). Family loyalties have helped engender broader feelings of solidarity in circumstances of oppression. The mutual dependence involved in family ties may well have helped to counter economic individualism among wage workers and often may have served to transmit radical sentiments from generation to generation. To the extent that this occurs, it may well be, however, at the expense of the position and rights of women. It is debatable, therefore, whether the interests of working-class women can be conflated with working-class interests in general.

# · 21 ·

# Women's Work and Theories of Class and Stratification

## Elizabeth Garnsey

### Introduction[1]

No consensus exists as to the proper scope and subject matter of social stratification studies in spite of a common concern with the following issues in the recent literature:

(a) institutionalized inequalities in access to and control over valued resources by individuals and groups in society, and,

(b) the relations between groups and individuals having differential access to and control over valued resources.[2]

Diversity of opinion is nowhere greater than on the question of whether the causes and effects of inequalities between the sexes come within this area of inquiry.

Two main positions are taken on the issue:

---

• From *Sociology* 12(2) (1978): 223–243; slightly revised for this volume.

1. I would like to acknowledge support from the SSRC which enabled me to write this paper.

2. These are sometimes described as the distributional and relational aspects of stratification. The distributional aspect of stratification has been described by Goldthorpe as involving the distribution of social power and advantage; power being defined as the capacity to mobilize resources to bring about a desired state of affairs, and advantage as the possession of, or control over, whatever in society is valued and scarce. Goldthorpe defines systems of social stratification as 'structures of inequality of both condition and opportunity' (Goldthorpe, in Wedderburn 1974: 218). See also Smelser and Lipset 1966: 6; our description differs from theirs to allow for the views of theorists who do not see power as a separate dimension of stratification.

(1) Stratification theory is concerned neither with the causes nor with the effects of inequalities between the sexes;

(2) The analysis of some of the effects of these inequalities is relevant, but stratification theory is not concerned with their causes.

It will be argued in this paper that the analysis of the class system calls for an examination both of the socio-economic causes of inequalities based on the division of labour between the sexes and of their effects.[3] Analysis of this kind involves a break with the traditional concerns of stratification theory.

Most writers adopting the first position in the recent literature recognize some degree of inequality between the sexes but deny its relevance to stratification theory.[4] Parkin, for example, maintains that 'inequalities associated with sex differences are not usefully thought of as components of stratification' (Parkin, 1971: 14). This statement could imply two separate points; either that these inequalities are not among those which need to be explained by stratification theory, or that the different social and economic circumstances of men and women should not be treated as explanatory factors in the analysis of social stratification. Parkin intends the first sense, but like most writers in this group he also refrains from treating the division of labour between men and women as an independent or explanatory variable in analysing the system of social stratification. Writers in this group discuss the effects of the changing occupational structure, 'the backbone of the reward system' (Parkin, 1971: 19), without emphasizing the differences in the occupational distribution of the male and female labour force.

Writers in the second category find it necessary to take account of women's occupations in their theories and explanations. They tend to be critical of theories in which the labour force is treated as homogeneous and they regard the sex composition of various occupational categories as a relevant factor in their analysis. But while recognizing the collective impact of women's employment on the occupational structure, they argue that women's work is subsidiary and peripheral to the class system.[5]

Some of the logical and empirical problems raised by the treatment of these and related issues in the recent literature will be examined in this paper. It will be seen that there are inconsistencies in the treatment of women's work which create difficulties for the analysis of questions which do come within the terms of reference adopted. These problems cannot be resolved simply by introducing gender as yet another dimension of social stratification, because of the great

---

3. Watson and Barth 1964 and Acker 1973 have criticized American stratification studies for their treatment of the position of women. There are an increasing number of empirical studies in the U.S. literature in this area, e.g. Ritter and Hargens 1975.

4. Functionalist theorists commonly maintain that 'husband and wife are always social equals' (K. Davis 1950: 364). This is held to be necessary if the family is to fulfil the function of status ascription. Thus, by definition, the family is a 'unit of equivalent evaluation'. For a critique of this view see M. G. Smith, 'Pre-Industrial Stratification Systems' in Smelser and Lipset 1966: 154–160; also Watson and Barth 1964 and Middleton 1974.

5. E.g. 'Given that women still have to await their liberation from the family it remains the case in capitalist societies that female workers are largely peripheral to the class system, or expressed differently, women are in a sense the "underclass" of the white-collar sector' (Giddens 1972: 288).

diversity in the conditions of life and opportunities of women variously placed in the class structure. Nor can the question be evaded on these grounds, because inequalities which stem from the division of labour between men and women pervade all levels of society and impinge on other aspects of inequality.

If it can be shown that evading the issue inevitably gives rise to inconsistencies and gaps in the treatment of important issues, it will follow that investigation of the position of women in society must be integrated with the analysis of stratification. This, however, requires a reconceptualization of the tasks of statification theory.

The dominant approach in stratification studies is to view the occupational system as a framework within which to locate individuals and groups and trace their movement in the hierarchy of skills and rewards which it represents. The social hierarchy, whether viewed in terms of one or many dimensions, is taken as given, as exogenously determined. Women's work is conceptually anomalous and methodologically inconvenient for the approach which aims to identify the relative ranking of individuals and groups in the structure of rewards and opportunities, of social advantages however defined. The occupational structure, which forms the 'backbone' of the reward system, includes positions filled by women, but the social and economic rewards available to the majority of women differ from those derived by most men from their occupational position. It is difficult to synchronize the ranking of 'positions and persons' in such a way as to describe the condition of both men and women (hence the difficulty of ranking clerical workers in relation to skilled manual workers), and yet the occupational positions which they fill cannot be isolated from each other; the occupational framework of society is common to both.

Implicit in the approach of mainstream stratification theories, however much they differ in other respects, is the notion that the occupational structure is determined by factors lying outside the scope of sociological analysis, by technological exigencies and the demands of economic efficiency. But the brief of stratification analysis can be extended beyond the task of mapping inequalities of position and person to the investigation of the formation and reproduction of the positions to which unequal advantages accrue. Thus the process of change in the occupational division of labour becomes part of the problematic.

Technological exigencies cannot be treated as autonomous factors, unrelated to the terms on which labour is obtainable. Wage rates and employment conditions are influenced by the inferior bargaining position of most women workers, which their unpaid domestic work entails. This outcome of the division of labour between men and women in domestic work and childcare is a determinant of wage structures for both men and women. Because of the connection between labour costs and incentives to introduce technological innovations, the supply of women workers available at relatively low wages (justified by the notion that their contribution to the family's resources is subsidiary to that of male workers) is a factor influencing investment decisions. The availability of women workers affects the ways in which labour processes are transformed and is thus among the determinants of change in the occupational structure. The division of labour between men and women in the household and labour market is in itself a factor contributing to change in those inequalities of condition and opportunity to which both men and women are subject, not simply by virtue of their gender, but as members of a class society. It is from this perspective that both causes and effects of inequalities between the sexes are seen to be integral to the subject matter of stratification studies.

Before an analysis of this kind can be developed, it is necessary to consider objections to including inequalities between men and women within the scope of analysis and difficulties which the exclusion of the topic creates. These and related issues will be discussed in terms of the unit of analysis adopted in studies of stratification and in relation to the different levels of analysis at which investigations are carried out.

I will start from the position that work and market situation are, for the bulk of the population, of primary importance in determining access to and control over valued resources (Lockwood, 1958: 202–208). I cannot in this paper explore the complex relationships between property ownership and class, but I do not hold that position in the occupational division of labour is the sole or invariably the most significant determinant of class position. My argument is that investigation of the dynamics of the occupational division of labour is the key to integrating the analysis of the position of women with the analysis of class.[6]

## Women's Work and the Unit of Analysis in Stratification Studies

Among the reasons frequently given for excluding the question of inequalities between men and women from the scope of stratification studies is the argument that the family, not the individual, is the proper unit of the stratification system (Parkin, 1971: 14). In my view the attempt to identify a unique and exclusive base of analysis is misplaced.[7] If the complexities of the stratification system are to be explored it is necessary to work with different bases for different purposes of enquiry. The salience of the family in the class system is not in question.[8] Its importance in the transmission of social advantage to the next generation through the inheritance of property and preparation for occupational position is indisputable. It does not follow, however, that the family must be

---

6. It will not be possible to discuss the attitudes and conventions associated with sexual distinctions in the present paper; these are more familiar than are the economic implications of the division of labour between men and women for the structural determination of class positions. However it is evident that structural factors maintain and are reinforced by the expectations and consciousness of individuals interacting in socially approved ways.

7. For a discussion of other categories in terms of which social stratification can be conceptualized, see Smelser and Lipset 1966: 6. In practice stratification theorists focus on the social unit appropriate to the particular problems with which they are concerned. Thus Parkin, having started by focusing on the family, speaks later in his study of 'broad occupational categories as our unit of analysis' (1971: 23).

8. The idea goes back to Schumpeter: 'The family, not the physical person, is the true unit of class theory' (Schumpeter 1951: 148). But Schumpeter goes on to relax this assumption as his analysis proceeds: 'the occasional cases [where the individual is able to move into a higher social class on his own account] can no longer be put aside' (p. 164). And 'success brings in its wake important functional positions and powers over material resources. The position of the physical individual becomes entrenched and with it that of the family' (p. 218). He also states: 'Only the physical individual, not the family, is class-born', a notion central to his analysis of mobility (p. 171).

taken as the exclusive unit of analysis. In a system of individual wage labour, families are not engaged as units in the occupational division of labour. The family is in some respects a unit of consumption; its members may own property in common; but it is as individuals that its members are engaged in roles in the system of economic production. In recent British studies it is these roles, rather than consumption patterns, which are held to be the components of class situation (Mackenzie, 1973: 175). Market and work situation deriving from occupation are essentially individual attributes.[9]

There are two possible ways of approaching the problems of the articulation of relevant individual attributes, in particular occupation, with attributes of families. One line of approach would inquire into the ways in which different members of the family, both men and women, contribute resources of value to other members and the family as a group. These contributions would be seen to stem not only from occupation but from inherited property, social connections and unpaid work in the household and community. This would also open to inquiry the functionalist axiom that the family is a unit of equivalent evaluation, on which doubt has been cast by recent research outside Britain (Ritter and Hargens, 1975). The second alternative involves aligning the class position of the family with the situation of one of its members. This is the approach which prevails where it is assumed that the male head of household acts as the family's sole agent in the class system. This assumption, though superficially convenient, creates difficulties of analysis.

The effects of demographic factors such as age structure, marriage, divorce and economic activity rates cannot be dealt with within a framework which assumes that the male head of household determines the class position of the family unit. A sizable proportion of the population consists of single adults having no identifiable families, of families which do not have a male head of household, or where the adult male has no obvious occupation. The available evidence refers mainly to household composition. In Britain, in 1971, over three million people were living on their own, making up nearly a fifth of all households. Over 30% of households did not consist of an adult male, wife and children (*Social Trends*, 1975: 62). One in five males over the school-leaving age was not economically active because in full-time education, retired or disabled; this figure does not include those unemployed and seeking work (*Social Trends*, 1975: 82; definitions: 242).

The assumption also prevents systematic consideration of the contribution of women's work to the resources of the family and the outlook of its members. In at least some of the cases where the category of male head of household is inapplicable, women's occupations must be held to determine class position; it is then inconsistent to disregard the significance of women's work in the majority of cases where there is also a male wage earner in the family. Table 1 shows the 'social class' composition of men and women in Britain on the basis of the occupational categories used for the Registrar General's classification (summa-

---

9. Work situation refers to the fact that 'in occupying given roles in the division of labour individuals are involved in distinct socio-technical environments' and in distinct patterns of social relationships. (Mackenzie 1974: 238). For a discussion of market situation see section 5 of the present paper.

**Table 1.** Social Class Composition of People Aged 15 and over, 1971, for Various Groups

| | GREAT BRITAIN | | | | | | PERCENTAGES AND THOUSANDS | | |
| --- | --- | --- | --- | --- | --- | --- | --- | --- | --- |
| | Men only | | | Women only | | | Men and women aged 15 and over | | |
| | Economically active | Retired | Economically active and retired | Married Own[1] class | Married Husband's[2] class | Single, widowed and divorced Own[3] class | 'Own' occupation of economically active and retired | Head of family | Chief economic supporter |
| | (1) | (2) | (3) | (4) | (5) | (6) | (7) | (8) | (9) |
| Percentage in each Social Class: | | | | | | | | | |
| I | 5.2 | 3.0 | 5.0 | 0.9 | 5.3 | 1.2 | 3.6 | 5.1 | 4.9 |
| II | 17.8 | 19.1 | 18.0 | 16.2 | 19.8 | 19.2 | 17.8 | 20.0 | 19.8 |
| IIIN | 11.9 | 12.1 | 11.9 | 35.4 | 11.3 | 41.2 | 21.1 | 11.9 | 14.2 |
| IIIM | 39.0 | 34.2 | 38.5 | 10.0 | 39.0 | 10.8 | 28.4 | 37.9 | 34.8 |
| IV | 17.8 | 20.3 | 18.1 | 28.2 | 17.5 | 22.7 | 20.9 | 18.0 | 18.6 |
| V | 8.2 | 11.2 | 8.6 | 9.4 | 7.1 | 4.9 | 8.2 | 7.3 | 7.7 |
| Total classified (=100%) | 15,368 | 1,911 | 17,279 | 5,697 | 12,365 | 3,834 | 26,809 | 13,150 | 15,907 |
| Total[4] unclassified | 516 | 323 | 909 | 1,101 | 471 | 1,549 | 3,488 | 694 | 1,374 |
| Total in Great Britain | 15,884 | 2,304 | 18,188 | 6,797 | 12,835 | 5,383 | 30,367 | 13,844 | 17,281 |

Source: Census of Population, 1971. Economic Activity Tables.
Reproduced from *Social Trends*, 1975: 11.

[1] Economically active and retired married women by own social class.

[2] Married women enumerated with their husbands by the social class of husband including both the economically active and retired, and those economically active.

[3] Economically active and retired single, widowed, and divorced women.

[4] Unclassified persons: those for whom no occupation or adequate information was reported in the Census. A large proportion of this group were out of

rized in notes to Table 2). In 1971, 12.9 million women could be classified on the basis of the occupation of their husbands (column 5), but no fewer than 5.4 million were single, widowed or divorced, and could not be so classified. Moreover, if women are automatically assigned to their husband's social class, the contrast between the distribution of married women according to their own and their husband's occupation (columns 4 and 5) is obscured. On the basis of their own occupation, over half of the women are classed in non-manual categories; only a third are so classed by their husband's occupations. This suggests an important disparity in the work experiences of many husbands and wives.

More evidence on the extensiveness of disparities between the occupations of husbands and wives is presented in Table 2. For husbands in Social Class I (professionals) having working wives, only 6% had wives in the same class as themselves, and 14% had wives in manual employment. For husbands in Social Class II (managers and administrators, including small proprietors) 34% had wives in the same social class as themselves, and nearly 20% had wives in manual occupations. The smaller group of husbands in non-manual Class III were most likely to have wives in the same social class as themselves (51%), but for this group of husbands over a third had wives in manual employment. Among husbands in manual occupations having working wives, the disparities were equally great; for no category did the majority of husbands have wives in the same social class as themselves, and a significant proportion of wives were on the other side of the manual/non-manual divide.

Disparities of this kind are difficult to interpret. Information on qualifications, experience, hours worked and length of service on the job for husband and wife is needed to give meaning to contrasts in their occupational position. However, the significance of these disparities is lost altogether when women's work is assumed to be of a different order from men's work and then left out of account in studies of class identification and consciousness. A specification of the factors influencing women's orientation to work would provide a starting point for the analysis of its effects. Brown outlines some of these factors in his review of the treatment of women as employees in industrial sociology (Brown, 1976). Both the structure of roles in the family and the response of women to the structure of labour markets is relevant. It is necessary to take into account the effects of changes in women's domestic work-load over the course of the life-cycle on their orientation to work. The effects of occupational segregation in the labour market on women's work and market situation are also relevant; few women are likely to be found in work situations identical to those of men, but certain features of work are experienced in common. To this extent typologies classifying aspects of work and associated social imagery should apply to both men and women (Mackenzie, 1975). At the same time, recognition of the limited job opportunities in routine low paid employment open to most women lowers their expectations and incentives to acquire qualifications, reinforcing their commitment, inculcated by social values, to their domestic role. These are among the factors which influence the type of work and pay which a large proportion of women are prepared or forced to accept.

**Table 2.** Married Couples Both Economically Active, 1971

| | GREAT BRITAIN SOCIAL CLASS OF HUSBAND | | | | PERCENTAGES | | | |
| --- | --- | --- | --- | --- | --- | --- | --- | --- |
| | I | II | IIIN | IIIM | IV | V | NC | Total (thousands) |
| Social Class of wife: | | | | | | | | |
| I | 6 | 2 | — | — | — | — | 1 | 44 |
| II | 31 | 34 | 15 | 9 | 8 | 5 | 12 | 806 |
| IIIN | 46 | 40 | 51 | 32 | 25 | 19 | 29 | 1,868 |
| IIIM | 3 | 4 | 7 | 12 | 11 | 10 | 7 | 502 |
| IV | 9 | 13 | 19 | 32 | 36 | 37 | 26 | 1,443 |
| V | 2 | 2 | 5 | 11 | 14 | 22 | 10 | 518 |
| Not classified | 4 | 4 | 3 | 4 | 4 | 6 | 16 | 232 |
| Total (=100%) (thousands) | 242 | 1,031 | 647 | 2,111 | 955 | 339 | 92 | 5,414 |

Social class categories are as follows:

Class I  Professional and similar occupations
II  Intermediate occupations
III(N)  Skilled occupations (non-manual)
III(M)  Skilled occupations (manual)
IV  Partly skilled occupations
V  Unskilled occupations
NC  Not classified

Source: Census of Population, 1971, Economic Activity Tables. *Social Trends*, 1975:12.

Investigation into the effects of dissimilar work and market situations of men and women is necessary for the solution of problems posed in recent stratification studies, where the importance of women's earnings and exposure to work environments is recognized. The authors of the *Affluent Worker* studies saw that crosscutting class affiliations among members of the same family affected class identification and outlook of their male respondents:

The long-run trends for white-collar employment to expand more rapidly than blue-collar work and for women to take up an increasing proportion of white-collar jobs must mean that more manual wage-earners will have siblings and wives who are "middle class" in terms at least of occupational status. Consequently it is precisely such changes in the occupational structure, rather than affluence itself, that must be regarded as possibly the most influential factor in encouraging the spread of middle-class values and life-styles among the working class'. (Vol. 3: 81).

It is shown that changes in occupational structure are likely to affect the work and market situation of women; the factors shaping their orientation to work, a crucial set of variables for the male manual workers, and the specific ways in which women's work experiences affect their outlook remain to be explored.

The response of women to job opportunities and the limitations imposed on them from within and outside the family are not analysed in the stratification literature. Neglect of this perspective accounts in large part for the 'piecemeal analysis of the interplay between the divisions of labour and community and family structure' of which Mackenzie complains (1974: 243). The benefits to employers and certain unions of a 'primary' workforce committed to full-time, long-term employment, and a low paid subsidiary labour force has been explored in models of a segmented labour market (Doeringer and Piore, 1971). Internal forces within the family facilitate the distinction between primary and secondary employment as it applies to men and women's work. ('Primary labour markets' are those in which employment is characterized by high earnings, relative security of tenure and chances of promotion: 'secondary markets' are those in which these conditions are absent (Giddens, 1973: 219)). We will consider the relevance of the structure of labour markets in a later section. However the notion of secondary employment cannot apply in the same way to all women workers. The situation of women in clerical and unskilled manual jobs differs. Whether the difference is less for women than for men because of the routinization of much of the clerical work in which women are engaged can only be ascertained through further research. The debate on the significance of the de-skilling and feminization of lower white collar employment, which has been identified as a crucial issue in class theory, cannot advance without detailed consideration of the factors affecting women's work and market situation, their orientation to work and class consciousness.

## Power, Conflict, and Cohesion

In contrast to most stratification theories which exclude inequalities based on gender from the scope of analysis, it has been argued by Lenski that women constitute a distinct class by virtue of their lack of power (Lenski, 1966). Because of the great diversity of circumstances in which women find themselves this is not a useful formulation. It is true that women frequently derive benefits such as wealth or prestige without exerting control over the source of such advantages. The nature of derived advantages and the ways in which they can be converted into resources over which the beneficiary has direct control is not dealt with in most stratification theories. This process is an important feature of patron-client, sponsor-protegé, master-slave and other relationships, in addition to those of kinship. But to assume that women benefit exclusively from derived advantages is to take as given what is problematic.

A number of theorists maintain that stratification theory is concerned only with social divisions which are 'the foci of group conflict' (Lockwood, 1970: 58). But though the analysis of conflict is an important aspect of stratification studies it is not the exclusive focus of analysis. And the conditions which inhibit open conflict in spite of manifest social inequalities are as important as those stimulating it. Barron and Norris have argued that because of the lack of friction associated with social differences between men and women 'sex as a criterion for labour market segregation is more useful than any other social difference' (Barron and Norris, 1976: 58). This aspect of occupational segregation is an important feature of labour market and occupational structure and hence of class relations in society.

It is indisputable that distinctions of race and gender are not class distinctions (Lockwood, 1970). This is not the question at issue. What needs to be considered is whether the failure to deal systematically with the question of inequalities based on race and gender impairs the usefulness of models of stratification. It may well be essential to know the social characteristics of those who predominate in specific economic roles in a society (e.g., whether they are immigrant workers, members of ethnic minorities, women) in order to understand the relations of production and property and thus the class structure. This becomes clear when attempts are made to look at class structure in different societies; criteria of race and gender exclude individuals from roles in the occupational division of labour in different ways with dissimilar effects. These distinctions need not and should not be subsumed under the category of class divisions, but the analysis of class relations cannot properly proceed if these aspects of social inequality are excluded from the analysis by the simplifying assumptions of the model of stratification proposed. While the salience of criteria of race, religion and culture varies from country to country and over time, the division of labour by sex is invariably relevant to the analysis of class.

The argument that inequalities based on sex are irrelevant to stratification studies because women do not form a 'cohesive social collectivity' (Parkin, 1971: 14) fails to take account of the different levels of analysis at which the study of class must be conducted. These inequalities are relevant precisely because they pervade the social structure. Women do not form a social stratum, but they are concentrated in the lowest band of every occupational category, and underrepresented in all positions commanding economic and political power. In the remainder of this paper we will consider some of the collective effects of limitations on the access to and control over valued resources experienced by women as individuals.

## The Collective Effects of Women's Work on the Class System

While there has been no serious reconsideration of the framework of analysis which assumed that the occupation of the male head of household determines the class position of the family, stratification theorists have had to take into account the collective effects of women's employment on income distribution and occupational structure. The effects of women's employment has been cited in support of the embourgeoisement thesis, which holds that an erosion of income differentials is a feature of neo-industrial societies (Lipset and Zetterberg 1953: 563). It has been argued that women's earnings exert a levelling effect on class inequalities by evening out differences in total household income. This argument can be turned the other way: women's earnings are of greatest importance in households where wage earners are in the less skilled and well-paid occupations, and this in itself is a reflection of inequalities of condition (Westergaard and Resler, 1975: 97). Either way, the importance of women's wages and the impact of the increasing proportion of married women in employment is acknowledged.

In Britain there was a doubling of the labour force participation rate for married women of all ages between 1951 and 1971, from 24% to 50% of the relevant population (*Social Trends,* 1974: 15). It is true that income differentials for households (classified by the occupation of the male wage-earner) are less marked where there is more than one wage-earner than where the husband is the sole wage earner.[10] But among all women, occupational differentials in earnings are greater than for men, and pay differentials between men and women are greatest at the base of the occupational hierarchy (Westergaard and Resler, 1976: 97). Women's earnings in clerical and sales jobs are lower than for men in skilled manual occupations and, as was seen in Table 2, of those husbands in manual occupations who have working wives, the majority have wives in manual occupations. The position of these women in the labour market is very unfavourable. They are predominantly in low paid unskilled jobs (Hunt, 1975). Women's earnings cannot offset differentials in household income, and the fact that they reduce these differentials does not substantiate the embourgeoisement thesis.

The effects of women's employment on income differentials must be considered in connection with the occupational distribution of men and women. This issue has come up in relation to data on the occupations of husbands and wives (Tables 1 and 2). In Britain as in other countries the distribution of the male labour force between manual and non-manual occupations has changed less over the century than the distribution of the female labour force. Table 3 shows that in 1911 approximately threequarters of the total labour force was

---

10. *Family Expenditure Survey* 1973; *Social Trends* 1975: 21.

*Table 3.* **Distribution of the Economically Active Population by Manual and Non-Manual Occupational Category, Great Britain, 1911, 1971, Men and Women Shown Separately and Together (In percentages[1] and millions)**

| | WOMEN | | MEN | | BOTH MEN AND WOMEN | |
| | 1911 | 1971 | 1911 | 1971 | 1911 | 1971 |
|---|---|---|---|---|---|---|
| Non-Manual[2] | 23.3 | 57.0 | 26.4 | 41.2 | 25.6 | 46.7 |
| Manual[3] | 76.7 | 43.0 | 73.6 | 58.8 | 74.3 | 53.2 |
| | 100.0 | 100.0 | 100.0 | 100.0 | 100.0 | 100.0 |
| Millions | 5.4 | 8.8 | 12.9 | 15.6 | 18.3 | 24.4 |

Source: Calculated from Goldthorpe and Llewellyn, 'Class Mobility in Britain: Three Theses Examined', *Sociology,* Vol. 11, No. 2, May 1977, p. 279.

[1]Percentages do not sum to total due to rounding error.

[2]Includes inspectors, supervisors and foremen.

[3]Comprises skilled manual workers (including self-employed artisans); semi-skilled manual workers and unskilled manual workers.

employed in manual occupations. Sixty years later the total labour force was almost evenly divided between manual and non-manual occupations. But a majority of the male labour force (58.8%) was to be found in manual occupations, while only 43% of the female labour force was so placed. A more detailed breakdown than that shown in Table 3 reveals that the rise in the proportion of women in sales and clerical occupations (from 9.7% in 1911 to 37.4% in 1971) accounted for a large part of the increase in the proportion of the total labour force in non-manual occupations. For men, the major expansion in non-manual occupations has come about in managerial, administrative and professional occupations, in which 6.8% of the male labour force were employed in 1911, and 21.5% of the male labour force in 1971 (Goldthorpe and Llewellyn, 1977: 279).

Proponents of the view that the expansion of white collar occupations heralds the arrival of a new middle class society (e.g., Bell, 1974) have not considered the implications of the fact that the clerical and sales jobs which account for the major part of this expansion are largely women's occupations. The routinization and feminization of lower-level white collar work calls into question the appropriateness of taking conventional distinctions between manual and non-manual work as class demarcations. The difficulties of applying a manual, non-manual dichotomy have stimulated reformulations of the study of class and the analysis of processes of 'class structuration' and strategies of 'social closure' (Giddens, 1973; Parkin, 1975). To this extent, implicit recognition of the complexities of men and women's employment patterns has led to new conceptualizations of the dynamics of stratification. The place of women's work in these analyses is still uncertain however. Parkin disregards social closure practised against women, and Giddens concludes that 'female workers are largely peripheral to the class system' (Giddens 1972: 288).

## The Level of Analysis

Some of the problems experienced in interpreting the significance of women's work arises from a failure to distinguish clearly between levels of analysis. There is a tendency to commit 'the fallacy of the wrong level' over this issue, to make 'direct translation of properties or relations from one level of analysis to another' (Galtung, 1967: 49). A different order of relations prevails at the individual and societal levels. In particular, it is not justifiable to 'translate' from relationships between male and female wage earners in the family, which are mediated by features of the division of labour in the family, to relations between the male and female labour force in society, which are mediated by a different range of factors. For this reason, the notion that it is the occupational composition of the male labour force, rather than that of the female labour force, which is of significance for the class structure cannot be derived from the principle that the man's occupation tends to determine the class position of the family, even by those who accept this tenet.

Westergaard and Resler preface their useful review of the employment position of women in Britain with the statement: '. . . the socio-economic position of men is still far more important than that of women for the class structure' (1975: 97). This is a statement about class structure based on considerations applicable at the individual levels of analysis (the importance of the occupational position of the male wage earner for his family). They do not investigate the collective impact of women's work on the dynamics of the class system.

## Complementary Employment Trends

The view that, from the point of view of class analysis, the female labour force constitutes a residual category, serving to accommodate changes in the distribution of the male labour force, leaves out of account the importance for the class system of the factors which shape the relationship between male and female employment patterns. It is on these grounds that Braverman criticised those who view '. . . female labour employment as temporary, incidental and fortuitous when it should actually be placed at the very centre of all occupational studies today' (Braverman 1974: 396). One need not, however, assume that trends in women's employment are more central than those of men. All that is necessary is to recognize that the participation of women in the labour market affects the condition of both men and women; changes in the occupational and industrial distribution of male and female workers are complementary and interdependent.

Braverman's analysis is based on the application of Marx's account of the process of capitalist accumulation to the conditions of twentieth century America. He argues that women form the prime source of the 'supplementary reservoir of labour' required for the functioning of the economy. Technical innovations in industry promote the polarization of the labour force into a minority of skilled and professional and a mass of unskilled workers. These innovations reduce the demand for labour in manufacturing, but there is an expansion of service activities ancillary to industry in marketing, retailing and commerce. 'The fastest growing industrial and occupational sectors in the 'automated' age tend, therefore, in the long run, to be those labour intensive areas which have not yet been or cannot be subject to high technology' (Braverman, 1974: 382). Those employed in the 'new mass occupations', he argues, are largely women: '. . . those who keep coming into the employment market at a time when traditional opportunities in industrial employment are shrinking furnish the labour supply for the clerical, service and sales fields' (Braverman, 1974: 384).

Wage rates are kept low by the influx of women into the 'new mass occupations' and this affects incentives to mechanize; this trend encourages 'the investment of capital in forms of the labour process which require masses of low-wage hand labour' (Braverman, 1974: 384). Hence women are employed largely in routine work. The 'reservoir of female labour' is released partly by the provision of commercial alternatives to goods and services previously produced in the household. New patterns of domestic consumption provide the market for new forms of product. Meanwhile an increasing proportion of households become dependent on women's earnings to meet subsistence needs, especially in the face of the shrinkage of job opportunities in traditionally male occupations in industry.

Braverman's application of analytic tools created by Marx to examine nineteenth century Britain is the source of the strength of his argument, but it opens his thesis to criticism, especially for his neglect of the implications of the growth of government intervention and the response of organized labour to management policies. For the present argument, however, the book is important in contrasting the critique of capitalism as a system of distribution with the critique of capitalism as a system of production. The force of the thesis is such that any response to it must take shifts in the occupational division of labour as problematic in the analysis of class; these shifts cannot be regarded as exogeneously determined, as a backdrop to the study of the distribution of advantages. Changes in women's employment are integral to the processes by which the occupational division of labour is transformed, and, with it, the distribution of advantages and 'life circumstances' of both men and women.

Braverman points to the importance of the extension of the market and new patterns of domestic consumption in 'releasing' women for employment. Consumption patterns, and more especially, demographic trends (fewer children born per woman and child-bearing completed at an earlier age) have facilitated the rise in labour force participation of married women (Oppenheimer, 1969). Nevertheless, these trends have not fundamentally altered the division of labour in the household between men and women. This must be recognized if the position of women in employent is to be differentiated analytically from that of other workers unfavourably placed in the labour market as members of ethnic, religious or linguistic groups. We have already seen that in most of the literature women are excluded from the analysis precisely because, as a group, they do not form a potentially cohesive social community (Parkin, 1971, 1974). Even where the importance of women's earnings or occupational distribution is recognized by those writing on class stratification (Westergaard and Resler, 1975), it is not made clear what sets women off from other groups of workers who are at a disadvantage in the labour market.

The unfavourable position of most women in the labour market cannot be attributed entirely to the influence of convention or the effects of discrimination, important though these factors are. The crucial factor for the analysis of the role of women's work in the class system is that limitations are placed on women's employment opportunities and their bargaining power in the labour market is weakened as a result of the division of labour in the household. It is, therefore, necessary to investigate and identify the effects of the work performed by women in the household on their position in the labour market.

A considerable body of relevant academic and government research is already available which can be drawn upon for this purpose. In the present paper I can only point to the relevance of some of the research on the structure of labour markets and of the discussion on the economic significance of women's domestic labour.

## Labour Market Structure and Women's Employment

Models of the structure of labour markets can be useful in a number of ways.

(1) These models examine the structural determinants of the market and work situation characterizing specific occupations in particular industries.

(2) They reveal the interdependence of wage structures and employment conditions in the various sectors of the labour market, including those sectors characterized by a high or low proportion of female employees.

(3) The models should draw attention to the social characteristics of workers who predominate in certain sectors of the labour market. For this reason they are relevant to the question of the social recruitment to occupational positions and to processes of social exclusion (Parkin, 1974: 11).

Consideration of the position of women in the labour market illustrates the usefulness of the notion of 'market capacity' as 'all forms of relevant attributes which individuals may bring to the bargaining encounter' in the labour market (Giddens, 1972: 103). Market capacity as a personal attribute can be contrasted with market situation as an attribute of a position in the occupational division of labour, with which certain earnings, security and prospects are associated. For women, bargaining capacity is likely to change over the life-cycle, and this in itself will influence the occupational positions that they are able to take up and the market situations in which they are thereby placed.

Differences in market situation which cut across the conventional manual/ non-manual distinction suggest the advantages of an analysis in terms of primary and secondary sector employment. But it is likely that difficulties will arise in another form if a new dichotomy is introduced, as was suggested earlier. Analysis of labour market structure as segmental rather than dual does more to reveal the complexity of the distinctions that break the work force up into non-competing groups (Rubery, 1978). Nevertheless, it is possible to identify certain kinds of employment which are characterized by internal promotion ladders and relative security of tenure, and to contrast these with other forms of employment in which less protection is afforded to workers against economic uncertainties.

Employers have an incentive to provide conditions which will encourage employment stability among those workers whose productivity is directly related to length of service. As a result of trade union and other pressures these conditions are extended to cover other groups of workers and come to characterize certain types of firm and organization. For individual firms the availability of employees to whom these favourable conditions are *not* extended enables them to have at their disposal a flexible workforce; long term planning is facilitated and economic fluctuations can be accommodated (Barron and Norris, 1976). The reasons for the establishment of favourable employment conditions for a sector of the workforce are explored in the expanding literature on labour market structure (Rubery, 1978). What is relevant for the present argument is that certain requirements must be met by workers if they are to qualify for and remain in employment in the 'protected' sector. It is not so much the intrinsic demands of the work to be performed as the organization of work and of the internal labour market which make it necessary for employees to be able to meet the requirements of: (a) long-term, uninterrupted employment, (b) full-time work, (c) geographic mobility, in order to qualify for and remain in employment in the 'protected sectors' of the labour market. These are precisely the conditions which the majority of women cannot meet because of the demands of their work in the household and family. In particular part-time work is treated as incompatible with enjoyment of the benefits of 'protected' employment; this is in the interests of employers and the majority of union membership. These are among the reasons why women are concentrated in those industries and occupations which are manifestly not part of the 'protected' employment sector (Hunt, 1974: 43, 55).

Barron and Norris set out the reasons why women are, from the employer's viewpoint, especially well suited as employees in the 'secondary labour market' (1976: 54ff). They show that employment patterns are self-reinforcing. Thus it is apparent that the propensity to join unions is in large part a function of position in the occupational division of labour rather than the result of the social attributes of job-holders. Women are concentrated in jobs characterized by high turnover rates, in smaller establishments where unions are weak and membership small. Absence of union pressure keeps earnings and employment conditions unfavourable in many of the industries and occupations into which, by convention and policy, employers recruit women workers. It is worth investigating why 'collective strategies' to improve their position have not been open to most women, to extend the analysis suggested by Parkin's theory of social closure (Parkin, 1974).

## Domestic and Wage Labour

The neo–Marxist literature on women's domestic labour holds that unpaid work by women in the household is productive labour (labour productive of surplus value) because it is required to maintain and reproduce the labour force. One can take issue with a number of features of these theories (Himmelweit and Mohun,

1977). The view that women stand in a specific relation to the mode of production in capitalist society does not meet the objection that not all women and not only women provide unpaid household services, process goods for final consumption and care for dependents.[11] Nevertheless, the issues dealt with in this debate demonstrate that domestic labour is socially necessary labour of considerable significance in the class system. This is in contrast to the perspective adopted in most studies of class stratification, where domestic 'activities' and consumption patterns are treated as cultural factors, making for differences in life-styles among the population.[12] Women's work has economic significance at both the micro and macro levels. It is at the micro level, in the household, that domestic labour, domestic consumption and women's wage labour articulate, partly as a result of the initiatives and responses women adopt and their perception of the opportunities and constraints facing them. The factors giving rise to the structure of incentives and constraints facing individual social actors are multiple. There are pressures in capitalist societies to expand markets for consumption of commercial alternatives to domestically produced goods and services and to expand low-wage female employment. There are conflicting pressures to reduce public and private expenditure on communal services which would facilitate women's employment (Gardiner, 1975). Attempts are made by trade unions to protect job structures threatened by the expansion of low-paid female employment (Rubery, 1978). The combined effects of these pressures alter over the course of major economic cycles, influencing consumption patterns and the structure of the labour market in ways which are to some extent irreversible.

Analysis along these lines would show that the disadvantages from which the majority of women suffer on the labour market are not incidental handicaps, but represent important features of the organization of the economy and of the labour performed in the 'subsistence sector' of neo-industrial societies. This is true not only in capitalist but in state socialist societies, which have been heavily dependent on the unpaid labour of women in the household to subsidize economic growth.

Wage structures which make women's earnings necessary for family subsistence ensure that labour force participation rates of women are high in these countries: about 85% of Soviet women aged 20 to 55 are in paid employment (Lapidus, 1975: 182). But the burden of housework is considerable because of persistent shortages of consumer goods and of communally organized alternatives to household services. These areas have been of low priority in the allocation of investment resources under the Soviet pattern of industrial development (Ofer, 1973). Although women are more evenly distributed throughout the occupational system, and a much higher proportion of professional workers are women than in the West, there is a considerable degree of occupational segregation and marked inequalities in levels of seniority and earnings of men and women (Lapidus, 1975: 193). Discrimination in employment is less apparent

---

11. For some British evidence on the extent to which work in the household is carried out predominantly by women, including those in full time employment, see Hunt 1968, vol. I: 130.

12. The new 'economics of the family' also calls into question the assumption that households are simply consuming units in industrial societies (Schulz 1975).

than in the West; a major factor accounting for these inequalities in the occupational system appears to be the division of labour in the household between men and women (Scott, 1976). This topic cannot be adequately treated in the present paper, but it is clear that the distinctive features of the organization of production, distribution and consumption in centrally planned socialist societies are made possible in part by the character of women's labour in these societies.[13] The structure of occupational positions and the rewards accruing to them are affected accordingly.[14]

## Conclusion

I have tried to show why the analysis of women's work raises problems for many studies of social stratification. I have argued that in order to give an account of the significance of women's work, a reconceptualization of the tasks of stratification theory is required. It is insufficient to take the occupational division of labour as given; it is necessary to investigate the formation and reproduction of positions in labour markets and occupational systems to which unequal advantages accrue. The division of labour is the vital link between changing economic processes and social relations. But because economic change is not autonomous, the analysis of class cannot be divorced from the analysis of changing economic processes, 'of the economic forms in which people produce, consume and exchange'.[15]

Women's work in the household and labour market cannot be dealt with simply in terms of the organisation of the family. When work in the subsistence sector and the distribution of female workers throughout the occupational and

---

13. Thus in state socialist societies clerical and sales work has a higher concentration of female employees than in the West—over 90% according to the Soviet census of 1970 (Tsentral'noe statisticheskoe upravlenie SSSR. *Itogi vsesoiuznoe perepisi naselenia* 1970 goda, Moscow, *Statistika* 1973, vol. VI Table 18). But the proportion of the total labour force employed in clerical and sales work is only a fraction of that found in the West (Garnsey 1975). The small size of the commercial sector and organizational patterns which discourage the employment of clerical workers have significant effects on women's occupations and on the occupational structure as a whole in state socialist societies.

14. We have already noted the contributions of Giddens (1972) and Parkin (1974). The primacy of the problem of the structural determination of class positions is stressed by Poulantzas (1975), but in his work preoccupation with the analysis of ideology and the state preclude a Marxist analysis of the political economy of change in the division of labour, of the kind presented by Braverman (1974). From a different direction we find the call for investigation into 'the sources and consequences of transformation of the occupational structure' based on the findings of the most recent round of social mobility studies (Hauser *et al.* 1975: 585).

15. Letter to Annenkov, 1846; MESW I: 519.
Marx maintained that '. . . the existence of classes is only bound up in (i.e. cannot be considered apart from) particular phases in the development of production' (Marx to Weydermeyer, 1852; MESW I: 528). 'Assume particular degrees of development of production, commerce and consumption and you will have a corresponding form of social constitution, a corresponding organization of the family, of orders and of classes . . . ' (Marx to Annenkov, 1846; MESW I: 518).
Marx did not treat the question of the connections between women's work and the class structure in any detail. His references to the issue are scattered; the matter comes up in his discussion of the use of low paid female labour to displace male workers (e.g. *Wage Labour and Capital* 1849; MESW I: 171). But any analysis of class which aims to examine 'the mode of production and the relations of production and exchange corresponding to that mode' (MESW II: 519) must confront the issue. Women's work in the household and labour market cannot be analysed simply.

industrial structure are analysed as factors in economic development (Boserup 1974), it becomes clear that women's labour is integral to the economic life and class systems of the societies in question. Production, distribution and consumption provide the impetus for changes in the class system in part through their effects on the division of labour between men and women, both in the household and in the occupational system. From this perspective the division of labour between men and women and the inequalities associated with it provide insight into some basic causes of change in occupational and class structure.

## References

Acker, J. 1973. 'Women and Social Stratification'. *American Journal of Sociology* 78, 4:936–945.

Allen, S. and Barker, D., eds. 1976. *Dependence and Exploitation in Work and Marriage*. London: Longmans.

Barron, R. D. and Norris, G. M. 'Sexual Divisons and the Dual Labour Market' in Allen and Barker, eds.

Bendix, R. and Lipset, S., eds. 1953. *Class, Status and Power*. New York: Free Press.

Bell, D. 1974. *The Coming of Post-Industrial Society*. London: Heinemann.

Blau, P. and Duncan, O. 1967. *The American Occupational Structure*. New York: Free Press.

Boserup, E. 1970. *Woman's Role in Economic Development*. London: Allen and Unwin.

Braverman, H. 1974. *Labor and Monopoly Capitalism*. New York: Monthly Review Press.

Brown, R. 1976. 'Women as Employees' in Allen and Barker, eds.

Castles, S. and Kosack, G. 1973. *Immigrant Workers and Social Class in Europe*. London: Oxford University Press.

Central Statistical Office. *Social Trends* No. 5, 1974; No. 6, 1975. H.M.S.O.

Coulson, M., et al. 1975. 'The Housewife and her Labour under Capitalism'. *New Left Review* No. 89.

Davis, K. 1950. *Human Society*. New York: Macmillan.

Doeringer, P. and Piore, M. 1971. *Internal Labor Markets and Manpower Analysis* New York: Heath & Co.

Galtung, J. 1967. *Theory and Methods of Social Research*. Oslo: Universitetsforlag.

Gardiner, J. 1975. 'The Political Economy of Female Labour in Capitalist Society'. *New Left Review*, No. 89.

Garnsey, E. 1975. 'Occupational Structure in Industrial Societies'. *Sociology* 9, 3:437–458.

Giddens, A. 1972. *The Class Structure of the Advanced Societies*. London: Heinemann.

Goldthorpe, J. H. and Lockwood, D. 1963. 'Affluence and the British Class Structure'. *British Journal of Sociology* 2: 337–361.

———, Lockwood, D., Bechofer, F., Platt, J. 1968. *The Affluent Worker* Vols. 1–3. Cambridge: Cambridge University Press.

———. 1974. 'Social Inequality and Social Integration' in Wedderburn, D., ed.: 217–238.

Hauser, R. M. and others, 1975. 'Structural Changes in the Occupational Mobility Among Men in the United States'. *American Sociological Review* 40, 5: 585–598.

Himmelweit, S. and Mohun, S. 1977. 'Domestic Labour and Capital', *Cambridge Journal of Economics* 1, 1:15–31.

Hunt, A. 1968. *A Survey of Women's Employment*. Government Survey. London H.M.S.O.

———. 1974. *Women and Work, A Statistical Survey*. Department of Employment. Manpower Paper No. 9. H.M.S.O.

Lapidus, G. 1975. 'USSR Women at Work: Changing Patterns'. *Industrial Relations* 14, 2.

Lenski, G. 1960. *Power and Privilege*. New York: McGraw-Hill.

Lipset, S. and Zetterberg, H. 1953. 'A Theory of Social Mobility' in R. Bendix, S. Lipset, eds., *Class, Status and Power*. New York: Free Press, 1967.

Lockwood, D. 1958. *The Blackcoated Worker: A Study in Class Consciousness*. London: Allen & Unwin.

———. 1970. 'Race, Class and Conflict' in S. Zubaida, ed., *Race and Racialism*. London: Tavistock.

Marx, K. and Engels, F. *Selected Works* (3 Vols.). Moscow: Progress Publishers, 1969–1970. (Abbreviated as MESW.)

Mackenzie, G. 1973. *The Aristocracy of Labour*. Cambridge: Cambridge University Press.

———. 1974. 'The Affluent Worker Study: An Evaluation and Critique' in Parkin, ed.

———. 1975. 'World Images and the World of Work' in Esland, G., *et al.*, eds., *People and Work,* Milton Keynes: Open University Press.

Middleton, C. 1974. 'Sexual Inequality and Stratification Theory' in Parkin, ed.

Oakley, A. 1974. *The Sociology of Housework*. London: M. Robertson.

Ofer, G. 1973. *The Service Sector in Soviet Economic Development*. Cambridge, Mass.: Harvard University Press.

Oppenheimer, V. 1970. *The Female Labour Force in the United States*. Berkeley: University of California Press.

Parkin, F. 1971. *Class Inequality and Political Order*. London: MacGibbon & Kee.

———. 1974. 'Strategies of Social Closure in Class Formation' in Parkin, ed. *The Social Analysis of Class Structure*. London: Tavistock.

Poulantzas, N. 1975. *Classes in Contemporary Capitalism*. London: New Left Books.

Ritter, K. and Hargens, L. 1975. 'Occupational Positions and Class Identifications of Married Women: A Test of the Assymetry Hypothesis'. *American Journal of Sociology*, 30: 934–948.

Rubery, J. 1978. 'Structured Labour Markets, Worker Organization and Low Pay' *Cambridge Journal of Economics* 2, 1:1–19.

Schulz, Th., ed. 1974. *Economics of the Family*. Chicago: Chicago University Press.

Schumpeter, J. 1951. *Imperialism and Social Classes*. Oxford: Blackwell.

Scott, H. 1976. *Women and Socialism: Experiences from Eastern Europe*. London: Allison and Busby.

Seccombe, W. 1974. 'The Housewife and her Labour under Capitalism'. *New Left Review* No. 83.

Smelser, N. J. and Lipset, S. M., eds. 1966. *Social Structure and Mobility in Economic Development:* Chicago: Aldine Publishing Co.

Watson, W., Barth, E. 1964. 'Questionable Assumptions in the Theory of Social Stratification'. *Pacific Sociological Review* 7, 1: 10–16

Wedderburn, P. 1974. *Poverty, Inequality and Class Structure*. Cambridge: Cambridge University Press.

Westergaard, J. and Resler, H. 1975. *Class in a Capitalist Society*. London: Heinemann.

# · 22 ·

# Capitalism, Patriarchy, and Job Segregation by Sex

## Heidi Hartmann

The division of labor by sex appears to have been universal throughout human history. In our society the sexual division of labor is hierarchical, with men on top and women on the bottom. Anthropology and history suggest, however, that this division was not always a hierarchical one. The development and importance of a sex-ordered division of labor is the subject of this paper. It is my contention that the roots of women's present social status lie in this sex-ordered division of labor. It is my belief that not only must the hierarchical nature of the division of labor between the sexes be eliminated, but the very division of labor between the sexes itself must be eliminated if women are to attain equal social status with men and if women and men are to attain the full development of their human potentials.

The primary questions for investigation would seem to be, then, first, how a more sexually egalitarian division became a less egalitarian one, and second, how this hierarchical division of labor became extended to wage labor in the modern period. Many anthropological studies suggest that the first process, sexual stratification, occurred together with the increasing productiveness, specialization, and complexity of society; for example, through the establishment of settled agriculture, private property, or the state. It occurred as human society

· Abridged from *Signs* 1(3) (1976): 137–55, 159–61, 164–68.

NOTE: I would like to thank many women at the New School for sharing their knowledge with me and offering encouragement and debate, in particular, Amy Hirsch, Christine Gailey, Nadine Felton, Penny Ciancanelli, Rayna Reiter, and Viana Muller. I would also like to thank Amy Bridges, Carl Degler, David Gordon, Fran Blau, Grace Horowitz, Linda Gordon, Suad Joseph, Susan Strasser, and Tom Vietorisz for helpful comments.

emerged from the primitive and became "civilized." In this perspective capitalism is a relative latecomer, whereas patriarchy,[1] the hierarchical relation between men and women in which men are dominant and women are subordinate, was an early arrival.

I want to argue that, before capitalism, a patriarchal system was established in which men controlled the labor of women and children in the family, and that in so doing men learned the techniques of hierarchical organization and control. With the advent of public-private separations such as those created by the emergence of state apparatus and economic systems based on wider exchange and larger production units, the problem for men became one of maintaining their control over the labor power of women. In other words, a direct personal system of control was translated into an indirect, impersonal system of control, mediated by society-wide institutions. The mechanisms available to men were (1) the traditional division of labor between the sexes, and (2) techniques of hierarchical organization and control. These mechanisms were crucial in the second process, the extension of a sex-ordered division of labor to the wage-labor system, during the period of the emergence of capitalism in Western Europe and the United States.

The emergence of capitalism in the fifteenth to eighteenth centuries threatened patriarchal control based on institutional authority as it destroyed many old institutions and created new ones, such as a "free" market in labor. It threatened to bring all women and children into the labor force and hence to destroy the family and the basis of the power of men over women (i.e., the control over their labor power in the family).[2] If the theoretical tendency of pure capitalism would have been to eradicate all arbitrary differences of status among

---

1. I define patriarchy as a set of social relations which has a material base and in which there are hierarchical relations between men, and solidarity among them, which enable them to control women. Patriarchy is thus the system of male oppression of women. Rubin argues that we should use the term "sex-gender system" to refer to that realm outside the economic system (and not always coordinate with it) where gender stratification based on sex differences is produced and reproduced. Patriarchy is thus only one form, a male dominant one, of a sex-gender system. Rubin argues further that patriarchy should be reserved for pastoral nomadic societies as described in the Old Testament where male power was synonomous with fatherhood. While I agree with Rubin's first point, I think her second point makes the usage of patriarchy too restrictive. It is a good label for most male-dominant societies (see Gayle Rubin, "The Traffic in Women," in *Toward an Anthropology of Women,* ed. Rayna Reiter [New York: Monthly Review Press, 1975]). Muller offers a broader definition of patriarchy "as a social system in which the status of women is defined primarily as wards of their husbands, fathers, and brothers," where wardship has economic and political dimensions (see Viana Muller, "The Formation of the State and the Oppression of Women: A Case Study in England and Wales," mimeographed [New York: New School for Social Research, 1975], p. 4, n. 2). Muller relies on Karen Sacks, "Engels Revisited: Women, the Organization of Production, and Private Property," in *Woman, Culture and Society,* ed. Michelle Z. Rosaldo and Louise Lamphere (Stanford, Calif.: Stanford University Press, 1974). Patriarchy as a system between and among men as well as between men and women is further explained in a draft paper, "The Unhappy Marriage of Marxism and Feminism: Towards a New Union," by Amy Bridges and Heidi Hartmann.

2. Marx and Engels perceived the progress of capitalism in this way, that it would bring women and children into the labor market and thus erode the family. Yet despite Engels's acknowledgment in *The Origin of the Family, Private Property, and the State* (New York: International Publishers, 1972), that men oppress women in the family, he did not see that oppression as based on the control of women's labor, and, if anything, he seems to lament the passing of the male-controlled family (see his *The Condition of the Working Class in England* [Stanford, Calif.: Stanford University Press, 1968], esp. pp. 161–64).

laborers, to make all laborers equal in the marketplace, why are women still in an inferior position to men in the labor market? The possible answers are legion; they range from neoclassical views that the process is not complete or is hampered by market imperfections to the radical view that production requires hierarchy even if the market nominally requires "equality."[3] All of these explanations, it seems to me, ignore the role of men—ordinary men, men as men, men as workers—in maintaining women's inferiority in the labor market. The radical view, in particular, emphasizes the role of men as capitalists in creating hierarchies in the production process in order to maintain their power. Capitalists do this by segmenting the labor market (along race, sex, and ethnic lines among others) and playing workers off against each other. In this paper I argue that male workers have played and continue to play a crucial role in maintaining sexual divisions in the labor process.

Job segregation by sex, I will argue, is the primary mechanism in capitalist society that maintains the superiority of men over women, because it enforces lower wages for women in the labor market. Low wages keep women dependent on men because they encourage women to marry. Married women must perform domestic chores for their husbands. Men benefit, then, from both higher wages and the domestic division of labor. This domestic division of labor, in turn, acts to weaken women's position in the labor market. Thus, the hierarchical domestic division of labor is perpetuated by the labor market, and vice versa. This process is the present outcome of the continuing interaction of two interlocking systems, capitalism and patriarchy. Patriarchy, far from being vanquished by capitalism, is still very virile; it shapes the form modern capitalism takes, just as the development of capitalism has transformed patriarchal institutions. The resulting mutual accommodation between patriarchy and capitalism has created a vicious circle for women.

My argument contrasts with the traditional views of both neoclassical and Marxist economists. Both ignore patriarchy, a social system with a material base. The neoclassical economists tend to exonerate the capitalist system, attributing job segregation to exogenous *ideological* factors, like sexist attitudes. Marxist economists tend to attribute job segregation to capitalists, ignoring the part played by male workers and the effect of centuries of patriarchal social relations. In this paper I hope to redress the balance. The line of argument I have outlined here and will develop further below is perhaps incapable of proof. This paper, I hope, will establish its plausibility rather than its incontrovertability.

The first part of this paper briefly reviews evidence and explanations offered in the anthropological literature for the creation of dominance-dependence relations between men and women. The second part reviews the historical literature on the division of labor by sex during the emergence of capitalism and the Industrial Revolution in England and the United States. This part focuses on the extension of male-female dominance-dependence relations to the wage-labor market and the key role played by men in maintaining job segregation by sex and hence male superiority.

---

3. See Richard C. Edwards, David M. Gordon, and Michael Reich, "Labor Market Segmentation in American Capitalism," draft essay, and the book they edited, *Labor Market Segmentation* (Lexington, Ky.: Lexington Books, forthcoming) for an explication of this view.

## Anthropological Perspectives on the Division of Labor by Sex

Some anthropologists explain male dominance by arguing that it existed from the very beginning of human society. Sherry Ortner suggests that indeed "female is to male as nature is to culture."[4] According to Ortner, culture devalues nature; females are associated with nature, are considered closer to nature in all cultures,[5] and are thus devalued. Her view is compatible with that of Rosaldo,[6] who emphasizes the public-private split, and that of Lévi-Strauss, who assumes the subordination of women during the process of the creation of society.

According to Lévi-Strauss, culture began with the exchange of women by men to cement bonds between families—thereby creating *society*.[7] In fact, Lévi-Strauss sees a fundamental tension between the family (i.e., the domestic realm in which women reside closer to nature) and society, which requires that families break down their autonomy to exchange with one another. The exchange of women is a mechanism that enforces the interdependence of families and that creates society. By analogy, Lévi-Strauss suggests that the division of labor between the sexes is the mechanism which enforces "a reciprocal state of dependency between the sexes."[8] It also assures heterosexual marriage. "When it is stated that one sex must perform certain tasks, this also means that the other sex is forbidden to do them."[9] Thus the existence of a sexual division of labor is a universal of human society, though the exact division of the tasks by sex varies enormously.[10] Moreover, following Lévi-Strauss, because it is men who ex-

---

4. Sherry B. Ortner, "Is Female to Male as Nature Is to Culture?" *Feminist Studies* 1, no. 2 (Fall 1972): 5–31. "The universality of female subordination, the fact that it exists within every type of social and economic arrangement, and in societies of every degree of complexity, indicates to me that we are up against something very profound, very stubborn, something that cannot be remedied merely by rearranging a few tasks and roles in the social system, nor even by rearranging the whole economic structure" (pp. 5–6).

5. Ortner specifically rejects a biological basis for this association of women with nature and the concomitant devaluation of both. Biological differences "only take on significance of superior/inferior within the framework of culturally defined value systems" (ibid., p. 9). The biological explanation is, of course, the other major explanation for the universality of female subordination. I, too, deny the validity of this explanation and will not discuss it in this paper. Female physiology does, however, play a role in supporting a cultural view of women as closer to nature, as Ortner argues persuasively, following DeBeauvoir (ibid., pp. 12–14). Ortner's article was reprinted in *Woman, Culture, and Society* in slightly revised form.

6. Michelle Z. Rosaldo, "Woman, Culture, and Society: A Theoretical Overview," in *Woman, Culture, and Society.*

7. Claude Lévi-Strauss, "The Family," in *Man, Culture and Society,* ed. by Harry L. Shapiro (New York: Oxford University Press, 1971).

8. Ibid., p. 348.

9. Ibid., pp. 347–48. "One of the strongest field recollections of this writer was his meeting, among the Bororo of central Brazil, of a man about thirty years old: unclean, ill-fed, sad, and lonesome. When asked if the man was seriously ill, the natives' answer came as a shock: what was wrong with him?—nothing at all, he was just a bachelor. And true enough, in a society where labor is systematically shared between men and women and where only the married status permits the man to benefit from the fruits of woman's work, including delousing, body painting, and hairplucking as well as vegetable food and cooked food (since the Bororo woman tills the soil and makes pots), a bachelor is really only half a human being" (p. 341).

10. For further discussion of both the universality and variety of the division of labor by sex, see Melville J. Herskovits, *Economic Anthropology* (New York: W. W. Norton & Co., 1965), esp. chap. 7; Theodore Caplow, *The Sociology of Work* (New York: McGraw-Hill Book Co., 1964), esp. chap. 1.

change women and women who are exchanged in creating social bonds, men benefit more than women from these social bonds, and the division of labor between the sexes is a hierarchical one.[11]

While this first school of anthropological thought, the "universalists," is based primarily on Lévi-Strauss and the exchange of women, Chodorow, following Rosaldo and Ortner, emphasizes women's confinement to the domestic sphere. Chodorow locates this confinement in the mothering role. She constructs the universality of patriarchy on the universal fact that women mother. Female mothering reproduces itself via the creation of gender-specific personality structures.[12]

Two other major schools of thought on the origins of the sexual division of labor merit attention. Both reject the universality, at least in theory if not in practice, of the sex-ordered division of labor. One is the "feminist-revisionist" school which argues that we cannot be certain that the division of labor is male supremacist; it may be separate but equal (as Lévi-Strauss occasionally seems to indicate), but we will never know because of the bias of the observers which makes comparisons impossible. This school is culturally relativist in the extreme, but it nevertheless contributes to our knowledge of women's work and status by stressing the accomplishments of females in their part of the division of labor.[13]

The second school also rejects the universality of sex-ordered division of labor but, unlike relativists, seeks to compare societies to isolate the variables which coincide with greater or lesser autonomy of women. This school, the "variationist," is subdivided according to the characteristics members emphasize: the contribution of women to subsistence and their control over their contribution, the organization of tribal versus state societies, the requirements of the mode of production, the emergence of wealth and private property, the boundaries of the private and public spheres.[14] A complete review of these approaches is impossible here, but I will cite a few examples from this literature to illustrate the relevance of these variables for the creation of a sex-ordered division of labor.

---

11. For more on the exchange of women and its significance for women, see Rubin.

12. Nancy Chodorow, *Family Structure and Feminine Personality: The Reproduction of Mothering* (Berkeley: University of California Press, forthcoming). Chodorow offers an important alternative interpretation of the Oedipus complex (see her "Family Structure and Feminine Personality" in *Woman, Culture, and Society*).

13. Several of the articles in the Rosaldo and Lamphere collection are of this variety (see particularly Collier and Stack). Also, see Ernestine Friedl, "The Position of Women: Appearance and Reality," *Anthropological Quarterly* 40, no. 3 (July 1967): 97–108.

14. For an example of one particular emphasis, Leavitt states: "The most important clue to woman's status anywhere is her degree of participation in economic life and her control over property and the products she produces, both of which factors appear to be related to the kinship system of a society" (Ruby B. Leavitt, "Women in Other Cultures," in *Woman and Sexist Society,* ed. Vivian Gornick and Barbara K. Moran [New York: New American Library, 1972], p. 396). In a historical study which also seeks to address the questions of women's status, Joanne McNamara and Suzanne Wemple ("The Power of Woman through the Family in Medieval Europe: 500–1100," *Feminist Studies* 1, nos. 3–4 [Winter–Spring 1973]: 126–41) emphasize the private-public split in their discussion of women's loss of status during this period.

Among the !Kung, a hunting and gathering people in South West Africa, the women have a great deal of autonomy and influence.[15] Draper argues that this is the result of (1) the contribution of 60–80 percent of the community's food by the women and their retention of control over its distribution; (2) equal absence from the camp and equal range and mobility of the male hunters and the female gatherers (the women are not dependent on the men for protection in their gathering range); (3) the flexibility of sex roles and the willingness of adults to do the work of the opposite sex (with the exception that women did not hunt and men did not remove nasal mucous or feces from children!); (4) the absence of physical expression of aggression; (5) the small size (seventeen to sixty-five) of and flexible membership in living groups; (6) a close, public settlement arrangement, in which the huts were situated in a circle around the campfire.

In the late 1960s when Draper did her fieldwork, some of the !Kung were beginning to settle in small villages where the men took up herding and the women agriculture, like other groups (e.g., the Bantu) who were already settled. The agriculture and the food preparation were more time consuming for the women than gathering had been and, while they continued to gather from time to time, the new agricultural pursuits kept the women closer to home. The men, in contrast, through herding, remained mobile and had greater contact with the world outside the !Kung: the Bantus, politics, wage work, and advanced knowledge (e.g., about domesticated animals). These sex roles were maintained with more rigidity. Boys and girls came to be socialized differently, and men began to feel their work superior to the women's. Men began to consider property theirs (rather than jointly owned with the women), and "[r]anking of individuals in terms of prestige and differential worth ha[d] begun. . . ."[16] Houses, made more permanent and private, were no longer arranged in a circle. The women in particular felt that the group as a whole had less ability to observe, and perhaps to sanction, the behavior of people in married couples. Doubtless these changes occurred partly because of the influence of the male-dominated Western culture on the !Kung. The overall result, according to Draper, was a decrease in the status and influence of women, the denigration of their work, and an increase, for women, in the importance of the family unit at the expense of the influence of the group as a whole. The delineation of public and private spheres placed men in the public and women in the private sphere, and the public sphere came to be valued more.

Boserup, in *Woman's Role in Economic Development*, writes extensively of the particular problems caused for women when Third World tribal groups came into contact with Western colonial administrations.[17] The usual result was the creation or strengthening of male dominance as, for example, where administrations taught men advanced agricultural techniques where women were

---

15. Patricia Draper, "!Kung Women: Contrasts in Sexual Egalitarianism in Foraging and Sedentary Contexts," in *Toward an Anthropology of Women*.

16. Ibid., p. 108.

17. Ester Boserup, *Woman's Role in Economic Development* (London: George Allen & Unwin, 1970).

farmers, or schooled men in trading where women were traders. The Europeans encouraged men to head and support their families, superseding women's traditional responsibilities. Previous to colonization, according to Leavitt: "In regions like Africa and Southeast Asia, where shifting agriculture and the female farmer predominate, the women work very hard and receive limited support from their husbands, but they also have some economic independence, considerable freedom of movement, and an important place in the community. . . . In traditional African marriages the woman is expected to support herself and her children and to feed the family, including her husband, with the food she grows."[18] Boserup supports this view of the economic role of women before the influence of Europeans began to be felt.

Europeans also entrusted local governance to male leaders and ignored women's traditional participation in tribal society. That the women had highly organized and yet nonhierarchical governmental structures, which were unknown and ignored by the colonists, is illustrated by the case of the Igbo in Nigeria. Allen reports that Igbo women held *mikiri,* or meetings, which were democratic discussions with no official leaders and "which articulated women's interests *as opposed* to those of men."[19] The women needed these meetings because they lived in patrilocal villages and had few kinship ties with each other, and because they had their own separate economic activities, their own crops, and their own trading, which they needed to protect from men. When a man offended the women, by violating the women's market rules or letting his cows into the women's yam fields, the women often retaliated as a group by "sitting on a man"—carrying on loudly at his home late at night and "perhaps demolishing his hut or plastering it with mud and roughing him up a bit."[20] Women also sometimes executed collective strikes and boycotts. With the advent of the British administrators, and their inevitably unfavorable policies toward women, the Igbo women adapted their tactics and used them against the British. For example, in response to an attempt to tax the women farmers, tens of thousands of women were involved in riots at administrative centers over an area of 6,000 square miles containing a population of 2 million people. The "Women's War," as it was called, was coordinated through the market *mikiri* network.[21] Allen continues to detail the disintegration of the *mikiri* in the face of British colonial and missionary policies.

In a study of a somewhat different process of state formation, Muller looks at the decline of Anglo-Saxon and Welsh tribal society and the formation of the English nation-state, a process which occurred from the eighth to the fifteenth century. Muller writes:

The transition from tribe to state is historically probably the greatest watershed in the decline in the status of women. . . . This is not to deny that in what we call "tribal," that is,

---

18. Leavitt, pp. 412, 413.

19. Judith Van Allen, "'Sitting on a Man': Colonialism and the Lost Political Institutions of Igbo Women," *Canadian Journal of African Studies* 6, no. 2 (1972): 169.

20. Ibid., p. 170.

21. Ibid., pp. 174–75. The British naturally thought the women were directed in their struggle by the men, though very few men participated in the riots.

pre-state, society there is not a wide variation in the status of women and even that in certain pre-state societies, women may be in what we would consider an abject position *vis à vis* the men in that society. . . . We believe that the causes for these variations in status can be found, as in the case of State Societies, in the material conditions which give rise to the social and economic positions therein.[22]

Muller stresses that, in the Welsh and Anglo-Saxon tribes, "the right of individual maintenance was so well entrenched that these rights were not entrusted to a patriarchal head of a nuclear family, but were, rather, vested in the larger social group of the *gwely* [four-generation kinship group]."[23] Both men and women upon adulthood received a share of cattle from the *gwely*. The cattle provided their personal maintenance and prevented an individual from becoming dependent upon another. Thus, although in the tribal system land inheritance was patrilineal and residence patrilocal, a married woman had her own means of economic subsistence. Women were political participants both in their husbands' and in their natal lineages. Like a man, a woman was responsible for her children's crimes, and she and her natal lineages (*not* her spouse's) were responsible for her crimes. Tribal customs were, however, undermined by the emergence of the state: ". . . we can observe the development of public—as opposed to social—male authority, through the political structure imposed by the emerging state. Since the state is interested in the alienation of the tribal resource base—its land and its labor power—it finds it convenient to use the traditional gender division of labor and resources in tribal society and places them in a hierarchical relationship both internally (husband over wife and children) and externally (lords over peasants and serfs)."[24] The king established regional administrative units without regard to tribal jurisdictions, appointed his own administrators, bypassed the authority of the tribal chiefs, and levied obligations on the males as "heads" of individual households. Tribal groups lost collective responsibility for their members, and women and children lost their group rights and came under the authority of their husbands. Woman's work became private for the benefit of her husband, rather than public for the benefit of the kin group. As Muller points out, there must have been tendencies evident in tribal society that created the preconditions for a hierarchical, male-dominated state, for it was not equally likely that the emerging state would be female. Among these tendencies, for example, were male ownership of land and greater male participation in military expeditions, probably especially those farther away.[25]

---

22. Muller, p. 1. I am very grateful to Viana Muller for allowing me to summarize parts of her unpublished paper.

23. Ibid., p. 14.

24. Ibid., p. 25.

25. The examples of the !Kung, the Igbo, the Anglo-Saxons, and the groups discussed by Boserup all suggest that the process of expansion of state or emerging-state societies and the conquest of other peoples was an extremely important mechanism for spreading hierarchy and male domination. In fact, the role of warfare and imperialism raises the question of whether the state, to establish itself, creates the patriarchal family, or the patriarchal family creates the state (Thomas Vietorisz, personal communication). Surely emerging patriarchal social relations in prestate societies paved the way for both male public power (i.e., male control of the state apparatus) and the privatization of patriarchal power in the family. Surely also this privatization—and the concomitant decline of tribal power—strengthened, and was strengthened by, the state.

This summary of several studies from the third school of anthropology, the variationist school, points to a number of variables that help to explain a decrease in woman's social status. They suggest that increased sexual stratification occurs along with a general process of social stratification (which at least in some versions seems to depend on and foster an increase in social surplus—to support the higher groups in the hierarchy). As a result, a decrease in the social status of woman occurs when (1) she loses control of subsistence through a change in production methods and devaluation of her share of the division of labor; (2) her work becomes private and family centered rather than social and kin focused; and/or (3) some men assert their power over other men through the state mechanism by elevating these subordinate men in their families, using the nuclear family against the kin group.[26] In this way the division of labor between men and women becomes a more hierarchical one. Control over women is maintained directly in the family by the man, but it is sustained by social institutions, such as the state and religion.

The work in this school of anthropology suggests that patriarchy did not always exist, but rather that it emerged as social conditions changed. Moreover, men participated in this transformation. Because it benefited men relative to women, men have had a stake in reproducing patriarchy. Although there is a great deal of controversy among anthropologists about the origins of patriarchy, and more work needs to be done to establish the validity of this interpretation, I believe the weight of the evidence supports it. In any case, most anthropologists agree that patriarchy emerged long before capitalism, even if they disagree about its origins.

In England, as we have seen, the formation of the state marks the end of Anglo-Saxon tribal society and the beginning of feudal society. Throughout feudal society the tendencies toward the privatization of family life and the increase of male power within the family appear to strengthen, as does their institutional support from church and state. By the time of the emergence of capitalism in the fifteenth through eighteenth centuries, the nuclear, patriarchal peasant family had become the basic production unit in society.[27]

---

26. This point is stressed especially by Muller but is also illustrated by the !Kung. Muller states: "The men, although lowered from clansmen to peasants, were elevated to heads of nuclear families, with a modicum of both public power [through the state and religion] and a measure of private power through the decree of the Church-State that they were to be lords over their wives" (p. 35).

27. Both Hill and Stone describe England during this period as a patriarchal society in which the institutions of the nuclear family, the state, and religion, were being strengthened (see Christopher Hill, *Society and Puritanism* [New York: Schocken Books, 1964], esp. chap. 13; Lawrence Stone, *The Crisis of the Aristocracy, 1558–1641,* abridged ed. [New York: Oxford University Press, 1967], esp. chap. 11). Recent demographic research verifies the establishment of the nuclear family prior to the industrial revolution (see Peter Laslett, ed., *Household and Family in Past Time* [Cambridge: Cambridge University Press, 1972]). Because of limitations of my knowledge and space, and because I sought to discuss, first, the concept and establishment of patriarchy and second, its transformation in a wage-labor society, I am skipping over the rise and fall of feudal society and the emergence of family-centered petty commodity production and focusing in the next section on the disintegration of this family-centered production, creation of the wage-labor force, and the maintenance of job segregation in a capitalist context.

## The Emergence of Capitalism and the Industrial Revolution in England and the United States

The key process in the emergence of capitalism was primitive accumulation, the prior accumulation that was necessary for capitalism to establish itself.[28] Primitive accumulation was a twofold process which set the preconditions for the expansion of the scale of production: first, free laborers had to be accumulated; second, large amounts of capital had to be accumulated. The first was achieved through enclosures and the removal of people from the land, their subsistence base, so that they were forced to work for wages. The second was achieved through both the growth of smaller capitals in farms and shops amassed through banking facilities, and vast increases in merchant capital, the profits from the slave trade, and colonial exploitation.

The creation of a wage-labor force and the increase in the scale of production that occurred with the emergence of capitalism had in some ways a more severe impact on women than on men. To understand this impact let us look at the work of women before this transition occurred and the changes which took place as it occurred.[29] In the 1500s and 1600s, agriculture, woolen textiles (carried on as a by-industry of agriculture), and the various crafts and trades in the towns were the major sources of livelihood for the English population. In the rural areas men worked in the fields on small farms they owned or rented and women tended the household plots, small gardens and orchards, animals, and dairies. The women also spun and wove. A portion of these products were sold in small markets to supply the villages, towns, and cities, and in this way women supplied a considerable proportion of their families' cash income, as well as their subsistence in kind. In addition to the tenants and farmers, there was a small wage-earning class of men and women who worked on the larger farms. Occasionally tenants and their wives worked for wages as well, the men more often than the women.[30] As small farmers and cottagers were displaced by larger farmers in the seventeenth and eighteenth centuries, their wives lost their

---

28. See Karl Marx, "The So-called Primitive Accumulation," in *Capital,* 3 vols. (New York: International Publishers, 1967), vol. 1, pt. 8; Stephen Hymer, "Robinson Crusoe and the Secret of Primitive Accumulation," *Monthly Review* 23, no. 4 (September 1971): 11–36.

29. This account relies primarily on that of Alice Clark, *The Working Life of Women in the Seventeenth Century* (New York: Harcourt, Brace & Howe, 1920). Her account is supported by many others, such as B. L. Hutchins, *Women in Modern Industry* (London: G. Bell & Sons, 1915); Georgiana Hill, *Women in English Life from Medieval to Modern Times,* 2 vols. (London: Richard Bentley & Son, 1896); F. W. Tickner, *Women in English Economic History* (New York: E. P. Dutton & Co., 1923); Ivy Pinchbeck, *Women Workers and the Industrial Revolution, 1750–1850* (London: Frank Cass & Co., 1930; reprinted 1969).

30. Women and men in England had been employed as agricultural laborers for several centuries. Clark found that by the seventeenth century the wages of men were higher than women's and the tasks done were different, though similar in skill and strength requirements (Clark 1920, p. 60). Wages for agricultural (and other work) were often set by local authorities. These wage differentials reflected the relative social status of men and women and the social norms of the time. Women were considered to require lower wages because they ate less, for example, and were expected to have fewer luxuries, such as tobacco (see Clark and Pinchbeck throughout for substantiation of women's lower standard of living). Laura Oren has substantiated this for English women during the period 1860–1950 (see n. 60 below).

main sources of support, while the men were able to continue as wage laborers to some extent. Thus women, deprived of these essential household plots, suffered relatively greater unemployment, and the families as a whole were deprived of a large part of their subsistence.[31]

In the 1700s, the demand for cotton textiles grew, and English merchants found they could utilize the labor of the English agricultural population, who were already familiar with the arts of spinning and weaving. The merchants distributed materials to be spun and woven, creating a domestic industrial system which occupied many displaced farm families. This putting-out system, however, proved inadequate. The complexities of distribution and collection and, perhaps more important, the control the workers had over the production process (they could take time off, work intermittently, steal materials) prevented an increase in the supply of textiles sufficient to meet the merchants' needs. To solve these problems first spinning, in the late 1700s, and then weaving, in the early 1800s, were organized into factories. The textile factories were located in the rural areas, at first, in order both to take advantage of the labor of children and women, by escaping the restrictions of the guilds in the cities, and to utilize waterpower. When spinning was industrialized, women spinners at home suffered greater unemployment, while the demand for male handloom weavers increased. When weaving was mechanized, the need for handloom weavers fell off as well.[32]

In this way, domestic industry, created by emerging capitalism, was later superseded and destroyed by the progress of capitalist industrialization. In the process, women, children, and men in the rural areas all suffered dislocation and disruption, but they experienced this in different ways. Women, forced into unemployment by the capitalization of agriculture more frequently than men, were more available to labor, both in the domestic putting-out system and in the early factories. It is often argued both that men resisted going into the factories because they did not want to lose their independence and that women and children were more docile and malleable. If this was in fact the case, it would appear that these "character traits" of women and men were already established

31. The problem of female unemployment in the countryside was a generally recognized one which figured prominently in the debate about poor-law reform, for example. As a remedy, it was suggested that rural families be allowed to retain small household plots, that women be used more in agricultural wage labor and also in the putting-out system, and that men's wages be adjusted upward (see Ivy Pinchbeck, *Women Workers and the Industrial Revolution, 1750–1850,* pp. 69–84).

32. See Stephen Marglin, "What Do Bosses Do? The Origins and Functions of Hierarchy in Capitalist Production," *Review of Radical Political Economics* 6, no. 2 (Summer 1974): 60–112, for a discussion of the transition from putting out to factories. The sexual division of labor changed several times in the textile industry. Hutchins writes that the further back one goes in history, the more was the industry controlled by women. By the seventeenth century, though, men had become professional handloom weavers, and it was often claimed that men had superior strength or skill— which was required for certain types of weaves or fabrics. Thus, the increase in demand for handloom weavers in the late 1700s brought increased employment for men. When weaving was mechanized in the factories women operated the power looms, and male handloom weavers became unemployed. When jenny and waterframe spinning were replaced by mule spinning, supposedly requiring more strength, men took that over and displaced women spinners. A similar transition occurred in the United States. It is important to keep in mind that as a by-industry, both men and women engaged in various processes of textile manufacture, and this was intensified under putting out (see Pinchbeck 1969, chaps. 6–9).

before the advent of the capitalistic organization of industry, and that they would have grown out of the authority structure prevailing in the previous period of small-scale, family agriculture. Many historians suggest that within the family men were the heads of households, and women, even though they contributed a large part of their families' subsistence, were subordinate.[33]

We may never know the facts of the authority structure within the preindustrial family, since much of what we know is from prescriptive literature or otherwise class biased, and little is known about the point of view of the people themselves. Nevertheless, the evidence on family life and on relative wages and levels of living suggests that women were subordinate within the family. This conclusion is consonant with the anthropological literature, reviewed in Part I above, which describes the emergence of patriarchial social relations along with early societal stratification. Moreover, the history of the early factories suggests that capitalists took advantage of this authority structure, finding women and children more vulnerable, both because of familial relations and because they were simply more desperate economically due to the changes in agriculture which left them unemployed.[34]

The transition to capitalism in the cities and towns was experienced somewhat differently than in the rural areas, but it tends to substantiate the line of argument just set out: men and women had different places in the familial authority structure, and capitalism proceeded in a way that built on that authority structure. In the towns and cities before the transition to capitalism a system of family industry prevailed: a family of artisans worked together at home to produce goods for exchange. Adults were organized in guilds, which had social and religious functions as well as industrial ones. Within trades carried on as family industries women and men generally performed different tasks: in general, the men worked at what were considered more skilled tasks, the women at processing the raw materials or finishing the end product. Men, usually the heads of the production units, had the status of master artisans. For though women usually belonged to their husbands' guilds, they did so as appendages; girls were rarely apprenticed to a trade and thus rarely become journeymen or masters. Married women participated in the production process and probably acquired important skills, but they usually controlled the production process only if they were widowed, when guilds often gave them the right to hire apprentices and journeymen. Young men may have married within their guilds (i.e., the daughters of artisans in the same trade). In fact, young women and girls had a unique and very important role as extra or casual laborers in a system where the guilds prohibited hiring additional workers from outside the family, and undoubtedly they learned skills which were useful when they married.[35]

---

33. See Clark: Pinchbeck; E. P. Thompson, *The Making of the English Working Class* (New York: Vintage Books, 1963).

34. In fact, the earliest factories utilized the labor of poor children, already separated from their families, who were apprenticed to factory owners by parish authorities. They were perhaps the most desperate and vulnerable of all.

35. Hutchins, p. 16 (see also Olive J. Jocelyn, *English Apprenticeship and Child Labor* [London: T. Fisher Unwin, 1912], pp. 149–50, on the labor of girls, and Clark, chap. 5, on the organization of family industry in towns).

Nevertheless, girls appear not to have been trained as carefully as boys were and, as adults, not to have attained the same status in the guilds.

Although in most trades men were the central workers and women the assistants, other trades were so identified by sex that family industry did not prevail.[36] Carpentry and millinery were two such trades. Male carpenters and female milliners both hired apprentices and assistants and attained the status of master craftspersons. According to Clark, although some women's trades, such as millinery, were highly skilled and organized in guilds, many women's trades were apparently difficult to organize in strong guilds, because most women's skills could not be easily monopolized. All women, as part of their home duties, knew the arts of textile manufacturing, sewing, food processing, and to some extent, trading.

In the seventeenth and eighteenth centuries the family industry system and the guilds began to break down in the face of the demand for larger output. Capitalists began to organize production on a larger scale, and production became separated from the home as the size of establishments grew. Women were excluded from participation in the industries in which they had assisted men as they no longer took place at home, where married women apparently tended to remain to carry on their domestic work. Yet many women out of necessity sought work in capitalistically organized industry as wage laborers. When women entered wage labor they appear to have been at a disadvantage relative to men. First, as in agriculture, there was already a tradition of lower wages for women (in the previously limited area of wage work). Second, women appear to have been less well trained than men and obtained less desirable jobs. And third, they appear to have been less well organized than men.

Because I think the ability of men to organize themselves played a crucial role in limiting women's participation in the wage-labor market, I want to offer, first, some evidence to support the assertion that men were better organized and, second, some plausible reasons for their superiority in this area. I am not arguing that men had greater organizational abilities at all times and all places, or in all areas or types of organization, but am arguing here that it is plausible that they did in England during this period, particularly in the area of economic production. As evidence of their superiority, we have the guilds themselves, which were better organized among men's trades than women's, and in which, in joint trades, men had superior positions—women were seldom admitted to the hierarchical ladder of progression. Second, we have the evidence of the rise of male professions and the elimination of female ones during the sixteenth and seventeenth centuries. The medical profession, male from its inception, established itself through hierarchical organization, the monopolization of new, "scientific" skills, and the assistance of the state. Midwifery was virtually wiped out by the men. Brewing provides another example. Male brewers organized a fellowship, petitioned the king for monopoly rights (in exchange for a tax on

---

36. The seventeenth century already found the crafts and trades sex divided. Much work needs to be done on the development of guilds from the point of view of shedding light on the sexual division of labor and on the question of the nature of women's organizations. Such work would enable us to trace more accurately the decline in women's status from the tribal period, through feudalism, to the emergence of capitalism.

every quart they brewed), and succeeded in forcing the numerous small-scale brewsters to buy from them.[37] Third, throughout the formative period of industrial capitalism, men appear to have been better able to organize themselves as wage workers. And as we shall see below, as factory production became established men used their labor organizations to limit women's place in the labor market.

As to why men might have had superior organizational ability during this transitional period, I think we must consider the development of patriarchal social relations in the nuclear family, as reinforced by the state and religion, a process briefly described above for Anglo-Saxon England. Since men's superior position was reinforced by the state, and men acted in the political arena as heads of households and in the households as heads of production units, it seems likely that men would develop more organizational structures beyond their households. Women, in an inferior position at home and without the support of the state, would be less likely to be able to do this. Men's organizational knowledge, then, grew out of their position in the family and in the division of labor. Clearly, further investigation of organizations before and during the transition period is necessary to establish the mechanisms by which men came to control this public sphere.

Thus, the capitalistic organization of industry, in removing work from the home, served to increase the subordination of women, since it served to increase the relative importance of the area of men's domination. But it is important to remember that men's domination was already established and that it clearly influenced the direction and shape that capitalist development took. As Clark has argued, with the separation of work from the home men became less dependent on women for industrial production, while women became more dependent on men economically. From a position much like that of the African women discussed above, English married women, who had supported themselves and their children, became the domestic servants of their husbands. Men increased their control over technology, production, and marketing, as they excluded women from industry, education, and political organization.[38]

When women participated in the wage-labor market, they did so in a position as clearly limited by patriarchy as it was by capitalism. Men's control over women's labor was altered by the wage-labor system, but it was not eliminated. In the labor market the dominant position of men was maintained by sex-ordered job segregation. Women's jobs were lower paid, considered less skilled, and often involved less exercise of authority or control.[39] Men acted to enforce

---

37. See Clark, pp. 221–31, for the brewers, and pp. 242–84, for the medical profession.

38. Ibid., chap. 7. Eli Zaretsky ("Capitalism, the Family, and Personal Life," *Socialist Revolution,* nos. 13, 14 [1973]), follows a similar interpretation of history and offers different conclusions. Capitalism exacerbated the sexual division of labor and created the *appearance* that women work for their husbands; in reality, women who did domestic work at home were working for capital. Thus according to Zaretsky the present situation has its roots more in capitalism than in patriarchy. Although capitalism may have increased the consequence for women of the domestic division of labor, surely patriarchy tells us more about why men didn't stay home. That women worked for men in the home, as well as for capital, is also a reality.

39. William Lazonick argues in his dissertation, "Marxian Theory and the Development of the Labor Force in England" (Ph.D. diss., Harvard University, 1975), that the degree of authority

job segregation in the labor market; they utilized trade-union associations and strengthened the domestic division of labor, which required women to do housework, child care, and related chores. Women's subordinate position in the labor market reinforced their subordinate position in the family, and that in turn reinforced their labor-market position.

The process of industrialization and the establishment of the factory system, particularly in the textile industry, illustrate the role played by men's trade-union associations. Textile factories employed children at first, but as they expanded they began to utilize the labor of adult women and of whole families. While the number of married women working has been greatly exaggerated,[40] apparently enough married women had followed their work into the factories to cause both their husbands and the upper classes concern about home life and the care of children. Smelser has argued that in the early factories the family industry system and male control could often be maintained. For example, adult male spinners often hired their own or related children as helpers, and whole families were often employed by the same factory for the same length of working day.[41] Technological change, however, increasingly made this difficult, and factory legislation which limited the hours of children, but not of adults, further exacerbated the difficulties of the "family factory system."

The demands of the factory laborers in the 1820s and 1830s had been designed to maintain the family factory system,[42] but by 1840 male factory operatives were calling for limitations on the hours of work of children between nine

---

required of the worker was often decisive in determining the sex of the worker. Thus handloom weavers in cottage industry were men because this allowed them to control the production process and the labor of the female spinners. In the spinning factories, mule spinners were men because mule spinners were required to supervise the labor of piecers, usually young boys. Men's position as head of the family established their position as heads of production units, and vice versa. While this is certainly plausible, I think it requires further investigation. Lazonick's work in this area (see chap. 4, "Segments of the Labour Force: Women, Children, and Irish") is very valuable.

40. Perhaps 25 percent of female textile factory workers were married women (see Pinchbeck, p. 198; Margaret Hewitt, *Wives and Mothers in Victorian Industry* [London: Rockliff, 1958], pp. 14 ff.). It is important to remember also that factory employment was far from the dominant employment of women. Most women worked as domestic servants.

41. Neil Smelser, *Social Change and the Industrial Revolution* (Chicago: University of Chicago Press, 1959), chaps. 9–11. Other researchers have also established that in some cases there was a considerable degree of familial control over some aspects of the work process. See Tamara Hareven's research on mills in New Hampshire; e.g., "Family Time and Industrial Time: The Interaction between Family and Work in a Planned Corporation Town, 1900–1924," *Journal of Urban History* 1, no. 3 (May 1975): 365–89. Michael Anderson, *Family Structure in Nineteenth Century Lancashire* (Cambridge: Cambridge University Press, 1971), argues, based on demographic data, that the "practice of allowing operatives to employ assistants, though widespread, can at no period have resulted in a predominantly parent-child pattern of employment" (p. 116). Also see Amy Hirsch's treatment of this question in her "Capitalism and the Working Class Family in British Textile Industries during the Industrial Revolution," mimeographed (New York: New School for Social Research, 1975).

42. "[The factory operatives'] agitation in the 1820's and 1830's was one avenue taken to protect the traditional relationship between adult and child, to perpetuate the structure of wages, to limit the recruitment of labourers into industry, and to maintain the father's economic authority" (Smelser, p. 265). Lazonick argues that the workers' main interest were not in maintaining their familial dominance in industry but in maintaining their family life outside industry. According to Smelser, agitation before 1840 sought to establish equal length days for all workers, which would tend to maintain the family in the factory, whereas after 1840 male workers came to accept the notion that married women and children should stay at home.

and thirteen to eight a day, and forbidding the employment of younger children. According to Smelser this caused parents difficulty in training and supervising their children, and to remedy it male workers and the middle and upper classes began to recommend that women, too, be removed from the factories.[43]

The upper classes of the Victorian Age, the age that elevated women to their pedestals, seem to have been motivated by moral outrage and concern for the future of the English race (and for the reproduction of the working class): "In the male," said Lord Shaftesbury, "the moral effects of the system are very sad, but in the female they are infinitely worse, not alone upon themselves, but upon their families, upon society, and, I may add, upon the country itself. It is bad enough if you corrupt the man, but if you corrupt the woman, you poison the waters of life at the very fountain."[44] Engels, too, appears to have been outraged for similar reasons: ". . . we find here precisely the same features reappearing which the Factories' Report presented,—the work of women up to the hour of confinement, incapacity as housekeepers, neglect of home and children, indifference, actual dislike to family life, and demoralization; further the crowding out of men from employment, the constant improvement of machinery, early emancipation of children, husbands supported by their wives and children, etc., etc."[45] Here, Engels has touched upon the reasons for the opposition of the male workers to the situation. Engels was apparently ambivalent about whose side he was on, for, while he often seems to share the attitudes of the men and of the upper classes, he also referred to the trade unions as elite organizations of grown-up men who achieved benefits for themselves but not for the unskilled, women, or children.[46]

That male workers viewed the employment of women as a threat to their jobs is not surprising, given an economic system where competition among workers was characteristic. That women were paid lower wages exacerbated the threat. But why their response was to attempt to exclude women rather than to organize them is explained, not by capitalism, but by patriarchal relations between men and women: men wanted to assure that women would continue to perform the appropriate tasks at home. . . .

In 1846 the *Ten Hours' Advocate* stated clearly that they hoped for the day

---

43. The question of the motives of the various groups involved in passing the factory acts is indeed a thorny one. Women workers themselves may have favored the legislation as an improvement in their working conditions, but some undoubtedly needed the incomes longer hours enabled. Most women working in the mills were young, single women who perhaps benefited from the protection. Single women, though "liberated" by the mills from direct domination in their families (about which there was much discussion in the 1800s), were nevertheless kept in their place by the conditions facing them in the labor market. Because of their age and sex, job segregation and lower wages assured their inability to be completely self-sufficient. Ruling-class men, especially those associated with the larger firms, may have had an interest in factory legislation in order to eliminate unfair competition. Working-class and ruling-class men may have cooperated to maintain men's dominant position in the labor market and in the family.

44. From Mary Merryweather, *Factory Life,* cited in *Women in English Life from Medieval to Modern Times,* 2: 200. The original is recorded in *Hansard Parliamentary Debates,* 3d ser., House of Commons, June 7, 1842.

45. Frederick Engels, *The Condition of the Working Class in England in 1844* (London: Geo. Allen & Unwin, 1892), p. 199.

46. Ibid., p. xv.

when such threats would be removed altogether: ". . . It is needless for us to say, that all attempts to improve the morals and physical condition of female factory workers will be abortive, unless their hours are materially reduced. Indeed we may go so far as to say, that married females would be much better occupied in performing the domestic duties of the household, than following the never-tiring motion of machinery. We therefore hope the day is not distant, when the husband will be able to provide for his wife and family, without sending the former to endure the drudgery of a cotton mill."[47] Eventually, male trade unionists realized that women could not be removed altogether, but their attitude was still ambivalent. One local wrote to the Women's Trade Union League, organized in 1889 to encourage unionization among women workers: "Please send an organizer to this town as we have decided that if the women here cannot be organized they must be exterminated."[48] . . .

Turning to the United States experience provides an opportunity, first, to explore shifts in the sex composition of jobs, and, second, to consider further the role of unions, particularly in establishing protective legislation. . . .

Conditions in the United States differed from those in England. First, the division of labor within colonial farm families was probably more rigid, with men in the fields and women producing manufactured articles at home. Second, the early textile factories employed young single women from the farms of New England; a conscious effort was made, probably out of necessity, to avoid the creation of a family labor system and to preserve the labor of men for agriculture.[49] This changed, however, with the eventual dominance of manufacture over agriculture as the leading sector in the economy and with immigration. Third, the shortage of labor and dire necessity in colonial and frontier America perhaps created more opportunities for women in nontraditional pursuits outside the family; colonial women were engaged in a wide variety of occupations.[50] Fourth, shortages of labor continued to operate in women's favor at various points throughout the nineteenth and twentieth centuries. Fifth, the constant arrival of new groups of immigrants created an extremely heterogeneous labor force, with varying skill levels and organizational development and rampant antagonisms.[51]

Major shifts in the sex composition of employment occurred in boot and shoe manufacture, textile manufacture, teaching, cigar making, and clerical

---

47. Smelser, p. 301. Similarly, Pinchbeck quotes from a deputation of the West Riding Short-Time Committee which demands "the gradual withdrawal of all females from the factories" because "home, its cares, its employments, is woman's true sphere." Gladstone thought this a good suggestion, easily implemented by appropriate laws, e.g., "forbidding a female to work in a factory after her marriage and during the life-time of her husband" (Pinchbeck, p. 200, n. 3, from the *Manchester and Salford Advertiser* [January 8, 15, 1842]).

48. Quoted in G. D. H. Cole and Raymond Postgate, *The Common People, 1746–1946,* 4th ed. (London: Methuen, 1949), p. 432.

49. Edith Abbott, *Women in Industry* (New York: Arno Press, 1969), esp. chap. 4.

50. Ibid., chap. 2.

51. These antagonisms were often increased by employers. During a cigar-makers strike in New York City in 1877 employers brought in unskilled native American girls. By printing on the boxes, "These cigars were made by American girls," they sold many more boxes of the imperfect cigars than they had expected to (Abbott, p. 207).

work.[52] In all of these, except textiles, the shift was toward more women. New occupations opened up for both men and women, but men seemed to dominate in most of them, even though there were exceptions. Telephone operating and typing for example, became women's jobs.

In all of the cases of increase in female employment, the women were partially stimulated by a sharp rise in the demand for the service or product. During the late 1700s and early 1800s, domestic demand for ready-made boots went up because of the war, a greater number of slaves, general population expansion, and the settling of the frontier. Demand for teachers increased rapidly before, during, and after the Civil War as public education spread. The demand for cheap, machine-made cigars grew rapidly at the end of the nineteenth century. The upward shift in the numbers of clerical workers came between 1890 and 1930, when businesses grew larger and became more centralized, requiring more administration, distribution, transportation, marketing, and communication.

In several cases the shift to women was accompanied by technical innovations, which allowed increased output and sometimes reduced the skill required of the worker. By 1800, boot- and shoemakers had devised a division of labor which allowed women to work on sewing the uppers at home. In the 1850s, sewing machines were applied to boots and shoes in factories. In the 1870s, the use of wooden molds, rather than hand bunching, simplified cigar making, and in the 1880s, machinery was brought in. And in clerical work, the typewriter, of course, greatly increased the productivity of clerical labor. The machinery introduced in textiles, mule spinners, was traditionally operated by males. In printing, where male unions were successful in excluding women, the unions insisted on staffing the new linotypes.[53]

The central purposes of subdividing the labor process, simplifying tasks, and introducing machines were to raise production, to cheapen it, and to increase management's control over the labor process. Subdivision of the labor process ordinarily allowed the use of less skilled labor in one or more subportions of the task. Cheapening of labor power and more control over labor were the motive forces behind scientific management and earlier efforts to reorganize

---

52. This summary is based on Abbott and is substantiated by both Elizabeth F. Baker, *Technology and Women's Work* (New York: Columbia University Press, 1964), and Helen L. Sumner, *History of Women in Industry in the United States, 1910,* United States Bureau of Labor, *Report on Condition of Women and Child Wage-Earners in the United States* (Washington, D.C.: Government Printing Office, 1911), vol. 9.

53. Baker and Abbott rely heavily on technological factors coupled with biological sex differences as explanations of shifts in the sex composition of jobs. Increased speed of machines and sometimes increased heaviness are cited as favoring men, who are stronger and have longer endurance, etc. Yet often each cites statistics which indicate that the same types of machines are used by both sexes; e.g., mule spinning machines. I would argue that these perceived differences are merely rationalizations used to justify the current sex assignment of tasks. Social pressures were powerful mechanisms of enforcement. Abbott gives several examples of this. A woman had apparently learned the mule in Lawrence and went to Waltham when mules were introduced there. She had to leave, however, because according to a male operative: "The men made unpleasant remarks and it was too hard for her, being the only woman" (p. 92). And: "Some of the oldest employees in the New England mills to-day [1910] say they can remember when weaving was so universally considered women's work that a 'man weaver' was held up to public ridicule for holding a 'woman's job'" (p. 95).

labor.[54] Machinery was an aid in the process, not a motive force. Machinery, unskilled labor, and women workers often went together.

In addition to greater demand and technical change, often a shortage of the usual supply of labor contributed to a change in the labor force. In textiles, for example, in the 1840s the young New England farm women were attracted to new job opportunities for middle-class women, such as teaching. Their places in the mills were taken by immigrants. In boots and shoes the increased demand could not be met by the available trained shoemakers. And in clerical work the supply of high school educated males was not equal to the increase in demand. Moreover, in clerical work in particular the changes that occurred in the job structure reduced its attractiveness to men—with expansion, the jobs became dead-end ones—while for women the opportunities compared favorably with their opportunities elsewhere.[55]

Cigar making offers ample opportunity to illustrate both the opposition of male unionists to impending sex changes in labor-force composition in their industries and the form that opposition took: protective legislation.[56] Cigar making was a home industry before 1800, when women on farms in Connecticut and elsewhere made rather rough cigars and traded them at village stores. Early factories employed women, but they were soon replaced by skilled male immigrants whose products could compete with fancy European cigars. By 1860, women were only 9 percent of the employed in cigar making. This switch to men was followed by one to women, but not without opposition from the men. In 1869, the wooden mold was introduced, and so were Bohemian immigrant women (who had been skilled workers in cigar factories in Austria-Hungary).[57] The Bohemian women, established by tobacco companies in tenements, perfected a division of labor in which young girls (and later their husbands)[58] could use the molds. Beginning in 1873 the Cigarmakers International Union agitated vociferously against home work, which was eventually restricted (for example, in New York in 1894). In the late 1880s machinery was introduced into the factories, and women were used as strikebreakers. The union turned to protective legislation.

The attitude of the Cigarmakers International Union toward women was

54. See Harry Braverman, *Labor and Monopoly Capital* (New York: Monthly Review Press, 1974), esp. chaps. 3–5.

55. Elyce J. Rotella, "Occupational Segregation and the Supply of Women to the American Clerical Labor Force, 1870–1930" (paper presented at the Berkshire Conference on the History of Women, Radcliffe College, October 25–27, 1974). Despite the long-standing recognition of job segregation and shifts in sex composition, there are surprisingly few studies of the process of shifting. In addition to Rotella for clerical workers there is Margery Davies, "Woman's Place Is at the Typewriter," *Radical America* 8, no. 4 (July–August 1974): 1–28. Valerie K. Oppenheimer discusses the shift in elementary teaching in *The Female Labor Force in the United States* (Berkeley: Institute of International Studies, University of California, 1970). And Abbott and Baker also discuss several shifts.

56. This account is based primarily on Abbott, chap. 9, and Baker, pp. 31–36.

57. According to Abbott, Samuel Gompers claimed the Bohemian women were brought in for the express purpose of strikebreaking (p. 197, n.).

58. Bohemian women came to America first, leaving their husbands behind to work on the fields. Their husbands, who were unskilled at the cigar trade, came over later (ibid., p. 199).

ambivalent at best. The union excluded women in 1864, but admitted them in 1867. In 1875 it prohibited locals from excluding women, but apparently never imposed sanctions on offending locals.[59] In 1878 a Baltimore local wrote Adolph Strasser, the union president: "We have combatted from its incipiency the movement of the introduction of female labor in any capacity whatever, be it bunch maker, roller, or what not."[60] Lest these ambiguities be interpreted as national-local conflicts, let Strasser speak for himself (1879): "We cannot drive the females out of the trade, but we can restrict their daily quota of labor through factory laws. No girl under 18 should be employed more than eight hours per day; all overwork should be prohibited. . . ."[61]

Unions excluded women in many ways,[62] not the least among them protective legislation. In this the unions were aided by the prevailing social sentiment about work for women, especially married women, which was seen as a social evil which ideally should be wiped out,[63] and by a strong concern on the part of "social feminists"[64] and others that women workers were severely exploited because they were unorganized. The social feminists did not intend to exclude women from desirable occupations but their strategy paved the way for

---

59. In 1877 a Cincinnati local struck to exclude women and was apparently successful. The *Cincinnati Inquirer* said: "The men say the women are killing the industry. It would seem that they hope to retaliate by killing the women" (ibid., p. 207).

60. Baker, p. 34.

61. John B. Andrews and W. D. P. Bliss, *History of Women in Trade Unions* in *Report on Condition of Woman and Child Wage-Earners in the United States,* vol. 10. Although the proportion of women in cigar making did increase eventually, in many other manufacturing industries the proportion of women decreased over time. Textiles and clothing are the outstanding examples (see Abbott, p. 320, and her "The History of Industrial Employment of Women in the United States," *Journal of Political Economy* 14 [October 1906]: 461–501). Sumner, cited in U.S. Bureau of Labor Statistics, Bulletin 175, concluded that men had taken over the skilled jobs in women's traditional fields, and women had to take unskilled work wherever they could find it (p. 28).

62. Gail Falk noted that unions used constitutional exclusion, exclusion from apprenticeship, limitation of women to helper categories or nonladder apprenticeships, limitation of proportion of union members who could be women, i.e., quotas, and excessively high fees. Moreover, the craft unions of this period, pre-1930, had a general hostility toward organizing the unskilled, even those attached to their crafts. See "Women and Unions: A Historical View," mimeographed [New Haven, Conn.: Yale Law School, 1970]. Published in somewhat shortened form in *Women's Rights Law Reporter* 1 [Spring 1973]: 54–65).

63. Such a diverse group as Caroll Wright, first U.S. Labor Commissioner (Baker, p. 84), Samuel Gompers and Mother Mary Jones, traditional and radical labor organizers, respectively (Falk), James L. Davis, U.S. Secretary of Labor, 1922 (Baker, p. 400), Florence Kelley, head of the National Consumers League (Hill), all held views which were variations of this theme. (Hill is Ann C. Hill, "Protective Labor Legislation for Women: Its Origin and Effect," mimeographed [New Haven, Conn.: Yale Law School, 1970], parts of which have been published in Barbara A. Babcock, Ann E. Freedman, Eleanor H. Norton, and Susan C. Ross, *Sex Discrimination and the Law: Causes and Remedies* [Boston: Little, Brown & Co., 1975], a law text which provides an excellent analysis of protective legislation, discrimination against women, etc.)

64. William O'Neill characterized those women who participated in various reform movements in the late nineteenth and early twentieth centuries "social feminists" to distinguish them from earlier feminists like Stanton and Anthony. The social feminists came to support women's rights because they thought it would help advance the cause of their reforms; they were not primarily interested in advancing the cause of women's rights (*Everyone Was Brave* [Chicago: Quadrangle Books, 1969], esp. chap. 3). William H. Chafe, *The American Woman* (New York: Oxford University Press, 1972), also provides an excellent discussion of the debate around protective laws.

this exclusion, because, to get protection for working women—which they felt was so desperately needed—they argued that women, as a sex, were weaker than men and more in need of protection.[65] Their strategy was successful in 1908 in *Muller v. Oregon,* when the Supreme Court upheld maximum hours laws for women, saying: "The two sexes differ in structure of body, in the capacity for long-continued labor particularly when done standing, the influence of vigorous health upon the future well-being of the race, the self-reliance which enables one to assert full rights, and in the capacity to maintain the struggle for subsistence. This difference justifies a difference in legislation and upholds that which is designed to compensate for some of the burdens which rest upon her."[66]

In 1916 in *Bunting v. Oregon* Brandeis used virtually the same data on the ill effects of long hours of work to argue successfully for maximum-hours laws for men as well as women. *Bunting* was not, however, followed by a spate of maximum-hours law for men, the way *Muller* had been followed by laws for women. In general, unions did not support protective legislation for men, although they continued to do so for women. Protective legislation, rather than organization, was the preferred strategy only for women.[67]

The effect of the laws was limited by their narrow coverage and inadequate enforcement, but despite their limitations, in those few occupations where night work or long hours were essential, such as printing, women were effectively excluded.[68] While the laws may have protected women in the "sweated" trades, women who were beginning to get established in "men's jobs" were turned back.[69] Some of these women fought back successfully, but the struggle is still being waged today along many of the same battle lines. As Ann C. Hill argued, the effect of these laws, psychically and socially, has been devastating. They confirmed woman's "alien" status as a worker.[70]

Throughout the above discussion of the development of the wage-labor force in England and the United States, I have emphasized the role of male workers in restricting women's sphere in the labor market. Although I have

---

65. What was achievable, from the legislatures and the courts, was what the social feminists aimed for. Because in Ritchie v. People (155 Ill 98 [1895]), the court had held that sex alone was not a valid basis for a legislature to abridge the right of an adult to contract for work and, thus, struck down a maximum-hours law for women, and because a maximum-hours law for baking employees had been struck down by the U.S. Supreme Court (Lockner), advocates of protective labor legislation believed their task would be difficult. The famous "Brandeis Brief" compiled hundreds of pages on the harmful effects of long hours of work and argued that women needed "especial protection" (see Babcock et al.).

66. Ibid., p. 32.

67. In 1914 the AFL voted to abandon the legislative road to reform (see Ann C. Hill).

68. Some states excluded women entirely from certain occupations: mining, meter reading, taxicab driving, core making, streetcar conducting, elevator operating, etc. (ibid.).

69. These conclusions are based on Ann C. Hill and are also supported by Baker.

70. At the same time that women were being excluded from certain skilled jobs in the labor force and otherwise protected, the home duties of women were emphasized in popular literature, through the home economics movement, in colleges and high schools, etc. A movement toward the stabilization of the nuclear family with one breadwinner, the male, is discernible (see Hartmann).

emphasized the role of men, I do not think that of employers was unimportant. Recent work on labor-market segmentation theory provides a framework for looking at the role of employers.[71] According to this model, one mechanism which creates segmentation is the conscious, though not necessarily conspiratorial, action of capitalists; they act to exacerbate existing divisions among workers in order to further divide them, thus weakening their class unity and reducing their bargaining power.[72] The creation of complex internal job structures is itself part of this attempt. In fact, the whole range of different levels of jobs serves to obfuscate the basic two-class nature of capitalist society.[73] This model suggests, first, that sex segregation is one aspect of the labor-market segmentation inherent in advanced capitalism, and, second, capitalists have consciously attempted to exacerbate sex divisions. Thus, if the foregoing analysis has emphasized the continuous nature of job segregation by sex—present in all stages of capitalism and before[74]—and the conscious actions of male workers, it is important to note that the actions of capitalists may have been crucial in calling forth those responses from male workers.

Historically, male workers have been instrumental in limiting the participation of women in the labor market. Male unions have carried out the policies and attitudes of the earlier guilds, and they have continued to reap benefits for male workers. Capitalists inherited job segregation by sex, but they have quite often been able to use it to their own advantage. If they can supersede experienced men with cheaper women, so much the better; if they can weaken labor by threatening to do so, that's good, too; or, if failing that, they can use those status differences to reward men, and buy their allegiance to capitalism with patriarchal benefits, that's okay too.[75]

But even though capitalists' actions are important in explaining the current virility of sex segregation, labor-market-segmentation theory overemphasizes

---

71. Edwards, Gordon, and Reich, *Labor Market Segmentation,* use labor-market segmentation to refer to a process in which the labor market becomes divided into different submarkets, each with its own characteristic behaviors; these segments can be different layers of a hierarchy or different groups within one layer.

72. Michael Reich's thesis, "Radical Discrimination and the White Income Distribution" (Ph.D. diss., Harvard University, 1973), sets forth this divide-and-rule model more thoroughly. In the labor-market-segmentation model there is another tendency toward segmentation in addition to the divide-and-rule mechanism. It arises out of the uneven development of advanced capitalism, i.e., the process of creation of a core and a peripheral economy. In fact, in the Edwards, Gordon, and Reich view, labor-market segmentation only comes to the fore under monopoly capitalism, as large corporations seek to extend control over their labor markets.

73. Thomas Vietorisz, "From Class to Hierarchy: Some Non-Price Aspects on the Transformation Problem" (paper presented at the Conference on Urban Political Economy, New School for Social Research, New York, February 15–16, 1975).

74. The strong divisions of the labor market by sex and race that existed even in the competitive phase of capitalism call into question the dominance of labor homogenization during that phase—as presented by Gordon, Edwards, and Reich.

75. Capitalists are not always able to use patriarchy to their advantage. Men's ability to retain as much of women's labor in the home as they have may hamper capitalist development during expansive phases. Men's resistance to female workers whom capitalists want to utilize also undoubtedly slows down capitalist advance.

the role of capitalists and ignores the actions of workers themselves in perpetuating segmentation. Those workers in the more desirable jobs act to hang onto them, their material rewards, and their subjective benefits.[76] Workers, through unions, have been parties to the creation and maintenance of hierarchical and parallel (i.e., separate but unequal) job structures. Perhaps the relative importance of capitalists and male workers in instituting and maintaining job segregation by sex has varied in different periods. Capitalists during the transition to capitalism, for example, seemed quite able to change the sex composition of jobs—when weaving was shifted to factories equipped with power looms women wove, even though most handloom weavers had been men, and mule spinning was introduced with male operators even though women had used the earlier spinning jennies and water frames. As industrialization progressed and conditions stabilized somewhat, male unions gained in strength and were often able to preserve or extend male arenas. Nevertheless, in times of overwhelming social or economic necessity, occasioned by vast increases in the demand for labor, such as in teaching or clerical work, male capitalists were capable of overpowering male workers. Thus, in periods of economic change, capitalists' actions may be more instrumental in instituting or changing a sex-segregated labor force—while workers fight a defensive battle. In other periods male workers may be more important in maintaining sex-segregated jobs; they may be able to prevent the encroachment of, or even to drive out, cheaper female labor, thus increasing the benefits to their sex.[77]

## Conclusion

The present status of women in the labor market and the current arrangement of sex-segregated jobs is the result of a long process of interaction between patriarchy and capitalism. I have emphasized the actions of male workers throughout this process because I believe that emphasis to be correct. Men will have to be forced to give up their favored positions in the division of labor—in the labor market and at home—both if women's subordination is to end and if men are to begin to escape class oppression and exploitation.[78] Capitalists have indeed used women as unskilled, underpaid labor to undercut male workers, yet this is only a case of the chickens coming home to roost—a case of men's co-optation by and support for patriarchal society, with its hierarchy among men, being turned

76. Engels, Marx, and Lenin all recognized the *material* rewards the labor aristocracy reaps. It is important not to reduce these to *subjective* benefits, for then the problems arising out of intraclass divisions will be minimized. Castles and Kosack appear to make this error (see their "The Function of Labour Immigration in Western European Capitalism," *New Left Review*, no. 73 [May–June 1972], pp. 3–12, where references to Marx et al. can be found).

77. David Gordon suggested to me this "cyclical model" of the relative strengths of employer and workers.

78. Most Marxist-feminist attempts to deal with the problems in Marxist analysis raised by the social position of women seem to ignore these basic conflicts between the sexes, apparently in the interest of stressing the underlying class solidarity that should obtain among women and men workers. Bridges and Hartmann's draft paper (n. 1 above) reviews this literature. . . .

back on themselves with a vengeance. Capitalism grew on top of patriarchy; patriarchal capitalism is stratified society par excellence. If non-ruling-class men are to be free they will have to recognize their co-optation by patriarchal capitalism and relinquish their patriarchal benefits. If women are to be free, they must fight against both patriarchal power and capitalist organization of society. . . .

# · 23 ·

# Class Struggle and the Persistence of the Working-Class Family

Jane Humphries

Marxist analyses have generally failed to explain the persistence of the working-class family as a central feature of capitalist social formations. The theoretical perspective of Marx and Engels denied that the kinship ties of the working class had any material basis, and led them to postulate the immanent decay of the traditional working-class family.

More recently certain authors have attempted to remedy this deficiency and to explain the continued existence of the working-class family by directing attention to its role in the reproduction of labour-power. They emphasize that capital derives certain benefits from the existence of family structures, in the form of both additional surplus value and of political stability. From this they deduce that the family survives because it is in the interests of capital that it should do so. This is an unbalanced approach, for it assumes the power of capital to be unlimited and fails to recognize that capital's ability to transform existing social institutions, like the family, is circumscribed by the opposition of those concerned. The theme of this paper is that the resilience of the family derives in part from workers' defence of an institution which affects their standard of living, class cohesion and ability to wage the class struggle.

The plan of the paper is as follows. The first section contains a brief critique

---

• From *Cambridge Journal of Economics* 1 (1977): 241–58.

NOTE: I would like to thank Sam Bowles, Jean Elshtain and Michelle Naples for their comments on an earlier draft of this paper. The students and faculty of the Cambridge Social and Political Science 'Women in Society' course provided many supportive discussions and interesting suggestions. The journal editors gave much valued editorial help. Special thanks are due to Michael Best.

of the perspective on the working-class family found in the writings of Marx and Engels. Marx is shown to abstract from issues crucial to an understanding of the material base of working-class kinship. The second section deals with attempts in the recent literature to develop a Marxist analysis of the role of domestic labour in the reproduction of labour-power, an issue not investigated by Marx himself. Criticism of this literature for its neglect of the possible benefits accruing to labour from kinship networks leads to the alternative hypothesis. The kinds of advantages appropriated by the working class are subsequently analysed in the specific context of early industrial capitalism in nineteenth-century England. The major conclusion is that the anti-family position of most Marxists is ill-informed, in that it ignores the connections between the material conditions of the working class and familial relationships. The theoretical ideas presented suggest a reassessment of the historic role played by the family.

## Marx, Engels and the Working-Class Family

The approach inherited from Marx and Engels explains the family as an outgrowth of property relations, and in the last analysis as itself constituting a property relation.[1] As early as 1845 Marx, arguing that the family was in decay, admitted its survival among the bourgeoisie only as a formal property relation, and among the proletariat declared the family already abolished! 'There the concept of the family does not exist at all.'[2] Although elsewhere Marx and Engels document the contemporary deterioration of working-class life, this particular conclusion was independent of observation and was derived *theoretically* from Marx's idea of the family as a property relation. Since the proletariat was by definition propertyless, the working-class family could not act as an instrument for the concentration of wealth. According to Marx there was therefore no material reason for its existence, and he concluded without empirical evidence that it had already ceased to exist. In *The Origin of the Family, Private Property and the State* Engels discusses the property relation more explicitly and argues that 'monogamy', involving fidelity for the woman only, afforded the means through which private property could be individually bequeathed.[3]

This vision of the family suffers from an ahistoric interpretation of property relations. Private property exists in almost all modes of production, but its form, extent and implications differ fundamentally according to the dominant mode of production. Is it then likely to have identical implications for social relations in all social formations? The equation of the family with monogamy is also invalid. Monogamy is neither a necessary nor a sufficient condition for the existence of the family, which encompasses, but is not necessarily defined by,

---

1. The connection between property and bourgeois forms of family is made in several places in the writings of Marx and Engels, but most clearly in Engels (1972).

2. Marx and Engels (1976), p. 181; quoted in Draper (1970). This article provides a useful survey illustrating the complex perspectives on 'the woman question' found in the writings of Marx and Engels.

3. Engels (1972). This work should be treated as a collaboration, since it was drawn from Marx's as well as Engels' notes on Lewis Henry Morgan's *Ancient Society*.

the man-woman relationship. The family commonly describes a network of social relationships which may be based on genealogical relationships but which also needs to be produced and sustained by social practices reinforcing reciprocal kinship relations. Most important of all, to emphasize the family as a bourgeois phenomenon, as an instrument for the concentration of wealth, diverts attention from the working-class family.[4] The latter then seems historically empty, a superficial reflection of an upper-class institution, without foundation and doomed to wither away under the strains of proletarianization and capitalist expansion.

This invisibility of the proletarian family is reflected in Marx's analyses of the determination of the working-class standard of living, class cohesion and the terms of class struggle. Specifically, the treatment of the reproduction of labour-power in *Capital* abstracts from two issues which are crucial in any investigation of the material base of working-class family life.

First, the working-class family constitutes an arena of production, the inputs being the commodities purchased with family wages, and one of the outputs being the renewed labour-power sold for wages on the market. Neither the material aspects nor the social forms of household productive activity, family relations and family activity are capitalistic. But household activity is welded to the capitalist mode of production through the reproduction cycle of labour-power.

Marx recognized the importance of the latter to capitalism, but did not investigate the process within the working-class household.

The maintenance and reproduction of the working class is, and must ever be, a necessary condition to the reproduction of capital. But the capitalist may safely leave its fulfillment to the labourer's instincts of self-preservation and of propagation (Marx, 1967, p. 572).

The working-class family in Marx is like the firm in neoclassical economics—a black box whose inner workings are simultaneously neglected and mystified.

Marx abstracts from the problem of domestic labour by dealing with a situation in which all workers are engaged in capitalist production and perform no domestic labour whatsoever. No use-values are produced within the household and the capitalist sector provides everything required to replace the labour-power used up in production. This gives the reproduction cycle of labour-power a distinctive feature in that value is neither created nor destroyed but merely recycled. Wages are used to purchase a subsistence bundle of commodities whose 'consumption' mysteriously leads to the replacement of used-up labour-power. This new labour-power is then exchanged for a new bundle of commodities, which is in its turn consumed, and so the process continues indefinitely, with labour-power being used up in capitalist production and replaced through the act of consumption.[5]

---

4. For a similar criticism, see Leacock's introduction to Engels (1972).

5. One consequence of Marx's neglect of domestic labour can be seen in his discussion of the value of labour-power. In the case of other commodities he determines their value by considering the way in which they are produced. In the case of labour-power, however, he adopts a quite different approach and begins not with production but with consumption. The wages of the average worker are used to purchase a given bundle of capitalistically produced commodities. To produce

While abstraction from the problem of domestic labour is acceptable within the terms of reference of *Capital,* its analysis is crucial not only for an explanation of the continued existence of the working-class family, but also for an understanding of the relationship between women's oppression and capitalism. Thus this issue has received considerable attention in the recent literature, which is discussed below.

The second issue from which Marx abstracts in *Capital* is the sensitivity of the value of labour-power to the employment structure of the working-class family. He acknowledges this connection:

> There are, besides, two other factors that enter into the determination of the value of labour-power. One, the expenses of developing that power, which expenses vary with the mode of production; the other, its natural diversity, the difference between the labour-power of men and women, of children and adults. The employment of these different sorts of labour-power, an employment which is, in its turn, made necessary by the mode of production, makes a great difference in the cost of maintaining the family of the labourer, *and in the value of the labour power of the adult male* (Marx, 1967, p. 519, my emphasis).

It is not, however, pursued. Instead Marx assumes a situation in which the male worker is supporting a wife and children, none of whom are wage labourers. This entails a redefinition of necessary labour-time, which is no longer the labour-time necessary to secure the conditions of reproduction of the labourer, but has become that necessary to secure the conditions of reproduction of the working-class family. In the circumstances discussed by Marx this also involves a parallel change in the value of labour-power. 'The value of labour-power was determined not only by the labour-time necessary to maintain the individual adult labourer but also by that necessary to maintain his family' (Marx, 1967, p. 395). But Marx also emphasized that the widespread contemporary phenomenon of working women and children, which he saw as a long-run tendency towards universal proletarianization, would spread the value of labour-power over the whole working-class family and so reduce the value of any one member's labour-power. His assignment of a crucial role in this process to machinery introduces an element of technological determinism.

Although Marx does not develop the argument, a reduction in the value of labour-power, caused by universal proletarianism, provided the working-class with a strong motive for defending traditional family structures during certain periods of capitalist development. Within these structures the working class was better equipped to exercise some jurisdiction and control over the supply of labour. The withdrawal of certain members of the working class from the labour market, in conjunction with a campaign for 'a family wage', supported by a bourgeois ideology which emphasized the fragility of women and integrity of the family, could, by raising the real wages of the remaining workers, improve the working-class standard of living. In this case the pursuit of class interest would promote labour's defence of the family, a defence which could

---

this subsistence bundle requires a certain amount of labour and Marx calls this amount the 'value' of labour-power. So the value of labour-power, in contrast with that of other commodities, is defined without any reference to its own conditions of production (and reproduction). Instead it is based on the conditions of production of those commodities for which it is exchanged.

have been critical in the latter's resilience. This argument will be further developed below.

## The Working–Class Family in the Contemporary Marxist Literature

Recent Marxist writing has focused almost exclusively on extensions of value theory which abandon Marx's first abstraction and so accommodate the existence of domestic labour.[6] The latter undermines the unique correspondence between the level of wages and the historically given working-class standard of living, which now depends not only on purchased commodities but also on household activity. The abstract labour-time embodied in the goods purchased with the wage can no longer be regarded as equivalent to the labour-time necessary to secure the maintenance and reproduction of the working class, either from day to day or from generation to generation. Wages have to be transformed into the use-values consumed in the home, a transformation embodying not inconsiderable labour-time.

Despite the heterogeneity of the approaches (in terms of the definition of domestic labour, the particular generalization of value theory, etc.), there are significant agreements. It is usually assumed that the payment made by capital to labour is premised on the existence of a certain volume of domestic work and state services. The power of capital is such that in the presence of domestic labour the wage is lower than it would have been had the standard of living of the working class been solely dependent on purchased commodities. In this way surplus labour is extracted from the housewife and ultimately transformed into surplus value.[7]

However, even within the above analyses of the relationship between domestic labour and the capitalist mode of production, there exists at least the *possibility* that domestic labour permits the working class to enjoy a higher standard of living. The ability or inability of capital to capture the benefits of household activity surely depends on the state of the class struggle.

This possiblity is ignored in the literature because labour-power is considered only from the viewpoint of capital. To understand the relationship between domestic labour and capitalism, it is necessary to begin not with capital but with the capitalist mode of production, essential aspects of which are antagonistic

---

6. For a recent review of this literature which illustrates the points to be made, see Himmelweit and Mohun (1977).

7. This idea is widespread in the literature, but it should be emphasized that the authors listed do not agree on the *precise* characterization of the transfer. See Althusser (1971), Benston (1969), Dalla Costa (1972), Gardiner (1975), Rowbotham (1973). Although John Harrison's approach is distinguished by his adherence to the concept of a domestic mode of production, it too could be included here (see Harrison, 1974). Similarly, although Gardiner, Himmelweit and Mackintosh's work is notable for its rejection of the comparability of domestic labour-time and labour-time expended in capitalist commodtiy production, they too postulate an ultimate and indirect effect on profits (see Gardiner, Himmelweit and Mackintosh, 1975). Even Seccombe, who argues that the housewife 'creates value embodied in the labour-power sold to capital, equal to the value she consumes in her own upkeep' and therefore that surplus value is unaffected, also believes that the pressure of capital is such that she is 'without leeway in converting the wage into renewed labour-power' (Seccombe, 1974 and 1975).

relations of production and class struggle. To consider *only* the perspective of capital is to compound Marx's original mistake, and leads, ultimately, to a kind of technological determinism. On the one hand, the fate of the working-class family is seen as dependent upon capital's ability to produce cheap substitutes for domestic labour, and/or its need to augment the industrial reserve army. If this were solely the case the proletarian family would indeed be long gone. This is recognized, in that the quest for surplus value, through its erosion of an institution which is viewed as vital in the reproduction of the forces and relations of production, is seen as endangering the conditions under which surplus value is created and realized—and indeed the existence of the capitalist mode of production itself. Thus the persistence of the working-class family is a product of the contradiction implicit in its relationship with capital.

Capitalism's dependence on the family and inability to generate alternative institutions never seem to be adequately explained. The intrinsic contradiction does not seem to be sufficiently strong to have guaranteed the working-class family two centuries of survival in capitalism. This enigma cannot be resolved without broadening the perspective on the working-class family to encompass a materialist analysis based on a non-individualistic theory of human needs.

Marx's abstraction from the sensitivity of the value of labour-power to the employment structure of the working-class family has received much less attention in the recent literature than his neglect of domestic labour. This is surprising, since it suggests a similar reappraisal of value theory. The remainder of this paper is concerned with the integration of such an approach into the theoretical perspective described above. The intention is to complement the existing literature by beginning from the capitalist mode of production, but nevertheless looking at the proletarian family from its own perspective. From this perspective it is of secondary importance whether or not the working-class family is essential to the existence of the capitalist mode of production. What matters is that the working class has always resisted alternatives to the family, recognizing in the erosion of traditional family structures an infringement of its standard of living and a deterioration in the position from which it engages in class struggle. This position is elaborated below.

## The Material Bases of the Working-Class Family

An investigation of the abstract nature of traditional family forms must preface any discussion of the material benefits derived by the working class from those family forms.

Apart from Seccombe, there is some agreement in the literature discussed above on the proposition that domestic labour produces a surplus. This takes the form of labour by the domestic worker beyond that necessary for her own subsistence. The immediate beneficiaries of this surplus labour are the other members of her family; but ultimately through a reduction in the wages earned by the family, it is captured, wholly or partly, by the capitalist, who by increased exploitation of the family's wage earners adds to surplus value.

New light may be cast on this process by reference to the ambiguity in the concept of necessary labour. Is this the labour necessary to secure the conditions of existence of the individual, or the labour necessary to secure the conditions of existence of the family to which the individual belongs?

This question is emphatically resolved in Marx's writings, which contain a recurring vision of humanity as 'the ensemble of the social relations' (Marx, 1967, p. 7). This definition of human existence has the important implication that labour has to relate to the maintenance and reproduction of the individual *in certain definite relationships with his community*. This in turn requires the existence of some surplus labour over and above necessary labour, as traditionally defined, *in all modes of production,* because the conditions of reproduction of the individual labourer are not equivalent to the conditions of reproduction of the economy as a whole.[8]

It follows that surplus labour does not exist solely to provide for a class of non–labourers. While the latter may or may not exist, non–labouring *individuals* can be found in all social formations, including children, the old, the sick and those who do unproductive but socially necessary work. Social functions in which there is no allowance for these individuals are unlikely to be resilient or evolutionary. Thus in all interesting cases the appropriation of surplus labour necessary to secure the reproduction of the economy and its conditions of existence in the totality of social relationships has to include an allowance, in some cases minimal, for these individuals.

It is instructive to remember how the surplus is appropriated in primitive communism. Here collective appropriation, manifested in the communal form of property, is achieved by denying any necessary correspondence between labour expended in a particular labour process and the share of the product received in reward. Instead the product is distributed among the producers and others according to established social relations. For redistribution to ensure the reproduction of the conditions of existence of the social formation, it has to involve a network of individuals extending beyond those engaged in the immediate labour. By the simple extension of shares in the community's product to those who have little to contribute in terms of 'the mutual exchange of activities', surplus is appropriated, and the non–labouring individuals given sustenance.

Redistribution requires a communal network defining precise reciprocal relationships between all pairs of individuals. These relationships then correspond to definite mutual responsibilities. The correspondence, when made effective by ideological conviction and commitment, maps out the flows of labour–time socially demanded from each individual and each individual's relative share in the social product. So the community simultaneously possesses and allocates the surplus.

The historical basis for such a network of definite relationships is kinship. Family ties are thus a basic element in this mode of appropriation, as the ideological interpretation of these ties constitutes the basis of the redistribution by which the surplus is appropriated.

These observations may appear unremarkable as long as they are directed

---

8. For a careful statement of this position see Hindess and Hirst (1975), pp. 23 ff. The following discussion of the primitive communist mode of production owes much to this exposition.

towards primitive communism. Their generalization to other modes of production is more controversial. The argument is that family ties, vitalized by ideology, bind together labouring and non-labouring individuals, and secure for the latter a share in the product of the former, not only in primitive communism, but also in more developed modes of production.

According to this perspective the wage earner, while receiving the value of his labour-power, if this includes a contribution to the maintenance and reproduction of his family as well as his own, must receive some surplus over and above the value of his labour-power individualistically defined. Similarly the domestic worker engages in surplus labour if her labour is related to the abstract labour-time involved in her own subsistence. Her surplus labour is embodied in use-values which contribute to the maintenance and reproduction of her family. In total she produces use-values embodying the socially necessary labour-time to secure the conditions of reproduction of herself *in relation to her community,* which is, immediately, her family.

In pre-capitalist societies all members of the family helped to produce the family subsistence, which included the support of non-labouring members and those whose productivity was insufficient to ensure their survival. The surplus labour involved in this support was appropriated by the family members themselves in the process of family production. The analogy with primitive communism is obvious.

The conditions of existence of the capitalist mode of production made this process more difficult and less transparent, as the direct producer was now separated from the means of production and appropriation was in the form of surplus value. Proletarianization of some members of the family became a prerequisite for survival. In capitalism the family can dispose of commodities purchased by the family's wages, and use-values produced by domestic labour. But the extension of shares in their product to family members who are unproductive, or not sufficiently productive to secure their own subsistence, still ensures their survival. Both wage workers and domestic workers participate in this 'mutual exchange of activities'.

Even in primitive societies a division of labour is likely to be associated with the development of hierarchy. Under capitalism the division of labour becomes extremely marked. The domestic labour process is isolated from the dominant mode of production, and its separation from the means of exchange has the effect of rendering it invisible and 'valueless'. This stands in sharp contrast to the 'distinctness' of the wage. Thus, whatever the origins of the sexual division of labour, the resulting differential experience of men and women cumulatively reinforces the differences between the marketability of different skills. The productivity of wage labour rises relative to that of domestic work, encouraging the tendency to hierarchy among specialized workers, which is further stimulated by the personal service characteristic of domestic work. Relations of dominance and subordination relating to age, sex, and division of labour exist within the family in primitive communism, but they take on their contemporary character under capitalism. The dominant capitalist mode of production corrupts the primitively communal family relations, and simultaneously hides the primitively communal core which the family retains in the union of labouring and non-labouring individuals which secures the survival of the latter.

## The Family as a Popular Support System During
## Early Industrialization

Why is it important to expose the primitively communal aspects of the family? Are they simply grotesque remnants of a less developed mode of production, protected from disintegration by the preservative of capitalist ideology only because they make it easy to shift responsibility from capital to labour?

Non-labouring individuals among the working class have to be supported. If their sustenance is not forthcoming from labour, via the primitive communism of the family, then it must come from capital in the form of state supplied services or individual charitable impulses. The usual argument is that capital generally finds it cheaper, more convenient, and less politically unsettling to maintain the historically given working-class autonomy, allowing a sufficient element of surplus in wages to sustain the non-labouring family members. Doubts have been expressed above about capital's long-run vested interest in the family, but the question of political stability provides a clue to another explanation of the latter's resilience. Presumably this course is less politically disruptive because any concerted attempt by capital to take over these functions, and to reduce the non-labouring members of the working class to more direct and obvious dependence on capital, would encounter resistance. Labour's opposition would arise from the realization (which might be imperfect) that the traditional arrangements can operate to its advantage, in terms of the determination of the standard of living and the development of class consciousness and cohesion, at least in certain periods of capitalist development.

Bureaucratic methods of support for non-labouring members of the working class are usually alienating and demoralizing, and have been chronically so in the past. While the implications of this fact for the interests of capital are not clear, it would seem that it is not in the interests of labour. From a purely materialistic point of view, it may be that the welfare of the non-labouring members of the working class is better secured by informal mechanisms than by more formal institutional channels, especially in periods of parsimonious and primitive capitalism. The humanity of the traditional methods, in comparison with the brutal and degrading alternatives, must have had positive implications for the development of working-class consciousness.

A full investigation of this approach requires detailed research into the changing structure of support for non-labouring members of the working class, and the attitudes of capital and labour to these changes. However, some support for such a perspective is provided by existing historical evidence.

For the working-class family in nineteenth-century England, kinship ties provided a major source of non-bureaucratic support in conditions of chronic uncertainty. Agriculture had always involved uncertainty associated with the vagaries of climate and crop, as well as seasonally related periods of dependence on stored produce. Now there were also cyclical fluctuations in industrial output and employment, which, in a mode of production where the direct producers are separated from the means of production, impose considerable insecurity. Wage dependence also aggravates other 'critical life situations,' i.e., situations in which the individual is unlikely to be competent to cope without help, such as sickness, death, disaster, old age, marriage and childbirth.

The view that industrialization typically disrupts pre-existing wider kinship ties has been called into question by recent discoveries about the pre-industrial family (Laslett, 1965). A comparison of the latter with modern traditional working-class communities, characterized by well developed kinship ties, as described by Willmott and Young (1957), suggests, superficially at least, that in Britain 'modernization' did not reduce kinship cohesion. The same conclusion is reached in Michael Anderson's investigation of kinship structures during the industrial revolution, which documents the retention, indeed the strengthening, of certain kinship connections (Anderson, 1971). The picture is one of a world where despite 'migration, residential mobility, industrial employment and high mortality rates most people managed to maintain relationships with their family, both the current nuclear family and the family as a web of wider kinship ties' (Anderson, 1971, p. 66).

Anderson's study clearly illustrates the material base of such relationships, in the importance of the family to non-labouring members of the working class. The help given to orphans, widows and widowers, and those temporarily unable to secure their own livelihood as a result of one or another of life's critical situations, is amply documented. Rowntree's classic study of the working class in York at the end of the nineteenth century tells a similar story (Rowntree, 1902). Migrants into the new industrial towns provided another group of temporarily non-labouring members of the working class, who sought to turn to their own account kinship ties with established residents.

Anderson emphasizes what he calls the 'instrumentalist' attitude to family ties, i.e., that most of the kinship relations maintained were mutually advantageous within a rather short period of time. Nevertheless, he shows that the working class exhibited a fierce element of dependence on low-cost kinship relations. The kinds of family ties described are exactly what would be expected in the context of primary poverty and universal insecurity, when responsibilities cannot always be met and must always be limited. It is clear that, although blood ties constitute a basis for possible kinship ties, the latter have to be created and maintained by social practices related to a specific material base. The latter, therefore, decisively influences the nature and extent of the kinship system that results.

That kinship ties provided a structure for reciprocal relationships among the early industrial working class, just as they did in primitive society is reflected in the way they were moulded to meet particular circumstances. For example, in the period when the family structure was integral to the capitalistic labour process, if spinners had no children they would frequently employ younger siblings, or children of neighbours and relatives, who were then taken into the family in a quasi-familial way (Anderson, 1971, p. 117, Smelser, 1959, p. 191). Similarly in mining communities, when it was common for colliers to employ their own children as 'hurriers', if an individual's family structure could not provide the labour-power needed, parish children would be employed as apprentices. It was not unusual for these children to be well treated by the standard of the times and to have obvious respect and affection for their quasi-family (Parliamentary Papers, 1842, pp. 120 and 138).

It was also common, because of housing shortages in the early industrial towns and the migration into these centres, for individuals to board with families with whom they had only distant kin connections or no such ties at all (Foster, 1974, p. 96; McGeown, 1967, p. 20; Rowntree, 1902, p. 391). Frequently these relationships would then assume fictive kin status. The lodger who lived in such close proximity was symbolically addressed as 'brother' and 'uncle'. Such quasi-kin ties ensured the development of community in the early industrial towns, binding together unrelated adults and thereby infusing such communities with conceptions of obligation which had flowed initially from family ties rooted in blood and marriage. The strength of neighbourhood ties among the nineteenth-century working class and their role in reciprocal assistance has been remarked upon by many contemporary commentators (Booth, 1902, p. 51; Rowntree, 1902, p. 43) and recent social historians (Stedman Jones, 1971, p. 87), as well as illustrated in surviving working-class autobiographies (Burnett, 1974, p. 62).

In areas where women were habitually wage workers the proportion of old women on relief was lower than elsewhere, which suggests that they were able to support themselves by childminding, laundering and so on. Anderson quotes the example of one old lady of seventy who lived with a family to which she was not related, but which supported her because she was able to contribute within their family configuration. Her explanation vividly illustrates the extension of the primitive communism of the family to include such quasi-kin, and thus the extension of mutual obligation to unrelated adults in the community. 'They cannot afford to pay me nought but aw fare as they fare'n, and they dunnot want to part wi' me' (Anderson, 1971, p. 143).

The official position in the early nineteenth century promoted family integrity and autonomy with respect to the care of the young, the old and the destitute. Legally, families were still governed by the '43 Elizabeth' which enjoined them to care for their dependents (Checkland and Checkland, 1974). But in an era of wage dependence, increased longevity and rising labour mobility, the traditional responsibilities could not be enforced. Industrialization and the concomitant changes produced a pressing need for the state to provide safety nets. At first the old Poor Law was stretched accommodatingly, but eventually, in 1834, new institutions had to be created. Capital's provision for the non-labouring members of the working class was neither magnanimous nor genial, and significantly involved a bitterly resented attack on the family (Hart, 1965, p. 208; Hobsbawm, 1964, p. 188); nevertheless it did exist.

The harshness of the 1834 Poor Law was an attempt to discourage recourse to the official channels and to make the poor 'self-sufficient'. It has been suggested above that individuals can never be 'self-sufficient'. What was promoted was 'class-sufficiency' via mutually reciprocal kinship ties. In the context of primary poverty the family could not always bear the weight of these ties. As a result they were rationalized as described above, and family members were put on relief even under conditions of 'less eligibility'.[9] But the Poor Law was a

---

9. This phrase was used to describe the requirement that life in the workhouse be less pleasant than the life of the poorest independent worker. Only if this 'principle' was maintained could the workhouse provide 'a test', in the sense of screening out all those capable of earning their own living. The intention was to provide a workhouse so uncomfortable as to deter from entrance anybody who could possibly earn a bare living. It might be thought that the application of such a test is only

refuge of last resort, to be submitted to only in times of dire distress. This can be seen from the rise in the numbers of old and infirm on relief in the crisis years 1839–46, as families which had shouldered their responsibilities bravely enough in better times found that they could no longer cope. Because of the deprivation and degradation of the workhouse, bureaucratic forms of assistance were hated and feared by the working class, whose *class* resistance was thereby enhanced (Hanson, 1975, p. 245; Smelser, 1959; Thompson, 1963). Kinship ties were strengthened because they provided the only framework controllable by the working class, within which reciprocation could occur that was sufficiently defined to provide an adequate guarantee of assistance in crisis situations.

According to this perspective the endurance of the family reflects a struggle by the working class for popular ways of meeting the needs of non-labouring comrades within a capitalist environment. Such a struggle could not but promote social obligation, i.e., concern among workers for non-kin. Social obligation is not of course identical with class consciousness; but it is a necessary condition for the development of such consciousness.

Thus, the family, as an institution, has been shaped by the aspiration of people for personalized non-market methods of distribution and social interaction. To ignore the role that these aspirations and beliefs have played in guiding human conduct and in shaping the class struggle is to fail to understand the proletarian family and its persistence.

### The Value of Labour-Power and the Family Labour Supply

A second important reason for the working class preference for traditional family forms relates to their implications for the control of the labour supply. Marx's prediction of the proletarianization of all members of the working-class family was not vindicated by nineteenth-century British history. Child labour was regulated and the age of entry into the labour force rose steadily. Incomplete data suggest that married women's participation rates fell from the high levels reached in the early phase of industrialization and the Napoleonic wars and thereafter slowly recovered (Hewitt, 1958). Female participation rates remained remarkably constant throughout the late nineteenth century, at around 26% of the female population. Mass proletarianization of married women never occurred (Best, 1971, p. 100; Burnett, 1974, p. 19).

Most explanations of this phenomenon have emphasized the changing needs of expansionary capitalism in terms of the quality and quantity of labour, its inability to provide substitutes for the use-values produced in the home, and the association between the maintenance of the family structure and political stability. Again the stress is on capital's restraint in its attack on the family. An alternative perspective is presented here in that the family is seen to be defended

---

relevant to the able-bodied poor, whereas the majority of people relieved were unable to work. But 'less eligibility' was extended to prescribe more miserable lives for aged paupers, sick paupers and orphans, lest the incentive to provide for old age, infirmity or dependent childhood be diminished. The 'principle' illustrates the obsession of the Commissioners with the able-bodied poor, and their intention of setting up institutions conducive to the unfettered workings of a free labour market. See Webb and Webb (1929).

by the working class, which recognizes that it can act as an obstacle to the cheapening of labour-power.

Compare two extreme situations:

(1) There is a single wage earner who receives the historic subsistence *family* wage. The activities of the other household members remain outside the jurisdiction of the capitalist and can be directed to the production of use-values, raising the family's standard of living.

(2) All the able-bodied family members are proletarianized, including the children, and the family wage is received piecemeal.

In both cases the non-labouring family members are supported out of the family product, distribution taking place according to non-market criteria. Under the assumption that the *same* family wage is received in both situations, the standard of living of the working class must be higher in (1) and surplus value creation (per family) greater in (2).

How valid is the assumption that the same family wage would be received in both situations? First it can be argued that the wage bargain in (1) would take into account the existence of domestic labour, and so be premised on a certain level of use-value production. The value of labour, in terms of the labour-time embodied in commodities purchased by the wage, could then be reduced below family subsistence by the amount of labour-time embodied in use-value production. Capital would gain control of the level and intensity of domestic production and indirectly drain value out of the working-class household.

While this appears to be a valid *possibility*—certainly in periods of falling real wages the working-class housewife tries to defend her family's standard of living by increasing her own efforts—it is not the *only* possibility. The extent to which capital can take advantage of domestic labour in this way surely depends on the success of the working-class defence of its standard of living, as given by the level of wages *and* the domestic production of use-values.

Secondly, is it probable that the total family wage would be unrelated to the number of family wage earners? Clearly, the more members of the family undertake wage employment the lower would be the value of any one member's labour-power; but the total family wage would be larger unless the fall in the value of labour-power was so great as to offset the incremental income earned by the additional wage workers. What do nineteenth-century labour market conditions indicate in this respect? Three observations may be considered relevant.

First, during the Ten Hours Campaign it was widely believed among the working class that limitations on hours would not permanently reduce wages, but that ultimately the same earnings would be realized in ten hours as had previously required twelve hours of work (Parliamentary Papers, 1833). Generalization from the labour demand conditions implicit in this argument suggests that widespread proletarianization of married women and children, while raising the number of hours worked by each family, could not in the long run expand family earnings.

Secondly, there is evidence that in certain trades over-stocked labour markets caused wages to be reduced to family subsistence level. Under these conditions proletarianization of additional family members was futile.

The same pressure that leads to the employment of the childen presently leads in a slack time to the acceptance of yet lower pay for the sake of securing work . . . Thus, by and by, mother and children come to receive no more than did the mother working alone. The employer . . . has in fact obtained the labour of the children without extra payment (Black, 1907, p. 148).

Thirdly, it must be clear that it is invalid to compare one working-class family with a single breadwinner with another family with multiple wage earners. In a situation where most families contained several wage workers, competition would have driven down the price of labour-power and each worker would receive only a fraction of the family subsistence. With labour-power so cheapened, a family with only one earner would be in an unfortunate position indeed. Poverty would force other family members into wage labour, the value of labour-power would sink even lower, and the vicious circle would be complete (Black, 1907; Mayhew, 1861, pp. 301–4).

The relevant comparison is between two general social settings, each characterized by a particular family employment structure, and an associated wage level. This approach exposes the material interest of the working class in the maintenance of a family structure and explicates the motivation for class struggle on this issue, since it seems at least possible that a retreat of certain family members from the labour force, in conjunction with an organized attempt to secure a 'family wage', would raise the standard of living of the working class. This view was expressed by a labourer in the *Trades Newspaper* of 16 October 1825.

Wages can never sink below the sum necessary to rear up the number of labourers the capitalists want. The weaver, his wife and children all labour to obtain this sum; the blacksmith and the carpenter obtain it by their single exertions . . . The labouring men of this country . . . should return to the good old plan of subsisting their wives and children on the wages of their *own* labour, and they should demand wages high enough for this purpose . . . By doing this, the capitalist will be obliged to give the same wages to men alone which they now give to men, women and children . . . I recommend my fellow labourers, in preference to every other means of limiting the number of those who work for wages, to prevent their wives and children from competing with them in the market, and beating down the price of labour (Hollis, 1973, pp. 193–4).

Working-class movements in the nineteenth century seem to be characterized by elements of this strategy, the demand for a family wage being only one example. Notions of endangered family integrity, the 'unsexing' of working-class men and women, and the adverse effects likely to become apparent in future generations of workers, were also used in the battle for factory legislation on conditions and hours; in the latter case to such an extent that Hutchins and Harrison conclude: 'the battle for the limitation of the hours of adults in general was fought from behind the women's petticoats' (Hutchins and Harrison, 1903, p. 186).

How can this working-class use of sexist ideology be judged in retrospect? It has been argued that the male-dominated trade unions selfishly sought to impede the employment of women, with whom they felt competitive in the labour market and whom they preferred to retain as dependent domestic workers. Undoubtedly the regulation of hours and occupations caused acute misery in individual cases, when women lost jobs that were vital to their survival. More important still, the opportunistic use of sexist ideology by labour must have reinforced sexism among workers and employers and so in the long run made the attainment of economic equality more difficult.

But to condemn this strategy out of hand is to be insensitive to the material conditions of nineteenth-century labour. One of the few sources of working-class control over the supply of labor lay in the levers that could be brought to bear on the labour supplied by married women. This was also one of the few tactics that could be accompanied by a supportive mobilization of bourgeois ideology. Both these points are apparent in the following contemporary description of the trade union perspective on female wage labour:

it [the trade union perspective] recognizes the danger of intolerable strain both to women themselves and to their actual and possible offspring, and it sees in the frantic efforts of the unskilled, unorganized woman to work for impossible hours, to undersell her competitors and lower both her and their standard of life, an 'offence', which, however pardonable in an individual, must in a member of society, by some means, be controlled or prevented for the general good. We cannot discuss these matters on purely individualistic lines . . . The one worker, whether man or woman, who works-excessive hours sets the pace, compels others to work long hours also, and inevitably lowers the rate of pay for all (Hutchins and Harrison, 1903, p. 185).

The tragedy is that action could not be controlled on a class basis, but had to be regulated *systematically* on the basis of *female* labour, and theoretically of *married* female labour, so reinforcing sex-based relations of dominance and subordination.

Nevertheless, the strategy was not entirely disadvantageous to working women. To think so is again to misunderstand the material conditions of working-class experience. First, the argument that male workers gained from regulation at the expense of 'protected' workers (female) is not easily substantiated. Hutchins and Harrison argue that, as men were then earning higher wages and working shorter hours, they had little to gain from 'supplanting' women. Gains were mainly at the lower end of the labour hierarchy, where women themselves were concentrated. There does not seem to have been a trend to replace protected workers by unprotected workers.

Secondly, women workers as well as being female are also members of the working class. Class action which tries to raise the price of labour usually had beneficial effects, if not directly on women's wages, then indirectly through increased *family* wages. This exposes the fallacy in the argument that women workers might be subject to disabilities in the guise of protective legislation. Such misunderstanding results from conflating the social and customary disabilities encountered by women in the professions with the constraints placed by law on women's work in industry. The two are very different. Their confusion illustrates the inability of protagonists of such views to understand the material conditions of the working class, especially as manifested in the industrial labour process.

The mistake that some of them [i.e., liberal women's groups making such charges] have made is in transferring their own grievances to a class whose troubles are little known and less understood . . . in supposing that while they pined to spend themselves in some intolerable toil of thought Mary Brown or Jane Smith should also pine to spend herself in fourteen hours a day washing or tailoring (Hutchins and Harrison, 1903, p. 184).

Hutchins and Harrison's verdict on this issue may be considered relevant.

The Trade Unions, whatever the faults in their economics or the lacunae in their reasoning, have never fallen into the blank and unfruitful individualism that has blighted the women's movement in the middle class; and the working woman we would submit has a far better chance to work out her economic salvation through solidarity and co-operation with her own class than by adopting the tactics and submitting to the tutelage of middle or upper class organizations (Hutchins and Harrison, 1903, p. 198).

## Class Cohesion and Class Consciousness

All too frequently in the modern literature the family is seen as engendering false consciousness, promoting capitalist ideology, undermining class cohesion and threatening the class struggle. In short, it stands charged with being a bourgeois institution acting in collaboration with capital against the real interests of the working class.[10] But superficial plausibility and anecdotal substantiation are no substitutes for thorough-going investigation. Many of the scenarios depicted in this literature seem coloured by preconceived ideas of working-class existence. The prosecution's case can be confronted with equally plausible counterarguments and comparable (if fragmentary) evidence.

Some connections have already been suggested between the existence of family ties and the growth of community and social obligation, important events in the development of class consciousness. For example, the existence of fictive kin involved an extension of family ties outwards into the community. In addition the struggles around the family, such as the resistance to 'in house relief' and the battle for a family wage, united families in *class* endeavours.

The bourgeoisie made repressive use of its provision for the working class. Poor relief was withheld during lockouts (Clements, 1961, p. 102), and denied to those who subscribed to the Chartist Fund (Hollis, 1973, p. 211). Truculent workers who lived in 'tied' cottages were evicted, and in general employers 'were suspected of the manipulation of charitable activity as yet another weapon in their disciplinary armour' (Denson, 1975, p. 402). Under these circumstances family and community-based assistance, both formal and informal, played a vital role in maintaining working-class integrity and autonomy.

Heroic family loyalties undoubtedly sustained many individuals through the turbulent period of industrialization, and engendered a feeling of comradeship in oppression. This must have been important. Class solidarity does not

---

10. The orthodox view is that the family promotes values and associated behaviour compatible with the capitalist mode of production: '. . . the nature of the relation is such that the performance of the respective sex-roles is seen as signs of love by the rest of the family. A good and loving husband is also a good factory worker, one who gets a large pay packet; a good and loving wife is one who spends much time on domestic work of one sort or another' (Gardiner, Himmelweit and MacKintosh, 1975, p. 6).

materialize out of a sudden recognition by isolated individuals that their situation is shared and that though weak individually they have collective power. It develops slowly over time, as a result of real-life experiences. Rather than promoting individualism, the mutual dependence of the family could well point up class community and class interest.[11]

Kinship ties are known to have been important instruments ensuring community solidarity in the eighteenth-century resistance to unpopular authorities, and legislation which redefined traditional rights in the light of the new overwhelming value placed upon property. Douglas Hay's study of poachers on Cannock Chase acknowledges that the 'virtually complete' solidarity against the keepers arose partly from 'bonds of blood and marriage, the tangled skein of alliances in small communities where degrees of kinship merged imperceptibly into those of friendship and acquaintance' (Hay, 1975, p. 200). Similarly the villagers of Hoylake on the Wirral, said to be unanimously engaged in wrecking and coastal plunder, were described as intermarried and 'nearly all related to each other' (Rule, 1975, p. 173). The reporter presumably believed this to be important for an understanding of their unity.

In contrast with the idea that the family socializes its members into acceptance of the dominant values stands the *possibility* that the family can, and sometimes does, promote 'deviant' ideas and behaviour. Evidence supporting this perspective is easy to find; witness the maternal indoctrination additive specific to the first all-female offshoot of union societies, which listed among its objectives 'to instill into the minds of our children a deep and rooted hatred of our corrupt and tyrannical rulers' (Marlow, 1971, p. 79).

Such unconventional idealism could be preserved within the family in periods of oppression and perpetuated intergenerationally. Joseph Arch is a good example of a working-class leader influenced not only by the experiences and reactions of his father, but also by the attitudes of his mother (Arch, 1898). John Foster's analysis of Oldham's working-class leadership documents other connections. The two Cleggs listed by Foster (1974, p. 151), were cousins, John Earnshaw, active in the 1816–19 period had a nephew, John Lees, who was killed at Peterloo. Foster's summary assigns to the family a crucial role in the growth and development of working-class consciousness and struggle.

Though there were always tactical disagreements and a constant stream of new recruits, what strikes one most from the descriptive evidence is the degree to which members saw themselves as part of a continuing tradition. Radical allegiances tended to be inherited within families and associated with particular neighbourhoods. The Swires, Earnshaws and Warwicks were all families that produced at least two generations of radicals (p. 138).

Similarly, family responsibilities did not always discipline working men, but sometimes promoted their radicalization. The experience of watching the suffering and oppression of their families could instigate class action. As Richard Marsden, a hand-loom weaver from Preston, put it: 'There is something in the effects of hunger and the sight of your family suffering from it which none can

---

11. The author believes that there is a class difference in the relationship between the family and the promotion of individualism or class solidarity. The middle-class family undoubtedly does promote individualism. The argument pursued in the text is not true of the working-class family.

judge of but those who have felt it. The equilibrium of temper and judgement is deranged' (Hollis, 1973, p. 227). Richard Pillings, another Chartist, at his trial in 1843 described how the sufferings of his family and his desire to keep them from the workhouse provided his action (Hollis, 1973, p. 293).

The working-class standard of living depends not only on the level of wages, the traditional trade union concern, but also on the cost of living, which is the primary concern of the administrator of the wage—the housewife. Attacks on the working-class situation through price increases have historically produced concerted action.

E. P. Thompson states that in the early nineteenth century the cost of bread was the most sensitive indicator of popular discontent and that, consumer consciousness was positively related to the evolution of class consciousness (Thompson, 1963). The bread riot predates the strike as an expression of workers' community of interest, and has remained in various more modern guises an important weapon in labour's arsenal down to the present day. The prominence of working-class women in these class struggles of the marketplace derives precisely from their family roles as the executors of consumption.

So, although women undoubtedly felt divided loyalties with respect to class action that incidentally imposed deprivation on their families,[12] their concern for the latter could also promote a class response, the effects of which were not inconsequential. Recent historical research has documented working women's early and widespread involvement in the class struggle (Thompson, 1963; Rowbotham, 1974). The charge that the nineteenth-century working-class mother was apathetic about, if not opposed to, class action depends crucially on the definition of the latter, and the particular historical circumstances considered. It certainly remains to be demonstrated. Similarly the case against the working-class family is not proven.

## Conclusion

An analysis of the role of the family in the maintenance and reproduction of labour-power is inadequate to explain the survival of working-class kinship structures under capitalism. Alternative private or state childrearing agencies, benefiting from economies of scale, could be envisaged which would meet capital's need for a passive labour force. The centralization of support involved in the substitution of state for family services would certainly give capital greater control over the administration of resources, which could then be streamlined and modified in the interests of capitalist production.

Capitalism has a history of market relations inexorably replacing social relations, as capitalist expansion leads to the rationalization of production according to the dictates of production for profit. The working-class family has escaped the disciplinary power of the market only because it has resisted that

---

12. Olwen Hufton's fascinating article (Hufton, 1971) illustrates the cyclical operation of these divided loyalties during the course of the French Revolution. An up-to-date example of the same phenomenon, the infamous 'wives revolt' at the Cowley complex of British Leyland in 1974, is described in Coulson, Magas and Wainwright (1975), p. 63.

power. A comprehensive explanation of labour's opposition to a total universalization of markets requires a theoretical framework based on a non-material as well as a material theory of human needs. The purpose of this paper was more modest: it was to demonstrate that in a capitalist environment the working class has certain well-defined reasons for defending the family which have been ignored in the literature. The preservation of non-market relations within the family emerges as neither an obsolete remnant of a less developed mode of production, nor a sociological anomaly, but a result of labour's struggle.

Family life has not been idealized here; there has been recognition that patterns of dominance relating to age, sex and the division of labour existed long before capitalism, and remain characteristic of family relations today. Their existence, however, should not blind observers to the material benefits that the family imparts to the working class in its struggle for a better life.

## References

Althusser, L., *Lenin and Philosophy,* Monthly Review Press, 1971.

Anderson, M., *Family Structure in Nineteenth Century Lancashire,* CUP, 1971.

Arch, J., *The Life of Joseph Arch by Himself,* Hutchinson, 1898.

Benson, J., 'English coal miners' trade union accident funds, 1850–1900', *Economic History Review,* Vol. XXVIII, No. 3, 1975.

Benston, M., 'The political economy of women's liberation', *Monthly Review,* September 1969.

Best, G., *Mid-Victorian Britain, 1857–1875,* Weidenfeld and Nicolson, 1971.

Black, C., *Sweated Industry and the Minimum Wage,* Duckworth, 1907.

Booth, C., *Life and Labour of the People in London,* Macmillan, 1902.

Burnett, J., ed., *Useful Toil: Autobiographies of Working People from the 1820's to the 1920's,* Allen Lane, 1974.

Checkland, S. G., and Checkland, E. O. A., eds., *The Poor Law of 1834,* Penguin, 1974.

Clements, R. V., 'British trade unions and popular political economy, 1850–1875', *Economic History Review,* Vol. XIV, No. 1, 1961.

Coulson, M., Magas, B., and Wainwright, H., 'The housewife and her labour under capitalism', *New Left Review,* No. 89, 1975.

Dalla Costa, M., 'Women and the subversion of the community', in *The Power of Women and the Subversion of the Community,* Falling Wall Press, 1972.

Drake, B., *Women in Trade Unions,* Special Edition for the Labour Movement, Trade Union Series No. 6, 1921.

Draper, H., 'Marx and Engels on women's liberation', *International Socialism,* July–August 1970.

Engels, F., *The Origin of the Family, Private Property and the State,* International Publishers, New York, 1972.

Foster, J., *Class Struggle and the Industrial Revolution: Early Capitalism in Three English Towns,* Weidenfeld and Nicolson, 1974.

Gardiner, J., 'Women's domestic labour', *New Left Review,* No. 89, 1975.

Gardiner, J., Himmelweit, S., and Mackintosh, M., 'Women's domestic labour, *Bulletin of the Conference of Socialist Economists,* Vol. IV, No. 2, 1975 (reprinted in *On the Political Economy of Women,* CSE Pamphlet No. 2, Stage One, 1976).

Hanson, C. G., 'Craft unions, welfare benefits, and the case for trade union law reform, 1867–75', *Economic History Review,* Vol. 28, No. 2, 1975.

Harrison, J., 'Political economy of housework', *Bulletin of the Conference of Socialist Economists,* Spring, 1974.

Hart, J., 'Nineteenth century social reform: a Tory interpretation of history', *Past and Present, A Journal of Historical Studies,* No. 31, 1965.

Hay, D., 'Poaching and the game laws on Cannock Chase', in *Albion's Fatal Tree: Crime and Society in Eighteenth Century England,* D. Hay, P. Linebaugh, J. G. Rule, E. P. Thompson and C. Winslow, eds., Pantheon Books, 1975.

Hewitt, M., *Wives and Mothers in Victorian Industry,* Rockliff, 1958.

Himmelweit, S., and Mohun, S., 'Domestic labour and capital', *Cambridge Journal of Economics,* Vol. 1, No. 1, 1977.

Hindess, B., and Hirst, P. W., *Precapitalist Modes of Production,* Routledge and Kegan Paul, 1975.

Hobsbawm, E. J., *Labouring Men: Studies in the History of Labour,* Weidenfeld and Nicolson, 1964.

Hollis, P., ed., *Class and Conflict in Nineteenth Century England: 1815–1850,* Routledge and Kegan Paul, 1973.

Hufton, O., 'Women in revolution, 1789–1796', *Past and Present,* No. 53, 1971.

Hutchins, B. L., and Harrison, A., *A History of Factory Legislation,* P. S. King and Son, 1903.

Laslett, P., *The World We Have Lost,* Charles Scribners' Sons, 1965.

Marlow, J., *The Peterloo Massacre,* Panther Books, 1971.

Marx, K., *Capital,* Vol. I, International Publishers, New York, 1967.

Marx, K., and Engels, F., *Collected Works,* Vol. 5, Lawrence and Wishart, 1976.

Mayhew, H., *London Labour and the London Poor,* Griffin, Bohn and Company, 1861.

McGeown, P., *Heat the Furnace Seven Times More,* Hutchinson, 1967.

Parliamentary Papers, Vol. XX. Reports from Commissioners, Factories Inquiry Commission, His Majesty's Stationery Office, 1833.

Parliamentary Papers, Vol. XVII. Reports from Commissioners, Children's Employment (Mines), William Clowes and Sons, for Her Majesty's Stationery Office, 1842.

Rowbotham, S., *Women's Consciousness, Man's World,* Penguin, 1973.

Rowbotham, S., *Women, Resistance and Revolution,* Vintage Books, New York, 1974.

Rowntree, B. S., *Poverty, A Study of Town Life,* Macmillan, 1902.

Rule, J. G., 'Wrecking and coastal plunder', in *Albion's Fatal Tree: Crime and Society in Eighteenth Century England,* D. Hay, P. Linebaugh, J. G. Rule, E. P. Thompson and C. Winslow, eds., Pantheon Books, 1975.

Seccombe, W., 'The housewife and her labour under capitalism', *New Left Review,* No. 83, 1974.

Seccombe, W., 'Domestic labour—reply to critics', *New Left Review,* No. 94, 1975.

Smelser, N. J., *Social Change in the Industrial Revolution: An Application of Theory to the British Cotton Industry,* University of Chicago Press, 1959.

Stedman Jones, G., *Outcast London: A Study in the Relationship between Classes in Victorian Society,* Penguin, 1971.

Thompson, E. P., *The Making of the English Working Class,* Vintage Books, New York, 1963.

Webb, S., and Webb, B., *English Poor Law History, Part II: The Last Hundred Years,* Private Subscription Edition, 1929.

Willmott, P., and Young, M., *Family and Kinship in East London,* Routledge and Kegan Paul, 1957.

# Selective Further Reading

Amsden, Alice H., ed., *The Economics of Women and Work* (Harmondsworth: Penguin, 1980).

Anderson, M., *Family Structure in the Nineteenth Century* (Cambridge: Cambridge University Press, 1971).

Barker, D., and S. Allen, eds., *Dependence and Exploitation in Work and Marriage* (London: Longmans, 1976).

Barrett, Michèlle, *Women's Oppression Today* (London: Verso Eds. and NLB, 1980).

Barrett, Michèlle, and Mary McIntosh, 'The "Family Wage": Some Problems for Socialists and Feminists', *Capital and Class* 2 (1980).

Beechey, Veronica, 'Some Notes on Female Wage Labour in Capitalist Production', *Capital and Class* 3 (1977).

Blaxall, Martha, and Barbara Reagan, eds., *Women and the Workplace* (Chicago: University of Chicago Press, 1976).

Bruegal, Irene, 'Women as a Reserve Army of Labour: A Note on Recent British Experience', *Feminist Review* 3 (1979).

Delamont, Sara, *The Sociology of Women* (London: Allen & Unwin, 1980).

Donzelot, Jacques, *The Policing of Families: Welfare Versus the State* (London: Hutchinson, 1980).

Eisenstein, Zillah R., ed., *Capitalist Patriarchy and the Case for Socialist Feminism* (New York: Monthly Review Press, 1979).

Engels, F., *The Origin of the Family, Private Property, and the State* (New York: International Publishers, 1972).

Gardiner, J., S. Himmelweit, and M. Mackintosh, *Conference of Socialist Economists,* CSE Pamphlet 2 (1976).

Herzog, Marianne, *From Hand to Mouth: Women and Piecework* (Harmondsworth: Penguin, 1980).

Hunt, Pauline, *Gender and Class Consciousness* (London: Macmillan, 1980).

Land, Hilary, 'The Family Wage', *Feminist Review* 6 (1980).

Lloyd, C., ed., *Sex, Discrimination, and the Division of Labour* (New York: Columbia University Press, 1975).

Malos, Ellen, ed., *The Politics of Housework* (London: Allen & Busby, 1980).

Mitchell, Juliet, and Ann Oakley, eds., *The Rights and Wrongs of Women* (Harmondsworth: Penguin, 1976).

Molyneux, M., 'Beyond the Domestic Labour Debate', *New Left Review* 116 (1979).

Oakley, A., *The Sociology of Housework* (Oxford: M. Robertson, 1974).

Reiter, Rayna, ed., *Toward an Anthropology of Women* (New York: Monthly Review, 1975).

Rowbotham, S., *Woman's Consciousness, Man's World* (Harmondsworth: Penguin, 1973).

―――――, *Women, Resistance, and Revolution* (New York: Vintage Books, 1974).

Schreiner, Olive, *Woman and Labour,* (London: Virago, 1978).

Tilley, Louis A., and Joan W. Scott, *Women, Work, and Family* (New York: Holt, Reinhart and Winston, 1978).

Wainwright, Hilary, 'Women and the Division of Labour', in *Work, Urbanism, and Inequality,* ed. P. Abrams (London: Weidenfeld, 1978).

Zaretsky, Eli, *Capitalism, the Family, and Personal Life* (London: Pluto, 1976).

# · VII ·

# Class, Race, and the City

# Introduction

Class analysis, as the contributions in the preceding section help to illustrate, cannot be confined to the study either of the workplace or of economic relations more generally. A variety of other sources of schism and solidarity have to be studied in close association with class structuration. Race or ethnicity is of major importance in this respect. Like sex divisions, these are not phenomena that brook large in the classical Marxian texts, although they are discussed by Weber in relation to 'status groups'.

In this section we offer two contrasting—although not necessarily mutually inconsistent—recent discussions of the intersection of ethnic and class relations. Robert Blauner adopts a strongly historical approach, arguing that ethnic diversity in the United States should be understood from a 'third world perspective' of the movement, forced or voluntary, of ethnic groups in terms of colonialism and immigration. Erik Olin Wright's analysis is more statistical, attempting to chart and to explicate established connections between ethnicity and class in respect of whites and blacks in the American occupational structure (one might note, in relation to Section Six, that his study is again confined to male workers).

According to Blauner, colonialism and immigration represent the two principal ways in which 'plural societies'—societies having ethnically diversified populations—come into being. Colonialism refers to processes whereby powerful countries incorporate other peoples through conquest or other means of coercion. Immigration refers to the 'free' or voluntary movement of ethnic groups into a particular country. The two are obviously not always entirely separable. Immigrants may be more or less compelled to leave their country of origin through factors outside their control, for example, but still choose to come to one country rather than another where alternative possibilities are open to them.

In the United States, native American Indians, blacks, and Chicanos are those groups, Blauner says, whose experience has been largely the outcome of coercion and who thus best exemplify the colonial model. 'Colonialism', Blauner insists, is an apt term to apply to the experience of blacks in the United States, in spite of the fact that the Africans were transported rather than colonised in Africa itself—as was their fate, of course, at the hands of the European nations. Colonial oppression which is 'imported' into the host nation remains colonial oppression: it is an instance of what the Mexican sociologist Casanova has labelled 'internal colonialism'. The conquest of the indigenous American population is a straightforward instance of colonialism, as was that of the American Southwest.

Some Third World groups in the United States can be regarded as part colonial, part immigrant. The Puerto Ricans, according to Blauner, are a case in point. The island of Puerto Rico has been colonised, but Puerto Ricans have also been able to move fairly freely between their homeland and the United States. The position of groups such as the Chinese and Japanese is more ambiguous, being first of all fairly coercive, but then yielding to a pattern of voluntary migration.

The differences between the mode of entry, and the subsequent fate, of these Third World groups as compared with European immigrants are quite clear-cut. By no means all the Europeans came 'voluntarily', but they characteristically had other options potentially open to them: in Canada, Australia, or some of the Latin American countries. As relatively free migrants, the European ethnic groups were able, in principle if not always effectively in practice, to be both geographically and socially mobile within American society. 'Though they faced great hardships', Blauner says, 'and even prejudice and discrimination on a scale that must have been disillusioning, the Irish, Italians, Jews, and other groups had the advantage of European ancestry and white skins'. As immigrants attracted by the promise of American liberalism, however harsh the realities they encountered, the Europeans had the chance to see the United States in positive terms rather than as an oppressive, alien culture.

Analysts of race relations in the United States, Blauner claims, have been loath to accept the significance of these contrasts. The immigrant model has been used as the main basis for studying ethnic diversity in America. The progressive assimilation of immigrant groups in a cultural 'melting pot' has become the baseline against which ethnicity has been analysed. Blacks especially provided the most obvious exception to this, but even they have been compressed into the same scheme, the idea being that migration from the South to the Northern cities can be regarded as the first phase of the process of assimilation followed by other immigrant groups.

Such a conception, in Blauner's view, is quite inadequate; we must trace through how the differences between colonialised and immigrant peoples have helped create some generic features of the American class system. Both types of groups, of course, were overwhelmingly poor and were employed as unskilled workers. But the modes of their incorporation into the economy involved important contrasts. The main element in these contrasts, Blauner emphasises, was that whereas the European immigrants were 'free' wage workers, the colonised peoples were involved in unfree, coerced labour. Early attempts to force the native Indians into some form of *corvée* or even slave labour were unsuccessful, and their armed resistance led to their being wiped out or herded into settlement areas. Africans in the Southeast were slaves, forbidden to own property or to enter into wage contracts; Mexicans in the Southwest were made dependent peon labourers. These phenomena have to be seen as part of a much broader process of European imperialism; slavery, serfdom, and peonage have been the lot of nonwhite peoples rather than 'equal' initiation into the labour force of capitalism. The significance of this, Blauner suggests, has been rather obscured in Marxist theory, with its concentration upon the 'wage slavery' of the industrial worker.

The differences between immigrant and colonised peoples, in Blauner's argument, have had long-term consequences for the class structure of the United States. Whereas European workers have been clustered in the manufacturing and state administration sectors, the colonised groups have been concentrated in mining and transport. The latter were then 'frozen' for a long period of time in economic sectors involving the harshest labour conditions and poorest chances of social mobility. The immigrants, on the other hand, were able to become socially mobile across the generations.

Whereas Blauner questions the use of a Marxist class model in understanding ethnic diversity and discrimination in the United States, the declared objective of Wright's discussion is to interpret persisting income inequalities between whites and blacks in terms of just such a model. A great deal of research, he says, has been carried out showing that blacks of similar educational level to whites nevertheless end up in more poorly paid jobs. Such research, however, has not been organised in terms of Marxist class analysis, and Wright seeks to demonstrate a strong influence of class division upon ethnic inequalities. His formulation of class follows the same lines as that to be found in his work as summarised in Section Two. 'Class', he emphasises, is not the same as 'occupation'. 'Occupation' refers to the tasks individuals carry out in the division of labour, 'class' to the social relations of production within which those tasks are performed. He recognises four basic class categories: employers, managers or supervisors, the petty bourgeoisie, and the working class.

Wright then sets out to test six main hypotheses, using material on income distribution. Each is found to be valid. These six hypotheses are the following: (1) Managers (regardless of colour) receive higher returns in relation to education than workers. This differentiation operates on two levels. Because of their controlling position in administrative hierarchies, managers are in any case, whatever their educational background, able to achieve higher material returns than workers. But in the managerial category educational qualifications also serve to facilitate promotion up a career hierarchy. (This is the 'credentialism' upon which Parkin, in Section Two, lays considerable emphasis). (2) There is a higher relative proportion of blacks than whites in the working class as a whole. This is hardly a startlingly novel proposition, but Wright provides a statistical documentation of it. (3) When class position is put to one side, blacks obtain lower returns, in respect of educational level, than whites. As has been indicated above, this is the 'standard' finding, but Wright wishes to show that it applies to the data that forms the empirical basis of his study. (4) There is less divergence between the economic returns of whites and blacks within the working class, in relation to education, than there is between whites and blacks overall. That this is so indicates common factors acting to regulate income among wage labourers whose labour is controlled by others, the two criteria of being in the 'working class' category for Wright. (5) The same relationship as in (4) holds among supervisors, that is, those in lower managerial positions without much executive authority. That such is found to be the case again tends to indicate the dominance of class categories over ethnic categories. And (6) among managers, blacks have substantially lower returns to education than whites. Wright's finding here is in fact rather different from that he anticipated; the return to education among black managers was virtually nil. This seems to be an expression of the fact that a high proportion of Wright's 'black managers' are college or university teachers, but Wright has no particular explanation of its significance.

How should we interpret these findings as a whole? There can be no question, Wright accepts, of reducing ethnic discrimination to class exploitation; we must try rather to explicate the relations between the two. One rather obvious connecting factor, supported by the empirical analysis, is that the ethnic differences between whites and blacks strongly influences the distribution of those occupying variant class positions. We should avoid the facile idea of some Marxists, Wright argues, that white/black ethnic discrimination is 'functional' for capitalism and therefore in some way directly fostered by capital. Capitalist economic relations are predicated upon the hiring of labour power, to which any other considerations are irrelevant: capitalism from this aspect expunges any 'qualitative' differences between categories of labour. But at the same time the dynamics of class conflict tend to intensify discriminatory attitudes and practices, both from the side of employers and from that of white workers. Ethnic divisions within the labour force, as Rubery has pointed out in Section Four, may facilitate the power of employers via the creation of segmented labour markets internally and externally.

The relationship between class and ethnic divisions is certainly a phenomenon which concerns other features of social life than those mentioned either by Blauner or Wright. Especially important here are the modes in which ethnic discrimination influences housing markets and, thus, the general distribution of neighbourhoods in urban areas. Although there have been many pieces of research work focussed on processes creating ghettos, the flight of whites from the 'inner city' and so on, we have opted to include here a study that approaches the relation between class structure and urbanism from a more general perspective.

David Harvey's work is part of a new wave of urban analysis, to which writers such as Castells and his followers have also made important contributions. Such authors have sought to criticise the idea that 'urban sociology' can be just a branch of social science among others. Urbanism is such an overwhelming feature of the social environments in which the majority of the population in capitalist societies live, that its study has a general importance for the social sciences. Also, these writers have argued forcibly that 'the city' cannot be studied, as has characteristically been presumed in 'urban sociology', as an entity or type of entity in itself. Cities have to be understood in the context of much more extensive social processes involving whole societies. Finally, they have stressed that 'the city', or 'urbanism', cannot be properly regarded as unitary phenomena, similar in all types of society. Such an assumption has often been made by those studying the early phases of industrial capitalism, who have analysed migrations from rural to urban areas. According to Harvey, Castells, and others, this is an inadequate conception because the very *nature* of what 'urbanism' is became radically transformed with the emergence of industrial capitalism. The 'built environment' became determined by new influences, deriving from its integration into capitalist product markets.

In the article reproduced here, Harvey tries to characterise some of these influences connecting the dynamics of urbanism to class structure. Class conflict is frequently expressed in struggles over the character of the built environment and in urban social movements. The intervention of capitalistic interests in the distribution of urban space, he asserts, takes various forms. There are specific capitalist interests seeking a return on rent, such as landlords, property companies, and other investors; sectors of capital concerned with the construction of houses, highways, etc; and 'general capital', which has diffuse interests in utilising the built environment via the placement of factories, shops, etc. Various sections of the population who are not 'capitalists' in any other sense participate directly on one or more of these levels, especially in the buying and selling of owner-occupied homes. For all classes, the built environment is also, of course, a set of spatial configurations in which daily life, work, and leisure pursuits are carried on.

Capitalism creates a separation between work and the place of residence. This leads to dislocations between struggles in the setting of the industrial enterprise and those concerned with housing and neighbourhood organisation; but there are actually strong relationships between these examined in the broad context of class structure. The control which ownership of capital yields in the workplace extends to what Harvey calls a 'natural monopoly' of urban space. According to him, there is a threefold intersection involved here, among the appropriators of rent, those involved in construction industry, and owner- or tenant-occupiers. The price and distribution of housing is determined by various possible conflicts and alliances among these three groupings or subsectors of them. The power or sanctions available to each grouping differs. Rentiers or landlords may be restricted by state legislation (via rent controls, etc.), but they normally have the capacity to transfer their capital investments when they become unprofitable—perhaps out of housing altogether—and will ordinarily do so. Rents are in turn affected by the allocation of capital in construction or renewal of housing stocks. This capital is also in principle 'mobile'—it can be transferred to other spheres or its investment patterns altered if levels of profitability are low. But the choices open to the third sector, the 'consumers' of urban space, are much more confined; people must have somewhere to live. Their main source of influence is through the mobility permitted by the sale of owner-occupied homes or by pressure to achieve rent controls on the part of tenants. But these capabilities tend to be largely dominated by the overall allocation of investment capital in the other two spheres. Moreover, as Harvey emphasises, most private home-ownership is based on mortgage payments, making the 'owner' deeply dependent upon finance capital.

Several different scenarios emerge from this analysis in respect of the nature of conflicts over the use of urban space. All are real possibilities, but each tends to merge into the others. We can envisage a situation in which every urban consumer acts as an individual, pursuing his or her best interests in competition with others in housing markets. Such a circumstance corresponds to neoclassical models of land use in economic theory. A second situation is that in which consumers act collectively, via some form of community action. Such activity does not by any means imply a direct struggle against the powers of capital but, on the contrary, tends to produce a privileged stratum of home owners who may be able to protect or enhance the value of their particular properties. The third type of circumstance is that of general class struggle, in which housing consumers act uniformly to confront exploitative control of the built environment by capital. These three situations appear in varying relations in differing societies; but there are always powerful influences that tend to inhibit the third scenario from developing in any full-blown way.

# · 24 ·

# Colonised and Immigrant Minorities

## Robert Blauner

### Group Entry and Freedom of Movement[1]

Colonialism and immigration are the two major means by which heterogeneous or plural societies, with ethnically diverse populations, develop. In the case of colonialism, metropolitan nations incorporate new territories or peoples through processes that are essentially involuntary, such as war, conquest, capture, and other forms of force or manipulation. Through immigration, new peoples or ethnic groups enter a host society more or less freely. These are ideal-types, the polar ends of a continuum; many historical cases fall in between. In the case of America's racial minorities, some groups clearly fit the criterion for colonial entry; others exemplify mixed types.

Native Americans, Chicanos, and blacks are the third world groups whose entry was unequivocally forced and whose subsequent histories best fit the colonial model. Critics of the colonial interpretation usually focus on the black experience, emphasizing how it has differed from those of traditional colonialism. Rather than being conquered and controlled in their native land, African

---

• From Robert Blauner, *Racial Oppression in America* (New York: Harper & Row, 1972), pp. 53–81.

1. [This article was in part inspired by the desire to assess the claims and activities of the movement—referred to as the 'Third World Movement'—that emerged during the late 1960s pressing for greater ethnic freedoms and control over everyday life—eds.] For accounts of this movement at San Francisco State, see James McEvoy and Abraham Miller, eds., *Black Power and Student Rebellion* (Belmont, Calif.: Wadsworth, 1969), especially the articles by Barlow and Shapiro, Gitlin, Chrisman, and the editors; and Bill Barlow and Peter Shapiro, *An End to Silence* (New York: Pegasus Books, Division of Bobbs-Merrill), 1971.

people were captured, transported, and enslaved in the Southern states and other regions of the Western hemisphere. Whether oppression takes place at home in the oppressed's native land or in the heart of the colonizer's mother country, colonization remains colonization. However, the term *internal colonialism* is useful for emphasizing the differences in setting and in the consequences that arise from it.[2] The conquest and virtual elimination of the original Americans, a process that took three hundred years to complete, is an example of classical colonialism, no different in essential features from Europe's imperial control over Asia, Africa, and Latin America. The same is true of the conquest of the Mexican Southwest and the annexation of its Spanish-speaking population.

Other third world groups have undergone an experience that can be seen as part colonial and part immigrant. Puerto Rico has been a colony exploited by the mainland, while, at the same time, the islanders have had relative freedom to move back and forth and to work and settle in the States. Of the Asian-American groups, the situation of the Filipinos has been the most colonial. The islands were colonies of Spain and the United States, and the male population was recruited for agricultural serfdom both in Hawaii and in the States. In the more recent period, however, movement to the States has been largely voluntary.

In the case of the Chinese, we do not have sufficient historical evidence to be able to assess the balance between free and involuntary entry in the nineteenth century. The majority came to work in the mines and fields for an extended period of debt servitude; many individuals were "shanghaied" or pressed into service; many others evidently signed up voluntarily for serflike labor.[3] A similar pattern held for the Japanese who came toward the end of the century, except that the voluntary element in the Japanese entry appears to have been considerably more significant.[4] Thus, for the two largest Asian groups, we have an original entry into American society that might be termed semicolonial, followed in the twentieth century by immigration. Yet the exclusion of Asian immigrants and the restriction acts that followed were unique blows, which marked off the status of the Chinese and Japanese in America, limiting their numbers and potential power. For this reason it is misleading to equate the Asian

---

2. In addition to its application to white-black relations in the United States—see for example, Stokely Carmichael and Charles Hamilton, *Black Power* (New York: Vintage, 1967), esp. chap. 1—the concept of internal colonialism is a leading one for a number of students of Indian-white and Indian-mestizo relations in Latin America. Representative statements are Pablo Gonzalez Casanova, "Internal Colonialism and National Development," Rodolfo Stavenhagen, "Classes, Colonialism and Acculturation," and Julio Cotler, "The Mechanics of Internal Domination and Social Change in Peru," *Studies in Comparative International Development*, vol. 1, 1965, no. 4, vol. 1, 1965, no. 6, vol. 3, 1967–1968, no. 12. The Stavenhagen and Cotler papers are found also in Irving L. Horowitz, ed., *Masses in Latin America* (New York: Oxford University Press, 1970). See also André Gunder Frank, *Capitalism and Underdevelopment in Latin America* (New York: Monthly Review Press, 1967), and Eugene Havens and William Flinn, eds., *Internal Colonialism and Structural Change in Colombia* (New York: Praeger, 1970).

3. Gunther Barth, *Bitter Strength, A History of the Chinese in the United States, 1850–1870* (Cambridge: Harvard University Press, 1964).

4. Harry H. L. Kitano, *Japanese-Americans: The Evolution of a Subculture* (Englewood Cliffs, N.J.: Prentice-Hall, 1969).

experience with the European immigrant pattern. Despite the fact that some individuals and families have been able to immigrate freely, the status and size of these ethnic groups have been rigidly controlled.

There is a somewhat parallel ambiguity in the twentieth-century movement from Mexico, which has contributed a majority of the present Mexican-American group. Although the migration of individuals and families in search of work and better living conditions has been largely voluntary, classifying this process as immigration misses the point that the Southwest is historically and culturally a Mexican, Spanish-speaking region. Moreover, from the perspective of conquest that many Mexicans have retained, the movement has been to a land that is still seen as their own. Perhaps the entry of other Latin-Americans approaches more nearly the immigrant model; however, in their case, too, there is a colonial element, arising from the Yankee neo-colonial domination of much of South and Central America; for this reason, along with that of racism in the States, many young Latinos are third world oriented.

Thus the relation between third world groups and a colonial-type entry into American society is impressive, though not perfect or precise. Differences between people of color and Europeans are shown most clearly in the ways the groups first entered. The colonized became ethnic minorities *en bloc,* collectively, through conquest, slavery, annexation, or a racial labor policy. The European immigrant peoples became ethnic groups and minorities within the United States by the essentially voluntary movements of individuals and families. Even when, later on, some third world peoples were able to immigrate, the circumstances of the earlier entry affected their situation and the attitudes of the dominant culture toward them.

The essentially voluntary entry of the immigrants was a function of their status in the labor market. The European groups were responding to the industrial needs of a free capitalist market. Economic development in other societies with labor shortages—for example, Australia, Brazil, and Argentina—meant that many people could at least envision alternative destinations for their emigration. Though the Irish were colonized at home, and poverty, potato famine, and other disasters made their exodus more of a flight than that of other Europeans, they still had some choice of where to flee.[5] Thus, people of Irish descent are found today in the West Indies, Oceania, and other former British colonies. Germans and Italians moved in large numbers to South America; Eastern Europeans immigrated to Canada as well as to the United States.

Because the Europeans moved on their own, they had a degree of autonomy that was denied those whose entry followed upon conquest, capture, or involuntary labor contracts. They expected to move freely within the society to the extent that they acquired the economic and cultural means. Though they faced great hardships and even prejudice and discrimination on a scale that must have been disillusioning, the Irish, Italians, Jews, and other groups had the advantage of European ancestry and white skins. When living in New York became too difficult, Jewish families moved on to Chicago. Irish trapped in Boston could get land and farm in the Midwest, or search for gold in California. It is obvious

---

5. Oscar Handlin, *Boston's Immigrants* (Cambridge: Harvard University Press, 1959), chap. 2.

that parallel alternatives were not available to the early generations of Afro-Americans, Asians, and Mexican-Americans, because they were not part of the free labor force. Furthermore, limitations on physical movement followed from the purely racial aspect of their oppression.

Thus, the entrance of the European into the American order involved a degree of choice and self-direction that was for the most part denied people of color. Voluntary immigration made it more likely that individual Europeans and entire ethnic groups would identify with America and see the host culture as a positive opportunity rather than an alien and dominating value system. It is my assessment that this element of choice, though it can be overestimated and romanticized, must have been crucial in influencing the different careers and perspectives of immigrants and colonized in America, because choice is a necessary condition for commitment to any group, from social club to national society.

Sociologists interpreting race relations in the United States have rarely faced the full implications of these differences. The *immigrant model* became the main focus of analysis, and the experiences of all groups were viewed through its lens.[6] It suited the cultural mythology to see everyone in America as an original immigrant, a later immigrant, a quasi-immigrant or a potential immigrant. Though the black situation long posed problems for this framework, recent developments have made it possible for scholars and ordinary citizens alike to force Afro-American realities into this comfortable schema. Migration from rural South to urban North became an analog of European immigration, blacks became the latest newcomers to the cities, facing parallel problems of assimilation. In the no-nonsense language of Irving Kristol, "The Negro Today Is Like the Immigrant of Yesterday."[7]

### The Colonial Labor Principle in the United States

European immigrants and third world people have faced some similar conditions, of course. The overwhelming majority of both groups were poor, and their early generations worked primarily as unskilled laborers. The question of how, where, and why newcomers worked in the United States is central, for the differences in the labor systems that introduced people of color and immigrants to America may be the fundamental reason why their histories have followed disparate paths.

The labor forces that built up the Western hemisphere were structured on the principle of race and color. The European conquest of the Native Americans

---

6. A crucial treatment of the model of immigration and assimilation is Oscar Handlin, *The Uprooted* (New York: Grosset & Dunlap, 1951).

7. *New York Times Magazine* (September 11, 1966), reprinted in Nathan Glazer, ed., *Cities in Trouble* (Chicago: Quadrangle, 1970), pp. 139–157. Another influential study in this genre is Edward Banfield, *The Unheavenly City* (Boston: Little, Brown, 1970). For a critical discussion of this thesis and the presentation of contrary demographic data, see Karl E. Taueber and Alma F. Taueber, "The Negro as an Immigrant Group: Recent Trends in Racial and Ethnic Segregation in Chicago," *American Journal of Sociology, 69* (1964), 374–382. The Kerner Report also devotes a brief chapter to "Comparing the Immigrant and Negro Experience," *Report of the National Advisory Commission on Civil Disorders* (New York: Bantam, 1968), chap. 9.

and the introduction of plantation slavery were crucial beginning points for the emergence of a worldwide colonial order. These "New World" events established the pattern for labor practices in the colonial regimes of Asia, Africa, and Oceania during the centuries that followed. The key equation was the association of free labor with people of white European stock and the association of unfree labor with non-Western people of color, a correlation that did not develop all at once; it took time for it to become a more or less fixed pattern.

North American colonists made several attempts to force Indians into dependent labor relationships, including slavery.[8] But the native North American tribes, many of which were mobile hunters and warrior peoples, resisted agricultural peonage and directly fought the theft of their lands. In addition, the relative sparsity of Indian populations north of the Rio Grande limited their potential utility for colonial labor requirements. Therefore Native American peoples were either massacred or pushed out of the areas of European settlement and enterprise. South of the Rio Grande, where the majority of Native Americans lived in more fixed agricultural societies, they were too numerous to be killed off or pushed aside, though they suffered drastic losses through disease and massacre.[9] In most of Spanish America, the white man wanted both the land and the labor of the Indian. Agricultural peonage was established and entire communities were subjugated economically and politically. Either directly or indirectly, the Indian worked for the white man.

In the Caribbean region (which may be considered to include the American South),[10] neither Indian nor white labor was available in sufficient supply to meet the demands of large-scale plantation agriculture. African slaves were imported to the West Indies, Brazil, and the colonies that were to become the United States to labor in those industries that promised and produced the greatest profit: indigo, sugar, coffee and cotton. Whereas many lower-class Britishers submitted to debt servitude in the 1600s, by 1700 slavery had crystallized into a condition thought of as natural and appropriate only to people of African descent.[11] White men, even if from lowly origins and serflike pasts, were able to own land and property, and to sell their labor in the free market. Though there were always anomalous exceptions, such as free and even slave-owning Negroes, people of color within the Americas had become essentially a class of unfree laborers. Afro-Americans were overwhelmingly bondsmen; Native Americans were serfs and peons in most of the continent.

Colonial conquest and control has been the cutting edge of Western capitalism in its expansion and penetration throughout the world. Yet capitalism and free labor as Western institutions were not developed for people of color; they were reserved for white people and white societies. In the colonies European

---

8. W. C. Macleod, *The American Indian Frontier* (London: Routledge & Kegan Paul, 1928).

9. For a discussion of these differences in ecological and material circumstances, see Marvin Harris, *Patterns of Race in America* (New York: Walker, 1964), esp. chaps. 1–4. Compare also John Collier, *The Indians of the Americas* (New York: Mentor, 1947), pp. 100–103.

10. H. Hoetink, *The Two Variants of Race Relations in the Caribbean* (London: Oxford University Press, 1967), presents a strong argument on this point.

11. For an historical account of this development, see Winthrop Jordan, *White over Black* (Chapel Hill: University of North Carolina Press, 1968), chap. 2.

powers organized other systems of work that were noncapitalist and unfree: slavery, selfdom, peonage. Forced labor in a myriad of forms became the province of the colonized and "native" peoples. European whites managed these forced labor systems and dominated the segments of the economy based on free labor. [12] This has been the general situation in the Western hemisphere (including the United States) for more than three out of the four centuries of European settlement. It was the pattern in the more classical colonial societies also. But from the point of view of labor, the colonial dynamic developed more completely within the United States. Only here emerged a correlation between color and work status that was almost perfect. In Asia and Africa, as well as in much of Central and South America, many if not most of the indigenous peoples remained formally free in their daily work, engaging in traditional subsistence economies rather than working in the plantations, fields, and mines established by European capital. The economies in these areas came within the orbit of imperial control, yet they helped maintain communities and group life and thus countered the uprooting tendencies and the cultural and psychic penetration of colonialism. Because such traditional forms of social existence were viable and preferred, labor could only be moved into the arenas of Western enterprise through some form of coercion. Although the association of color and labor status was not perfect in the classical colonial regimes, as a general rule the racial principle kept white Europeans from becoming slaves, coolies, or peons.

Emancipation in the United States was followed by a period of rapid industrialization in the last third of the nineteenth century. The Civil War and its temporary resolution of sectional division greatly stimulated the economy. With industrialization there was an historic opportunity to transform the nation's racial labor principle. Low as were the condition and income of the factory laborer, his status was that of a free worker. The manpower needs in the new factories and mines of the East and Middle West could have been met by the proletarianization of the freedmen along with some immigration from Europe.

---

12. Pedro Carrasco, cited in Sidney W. Mintz, "The Plantation as a Socio-Cultural Type," in Pan American Union, "Plantation Systems of the New World," *Social Science Monographs,* 7 (1959), 52–53.

It is an equally regular feature of the absorption of colonial peoples into the wider capitalistic system, that such absorption has often been limited to the introduction of the minimum changes necessary for production of staples required by the Western economy, while otherwise leaving practically untouched the non-capitalistic economic system prevalent in the colonial areas. The sharp separation of worker and employer classes and the colonial status of plantation areas, that is, the limited social and political absorption of plantation populations are the usual correlates of the limited economic absorption.

The systems of labor by which these colonial populations come to participate in the world capitalist system are usually described in terms of a dichotomy of compulsory versus free labor which generally results in a typological and developmental continuum: slavery, forced or conscripted labor of subject populations, various forms of contract labor with elements of compulsion such as indentured labor or peonage, and finally free labor.

Also see W. Kloosterboer, *Involuntary Labour Since the Abolition of Slavery* (Leiden: Brill, 1960), for a general account and a specific analysis of 13 different societies. This survey found the racial principle to be the prevailing rule with the following exceptions: the forced labor camps in the Soviet Union during the Stalin era, the peonage of white labourers by Maine lumber companies around 1900, and two situations where people of African descent oppressed unfree black labor, Haiti and Liberia. In addition, Portuguese have at times served as semifree agricultural workers in Brazil and the Caribbean.

But the resurgent Southern ruling class blocked the political and economic democratization movements of Reconstruction, and the mass of blacks became sharecroppers and tenant farmers, agricultural serfs little removed from formal slavery.[13] American captains of industry and the native white proletariat preferred to employ despised, unlettered European peasants rather than the emancipated Negro population of the South, or for that matter than the many poor white Southern farmers whose labor mobility was also blocked as the entire region became a semi-colony of the North.

The nineteenth century was the time of "manifest destiny," the ideology that justified Anglo expansionism in its sweep to the Pacific. The Texan War of 1836 was followed by the full-scale imperialist conquest of 1846–1848 through which Mexico lost half its territory. By 1900 Anglo-Americans had assumed economic as well as political dominance over most of the Southwest. As white colonists and speculators gained control (often illegally) over the land and livelihood of the independent Hispano farming and ranching villages, a new pool of dependent labor was produced to work the fields and build the railroads of the region.[14] Leonard Pitt sums up the seizure of California in terms applicable to the whole Southwest:

In the final analysis the Californios were the victims of an imperial conquest. . . . The United States, which had long coveted California for its trade potential and strategic location, finally provoked a war to bring about the desired ownership. At the conclusion of fighting, it arranged to "purchase" the territory outright, and set about to colonize, by throwing open the gates to all comers. Yankee settlers then swept in by the tens of thousands, and in a matter of months and years overturned the old institutional framework, expropriated the land, imposed a new body of law, a new language, a new economy, and a new culture, and in the process exploited the labor of the local population whenever necessary. To certain members of the old ruling class these settlers awarded a token and symbolic prestige, at least temporarily; yet with that status went very little genuine authority. In the long run Americans simply pushed aside the earlier ruling elite as being irrelevant.[15]

Later, the United States' economic hegemony over a semicolonial Mexico and the upheavals that followed the 1910 revolution brought additional mass migrations of brown workers to the croplands of the region. The Mexicans and Mexican-Americans who created the rich agricultural industries of the Southwest were as a rule bound to contractors, owners, and officials in a status little above peonage. Beginning in the 1850s, shipments of Chinese workmen—who

---

13. This pattern was not unique to the United States. The emancipation of slaves in other societies has typically led to their confinement to other forms of unfree labor, usually sharecropping. In this context Kloosterboer cites the examples of the British West Indies, South Africa, the Dutch West Indies, the Dutch East Indies (Java), Portuguese Africa, Madagascar, the Belgian Congo, and Haiti (ibid.). The great influx of European immigration to Brazil also followed the abolition of slavery, and the new white Brazilians similarly monopolized the occupational opportunities brought by the industrialization that might have otherwise benefited the black masses (F. Fernandes, "The Weight of the Past," in John Hope Franklin, ed., Color and Race [Boston: Beacon, 1969], pp. 283–286).

14. See Carey McWilliams, The Mexicans in America, A Student's Guide to Localized History (New York: Teacher's College, Columbia University Press, 1968), for a summary discussion.

15. Leonard Pitt, The Decline of the Californios, A Social History of the Spanish-Speaking Californians, 1846–1890 (Berkeley and Los Angeles: University of California Press, 1970), p. 296.

had sold themselves or had been forced into debt servitude—were imported to build railroads and to mine gold and other metals. Later other colonized Asian populations, Filipinos and East Indians, were used as gang laborers for Western farm factories.[16] Among the third world groups that contributed to this labor stream, only the Japanese came from a nation that had successfully resisted Western domination. This may be one important reason why the Japanese entry into American life and much of the group's subsequent development show some striking parallels to the European immigrant pattern. But the racial labor principle confined this Asian people too; they were viewed as fit only for subservient field employment. When they began to buy land, set up businesses, and enter occupations "reserved" for whites, the outcry led to immigration restriction and to exclusion acts.[17]

A tenet central to Marxian theory is that work and systems of labor are crucial in shaping larger social forces and relations. The orthodox Marxist criticism of capitalism, however, often obscures the significance of patterns of labor status. Since, by definition, capitalism is a system of wage slavery and the proletariat are "wage slaves," the varied degrees of freedom within industry and among the working class have not been given enough theoretical attention. Max Weber's treatment of capitalism, though based essentially on Marx's framework, is useful for its emphasis on the unique status of the free mobile proletariat in contrast to the status of those traditional forms of labor more bound to particular masters and work situations. Weber saw "formally free" labor as an essential condition for modern capitalism.[18] Of course, freedom of labor is always a relative matter, and formal freedoms are often limited by informal constraint and the absence of choice. For this reason, the different labor situations of third world and of European newcomers to American capitalism cannot be seen as polar opposites. Many European groups entered as contract laborers,[19] and an ethnic stratification (as well as a racial one) prevailed in industry. Particular immigrant groups dominated certain industries and occupations: the Irish built the canal system that linked the East with the Great Lakes in the early nineteenth century; Italians were concentrated in roadbuilding and other construction; Slavs and East Europeans made up a large segment of the labor force in steel and heavy metals; the garment trades was for many years a Jewish enclave. Yet this ethnic stratification had different consequences than the racial labor principle had, since the white immigrants worked within the wage system

---

16. Carey McWilliams, *Factories in the Fields* (Boston: Little, Brown, 1934), and *Ill Fares the Land* (Boston: Little, Brown, 1942). See also McWilliams, *North from Mexico* (Philadelphia: Lippincott, 1948). Recently two papers have applied the colonial model to Mexican-Americans. See Joan W. Moore, "Colonialism: The Case of the Mexican Americans," *Social Problems*, 17 (Spring 1970), 463–472; and Mario Barrera, Carlos Muñez, and Charles Ornelas, "The Barrio as Internal Colony," in Harlan Hahn, ed., *Urban Affairs Annual Review*, 6 (1972).

17. Roger Daniels and Harry Kitano, *American Racism* (Englewood Cliffs, N. J.: Prentice-Hall, 1970), pp. 45–66. See also R. Daniels, *The Politics of Prejudice* (Berkeley and Los Angeles: University of California Press, 1962). The most comprehensive study of American racist attitudes and practices toward the Chinese is Stuart Miller, *The Unwelcome Immigrant: The American Image of the Chinese, 1785–1882* (Berkeley and Los Angeles: University of California Press, 1969).

18. Max Weber, *General Economic History* (New York: The Free Press, 1950), p. 277.

19. John Higham, *Strangers in the Land* (New York: Atheneum, 1969), pp. 45–52.

whereas the third world groups tended to be clustered in precapitalist employment sectors.[20]

The differences in labor placement for third world and immigrant can be further broken down. Like European overseas colonialism, America has used African, Asian, Mexican and, to a lesser degree, Indian workers for the cheapest labor, concentrating people of color in the most unskilled jobs, the least advanced sectors of the economy, and the most industrially backward regions of the nation. In an historical sense, people·of color provided much of the hard labor (and the technical skills) that built up the agricultural base and the mineral-transport-communication infrastructure necessary for industrialization and modernization, whereas the Europeans worked primarily within the industrialized, modern sectors.[21] The initial position of European ethnics, while low, was therefore strategic for movement up the economic and social pyramid. The placement of nonwhite groups, however, imposed barrier upon barrier on such mobility, freezing them for long periods of time in the least favorable segments of the economy.

### Rural Versus Urban

European immigrants were clustered in the cities, whereas the colonized minorities were predominantly agricultural laborers in rural areas. In the United States, family farming and corporate agriculture have been primarily white industries. Some immigrants, notably German, Scandinavian, Italian, and Portuguese, have prospered through farming. But most immigrant groups did not contribute to the most exploited sector of our industrial economy, that with the lowest status: agricultural labor. Curiously, the white rural proletariat of the South and West was chiefly native born.

### Industry: Exclusion from Manufacturing

The rate of occupational mobility was by no means the same for all ethnics. Among the early immigrants, the stigmatized Irish occupied a quasi-colonial status, and their ascent into a predominantly middle-class position took at least a generation longer than that of the Germans. Among later immigrants, Jews, Greeks, and Armenians—urban people in Europe—have achieved higher social and economic status than Italians and Poles, most of whom were peasants in the old country.[22] But despite these differences, the immigrants as a whole had a key

20. In a provocative paper which contains a comparison of black and European immigrant experience, Melvin Posey argues that Afro-Americans were never permitted to enter the nation's class system. "Toward a More Meaningful Revolution: Ideology in Transition," in McEvoy and Miller, eds., *Black Power and Student Rebellion, op. cit.,* esp. pp. 264–271.

A contrast between Mexican and European immigrant patterns of work and settlement, and their consequences for social mobility is found in Lee Grebler, Joan W. Moore, and Ralph C. Guzman, in *The Mexican-American People* (New York: The Free Press, 1970), chap. 5.

21. I do not imply a perfect correlation between race and industrial type, only that third world workers have been strikingly overrepresented in the "primary sector" of the economy. Unlike in classical colonialism, white labor has outnumbered colored labor in the United States, and therefore white workers have dominated even such industries as coal mining, non-ferrous metals, and midwestern agriculture.

22. Analyzing early twentieth-century data on European immigrant groups, Stephen Steinberg has found significant differences in occupational background, literacy, and other mobility-re-

advantage over third world Americans. As unskilled laborers, they worked within manufacturing enterprises or close to centers of industry. Therefore they had a foot in the most dynamic centers of the economy and could, with time, rise to semiskilled and skilled positions.[23]

Except for a handful of industrial slaves and free Negroes, Afro-Americans did not gain substantial entry into manufacturing industry until World War I,[24] and the stereotype has long existed that Asians and Indians were not fit for factory work. For the most part then, third world groups have been relegated to labor in preindustrial sectors of the nonagricultural economy. Chinese and Mexicans, for example, were used extensively in mining and building railroads, industries that were essential to the early development of a national capitalist economy, but which were primarily prerequisites of industrial development rather than industries with any dynamic future.[25]

### Geography: Concentration in Peripheral Regions

Even geographically the Europeans were in more fortunate positions. The dynamic and modern centers of the nation have been the Northeast and the Midwest, the predominant areas of white immigration. The third world groups were located away from these centers: Africans in the South, Mexicans in their own Southwest, Asians on the Pacific Coast, the Indians pushed relentlessly "across the frontier" toward the margins of the society. Thus Irish, Italians, and Jews went directly to the Northern cities and its unskilled labor market, whereas Afro-Americans had to take two extra "giant steps," rather than the immigrants' one, before their large-scale arrival in the same place in the present century: the emancipation from slavery and migration from the underdeveloped semicolonial Southern region. Another result of colonized entry and labor placement is that the racial groups had to go through major historical dislocations within this country before they could arrive at the point in the economy where the immigrants began! When finally they did arrive in Northern cities, that economy had changed to their disadvantage. Technological trends in industry had drastically reduced the number of unskilled jobs available for people with little formal education.[26]

---

lated factors. The Jews were consistently advantaged on these points, Catholic ethnic groups such as Poles and Italians disadvantaged. S. Steinberg, "The Religious Factor in Higher Education," Doctoral dissertation, Department of Sociology, University of California, Berkeley (1971).

23. Even in the first generation, immigrants were never as thoroughly clustered in unskilled labor as blacks, Mexicans, and Chinese were in their early years. In 1855, when New York Irishmen dominated the fields of common labor and domestic service, there were sizable numbers (more than a thousand in each category) working as blacksmiths, carpenters, masons, painters, stonecutters, clerks, shoemakers, tailors, food dealers and cartmen. (Robert Ernst, *Immigrant Life in New York City, 1625–1863* [Port Washington, N. Y.: Friedman, 1965], pp. 214–217).

24. Robert Starobin, *Industrial Slavery in the Old South* (New York: Oxford University Press, 1970), and Leon Litwack, *North of Slavery* (Chicago: University of Chicago Press, 1961). For a recent interpretation, see Harold M. Baron, "The Demand for Black Labor: Historical Notes on the Political Economy of Racism," *Radical America, 5* (March–April 1971), 1–46.

25. Of course some Europeans did parallel labor in mining and transportation construction. But since they had the freedom of movement that was denied colored laborers, they could transfer the skills and experience gained to other pursuits.

26. *Report of the National Advisory Commission on Civil Disorders, op. cit.*

## Racial Discrimination

To these "structural" factors must be added the factor of racial discrimination. The argument that Jews, Italians, and Irish also faced prejudice in hiring misses the point. Herman Bloch's historical study of Afro-Americans in New York provides clear evidence that immigrant groups benefited from racism. When blacks began to consolidate in skilled and unskilled jobs that yielded relatively decent wages and some security, Germans, Irish, and Italians came along to usurp occupation after occupation, forcing blacks out and down into the least skilled, marginal reaches of the economy.[27] Although the European immigrant was only struggling to better his lot, the irony is that his relative success helped to block the upward economic mobility of Northern blacks. Without such a combination of immigration and white racism, the Harlems and the South Chicagos might have become solid working-class and middle-class communities with the economic and social resources to absorb and aid the incoming masses of Southerners, much as European ethnic groups have been able to do for their newcomers. The mobility of Asians, Mexicans, and Indians has been contained by similar discrimination and expulsion from hard-won occupational bases.[28]

Our look at the labor situation of the colonized and the immigrant minorities calls into question the popular sociological idea that there is no fundamental difference in condition and history between the nonwhite poor today and the ethnic poor of past generations. This dangerous myth is used by the children of the immigrants to rationalize racial oppression and to oppose the demands of third world people for special group recognition and economic policies—thus the folk beliefs that all Americans "started at the bottom" and most have been able to "work themselves up through their own efforts." But the racial labor principle has meant, in effect, that "the bottom" has by no means been the same for all groups. In addition, the cultural experiences of third world and immigrant groups have diverged in America, a matter I take up in the next section.

## Culture and Social Organization

Labor status and the quality of entry had their most significant impact on the cultural dynamics of minority people. Every new group that entered America experienced cultural conflict, the degree depending on the newcomers' distance from the Western European, Anglo-Saxon Protestant norm. Since the cultures of people of color in America, as much as they differed from one another, were non-European and non-Western, their encounters with dominant institutions

---

27. Herman Bloch, *The Circle of Discrimination* (New York: New York University Press, 1969), esp. pp. 34–46. That discrimination in the labor market continues to make a strong contribution to income disparity between white and nonwhite is demonstrated in Lester Thurow's careful study, *Poverty and Discrimination* (Washington, D. C.: Brookings, 1969).

28. As far as I know no study exists that has attempted to analyze industrial and occupational competition among a variety of ethnic and racial groups. Such research would be very valuable. With respect to discrimination against Asians and Mexicans, Pitt, for example, describes how white and European miners were largely successful in driving Chinese and Mexican independent prospectors out of the gold fields. *The Decline of the Californios, op. cit.,* chap. 3.

have resulted in a more intense conflict of ethos and world view than was the case for the various Western elements that fed into the American nation. The divergent situations of colonization and immigration were fateful in determining the ability of minorities to develop group integrity and autonomous community life in the face of WASP ethnocentrism and cultural hegemony.

Voluntary immigration and free labor status made it possible for European minorities to establish new social relationships and cultural forms after a period of adjustment to the American scene. One feature of the modern labor relationship is the separation of the place of work from the place of residence or community. European ethnics were exploited on the job, but in the urban ghettos where they lived they had the insulation and freedom to carry on many aspects of their old country cultures—to speak their languages, establish their religions and build institutions such as schools, newspapers, welfare societies, and political organizations. In fact, because they had been oppressed in Europe—by such imperial powers as England, Tsarist Russia, and the Hapsburg Monarchy—the Irish, Poles, Jews, and other East Europeans actually had more autonomy in the New World for their cultural and political development. In the case of the Italians, many of their immigrant institutions had no counterpart in Italy, and a sense of nationality, overriding parochial and regional identities, developed only in the United States.[29]

But there were pressures toward assimilation; the norm of "Anglo-conformity" has been a dynamic of domination central to American life.[30] The early immigrants were primarily from Western Europe. Therefore, their institutions were close to the dominant pattern, and assimilation for them did not involve great conflict. Among later newcomers from Eastern and Southern Europe, however, the disparity in values and institutions made the goal of cultural pluralism attractive for a time; to many of the first generation, America's assimilation dynamic must have appeared oppressive. The majority of their children, on the other hand, apparently welcomed Americanization, for with the passage of time many, if not most, European ethnics have merged into the larger society, and the distinctive Euro-American communities have taken on more and more of the characteristics of the dominant culture.

The cultural experience of third world people in America has been different. The labor systems through which people of color became Americans tended to destroy or weaken their cultures and communal ties. Regrouping and new institutional forms developed, but in situations with extremely limited possibilities. The transformation of group life that is central to the colonial cultural dynamic took place most completely on the plantation. Slavery in the United States appears to have gone the farthest in eliminating African social and cultural forms; the plantation system provided the most restricted context for the development of new kinds of group integrity.[31]

29. Humbert S. Nelli, *Italians in Chicago 1880–1930: A Study in Ethnic Mobility* (New York: Oxford University Press, 1970).

30. Milton Gordon, *Assimilation in American Life* (New York: Oxford University Press, 1964).

31. Beltran makes the point that the plantation system was more significant than enforced migration in affecting African cultural development in the new world. "This system, which had created institutionalized forms of land tenure, work patterns, specialization of labor, consumption

In New York City, Jews were able to reconstruct their East European family system, with its distinctive sex roles and interlocking sets of religious rituals and customs. Some of these patterns broke down or changed in response, primarily, to economic conditions, but the changes took time and occurred within a community of fellow ethnics with considerable cultural autonomy. The family systems of West Africans, however, could not be reconstructed under plantation slavery, since in this labor system the "community" of workers was subordinated to the imperatives of the production process. Africans of the same ethnic group could not gather together because their assignment to plantations and subsequent movements were controlled by slaveholders who endeavored to eliminate any basis for group solidarity. Even assimilation to American kinship forms was denied as an alternative, since masters freely broke up families when it suited their economic or other interests.[32] In the nonplantation context, the disruption of culture and suppression of the regrouping dynamic was less extreme. But systems of debt servitude and semifree agricultural labor had similar, if less drastic, effects. The first generations of Chinese in the United States were recruited for gang labor; they therefore entered without women and children. Had they been free immigrants, most of whom also were male initially, the group composition would have normalized in time with the arrival of wives and families. But as bonded laborers without even the legal rights of immigrants, the Chinese were powerless to fight the exclusion acts of the late nineteenth century, which left predominantly male communities in America's Chinatowns for many decades. In such a skewed social structure, leading features of Chinese culture could not be reconstructed. A similar male-predominant group emerged among mainland Filipinos. In the twentieth century the migrant work situation of Mexican-American farm laborers has operated against stable community life and the building of new institutional forms in politics and education. However, Mexican culture as a whole has retained considerable strength in the Southwest because Chicanos have remained close to their original territory, language, and religion.

Yet the colonial attack on culture is more than a matter of economic factors such as labor recruitment and special exploitation. The colonial situation differs from the class situation of capitalism precisely in the importance of culture as an instrument of domination.[33] Colonialism depends on conquest, control, and the imposition of new institutions and ways of thought. Culture and social organization are important as vessels of a people's autonomy and integrity;

---

and distribution of produce, destroyed African economic forms by forceably imposing Western forms. . . .Negro political life along with African social structure, was in a position of subordination." Gonzalo Aguirre Beltran, "African Influences in the Development of Regional Cultures in the New World," in Pan American Union, *Plantation Systems of the New World, op. cit.,* p. 70.

32. I do not imply here that African culture was totally eliminated, nor that Afro-Americans have lived in a cultural vacuum. A distinctive black culture emerged during slavery. From the complex vicissitudes of their historical experience in the United States, Afro-American culture has continued its development and differentiation to the present day, providing an ethnic content to black peoplehood. . . .

33. According to Stokely Carmichael, capitalism exploits its own working classes, while racist systems colonize alien peoples of color. Here colonization refers to dehumanization, the tendency toward the destruction of culture and peoplehood, above and beyond exploitation. S. Carmichael, "Free Huey," in Edith Minor, ed., *Stokely Speaks* (New York: Vintage, 1971).

when cultures are whole and vigorous, conquest, penetration, and certain modes of control are more readily resisted.[34] Therefore, imperial regimes attempt, consciously or unwittingly, either to destroy the cultures of colonized people or, when it is more convenient, to exploit them for the purposes of more efficient control and economic profit. As Mina Caulfield has put it, imperialism exploits the cultures of the colonized as much as it does their labor.[35] Among America's third world groups, Africans, Indians, and Mexicans are all conquered peoples whose cultures have been in various degrees destroyed, exploited, and controlled. One key function of racism, defined here as the assumption of the superiority of white Westerners and their cultures and the concomitant denial of the humanity of people of color, is that it "legitimates" cultural oppression in the colonial situation.

The present-day inclination to equate racism against third world groups with the ethnic prejudice and persecution that immigrant groups have experienced is mistaken. Compare, for example, intolerance and discrimination in the sphere of religion. European Jews who followed their orthodox religion were mocked and scorned, but they never lost the freedom to worship in their own way. Bigotry certainly contributed to the Americanization of contemporary Judaism, but the Jewish religious transformation has been a slow and predominantly voluntary adaptation to the group's social and economic mobility. In contrast, the U.S. policy against Native American religion in the nineteenth century was one of all-out attack; the goal was cultural genocide. Various tribal rituals and beliefs were legally proscribed and new religious movements were met by military force and physical extermination. The largest twentieth-century movement, the Native American Church, was outlawed for years because of its peyote ceremony.[36] Other third world groups experienced similar, if perhaps less concerted, attacks on their cultural institutions. In the decade following the conquest, California prohibited bullfighting and severely restricted other popular Mexican sports.[37] In the same state various aspects of Chinese culture, dress, pigtails, and traditional forms of recreation were outlawed. Although it was tolerated in Brazil and the Caribbean, the use of the drum, the instrument that was the central means of communication among African peoples, was successfully repressed in the North American slave states.[38]

American capitalism has been partially successful in absorbing third world

---

34. An historical study of Brazilian coffee plantations illustrates how African cultural institutions were the focal point for the slave's resistance to intensified exploitation. Stanley Stein, *Vassouras* (Cambridge: Harvard University Press, 1957), pt. 3.

35. Mina Davis Caulfield, "Culture and Imperialism: Proposing a New Dialectic," in Dell Himes, ed., *Reinventing Anthropology* (New York: Pantheon, 1972).

36. Collier, *op. cit.*, pp. 132–142.

37. Pitt, *The Decline of the Californios, op. cit.*, pp. 196–197.

38. Janheinz Jahn, *Muntu* (New York: Grove, n.d.), p. 217:

The peculiar development of African culture in North America began with the loss of the drums. The Protestant, and often Puritan, slave owners interfered much more radically with the personal life of their slaves than did their Catholic colleagues in the West Indies or in South America . . . And to forbid the drums was to show a keen scent for the essential: for without the drums it was impossible to call the orishas, the ancestors were silent, and the proselytizers seemed to have a free hand. The Baptists and Methodists, whose practical maxims and revivals were sympathetic to African religiosity quickly found masses of adherents.

groups into its economic system and culture. Because of the colonial experience and the prevalence of racism, this integration has been much less complete than in the case of the ethnic groups. The white ethnics who entered the class system at its lowest point were exploited, but not colonized. Because their group realities were not systematically violated in the course of immigration, adaptation, and integration, the white newcomers could become Americans more or less at their own pace and on their own terms. They have moved up, though slowly in the case of some groups, into working-class and middle-class positions. Their cultural dynamic has moved from an initial stage of group consciousness and ethnic pluralism to a present strategy of individual mobility and assimilation. The immigrants have become part of the white majority, partaking of the racial privilege in a colonizing society; their assimilation into the dominant culture is now relatively complete, even though ethnic identity is by no means dead among them. In the postwar period it has asserted itself in a third-generation reaction to "overassimilation"[39] and more recently as a response to third world movements. But the ethnic groups have basically accepted the overall culture's rules of "making it" within the system, including the norms of racial oppression that benefit them directly or indirectly.

The situation and outlook of the racial minorities are more ambiguous. From the moment of their entry into the Anglo-American system, the third world peoples have been oppressed as groups, and their group realities have been under continuing attack. Unfree and semifree labor relations as well as the undermining of non-Western cultures have deprived the colonized of the autonomy to regroup their social forms according to their own needs and rhythms. During certain periods in the past, individual assimilation into the dominant society was seen as both a political and a personal solution to this dilemma. As an individual answer it has soured for many facing the continuing power of racism at all levels of the society. As a collective strategy, assimilation is compromised by the recognition that thus far only a minority have been able to improve their lot in this way, as well as by the feeling that it weakens group integrity and denies their cultural heritage. At the same time the vast majority of third world people in America "want in." Since the racial colonialism of the United States is embedded in a context of industrial capitalism, the colonized must look to the economy, division of labor, and politics of the larger society for their individual and group aspirations. Both integration into the division of labor and the class system of American capitalism as well as the "separatist" culture building and nationalist politics of third world groups reflect the complex realities of a colonial capitalist society.[40]

---

Thus the long-term interest of many Afro-American youth in the playing of drums, as well as the more recent and general embracing of African and black cultural forms, might be viewed as *the return of the repressed* —to borrow a leading concept from Freudian psychology.

For a discussion of the attack on culture in the context of classical colonialism, see K. M. Panikkar, *Asia and Western Dominance* (New York: Collier, 1969); H. Alan C. Cairns, *The Clash of Cultures: Early Race Relations in Central Africa* (New York: Praeger, 1965), originally published in England as *Prelude to Imperialism,* and my brief introduction to Part 2 of *Racial Oppression in America*.

39. The standard discussion of this phenomenon is Will Herberg, *Protestant-Catholic-Jew* (Garden City, N. Y.: Doubleday, 1955).

40. These two poles of the pendulum, integration and nationalism, have long been recognized

The colonial interpretation of American race relations helps illuminate the present-day shift in emphasis toward cultural pluralism and ethnic nationalism on the part of an increasing segment of third world people. The building of social solidarity and group culture is an attempt to complete the long historical project that colonial domination made so critical and so problematic. It involves a deemphasis on individual mobility and assimilation, since these approaches cannot speak to the condition of the most economically oppressed, nor fundamentally affect the realities of colonization. Such issues require group action and political struggle. Collective consciousness is growing among third world people, and their efforts to advance economically have a political character that challenges longstanding patterns of racial and cultural subordination.

### Conclusion: The Third World Perspective

Let us return to the basic assumptions of the third world perspective and examine the idea that a common oppression has created the conditions for effective unity among the constituent racial groups. The third world ideology attempts to promote the consciousness of such common circumstances by emphasizing that the similarities in situation among America's people of color are the essential matter, the differences less relevant. I would like to suggest some problems in this position.

Each third world people has undergone distinctive, indeed cataclysmic, experiences on the American continent that separate its history from the others, as well as from whites. Only Native Americans waged a 300-year war against white encroachment; only they were subject to genocide and removal. Only Chicanos were severed from an ongoing modern nation; only they remain concentrated in the area of their original land base, close to Mexico. Only blacks went through a 250-year period of slavery. The Chinese were the first people whose presence was interdicted by exclusion acts. The Japanese were the one group declared an internal enemy and rounded up in concentration camps. Though the notion of colonized minorities points to a similarity of situation, it should not imply that black, red, yellow, and brown Americans are all in the same bag. Colonization has taken different forms in the histories of the individual groups. Each people is strikingly heterogeneous, and the variables of time, place, and manner have affected the forms of colonialism, the character of racial domination, and the responses of the group.

Because the colonized groups have been concentrated in different regions, geographical isolation has heretofore limited the possibilities of cooperation.[41] When they have inhabited the same area, competition for jobs has fed ethnic antagonisms. Today, as relatively powerless groups, the racial minorities often find themselves fighting one another for the modicum of political power and

---

as central to the political dynamics of American blacks. As early as 1903 in *The Souls of Black Folk* W. E. B. Du Bois analyzed the existential "twoness" of the American Negro experience which lies behind this dilemma. However it is a general phenomenon applicable to all third world people in the United States, to the extent that their history has been a colonial one.

41. The historical accounts also indicate a number of instances of solidarity. A serious study of the history of unity and disunity among third world groups in America is badly needed.

material resources involved in antipoverty, model-cities, and educational reform projects. Differences in culture and political style exacerbate these conflicts.

The third world movement will have to deal with the situational differences that are obstacles to coalition and coordinated politics. One of these is the great variation in size between the populous black and Chicano groups and the much smaller Indian and Asian minorities. Numbers affect potential political power as well as an ethnic group's visibility and the possibilities of an assimilative strategy. Economic differentiation may be accelerating both between and within third world groups. The racial minorities are not all poor. The Japanese and, to a lesser extent, the Chinese have moved toward middle-class status. The black middle class also is growing. The ultimate barrier to effective third world alliance is the pervasive racism of the society, which affects people of color as well as whites, furthering division between all groups in America. Colonialism brings into its orbit a variety of groups, which it oppresses and exploits in differing degrees and fashions; the result is a complex structure of racial and ethnic division.[42]

The final assumption of the third world idea remains to be considered. The new perspective represents more than a negation of the immigrant analogy. By its very language the concept assumes an essential connection between the colonized people within the United States and the peoples of Africa, Asia and Latin America, with respect to whom the idea of *le tiers monde* originated. The communities of color in America share essential conditions with third world nations abroad: economic underdevelopment, a heritage of colonialism and neocolonialism, and a lack of real political autonomy and power.[43]

This insistence on viewing American race relations from an international perspective is an important corrective to the parochial and ahistorical outlook of our national consciousness. The economic, social, and political subordination of third world groups in America is a microcosm of the position of all peoples of color in the world order of stratification. This is neither an accident nor the result of some essential racial genius. Racial domination in the United States is part of a world historical drama in which the culture, economic system, and political power of the white West has spread throughout virtually the entire globe. The expansion of the West, particularly Europe's domination over non-Western people of color, was the major theme in the almost five hundred years

---

42. The ethnic and racially "plural society" is another characteristic colonial phenomenon. See J.S. Furnivall, *Colonial Policy and Practice* (New York University Press, 1956), and M. G. Smith, *The Plural Society in the British West Indies* (Berkeley and Los Angeles: University of California Press, 1965).

43. The connection has been cogently argued by Dale L. Johnson, "On Oppressed Classes and the Role of the Social Scientist in Human Liberation," in Frank Cockcroft and Dale Johnson, eds., *The Political Economy of Underdevelopment in Latin America* (Garden City, N. Y.: Doubleday, 1971), and by William K. Tabb, *The Political Economy of the Black Ghetto* (New York: Norton, 1970), esp. chap. 2.

However, the international perspective on American racial problems is by no means new. W. E. B. Du Bois was one of its early exponents, and in more recent years Malcolm X placed domestic racism and strategies of liberation in a worldwide context. For a discussion of the internationalizing of Malcolm's politics, see Robert L. Allen, *Black Awakening in Capitalist America* (Garden City, N. Y.: Doubleday, 1969), pp. 31–34.

that followed the onset of "The Age of Discovery." The European conquest of Native American peoples, leading to the white settlement of the Western hemisphere and the African slave trade, was one of the leading historical events that ushered in the age of colonialism.[44] Colonial subjugation and racial domination began much earlier and have lasted much longer in North America than in Asia and Africa, the continents usually thought of as colonial prototypes. The oppression of racial colonies within our national borders cannot be understood without considering worldwide patterns of white European hegemony.

The present movement goes further than simply drawing historical and contemporary parallels between the third world within and the third world external to the United States. The new ideology implies that the fate of colonized Americans is tied up with that of the colonial and former colonial peoples of the world. There is at least impressionistic evidence to support this idea. If one looks at the place of the various racial minorities in America's stratified economic and social order, one finds a rough correlation between relative internal status and the international position of the original fatherland. According to most indicators of income, education, and occupation, Native Americans are at the bottom. The Indians alone lack an independent nation, a center of power in the world community to which they might look for political aid and psychic identification. At the other pole, Japanese-Americans are the most successful nonwhite group by conventional criteria, and Japan has been the most economically developed and politically potent non-Western nation during most of the twentieth century. The transformation of African societies from colonial dependency to independent statehood, with new authority and prestige in the international arena, has had an undoubted impact on Afro-Americans in the United States; it has contributed both to civil rights movements and to a developing black consciousness.[45]

What is not clear is whether an international strategy can in itself be the principle of third world liberation within this country. Since the oppression, the struggle, and the survival of the colonized groups have taken place within our society, it is to be expected that their people will orient their daily lives and their political aspirations to the domestic scene. The racial minorities have been able to wrest some material advantages from American capitalism and empire at the same time that they have been denied real citizenship in the society. Average levels of income, education, and health for the third world in the United States are far above their counterparts overseas; this gap will affect the possibility of

---

44. The other major event was instituting trade with India.

45. In the early 1970s Pan-Africanism seems to be gaining ground among black American militants and intellectuals. The most celebrated spokesman has been Stokely Carmichael who has virtually eschewed the struggle in the United States. The *Black Scholar* devoted its February and March (1971) issues to Pan-Africanism. Afro-American organizations have been challenging the South African involvements of U. S. business and government, as, for example, in the action of black employees against the Polaroid Corporation. Chicano groups have been taking an active political interest in Mexico and Latin America. On some university campuses Asian militants have taken the lead in protesting American imperialism and genocide in Southeast Asia. Whereas only recently black and brown nationalists tended to see antiwar protest as a white middle-class "trip," the third world perspective has led to an aggressive condemnation of the war in Indochina and a sense of solidarity with the Vietnamese people.

internationalism. Besides which, group alliances that transcend national borders have been difficult to sustain in the modern era because of the power of nationalism.

Thus, the situation of the colonized minorities in the United States is by no means identical with that of Algerians, Kenyans, Indonesians, and other nations who suffered under white European rule. Though there are many parallels in cultural and political developments, the differences in land, economy, population composition, and power relations make it impossible to transport wholesale sociopolitical analyses or strategies of liberation from one context to another. The colonial analogy has gained great vogue recently among militant nationalists—partly because it is largely valid, partly because its rhetoric so aggressively condemns white America, past and present. Yet it may be that the comparison with English, French, and Dutch overseas rule lets our nation off too easily! In many ways the special versions of colonialism practiced against Americans of color have been more pernicious in quality and more profound in consequences than the European overseas varieties.

In traditional colonialism, the colonized "natives" have usually been the majority of the population, and their culture, while less prestigious than that of the white Europeans, still pervaded the landscape. Members of the third world within the United States are individually and collectively outnumbered by whites, and Anglo-American cultural imperatives dominate the society—although this has been less true historically in the Southwest where the Mexican-American population has never been a true cultural minority.[46] The oppressed masses of Asia and Africa had the relative "advantage" of being colonized in their own land.[47] In the United States, the more total cultural domination, the alienation of most third world people from a land base, and the numerical minority factor have weakened the group integrity of the colonized and their possibilities for cultural and political self-determination.

Many critics of the third world perspective seize on these differences to question the value of viewing America's racial dynamics within the colonial framework. But all the differences demonstrate is that colonialisms vary greatly in structure and that political power and group liberation are more problematic in our society than in the overseas situation. The fact that we have no historical models for decolonization in the American context does not alter the objective realities. Decolonization is an insistent and irreversible project of the third world groups, although its contents and forms are at present unclear and will be worked out only in the course of an extended period of political and social conflict.

---

46. McWilliams, *North From Mexico, op. cit.*

47. Within the United States, Native Americans and Chicanos, in general, retain more original culture than blacks and Asians, because they faced European power in their homelands, rather than being transported to the nation of the colonized. Of course the ecological advantage of colonization at home tends to be undermined to the extent to which large European settlements overwhelm numerically the original people, as happened in much of Indo-America. And in much of the Americas a relative cultural integrity among Indian peoples exists at the expense of economic impoverishment and backwardness.

# · 25 ·

# Race, Class, and Income Inequality

## Erik Olin Wright

One of the most consistent findings of research on racial inequality is that black males receive considerably lower income returns to education than white males. Weiss (1970, p. 154) found that, within specific age groups, black males received significantly lower returns to education than white males, whether education was measured as years of schooling or as achievement level. Siegel (1965) found that, net of occupation and region of the country, the difference in expected incomes of black and white males increased monotonically with education: at less than elementary education, blacks earned $700 less than whites (net of occupation and region) in 1960; at the high school level this increased to $1,400, and at the college level, to $3,800. Duncan (1969) has shown that even after controlling for family background, number of siblings, and occupational status black males still receive lower returns to education than white males.[1]

---

· Abridged from *American Journal of Sociology* 83(6) (1978): 1368–82, 1386–97.

NOTE: This research was supported by funds granted to the Institute for Research on Poverty at the University of Wisconsin—Madison by the Department of Health, Education, and Welfare, pursuant to the provisions of the Economic Opportunity Act of 1964. I would like to express my gratitude to Arthur Stinchcombe, Barbara Heyns, Michael Reich, and Luca Perrone for their comments and criticisms on various aspects of this work and to Aage Sørenson for his skepticism about an earlier draft of this paper. I would also like to thank James N. Morgan of the Institute for Social Research for making the data for this study available. The opinions expressed herein are the responsibility solely of the author.

1. To my knowledge, the only study which claims to present findings different from these results is the research of Ross Stolzenberg (1973, 1975). Stolzenberg estimates a rather complicated income-determination equation within 67 detailed occupational categories for both black and white males. He then compares the partial derivatives of income with respect to education for the equations and finds that in nearly one-half of the occupational categories the partial derivative is larger for

None of these studies, however, has controlled for class position as under-stood within the Marxist tradition, the position of individuals within the social relations of production. The underlying premise of a Marxist class analysis is that, while the diverse dimensions of social inequality cannot be reduced to class inequality, class relations nevertheless play a decisive role in shaping other forms of inequality. In the study of income inequality, this implies that class relations organize the structure of income inequality in the sense that class position shapes the ways in which other causes influence income. If this notion is correct, then an analysis of racial differences in income that ignores positions within the social relations of production is incomplete. More concretely, if it is true that the returns to education vary substantially across class positions, and if it is true that black and white males are distributed quite differently across class positions, then much of the racial difference in returns to education could in fact be a consequence of the class distribution of races. This paper will explore such a possibility.

## Operationalizing Class

Before developing a series of explicit hypotheses about the interactions of race and class in the income-determination process, it is necessary to discuss briefly how the Marxist notion of class will be operationalized in this study.[2] When non-Marxists use the term "class," it generally designates a group of people who share common "life chances" or market positions (Weber 1968, p. 927; Giddens 1973; Parkin 1971, pp. 18–23), common positions within status hierarchies (Warner 1960; Parsons 1970, p. 24), or common positions within authority or power structures (Dahrendorf 1959, p. 138; Lenski 1966, p. 95). In contrast to these usages, Marxists define classes primarily in terms of common structural positions within the social organization of production. In contemporary Ameri-can society, this means defining classes in terms of positions within capitalist social relations of production.

For the purposes of the present analysis, position within the social relations

---

blacks than for whites. Thus, he concludes, "Earlier findings suggesting high within-occupation racial differences in wage returns to schooling . . . were probably artifacts of the gross occupational classifications used. These past findings appear to have been produced by the tendency of black men to be concentrated in the lowest-paying *detailed* occupation categories within the major occupational group in which they are employed" (1975, p. 314). The problem with this conclusion is that Stolzenberg uses a natural logarithmic transformation of income, whereas Siegel (1965) uses raw dollars. This means that Stolzenberg is estimating rates of returns to education rather than absolute returns. The absolute returns to education within the detailed occupational categories may still not have differed significantly between blacks and whites, but Stolzenberg's results do not demonstrate this. I ran Stolzenberg's equation using the data in the present study, calculated the partial derivatives for all blacks and all whites, and discovered that the rates of return for all blacks were significantly greater than for all whites (Stolzenberg does not report the results for all blacks and all whites). Stolzenberg's results thus indicate that these higher rates of return to education for black men as a whole can also be found within about one-half of the detailed occupations held by black men. His results do not indicate that the absolute returns for black and white men are the same within detailed occupations.

2. For a more detailed discussion of this operationalization of class, see Wright (1976*b*, pp. 137–39). For an extended discussion of the concept of class within the Marxist tradition, see Wright (1976*a*; 1976*b*, pp. 20–90) and Poulantzas (1975).

Ownership of the Means of Production

|  | | YES | NO |
|---|---|---|---|
| Control over the labor power of others | YES | Employers | Managers/Supervisors |
| | NO | Petty Bourgeoisie | Workers |

*Figure 1.* Criteria for class position. In the upper left hand quadrant, the term "Employers" is used rather than "Capitalists," since in the present study most of the individuals in this category employ fewer than 10 workers. See Wright (1976a, pp. 35–36) for a discussion of small employers as a contradictory class location between the capitalist class and the petty bourgeoisie.

of production will be defined according to two basic criteria: whether or not the individual owns his or her own means of production, and whether or not the individual controls the labor power of others (i.e., supervises people on the job). These two criteria generate four basic class positions, as illustrated in Figure 1. "Ownership of the means of production" is operationalized by the question, "Do you work for yourself or someone else?" For self-employed individuals, "control of the labor power of others" is operationalized in terms of having employees; for individuals who are not self-employed, this criterion is operationalized by the question, "Do you supervise the work of others, or tell other employees what work to do?"

One further distinction will be made within this basic class schema. Clearly, some of the people who are placed in the manager/supervisor category are nominal supervisors. This would be the case, for example, for the head of a work team who serves as the conduit for orders from above but who lacks any capacity whatsoever to invoke sanctions on his or her fellow workers. Proper managers are thus distinguished from nominal supervisors by the question, "Do you have any say in the pay and promotions of your subordinates?"

It is important to be clear about the logic underlying these class categories. They are not simply proxies for occupations. "Occupation" designates the technical function performed by individuals within the labor process; "class" designates the social relationship within which those technical functions are performed. While, of course, different class positions include different mixes of occupations, every broad category of occupations is represented within each class category (Wright 1976b, pp. 168–73; Wright and Perrone 1977).

## Hypotheses

The empirical investigation will revolve around six hypotheses.[3]

1. *Managers as a whole will receive much higher returns to education than workers.*

---

3. All of the hypotheses that follow center on the relationship of the working class and the managerial category to racial differences in returns to education. Since such a small percentage of black males are either capitalists or petty bourgeois it is impossible, using the sample available for this study, to examine systematically the interactions of these class positions with race.

This basic result has already been established in an earlier study (Wright and Perrone 1975, 1977). The rationale underlying this hypothesis is based on an analysis of the specific position of managers within capitalist social relations of production. Specifically, this analysis suggests that within the managerial category there will be a strong link between income and hierarchical position on the one hand and hierarchical position and education on the other. The high returns to education within the managerial category are a result of this double link.

First, examine the link between hierarchy and income. The behavior of all employees within a capitalist organization is controlled by a combination of repressive sanctions and positive inducements. As one moves up the managerial hierarchy, however, the balance shifts between these two modes of control. While repressive controls may be effective in creating conformity to explicit rules, they are not terribly well suited to generating responsible and enthusiastic job performance. Because the managerial hierarchy is one of increasing responsibility (and, in a limited way, increasing power as well), there will be a tendency for the behavior of higher managers to be controlled more exclusively through a structure of inducements. The result is that managerial hierarchies will be characterized by a steep income gradient attached to authority position (Tannenbaum et al. 1974, p. 107), even when the education of managers is held constant (Wright 1976b, pp. 235–38).

Second, examine the relationship between educational credentials and hierarchical position. In both the working class and the managerial category, education is in part a determinant of the value of the labor power of the individual (or what non-Marxist economists typically call "human capital"). It is therefore to be expected that both workers and managers would receive a positive income return to their education. However, among managers, educational credentials serve a second function. In addition to creating genuine skills, education also serves as an institutional mechanism for legitimating inequalities of power within capitalist organizations. In practice, this means that there will be a general tendency for people with lower credentials not to be promoted above people with higher credentials, and thus there will be a tendency for managerial hierarchies to be characterized by rather steep educational credential gradients (Tannenbaum et al. 1974, p. 112).

The combination of this steep education gradient and steep income gradient associated with hierarchy means that the managerial category as a whole will be characterized by an especially high return to education. That is, in addition to the direct return to education resulting from increases in the market value of labor power (skills), which both managers and workers receive, managers receive an additional increment of income for education, stemming from the link between the legitimation function of education within hierarchies and the use of income as a control mechanism within authority hierarchies. (For a more detailed discussion of this interpretation, see Wright and Perrone 1977; Wright 1976b, pp. 105–10.)

2. *Black males will be more concentrated in the working class than white males.* While we will not explore the actual mechanisms by which individuals are sorted into class positions, it is nevertheless predicted that one outcome of this sorting process is that blacks will be more heavily concentrated in the working class than whites.

3. *When class position is ignored, black males will receive lower returns to education than white males.* This is the standard finding in sociological studies of racial differences in returns to education. It will be formally tested in order to show that the usual results hold for the data used in the present study.

4. *Within the working class, the returns to education for black and white males will be much more similar than for all blacks and all whites.* If at least part of the overall difference in returns to education for blacks and whites is a consequence of the class distributions of the two racial categories, then it would be expected that within the working class itself the returns should be much more similar. While white workers may be in relatively privileged working situations as compared with black workers, neither white nor black workers occupy positions of authority (by definition) and, thus, neither receive the legitimation increment of returns to education discussed in hypothesis 1.

5. *Within the supervisor category, the returns to education for black and white males will be more similar than for all blacks and all whites.* The argument here is essentially the same as that presented in hypothesis 4. To the extent that the overall racial differences in returns to education are a consequence of class distribution, within a single class position—in this case, the very bottom level of the managerial hierarchy—the returns for blacks and whites should be much more similar than for all blacks and whites.

6. *Within the managerial category, black males will have lower returns to education than white males.* The argument in hypothesis 1 concerning the high returns to education of managers hinges on the dual link between education and hierarchical position and between income and hierarchical position. If a particular category of managers is highly concentrated at the bottom of the authority structure, then this education-hierarchy legitimation mechanism will tend to be attenuated. Although no data are available in the present study concerning the hierarchical distribution of race within the manager category, white males can be expected to be much more evenly distributed throughout the hierarchy than black males. If this is the case, then within the managerial category the returns to education for black males should be considerably smaller than returns for white males.

## Data

The data for this study come from the eighth wave of the *Panel Study of Income Dynamics* (Institute for Social Research 1975) conducted by the Institute for Social Research (ISR) at the University of Michigan. While in the original year of the panel study the sample was a random sample of 5,000 households, by the eighth year of the study, because of successive nonresponses, the sample was no longer genuinely random.[4] While this probably will not seriously affect the

---

4. Two things need to be noted concerning nonrandomness of the sample in the *Panel Study of Income Dynamics*. First, whenever an individual left the original household in the study (because of divorce, high school graduation, etc.), the "split-off" was also included in the subsequent years of the panel. Thus, the sample is not particularly skewed on age distribution. Second, a fairly complex system of weights has been devised to correct, at least partially, for nonrandomness in nonresponse. Thus, the regression results in the present study are probably reasonably reliable in spite of the nonrandomness of the sample.

regression results, it certainly may affect hypothesis 2, concerning class distribution of races. Two other data sets, the 1969 Survey of Working Conditions and the 1973 Quality of Employment Survey (both from ISR), will thus be used for hypothesis 2.[5] Throughout the analysis, the samples will be restricted to active participants in the labor force.

## Equations

In order to test the hypotheses about class and race interactions with returns to education, two regression equations will be estimated for each of the race-class groups being compared:[6]

$$\text{Income} = a + b_1\text{Education}, \tag{1}$$

and

$$\begin{aligned}
\text{Income} = a &+ b_1\text{Education} = b_2\text{Occupational Status} = b_3\text{Age} \\
&+ b_4\text{Seniority} + b_5\text{Father's Status} + b_6\text{Father's} \\
&\text{Education} + b_7\text{Parental Economic Condition} \\
&+ b_8\text{Annual Hours Worked}.
\end{aligned} \tag{2}$$

While the present study will not investigate the more complex structural equation model which underlies the second equation, this equation is nevertheless important in assessing the extent to which the class interactions observed in equation (1) may be consequences of the class distributions of the various control variables in equation (2). Thus, for example, if in hypothesis 1 the greater returns to education for managers were entirely due to the occupational status distribution across class categories, then, when occupational status is included in the equation, the differential returns to education between classes should be substantially reduced. All of the control variables in equation (2) are to a greater or lesser extent either causes or consequences of education, and all of them can also be plausibly thought to vary with class position. By controlling for these variables in equation (2), we will be able to see if the differences in education coefficients between the various groups being compared can be considered direct consequences of class and race.[7]

---

5. A discussion of these data sets can be found in Wright (1976*b*, pp. 132–35).

6. The significance of the slope differences between groups will be assessed using the conventional dummy-variable interaction model (Kmenta 1971, pp. 419–23). This means that, if we are comparing the education slopes for two groups, the *t*-test would be:

$$t = (B_{11} - B_{12})/\sqrt{(V_1 S^2 B_{11} + V_2 S^2 B_{12})/(V_1 + V_2)},$$

where $B_{11}$ is the education coefficient for group 1, $B_{12}$ is the education coefficient for group 2, $S^2 B_{11}$ and $S^2 B_{12}$ are the standard errors of the coefficients for groups 1 and 2, respectively, and $V_1$ and $V_2$ are the degrees of freedom for groups 1 and 2, respectively. The denominator in this *t*-test is the standard error of the education × class-dummy interaction term in the usual dummy-variable interaction model. It can be computed equally well from the separate regression equations for the two groups using the above formula.

7. A brief comment about the kind of information contained in these regression equations might clarify the logic of eq. (2). These equations describe characteristics of positions in a social structure. While the data are tagged onto individuals, the equations themselves do not adequately describe individual income-attainment processes, but only the income-determination process for certain structural locations. Since we have no data on how individuals are sorted into structural

## Variables

The variables to be included in the analysis are measured as follows.

1. *Income* is measured by total annual taxable income received by the individual. In addition to wage and salary income, this variable includes income from assets, interest, and other sources of unearned income. Both regression equations were also estimated for three other income variables: annual earnings, an estimate of "permanent income" (an average of income over the previous seven years), and imputed hourly wage (wage and salary income divided by total annual hours worked). In none of the comparisons of racial differences in returns to education did the results differ significantly for these alternative income variables (see Wright 1976*b*, pp. 328–39).

2. *Education* is operationalized by a quasi-credential scale in which:

0 = no schooling or illiterate,
1 = less than elementary school,
2 = elementary school,
3 = some high school,
4 = completed high school,
5 = high shool plus some nonacademic training,
6 = some college,
7 = college degree, and
8 = graduate training.

3. *Occupational Status* is measured by the standard Duncan SEI scores. These scores were available only for the seventh wave of the panel study (1974), while the class position questions were asked only in the eighth wave. This means, in effect, that we have the individual's occupational status score at the beginning of the year in which income was earned and his class position at the end of the year (i.e., the beginning of the following year).[8]

4. *Age* is included in the regression both as a rough control for cohort effects and as a rough measure of years of experience in the labor market.

5. *Seniority* designates the number of years the individual has worked for

---

positions, and since education obviously may play an important role in this sorting process, the education coefficients in the various equations may say very little about individual returns to education. What they describe is the return to education which characterizes the position "worker," "manager," "black worker," etc. Now, positions within a social structure can be characterized along many dimensions. Marxists assert that the critical dimension of position within social structures is class relations. Other social scientists have argued explicitly or implicitly that occupational status or the social backgrounds selected into positions are the key dimensions. Equation (2) in effect holds constant a variety of positional dimensions which have some claim to being important determinants of the relationship between education and income. To the extent that class and race positions differ on education coefficients even when all of these factors are held constant, these coefficient differences can be considered direct, unmediated consequences of the class-race positions themselves. (See Wright and Perrone 1977, p. 38, for a further discussion of this issue.)

8. One other minor point concerning the status variable needs mentioning: about 6% of the sample represents "split-offs" in the 1975 year of the survey, that is, those who left a household after the 1974 survey and set up a new family unit. For these people a three-digit occupation classification was not available, and thus in these cases the Duncan score is based on the average SEI value for the gross-census occupation categories.

the same employer, or the number of years an individual has been self-employed in the same business.

6. *Father's Status* is measured by the average SEI score for the father's gross-census occupation category. While this is clearly a much weaker variable than a status score based on the three-digit occupation classification, it is the best available from the panel study data.

7. *Father's Education* is measured by the same scale as respondent's education.

8. *Parental Economic Condition* is a scale reflecting the respondent's subjective perception of parents' economic status in which:

1 = parents generally poor
2 = parents generally about average, and
3 = parents generally well-off.

9. *Annual Hours Worked* is a product of the number of weeks worked in the previous year and the average number of hours worked per week.

The means and standard deviations for each of these variables for each of the race and class groups included in this study are given in Table 1.

## Results

*Hypothesis 1: Managers as a whole will receive much higher returns to education than workers.* Table 2 indicates that, in the simple regression of income on education, workers receive $851 for each increment in education while managers/supervisors receive $1,689. When the various control variables in equation (2) are added, the returns for workers are $655, while the returns for managers/supervisors are $1,169. In both cases, the difference in returns is significant at the .001 level. This hypothesis is thus strongly confirmed.

The theoretical rationale for this hypothesis centers on the relationships among hierarchical position, education, and income. If this rationale is correct, then it would be expected that the high returns to education among managers/supervisors would disappear if we examined a single hierarchical level within the managerial hierarchy. In a limited way, we can test this proposition by examining separately the returns to education among mere supervisors (positions which involve no say over pay and promotions) and proper managers, since mere supervisors can be considered the bottommost level of the hierarchy. As can be seen in Table 2, mere supervisors differ hardly at all from workers in returns to education (although they receive more income at every level of education), whereas proper managers receive much higher returns.

One obvious objection to these results is that the true relationship between educational credentials and income might be curvilinear. Thus, what appear to be slope differences between workers and managers might in fact simply be a consequence of the two linear regressions reflecting different parts of a single, nonlinear credential-income function. Figure 2 presents the relationship between the linear regressions in Table 2 and the mean incomes for each educational level for workers, managers, and supervisors. Table 3 indicates the $R^2$ for

*Table 1.* **Means and Standard Deviations of Variables Used in Regression Equations**

| | Annual Taxable Income ($) | Education | Occupational Status | Age (Years) | Seniority (Years) | Father's Education | Father's Status | Parents' Economic Condition | Annual Hours Worked |
|---|---|---|---|---|---|---|---|---|---|
| Workers ......... | 10,976 | 4.4 | 34.0 | 36.5 | 6.7 | 2.9 | 29.5 | 2.5 | 2,047 |
| | (5,929) | (1.8) | (21.8) | (13.0) | (7.5) | (1.7) | (18.4) | (1.5) | (591) |
| Managers/supervisors | 15,257 | 5.3 | 49.5 | 39.1 | 7.7 | 3.2 | 34.3 | 2.6 | 2,300 |
| | (8,111) | (1.8) | (23.4) | (12.3) | (8.0) | (1.8) | (20.3) | (1.5) | (581) |
| Supervisors......... | 12,266 | 4.9 | 42.2 | 38.3 | 7.4 | 3.1 | 32.4 | 2.6 | 2,189 |
| | (6,081) | (1.8) | (23.5) | (13.2) | (7.9) | (1.7) | (19.7) | (1.5) | (578) |
| Managers ......... | 18,090 | 5.6 | 56.6 | 40.0 | 8.0 | 3.4 | 36.2 | 2.7 | 2,412 |
| | (8,770) | (1.7) | (20.7) | (11.2) | (8.1) | (1.8) | (20.7) | (1.5) | (559) |
| Whites......... | 14,615 | 5.0 | 43.8 | 38.7 | 8.0 | 3.1 | 33.1 | 2.7 | 2,231 |
| | (11,133) | (1.8) | (24.0) | (13.0) | (8.8) | (1.7) | (19.7) | (1.5) | (657) |
| Blacks......... | 9,307 | 3.8 | 28.0 | 37.4 | 7.3 | 2.4 | 22.4 | 2.1 | 2,050 |
| | (5,408) | (1.8) | (20.5) | (13.1) | (7.6) | (1.4) | (16.3) | (1.5) | (630) |
| White workers ......... | 11,339 | 4.6 | 36.0 | 36.6 | 6.8 | 3.0 | 31.0 | 2.6 | 2,055 |
| | (6,020) | (1.8) | (22.0) | (13.0) | (7.6) | (1.7) | (18.5) | (1.5) | (589) |
| Black workers ......... | 8,469 | 3.6 | 24.1 | 36.1 | 6.8 | 2.3 | 20.2 | 2.2 | 1,964 |
| | (4,411) | (1.6) | (16.8) | (13.3) | (7.3) | (1.2) | (13.5) | (1.6) | (555) |
| White supervisors ..... | 12,519 | 5.0 | 43.1 | 38.4 | 7.5 | 3.2 | 32.8 | 2.7 | 2,189 |
| | (6,111) | (1.8) | (23.4) | (13.5) | (8.0) | (1.7) | (19.6) | (1.5) | (584) |
| Black supervisors...... | 8,646 | 3.6 | 28.2 | 36.7 | 7.1 | 2.4 | 25.2 | 2.0 | 2,191 |
| | (4,071) | (1.8) | (20.3) | (10.2) | (7.2) | (1.7) | (19.2) | (1.4) | (596) |
| White managers ...... | 18,301 | 5.6 | 57.3 | 40.0 | 7.8 | 3.4 | 36.6 | 2.7 | 2,412 |
| | (8,708) | (1.6) | (20.0) | (11.3) | (8.0) | (1.8) | (20.6) | (1.5) | (539) |
| Black managers ...... | 13,250 | 4.8 | 46.2 | 39.9 | 11.4 | 2.7 | 31.1 | 1.6 | 2,321 |
| | (6,090) | (1.9) | (28.8) | (11.5) | (9.4) | (1.8) | (23.6) | (1.1) | (841) |

Note. Standard deviations are numbers in parentheses.

## Table 2. Comparison of Returns to Education for Workers, Managers/Supervisors, and Supervisors

### A. REGRESSION EQUATIONS

| Dependent Variable (Total Annual Taxable Income) | Unadjusted Constant | Education | Occupational Status | Age (Years) | Seniority (Years) | Father's Education | Father's Occupational Status | Parents' Economic Condition | Annual Hours Worked | $R^2$ |
|---|---|---|---|---|---|---|---|---|---|---|
| Workers (N=1,715):[a] | | | | | | | | | | |
| Eq. (1): | | | | | | | | | | |
| B | 7,193 | 851.4 | ... | ... | ... | ... | ... | ... | ... | .066 |
| (SE) | | (77.3) | ... | ... | ... | ... | ... | ... | ... | ... |
| Beta | | .26 | ... | ... | ... | ... | ... | ... | ... | ... |
| Eq. (2): | | | | | | | | | | |
| B | -6,627 | 655.1 | 67.9 | 122 | 124 | 249 | -30 | 263 | 3.2 | .369 |
| (SE) | | (92.8) | (7.0) | (11) | (18) | (89) | (7.6) | (87) | (.19) | ... |
| Beta | | .20 | .25 | .27 | .16 | .07 | -.09 | .07 | .32 | ... |
| Managers/ supervisors (N=1,014): | | | | | | | | | | |
| Eq. (1): | | | | | | | | | | |
| B | 6,382 | 1,689.1 | ... | ... | ... | ... | ... | ... | ... | .135 |
| (SE) | | (133.5) | ... | ... | ... | ... | ... | ... | ... | ... |
| Beta | | .37 | ... | ... | ... | ... | ... | ... | ... | ... |
| Eq. (2): | | | | | | | | | | |
| B | -7,145 | 1,168.7 | 98.6 | 140 | 127 | -251 | 29 | -422 | 2.6 | .373 |
| (SE) | | (153.4) | (11.0) | (21) | (29) | (143) | (12) | (152) | (.35) | ... |
| Beta | | .25 | .28 | .21 | .13 | -.05 | .07 | -.08 | .18 | ... |
| Supervisors (N=535): | | | | | | | | | | |
| Eq. (1): | | | | | | | | | | |
| B | 8,065 | 854.6 | ... | ... | ... | ... | ... | ... | ... | .065 |
| (SE) | | (140.4) | ... | ... | ... | ... | ... | ... | ... | ... |
| Beta | | .25 | ... | ... | ... | ... | ... | ... | ... | ... |

**Table 2. (Continued)**

| Dependent Variable (Total Annual Taxable Income) | Unadjusted Constant | Education | Occupational Status | Age (Years) | Seniority (Years) | Father's Education | Father's Occupational Status | Parents' Economic Condition | Annual Hours Worked | $R^2$ |
|---|---|---|---|---|---|---|---|---|---|---|
| Eq. (2): | | | | | | | | | | |
| $B$ | −3,468 | 855.8 | 54.5 | 78 | 176 | −157 | 28 | −512 | 2.7 | .349 |
| (SE) | ... | (161) | (11.4) | (21) | (31) | (170) | (14) | (166) | (.37) | ... |
| Beta | ... | .26 | .21 | .17 | .23 | −.05 | .09 | −.13 | .25 | ... |
| Managers ($N=479$): | | | | | | | | | | |
| Eq. (1): | | | | | | | | | | |
| $B$ | 6,481 | 2,081.6 | ... | ... | ... | ... | ... | ... | ... | ... | .155 |
| (SE) | ... | (222) | ... | ... | ... | ... | ... | ... | ... | ... |
| Beta | ... | .39 | ... | ... | ... | ... | ... | ... | ... | ... |
| Eq. (2): | | | | | | | | | | |
| $B$ | −6,903 | 1,402.7 | 115.8 | 184 | 80 | −379 | 29 | −291 | 1.5 | .339 |
| (SE) | ... | (258) | (20) | (37) | (48) | (216) | (18) | (246) | (.60) | ... |
| Beta | ... | .27 | .27 | .24 | .07 | −.08 | .07 | −.05 | .10 | ... |

**B. COMPARISON OF RETURNS TO EDUCATION**

| | Workers Compared to Managers and Supervisors | | Workers Compared to Managers Only | | Workers Compared to Supervisors Only | |
|---|---|---|---|---|---|---|
| | Eq. (1) | Eq. (2) | Eq. (1) | Eq. (2) | Eq. (1) | Eq. (2) |
| Difference in education coefficients | 838 | 514 | 1,231 | 748 | 4 | 201 |
| t-value of difference | 8.2* | 4.3* | 9.9* | 5.1* | <1 | 1.7 |
| Workers slope as % of other | 50 | 56 | 41 | 47 | 99 | 77 |

equation (1) using the credential scale and using a series of dummy variables to represent the individual levels of the scale. Both the visual inspection of Figure 2 and the closeness of the $R^2$ using the dummy variables and a single scale in table 3 indicate that the relationship of credentials to income is reasonably linear within each class category. The differences in slopes thus cannot be interpreted as artifacts of a single curvilinear relationship between income and credentials for both classes.

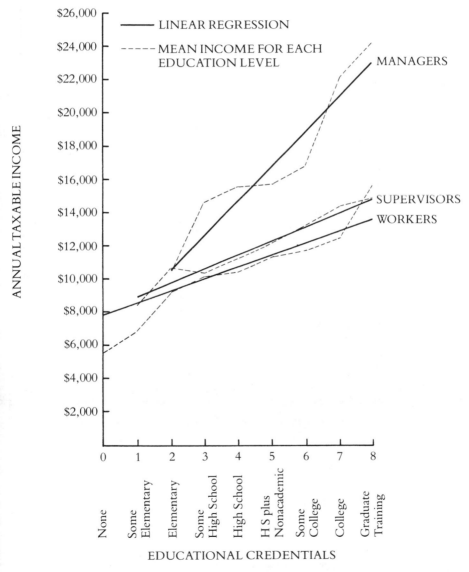

*Figure 2.* Relationship of income to education for workers, supervisors, and managers.

*Table 3.* **Comparison of Explained Variance Using Education
Scale and Education Dummies
(Annual Income = Dependent Variable)**

|  | $R^2$ USING EDUCATION CREDENTIAL SCALE | $R^2$ USING EDUCATION DUMMIES |
|---|---|---|
| Equation for: |  |  |
| Workers............... | .066 | .069 |
| Managers/supervisors.... | .135 | .154 |
| Supervisors ............ | .065 | .065 |
| Managers.............. | .155 | .180 |

*Hypothesis 2: Black males will be more concentrated in the working class than white males.* Table 4 gives the class distribution of black and white males based on an average of the 1969 Survey of Working Conditions and the 1973 Quality of Employment Survey and the distribution for the panel study. Because of the problems of nonrandomness in the panel study, the average of the two earlier surveys is undoubtedly a more accurate estimate of the actual class distribution of races. It is clear from these results that black males are indeed more concentrated in the working class than white males: 61% of all black males compared with only 40% of white males fall within the working class.[9]

*Hypothesis 3: When class position is ignored, black males will receive lower returns to education than white males.* . . . Figure 3 graphically presents the results for the simple regression of income on education. Table 5 presents the statistical tests for significance of the differences in returns to education for various race-class comparisons. In the simple regression of income on education, white males receive $1,419 for each increment in education; black males receive only $860. When the controls in equation (2) are added, the returns among white males decrease to $1,147 and among black males to $614. Both of these differences are significant at the .001 level. Thus, as in most studies of black-white differences in returns to education, black males as a whole do receive lower returns than white males as a whole.

*Hypothesis 4: Within the working class, the returns to education for black and white males will be much more similar than for all blacks and all whites.* In the simple regression of income on education, the returns for all black males are less than one-half of the returns for all white males; within the working class, on the other hand, the returns for black males are slightly over 75% of the returns for white males. What is more, when the controls in equation (2) are added, the returns for black male workers become virtually identical to the returns for all white

9. If anything, these figures underestimate the proportion of the black male population in the working class, since unemployed persons are excluded from both the Survey of Working Conditions and the Quality of Employment Survey. If one assumes that most unemployed black males belong in the working class, then the actual proportion of black males who are workers would probably be closer to 70% or 75%, and of white males closer to 45% or 50%.

## Table 4. Class Distribution Within Race Categories

| | AVERAGE OF SURVEY OF WORKING CONDITIONS, 1969, AND QUALITY OF EMPLOYMENT SURVEY, 1973, DISTRIBUTION | | PANEL STUDY OF INCOME DYNAMICS, 1975[a] | | | | | |
| --- | --- | --- | --- | --- | --- | --- | --- | --- |
| | | | White Males | | | Black Males | | |
| | White Males | Black Males | Weighted N | Unweighted N | % | Weighted N | Unweighted N | % |
| | % | % | | | | | | |
| Employers .......... | 11.5 | 4.9 | 302 | 217 | 10.9 | 11 | 31 | 4.1 |
| Supervisors and managers | 40.2 | 32.5 | 1,090 | 812 | 39.3 | 66 | 198 | 24.7 |
| Supervisors ....... | ... | ... | 524 | 401 | 18.9 | 35 | 126 | 13.1 |
| Managers ......... | ... | ... | 566 | 411 | 20.4 | 31 | 72 | 11.6 |
| Workers .......... | 43.5 | 61.4 | 1,225 | 984 | 44.2 | 186 | 657 | 69.7 |
| Petty bourgeoisie ...... | 4.9 | 1.2 | 153 | 117 | 5.5 | 4 | 15 | 1.5 |
| Total ......... | 100 | 100 | ... | ... | 100 | ... | ... | 100 |
| N ........ | 2,100 | 168 | 2,770 | 2,130 | ... | 267 | 901 | ... |

[a]Percentages are calculated on the basis of the weighted N. The weights are designed to correct for oversampling in the original sample design and differential attrition rates during the first four waves of the panel.

workers, while the returns for all black males are still only 54% of the returns for all white males. This suggests that, within the working class, most of the difference between black and white males in returns to education observed in the simple regression of income on education is mediated by the control variables in equation (2), whereas this is not the case for all blacks and all whites.

*Hypothesis 5: Within the supervisor category, the returns to education for black and white males will be more similar than for all blacks and all whites.* As in the case of

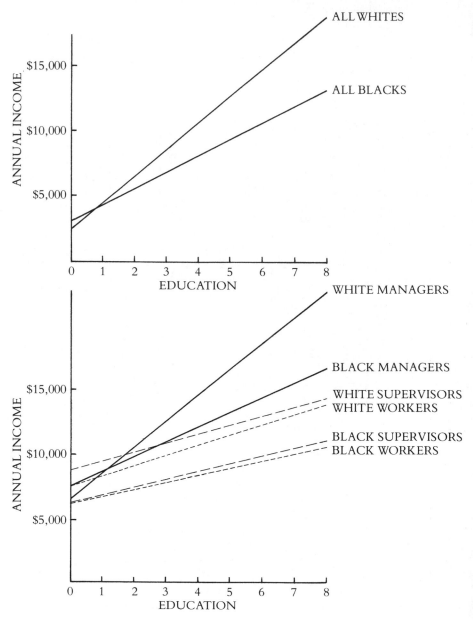

*Figure 3.* Returns to education for blacks and whites in different class positions

***Table 5.*** **Comparison of Returns to Education for Black and White Males Across Class Categories and Within Class Categories**

| | RETURNS TO EDUCATION | |
| --- | :---: | :---: |
| | **Eq. (1)** | **Eq. (2)** |
| All black and white males: | | |
| Slope difference . . . . . . . . | 959 | 533 |
| *t*-value of difference . . . . | 8.1★ | 3.6★ |
| Black slope as % white slope . . . . . . . . . . . . . . . . | 49 | 54 |
| % difference in eq. (1) eliminated by the controls in eq. (2) . . . . . . | . . . | 44 |
| Workers: | | |
| Slope difference . . . . . . . . | 192 | 7 |
| *t*-value of difference . . . . | 1.8 | <1 |
| Black slope as % white slope . . . . . . . . . . . . . . . . | 76 | 99 |
| % difference in eq. (1) eliminated by the controls in eq. (2) . . . . . . | . . . | 97 |
| Supervisors: | | |
| Slope difference . . . . . . . . | 93 | −216 |
| *t*-value of difference . . . . | <1 | <1 |
| Managers: | | |
| Slope difference . . . . . . . . | 938 | 1,991 |
| *t*-value of difference . . . . | 3.5★ | 6.3★ |

★Significant at the .001 level (one-tailed test).

black and white workers, this expectation is strongly supported by the results. In the simple regression, black male supervisors receive only $93 less returns to education than do white male supervisors, and in equation (2) they actually receive returns $200 greater (although the difference is statistically insignificant).

*Hypothesis 6: Within the managerial category, black males will have lower returns to education than white males.* As predicted, in both regression equations black male managers receive significantly lower returns to education than white male managers. However, it was not expected that the returns to education among black male managers would be essentially zero in the multiple regression equation. The expectation was merely that, because of restrictions of blacks to lower levels of the authority hierarchy, the hierarchical-promotion mechanism would be blunted among black managers, and thus the returns to education would be less among black than among white male managers. There was no a priori expectation that those returns would disappear entirely in equation (2).

One possible clue to these results might be found in the occupational distribution among white and black managers (Table 6). As would be expected, black male managers are considerably more concentrated than white male managers among unskilled and semiskilled manual occupations (38.5% compared with

*Table 6.* **Occupational Distribution Among Managers for Black and White Males (%)**

|  | WHITE MALES | BLACK MALES |
| --- | --- | --- |
| Professional, technical, and kindred .......... | 24.6 | 22.5 |
| Professionals .......... | 19.3 | 9.3 |
| Technicians .......... | 3.0 | 0 |
| Teachers .............. | 2.3 | 13.2 |
| Managers and administrators .......... | 35.2 | 25.0 |
| Sales .................. | 4.7 | .8 |
| Clerks ................. | 1.9 | 1.7 |
| Craftsmen and kindred .... | 20.5 | 11.5 |
| Operatives, laborers, and miscellaneous .......... | 13.1 | 38.5 |
| Total ................. | 100 | 100 |

13%, respectively). What is somewhat surprising is the much higher proportion of black managers who are teachers compared with white managers (13% compared with 2%, respectively). Expressed in a different way, nearly 60% of the black managers in professional or technical occupations are teachers as compared with less than 10% of white professional-technical managers. Remember, these are proper managers, people who, unlike mere supervisors, state that they have some say in the pay and promotions of their subordinates. This implies that teacher-managers either occupy administrative positions within their educational institutions or direct research projects in which they authorize the pay and promotions of research staff (all but one of the teacher-managers were college or university teachers).

If the regressions . . . [which are the basis of Figure 3—eds.] are rerun excluding teachers from the managerial category, the results conform much more to expectation (Table 7). Black male managers still have significantly lower returns to education than do white male managers, but the returns are not nearly as small as returns in the regressions that included teachers.

I cannot offer a particularly coherent explanation for why the presence of so many teachers among black managers should have such a drastic effect on the education coefficient in equation (2). Most likely, this result has something to do with the interrelationship of education, occupational status, and income among this specific subgroup of managers. To say this, however, merely describes the problem; it does not provide a theoretical explanation.

## Discussion: The Interplay of Racism and Class Relations

It would be a mistake to interpret these results as indicating that all racial discrimination is really disguised class oppression. While it is true that the

**Table 7.** **Returns to Education for Blacks and Whites Within the Manager/Supervisor Category, Excluding Teachers**

| | TOTAL ANNUAL INCOME | |
| --- | --- | --- |
| | Eq. (1) | Eq. (2) |
| Supervisors: | | |
| White males .......... | 732 | 761 |
| | (182) | (208) |
| Black males .......... | 506 | 934 |
| | (217) | (350) |
| Difference ........... | 226 | −173 |
| $t$-value .............. | 1.1 | <1 |
| Managers: | | |
| White males ($N$ =385) .. | 2,154 | 1,570 |
| | (256) | (293) |
| Black males ($N$ =60) ... | 1,582 | 880 |
| | (476) | (473) |
| Difference ........... | 572 | 690 |
| $t$-value............... | 2.0* | 2.1* |

Note. Numbers in parentheses are standard errors.
*Significant at .05 level.

differential returns to education for blacks and whites largely disappear when we control for class (except in the case of managers), this does not imply that race is an insignificant dimension of inequality in American life. The empirical and theoretical problem is to sort out the complex interplay of racism and class relations, not to absorb the former into the latter.

The most obvious way in which racism intersects class relations is in the social processes which distribute people into class positions in the first place. In recent years, sociologists have devoted considerable attention to the effects of racial discrimination on occupational mobility chances of blacks as compared with whites. To my knowledge, there have been no studies which systematically explore the role of racism in the distribution of individuals into different positions within the social relations of production. Of particular importance in such a study would be the social processes which select people into the managerial/supervisory category and the mechanisms which regulate the promotion patterns in managerial hierarchies. Racism would affect the distribution of races within authority structures in two general ways. First, as in the sorting process for occupations, various forms of racial discrimination affect access to the mechanisms which sort people into the managerial hierarchy (educational credentials, connections, etc.). Since, as was argued earlier, people with lower credentials will tend not to be promoted above people with higher credentials, the result will be a higher concentration of blacks at lower levels of the managerial structure and a higher concentration of blacks in the working class. Second, and perhaps more important, because of the necessity to legitimate the social relations of domination embodied in managerial hierarchies, racism will tend directly to prevent the promotion of blacks above whites. Of course, this does not mean that blacks will never be promoted above whites. Particularly when strong political struggles against racism occur, corporations and bureaucracies may see the imperatives of legitimation as requiring the acceptance of some blacks into "token" positions of authority within managerial structures. But in the absence of such struggles, it would be expected that the logic of hierarchical domination within capitalist production relations and the necessity of legitimating that domination would generate racist patterns of recruitment into and promotion up managerial hierarchies.

The above argument about recruitment and promotion presupposes the existence of racism. Given the presence of intense racist beliefs, it is easy to explain why blacks will not be promoted above whites within hierarchies; but this begs the question about the existence of racism in the first place. It is beyond the scope of this paper to attempt a systematic account of the origins of racism and the social processes which reproduce it in contemporary American society. What I will do is very briefly indicate the essential thrust of a class analysis of the role of racism in American capitalism and show how the present study relates to that analysis.

A common mistake made by Marxists in analyzing racism is to assume that all forms of racial discrimination are unequivocally functional for the capitalist class. This is similar to analyses of the capitalist state which argue that every policy of the state is orchestrated by the capitalist class to serve its interests. Such "instrumentalist" views of the state and ideology minimize the intensely contradictory character of capitalist society.[10] Capitalism simultaneously undermines and reproduces racism, and it is essential to disentangle these two tendencies if one is to genuinely understand the relationship between class and race in contemporary capitalism.

One of the basic dynamics of capitalist development stressed by Marx, as well as many non-Marxist theorists, is the tendency for capitalism to transform all labor into the commodity labor power and to obliterate all qualitative distinctions between different categories of labor. From the point of view of the capital accumulation process, the more labor becomes a pure commodity, regulated by pure market principles unfettered by personal ties and ascriptive barriers, the more rapidly can capitalism expand. In terms of the logic of accumulation developed by Marx in *Capital,* there will therefore be systemic tendencies in capitalism to reduce racial discrimination in the labor market and to treat black labor power as identical with any other labor power.

But this is only one side of the story. Capitalism is not just a system of capital accumulation; it is also a class system in which workers struggle against capitalists, both over their condition as sellers of labor power and potentially over the existence of the capitalist system itself. Whereas the essential dynamics of accumulation may lead to an undermining of racial differences in the labor market, the dynamics of class struggle tend to intensify racism. To the extent that the working class is divided along racial and ethnic lines, the collective power of the working class is reduced, and thus the capacity of workers to win

---

10. For a critique of instrumentalist views in Marxist theory, see Gold, Lo, and Wright (1975) and Esping-Anderson, Friedland, and Wright (1976).

demands against capital is decreased. The result will be an increase in the rate of exploitation of both white and black workers, although the effects may well be more intense for blacks and other minorities than for whites.[11] As a divide-and-conquer strategy, racism thus serves the interests of capitalists, both as individuals and as a class.[12]

We thus have a basic contradiction: capitalism tends to undermine all qualitative distinctions between categories of labor, but the capitalist class needs those qualitative divisions for its own reproduction as the dominant class.[13] Both forces operate. The actual balance between the two depends upon a variety of historical factors. For example, under conditions of extreme shortages of labor, obstacles to labor mobility in the labor market are likely to be rather costly to individual capitalists, and thus it would be expected that racial barriers would be more rapidly eroded by imperatives of accumulation. On the other hand, when the supply of labor is relatively abundant and when individual differences between laborers make little difference to productivity (because of routinization, automation, etc.), those strictly economic imperatives are likely to be weaker. The extent to which racial or ethnic divisions within the working class are being deepened or eroded in a given capitalist society cannot therefore be derived directly from the abstract theory of capitalist economic development. It is only when such abstract theory is linked to specific political and ideological developments that it becomes possible to assess the real dynamics of racism in a given society.

While the present study does not deal with this historical process, the data in the research nevertheless can be related to both sides of this contradictory ten-

---

11. While Marxists have often claimed that racism hurts white as well as black workers, until recently there have not been any systematic empirical investigations of this proposition. Two recent studies deal directly with this question. Reich (1971, 1973) shows that, in the 50 largest SMSAs, the greater the racial inequality in median family earnings, the greater the inequality of earnings among whites (as measured by the Gini coefficient for earnings among whites) and the weaker the level of unionization. Szymanski (1976) shows that, for the 50 states, the greater the inequality between black and white median earnings, the lower the median earnings of white males and the greater the inequality among whites (again, measured by Gini coefficients). Both of these sets of results indicate that racism, in dividing the working class, leads to an increase in exploitation of all workers.

12. The analysis of racism as a divide-and-conquer strategy has been perhaps the central theme in Marxist treatments of the subject. Marx emphasized this issue in his various discussions of the "Irish Question." In 1870, for example, he wrote, "The English bourgeoisie has not only exploited the Irish poverty to keep down the working class in England by forced immigration of poor Irishmen, but it has also divided the proletariat into two hostile camps. . . . In all the big industrial centers in England there is profound antagonism between the Irish proletariat and the English proletariat. The average English worker hates the Irish worker as a competitor who lowers wages and the standard of life. . . . This antagonism among the proletarians of England is artificially nourished and supported by the bourgeoisie. It knows that this scission is the true secret of maintaining its power" (Marx and Engels 1972, p. 162).

13. Both Marxist theory and neoclassical economics recognize that the inherent economic logic of capitalism is to reduce progressively economic divisions between races, in terms of both income and occupation. The difference (in these terms) between the two perspectives is that neoclassical economics treats capitalism solely as an economic system and ignores the fundamental class antagonisms within that system. Thus, the political and ideological imperatives of controlling the working class play no role in the theory. Instead of seeing the relationship of capitalism to racism as an intrinsically contradictory process, neoclassical economics typically treats racism as a problem of individual "tastes" for discrimination on the part of employers and workers (see Becker 1971, pp. 13–18).

*Table 8.*  **Income Gaps[a] Between Races Within Class Categories**

| | Mean Income | | |
| --- | --- | --- | --- |
| | ($) | Eq. (1)[b] | Eq. (2)[b] |
| **All respondents:** | | | |
| Gap in income ......... | 5,308 | 3,698 | 1,868 |
| Black expected income as % of white expected income .............. | 64 | 73 | 85 |
| % difference in means eliminated by controls .. | . . . | 30 | 65 |
| $t$-value of gap ......... | . . . | 16.4★ | 8.1★ |
| **Workers:** | | | |
| Gap in income ......... | 2,870 | 2,203 | 1,428 |
| Black expected income as % of white expected income .............. | 75 | 80 | 86 |
| % difference in means eliminated by controls .. | . . . | 23 | 49 |
| $t$-value of gap ......... | . . . | 11.9★ | 8.9★ |
| **Supervisors:** | | | |
| Gap in income ......... | 3,872 | 2,896 | 2,140 |
| Black expected income as % of white expected income .............. | 69 | 76 | 82 |
| % difference in means eliminated by controls .. | . . . | 25 | 45 |
| $t$-value of gap ......... | . . . | 8.6★ | 6.8★ |
| **Managers:** | | | |
| Gap in income ......... | 5,051 | 3,707 | 3,011 |
| Black expected income as % of white expected income .............. | 72 | 79 | 83 |
| % difference in means eliminated by controls .. | . . . | 27 | 40 |
| $t$-value of gap ......... | . . . | 8.0★ | 6.8★ |

[a]Income gaps represent the difference in expected incomes for two groups evaluated at a level of the independent variables in the regression equal to the average of their respective means on the independent variables.

[b]Independent variables in eq. (1) =education only; independent variables in eq. (2) =education, age, seniority, background, occupational status, and annual hours worked.

★Significant at the .001 level (one-tailed test).

dency within capitalism, that is, both to the perpetuation of important racial divisions within the working class and to the common situation of all workers as workers, regardless of race.

The data presented in Figure 3 . . . clearly indicate that, while black and white workers receive similar returns to education, black-worker income is less than white-worker income at every level of education. One way of assessing this gap in income is to see what the expected difference in income between a black and white male worker would be if they both had some intermediate value on the independent variables included in the equation. In Table 8 this gap is calculated at levels of the independent variables halfway between the means for each group in the comparison being made.[14] As can be seen from this table, the income gaps between races are large and statistically significant for both regression equations within each class category. Furthermore, the addition of the various controls in the multiple regression equations reduces the total difference in mean incomes between races within classes by no more than 50%, indicating that a substantial part of the difference in mean incomes between races within classes should probably be directly attributed to racial discrimination. In terms of Marxist theory, these results strongly suggest that black workers are exploited at a higher rate than white workers and that racism has generated real, material divisions between races within the working class.[15]

Ultimately, the political thrust of the Marxist theory of racism hinges on the other side of the contradiction: that, in spite of the divisive character of racism and in spite of the material differences between black and white workers which racism generates, workers of all races nevertheless share a fundamental class situation and thus share fundamental class interests.[16] The central finding of this study—that black and white workers have very similar returns to education—reflects this common class situation. . . .

---

14. Thus, in the simple regression of income on education for the comparison of black and white workers, the income gap is assessed at a value of education equal to $(E_{\text{black worker}} + E_{\text{white worker}})/2$. The statistical significance of this income gap can be tested in a way exactly analogous to the test of slope differences, only in this case a $t$-test is performed on the differences between constant terms adjusted to the appropriate values of the independent variables (see Wright 1976b, pp. 55–57).

15. In order to interpret these results as indicating a higher rate of exploitation of black labor, it is necessary to assume that two workers who have the same values on all of the variables in eq. (2) will have essentially similar complexities of labor (i.e., embodied labor in their own labor power) and intensities of labor (i.e., pace of work within the labor process). Since eq. (2) contains annual hours worked, if we accept the above two assumptions then two workers who have the same values on all the independent variables will produce the same amount of total value in a year. Any difference in their incomes would then reflect differences in the costs of reproduction of their labor power and thus differences in rates of exploitation. Two factors could undermine this conclusion. First of all, the reproductive costs of labor power are not represented simply by wages, but by fringe benefits, state subsidies for education and other services, etc. To the extent that such additional elements of the costs of reproducing labor power are themselves correlated with earnings, we are, if anything, underestimating the differences in rates of exploitation by looking exclusively at direct income. Second, if black workers as a whole are overqualified for the jobs which they hold, wage differences could reflect in part social waste of potential surplus value rather than superexploitation of black labor in the technical sense of the concept. If a college graduate works on an assembly line, he or she produces no more surplus value and is no more exploited than a high school dropout in the same production process. The complexity of the college graduate's potential labor is being socially wasted in such a situation. In the strategy used to compare black and white exploitation above, however, this situation would appear as a greater rate of exploitation of the college graduate. There is no way, in the present data, to differentiate between underemployment and more intense exploitation. For a much fuller discussion of the relationship between econometric models of income determination and the Marxist concept of exploitation, see Wright (1976b, pp. 120–31).

16. "Fundamental" class interests refer to interests defined across modes of production (i.e., interests in capitalism vs. interests in socialism), whereas "immediate" interests refer to interests defined within a given mode of production. Black and white workers may well have conflicting immediate interests under certain circumstances (as do many categories of labor within the working class) and still share fundamental class interests. For a discussion of the importance of the distinction between fundamental and immediate interests, see Wright (1978, chap. 2).

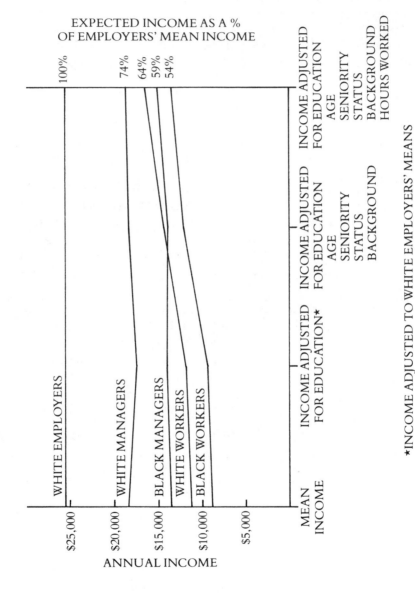

*INCOME ADJUSTED TO WHITE EMPLOYERS' MEANS

Figure 4.  Comparison of income differences between races and classes

Furthermore, it is easy to show that the income gaps between black and white workers, while significant, are much smaller than the gaps between either black or white workers and small employers. Figure 4 indicates the expected incomes of each race and class category assessed at the level of the independent variables of white employers.[17] The unadjusted mean income of white workers is less than one-half that of white employers; the mean income of black workers, on the other hand, is 75% of white workers' mean income. In absolute dollar amounts, the mean white workers' income is over $14,000 less than the mean white employers' income, whereas the mean black workers' income is only $2,900 less than the mean white workers' income. When the various controls in equation (2) are added, the expected incomes of both black and white workers (evaluated at the white employers' means on the independent variables) increase considerably. Yet, the difference between workers and employers is still considerably greater than the differences between workers of different races. These results indicate that compared with even small employers—let alone proper capitalists—the common position of black and white workers within the social relations of production generates a basic unity of economic situation. . . .

## References

Becker, Gary S. 1971. *The Economics of Discrimination*. Chicago: University of Chicago Press.

Dahrendorf, Ralf. 1959. *Class and Class Conflict in Industrial Society*. Palo Alto, Calif.: Stanford University Press.

Duncan, Otis Dudley. 1969. "Inheritance of Poverty or Inheritance of Race?" In *Understanding Poverty*, edited by Daniel P. Moynihan. New York: Basic.

Esping-Anderson, Gösta, Roger Friedland, and Erik Olin Wright. 1976. "Modes of Class Struggle and the Capitalist State." *Kapitalistate*, nos. 4–5, pp. 186–22.

Giddens, Anthony. 1973. *The Class Structure of the Advanced Societies*. New York: Harper & Row.

Gold, David, Clarence Y. H. Lo, and Erik Olin Wright. 1975. "Recent Developments in Marxist Theories of the State." *Monthly Review* 27 (5): 29–42; 27 (6): 36–51.

Institute for Social Research. 1975. *Panel Study of Income Dynamics: Procedures and Tape Codes for 1975 Interview Year, Wave VIII*. Ann Arbor, Mich.: Institute for Social Research.

Kmenta, Jan. 1971. *Elements of Econometrics*. New York: Macmillan.

Lenski, Gerhard. 1966. *Power and Privilege*. New York: McGraw-Hill.

Marx, Karl, and Frederick Engels. 1972. *Ireland and the Irish Question*. New York: International Publishers.

---

17. This procedure is basically similar to the familiar cross-substitution technique employed by Duncan (1969) and others.

Parkin, Frank. 1971. *Class Inequality and Political Order.* New York: Praeger.

Parsons, Talcott. 1970. "Equality and Inequality in Modern Society, or Social Stratification Revisited." In *Social Stratification: Research and Theory for the 1970s,* edited by E. O. Laumann. New York: Bobbs-Merrill.

Poulantzas, Nicos. 1975. *Classes in Contemporary Capitalism.* London: New Left.

Reich, Michael. 1971. "The Economics of Racism." In *Problems in Political Economy,* edited by David M. Gordon. Lexington, Mass.: Heath.

————. 1973. "Racial Discrimination and the White Income Distribution." Ph.D. dissertation, Harvard University.

Siegel, Paul. 1965. "On the Costs of Being a Negro." *Sociological Inquiry* 35 (Winter): 41–57.

Stolzenberg, Ross M. 1973. "Occupational Differences in Wage Discrimination against Black Men: The Structure of Racial Differences in Men's Wages, Returns to Schooling, 1960." Ph.D. dissertation, University of Michigan.

————. 1975. "Education, Occupation, and Wage Differences between White and Black Men." *American Journal of Sociology* 81 (September): 299–323.

Szymanski, Albert. 1976. "Racial Discrimination and White Gain." *American Sociological Review* 41 (3): 403–14.

Tannenbaum, Arnold S., Bodgon Kavcic, Menachem Rosner, Mino Vianello, and Georg Wiesner. 1974. *Hierarchy in Organizations.* San Francisco: Jossey-Bass.

Warner, W. Lloyd. 1960. *Social Class in America.* New York: Harper & Row.

Weber, Max. 1968. *Economy and Society,* edited by Guenther Roth. New York: Bedminster.

Weiss, Randall. 1970. "The Effect of Education on the Earnings of Blacks and Whites." *Review of Economics and Statistics* 52 (May): 150–59.

Wright, Erik Olin. 1976a. "Class Boundaries in Advanced Capitalism." *New Left Review* 98 (July–August): 3–42.

————. 1976b. "Class Structure and Income Inequality." Ph.D. dissertation, University of California, Berkeley.

————. 1978. *Class, Crisis and the State.* London: New Left.

Wright, Erik Olin, and Luca Perrone. 1975. "Classi sociale, scuola, occupazione e reddito in U.S.A.: una analisi quantitativa sulle disequaglianze sociale in una società postindustriale." *Quaderni di sociolegia* 24 (1–2): 57–91.

————. 1977. "Marxist Class Categories and Income Inequality." *American Sociological Review* 42 (1): 32–55.

# Labour, Capital, and Class Struggle Around the Built Environment in Advanced Capitalist Societies

## David Harvey

In this paper I will seek to establish a theoretical framework for understanding a facet of class struggle under advanced capitalism. The conflicts that will be scrutinized are those that relate to the production and use of the built environment, by which I mean the totality of physical structures—houses, roads, factories, offices, sewage systems, parks, cultural institutions, educational facilities, and so on. In general I shall argue that capitalist society must of necessity create a physical landscape—a mass of humanly constructed physical resources—in its own image, broadly appropriate to the purposes of production and reproduction. But I shall also argue that this process of creating space is full of contradictions and tensions and that the class relations in capitalist society inevitably spawn strong cross-currents of conflict.

I shall assume for purposes of analytic convenience that a clear distinction exists between (1) a faction of capital seeking the appropriation of rent either directly (as landlords, property companies, and the like) or indirectly (as financial intermediaries or others who invest in property simply for a rate of return), (2) a faction of capital seeking interest and profit by building new elements in the built environment (the construction interests), (3) capital "in general," which looks upon the built environment as an outlet for surplus capital and as a bundle of use values for enhancing the production and accumulation of capital, and (4) labor,

* Abridged from *Politics and Society* 5(3) (1976): 265–79, 288–93.

NOTE: I am much indebted to Dick Walker for critical comments upon an earlier draft of this paper. I should also add that his thought and work have contributed in many ways (some of which I am sure I am unaware of) to my understanding of the issues raised in this paper.

which uses the built environment as a means of consumption and as a means for its own reproduction. I shall also assume that the built environment can be divided conceptually into *fixed capital* items to be used in production (factories, highways, railroads, and so on) and *consumption fund* items to be used in consumption (houses, roads, parks, sidewalks, and the like).[1] Some items, such as roads and sewer systems, can function both as fixed capital and as part of the consumption fund depending on their use.

I will restrict attention in this paper to the structure of conflict as it arises in relation to labor's use of the consumption fund rather than its use of fixed capital in the immediate process of production. An analysis of this aspect of class struggle will do much to shed light, I believe, on the vexing questions that surround the relationship between community conflict and community organizing, on the one hand, and industrial conflict and work-based organizing on the other. In short, I hope to be able to shed some light on the position and experience of labor with respect to *living* as well as *working* in the historical development of those countries that are now generally considered to be in the advanced capitalist category. The examples will be taken from the United States and Great Britain. Some preparatory comments on the general theme to be pursued are in order.

The domination of capital over labor is basic to the capitalist mode of production—without it, after all, surplus value could not be extracted and accumulation would disappear. All kinds of consequences flow from this and the relation between labor and the built environment can be understood only in terms of it. Perhaps the single most important fact is that industrial capitalism, through the reorganization of the work process and the advent of the factory system, forced a separation between place of work and place of reproduction and consumption. The need to reproduce labor power is thus translated into a specific set of production and consumption activities within the household—a domestic economy that requires use values in the form of a built environment if it is to function effectively.

The needs of labor have changed historically and they will in part be met by work within the household and in part be procured through market exchanges of wages earned against commodities produced. The commodity requirements of labor depend upon the balance between domestic economy products and market purchases as well as upon the environmental, historical, and moral considerations that fix the standard of living of labor.[2] In the commodity realm, labor can, by organization and class struggle, alter the definition of needs to include "reasonable" standards of nutrition, health care, housing, education, recreation, entertainment, and so on. From the standpoint of capital, accumulation requires a constant expansion of the market for commodities, which means the creation of new social wants and needs and the organization of "rational consumption" on the part of labor. This last condition suggests theoretically what is historically observable—that the domestic economy must steadily give way before the expansion of capitalist commodity production. "Accumulation for accumulation's sake, production for production's sake," which jointly drive the capitalist system

---

1. This distinction derives from Marx. See Karl Marx, *Capital* (New York: 1967), 2: 210; and *idem., The Grundrisse* (Harmondsworth, Middlesex: 1973), pp. 681–7.
2. See Marx, *Capital,* 1: 171.

onwards, therefore entail an increasing integration of labor's consumption into the capitalist system of production and exchange of commodities.[3]

The split between the place of work and the place of residence means that the struggle of labor to control the social conditions of its own existence splits into two seemingly independent struggles. The first, located in the work place, is over the wage rate, which provides the purchasing power for consumption goods, and the conditions of work. The second, fought in the place of residence, is against secondary forms of exploitation and appropriation represented by merchant capital, landed property, and the like. This is a fight over the costs and conditions of existence in the living place. And it is this second kind of struggle that we focus on here, recognizing, of course, that the dichotomy between *living* and *working* is itself an artificial division that the capitalist system imposes.

## Labor Versus the Appropriators of Rent and the Construction Interest

Labor needs living space. Land is therefore a condition of living for labor in much the same way that it is a condition of production for capital. The system of private property that excludes labor from land as a condition of production also serves to exclude labor from the land as a condition of living. As Marx puts it, "the monstrous power wielded by landed property, when united hand in hand with industrial capital, enables it to be used against laborers engaged in their wage struggle as a means of practically expelling them from the earth as a dwelling place."[4] Apart from space as a basic condition of living we are concerned here with housing, transportation (to jobs and facilities), amenities, facilities, and a whole bundle of resources that contribute to the total living environment for labor. Some of these items can be privately appropriated (housing is the most important case) while others have to be used in common (sidewalks) and in some cases, such as the transportation system, even used jointly with capital.

The need for these items pits labor against landed property and the appropriation of rent as well as against the construction interest, which seeks to profit from the production of these commodities. The cost and quality of these items affect the standard of living of labor. Labor, in seeking to protect and enhance its standard of living, engages in a series of running battles in the living place over a variety of issues that relate to the creation, management, and use of the built environment. Examples are not hard to find—community conflict over excessive appropriation of rent by landlords, over speculation in housing market, over the siting of "noxious" facilities, over inflation in housing construction costs, over inflation in the costs of servicing a deteriorating urban infrastructure, over congestion, over lack of accessibility to employment opportunities and services, over highway construction and urban renewal, over the "quality of life" and aesthetic issues—the list seems almost endless.

---

3. This condition can be derived directly from Marxian theory by bringing together the analyses presented in Marx, *Capital*, 1: 591–640, 2: 437–48, 515–16.

4. Marx, *Capital*, 3: 773.

Conflicts that focus on the built environment exhibit certain peculiar characteristics because the monopoly power conferred by private property arrangements generates not only the power to appropriate rent but also yields to the owners command over a "natural monopoly" in space.[5] The fixed and immobile character of the built environment entails the production and use of commodities under conditions of spatial monopolistic competition with strong "neighborhood" or "externality" effects.[6] Many of the struggles that occur are over externality effects—the value of a particular house is in part determined by the condition of the houses surrounding it and each owner is therefore very interested in seeing to it that the neighborhood as a whole is well-maintained. In bourgeois theory, the appropriation of rent and the trading of titles to properties set price signals for new commodity production in such a way that a "rational" allocation of land to uses can be arrived at through a market process. But because of the pervasive externality effects and the sequential character of both development and occupancy, the price signals suffer from all manner of serious distortions. There are, as a consequence, all kinds of opportunities for both appropriators and the construction faction, for developers, speculators, and even private individuals, to reap windfall profits and monopoly rents. Internecine conflicts within a class and faction are therefore just as common as conflict between classes and factions.

We are primarily concerned here, however, with the structure of the three-way struggle between labor, the appropriators of rent, and the construction faction. Consider, as an example, the direct struggle between laborers and landlords over the cost and quality of housing. Landlords typically use whatever power they have to appropriate as much as they can from the housing stock they own and they will adjust their strategy to the conditions in such a way that they maximize the rate of return on their capital. If this rate of return is very high, then new capital will likely flow into landlordism, and, if the rate of return is very low, then we will likely witness disinvestment and abandonment. Labor will seek by a variety of strategies—for example, moving to where housing is cheaper or establishing rent controls and housing codes—to limit appropriation and to ensure a reasonable quality of shelter. How such a struggle is resolved depends very much upon the relative economic and political power of the two groups, the circumstances of supply and demand that exist at a particular place and time, and upon the options that each group has available to it.[7]

The struggle becomes three dimensional when we consider that the ability of appropriators to gain monopoly rents on the old housing is in part limited by the capacity of the construction interest to enter the market and create new housing at a lower cost. The price of old housing is, after all, strongly affected by the costs of production of new housing. If labor can use its political power to gain state subsidies for construction, then this artificially stimulated new development will force the rate of appropriation on existing resources downwards.

---

5. Ibid., chap. 37.

6. See David Harvey, *Social Justice and the City* (London and Baltimore: Edward Arnold, 1973), chaps. 2, 5.

7. For a more detailed argument see David Harvey, "Class-Monopoly Rent, Finance Capital and the Urban Revolution," *Regional Studies* 8 (1974): 239–55.

If, on the other hand, appropriators can check new development (by, for example, escalating land costs), or if, for some reason, new development is inhibited (planning permission procedures in Britain have typically functioned in this way), then the rate of appropriation can rise. On the other hand, when labor manages to check the rate of appropriation through direct rent controls, then the price of rented housing falls, new development is discouraged, and scarcity is produced. These are the kinds of conflicts and strategies of coalition that we have to expect in such situations.

But the structure of conflict is made more complex by the "natural monopoly" inherent in space. For example, the monopoly power of the landlord is in part modified by the ability of labor to escape entrapment in the immediate environs of the work place. Appropriation from housing is very sensitive to changes in transportation. The ability to undertake a longer journey to work is in part dependent upon the wage rate (which allows the worker to pay for travel), in part dependent upon the length of the working day (which gives the worker time to travel), and in part dependent upon the cost and availability of transportation. The boom in the construction of working-class suburbs in late nineteenth-century London, for example, can in large degree be explained by the advent of the railways and the provision of cheap "workman's special" fares and a shortening of the working day, which freed at least some of the working class from the need to live within walking distance of the workplace.[8] The rate of rental appropriation on the housing close to the centers of employment had to fall as a consequence. The "streetcar" suburbs of American cities and the working-class suburbs of today (based on cheap energy and the automobile) are further examples of this phenomenon.[9] By pressing for new and cheap forms of transportation, labor can escape geographical entrapment and thereby reduce the capacity of landlords in advantageous locations to gain monopoly rents. The problems that attach to spatial entrapment are still with us, of course, in the contemporary ghettos of the poor, the aged, the oppressed minorities, and the like. Access is still, for these groups, a major issue.[10]

The struggle to fight off the immediate depredations of the landlord and the continuous battle to keep the cost of living down do much to explain the posture adopted by labor with respect to the distribution, quantities, and qualities of all elements in the built environment. Public facilities, recreational opportunities, amenities, transportation access, and so on, are all subjects of contention. But underlying these immediate concerns is a deeper struggle over the very meaning of the built environment as a set of use values for labor.

The producers of the built environment, both past and present, provide labor with a limited set of choices of living conditions. If labor has slender

---

8. John R. Kellet, *The Impact of Railways on Victorian Cities* (London: Routledge & K. Paul, 1969), chap. 11.

9. G. R. Taylor, "The Beginnings of Mass Transportation in Urban America," *The Smithsonian Journal of History* 1, nos. 1–2: 35–50, 31–54; J. Tarr, "From City to Suburb: The 'Moral' Influence of Transportation Technology," in *American Urban History,* ed. Alexander B. Callow (New York: Oxford University Press, 1973); David R. Ward, *Cities and Immigrants* (New York: Oxford University Press, 1971).

10. The McCone Commission report on the Watts rebellion in Los Angeles in 1964 attributed much of the discontent to the sense of entrapment generated out of lack of access to transportation.

resources with which to exercise an effective demand, then it has to put up with whatever it can get—shoddily built, cramped, and poorly serviced tenement buildings, for example. With increasing effective demand, labor has the potential to choose over a wider range and, as a result, questions about the overall "quality of life" begin to arise. Capital in general, and that faction of it that produces the built environment, seek to define the quality of life for labor in terms of the commodities that they can profitably produce in certain locations. Labor, on the other hand, defines quality of life solely in use value terms and in the process may appeal to some underlying and very fundamental conception of what it is to be human. Production for profit and production for use are often inconsistent with each other. The survival of capitalism therefore requires that capital dominate labor, not simply in the work process, but with respect to the very definition of the quality of life in the consumption sphere. Production, Marx argued, not only produces consumption, it also produces the mode of consumption and that, of course, is what the consumption fund for labor is all about.[11] For this reason, capital in general cannot afford the outcome of struggles around the built environment to be determined simply by the relative powers of labor, the appropriators of rent, and the construction faction. It must, from time to time, throw its weight into the balance to effect outcomes that are favorable to the reproduction of the capitalist social order. It is to this aspect of matters that we must now turn.

## The Interventions of Capital in Struggles over the Built Environment

When capital intervenes in struggles over the built environment it usually does so through the agency of state power. A cursory examination of the history of the advanced capitalist countries shows that the capitalist class sometimes throws its weight to the side of labor and sometimes on the side of other factions. But history also suggests a certain pattern and underlying rationale for these interventions. We can get at the pattern by assembling the interventions together under four broad headings—private property and homeownership for the working class, the cost of living and the value of labor power, managed collective consumption of workers in the interest of sustained capital accumulation, and a very complex, but very important, topic concerning the relation to nature, the imposition of work discipline, and the like. A discussion of the pattern will help us to identify the underlying rationale, and in this manner we can identify a much deeper meaning in the everyday struggles in which labor engages in the living place.

### Private Property and Homeownership for Labor

The struggle that labor wages in the living place against the appropriation of rent is a struggle against the monopoly power of private property. Labor's fight against the principle of private property cannot easily be confined to the housing

---

11. Marx, *Grundrisse*, Introduction.

arena, and "the vexed question of the relation between rent and wages. . . . easily slides into that of capital and labor."[12] For this reason the capitalist class as a whole cannot afford to ignore it; they have an interest in keeping the principle of private property sacrosanct. A well-developed struggle between tenants and landlords—with the former calling for public ownership, municipalization, and the like—calls the whole principle into question. Extended individualized homeownership is therefore seen as advantageous to the capitalist class because it promotes the allegiance of at least a segment of the working class to the principle of private property, promotes an ethic of "possessive individualism," and brings about a fragmentation of the working class into "housing classes" of homeowners and tenants.[13] This gives the capitalist class a handy ideological lever to use against public ownership and nationalization demands because it is easy to make such proposals sound as if the intent is to take workers' privately owned houses away from them.

The majority of owner-occupants do not own their housing outright, however. They make interest payments on a mortgage. This puts finance capital in a hegemonic position with respect to the functioning of the housing market—a position that it is in no way loath to make use of.[14] The apparent entrance of workers into the petit form of property ownership in housing is, to a large degree, its exact opposite in reality—the entry of money capital into a controlling position within the consumption fund. Finance capital not only controls the disposition and rate of new investment in housing, but controls labor as well through chronic debt-encumbrance. A worker mortgaged up to the hilt is, for the most part, a pillar of social stability, and schemes to promote homeownership within the working class have long recognized this basic fact. And in return the worker may build up, very slowly, some equity in the property.

This last consideration has some important ramifications. Workers put their savings into the physical form of a property. Obviously, they will be concerned to preserve the value of those savings and if possible to enhance them. Ownership of housing can also lead to petty landlordism, which has been a traditional and very important means for individual workers to engage in the appropriation of values at the expense of other workers. But more importantly, every homeowner, whether he or she likes it or not, is caught in a struggle over the appropriation of values because of the shifting patterns of external costs and benefits within the built environment. A new road may destroy the value of some housing and enhance the value of others, and the same applies to all manner of new development, redevelopment, accelerated obsolescence, and so on.

The way in which labor relates to these externality effects is crucial if only

---

12. Quoted in Counter Information Services, *The Recurrent Crisis of London* (CIS, 52 Shaftesbury Ave., London, W.1).

13. C. B. McPherson, *The Political Theory of Possessive Individualism* (Oxford: Clarendon Press, 1962); J. Rex and T. Moore, *Race, Community and Conflict* (London: Oxford University Press, 1975).

14. M. Stone, "Housing and Class Struggle," *Antipode*, vol. 7, no. 2 (1975); David Harvey, "The Political Economy of Urbanization in Advanced Capitalist Societies: The Case of the United States," in *The Social Economy of Cities*, ed. G. Gappert and H. Rose (Beverly Hills: Urban Affairs Annual, no. 9 (1975).

because the housing market is in quantitative terms by far the most important market for any one particular element in the built environment. It would be very difficult to understand the political tension between suburbs and central cities in the United States without recognizing the fragmentation that occurs within the working class as one section of it moves into homeownership and becomes deeply concerned to preserve and if possible to enhance the value of its equity. The social tensions omnipresent within the "community structure" of American cities are similarly affected. Homeownership, in short, invites a faction of the working class to wage its inevitable fight over the appropriation of value in capitalist society in a very different way. It puts them on the side of the principle of private property and frequently leads them to appropriate values at the expense of other factions of the working class. With such a glorious tool to divide and rule at its disposal, it is hardly surprising that capital in general sides with labor in this regard against the landed interest. It is rather as if capital, having relied upon landed property to divorce labor from access to one of the basic conditions of production, preserves the principle of private property intact in the face of the class struggle by permitting labor to return to the face of the earth as a partial owner of land and property as a condition of consumption.

### The Cost of Living and the Wage Rate

Marx argued that the value of labor power was determined by the value of the commodities required to reproduce that labor power. This neat equivalence disappears in the pricing realm, but nevertheless there is a relation of some sort between wages and the cost of obtaining those commodities essential to the reproduction of the household.[15]

An excessive rate of appropriation of rent by landlords will increase the cost of living to labor and generate higher wage demands that, if won, may have the effect of lowering the rate of accumulation of capital. For this reason capital in general may side with labor in the struggle against excessive appropriation and attempt also to lower the costs of production of a basic commodity such as housing. Capitalists may themselves seek to provide cheap housing, as in the "model communities" typical of the early years of the industrial revolution, or they may even side with the demands of labor for cheap, subsidized housing under public ownership, provided that this permits the payment of lower wages. For the same reason the capitalist class may seek to promote, through the agency of the state, the industrialization of building production and the rationalization of production of the built environment through comprehensive land use planning policies, new town construction programs, and the like. Capitalists tend to become interested in such things, however, only when labor is in a position, through its organized collective power, to tie wages to the cost of living.

These considerations apply to all elements in the built environment (and to social services and social expenditures also) that are relevant to the reproduction

---

15. The relation between values and prices in Marxian theory is highly problematic and involves us in the celebrated "transformation problem." To avoid making silly mistakes it is important to bear in mind that the value of labor power is not automatically represented by the wage rate.

of labor power. Those that are publicly provided (which means the bulk of them outside of housing and until recently transportation) can be monitored by a cost-conscious municipal government under the watchful eye of the local business community, and, perhaps, in an emergency situation such as that experienced in New York both in the 1930s and the 1970s, even under direct supervision by the institutions of finance capital. In the interests of keeping the costs of reproduction of labor power at a minimum, the capitalist class as a whole may seek collective means to intervene in the processes of investment and appropriation in the built environment. In much the same way that the proletariat frequently sided with the rising industrial bourgeoisie against the landed interest in the early years of capitalism, so we often find capital in general siding with labor in the advanced capitalist societies against excessive appropriation of rent and rising costs of new development. The coalition is not forged altruistically but arises organically out of the relation between the wage rate and the costs of reproduction of labor power.

### "Rational," Managed, and Collective Consumption

Workers mediate the circulation of commodities by using their wages to purchase means of consumption produced by capitalists. Any failure on the part of workers to use their purchasing power correctly and rationally from the standpoint of the capitalist production and realization system will disrupt the circulation of commodities. In the early years of capitalist development this problem was not so important because trade with noncapitalist societies could easily take up any slack in effective demand. But with the transition to advanced capitalism, the internal market provided by the wage-labor force becomes of greater and greater significance. Also, as standards of living rise, in the sense that workers have more and more commodities available to them, so the potential for a breakdown from "irrationalities" in consumption increases. The failure to exercise a proper effective demand can be a source of crisis. And it was, of course, Keynes's major contribution to demonstrate to the capitalist class that under certain conditions the way out of a crisis manifest as a falling profit rate was not to cut wages but to increase them and thereby to expand the market.

This presumes, however, that workers are willing to spend their wages "rationally." If we assume, with Adam Smith, that mankind has an infinite and insatiable appetite for "trinkets and baubles," then there is no problem, but Malthus voiced another worry when he observed that the history of human society "sufficiently demonstrates [that] an efficient taste for luxuries and conveniences, that is, such a taste as will properly stimulate industry, instead of being ready to appear the moment it is required is a plant of slow growth."[16] Production may, as Marx averred, produce consumption and the mode of consumption, but it does not do so automatically, and the manner in which it does so is the locus of continuous struggle and conflict.[17]

Consider, first of all, the relationship between capitalist production and the household economy. In the United States in 1810, for example, "the best figures

---

16. T. R. Malthus, *Principles of Political Economy* (New York: Kelley Reprint, 1836), p. 321.
17. Marx, *Grundrisse*, Introduction.

available to historians show that . . . about two thirds of the clothing worn . . . was the product of household manufacture," but by 1860 the advent of industrial capitalism in the form of the New England textile industry had changed all that—"household manufactures had been eclipsed by the development of industrial production and a market economy."[18] Step by step, activities traditionally associated with household work are brought within the capitalist market economy—baking, brewing, preserving, cooking, food preparation, washing, cleaning, and even child-rearing and child socialization. And with respect to the built environment, house-building and maintenance become integrated into the market economy. In the United States in the nineteenth century a substantial proportion of the population built their own homes with their own labor and local raw materials. Now almost all units are built through the market system.

The advent of the factory system was a double-edged sword with respect to the household economy. On the one hand it extracted the wage earner(s) from the home. In the early years of industrial capitalism it did so for 12 or 14 hours a day and, under particularly exploitative conditions, forced the whole household—women and children as well as men—into the wage labor force (in this manner the wages of the *household* could remain stable in the face of a falling wage rate). Of these early years E. P. Thompson writes: "Each stage in industrial differentiation and specialization struck also at the family economy, disturbing customary relations between man and wife, parents and children, and differentiating more sharply between 'work' and 'life.' It was to be a full hundred years before this differentiation was to bring returns, in the form of labour-saving devices, back into the working woman's home."[19]

This "return" of commodities to the household is the other edge of the sword. The factory system produced use values for consumption more cheaply and with less effort than the household. The use values may be in the form of standardized products, but there should at least be more of them and therefore a material basis for a rising standard of living of labor. In the early years of industrial capitalism this did not in general happen. Laborers certainly worked longer hours and probably received less in the way of use values (although the evidence on this latter point is both patchy and controversial).[20] But the rising productivity of labor that occurs with accumulation, the consequent need to establish an internal market, and a century or more of class struggle have changed all of this. Consumer durables and consumption fund items (such as housing) have become very important growth sectors in the economy, and the political conditions and the material basis for a rising standard of living of labor have indeed been achieved.

The experience of labor in substituting work in the factory for work in the household has, therefore, both positive and negative aspects. But such substitu-

---

18. Thomas Bender, *Toward an Urban Vision: Ideas and Institutions in Nineteenth Century America* (Lexington, Kentucky: University Press of Kentucky, 1975), pp. 28–29; R. M. Tryon, *Household Manufactures in the United States, 1640–1860* (Chicago: University of Chicago Press, 1917).

19. E. P. Thompson, *The Making of the English Working Class* (Harmondsworth, Middlesex: 1968), p. 455.

20. Ibid., chap. 10; E. J. Hobsbawm, *Labouring Men* (London: Weidenfeld and Nicolson, 1964), chap. 7.

tions are not easily achieved because they involve the nature and structure of the family, the role of women in society, culturally entrenched traditions, and the like. The substitutions are themselves a focus of struggle. The rational consumption of commodities in relation to the accumulation of capital implies a certain balance between market purchases and household work. The struggle to substitute the former for the latter is significant because its outcome defines the very meaning of use values and the standard of living for labor in its commodity aspects. The construction of the built environment has to be seen, therefore, in the context of a struggle over a whole way of living and being.

Techniques of persuasion are widely used in advanced capitalist societies to ensure rational consumption. Moral exhortation and philanthropic enterprise are often put to work "to raise the condition of the laborer by an improvement of his mental and moral powers and to make a rational consumer of him."[21] The church, the press, and the schools can be mobilized on behalf of rational consumption at the same time as they can be vehicles for genuinely autonomous working-class development. And then, of course, there are always the blandishments of the ad-men and the techniques of Madison Avenue.

It would be idle to pretend that "the standard of living of labor" has been unaffected by these techniques. But, again, we are dealing with a double-edged sword. They may in fact also exert what Marx called a "civilizing influence" on labor and be used by labor to raise itself to a new condition of material and mental well-being that, in turn, provides a new and more solid basis for class struggle.[22] Conversely, the drive by labor to improve its condition may be perverted by a variety of stratagems into a definition of use values advantageous to accumulation rather than reflective of the real human needs of labor. The human demand for shelter is turned, for example, into a process of accumulation through housing production.

Rational consumption can also be ensured by the collectivization of consumption, primarily, although not solely, through the agency of the state.[23] Working-class demands for health care, housing, education, and social services of all kinds are usually expressed through political channels, and government arbitrates these demands and seeks to reconcile them with the requirements of accumulation. Many of these demands are met by the collective provision of goods and services, which means that everyone consumes them whether he or she likes it or not. Capitalist systems have moved more and more towards the collectivization of consumption because of the need, clearly understood in Keynesian fiscal policies, to manage consumption in the interests of accumulation. By collectivization, consumer choice is translated from the uncontrolled anarchy of individual action to the seemingly more controllable field of state

---

21. Marx, *Capital,* 2: 516; Dickens satirized the role of bourgeois philanthropy in relation to workers' consumption in *Hard Times.*

22. Marx, *Capital,* p. 408.

23. The theme of collective consumption has been examined in some detail by the French urbanists. See E. Preteceille, *Equipements Collectifs, Structures Urbaines et Consommation Sociale* (Paris: Centre de Sociologie Urbaine, 1975); and M. Castells, "Collective Consumption and Urban Contradictions in Advanced Capitalist Societies," in *Patterns of Advanced Societies,* ed. L. Lindberg (New York: 1975).

enterprise. This translation does not occur without a struggle over both the freedom of individual choice (which generates a strong antibureaucratic sentiment) and the definition of the use values involved (national defense versus subsidized housing for the poor, for example).

The built environment has a peculiar and important role in all of this. The bundle of resources that comprise it—streets and sidewalks, drains and sewer systems, parks and playgrounds—contains many elements that are collectively consumed. The public provision of such public goods is a "natural" form of collective consumption that capital can easily colonize through the agency of the state. Also, the sum of individual private decisions creates a public effect because of the pervasive externality effects that in themselves force certain forms of collective consumption through private action—if I fail to keep my yard neat then my neighbors cannot avoid seeing it. The built environment requires collective management and control, and it is therefore almost certain to be a primary field of struggle between capital and labor over what is good for accumulation and what is good for people.

The consumption fund has accounted for an increasing proportion of gross aggregate investment in the built environment since around 1890 in both Britain and the United States.[24] The housing sector in particular has become a major tool in macroeconomic policy for stabilizing economic growth, particularly in the United States where it has openly been used as a Keynesian regulator (not always, we should add, with success). And there are also strong multiplier effects to be taken into account. Housing construction, for example, requires complementary investments in other aspects of the built environment as well as in a wide range of consumer durables. The multipliers vary a great deal according to design and other considerations, but in all cases they are substantial.

These multipliers assume an added importance when we consider them in relation to the "coercive power" that the built environment can exercise over our daily lives. Its longevity and fixity in space, together with its method of financing and amortization, mean that once we have created it we must use it if the value that it represents is not to be lost. Under the social relations of capitalism, the built environment becomes an artifact of human labor that subsequently returns to dominate daily life. Capital seeks to mobilize it as a coercive force to help sustain accumulation. If our cities are built for driving, for example, then drive we must in order to live "normally" whether we like it or not. The highway lobby in the United States, the automobile, oil, and rubber industries and the construction interests, changed the face of America and used the coercive power of the built environment to ensure rational growth in the consumption of their products.[25] . . .

### The Interventions of Capital: A Conclusion

Capital seeks to discipline labor as much in the home as in the factory because it is only in terms of an all-embracing domination of labor in every facet of its life

---

24. S. Kuznets, *Capital in the American Economy: Its Formation and Financing* (Princeton, New Jersey: Princeton University Press, 1961).

25. See the accounts by J. Flink, *The Car Culture* (Cambridge, Massachusetts: M.I.T. Press, 1975); and H. Leavitt, *Superhighway—Super Hoax* (Garden City, New York: Doubleday, 1970).

that the "work ethic" and the "bourgeois values" necessarily demanded by the capitalist work process can be created and secured. The promotion of home-ownership for workers establishes the workers' allegiance to the principle of private property and therefore fits with this general stratagem. Sometimes conflicting with this drive we see that capital also needs to organize the consumption of the workers to ensure that it is cheap and rational from the standpoint of accumulation. The collectivization of consumption tends to take away the sense of individual responsibility and thereby undercuts the notion of bourgeois individualism if pushed too far. And running as a counterthread in all of this we see the need on the part of capital to promote in the workforce a sense of satisfaction and contentment that will lead to spontaneous cooperation and efficiency in the work place. This condition cannot be cultivated without giving the worker at least the illusion of freedom of choice in the living place and of healthy and satisfying relation to nature in the consumption sphere. Such illusions are pervasive but not always easy to sustain in the face of the realities enforced by the necessities of accumulation for accumulation's sake, production for production's sake. And the conditions in the work place can never be that easily concealed, no matter how mountainous the mystifications.

Nevertheless, the response of labor to its own condition is constantly subjected to the interventions and mediations of capital. As labor seeks to reorganize its mode of living to compensate for the degradations and disciplines of factory work, so capital seeks to colonize and pervert these efforts for its own purposes, sometimes to be turned cruelly against labor in the course of class struggle. Labor strives to raise its living standards by reducing the cost of living and increasing the use values it can command, but capital constantly seeks to subvert this drive, often through the agency of the state, into a reduction in the value of labor power and into "rational" modes of consumption understood from the standpoint of accumulation. As labor seeks relief from a degrading relation to nature in the work place, so capital seeks to parlay that into a mystified relation to nature in the consumption sphere. As labor seeks more control over the collective conditions of its existence, so capital seeks to establish collectivized forms of consumption and individual homeownership. The power of capital is omnipresent in the very definition of "a use value in the built environment for labor."

Conflicts in the living place are, we can conclude, mere reflections of the underlying tension between capital and labor. Appropriators and the construction faction mediate the forms of conflict—they stand between capital and labor and thereby shield the real source of tension from view. The surface appearance of conflicts around the built environment—the struggles against the landlord or against urban renewal—conceals a hidden essence that is nothing more than the struggle between capital and labor.

Capital may be omnipresent in such struggles, but it is neither omniscient nor omnipotent. The dynamics of accumulation require periodic rationalizations through crises that affect the working class in the form of bouts of widespread unemployment. At such moments the plans to coopt labor by the provision of "healthful and satisfying" living environments, by a contented relation to nature in the living place, go awry. In using the built environment as a coercive tool over consumption, capital ultimately coerces itself because it sets the conditions for the realization of values quite literally in a sea of concrete. And once committed, capital cannot go back. Pullman discovered this elemental fact in his ill-fated model town. When conditions of over-accumulation become apparent in the economy at large it became necessary to lay off workers, but Pullman could not do so because the profits to be had from the town were contingent upon full employment in the factory. The solution for the individual capitalist is to withdraw from the production of consumption fund items for the workers he or she employs. But the problem remains for the capitalist system as a whole. As problems of overaccumulation arise in capitalist societies—and arise they must—so the most well-laid plans of the capitalist fall by the wayside and the mechanisms for mystification, cooptation, disciplining labor, and inculcating the work ethic and bourgeois virtues, begin to crumble. And it is at just such times that labor recognizes that the bargain that it has struck with capital is no bargain at all but founded on an idealized mystification. The promises of capital are seen to be just that and incapable of fulfillment. And it also becomes evident that the needs of labor for use values in the built environment are incapable of being met by the captains of the system who promise so much but who can deliver so little.

## Class Consciousness, Community Consciousness, and Competition

The phrase, "the standard of living of labor," plainly cannot be understood outside of the context of actual class struggles fought over a long period in particular places around the organization of both work and living. This continuously shifting standard defines the needs of labor with respect to use values— consumption fund items—in the built environment. Individual workers have different needs, of course, according to their position in the labor force, their familial situation, and their individual requirements. At the same time, the processes of wage rate determination in the work place yield different quantities of exchange value to workers in different occupational categories. The social power that this money represents can be used to procure control over certain use values in the built environment. The way this money is used affects the appropriation of rent and the functioning of the price signals that induce the flow of capital into the production of new consumption fund items. We can envisage three general situations.

Consider, first, a situation in which each worker seeks independently to command for his or her own private use the best bundle of resources in the best location. We envisage a competitive war of all against all, a society in which the ethic of "possessive individualism" has taken root in the consciousness of workers in a very fundamental way. If the use values available in the built environment are limited, which is usually the case, then individuals make use of their market power and bid for scarce resources in the most advantageous locations. At its most elemental level this competition is for survival chances, for each worker knows that the ability to survive is dependent upon the ability to secure access to a particular bundle of resources in a reasonably healthy location. There is also competition to acquire "market capacity"—that bundle of attitudes, understandings, and skills that permits the worker to sell his or her labor power at a higher wage rate than the average.[26] Symbols of status, prestige, rank, and importance (even self-respect) may also be acquired by procuring command over particular resources in prestigious locations. These symbols may be useful in that they help a worker gain an easier entry into a particularly privileged stratum within the wage labor force. And finally we can note that if the relation to nature in the work place is felt to be as degrading as it truly is, then there is a positive incentive to seek a location far enough away that the "facts of production" are in no way represented in the landscape. In other words, workers may compete to get as far as possible away from the work place (the automobile proves particularly useful for this purpose).

The competitive situation that we have here outlined is in most respects identical to that assumed in neoclassical models of land use determination in urban areas.[27] Individual households, such models assume, attempt to maximize their utility by competing with each other for particular bundles of goods in particular locations subject to a budget constraint. If it is assumed that the two most important "goods" being competed for are locations with lower aggregate transportation costs and housing space, then it can be shown with relative ease that individuals will distribute themselves in space according to (1) the distribution of employment opportunities, usually assumed to be collected together in one central location, and (2) the relative marginal propensities to consume transportation services and living space in the context of the overall budget constraint. Competitive bidding under these conditions will generate a differential rent surface that, in the case of a single employment center, declines with distance from the center at the same time as it distributes individuals by income in space. In this case the ability to appropriate differential rent is entirely created by competitive behavior within the working class. Also, if new development is typically distributed in response to the pricing signals set by such differential rents, then it is easy to show that a spatial structure to the built environment will be created that reflects, to large degree, social and wage stratifications within the labor force.

The second situation that we wish to consider is one in which collective action in space—community action—is important. The pervasive externality effects and the collective use of many items in the built environment mean that it is in the self-interest of individuals to pursue modest levels of collective action.[28] Workers who are homeowners know that the value of the savings tied up in the house depends on the actions of others. It is in their common interest to collectively curb "deviant" behaviors, bar "noxious" facilities, and to ensure high standards of public service. This collectivization of action may go well beyond

---

26. See Anthony Giddens, *The Class Structure of the Advanced Societies* (London: Harper and Row, 1973), p. 103.

27. See, for example, W. Alonso, *Location and Land Use* (Cambridge: Harvard University Press, 1964); and E. S. Mills, *Studies in the Structure of the Urban Economy* (Baltimore: Johns Hopkins Press, 1972).

28. The theory of self-interested collective action is laid out in Mancur Olson, *The Logic of Collective Action* (Cambridge: Harvard University Press, 1965), but the theory of community is a mess that will require a good deal of sorting out.

that required out of pure individual self-interest. A consciousness of place, "community consciousness," may emerge as a powerful force that spawns competition between communities for scarce public investment funds, and the like. Community competition becomes the order of the day.

This process relates to the appropriation of rent in an interesting way. Community control enables those in control to erect barriers to investment in the built environment. The barriers may be selective—the exclusion of low-income housing, for example—or more or less across the board, a ban on all forms of future growth. Actions of this sort have been common in suburban jurisdictions in the United States in recent years. The cartel powers of local government are in effect being mobilized to control investment through a variety of legal and planning devices. Homeowners may use these controls to maintain or enhance the value of their properties. Developers may seek to use such controls for rather different purposes. But "community consciousness" typically creates small legal "islands" within which monopoly rents are appropriatable, often by one faction of labor at the expense of another faction. This latter situation gives rise to internecine conflicts within the working class along parochialist community-based lines. The spatial structure of the city is very different under these conditions compared to the product of individual competition.

The third kind of situation we can envisage is that of a fully class-conscious proletariat struggling against all forms of exploitation, whether they be in the work place or in the living place. Workers do not use their social power as individuals to seek individual solutions; they do not compete with each other for survival chances, for ability to acquire market capacity, for symbols of status and prestige. They fight collectively to improve the lot of all workers everywhere and eschew those parochialist forms of community action that typically lead one faction of labor to benefit at the expense of another (usually the poor and underprivileged).

Under such conditions the appropriation of rent cannot be attributed to the competitive behavior of individual workers or of whole communities. It has to be interpreted, rather, as something forced upon labor in the course of class struggle. A differential rent surface may arise in an urban area, but it does so not because labor automatically engages in competitive bidding, but because the class power of the appropriators is used to extract a rent to the maximum possible, given that resources are scarce and that they exist in a relative space. Because we witness a consequent social stratification (according to income) in space, and a development process that exacerbates this social ordering, we cannot infer that this is simply a reflection of individual workers expressing their "subjective utilities" through the market. Indeed, it may express the exact opposite—the power of the appropriators to force certain choices on workers no matter what the individual worker may think or believe. The power to appropriate rent is a class relation and we have to understand it that way if we are to understand how residential differentiation emerges within cities and the degree to which this phenomenon is the outcome of free or forced choices.[29]

---

29. I have attempted a preliminary analysis on this theme in David Harvey, "Class Structure in a Capitalist Society and the Theory of Residential Differentiation," in *Processes in Physical and Human Geography,* ed. M. Chisholm, P. Hagget, and R. F. Peel (London, 1975).

The three situations we have examined—competitive individualism, community action, and class struggle—are points on a continuum of possibilities. We cannot automatically assume labor to be at any particular point on this continuum. This is something to be discovered by concrete investigations of particular situations. The United States, for example, appears to be more strongly dominated by competitive individualism and community consciousness compared to the more class-conscious working class in Europe. From the standpoint of capital, individual and community competition is advantageous because it then seems as if the appropriation of rent results from labor's own actions rather than from the actions of the appropriators themselves. The overt forms of conflict around the built environment depend, therefore, upon the outcome of a deeper and often hidden ideological struggle for the consciousness of those doing the struggling. This deeper struggle between individual, community, and class alignments and consciousness, provides the context in which daily struggles over everyday issues occur.

# Selective Further Reading

Adam, H., *Modernizing Racial Domination* (Berkeley: University of California Press, 1971).

Baron, Harold, 'Racial Domination in Advanced Capitalism: A Theory of Nationalism and Divisions in the Labour Market', in *Labor Market Segmentation,* ed. R. C. Edwards et al. (Lexington, Mass.: D.C. Heath, 1975).

Berghe, P., van den, *Race and Racism* (New York: Wiley, 1967).

Blauner, R., *Racial Oppression in America* (New York: Harper & Row, 1972).

Castells, Manuel, *The Urban Question* (Cambridge, Mass.: M.I.T. Press, 1977).

Castles, S., and G. Kosak, *Immigrant Workers and Class Structure in Western Europe* (Oxford: Oxford University Press, 1973).

Cloward, R. A., and Frances F. Piven, *The Politics of Turmoil* (New York: Pantheon, 1974).

Daniels, Roger, and Harry Kitano, *American Racism* (Englewood Cliffs, N.J.: Prentice-Hall, 1970).

Davies, R., 'The White Working Class in South Africa', *New Left Review* 82 (1973).

Grappert, G., and H. Rose, eds., *The Social Economy of Cities, Urban Affairs Annual Review* no. 9 (Beverly Hills: Sage, 1975).

Glazer, N., and D. P. Moynihan, *Ethnicity* (Cambridge, Mass.: Harvard University Press, 1975).

Harvey, David, *Social Justice and the City* (London and Baltimore: Edward Arnold, 1973).

———, 'The Political Economy of Urbanization in Advanced Capitalist Societies: The Case of the United States', *Urban Affairs Annual Review* no. 9 (Beverly Hills: Sage, 1975).

Hecter, M., *Internal Colonialism* (London: Routledge, 1975).

Kapitalistate, San Francisco Bay Area Group, eds., *The Urban Crisis and the Capitalist State, Kapitalistate* 4–5 (Summer 1976).

Piven, Frances F., and Richard A. Cloward, *Poor People's Movements* (New York: Pantheon Books, 1977).

Reich, Michael, 'The Economics of Racism', in *Problems in Political Economy,* ed. David M. Gordon (Lexington, Mass.: D. C. Heath, 1971).

Rex, J., and T. Moore, *Race, Community, and Conflict* (Oxford: Oxford University Press, 1975).

Stone, M., 'Housing and Class Struggle', *Antipode* 7(2) (1975).

Tabb, Bill, and Larry Sawyer, eds., *Marxism and the Metropolis* (Oxford: Oxford University Press, 1977).

Wolpe, Harold, 'The Theory of Internal Colonialism: The South African Case', in *Beyond the Sociology of Development,* ed. I. Oxaal et al. (London: Routledge, 1975).

Zubaida, S., ed., *Race and Racialism* (London: Tavistock, 1970).

# · VIII ·

# Classes in Eastern Europe

# Introduction

In Marx's day, socialism was an anticipated form of society in which class divisions would be transcended, the division of labour and the state radically reorganised. In our times, socialism is no longer only a project for the future but an extant reality. The industrialised world is partitioned between capitalism and socialism, between the 'liberal democracies' of the West and Japan, and the 'peoples' democracies' of Eastern Europe. It is no longer adequate to analyse the class structure of the capitalist societies without reference to what Bahro has called the 'actually existing' socialist countries.

The question of how what we shall refer to as the 'state socialist' societies of Eastern Europe should be characterised has proved a highly controversial one. A welter of divergent viewpoints have been expressed, in both Marxist and non-Marxist traditions of thought, about to what extent and in what ways the state socialist societies differ from Western capitalism. These diverse views, however, tend to be clustered around one main line of disagreement. One type of standpoint tends to emphasise the similarities between the capitalist and state socialist societies, although there are major contrasts in the reasons that are given for this. The so-called 'convergence' thesis, expressed in its most unequivocal form by C. Kerr in his book *Industrialism and Industrial Man,* holds that industrialism necessarily produces similar sets of social changes across societies. Hence, as industrialism matures, the societies of East and West tend to become more alike in spite of supposedly having very distinct economic and political systems. A quite different version of this standpoint has been advanced by some Western Marxist writers. These authors (among whom, in this book, may be included Braverman and Marglin) argue that the Eastern European societies never really broke substantially with capitalism. The utilisation of 'scientific management' in the Soviet Union, according to this view, is symptomatic of the fact that the capitalist mode of production was not seriously undermined.

A second set of approaches tends to emphasise that there are basic differences between the capitalist societies and their state socialist counterparts. Again, however, there is dissensus over what these differences are and what accounts for them. One view is the orthodox ideology of the Eastern European societies themselves, that is, that these societies represent, in concrete form, the type of social order which Marx envisaged as succeeding capitalism. A more common version among Western analysts is that the divergencies between capitalist and state socialist societies result from the greater political control of economic life found in the latter as compared with the former. These are not societies in which either the state or the division of labour has been transcended. On the contrary, the state, dominated internally by the Communist Party, has a preeminent influence over economic activity. However, so this viewpoint runs, this does have the very important consequence that class is a less salient feature of state socialism than of capitalism. For the class structure of the capitalist countries depends upon the centrality of private property as capital, organised through labour and product markets. Private ownership of capital is either suppressed or strictly regulated in the Eastern European societies in favour of state direction of the economy. We should perhaps declare *parti pris* at this juncture: in using the phrase 'state socialist' societies, we imply our general concordance with this type of viewpoint.

Of the four contributions to this section, Frank Parkin's is the most generalised and ambitious. He attempts to elucidate some of the key features of state socialism in terms of Lockwood's distinction between 'social integration' and 'system integration'. The first of these terms refers to the relations between groups, strata, or classes within a society; the second refers to the relations between different institutional sectors of a society—somewhat analogous to the 'levels' recognised by Althusser and Poulantzas. According to Lockwood, both dimensions appear in Marx's analysis of capitalist development, but it is not evident what the relationship between them is. The first takes the form of class struggle between capital and wage labour, the second that of the contradiction between forces and relations of production (or, as we expressed this in Section One, between private appropriation and socialised production). The core of Parkin's argument is that the notion of contradiction in respect of system integration—'system contradiction'—can be usefully applied to the analysis of state socialist societies.

His case is based upon the idea that the notion of system contradiction can be usefully connected to social integration in respect of what he calls 'power equilibrium' and 'elite differentiation'. Power equilibrium refers to a situation in which the sources of power in a society are in some sort of stable alignment with one another, 'power disequilibrium' to where they are out of alignment. Where the second of these two conditions exists, there will tend to be a polarisation or fracturing of elites: 'elite differentiation'. Parkin's theory is that it is only where a society is characterised by elite differentiation that system contradictions are likely to produce substantial social change. He regards this as broadly consistent with what Marx has to say about the origins of transformations in class societies (save that he wishes to apply the scheme to state socialism). Marx's historical materialism, Parkin argues, could be represented in these terms as follows. A society becomes likely to undergo revolutionary change when there is disequilibrium between economic and political power: when a class that has achieved control of production does not hold the reins of government. The tensions thus created are resolved by a process of political transformation, by means of which the economically dominant class achieves political power.

The proletariat is the 'ascendant class' in the transformation of capitalism; it achieves economic power in an economy increasingly socialised 'from within'; and its acquisition of political power, creating socialism, brings power again into equilibrium. Leninism, in Parkin's view, involves a major deviation from Marx's ideas because it presumes that an economically weak class can first of all make the revolution and then fabricate the economic supremacy upon which its political rule would be founded. Here we find major sources of tension in the state socialist societies: the Bolshevik seizure of power in Russia and subsequent 'revolutions' in Eastern Europe after the Second World War introduced power disequilibrium. Political power is concentrated in the heads of the party apparatus; but as the Eastern European societies are increasingly developed economically, the economic 'base' becomes more and more distanced from, and out of alignment with, the monopoly of political power by the centralised party. A newly ascendant class—the intelligentsia and technical specialists—emerges which does not hold political power. On the level of elite differentiation, the result is the recurrence of conflicts between party officials and the leaders of these other groupings, which in principle could eventually lead to system transformation of the state socialist societies. Such a possibility is strengthened by the semicolonial status of the Eastern European countries in relation to the Soviet Union; for the intelligentsia, educated in the varying traditions of their specific countries, are the standard bearers of nationalistic sentiments.

The problem of the nature of political and economic rule in the state socialist societies is one of the most hotly debated issues of all. Has the Communist Party apparatus simply become another ruling class, different in character, but perhaps even more powerful than capitalist classes in the Western societies? Alec Nove offers a cogent summary of the major issues at stake here, concentrating his attention however on the Soviet Union. (An important qualification should be inserted here: the Soviet Union may be no more 'typical' of the state socialist societies in general than the United States is of capitalist ones. The reader should beware of assuming that the whole of Eastern Europe simply duplicates the social system of the USSR.)

In the Soviet Union, Nove points out, the economy, polity, and judiciary, as well as educational and cultural institutions, are acknowledged by all commentators to be in the hands of the Communist Party. The party is in turn a highly centralised organisation internally, in which rank-and-file party members have very little way of influencing decisions taken at the top. Those in the higher echelons of the party enjoy material rewards that set them apart from the mass of the population. Although there seems in some significant respects to be more vertical social mobility, especially into elite positions, than in the capitalist

societies, precise comparison is difficult. However, higher education has become virtually a prerequisite for access to top positions; and access to higher
education is certainly skewed in favour of the sons and daughters of those who
themselves have a degree or equivalent qualification.

Should these facts be taken to indicate that there is a 'ruling class' in the
USSR? Or should we speak rather of the existence of a powerful elite, which is
sufficiently different from dominant classes in the West that it would be misleading to call it a class? The matter is not, as it may sound, merely a trite issue of
terminology. For the way these questions are answered depends upon, and in
some part is an expression of, structural differences that may distinguish the
state socialist from the Western societies.

As Nove stresses, some such differences are so plain that they must be
involved in elucidating the questions just posed. Centralised planning of production is highly developed in the Soviet Union and goes well beyond anything
observed in the efforts of Western states to 'intervene' in economic life. This can
be easily illustrated. In Western economies, the production and distribution of
goods, even in monopolistic or oligopolistic sectors, is fundamentally ordered
through market mechanisms. In the Soviet Union, on the other hand, inputs
and outputs of the productive system are controlled by a centralised political
apparatus. The 'means of production' are not owned by party officials as private
property which can be bought and sold; but as against this point it could be
argued that their effective control over production is much greater than any
single grouping in Western societies.

A range of different theoretical tacks have been taken in trying to cope with
these circumstances conceptually. One view would have it that the Soviet Union is a 'single class society'. No one owns property in the means of production,
and hence everyone is a 'worker', although there remains a hierarchy of inequalities. Nove rejects this view because it fails to come to terms precisely with the
extraordinary concentration of power in the hands of the party elite. Another
approach is that developed by Trotsky and favoured by many others since.
Trotsky regarded the USSR as a 'degenerate workers' state': a society which
began along the right lines but which degenerated into a bureaucratic tyranny as
noxious as anything ever envisaged by Weber. Nove argues, however, that the
USSR was never a 'workers' state', in the sense that the mass of the working
population ever participated actively in the operations of political power.

A third position, and a very common one today among Eastern dissidents,
and both Marxists and non-Marxists in the West, is that the party rulers have in
fact become a new ruling class. Milovan Djilas's formulation of this view, in his
book *The New Class,* is one of the most well known. It has affinities with the
views of Poulantzas, as set out in Section Two. According to Djilas, legal
ownership of property is not particularly important to the existence of a class
system. What matters is whether a minority is able to control the means of
production, and the state, so as to exploit a majority. And this, according to
him, is exactly the situation in the Soviet Union. A similar claim is made by the
French economist Charles Bettelheim. His terminology is slightly different; a
'new bourgeoisie' is dominant in the Soviet Union. But the argument is parallel:
it is the fact that a minority control the (centralised) means of production which
counts, not the fact that private capital has legally been abolished.

Nove also has reservations about this type of standpoint. If there is a 'new class' which dominates economically and politically, and the nature of this class is to be explained in terms of an extension or adaptation of Marxist concepts, we must consider the issue of surplus production. There is a sense, Nove says, in which the privileges of the party elite are acquired through appropriation of surplus produced by the mass of the working population. But the *mechanism* of appropriation is via political power, not through surplus value as in capitalism. Moreover, only a small proportion of total surplus production finds its way into the pockets of the elite, even though they control the allocation of resources involved in creating and distributing the fruits of the productive activity of the rest of the population. Finally, it is misleading to speak of the Soviet Union, as Bettelheim does for instance, as a 'state capitalist' society. The rulers of the state are not capitalists, and the accumulation process they control is not produced via 'capitalistic enterprise', save in a very attenuated sense of that term.

Once more we come to that contentious word, 'control'—which the reader will note has turned up in a variety of contexts in the contributions to this book. Is 'ownership' simply a subcategory of 'control'? Nove effectively concludes not. Where ownership refers to *capital,* it implies not just power as such, but certain mechanics of how power operates, within a broader socioeconomic and political context. State officials cannot (legally, at least) make capital investments or inherit wealth; the 'means of production' in which they are the dominant power is not identical to the 'means of production' in capitalism. We therefore need a different terminology from that available in Marx, but Nove seems equivocal about what that terminology should be. If we are to persist with the term 'class', we should be clear that it cannot be used in the same way as it has been employed to describe the class structure of capitalist societies.

Nove is concerned with the upper echelons of political power in Soviet society, Murray Yanowitch with industrial hierarchy and the economic position of the working class. His discussion serves as an interesting counterbalance to the idea that in Soviet industrial management a version of Taylorism has reigned supreme. Soviet literature on industrial management recognises certain similarities with managerial systems in the West. But differences are also emphasised. According to official Soviet theory, in the USSR management is performed in the interests of 'society as a whole', not to further the interests of particular enterprises. It is also claimed that workers have substantial, and increasing, opportunities to influence managerial decisions. However, Leninist principles are still regarded as fundamental. Political and economic leadership are supposed to be unified—which, in practice, Yanowitch says, means that the party is responsible for formulating overall policy. The role of the party, however, is not supposed to be one of merely giving directives from above; 'democratic centralism' is held, in Soviet management theory, to encourage the combination of initiative from below with centralised policy formation. A further principle, that of 'one-man management', has to be looked at with some prudence: both because it has direct connections with how Soviet management actually operates and because it seems more authoritarian than it in fact is. What it means is that each level of an enterprise—those of top executive, shop, and section manager—is ultimately the responsibility of a single individual. This does not, in fact, imply the existence of a unilateral relation of power. For the accountability of the individual at each level is always 'upwards': subordinates are not to be blamed when things go wrong. Thus 'one-man management' is compatible with 'collegial' or consultative relations involving various levels of the enterprise. For this is a way in which the potential pitfalls of personal accountability can be avoided; a decision taken consensually has more weight than one taken purely individually, even if the individual is in the end accountable for its consequences.

The most interesting parts of Yanowitch's survey concern schemes initiated to 'humanise' Soviet management. The management principles described above were formulated at an early stage of Soviet industrial development, prior to World War II. The context in which they were constructed differs significantly from the present one since the Soviet economy has passed through its stage of 'forced industrialisation', employing large numbers of ex-peasants with little knowledge of, or skills in, industrial production. In more recent times, although Leninist rhetoric is still formally acknowledged, significant changes have occurred in management theory and practice. A version of 'human relations' ideology has appeared, explicitly indebted to Western literature, as Leninist principles were to Taylorism. As in the West this seems in some part due to a perceived need to accommodate to the demands of potentially recalcitrant workers who have a good deal of potential informal power on the shop floor.

The real influence of 'humanising management', Yanowitch says, is difficult to assess. Part of the problem is that participation in managerial decisions, in Soviet ideology, is supposed to be something that has already been substantially achieved, as compared with the capitalist West. But there is strong evidence of real processes of reorganisation in Soviet industrial relations. There is open recognition that, as one Soviet writer describes it, 'democratic centralism' has often in practice meant 'bureaucratic centralism' and that the abolition of private capital is not the same as the securing of industrial democracy. Soviet sociological studies of industrial organisations and collective farms have documented the implications of this for the actual distribution of power within these productive settings. Soviet social science no longer ignores completely the problem of what constitutes 'control'!

Elizabeth Garnsey's discussion provides something of a general backdrop to Yanowitch's analysis. She criticises both versions of the notion that Soviet industry is essentially similar to that of Western capitalism: the 'convergence' theory, on the one hand, and the view of Braverman, Marglin, etc., on the other. Her approach places particular emphasis upon the division of labour. Rather than asking how class inequalities are perpetuated by the division of labour, she argues, we should enquire into the factors that have influenced its specific development in the Soviet Union. These factors, she claims, have been little studied and show significant divergencies between the Soviet Union and the capitalist societies. In the Soviet Union, centralised planning decisions govern the accumulation process rather than those taken at the level of the industrial corporation. Market mechanisms play at best a subdued role, and the generation of profit is not the guiding element in investment policies. Shortage of labour rather than unemployment is a further distinctive feature of the Soviet economy.

As a consequence, the allocation of resources in the USSR shows quite a different pattern to the West, even though all the capitalist societies now have large public sectors. Soviet managers do not determine investment policies or the form which investment allocation takes; neither are modes of technological innovation determined at the level of the enterprise. Unlike the majority of their Western counterparts, Soviet managers tend to resist the introduction of novel technologies, as technological innovation may disrupt planning targets. The constant pressure to reduce labour costs through the technical reorganisation of production, so characteristic of capitalism, is less acutely felt. Soviet managers accept overmanning to a degree impossible in a capitalist economy, even though industrialists in the West may face strong union opposition to policies which reduce the size of the labour force.

We should distinguish, Garnsey suggests, three aspects of the division of labour. One is the character of labour tasks, the 'labour process'; the second is the sectoral distribution of workers in the economy; the third is the overall relation between occupations in the economy, the occupational structure. The intersections between these have developed differently in the Soviet Union as compared with the capitalist societies. In the Soviet pattern of industrial development, the expansion of manufacturing in the process of industrialisation was the result of state policy, not an outcome of rising demand for consumer goods. A labour force recruited largely from the peasantry was incorporated in developing heavy industries in which technology was copied from that of the West. The early Soviet labour force was subject to strict labour discipline at the same time as union control was substantially appropriated by the Communist Party. Taylorism was in a certain sense, in the relatively early stages of industrial development, more strongly inculcated than in the West. But the fact that it was not geared to technological innovation at enterprise level led to quite different consequences. On the one hand, entrenched workers' organisations were less able to resist its impact; on the other hand, managers were not able, or required, to link it to the furtherance of technological innovation. If Yanowitch is right, this pattern may be changing; but it remains to be seen how significant such changes might be.

# · 27 ·

# System Contradiction and Political Transformation

## Frank Parkin

### I

David Lockwood has drawn attention to two related but analytically distinct types of integration in society: social integration, referring to the relationship between groups—more especially classes or strata; and system integration referring to the degree of connectedness between institutional parts of the social order.[1] The former type of integration concerns the social relations between actors, so that the problem of order in society is posed in terms of moral or normative categories. The second type of integration directs attention to the somewhat more technical or non-normative aspects of order, concerning as it does the degree of 'fit' or compatibility between various functionally connected institutions. Both types of integration are of course central to Marx's theory of social change. For Marx, the antagonisms stemming from weaknesses in social integration (exemplified in the extreme case by class polarization) plus the weaknesses in system integration (the contradiction between the forces of production and the relations of production) are understood to be the twin mechanisms responsible for social transformation. As many critics have pointed out, the exact nature of the link between these two different processes was never clearly specified by Marx. But it does seem apparent that system contradiction is regarded as causally prior to the cleavage, and ultimate conflict, between classes,

---

· From *Archives enropéennes de sociologie* 13 (1972): 45–62.

1. David Lockwood, Social Integration and System Integration, *in* George K. Zollschan *and* Walter Hirsch (eds.), *Explorations in Social Change* (London, Routledge, 1964).

since it's not until these contradictions in the system become irresolvable that the stage is set for the final showdown between contending classes.

Given the importance that this notion of system contradiction occupies in Marx's whole theoretical scheme it is, as Lockwood points out, rather surprising that it should have been largely disregarded by sociologists—even by those specifically concerned with conflict models. Instead, the main preoccupation has been with class antagonism, which can in some respects be regarded as a derivative phenomenon. This is, perhaps, partly because of the difficulty in establishing clearly the "breakdown mechanisms" in different societies, including capitalism. Moreover, given the apparent ability of this particular system to survive the almost countless prophecies of imminent collapse, through crises of overproduction, the falling rate of profit, or whatever, it is understandable that sociologists should have come to regard the notion of system contradiction with some suspicion.

In this paper I try to show that the concept can be usefully employed in analysing certain aspects of the problem of order in industrial society. And there is a certain pleasing irony in the fact that it seems particularly appropriate to the understanding of state socialist societies, notwithstanding the official Marxist view that the overthrow of capitalism heralds the end of internal contradictions. The view advanced here is that the notion of system contradiction is only useful when considered in relation to certain aspects of the stratification order, and more particularly, with what could be referred to as "power equilibrium" and "elite differentiation". By power equilibrium is meant simply a high degree of congruence between the various dimensions of stratification, such that economic, social and political power follow roughly the same pattern of distribution. Power disequilibrium is said to occur where these three elements of the stratification order do not exhibit the same general profile. It may be suggested that under this condition there will typically be alternative or competing bases of elite legitimation, so giving rise to a differentiation or polarization of elites. In a nutshell my argument is that only when a society is characterized by elite differentiation do system contradictions become significant for the problem of social transformation. Where, on the other hand, the stratification order is in equilibrium, the elite structure will typically be one of uniformity, not differentiation. Under these conditions, weaknesses in system integration will not generally entail a threat to the social order.

In a sense, the whole of the scheme adopted here could be said to rest on some kind of equilibrium model; but not so much the equilibrium model derived from structural-functionalism, as that implicit in Marx's own formula. The difference is of course that the structural-functionalist approach is to treat the social system as a self-regulating mechanism operating in a timeless void. Whereas for Marx, the states of equilibrium and disequilibrium are understood as alternating processes by which societies are moved along in a sequence of historical change. One could say that, for Marx, a society becomes ripe for social transformation when the stratification order is in disequilibrium; that is, when the class which is (say) economically dominant through its control of the productive process is not the class which is politically dominant. The tensions which this imbalance generates can only be resolved by one and the same class winning mastery over all the elements of power—social, economic and political. The paradigm case is of course that of an ascendant bourgeoisie being politically subordinate to a declining aristocracy. The ideal-type bourgeois revolution can thus be seen as the mechanism which restores the stratification order to a state of equilibrium by concentrating all the dimensions of power in the hands of one social class. The next stage in the developmental sequence is then scheduled for that point in time when capitalism itself would give rise to new forms of disequilibrium which would be resolved in the same conclusive manner.

Crucial to the understanding of this whole conceptual scheme is the role of the ascendant class. For Marx, a social class only assumes dominance in society when it is the social embodiment of those institutional and material forces which define the essential character of the social system—or its "core institutional order". Thus the historical progression of societies through different stages is closely linked to the ascendance of that particular class whose members possess the qualities and attributes best fitted to cope with the newly emergent material forces and new institutional tasks.[2] In true Darwinian fashion a class dominant in one epoch is earmarked for liquidation as soon as the social forces on which its dominance rests have given way to new conditions, so preparing the ground for the ascendancy of a different class better able to respond to the new challenge. Not until a social class has reached this state of ascendancy within the framework of the old order is it able to bring about system change by assuming political mastery.

Now it is clear from all this that the successful transition from capitalism to socialism must, in terms of Marx's theory, presuppose the emergence of a class which embodies a distinctive set of social and productive relationships of a non-bourgeois kind which contain the promise of resolving the contradictions within capitalism. To use Marx's gynaecological metaphor, the embryo of the new socio-economic system must always mature in the womb of the old order. It was therefore necessary for Marx to show that embryonic forms of socialism were developing within the body of capitalism, just as bourgeois social relations and a market economy had been slowly nurtured within the old feudal order. And Marx did in fact detect two different tendencies within capitalism which he took to be early forms of the emergent productive forces which would come to replace private property relations, and so prepare the ground for the demise of the bourgeoisie. The first of these developments was the rise of the joint stock company. He saw the separation of ownership from control, and the expansion of the shareholding system, as a corrosive force at work on capitalist property relations; and although this in itself was not to be understood as social ownership in its pure form, it was a transitionary stage to this ideal.

In stock companies the function is divorced from capital ownership, hence also labour is entirely divorced from ownership of means of production and surplus labour. This result of the ultimate development of capitalist production is a necessary transitional phase

---

2. One must here surely agree with Lockwood that "there is nothing metaphysical about the general notion of social relationships being somehow implicit in a given set of material conditions" (Lockwood, *op. cit.* p. 251).

towards the reconversion of capital into the property of producers, although no longer as the private property of the individual producers, but rather as the property of associated producers, as outright social property. . . .[3]

As Marx saw it, this development heralded "the abolition of the capitalist mode of production within the capitalist mode of production itself" and could thus be understood as "a mere phase of transition to a new form of production".[4]

A second and parallel development was the growth of the workers' co-operative movement. For Marx, this movement brought into being a new kind of property in which "the antithesis between labour and capital is overcome".[5] The co-operative factory system demonstrated "how a new mode of production naturally grows out of an old one, when the development of the material forces of production, and of the corresponding forms of social production have reached a particular stage. Without the factory system arising out of the capitalist mode of production there could have been no co-operative factories".[6]

Here then is evidence for the kind of development that Marx was intent on discovering—a new social form arising within the shell of the old—which for him is always a precondition for the ascendancy of a new class (in this case the proletariat), the class which is the social embodiment of the emergent productive forces. It is no part of Marx's scheme to suggest that a class which has *not* reached such a position of ascendancy could effectively become the new dominant class. As Avinieri has recently pointed out, the notion that the proletariat could assume power while it was still the totally subordinate class is a purely Leninist one.[7] For Lenin, the proletariat could make the revolution first and then set about creating the social and economic foundations upon which its political supremacy would rest. This is a complete reversion of Marx's priorities. For Marx, political power can only *actualize* the potential already *existing* within the society; it cannot fashion social and material realities according to some abstract formula or design. It could be argued then, that the revolution failed to bring about socialism in the Soviet Union not simply because it occurred in an economically backward society (which is the standard explanation) but because the proletariat was not the ascendant class.[8] For even if a society was economically advanced, the transition could still not properly be made while the proletariat was the totally subordinate class. Indeed given the fact that proletarian ascendancy does not appear to coincide with advanced industrialism, and that the cooperative movement and joint stock ownership no longer seem to be transitionary or embryonic forms of a new social order, then the very possibility of the successful transformation from capitalism to socialism becomes highly problematic. Expressed somewhat differently, in so far as the bourgeoisie remain the socially, economically and politically dominant class, then the

---

3. *Capital* (Moscow 1961), III, p. 428.

4. *Capital*, III, p. 429.

5. *Capital*, III, p. 431.

6. *Loc. cit.*

7. Shlomo Avinieri, *The Social and Political Thought of Karl Marx* (Cambridge 1968), pp. 181–182.

8. Cf. Plekhanov's prediction that the premature seizure of power in the name of the proletariat would result in a system of "Peruvian tutelage".

stratification order is in equilibrium. And under this condition there is no internal tension that has to be resolved through radical social transformation. This point is touched upon again later when the elite structure of modern capitalism is under discussion.

## II

As far as state socialist societies are concerned, the same equilibrium condition does not prevail. One could say in fact that the seizure of power created disequilibrium in the stratification order where previously there was none. Moreover, it is precisely as a result of this that weaknesses in system integration are a more distinctive feature of socialist society than of modern capitalism. Now weaknesses at the system level tend to find expression at the social level in the form of conflict between groups or collectivities; indeed these opposing groups may be even thought of as personifying conflicting system elements—that is, as social typifications of diffuse structural processes. In socialist society the key antagonisms occurring at the social level are those between the party and state bureaucracy on the one hand and the intelligentsia on the other. The power of the former rests upon their control of the political and administrative apparatus of the state, giving them effective legal guardianship of socialized property. The social power of the latter group inheres in its command of the skills, knowledge and general attributes which are held to be of central importance for the development of productive and scientific forces in modern industrial society. Examples of weaknesses in system integration, of which these conflicts are the social symptom, have received ample documentation. Probably the most familiar are those problems associated with the attempt to maximise industrial efficiency within the framework of a highly centralized political economy. The command system appears to operate quite effectively during the early stages of development, when the primary emphasis is on capital accumulation; but at more advanced stages of growth, and with the emphasis shifting to light industry and consumer goods production, the dirigist system becomes increasingly dysfunctional. It is when the crucial phase of the "second industrial revolution" is reached that the command mechanism becomes unable to cope satisfactorily with the volume of information and detailed decisions necessary to the smooth working of the economy. The leading east German economist, Fritz Behrens, was only one among many who pointed to a "contradiction [. . .] between the form of state direction of the economy and the content of the quickly developing economic substructure".[9] Attempts to resolve this contradiction have raised the delicate problem of how to curtail the economic powers of the central apparatus without eroding the party's monopoly of political authority. Resistance to economic reforms has been strongest among members of the party apparatus and state administration, whose personal authority would be seriously undermined by a radical switch from plan criteria to market criteria. Seen in ideal-typical terms, the controversy over the economy is most sharply expressed in the form

---

9. Cited by Thomas A. Baylis, "The New Economic System: The Role of the Technocrats in the DDR", *Survey*, LXI (1966), p. 141.

of conflict between the apparatchiki and the intelligentsia, respectively the main opponents and advocates of reform.[10] Czechoslovakia was an exceptional case only in the extent to which the latent but ever-present tensions between these two groups erupted into open political conflict—a showdown precipitated by the inability of the existing system to cope with economic crisis.[11]

It is not in the least fanciful to suggest that the crisis came about as a result of the forces of production coming into direct conflict with the social relations of production; in other words, that the legal and political order buttressing the command system had become a 'fetter' on the further development of productive forces. The events leading up to and culminating in the "Prague spring" might thus be seen as a paradigm case of system contradiction leading to pressures for internal transformation in line with the classic Marxist formula. Furthermore, a latter-day Marx seeking to locate within socialist society an ascendant class closely identified with the transformation, and capable of pushing it through, would doubtless find the intelligentsia the obvious candidate for the post. It seems clear that in all socialist states the intelligentsia occupies a position of high social and material standing in the stratification hierarchy by virtue of its command over socially valued knowledge and expertise. In empirical studies of status ranking, moreover, they are invariably shown to be higher in the scale of social honour than the party bureaucrats. In a sense, then, this group is popularly regarded, and seems to regard itself, as the social embodiment of those scientific, economic and creative forces which are felt to be indispensable to the quest for modernity and social progress.[12]

However, as in previous epochs, the ascendant class in socialist society is not the class which wields political power. Indeed, it is because political authority is concentrated elsewhere—in the hands of the party apparatus—that the stratification order can be characterized as one of disequilibrium. And this is a social condition which generates internal tensions that can only be fully resolved through a reconstitution of the different elements of power in the hands of the same social group. Seen from this angle, equilibrium could be restored by the accession to political power of the intelligentsia and the displacement of the apparatchiki. Once this was achieved (and again the events in Czechoslovakia give some indication of possible lines of development) the new men of power would be in a position to de-politicize the economy by introducing strategic shifts from plan to market.[13]

---

10. The struggles over economic reform cannot be understood in terms of the clearcut categories of a morality play. Western social scientists tend to explain opposition to the reforms solely in terms of the bureaucrats' defence of their own power and privileges, whereas the advocates of reform are seen merely to be acting in the national interest. The situation is more complex. *Both* groups invoke notions of the public good which also conceal claims to power.

11. Initially the most advanced state in the socialist bloc, Czechoslovakia had by 1963 become "the only industrial country in the entire world to register a decrease in industrial output, national income and real wages". Harry G. Schaffer, Czechoslovakia's New Economic Model, *in* George R. Feiwel (ed.), *New Currents in Soviet-Type Economics* (Scranton 1968), p. 466.

12. For a trenchant affirmation of this view see the analysis of modern society produced by the Czech Academy of Arts and Sciences under the editorship of Radovan Richta, *Civilization at the Crossroads: Social and Human Implications of the Scientific and Technological Revolution* (Prague 1967).

13. Cf. Ota Sik, *Plan and Market under Socialism* (Prague 1966).

It must be emphasized here that contradictions in the productive system should be understood as a particular case of a more general condition. Dysfunctions in the economy are largely attributable to the informational blocks which a highly centralized political structure tends to set up. But the central control of economic and technical information is merely part of a more generalized political surveillance over the dissemination of knowledge in all its forms. The embargo on the free circulation of ideas and information is a strategy designed to enhance system stability through the suppression of all social knowledge which detracts from official versions of reality. The existing socialist order would in fact be seriously undermined by any relaxation of the controls on knowledge, since the party's criteria of what counts as social fact cannot often be squared with common-sense criteria. However, the party's claim to the monopoly of truth is in effect self-defeating in that it negates the regime's attempts to secure moral support and system legitimacy. Direct political censorship of knowledge and information results not in the desired conformity of outlook but in widespread scepticism or disbelief in the validity of officially blessed facts. The sanctification of revolutionary truth is especially difficult to achieve in east European societies because of the state's inability to seal off competing versions of reality which emanate from neighbouring western sources. The credibility, and hence the legitimacy, of the socialist regime is naturally most suspect in the eyes of those with greatest access to external information—the intelligentsia—although clearly the broad mass of the population does not lack opportunities to compare official claims against personal experience. Thus although the present system would be unlikely to survive under conditions of free enquiry and open debate, the regime's very attempt to suppress politically unacceptable knowledge destroys those claims to moral authority by which it seeks to rule. This contradiction seems irresolvable within the existing order and is probably of greater import for system stability than are the contradictions associated with the productive sphere. Indeed, it may be quite possible for socialist states eventually to overcome many of the dysfunctions of a command economy without dismantling the apparatus of political control, as in the case of east Germany. But this would not eradicate the basic contradiction between the political censorship of knowledge and the quest for legitimacy, as again the east German case illustrates all too vividly.

## III

As previously suggested, one important reason why disequilibrium in the stratification order leads to pressures for internal change is that this is the social condition most amenable to the differentiation of elites. And part of the argument advanced here is that only when elites exhibit a high degree of differentiation are weaknesses in system integration likely to result in pressures making for system change. The reason that social disequilibrium and elite differentiation go hand in hand is that a non-crystallized stratification order provides multiple bases for elite recruitment and legitimacy. Medieval society provides the archetypal illustration of this, though a similar situation prevails in many kinds of pre-industrial society. In the standard case, the society will contain groups like the clergy, whose claims to authority rest upon sacramental knowledge; a military caste basing itself on the possession of arms and warrior skills; a merchant class deriving wealth and influence from the monopoly of trade; and so forth. Each group seeks to legitimize its power and privileges by reference to different criteria, and there are no commonly accepted criteria which could provide the basis for a uniform status order. Thus, where there are multiple bases of social legitimacy within the same society, the scene is set for the diversification of elites, all basing their claims to power on the possession of different status attributes.

In industrial society, this situation does not usually occur to the same extent. The long run tendency is for the reward structure to become closely tied to the division of labour, so that occupational and educational criteria come to provide the cornerstone of the whole edifice of stratification. Now, both socialist and capitalist versions of industrial society each contain an alternative source of elite recruitment and legitimacy to that primary one associated with the division of labour. In capitalist society, property ownership is the one obvious alternative; while in socialist society it is party office. Party elites and propertied elites might thus be said to be in a roughly similar structural situation in so far as the values which underwrite their privileged position are different from the values which guarantee the position of most other groups in society. To the extent, then, that we can detect quite distinct bases of legitimacy, the way seems clear for elite differentiation or cleavage in both types of society.

However, it would seem to be the case that this particular development is much more characteristic of socialist society than of modern capitalism. At any rate, there is no obvious counterpart in western society to the kind of elite polarization which manifested itself in Czechoslovakia, and which typically exists in a rather less dramatic form in most east European states. The question is, then, why should elite structure be more unitary under capitalism than under socialism? Two reasons may be suggested. The first is to do with purely social aspects of elite recruitment. In socialist states the cleavage between the political bureaucracy and the intelligentsia is partly a matter of social background and education. The typical member of the party apparatus, especially in the important middle levels of the hierarchy, will be of peasant stock, and with no formal education beyond the elementary level. The typical member of the white collar elite will probably be of urban, middle class background, and of course a university graduate. These differences in social pedigree, formal education and culture tend to encourage differing perceptions of social and political problems notwithstanding the absence of sharp inequalities in the material condition of the two groups.

A second and much more important factor in elite polarization is that arising directly from functional differences between the two groups. Members of the party and state bureaucracy are dependent for their position and privileges on the centralized command system and the whole apparatus of political patronage which accompanies it. Any threat to the bureaucratic principle is a direct threat to those whose authority rests largely on the qualities of proven loyalty and obedience to political superiors. And in this category must be included the managers or directors of industrial firms, since under a command system they operate mainly as administrators—that is, middle level functionaries in the state apparatus. This immediate dependence on a higher chain of command means that the enterprise director is an entirely different animal from the manager of a capitalist firm, with altogether different tasks to perform and requiring different personal qualities to ensure success. The notion of the enterprise director as the spearhead of a potential managerial revolution is completely ludicrous in the context of socialist society; in fact the managers have generally allied themselves with the opponents of economic reform, since their political and administrative qualities would be of no use in a non-bureaucratic setting. Like most other members of the party and state administration their particular skills and attributes are highly specific to this *one particular version* of industrial society, and are not readily transferable to some alternative version. This entire group thus has an obvious stake in the preservation of the existing order, in a way that the intelligentsia does not. The latter have the kinds of skills which are at a premium in any type of modern society irrespective of its political make-up. And it is because the intelligentsia themselves are clearly aware of this fact that their virtual exclusion from political power is such a serious point of tension in the socialist system.

One further contributing factor here is that the socialist white-collar intelligentsia, immersed as they are in the mainstream of European science and culture, are in a position to contrast their lot with that of their west European counterparts—who do not on the whole appear to regard themselves as subordinate to a morally, socially and culturally inferior political class. Now if it were the case that the socialist intelligentsia did *not* in fact feel some sort of collective resentment over their political subordination, then the notion of equilibrium, as here employed, would be rendered useless. For the basic assumption on which this notion rests is that a social group or class which feels itself raised to a position of strategic social importance, will wish to acquire political authority for itself and to remove it from those who lack the technical and moral qualities which are felt to be the one legitimate source of all power. If such a group *did* emerge in a society but developed no consciousness of its own moral superiority, and was content to have its hands kept off the levers of political power, then no general claim could be advanced that disequilibrium in the stratification order is a major source of tension and of potential system change. But at any rate, as far as the particular case under review is concerned the assumption is a plausible one, in so far as the socialist intelligentsia does appear to have something approaching a common moral identity, and a sense of its own latent power being held in check illegitimately.

Two factors contributing to this moral distinctiveness of the intelligentsia may be singled out for special comment. The first concerns the quasi-colonial status of the east European countries. The intelligentsia in most of these countries has historically acted as the standard bearer of national consciousness. The literary and creative elements in particular have played a key role in preserving the sense of nationhood and cultural unity during periods of foreign domination and shifting political boundaries. There is perhaps more than a grain of truth in the elitist view that under these critical conditions the intelligentsia *is* the embodiment of nationhood and the watchdog of cultural and moral unity. The present fact of Soviet domination throughout eastern Europe ensures that the intelligentsia will continue to act as guardians of national identity within the limits imposed by political surveillance and offical displeasure. Moreover, the role and standing of the intelligentsia contrast markedly with that of the political bureaucracy, who are readily identified with the Soviet regime and whose very survival is guaranteed largely by the presence or threatened appearance of comradely tanks from the East. Thus it is not merely the intelligentsia's claim to functional importance which encourages a moral bond, but their symbolic role as guardians of national consciousness and the figureheads of independence.[14]

A second factor reinforcing this same tendency concerns the role of conflict as a unifying social force. Collective identity of a class or political kind emerges most strongly among members of a nominal group which is caught up in a process of continuing conflict with some other clearly demarcated social group. In the absence of such ongoing conflict the potentialities inherent in purely formal or structural similarities do not generally transcend the latency stage. A striking difference between the professional middle classes of capitalist society and their socialist counterparts in this respect is that the former are not confronted by powerful and clearly definable opponents analogous to the communist party bureaucracy. It is doubtless partly on account of this that the western members of what Galbraith has dubbed the "educational and scientific estate" significantly lack that sense of a shared moral identity implied by the self-designation 'intelligentsia'. In other words it is the close-knit and politically combative nature of the hegemonic party itself which helps to account for the special character of the socialist intelligentsia. It is thus on the basis of this combination of social, functional and moral differences between the two groups that one can describe the elite structure of socialist society as highly differentiated or polarized.

The contrast with modern capitalist society is instructive. Elites in this system have a much greater degree of uniformity, both in social and functional terms. In the first place, those recruited to elite positions are drawn from a far more restricted social circle than are their socialist counterparts. Upward mobility into these positions occurs on such a minor scale that it can always be accompanied by an intensive programme of assimilation into elite culture. The effect of all this is to preserve a remarkable degree of social homogeneity among those who staff positions of power and privilege in western society. Secondly, and more importantly, there is no functional separation between different elite groupings, arising from different principles of elite recruitment and legitimacy. As already acknowledged, there are two distinct sets of principles which serve to underwrite privileged positions in capitalist society; one associated with occu-

---

14. While the use of the blanket term 'intelligentsia' does not of course imply a completely homogeneous group it is probably misleading to insist upon drawing sharp internal distinctions—e.g. between scientific and creative categories. In critical situations such distinctions appear wholly artificial. It is instructive to note that even in the Soviet Union political protest against the trial and imprisonment of dissident writers has not been confined to the literary intelligentsia but has included many members of the scientific and technical elite. For documentation on this point see the detailed lists of signatories to protest petitions reproduced in *Problems of Communism*, XVII (1968), pp. 39–73.

pational achievement, and the other with private property. The crucial point is, though, that these two sets of legitimating principles do not give rise to separate and discrete groupings, one based solely on wealth and the other on the division of labour. A key characteristic of almost any given elite group in capitalist society is that it will have a social mix exemplifying both sets of principles. Political leadership for example is not the sole prerogative of men of property, nor is the industrial elite comprised only of men of qualifications—or vice versa. In fact it is highly artificial to attempt to draw sharp distinctions between a propertied bourgeoisie on the one hand and a professionally qualified middle class on the other. To begin with, those who inherit family wealth no longer constitute anything resembling a leisure class. Typically, those born into wealth will now use it to secure for themselves or their children educational privileges designed to ensure equally privileged entry into one of the professions. This is one way in which fusion has taken place between the two different bases of reward. The other way is through the opportunities available to the professionally qualified to become property owners themselves. The most striking instance of this is the case of industrial managers and executives becoming major shareholders in the companies they control. But share ownership is becoming increasingly common among the professional middle classes generally, as indicated by the rapid growth of unit trusts. These two parallel developments, then, have forestalled the emergence of two clearly demarcated elites, each seeking to establish legitimacy by reference to mutually exclusive principles of status and reward. When those born to wealth are gainfully employed, and the professionally skilled have access to unearned rewards, then property and qualifications can be accepted as complementary bases of privilege and not as antagonistic principles. Those who insist that the distinction between ownership and nonownership of property is still the major source of cleavage in the stratification order of capitalist society appear not to have grasped the significance of current developments.

One signal indication of the extent of elite fusion is the common allegiance of both propertied and qualified groups to the same political symbols and bourgeois parties. To be sure, the professional middle classes have become fully integrated into the ruling order not simply through their influence on the party system but, more tellingly, through their ability to dominate a power structure based on pluralism. Bourgeois democracy is in fact a system which is highly responsive to the demands of an educated middle class in so far as it ensures greatest political leverage to those who command the most privileged positions in the marketplace. This fact that western members of the educational and scientific estate have become so thoroughly assimilated into the power structure is, as hinted at above, one important reason for the lack of that sense of moral and social distinctiveness which is the hallmark of an intelligentsia.

The claim that modern capitalism has a unitary elite structure seems to have an important bearing on the whole problem of system contradiction and its relation to internal change. In brief, it may be suggested that system contradictions are most likely to generate pressures for change when elites are polarized, so that the unitary nature of elites under capitalism would give it rather more stability than could be predicted from the theory of system-crisis taken on its own. One reason for this is that a unified elite is able to respond more effectively to potential threats to the system. They can usually introduce ameliorative measures which avert or stave off impending crisis without dismantling the system itself in any serious way. A polarized elite, on the other hand, is much less responsive to the threat of crisis mainly because any adaptations will tend to bring advantages to one group and disadvantages to the other. Consider, for example, the readiness and facility with which capitalist society adopted Keynesian economic reforms, thereby counteracting the tendencies towards cyclical crisis—a move which among other things converted unemployment from a potential political threat to a "social problem". Contrast this adaptability with the relative inability of socialist states to implement the economic reforms designed to overcome their internal contradictions. Why, we may ask, was Keynes acceptable but not Liberman? The answer is that Libermanism threatens to alter the balance of authority between the political bureaucracy and the white-collar intelligentsia; whereas the interests of elites under capitalism are not sufficiently differentiated for Keynesianism to be construed in politically divisive terms. The notion of system contradiction must thus be set against the background of elite structure when assessing the potential for system change. This is a recommendation which is also implied in the Marxist notion that "a split in the ruling class" is a necessary precondition of radical social transformation. And on this score the survival value of capitalism should perhaps be rated somewhat higher than the proponents of all the various crisis theories would encourage one to expect.

## IV

Finally, then, we may turn to the question of whether the elites in socialist states are likely to become less polarized and to move towards a more unitary structure. Predictions that such a development must inevitably occur are frequently met with in the literature on Soviet systems. The argument is that the political bureaucracy cannot effectively control society if its own functionaries are less well equipped technically than members of the intelligentsia. Therefore the tendency will be for the party to ensure that new recruits to the bureaucracy will be men with the same kind of education and training as the intelligentsia. The end result of this process is that the apparatchiki will be virtually indistinguishable from the white-collar specialists; the two groups will have become fused even though the system of centralized command will remain more or less intact. Now there certainly is evidence that leaders of the bureaucracy have become concerned about the relatively low technical standards of the men who staff the apparatus, and that efforts are continually being made to improve these standards. The dilemma facing the leadership, however, is that any devaluation of political criteria in favour of technical criteria carries with it the risk of secularizing the party. If the party apparatus came to be controlled exclusively by men more noted for their paper qualifications than for their ideological loyalty, then this would be tantamount to ultimate political victory for the white-collar intelligentsia. One reason why the present political leadership would probably resist such a development is that a transfer of power of this kind would be likely to undermine the party's total domination of society. The *raison d'être* of the hegemonic party is to preserve political control in the hands of a social group which could not legitimate its power and privileges by reference to the same criteria which govern the distribution of rewards among the population at large. The skills and attributes of the political bureaucracy are useful mainly for the maintenance of the apparatus which is its own creation; they are not skills which are intrinsically necessary to an industrial society. This is perhaps another way of saying that the political bureaucracy cannot be regarded as the ascendant class within its own society. And where the political class is not also the ascendant class, its survival can only be guaranteed by a hegemonic party exercising total dominion over men and ideas. The tight censorship upon the circulation of knowledge and creative ideas is indicative of a ruling class which is uncertain of its own legitimacy, and for whom even poetry can be construed as a potential threat to political survival. A political class which is also the ascendant class has much less need to police the thoughts and activities of subordinate groups. The European bourgeoisie, for example, has generally regarded itself as politically secure and as having a 'natural' command of all the centres of power. This confidence in its own legitimacy was a precondition for the flowering of bourgeois liberal ideology, with its institutionalized support for civil liberties, including formal rights of political dissent and the free circulation of knowledge. The granting of such rights is felt to be possible only because no other class or group in the society is seen as a serious natural contender for political power. In this situation, the coercive machinery of the state can usually be kept in the background of social life, as a means of last resort, rather than as an instrument of day to day political survival.

What all this suggests, then, is that if the communist party apparatus was to undergo a process of what Weber would call 'usurpation' by the white-collar intelligentsia, the very rationale of a hegemonic party would be thrown into question. For once the ascendant class had become the political class, it would have no obvious need to protect itself by the strategy of total surveillance and the control of knowledge. It seems unlikely however that the present party leadership is unaware of the possible consequences of secularization. And unless one believes that ideology has no bearing on men's actions, it is difficult to envisage the leadership allowing the principles of recruitment to be changed in such a way as might weaken the party's grip on society—thereby, as they perceive it, putting at risk the future of communism.[15]

As long as the attainment of the party's historic mission is felt to depend on men with distinctive attributes of loyalty and obedience, then the party apparatus is likely to continue to choose its own successors with care. And men whose primary commitment is to the political bureaucracy, whose rewards and

---

15. Even in east Germany, where technical expertise and political authority are especially closely linked, there is a clear separation of the two spheres at the apex of power. As Baylis's study shows, the technical specialists control the Council of Ministers, but the apparatchiki still dominate the Politburo. "The peculiar division of labour between the 'political' Politburo and the 'economic' Council of Ministers may be seen as reflecting the present unstable equilibrium of east German politics". Moreover, in critical situations, "the apparatchiki are in a position to enforce political requirements at the expense of economic ones [. . .]" (Baylis, *op. cit.* p. 151).

privileges, authority and influence are dependent on this commitment are, by this very fact, a clearly demarcated social group, whatever purely technical qualities they may have in common with other men. It is this functional difference between the bureaucracy and the intelligentsia which lies at the root of the cleavage between the two elites, and which mere improvement in the former's technical qualities will not eradicate.

## V

In summary, this has been an attempt to show that Marx's concept of system contradiction can be usefully employed in the comparative analysis of industrial societies. The proviso entered here was that system contradictions have to be understood in relation to certain aspects of the stratification order—and more particularly to elite structure and the distribution of power. It was argued that socialist society is characterized by disequilibrium in the stratification order—a condition stemming from the fact that the seizure of power was carried out in the name of a class which was totally subordinate in society. The effect of this was to put political power in the hands of bureaucratic class, rather than an ascendant class, so creating a cleavage at the apex of the social system. This cleavage in the elite structure tends to exacerbate tensions arising from weaknesses in system integration, and makes adaptations to system deficiencies difficult to accomplish.

This situation was contrasted with that of modern capitalism, a society in which power in all its dimensions is monopolized by the same class. The unification of elites that this condition entails, means that the dominant class is usually able to respond effectively to potential system crisis.[16] At the same time, this does not permit one to dogmatize about the political invulnerability of modern capitalism. The seizure of power must always be accepted as an empirical possibility; but any judgement on the likelihood of this event, and of the kind of system that would result from it, may ultimately depend on whether one accepts the Leninist or Marxist view of the political capacities of a totally subordinate class.

---

16. Bauman's view that capitalist states in the pre-welfare period were inherently vulnerable to revolutionary seizure seems to be based more on predictions of collapse than on the event itself. Zygmunt Bauman, Social Dissent in the East-European Political System, *Europ. Journ. Sociol.*, XII (1971), 25–51. The European historical record contains in fact remarkably few instances of the successful overthrow of capitalism. The Soviet Union and Yugoslavia provide the only examples of revolutionary transformation from capitalism to socialism, and in both cases the *ancien régime* was already in a state of imminent collapse as a result of war.

By contrast, the brief post-war history of eastern Europe suggests that socialist states are considerably more vulnerable to the threat of internal dissolution. The survival of most of these states in their present form is guaranteed mainly by the authority of an external power. The typical European bourgeois state, on the other hand, has been required to accommodate to internal pressures in order to preserve its stability, since, with few exceptions, it has been unable to summon the aid of a greater sovereign power when threatened by internal revolt. Thus any proper assessment of the comparative stability of the two systems requires us to "think away" the Red Army when judging the viability of the ideal-typical socialist state.

# · 28 ·

# Is There a Ruling Class in the USSR?

## Alec Nove

This is a discussion article, not an inclusive survey of all, or even most, of the issues raised when one examines the Soviet social structure. Thus I will deliberately ignore so important a question as nationalities policy, and touch only briefly on problems of social mobility. This is not because they are either uninteresting or irrelevant, but because I wish to concentrate here on something else, which can be formulated as follows: *given* the existence of a ruling stratum, class or élite, why did it establish so dominant a position, and what should one call a stratum of this kind, a society so constituted? The last point is, for this article, the vital one.

There will probably be no major disagreement about the basic facts, though there may certainly be differences of interpretation. We are analysing a society in which almost all the means of production are owned by the state. (At the present level of generality, let us ignore the kolkhozy.) These means of production, and also the administrative, judicial, cultural and social institutions of the USSR, are controlled, managed, dominated, by a party which is itself a centralized and disciplined body. The party selects and appoints cadres, this function *(podbor i rasstanovka kadrov)* being carried out by the personnel or establishment department of the central committee—for more junior appointments the republican committees. Rank-and-file party members have very limited means of influencing affairs. The ruling stratum could perhaps be formally defined as all those persons holding appointments deemed to be significant enough to figure

• Abridged from *Soviet Studies* 27(4) (1975): 615–23, 624–35.

on the central committee's establishment nomenclature of such appointments, i.e. who are on the *nomenklatura*. They are, literally, the Establishment. As pointed out in an earlier article relating to this theme,[1] this covers all spheres of economic, social, cultural or political significance. It is this which distinguishes the Soviet Union from other bureaucratic or authoritarian societies: in a significant sense there is one centrally-administered hierarchy. Of course, within it there are not only gradations but differences of interest. Thus the sub-hierarchy concerned with primary education or with Kazakhstan may press for resources which officials responsible for artillery or the Leningrad oblast might desire to direct for *their* purposes, and such differences are reconciled at higher administrative levels. But few will disagree that the Soviet system has evolved into a hierarchical society within which status and power depends decisively on rank.

Indeed, one could, without too much exaggeration, fit Soviet society into a 'universal civil and military service' model. Everyone (almost) is employed by the state-and-party or one of their organizations, doing the work and getting the pay laid down for the rank they occupy. The questions we will have to ask are: What are the upper strata of such a society? What should they be called? Is Marxist 'class' analysis applicable to such a system? If not, what is?

To avoid misunderstandings, let it be said at once that the existence of the hierarchical structure, though certainly a fact, does not imply that everyone obeys his superior passively, nor yet that there is no upward pressure exerted upon the top leadership. No student of Soviet planning can fail to notice that instructions are often ambiguous, or contradictory, or evaded, and that the content of orders received is often influenced by the recipients of the orders. Interest and pressure groups exist, as already noted. Even ordinary workers and peasants can affect plans and income schedules, e.g. by 'voting with their feet' (by leaving occupations and areas where pay is poor or by not going where the authorities wish them to go unless there are sufficient inducements). Mass terror and forced labour cannot now provide a labour force for East Siberia, for instance. However, no autonomous organizations are allowed to exist, no effective trade unions, no uncontrolled organs of the press, and the KGB is active. The structure still accords with a basically unihierarchical model.

Is the élite hereditary, or perhaps becoming such? This is certainly an important question, and one highly relevant to the issue as to whether it is becoming a class or caste. Before considering any of the evidence, it is important to define who it is one has in mind. If by 'élite' is meant the apex of the state and party bureaucracy, say, the top 20,000, then one can assert with fair confidence that they are *not* hereditary. Indeed, it is hard to find a single instance of any member of the central committee, minister, party secretary or army general whose father held any of these ranks.

It is another matter if one extends one's attention to the privileged, a much larger group, defined perhaps by family income.[2] There is indeed downward

---

1. 'History, Hierarchy and Nationalities', *Soviet Studies*, vol. XXI, no. 1 (July 1969).

2. These include successful artists, dancers, professors of philology, and other well-paid persons who exercise no political, social or economic authority, and may be on no one's *nomenklatura*.

immobility, in the sense that the children not only of the élite narrowly defined but also of other privileged strata tend to receive higher education and to find jobs with reasonably good status, in scientific research institutes, for instance. Statistics in this field are, however, liable to misuse because some analysts shift their attention to yet another group, much larger than the upper élite or the *nomenklatura* officials, or the privileged strata, and use figures relating to the so-called 'intelligentsia' in its Soviet definition. This 'intelligentsia' (officially a stratum—*prosloika*) can include everyone who is not either a worker by hand or a peasant. Teachers, librarians, book-keepers, hospital nurses, shop assistants, as well as senior officials, fall within this remarkably wide and socially meaning-less definition. It includes a great many badly paid persons (many women among them), who could not in any circumstances be described as privileged, or influential, or élite. Movement into the élite proper out of the 'lower' intelli-gentsia so defined is plainly a form of upward social mobility.

This said, it must be stressed that higher education has now almost become a necessary (though not sufficient) condition to get into *nomenklatura* and into senior positions generally. Virtually every party leader or secretary of significance, nearly every industrial manager or minister, has a degree, most usually in engineering or technology. Consequently, access to higher education is vital for advancement. This is difficult for peasants, because of the persistent inadequacy of rural schooling and the low cultural level prevailing in rural areas, and efforts to remedy this have still borne little fruit. Talented children of workers have better opportunities, but the figures show quite clearly that a disproportionate number of places in higher education are occupied by children of the so-called intelligentsia. This whole subject is too complex to pursue here in any analytical and statistical detail, but a very few remarks are in order. The first is again to stress that many of the families of this 'intelligentsia' are not materially privileged. The majority of the group earn less, often very much less, than skilled workers. The second is that, owing to the very large expansion of higher education since 1928, the relative and absolute number of children of persons already educated is now much larger, as is obvious and natural. The third point is that, as our own experience demonstrates, children from educated homes have a clear 'academic' advantage in competition with children from a less cultured environment. We are all familiar with the reasons (books and conversation in the home, parental encouragement, greater motivation, coach-ing from parents or friends, and so on). But in recent years there has been a notable increase in the intensity of the scramble for higher education places, owing to the fact that full secondary education has expanded much more rapidly than have institutions of university status,[3] so that a greater number of students qualified through completing secondary school cannot find places. The short-age is, naturally, greatest in prestigious institutions. The use of backstairs

---

3. The following figures demonstrate this:

|  | 1960 | 1972 |
|---|---|---|
|  | *(millions)* | |
| Forms 9–10 (11) in secondary schools | 1.5 | 5.1 |
| Full-time students in higher education | 1.2 | 2.4 |

(*Narodnoe khozyaistvo SSSR v 1972 godu* (M., 1973), pp. 629, 637).

methods and stringpulling via influence has therefore become more important, and here the *nomenklatura* officials and their hangers-on have evident advantages, especially as abuses they commit seldom attract publicity. (Khrushchev's efforts to repress these abuses in the 1958 educational reforms were among his less successful actions.)

One needs more evidence before coming to any definite conclusion about recruitment of talent from below into the educational system, and ultimately co-option into the *nomenklatura* ranks, which might enable us to answer the question of whether it is an imperfect meritocracy or a closed corporation. An important point is that, while competitive entrance examinations are held for entry into higher education,[4] recruitment to public and party office is almost always a process hidden from any public eye, and is essentially appointment from above, or co-option. Roy Medvedev, in his excellent book,[5] complains that selection pays far too much attention to incidental factors such as personal acquaintance and connections, and far too little to efficiency, but this too we shall leave aside.

Finally, one must mention one feature of the system in its most recent evolution: the growth of job security in the *nomenklatura*. Under Stalin in the thirties there was a high death and arrest rate, though survivors of the Great Purge proved durable. Even under Khrushchev a fair number of officials were demoted. Since then, the 'civil service' habits familiar in all bureaucracies have become more firmly established, and the vast majority of *nomenklatura* officials are promoted or transferred in a routine manner, save in cases of quite outstanding failure or success. This is no more than to say that the bureaucratic machine functions in accordance with its own rules and habits, with less interference and disruption from a despotic ruler.

One objection to the use of the *nomenklatura* as a means of defining the ruling class or group is that we know little about it, apart from its existence and general function. Details and figures are unpublished in any systematic way. Consequently, even if accepting the *nomenklatura* in theoretical terms, we cannot readily translate it into concrete analysis. Does the central committee's list number 10,000 or 100,000? Just whom does it cover, or leave out? Faced with this problem, Mervyn Matthews, in an unpublished paper, tried to define what he called the 'élite' in terms of a combination of three indicators: income (including the value of 'extras') of over 500 rubles a month, the holding of a *nomenklatura* post, and access to various specific privileges (i.e. to the 'extras' just referred to). We may not wholly agree about concepts or numbers, but clearly Dr. Matthews was seeking to define the same sort of group as is here being discussed.

Such a system is not quite the kind of thing the original revolutionaries had in mind. It is a result of a historical evolution, from the libertarian enthusiasm of 1917 to the ordered 'establishment' of today. The causes of this development have been much debated, usually in the context of explaining the rise of Stalin-

---

4. I abstract here from complications arising out of nationality, which can be very significant. String-pulling and influence have been mentioned already.

5. R. Medvedev, *Kniga o sovetskoi demokratii* (Amsterdam, 1972), especially p. 352.

ism. Stalin did much to create the hierarchical-bureaucratic system, true enough, but it is proving durable long after his death. I will confine myself here to a bare listing of explanatory factors, each of which could be the subject of a long paper in itself.

First, there is the fact that this was Russia, with its autocratic-bureaucratic tradition and hypertrophy of the state, and relative weakness of spontaneous social forces, repeatedly noted by historians of many different ideologies and backgrounds. This could be expected to affect rulers and ruled, inclining the former to use traditional methods and the latter to accept the methods to which they were accustomed.

Secondly, one must mention the entire logic of change from above, inherent in a socialist-led revolution in a predominantly peasant country. A prolonged period of administered change, imposed upon a peasant majority (the 'petty-bourgeois morass', or *stikhiya,* so often referred to by Bolsheviks in the early twenties), had powerful bureaucratic implications. So did the one-party state, required to maintain Bolshevik rule in such an uncongenial environment. This point is too familiar to require elaboration.

Thirdly, the generally low level of education, culture, consciousness, the exhaustion after years of civil war. The few reliable and effective Bolsheviks had to be disposed in key sectors, subject to the discipline of their party superiors. This was when the *podbor i rasstanovka kadrov* was born. Fourthly, there was Soviet Russia's isolation in a largely hostile world, a point which is again too well known to pursue here.

Roy Medvedev put the argument as follows:

In a vast country such as Russia with its mainly peasant and petty-bourgeois population, its economic backwardness and ignorance . . . in such a country after a socialist revolution a mainly authoritarian regime was inevitable, and not only the old tsarist officials and specialists, who had perforce to be utilized by the new regime, were bureaucrats. Even yesterday's proletarian revolutionaries had to use authoritarian methods, to issue orders, i.e. adopt bureaucratic procedures. Sometimes it is said that the first generation of proletarian revolutionaries could not be bureaucrats. Just the opposite is true. In the conditions of Russia, they *had* to a considerable extent to be bureaucrats.[6]

Without the benefit of historical hindsight, Bukharin saw the danger, as early as 1922:

Even proletarian origin, even the most calloused hands . . . are no guarantee against turning into a new class. For if we imagine that a section of those who have risen out of the working class becomes detached from the mass of the workers and congeals into a monopoly position in its capacity of ex-workers, they too could become a species of caste, which could also become a 'new class'.

He noted the existence of 'worker bureaucrats' in Western trade unions, but saw particular dangers in Russia, because, in his words:

the cultural backwardness of the working masses, especially in conditions of general misery, when *nolens volens* the administrative and leadership apparatus has to receive many more consumer goods than the ordinary worker, gives rise to the danger of a very substantial divorce from the masses even of that part of the cadres which emerged from

---

6. *Ibid.,* p. 340.

the working masses themselves. . . . An appeal to working-class origin and proletarian goodness is not itself an argument against the existence of this danger.

He saw here the germ of a 'new ruling class'.[7] (Note in passing his use in this context, interchangeably, of the words 'class' and 'caste', reflecting a perplexity which still bothers us today in analysing these phenomena.)

Rakovsky, when in exile in 1929, noted that the new rulers had 'changed to such an extent that they have ceased, not only 'objectively' but 'subjectively', not only physically but morally, to be members of the working class, and that 'the Soviet and party bureaucracy is a phenomenon of a new order'.[8]

We need not enter here into the argument as to whether the bureaucratization which occurred was inevitable. We can surely all of us accept that the danger was there and the tendencies towards it were inherent in the situation, unless very strongly combated. Far from strongly combating them, Stalin and his faction utilized these trends for their own advantage, thereby providing a powerful additional impetus to the domination of the apparatus.

Then, next on the list of relevant factors must be the functional logic of a centrally planned economy. With the elimination of almost all private enterprise, and the imposition through the state planning system of centrally-determined priorities, the trends towards comprehensive bureaucratization were powerfully reinforced. This was not only because, by placing economic management within the party-state machine, its power and control were enhanced. It is also that the *modus operandi* of this species of centralized planning is inherently bureaucratic in nature. The replacement of the largely market economy of NEP by the directive planning of the thirties meant that decisions on resource allocation, production, investment, required to be consciously made and coordinated. A complex official apparatus issued the necessary instructions. In practice, the major part of the party-state apparatus, and most of the *nomenklatura* officials, have been engaged in operating some aspect of the economy.

I am, of course, aware that a school of thought exists which claims that central planning can be operated by the 'associated producers' (Mandel's phrase) or by workers' democracy without the great bureaucratic machine which, in actual Soviet history, in fact operated it. I have argued my own view on this matter elsewhere.[9] In *this* context it is surely enough to assert that the Soviet way of running the economy was, and is, bureaucratic, and that this is a very important part of any explanation of the all-pervasiveness and completeness of the bureaucratic-hierarchical system as a whole.

While competitive capitalism operates through conflict (for competition is conflict), a centrally planned economy requires hierarchy to ensure consistency and to resolve conflicting claims on resources by administrative decision. In this connection, the French left-wing theorist Claude Lefort is worth citing. His argument is interesting and (at least to English-speaking readers) little known.

---

7. 'Burzhuaznaya revolyutsiya i revolyutsiya proletarskaya' (1922). (The passage appears on p. 168 of *Put' k sotsializmu v Rossii*, a selection of Bukharin's works edited by S. Heitman.)

8. Rakovsky is quoted here from E. H. Carr, *Foundations of a Planned Economy*, vol. 2 (London, 1971), p. 433.

9. 'Market Socialism and Its Critics', *Soviet Studies*, vol. XXIV, no. 1 (July 1972).

'If the productive apparatus did not allow, permit, demand its unification, the role of the political apparatus would be inconceivable. Conversely, if the cadres of the old society had not been destroyed by the party, if a new social stratum had not been promoted to directing functions in all sectors, the transformation of productive relations would have been impossible. . . .' Stalinism made a 'new formation out of elements taken from all classes and pitilessly subordinated them to the task of direction (management) which the new economic system gave them. . . .' Whatever their social origin, they form part 'of a new hierarchy, whose common denominator is that it directs, controls, organizes at all levels of its functioning the apparatus of production and the living work force, that of the exploited classes'.[10] Terror is seen by Lefort as an essential part of the process of destroying the remnants of the older classes, disciplining the workers and peasants and disciplining also the new class so that it could fulfil its functions. 'The bourgeois class grows and develops as a *consequence* of the actions of individual capitalists, economically determined, whatever the conflicts among the actors. . . . The division of labour among capitalists, and the market, make capitalists dependent upon one another and act collectively *vis-à-vis* the labour force. By contrast, the bureaucrats form a class only by reason of the fact that their functions and their rules differentiate them collectively from the exploited classes, only because they are interlinked with a directing centre which decides what is produced. . . .' It is because production relations are dominated by the state, with the workers reduced to 'simple executants' of orders received, that the bureaucrats have a class position. 'It is not as individual actors that they weave the network of class relations; it is the bureaucratic class in its generality . . . by reason of the existing structure of production which converts the activities of individual bureaucrats (privileged activities among other such) into class activities. . . . The bureaucratic community is not guaranteed by the mechanism of economic activities; it is established by the integration of the bureaucrats around the state, in the total discipline with regard to the directing apparatus. Without this state, without this apparatus, the bureaucracy is nothing.'[11]

Clearly there *is* something to the proposition that the nature of the central planning system is both a functional justification of the great hierarchy and a precondition of its all-embracing nature. Let me illustrate this with the simplest of examples. In a competitive economy materials are 'allocated' in an uncoordinated way through a market, and entrepreneurs who find the price too high will switch to another material or another line of business, guided by profit considerations. The outcome may or may not be optimal, but no hierarchical-bureaucratic structure is needed.[12] In a centralized planning system, however, the decision as to who is to receive the materials requires to be taken at a level *above* that of the factories which are seeking to obtain them, in the light of social priorities, or of input-output consequences of prior policy decisions, i.e. of

---

10. C. Lefort, *Eléments d'une critique de la bureaucratie* (Geneva, 1971), pp. 145, 147.

11. *Ibid.,* pp. 150–1.

12. Yes, I know that large Western corporations also have bureaucracies. The point still has validity.

questions which cannot be resolved at factory-management levels—or indeed by those factories' workers. Hence the need for subordination, or hierarchy. I do not share Lefort's basic philosophy, but he surely has a point. In his interpretation, a supreme despot of the Stalin type is required by this economic system, and he argues that the party-state bureaucracy understood this, however much they may have deplored (as individuals) being shot on Stalin's orders.

One other feature, particularly of Stalinism, is worth a brief mention. This is the often brutal and crude relations between superior and subordinate in all spheres of life. The attitude became known as *Borzovshchina,* after a fictional rural official, Borzov, who bulldozed his way through the pages of Ovechkin's stories. In one sense this ruthless disregard of one's subordinates' feelings and interests seems to contradict the entire spirit and purpose of the Bolshevik revolution. But in another it is one consequence of promoting men of little culture into positions of authority, a process which was an integral part of the revolution. One requires to be a starry-eyed idealist indeed to imagine that working-class origin endows individuals with virtue. The civil war brought to the fore those who could get things done in the face of appalling obstacles and much resistance. The 'sergeant-major' type, well known in many armies, is not rendered less authoritarian by the fact that almost every sergeant-major rose from the ranks. It is, indeed, an elementary social observation that first-generation promotees tend to value greatly the privileges which promotion gives them. How well Stalin knew this! He certainly utilized these aspirations in his climb to power. Much of the urban labour force consisted of ex-peasants lacking both 'revolutionary initiative and power of resistance to authority', to cite Carr.[13] . . .

There are other points which could be made, including the dominance for long periods of military considerations, which affected both economic priorities and organizational-disciplinary methods. But I think enough has been said in the present context. One has only to add a rather obvious corollary: that the apparatus, once in existence, develops a strong vested interest in its own continuance, and, especially under conditions in which it is tightly in control of communications media, it is in a strong position to abuse its power by allocating to itself material and other privileges. It tends, like other rulers, to identify its interests with those of the people as a whole, and uses its monopoly role of interpreter of the ideology to defend its power. It mobilizes millions not only to vote at 'elections', but also to participate in low-level execution of policies decided in the upper echelons of the apparatus, as is demonstrated by the numbers engaged in local soviets and social organizations and committees, under the control and supervision of the appropriate party organs.

Let us now suppose that Soviet society is of the type described in the preceding pages, for the reasons there given. What should such a society be called? Does it possess a ruling *class*?

The official Soviet answer is that there are two classes, workers and peasants, and a *prosloika* (stratum)—the intelligentsia. We have noted the uselessness

---

13. Carr, *op. cit.,* vol. 2, p. 432.

of such labels as these, especially as their applicability to the Soviet economic and political structure is never discussed in Soviet publications.

In the West, David Lane has argued for the concept of a 'uni-class state', socialist because of state ownership of means of production, but 'bourgeois' because distribution is unequal. In this conception, everyone is a species of worker (hence 'uni-class'), indeed it is a workers' state, but there is inequality and privilege.[14] My belief is that this conception is misleading, because it obscures the qualitative distinction between (so to speak) officers and other ranks, between 'we' and 'they', between rulers and ruled, which not only exists in reality but also impregnates people's consciousness in the Soviet Union itself.

Another conception has a long historical lineage: this is the 'degenerated workers' state', which Trotsky favoured and to which some Trotskyists still cling. If by this is meant that there was once a workers' state and that it degenerated, it is an arguable position. E. H. Carr was more sceptical about a workers' state ever existing,[15] and so am I, since any worker appointed to run any part of the state apparatus ceases to be a worker. To this it can be objected that a workers' state no more requires workers to run it than a state in a capitalist society is run by capitalists, but this argument contains a fallacy. In the 'bourgeois state' model it matters little who the actual ministers or senior civil servants are; so long as the great capitalists and landlords own the bulk of property, they exercise power by virtue of the fact of ownership. This is not so in the 'workers' state' model; the workers have no power by the mere virtue of being workers, and can exercise it only through their control over their representatives who run the state (and economic) machine. If this control lapses, so does their influence on affairs. Surely no Trotskyist doubts that it has lapsed, and long ago. They can, and do, argue that something which could be called a workers' state existed in (say) 1920. Trotsky could claim that it had degenerated by the time of his own defeat. Now, 50 years after, is the *present* Soviet state really to be described as a workers' state, albeit a degenerate one? My own answer is in the negative.

A whole number of analysts assert the existence of a new class, or a new bourgeoisie. The most familiar argument is probably that of Milovan Djilas: 'Ownership is nothing other than the right of profit and control. If one defines class benefits by this right, the communist states have seen in the final analysis, the origin of a new form of ownership or of a new ruling and exploiting class. . . . The new class may be said to be made up of those who have special privileges and economic preferences because of the administrative monopoly they hold. . . . Membership in the new party class or political bureaucracy is reflected in larger economic and material goods and privileges than society should normally grant for such functions. In practice the ownership privilege of the new class manifests itself as an exclusive right, as a party monopoly for the political bureaucrat to distribute the national income, to set wages, direct economic

---

14. D. Lane, 'Marxist and neo-Marxist class theories of Soviet society' (unpublished seminar paper).

15. Carr, *op. cit.*, vol. 2, pp. 429–33.

development and dispose of nationalized and other property. . . . The so-called social ownership is a disguise for real ownership by the political bureaucracy.'[16]

The essence of the case rests on the proposition that what matters is *control*, and that the upper strata are in control; they decide what should be done with nationalized means of production. This too is the basis of Bettelheim's claim that there is a 'state bourgeoisie' which runs the Soviet Union. Bettelheim is, of course, aware that there is both state ownership and planning, but for him these are necessary but not sufficient preconditions for a socialist transformation; essential for progress towards socialism[17] is the domination of the workers. Instead, there is domination over the workers, the means of production and the product by a *class*.[18]

A variant of this approach is that of Castoriadis. He argues that the productive process has a class character because 'of the effective possession of the productive apparatus by the bureaucracy, which is in full charge of it, while the proletariat is fully dispossessed'. In common with Djilas, he argues that the bureaucracy enjoys 'surplus revenue', which is unjustified by its productive contribution to society and determined by the position of any given individual in the bureaucratic pyramid. This, according to him, is a form of exploitation of the masses. He asserts that 'bureaucratic property is neither individual nor collective; it is private property in so far as it exists only for the bureaucracy while the rest of society is dispossessed; it is private property managed in common by a class and collective within this class. . . . In this sense one can briefly define it as private collective property.'[19]

He concludes: 'It is not capitalism, it is not socialism, it is not even on its way to either of these two forms; the Soviet economy represents a historically new type, and its name matters little if its essential features are understood.'[20]

Lefort, whom we have already quoted and who is an ally of Castoriadis in the *Socialisme ou Barbarie* group, also speaks of a 'collective apparatus of appropriation' exercised by a 'new class' which does not dominate through *private* appropriation. For reasons which, as already shown, he finds within the relations of production, there takes place (in his view) a 'fusion of all the strata of the bureaucracy in the mould of a new directing class', whose unity is linked with 'the collective appropriation of surplus'.[21]

Chinese criticisms, usually worded in very strident terms, also tend to identify a new oppressive class in the USSR, which appropriates and exploits. (In sources available to me at least, this is backed by no serious historical and social analysis, and the allegation that this class came to power after the death of Stalin is absurd.)

All this raises some awkward questions, though it is none the worse for that:

---

16. M. Djilas, *The New Class* (London, 1957).
17. More will be said in a moment as to what he and others consider to be socialism.
18. See, for instance, Bettelheim's letter to Sweezy, *Monthly Review*, March 1969.
19. Castoriadis, *La Société bureaucratique* (Paris, 1973), pp. 84–85.
20. *Ibid.*, p. 67.
21. Lefort, *op. cit.*, pp. 148, 151.

we may be facing a qualitatively new phenomenon for which our customary categories (whether derived from Marx or from Parsons) may require substantial modification.

But before pursuing the argument further let us halt for a moment and consider the relationship of the *nomenklatura*-rulers to the means of production. They are in command of them. Marxists will then turn their attention to the *surplus* which they should be extracting. Do they derive an exploitation income? If so, in what does it consist? It is clear that, *qua* individuals (as Castoriadis duly noted), they do not pocket the profits.

The question of surplus in the Soviet economy can be handled basically in two different ways. One may assert that the surplus is equal to what the Soviet leaders themselves describe as the surplus product, or 'product for society', i.e. the total profit (including turnover tax, etc.) generated by productive labour and appropriated by the state or its enterprises. It is used for a variety of purposes: hospitals, schools, investments of all kinds, administration, defence, and so on. Plainly, a part of these expenditures (Brezhnev would say: all) is for the common weal. There are those who assert both that the USSR is an autocracy which pays no attention to people's needs *and* that the masses have no means of exerting pressure. If, then, there is an increase in minimum wages and old-age pensions, this must upset these assumptions: either the leaders *are* paying attention to people's needs, or they respond to pressure from below in their own self-interest (in which case such pressure does exist). In practice, surely, both these things are true. The leaders would like the citizens to live better, *and* it would be dangerous for their political security if there were no improvements. The essential point in the present context is that the surplus is disposed of by the *nomenklatura*-apparatus; it decides what happens to it. Naturally, some part of it benefits ordinary citizens, in their capacity as pensioners, patients, students, scientists, etc. etc. The 'collective owners' of Castoriadis's conception 'appropriate' *this* surplus in the sense of deciding on its use. They control it.

A different approach is contained in the quotation from Djilas. The 'new class' is held to divert for *its own use* 'a larger income in material goods and privileges than society should normally grant for such functions'. By this criterion, they appropriate an amount equal to the notional excess of what they earn (and receive in the form of 'perks') over what they ought to have received, an excess which control over the means of production enables them to acquire. I shall not discuss this further, but of course one must point out that *this* sense of surplus is statistically and conceptually quite different from, and much smaller than, the surplus product referred to above.

Anyhow, it behoves those who speak of a 'new class' to adopt one or the other of these definitions of what it is that this class appropriates. (My own preference is for the second definition, though it too presents difficulties.)

The doctrine of 'state capitalism' should, in my view, be seen as a variant of the above. In a functional sense, it is quite proper to speak of the state carrying out the role of capitalists, especially in growth and development. Presumably, this interpretation lends itself well to the notion that the ruling stratum that controls the state is, collectively, the equivalent of the capitalist class. It is all a question of how useful it is to use this term, whether it helps to clarify more than to confuse. Can one have state capitalism and no capitalists? Or can one call the ruling stratum 'collective capitalists'? This seems wrong to me. Lenin used to refer to state capitalism, but this term led to much misunderstanding among his comrades. Mao interprets it as referring to a workers' state domination over surviving capitalists.[22]

Popular among some neo-Marxists is the view that there is no ruling class in the Soviet Union, but that the USSR is a 'transitional society'. Let us examine this conception, of which Mandel is a well-known representative.

It is based on the belief that a society can be either capitalist or socialist, and that the Soviet system contains some elements of both and is neither. It has a centrally planned economy, the 'law of value' is severely constrained. There are no capitalists. However, it is not a workers' state, workers do not control the means of production, the plan contains many lacunae, and there is pressure to strengthen market elements, pressure which (on this interpretation) could lead to the restoration of capitalism. Alternatively, the assertion of the power of the working masses could or would lead on to socialism. Meanwhile, it is a transitional, mixed system, which must go one way or the other.

Mandel's view of socialism is a common one among the New Left: it is close to, if not identical with, Marx's vision of communism. In such a society, the market would vanish along with commodity relations, the state would wither away, and so would money, wages, the disparity between mental and physical labour; there would be no scarcity: we would have 'from each according to his abilities, to each according to his needs'. I have expressed elsewhere my scepticism about this conception of socialism, and this is not the place to pursue the matter. It is enough to assert, with (presumably) Mandel's agreement, that such a socialism is not immediately practicable, and that in any case there is no sign that Soviet society is in process of transition towards it. (Presumably, Mandel takes the position that a revolutionary overthrow of the ruling 'élite' is a prerequisite of progress in that direction.) Bettelheim adopts a less fundamentalist definition of socialism: in his letter to Sweezy he argues that socialism is characterized not by the presence or absence of commodity relations, money and prices, but by the existence of the domination of the proletariat. He therefore lays special stress on the decisive role of power. It is because in the Soviet Union power resides with what he calls the new bourgeoisie that he regards the Soviet Union as not socialist, and not because they use money, pay wages, etc. It must be added that Sweezy's reply includes the following sentence: 'My conception is that market relationships (which of course imply money and prices) are *inevitable* under socialism for a long time, but that they constitute a standing danger to the system . . .'[23] He too, then, has problems with defining the relationship to production of the managerial élite, which also in his eyes is tending to develop into a new type of bourgeoisie. He sees a conflict between this managerial élite and the old party bureaucracy. He fears that this might lead to a restoration of capitalism.

---

22. In 'Miscellany of Mao Tse-tung Thought (1949–68)', parts 1 and 2, reference no. JPRS 61269/1/2/, p. 308.

23. *Monthly Review*, March 1969.

If socialism is not on the agenda, why should capitalism be restored? Why, indeed, not assume that the existing system is as durable and stable as any other in a rapidly-changing world? Mandel's answer, if I understand it correctly, is that it is in the interests of the élite, or of an important segment of the élite, to strengthen market relations. All reform proposals in Eastern Europe tend in that direction. The implication of a market system is that there will be capitalists; managers will seek the advantages and security which ownership would bring. The 'law of value' re-enthroned will restore capitalist relations.

Is this a likely outcome? All things are possible, but I would like to question the assumption that administrators of state property have a predisposition to wish to own it. Is this so? Analysis of the interests of industrial managers can provide evidence for their desire for security and non-interference, for more autonomy (though some managers fear responsibility and like being given orders) and higher incomes. But ownership? Why is this in their interests as they conceive them? They are privileged members of the hierarchy. They see their own promotion as taking place within it. Thus, let us say, the manager of a medium-sized factory aims not so much at owning it as at being advanced to a managership of a larger factory, or to the rank of deputy-minister of 'his' industry. Indeed, most industrial deputy-ministers are senior managers, who can scarcely aspire to 'own' their ministry! This whole conception, like that of Burnham, over-concentrates on the factory manager: this level of the hierarchy is important, but it is only part of a complex whole.

The factor of ownership is surely crucial if capitalism is to be restored by the 'Mandel' route. 'Market' type reforms (à la Budapest, for instance) are not of themselves enough. It is also worth stressing that, with all their imperfections, market forces may express the desires of the masses more effectively than the plan, if the plan is drafted by a remote and irresponsible oligarchy. It is, surely, as foolish (in the Soviet context) to assume that the plan is right as against the market as to assume the opposite. We all know how often planners' programmes have failed to match consumer preferences, and indeed how often the actual product-mix fails to reflect the original intentions of the planners.[24]

Where has all this got us? One could go on citing other interpretations, but perhaps the heart of the matter is in the significance of *control* through a hierarchy, and the relation of this to the traditional Marxian analysis of class. Control relates to power, and power resides in ownership, so Marxists naturally look at property relations as a key to identifying a ruling class. This is a useful model for analysing capitalism. But what of other social formations?

Danilova, a Soviet anthropologist, boldly grappled with this question. Ernest Gellner should be thanked for drawing attention to her ideas, which are highly germane to the fundamental question just raised.[25] 'Does the ownership of the means of production constitute the determining element in all societies? Is it correct to extend the primacy of production relations to all stages of human

---

24. See my article 'Planners' Preferences, Priorities and Reforms', *Economic Journal,* vol. LXXVI, no. 302 (June 1966), pp. 267–77.

25. *Times Literary Supplement,* 18 October 1974, citing L. V. Danilova's writings on pre-capitalist societies.

history . . .? Contrary to the viewpoint widely diffused in Soviet science, the relations of domination-subjection conditioned by the development of the division of labour are themselves by no means relations of production. The dominant relationships in all pre-capitalist structures are non-economic ones.' In her view, 'the absolutization of the economic factor in due time became an obstacle to solving serious theoretical problems, notably the problem of socialist and pre-capitalist societies.' Gellner commented: 'The absolutization of the economic factor is applicable to the capitalist period only. Elsewhere, before and since, we must look to relations of domination-subjection.'

This, surely, means that there are circumstances in which power ('domination-subordination') determines relations of production rather than vice versa. The mention by Danilova in this connection of 'socialism' (which her readers would construe as the Soviet system) is, of course, most important. A similar or related point was made by Wlodzimierz Brus:

In my opinion, the traditionally accepted relationship between economy and policy as 'base' on the one hand and 'superstructure' on the other, and hence as 'in the last resort' the determining factor and the determined factor, needs, with respect to socialism, fundamental modification. Economy and politics are so intimately intertwined, especially when considered dynamically, that the continued use of the old conceptual apparatus of 'base' and 'superstructure' becomes more and more inadequate.[26] . . .

Trotsky wrote long ago, in relation to the Soviet system, that 'the character of the economy as a whole thus depends upon the character of state power'.[27]

Even longer ago Lenin wrote: 'Politics cannot but have dominance over economics. To argue otherwise is to forget the ABC of Marxism.' What, then, is the name to attach to an identifiable group which exercises state power, and achieves political and economic domination?

Let us attempt a few generalizations based upon the considerations set out above.

1. If the state owns the means of production, the nature of the state, its political processes, its power-relations, are essential determinants of production relations.

2. If such a state is in some sense a workers' state, i.e. the masses have a strong and continuous influence on public affairs and on economic policy, *and* if planning dominates in large-scale economic decision-making, I for one would accept that the system could be described as socialist. Probably, I would have Bettelheim, Brus and some other Marxist theorists on my side in doing so. . . .

3. If the Soviet state machine, the process of production and the producers, are directed by the party-state *nomenklatura* officials, who recruit by co-option from among the beneficiaries of higher education, and who in various ways benefit from privilege, it follows that this ruling stratum has *some* of the characteristics of a *ruling* class, though not that of ownership, except possibly in some collective sense (cf. Castoriadis). Medvedev argues, however, that 'it is evident

---

26. W. Brus, *The Economics and Politics of Socialism* (London, 1973), p. 88.
27. L. Trotsky, *The Revolution Betrayed* (London, 1937), p. 237.

that they are not owners of the means of production, do not possess lands and cannot bequeath their rights and their ranks *(dolzhnosti)* to their children'. He claims that, though their power is 'very great', none the less 'the position of these men is in many ways less secure than that of high officials of a church hierarchy, for instance the Catholic one'.[28] He prefers to regard the leadership as in a position analogous to that of a trustee, administering the property of a minor: while appearing to be in full charge, 'the trustee is not the owner of the property he controls. True, some trustees can succeed in prolonging the trustee-ship even after the real proprietor comes of age. None the less the trustee is still only a trustee, the administrator and not the boss, not the owner. This is known . . . by all society.' Medvedev quotes the view that 'the bureaucrats' power rests only on political equilibrium, and this is a much more fragile basis for a superior position in society than any of the known structures of property relations, hallowed by law, religion and tradition'.[29] This is indeed a serious argument, though surely it is only the power of the individual bureaucrat which rests on 'political equilibrium', rather than the power of the ruling group as a collectiv-ity. It still leaves one perplexed about how to define the ruling stratum.

An (anonymous) Soviet commentator, also cited by Medvedev, puts the dilemma in another way, very close to the ideas of Medvedev himself (and of the author of this article too). He notes a 'contradiction between the socialist form of production relations and the bureaucratic system of control. . . . For a scientist the question of the social nature of our bureaucracy is a vital and fundamental question. The Stalin and post-Stalin periods formed the bureaucracy into a separate social group, a separate stratum. . . . Of course our bureaucracy is not a new exploiting class, representing state capitalism, etc. But then what is it? It seems that we need more subtle intermediate categories, different from [con-ventional-Marxist] social-economic formations—although we note in paren-thesis that the fact of the appropriation of a part of the surplus product [by this stratum] is undeniable. It is not enough to talk of "elements of caste", when power is in the hands of a social group standing above society, self-sufficient, closed, which retains power in the hands of these same people. New recruits . . . enter only from the ranks of the "reliables", who satisfy the social requirements of the bureaucracy.'[30] Here again the search is for new categories, new labels to attach to a phenomenon which Marx did not analyse.

Rolf Dahrendorf distinguished 'class' and 'stratum' *(Schicht):* 'the concept class is an analytical tool that can only make sense in the context of a class theory. "Classes" are major interest groupings emerging from specific structural cir-cumstances, which intervene as such in social conflicts and play a part in changes of social structure.' Whereas a 'stratum' is merely an analytical category, identi-fying persons of a similar situation in the social hierarchy, who share some situational identities such as 'income, prestige, style of living, etc. . . .' So for him *classes* relate to groups which act together in a power context, about which

---

28. Medvedev, *op. cit.,* p. 347.
29. *Ibid.,* pp. 347–8.
30. *Ibid.,* pp. 349–50.

one speaks in terms of 'inclusion or exclusion from positions of power'.[31] Ownership is, of course, one means of acquiring power, but Dahrendorf, if I understand him correctly, would certainly not confine his definition of a ruling (or any other) class to any specific property relationship: there could be ownership with little power, or more commonly, power without ownership. In these terms, the Soviet 'establishment' would seem to qualify as a 'class'. This appears to be not Marxist, but then we are trying to deal with a society unlike any that Marx described.

Is the term 'power élite', associated with C. Wright Mills, more suitable? There is no doubt that it *can* be used to describe the Soviet dominant stratum. However, the term is most usually applied to the group that exercises power within a Western class society: thus it may consist of top officials, generals, senior advisers, a few influential industrialists and bankers, even some trade union officials. The common denominator is that they all have their hands on the levers of power. Yet in this society there are a great many others who may have as much (or more) wealth or social prestige, and the power élite itself lacks social cohesion or any definite relationship to the means of production. This is not to criticize Mills's use of the term, but merely to underline that the Soviet case is different: the rulers ('power élite') are at the same time the controllers of the bulk of state property, of almost all means of production, and can determine to a great extent the status, earnings and social position of various sub-groups in society. Thus in America there is a power élite *and* a class structure, while in the USSR the power élite *is* the class structure, or rather its apex. The use of the same term for these two distinct formations may mislead.

The word 'caste' is unsuitable because it suggests fixed hereditary status. So does the old Russian world *soslovie*, or 'estate', though the *dvoryanskoe soslovie* could be entered under tsarism by promotion in the civil and military service (Lenin's father was one of many). But some would argue that the term 'class' also implies heredity. Thus Bukharin wrote of the ancient Inca state, in which there was 'a gentry-priesthood *class* . . . which controlled everything, ran everything and operated the *state* economy as a dominant *class*, sitting on top of all the others'.[32] Note that Bukharin used 'class' in relation to a society without private *ownership*, but presumably the 'gentry-priesthood' were hereditary. We have seen that, despite some evidence advantages in being well born, the Soviet 'ruling class' is not hereditary. Does this destroy the validity of the 'class' label? I think not, though I see the force of objections to my position. . . .

It seems to me not greatly to matter that, in a unihierarchical system, the definition of where to draw the 'class' line is necessarily arbitrary. I do not insist on *nomenklaturnyi rabotnik*. There is no scientific reason why one should include only the top 10,000 or the top 100,000. The point about the *nomenklatura* is that it lists those whom the *system itself* regards as being important enough to require the special attention of the central committee's organization department. Consequently, unlike vague words about bureaucrats and élite, they represent some-

---

31. R. Dahrendorf, *Soziale Klassen und Klassenkonflikt* (Stuttgart, 1957), pp. ix, 139 (translation mine). Thanks are due to H. Adomeit for drawing my attention to these passages.
32. N. Bukharin, *Teoriya istoricheskogo materializma* (M., 1921), p. 69; emphasis added.

thing not only definable but defined, and defined not by the arbitrary whim of the foreign scholar but by the party machine itself (though this definition is not known to us in detail).

There is another dimension to the problem of 'class' analysis of Soviet society: that of consciousness. Do *they* regard themselves as a sort of class, *sui generis?* Some would certainly argue that they do. The poet-playwright Aleksandr Galich quotes a story of a woman patient at one of the special 'government' hospitals who, eating a smoked salmon sandwich, remarked: 'I visited a school friend, not one of us *(ne iz nashikh),* who gave me tea, and it was awkward to refuse, so I ate some town sausage, and got gastritis.'[33] The two key points are the concept of *iz nashikh,* and access to superior sausages (and smoked salmon) which are simply not on sale to ordinary townspeople. Galich speaks of a special official pass giving access to 'special buffets, smoked fish, caviare, American cigarettes, cheap dinners', and also 'dachas with paintings, Czech crystal, silver cutlery, service personnel', a separate existence with its own access to information ('the white TASS') and to politically spicy and sexy films, luxurious and cheap sanatoria and the opportunity to visit foreign countries. The beneficiaries of such privileges live in a world of their own, to which ordinary mortals are denied access. Surely they have a sense of belonging to some separate and high 'class', and their subordinates, and ordinary workers and peasants, regard them as a privileged group. David Lane . . . argues that the dominant values are in some sense working-class values, but I find this hard to follow. The *nominal* values of Soviet society indeed stress the working class, but has this more significance than did Christian poverty and humility in relation to a proud, rich, aristocrat–archbishop in Renaissance times? . . .

---

33. A. Galich, *General'naya repetitsiya* (Frankfurt, 1974), p. 188.

# · 29 ·

# Work Hierarchy and Management "Participation" in the Soviet Union

## Murray Yanowitch

### Managerial Ideology and the Formal Structure of Authority

Recent years have witnessed the emergence of a heightened interest in the "science of management" in the Soviet Union. The management literature which has accompanied this interest embodies a philosophy of management, a set of presuppositions concerning the functional requirements of "relations of management," which may serve as a useful introduction to our examination of the structure of authority in the Soviet enterprise. What follows is our attempt to convey the essence of these presuppositions as they appear in some of the more authoritative management literature. As illustrations of the latter we rely chiefly on the work of V. G. Afanas'ev and Iu. E. Volkov.[1]

Although all members of the socialist society are simultaneously "managers" and "managed," the effective functioning of any subsystem of this society—such as an economic enterprise—requires the clear delineation of "relations of subordination." These relations prevail between those who "direct" (or "manage") the organization and those who "execute" the directives of the former. This separation of functions between "the managers and the managed" (or the "subjects" and "objects" of management) is personified in the factory in

* From Murray Yanowitch, *Social and Economic Inequality in the Soviet Union* (London: Martin Robertson, 1977), pp. 135–64.

1. V. G. Afanas'ev, "The Management of Society as a Sociological Problem," in V. G. Afanas'ev ed., *Nauchnoe upravlenie obshchestvom*, No. 2, Moscow, 1968, pp. 190–97; Iu. E. Volkov, "The System of Management of Society and the Type of Social Structure," in L. A. Volovik ed., *Sotsiologiia i ideologiia*, Moscow, 1969, pp. 168–71.

the relations between ordinary workers, on the one hand, and the foreman, shop superintendent, and factory director, on the other. Relations among the latter groups, as well as between them and workers, may be characterized as relations of subordination. Thus the formal organization of the Soviet enterprise, as of the production system as a whole, is explicitly recognized as a hierarchical structure in which successively higher positions in the organization correspond to "functions . . . which are increasingly purely managerial."[2] Such functions are essentially those of planning, coordination, and control.

Although the Soviet management literature acknowledges the "surface similarity" between the general approach outlined here and traditional management philosophy in capitalist societies, it also stresses certain differences. The management function is not performed on behalf of a class of private owners of capital whose interests dominate the production process but on behalf of "society as a whole."[3] Moreover, the need to concentrate managerial functions in the hands of a special stratum of "professional managers" presumably does not conflict with steadily increasing opportunities for workers to influence and participate in management activity.[4] We shall examine this latter claim in some detail below but present it here merely as a frequently reiterated theme in Soviet management literature.

When we turn to the details of management organization and the authority structure in the enterprise, the language of Soviet organization theory is often supplemented or replaced by the more traditional "Leninist principles of management." While some of these are drawn from the political lexicon of Party history and may seem more rhetorical than substantive, they are as much part of the "tone" of Soviet management philosophy as the more "scientific" organization theory briefly reviewed above. Indeed, at least on the surface, there seems to be a striking similarity between the latter (with its explicit acceptance of hierarchy, relations of subordination, the dichotomy between managers and managed) and some of the "Leninist principles of management." What are these principles and what bearing do they have on the distribution of authority in the enterprise?

1. The principle of "unity of political and economic leadership." This is essentially a way of affirming that the production program and economic measures that are to be implemented by any level of management have their source in the economic policy of the Communist Party. This follows from the Party's leading role in directing Soviet economic development. Hence the manager must be guided by "general state interests," not by "narrow departmental, local interests." To perform his functions effectively,

the manager must know the policy of the Party, master Marxist–Leninist theory, have a broad political orientation, and be able to correctly combine current economic work with political activity. . . .[5]

---

2. G. V. Suvorov, "The Problem of Studying the Structure of Management of the Production Collective," in A. S. Pashkov, *Chelovek i obshchestvo,* Issue VIII, Leningrad, 1971, p. 76.

3. Iu. E. Volkov, pp. 168–69.

4. V. G. Afanas'ev, pp. 190, 192.

5. F. F. Aunapu, *Chto takoe upravlenie,* Moscow, 1967, p. 14.

The implementation of this principle requires close and continuing contact between managerial personnel and the Party organization at the enterprise. The latter serves simultaneously as a resource that management draws on in meeting plan assignments and as a "monitor" of management's performance. The discussions of the Party organization's role in the enterprise that appear in the management literature, however, stress that in no case does the Party assume the operational functions of managerial personnel, that it never becomes a "substitute" for management.[6] This point is related to principle 3 below.

2. The principle of "democratic centralism." This is a principle of Party organization which, in its application to enterprise management, is reducible to the idea that the "organizing and directing role" of management staffs must be combined with the encouragement of initiative "from below" and must take account of the peculiarities of particular enterprises and localities.[7] It is typically stated in such broad terms that it is difficult to see how it can be anything but a very general guide to managerial behavior. However, it is precisely its nonspecific and all-inclusive character that has made it possible to appeal to this principle to justify arguments for broadening the base of participation in decision-making at the enterprise.

3. The principle of "one-man management" (edinonachalie). This deserves more careful examination than the above two principles, partly because it moves us into the operational details of the authority structure at the enterprise, and partly because of the danger of too facile an interpretation based on the authoritarian image conveyed by the concept. That Soviet management has had a markedly authoritarian character can hardly be doubted, but the principle of one-man management is not reducible to the absolute rule of the factory director. Let us see how this principle is formulated in the management literature and applied in managerial practice.

The principle of one-man management in the management of production consists in the following: the leadership of each production unit (enterprise, shop, section) is assigned to a single executive who is endowed by the state with the necessary rights to manage, and who bears full responsibility for the work of the given unit. All individuals working in the unit are obligated to fulfill the instructions of the executive.

To correctly implement the principle of one-man management it is of great importance that there be a clear demarcation of obligations, rights, and responsibilities. . . . Every employee must be subordinate to only one individual, from whom he receives an assignment and to whom he is accountable.

In actual practice the principle of one-man management in industry is implemented as follows: the director of the enterprise is appointed by the ministry and directs the enterprise in the interests of the people on the basis of one-man management, answering to the ministry for the activity of the enterprise which he heads. The director of the plant is the highest one-man manager at the enterprise. On his instructions the superintendents of shops and departments, foremen, and other [managerial—M. Y.] personnel . . . are appointed and relieved of employment. His instructions must be fulfilled by all personnel at the plant without question.

The shop superintendent is the one-man manager for all individuals working in the

6. Ibid., p. 14.

7. Ibid., p. 15; S. Kamenitser et al., Organizatsiia i planirovanie promyshlennykh predpriiatii, Moscow, 1967, p. 45.

shop. The senior foreman, correspondingly, is the one-man manager at his section; the shift foreman—on his shift.[8]

What appears initially as a single "principle of management" is translated into an integrated set of organizational rules. A number of important features emerge from this lengthy quotation. Perhaps the most obvious point is that every level of the organization, not only the enterprise as a whole, has its own one-man manager. The authority of the foreman relative to the workers under his supervision appears to be of the same order (absolute) as that of the shop superintendent relative to his direct subordinates. Not only is authority individualized in one-man management but responsibility is as well. Indeed, the stress on fixing individual responsibility for the performance of a particular unit of the enterprise is no less than the emphasis on individual authority. This is symbolized by frequent warnings against *obezlichka*—the evasion of personal responsibility for a unit's performance. One-man management fixed this responsibility on the single source of authority in the unit. Reliance on "unity of command" (every employee must be directly subordinate to only one superior) is expressly designed to avoid both conflicting orders and the evasion of personal responsibility. Furthermore, accountability is always structured "upward," i.e., managerial personnel are always accountable to their superiors, never to those whom they manage, just as they are always appointed to their posts by a "higher" level of management (the ministry in the case of the director, the director in the case of the shop superintendent, etc.).

There is one qualification that must be introduced at this point. Our discussion thus far has been modeled on the industrial plant. There are no significant departures from this model of formal organization in the case of the state farm. In the case of the collective farm, however, the formal process of selection of top management differs from that in the industrial plant. The chairman and managing board of the collective farm are "elected" by the "highest organ" of the farm, the general membership meeting of collective farm members.[9] We will return later to the question of how much difference this makes for the distribution of effective power over the farm's affairs. For the present the point worth stressing is that, aside from the formal management selection process, the principle of one-man management is also acknowledged to be the guiding principle of farm administration, with emphasis on "the strict administrative subordination of the primary production units [brigades—M. Y.] to the leaders of the various farm subdivisions, and the latter to the collective farm chairman."[10]

It is apparent that, whatever the form of enterprise to which it is applied, one-man management is essentially a means of specifying the "relations of subordination" which in the Soviet view (although obviously not only in the Soviet view) are inherent in the effective management of all organizations. The stress on clearly defined areas of responsibility and lines of authority is all directed to one objective: ". . . the fulfillment of the production program, since under all conditions management must take as its point of departure the priority

---

8. F. F. Aunapu, pp. 16–17.

9. G. M. Loz, *Upravlenie v sovkhozakh i kolkhozakh,* Moscow, 1972, pp. 102, 108.

10. Ibid., p. 111.

of production requirements as the first and principal task of the enterprise."[11] The plant's production program itself, following its ratification—at least in its broad features—by the appropriate "superior" agency (ministry or combine), is transmitted from the director downward through the various one-man managers corresponding to each "level" of the organization. The number of such "levels" differs, of course, depending on the size and technological characteristics of the organization, but a typical Soviet organization chart for the "basic production" activity of the enterprise (excluding staff and auxiliary positions) will show the line of authority moving downward from plant director to shop superintendent to section foreman to brigade leaders to production workers.[12]

Seen in this light, as a specification of "relations of subordination," we may be surprised initially to learn that one-man management is compatible with "collegiality" in management. Although the notion of collegiality is typically not accorded the status of a "principle of management," it is frequently treated as a necessary supplement to one-man management. What meaning, if any, can we attach to this coupling of what, on the surface, appear to be diverse concepts? Although the notion of collegiality readily lends itself to empty rhetoric, the essential idea is that management is encouraged to involve all personnel of the enterprise "in the discussion of the most important problems of the operation of the enterprise, shop, and section."[13] In its more extreme formulations the concept of collegiality is reflected in the claim that "At the present time it is difficult to find any important problem which is decided by enterprise management exclusively on its own *(edinolichno)* without first ascertaining collective opinion."[14] The latter is normally interpreted to mean the views of the factory trade union organization, the Party, and Komsomol units and the resolutions adopted at production conferences. In its more concrete form the principle of collegiality in management may be illustrated by the expectation that in appointing and releasing a shop superintendent the plant director will "consider" the views of the factory union committee.[15]

We are not concerned for the moment with ascertaining the degree to which these prescriptions are realized in managerial practice or the sector of "collective opinion" which receives closest attention. What should be obvious from this brief review of the uses of the collegiality concept, however, is that the latter is certainly compatible with, and indeed may facilitate, one-man management. The function of collegiality is to help the manager make the "best" decision. But his authority to make the decision and the expectation that it will be followed "without question" remain unaffected. The point is simply that the recommendations made in the name of collegiality—at least those not emanating from the Party organization—are of a "consultative" rather than "binding" character.

Our preliminary examination of Soviet managerial philosophy and formal organizational structure is intended mainly to set the stage for our discussion of

11. V. G. Podmarkov, *Vvedenie v promyshlennuiu sotsiologiiu*, Moscow, 1973, p. 157.

12. Ibid., p. 46.

13. F. F. Aunapu, p. 18.

14. V. N. Ermuratskii, *Sotsial'naia aktivnost' rabotnikov promyshlennogo predpriiatiia*, Kishinev, 1973, p. 26.

15. F. F. Aunapu, p. 75.

the issue of participation in decisionmaking at the enterprise. What has already become apparent, however, is that despite its distinctive terminology (embodied in the Leninist principles of management), Soviet managerial ideology is not strikingly distinctive in content. In fact, it does not seem to depart significantly from some versions of what, in the West, has been labeled as the "classical theory of organization." It was not V. I. Lenin but H. Fayol, one of the founding fathers of classical theory, who, in reviewing some of the principles of management "which I have most frequently had to apply," formulated one of them as follows:

Subordination of individual interest to general interest. This principle calls to mind the fact that in a business the interest of one employee or group of employees should not prevail over that of the concern, that the interests of the home should come before that of its members, and that the interest of the State should have pride of place over that of one citizen or group of citizens.[16]

It seems clear that Soviet management ideology has had little difficulty assimilating some early examples of Western "classical" principles of management. It is not only Fayol's general formulation cited above that Soviet management philosophy would find congenial; his concepts of unity of command, unity of direction, and scalar chain, among others, have become part of the common parlance of Soviet management philosophy—sometimes under the general rubric of one-man management.

## The "Humanization" of Soviet Management

It is important to realize that most of the ideas we have just discussed, including one-man management, were originally enshrined as "principles of management" during a historically unique period, that of the prewar five-year plans. Although these principles remain an integral part of current management philosophy, they are rooted in a work situation which obviously differed in important respects from the present. The stress on the clear-cut delineation of lines of authority and responsibility, the expectation of unquestioning obedience to the instructions of superiors, the high degree of concentration of decision-making power combined with often perfunctory appeals for "initiative from below," all suggest an authoritarian style of management behavior which must have seemed especially appropriate for the early planning years. It is well to recall that this was a period in which the bulk of new entrants to the industrial work force consisted of unskilled, uprooted peasants or their children, unfamiliar with both the technology and work discipline of their new work sites. The enormous task of rapidly adapting this new labor force to the disciplined work routines of the factory seemed to require the strict ordering of formal authority relationships which is so much a part of one-man management. The apparent absence (beginning in 1931–32) of significant unemployment compounded the problem of maintaining effective work discipline. Nor were the turbulent years of war and postwar reconstruction which followed conducive to an easing of the "command" style of enterprise management.

---

16. D. S. Pugh ed., *Organization Theory* (Baltimore: Penguin Books, 1971), pp. 101, 108.

A striking feature of more recent years is that, without the explicit abandon-ment of the Leninist principles of management or significant alterations in the formal structure of authority within the enterprise, a new theme has begun to permeate Soviet management literature. This theme stresses that the effective performance of managerial functions has become increasingly complex, not only because of more advanced technology but because of changes in the "hu-man factor." The result has been the emergence of a Soviet version of the "human relations" approach to management. This has been accompanied by the acknowledgement that Western human relations' literature—just as the earlier writings on scientific management by Frederick Taylor—contain "rational ele-ments" which must be "assimilated, interpreted in a Marxist methodological framework, and be applied in practice."[17] Human relations in industry are not a peculiarity of capitalist society, and there is no reason for Marxist sociology to permit their study to become "a monopoly of bourgeois sociology."[18] Thus, as we shall see below, concepts drawn from or inspired by Western human rela-tions literature are in the process of becoming incorporated into Soviet manage-rial theory.

The legitimation of the theme of human relations signals the need for a modification of the traditional authoritarian management style. It reflects the recognition that the effective economic performance of an enterprise depends significantly on "the solidarity of the collective, the degree of confidence of the collective in its leadership, the quality of interpersonal relations, the attitude (nastroenie) of the workers. . . ."[19] It is not only the perfection of a formal structure of authority that counts but an "improvement in the psychological climate of the collective" through methods of supervision that stress dignified treatment of subordinates and increased reliance on methods of "self-regula-tion" rather than purely external controls. Even the manager's presumed duty to "fulfill the plan at any price" is no longer an excuse for ignoring the interests of the members of the collective. Moreover, managerial personnel must recognize that many jobs continue to be "uninteresting, arduous, dirty, monotonous . . ." and that workers must be imbued with a sense of the social significance of such work if it is to be performed adequately. This requires a "benevolent, comradely atmosphere" and supportive attitudes of managerial personnel.[20]

However moderate or even trivial some of these strictures may appear, they must be seen as part of a new "tone" in Soviet management philosophy, and they undoubtedly have had some impact on managerial behavior. Before turn-ing to some elaborations and illustrations of the human relations approach under Soviet circumstances, let us ask why it should have appeared at all.

Perhaps the most obvious explanation lies in the changed composition of the work force. Young people now entering the urban labor market are less likely to be displaced peasants or their children. They are mainly the offspring of

---

17. D. P. Kaidalov and E. I. Suimenko, *Aktual'nye problemy sotsiologii truda,* Moscow, 1974, p. 54.

18. V. G. Podmarkov, p. 31.

19. Iu. V. Kolesnikov, "On the Social Functions of a Leader of a Socialist Production Collec-tive," in V. G. Afanas'ev ed., *Nauchnoe upravlenie obshchestvom,* No. 6, Moscow, 1972, p. 108.

20. D. P. Kaidalov and E. I. Suimenko, pp. 59–60; Iu. V. Kolesnikov, pp. 103, 119–20, 129.

urban workers and have been reared under the "looser" controls of urban life. They are substantially more educated than their predecessors of the prewar industrialization period. As late as 1939 less than 10% of industrial workers had received seven years or more of schooling; by the late 1960s in excess of one-half had attained this level.[21] Crude and authoritarian methods of supervision at the work place—symbolized by the "peremptory command"[22]—which seemed appropriate in the past are less so now. In the words of two Soviet industrial sociologists:

While in the past people were capable of tolerating the "inconvenience' of rude interpersonal relations and even ignoring them—since they were under the pressure of material need—now, under changed circumstances, they are just as sensitive to rudeness, coarseness, bureaucratism as they were in the past to need and deprivation.[23]

But the problem is not simply that the extended schooling and urban upbringing of workers require a more "cultured" style of supervision at the work place. One of the principal findings of Soviet industrial sociology has been that the extension of education has created aspirations for a "creative" job content that the existing structure of job opportunities frequently cannot satisfy.[24] The result has been a "surplus" of educated workers in the special sense that their formal schooling is in excess of that required for effective performance of the many routine, manual, or assembly-line types of jobs that must be filled. Much of the recent Soviet concern with job dissatisfaction is explicitly centered on this issue of the apparent "disproportion" between the level of formal schooling and limited opportunities for intellectually rewarding work. The perennial problem of excessive labor turnover is no longer interpreted simplistically as largely reflecting the search for the "long ruble" or irrationalities in the wage structure but is seen as significantly affected by workers' aspirations for a "richer" job content.[25] The acknowledgement of substantial work dissatisfaction has posed the issue of how to "compensate" workers for the gap between their limited work content and the aspirations fostered by extended schooling. One means of offsetting this dissatisfaction, according to the sociologist whose work has probably contributed most to the discussion of this issue, is the

development of all types of participation of workers in the management of production. The highly educated worker now coming to the factory is prepared to assume greater responsibility for the affairs of production and the organization of labor. It is perfectly obvious that much more must be done to develop all forms of initiative in the sphere of management than we have done up to now. . . .[26]

Given the context of this statement, it should not be interpreted as a merely perfunctory appeal for "collegiality" in management, although the failure to spell out the form that worker participation in management might take obvi-

---

21. D. P. Kaidalov and E. I. Suimenko, p. 92.

22. Ibid., p. 62.

23. Ibid., p. 56.

24. V. A. Iadov, "Orientation—Creative Work," in G. M. Gusev et al. eds., *Obshchestvo i molodezh'*, Moscow, 1968, pp. 129–44.

25. D. P. Kaidalov and E. I. Suimenko, p. 92.

26. V. A. Iadov, p. 142.

ously weakens its force. It is, in any case, a proposal directed to meeting a serious problem. What must be stressed here is that under conditions in which the scope for genuine worker participation in managerial decisions is insignificant or nonexistent, this proposal becomes a persuasive argument for a more participatory, less authoritarian style of leadership at the plant. And it is primarily with matters of managerial style, rather than with the substance of decision-making power, that the Soviet human relations approach is concerned. In this sense Soviet sociologists' studies of work attitudes and the linking of work dissatisfaction to extended education have helped to legitimate a human relations approach to management.

We have seen that this approach stresses the importance of a solidaristic psychological climate and a higher "culture" of interpersonal relations at the enterprise. But these are rather broadly stated prescriptions. What are their more specific implications for managerial behavior? One illustration is provided by the "Recommendations to Managers" issued at large plants and designed to improve the work of supervision by equipping managerial staffs with "social-psychological knowledge." A Soviet volume on industrial sociology which urges the assimilation of human relations' techniques cites with obvious approval the following rules at a Dnepropetrovsk steel plant:

A good manager must not only think of the technology of production but also be a "guardian" of his subordinates; he must be aware of their frame of mind.

An inseparable feature of the style of leadership is courtesy, friendliness, and tact. Instructions issued in a firm but courteous manner always lead to better results than those issued rudely.

Do not wait for a subordinate to be the first to show friendship and affability, but take the initiative yourself. Even if the subordinate does not immediately respond, your affability will ultimately be worthwhile.

The subordinates of a poor manager live in a world of rumors, conjectures. . . . A good manager keeps his subordinates informed about the general state of affairs. . . .

Do not "throw yourself" on someone who has made a mistake. Even when you are about to reprimand someone, it is better to begin with praise. . . .[27]

Another illustration of the attempt to affect specific norms of managerial behavior is the suggestion that managers recognize and cultivate "informal relations" (and groups) at the enterprise. Exclusive reliance on the formal structures and instruments of authority generates a superfluous flow of official directives, instructions, written orders. Increased reliance on "informal" modes of communication can help to overcome the sense of "alienation" between managers and subordinates, make for frankness in their discussions of production problems—apparently something that is often not present—and improve the quality of information received by managers. Finally, in what must be regarded as a somewhat rhetorical flourish by the Soviet writers on whose work we rely here, "informal relations promote . . . the democratization of management."[28]

Despite the apparently trivial and obvious nature of some of these recom-

---

27. D. P. Kaidalov and E. I. Suimenko, pp. 67–68. We include a partial listing of the 16 rules cited in this source.

28. Ibid., pp. 73–74.

mendations and guidelines, their significance should not be dismissed. They are part of a relatively recent theme in Soviet management literature and a response to new problems. All of them have this in common: they point to an effort to inculcate a more "humane," looser, less rigid style of supervision in the enterprise while leaving the Leninist principles of management—and one-man management in particular—essentially undisturbed. We may take this as a hallmark of what might be called Soviet human relations theory. A nonauthoritarian style of management is encouraged, while the substance of managerial power—the exclusion of workers from significant decision-making—remains intact. Nowhere is this more clearly expressed than in a Soviet writer's (I. P. Volkov) recent attempt to elaborate a typology of management styles, specifying their various advantages and disadvantages. No single style, according to Volkov, is appropriate for all circumstances. A "directive" (authoritarian) style may be appropriate for wartime or other emergency situations, but under normal conditions it stifles initiative. A "permissive" style may be required in research institutes or where work is highly individualized. However, the "norm" should be ("is," according to Volkov) a collegial style of management. A collegial manager's subordinates "participate actively" in the decision-making process, but the manager "leaves to himself the right of final decision." Perhaps the most significant quality of this ideal type of Soviet manager is that "his art consists of the ability to use power without appealing to it."[29]

We can hardly judge from our review of the literature how frequently the various recommendations and models offered under the rubrics of human relations or collegiality are applied in managerial practice. There is some evidence of considerable resistance by managerial staffs to their implementation.[30] But their very emergence in the management literature testifies to the search for management methods more appropriate to the changing composition of the current Soviet work force and its aspirations. This search has gone beyond the issue of management style and has touched, sometimes hesitantly, on the more sensitive issue of the structure of power in the enterprise.

### Beyond "Humanization": The Issue of Participation in Management

The fog of rhetoric surrounding the theme of "democratization of management" is an obstacle to the analysis of an important issue in Soviet society: the search for more effective modes of organization in economic enterprises. The problem is, in part, that worker participation in management is regarded as something that has already been substantially attained and to which homage is constantly paid. Moreover, the further extension of such participation is an

---

29. I. P. Volkov, "The Style of Management in Solving Problems of the Social Development of Enterprise Collectives," in E. S. Kuz'min and A. A. Bodalev eds., *Sotsial'naia psikhologiia i sotsial'noe planirovanie,* Leningrad, 1973, p. 89.

30. D. P. Kaidalov and E. I. Suimenko, p. 59. A survey of managerial personnel of the Ukrainian Ministry of Ferrous Metallurgy found that about 35% "categorically insist on a hard *(zhestkii)* style of work with people and complained about excessive democratism which results in a weakening of the work discipline of their subordinates."

officially approved value. This often makes it difficult to distinguish between ritualistic celebrations of an alleged "achievement" and serious attempts to pose the problem. The latter almost invariably contain elements of the former. Concrete proposals for changing the distribution of managerial authority are typically presented as improvements in a system which is already highly participatory—when it obviously is not.

Nonetheless there is unmistakable evidence that recent years have witnessed an upsurge of efforts to broaden the social base of participation in management functions. These efforts appear to have been largely unsuccessful thus far. But the discussions which ensued were accompanied by specific proposals for the redistribution of managerial authority, revealing studies of the limited extent of worker (and peasant) participation in decision-making, and a remarkable but short-lived experiment in the democratization of management. What follows is a review of the limited but distinct forms recently assumed by the issue of "production democracy" in the Soviet Union.

The economic reforms of 1965 provided the setting in which serious public discussion of the democratization of management began to emerge. Among their other features, the reforms were intended to increase the autonomy of individual enterprises by reducing the number of centrally fixed plan assignments and increasing the share of profits that could be retained and allocated at the enterprise. They did not directly provide for changes in the structure of authority within enterprises. In this sense they appeared to offer promise of "decentralization" rather than "democratization" of management. But the Party resolutions which accompanied the reforms stressed that they "provide the economic prerequisites for wider participation by the masses in the running of production." A. N. Kosygin's speech at the time made the same point: "Better management is impossible unless it becomes more democratic and unless the participation of the masses is considerably extended. . . . Every worker should be made to feel that he is one of the owners of the factory."[31]

Indeed, there was a certain logic to linking the opportunities offered by the reform to the issue of the structure of authority in the plant. Under conditions in which the scope for autonomy by the enterprise was severely limited by a myriad of assignments and instructions from higher agencies (whether these were regional economic councils or industrial ministries), the possibility of effectively broadening the social base of participation in management could hardly be taken seriously. Worker participation could mean little more than conscientious performance of job tasks assigned by managerial personnel. The reform, by appearing to enlarge the scope of decisions that could be made at the enterprise (particularly by permitting increases in decentralized investment and premium payments out of retained profits), provided a kind of "platform" for reopening the issue of the structure of managerial authority at the enterprise.

One of the first questions to be raised in the years immediately following the reforms was the need to limit the applicability of one-man management. As one of the participants in this discussion put it, the increased involvement of workers

---

31. Cited from Roy A. Medvedev, *On Socialist Democracy* (New York: Alfred A. Knopf, 1975), p. 247.

in management required that "a clear line of demarcation be established between the rights and obligations of the one-man manager and the collective organs of management at enterprises."[32] In this context such "collective organs" included the factory trade union and production conferences through which the principles of "collegiality" and "democratic centralism" were formally implemented. The need for more clearly defining (i.e., restricting) the rights of management officials arose from the "considerable discrepancy" which had developed between the theory of participation by the masses in management and actual managerial practice. This was a heritage of the prereform period, when management would frequently ignore "rational" proposals of the collective organs and thereby even generate "hostility" among workers toward the factory administration. But the reforms would not automatically force management to cease ignoring "the will of the collective." What was required was a specification of those decisions which should fall within the authority of the collective organs and whose implementation would become "juridically obligatory" for the plant director.[33] The distribution of premiums was offered as one example of such a decision. The writer who offered this illustration hastened to add that it would not conflict with the principle of one-man management. The latter would continue to apply to all "operational" or "technical" decisions at the enterprise. The allocation of premiums was to be regarded as an aspect of "social management" falling within the competence of the plant's collective organs.

The point to be stressed here is not the specific, relatively modest proposal concerning the authority to allocate premium funds, but the fact that a much larger issue could now be treated as an open question:

which elements of managerial activity should be implemented solely by management, which through the obligatory participation of the collective, and which exclusively by the collective.[34]

Some of the literature urging the "democratization of management" in the years immediately following the economic reforms of 1965 exhibited an unprecedented boldness in criticizing prevailing interpretations of the Leninist principles of management. As an illustration we may consider a volume of essays by members of the philosophy faculty of Moscow State University edited by V. A. Fomin. One of the contributors noted that the concept of democratic centralism had been reduced by some to the idea of "initiative from below and leadership from above"; in other cases it was treated simply as the need to subordinate one level of an organization to another. This had unduly narrowed a concept whose real intent was to provide for "participation in management by *every* worker"[35] (emphasis in the original—M. Y.). The result was that democratic centralism

---

32. A. F. Sinel'nikov, "On the Relation between One-Man Management and the Participation of the Masses in the Management of the Production Process," in V. A. Fomin ed., *Nekotorye voprosy nauchnogo upravleniia obshchestvom,* Moscow, 1967, p. 51.

33. Ibid., pp. 48–50, 54–55.

34. P. M. Panov, "Problems of the Development of Democratic Principles in the Management of Production," in Iu. E. Volkov ed., *Sotsiologicheskie problemy upravleniia narodnym khoziaistvom,* Sverdlovsk, 1968, pp. 111–12.

35. L. Klepatskii, "On the Question of Forms of Organization and Management of Industry in the USSR," in V. A. Fomin, p. 63.

had often been transformed into "bureaucratic centralism," causing "harm which we cannot yet fully estimate."[36] Perhaps the most challenging aspect of such criticisms was directed against the simplistic identification of "democracy" with the existence of socialized property. The latter, however, was only a necessary condition for democratic management, not identical with it.[37] The very concept of property was typically viewed—mistakenly—from a "juridical" aspect only, i.e., from the standpoint of its legal form of ownership. In this view the greater the amount of socialized property and the more centralized its management, the "higher" the form of property. But for Marxists the juridical aspect of property is only an "external cover" for "real economic relations." The analysis of property systems in their broader, nonjuridical aspects must encompass "the totality of relations of production, exchange, and distribution."[38] The distinction made here (in a 1967 publication reporting on a 1966 conference) between the "juridical" and "real" aspects of property was to become a hallmark of the literature urging the democratization of management (pages 151 and 159 below). "Real" socialization implied not only some form of public (state or cooperative) "possession" *(vladenie)* of property but collective control over the utilization and "disposal" *(rasporiazhenie)* of property.

The very manner of posing the issue of evolving a more participatory mode of management in the postreform period suggests a seriousness of intent that was absent in earlier years. Some of the formulations of this issue in the work of Iu. E. Volkov may serve as an additional illustration. Writing in 1970, Volkov stressed that involving workers in management functions cannot mean simply providing opportunities for them to assist managerial personnel in the latter's efforts to strengthen work discipline, locate "production reserves," and generally to "improve production." While all this is necessary it is not enough, for the main feature of management is decision-making in the enterprise. Those who make decisions

possess the highest rights of management. And if we are to speak of democracy in management, its highest manifestation consists in the fact that decisions are made with the participation of the masses and are implemented under their control.[39]

This was not the usual participatory rhetoric, for Volkov was pointing out that to conceive of worker participation as exclusively an aid to managerial staffs in the performance of the latter's functions was to "stand things upside down." Workers must themselves assume managerial functions because in a socialist society "they are the masters" of the production process (Volkov's readers would understand that "are" meant "should be").[40] Volkov also called for sociological studies of the effectiveness of existing forms of participation and the working out of "specific recommendations" designed to extend them.

---

36. Ibid., p. 64.

37. Ibid., p. 65.

38. A. Tsipko, "On the Economic and Legal Concept of Property," in V. A. Fomin, p. 124.

39. Iu. E. Volkov, "Problems of Development of Democratic Principles in the Management of Socialist Production," in V. G. Afanas'ev ed., *Nauchnoe upravlenie obshchestvom*, No. 4, Moscow, 1970, pp. 152–53.

40. Ibid., p. 153, 158.

Although our discussion thus far has focused on the emergence of the theme of worker participation in management in an industrial setting, suffice it to note for the present that it also appeared in agriculture. The search for more effective modes of work organization was, if anything, more pressing there than in industry.[41]

It is all too easy to dismiss the increased attention paid in Soviet public discourse to the issue of "production democracy" as empty phrase-making or as a facade used by the Party to reinforce its authority over management at the plant and farm. But too much has occurred in this area during the postreform period that cannot be encompassed by such a facile explanation. This should become apparent from our examination of the studies, policy proposals, and experiments bearing on participation in management.

### Sociological Studies

Soviet empirical studies of decision-making in economic enterprises are of interest not only for what they reveal about the distribution of power in the producing unit but also because they have served as vehicles for an argument: the need for more participatory forms of economic organization. They obviously have also served as signals of themes which political authorities (or some faction among them) deem "legitimate" for public discussion.

Perhaps the most illuminating studies of this type have been conducted by Iu. V. Arutiunian in rural areas. Although the latter feature limits the applicability of his findings, Arutiunian included rural industrial enterprises as well as collective and state farms in his studies. He sought to determine the "distribution of rights and power within the collective" among six socio-occupational groups, ranging from common laborers at one extreme to higher-level managers and specialists at the other. Arutiunian's respondents were asked to indicate whether, in their judgment, they "exercised an influence in deciding major questions of the collective." Thus what emerged were subjective perceptions of influence in the enterprise, differentiated by occupational status of respondents. We show Arutiunian's findings in one of the three investigated regions in Table 1 (the results in the other two were essentially the same).

All forms of rural economic organization were obviously hierarchical in the sense that the frequency of perceived influence declined markedly as we move from the highest-ranking occupations to low-skilled and unskilled peasants and workers. Some two-thirds to three-fourths of the latter group—the most numerous rural stratum—perceived itself as without influence over important decisions in farms and other rural enterprises. Moreover, the majority of all respondents combined felt themselves to be without influence. Perhaps the most striking result was that the type of organization which in a strictly formal sense was the most participatory exhibited the lowest sense of participation among its members. The collective farm, it will be recalled, was presumably a cooperative that elected its own top management and held regular meetings of its members through which "control" over its operations was to be exercised.

---

41. See, for example, L. Nechaeva and A. Yanov, "Help the Strong," *Molodoi kommunist,* 1970, no. 2, pp. 55–63.

**Table 1.** Percentage of Individuals Having No Influence on Major
Decisions at the Work Place, Rural Areas, Tatar Republic, 1967
(by socio-occupational group)

| Socio-occupational groups | Percentage without influence on major decisions | | | |
| --- | --- | --- | --- | --- |
| | on collective farms | on state farms | in other enterprises | total |
| Higher-level managerial personnel and specialists | 13 | | 20 | 12 |
| Middle-level managerial personnel and specialists | 17 | 36 | | 20 |
| Nonmanual employees | 33 | 48 | 37 | 38 |
| Machine operators | 54 | 45 | 45 | 50 |
| Skilled manual workers | 64 | 51 | 58 | 58 |
| Low-skilled and unskilled manual workers | 69 | 72 | 68 | 69 |
| Total | 63 | 55 | 50 | 56 |

Source: Iu. V. Arutiunian, *Sotsial'naia struktura*, p. 108.

But the employees of state farms and rural industrial enterprises (in which "state" as distinct from "cooperative" property prevailed) experienced their roles as providing greater scope for participation in management than did collective farm members.[42]

Arutiunian did not hesitate to draw the obvious conclusion that differences in the legal form of property ownership in the Soviet setting had little impact on the distribution of control over the use of property.[43] Whatever the form of ownership, the typical worker or peasant could hardly feel himself "a master" of the production process. In a manner that departed from the typically simplistic definition of socialism, Arutiunian distinguished between "juridical" socialization (the elimination of private ownership) and "real" socialization (measured by the "degree to which the producers themselves perform the functions of management").[44] His findings clearly seemed to demonstrate that the latter kind of socialization was a long way from being achieved. In this context his formulation of the "task" ahead, although stated in general terms, flowed naturally from his research findings and illustrates the seriousness with which the issue of "production democracy" was regarded in some quarters: "The social task standing on the order of the day points to the necessity for the further democratization of the functions of control over property."[45]

---

42. Other studies of farm management in the more "popular" literature reinforced Arutiunian's findings. Collective farm membership meetings were often dominated by managerial staff, with farm specialists reporting to each other and with ordinary peasants rarely participating in discussions. The principal subject of these discussions was often the problem of work discipline rather than broad issues of economic policy. See the study of the Frunze Collective Farm in ibid., pp. 60–61.

43. Iu. V. Arutiunian, *Sotsial'naia struktura*, p. 111.

44. Ibid., p. 104.

45. Ibid., p. 109.

None of the recent studies of urban industrial enterprises of which we are aware has replicated Arutiunian's design. But several provide additional illustrations of the kind of empirical research whose findings—at least implicitly—served to buttress Arutiunian's conclusion cited above. Each points in its own way to the limited influence of workers outside their regular (nonmanagerial) job functions. One study of the sources of directives issued by plant management (in a Sverdlovsk machinery plant) over the course of a year sheds a revealing light on the limited nature of "collegiality" in decision-making. Some 90% of such directives were initiated by the management staff alone, less than 1% were based on proposals submitted by individual workers, and the remainder were based on the recommendations of the "collective organs." But of the latter the vast majority concerned safety regulations. It was hardly surprising that the author concluded that one-man management was not being adequately combined with "collegiality."[46]

Another recent study of an individual plant (a tractor factory in Kishinev) is of interest chiefly because it specifies the meaning that can be attached to the concept of "worker participation in deciding important problems of the collective" within the framework of centralized planning and existing legal procedures. Such "important problems" were identified as the revision of output norms, the distribution of premiums, the preparation of drafts of production plans, the distribution of housing facilities, and the selection of new lower-level managerial staff (foreman, brigade leader). The rate of participation by workers in such decisions was typically on the order of 30%, which the author of the study characterized as "relatively low."[47]

There is no need and no basis on which to accept such findings for individual plants as typical of a broader range of industrial enterprises. If anything, they probably overstate the typical rate of worker participation in managerial decisions. Their significance, like that of Arutiunian's work, lies elsewhere. They are part of a current in the management and sociological literature which recognizes that the traditional distribution of authority and influence in the enterprise is an obstacle to effective work performance. The same is true of those Soviet studies which have found that opportunities for participation in decisions on the organization of the work process and the distribution of its rewards have important psychological correlates: they increase work satisfaction and promote a feeling of "being a master of the work place" *(chuvstvo khoziaina)*.[48]

But are there any conceivable changes in decision-making power and work organization at enterprises that could stimulate this feeling and simultaneously be politically and economically acceptable?

### Specific Proposals for "Democratization" of Management

One of the proposals which emerged during the late 1960s called for selected categories of managerial personnel in industry to be "elected" by their subordi-

---

46. V. I. Oligin-Nesterov, *Ispol'zovanie ekonomicheskikh zakonov sotsializma i upravlenie proizvodstvom,* Moscow, 1973, pp. 94, 95.

47. V. N. Ermuratskii, pp. 102, 104.

48. N. I. Alekseev, "The Interaction of Social Factors in Determining the Attitude toward Work," *Sotsiologicheskie issledovaniia,* 1975, no. 3, pp. 120–21.

nates rather than appointed by their superiors. When the idea was raised in 1965 (prior to the economic reform announced in September of that year) by Iu. Volkov, it was presented as something that could not be implemented "today" but would mark the "completion" of self-management in the communist society of the future.[49] By 1968, however, one of the most authoritative Soviet spokesmen for "scientific management," V. G. Afanas'ev, proposed that the time had come to introduce such elections on an experimental basis as part of the search for more participatory forms of management. Afanas'ev couched his proposal in the following terms:

> The election of enterprise managers can become one of the forms of participation in management. . . .
>
> The fate of the manager is essentially in the hands of higher-level organs rather than in those of the collective which he manages. Hence the tactics adopted by some managers of orienting themselves not to those "below" them, not to gain the respect and confidence of the collective, but to those "above" them. It is not the respect of the collective which is important to them but primarily the good will of their superiors. This creates bureaucrats and zealous administrators, some of whom unfortunately have not yet been removed. This situation would be fundamentally changed if the masses had the right to elect enterprise managers. . . .
>
> Elections would be an effective form of direct participation of the masses in management of enterprises.[50]

At first glance there are obvious grounds for doubting the seriousness of this proposal. What meaning could be attached to elections of either plant directors or lower managerial staffs by a working population long unaccustomed to freely choosing its leadership at any level of economic or social organization? Could such elections be anything but a facade behind which the plant's Party organization would make its selections? Moreover, Arutiunian was shortly to show (his work was published in 1971) that the perception of influence on the enterprise was no more widespread in rural economic units in which management was formally elected than in those in which it was appointed. The proposal should not be dismissed as an empty gesture, however, for it was made at a time when even more far-reaching experiments were under consideration.

In any case the ensuing discussion of this proposal revealed considerable support for some new kind of mechanism which would give a plant's employees a direct role in selection or retention of managerial staffs. Even without formal "elections," factory trade union and Party organizations could appeal to the appropriate ministry to remove a factory director; but such appeals were apparently often ineffective. Cases were cited in which tyrannical directors had caused the firing, exclusion from the Party, and even imprisonment of workers criticizing managerial behavior. Such instances were cited to justify the desirability of giving employees the right to "independently" replace factory managers.[51] Support for the idea of electing lower-level management staffs (foremen, bri-

---

49. Iu. E. Volkov, *Tak rozhdaetsia kommunisticheskoe samoupravlenie*, Moscow, 1965, p. 176.

50. V. G. Afanas'ev, *Nauchnoe upravlenie obshchestvom*, Moscow, 1968, pp. 259–60. Earlier support for the idea of elections of managers appears in Ia. S. Kapeliush, "Democracy and Centralism," in V. A. Fomin, p. 44.

51. P. M. Panov, p. 114.

gade leaders, shop superintendents) was expressed by some who thought that employee selection of plant directors was "premature."[52] A scattering of sociological surveys sought to elicit the responses of different occupational groups to the proposal. Not surprisingly, the reactions were related to the social positions of the respondents. A Kiev study, published in 1968, showed that more than 70% of a sample of factory directors, chief engineers, chairmen of trade union committees, and Party secretaries opposed the principle of elections to managerial positions.[53] A study of a Cheliabinsk factory issued in 1970 revealed almost two-thirds of the workers holding the view that "the collective itself should choose its leader," while the comparable figure among foremen was only 13% Apparently the proper mix of "democracy" and "centralism" in democratic centralism was interpreted differently by workers and managerial personnel. The authors of the latter study concluded that "workers hold more radical views on democracy than managers."[54] The implication here that attitudes toward forms of organization differed markedly, depending on class position, was a rather remarkable feature of the brief discussion that followed Afanas'ev's proposal. It may even help to explain why the issue of "election" rather than appointment of managers largely evaporated by the early 1970s. To the extent that it reappeared at all, it was raised in the context of the "future society" rather than current experiments.[55]

Another illustration of the search for more participatory organizational forms appears in proposals to enhance the authority of trade unions and production conferences at the enterprise. Until 1965 the collective agreements between factory administrations and trade unions did little more than spell out the assignments embodied in the state plan for the given enterprise and some details of labor law applicable to it (rules governing overtime work, safety measures, etc.). As a recent Soviet commentary puts it, "It [the collective agreement—M.Y.] only reproduced the norms established for the given enterprise from 'above.' . . ."[56] Since the 1965 reform the increased availability of retained profits has provided some scope for at-plant decisions on the uses of various "incentive funds" drawn from these profits. Such funds may be used as wage supplements (about 5% of average earnings of workers in industry were drawn from these funds in 1973) or as sources of financing improvements in recreational and housing facilities. Collective agreements now incorporate provisions governing projected uses of such funds and specify that their precise allocation will be decided by management "jointly with" or "in agreement with" the factory trade union. This means that in a formal sense unions are regarded as having "parity rights," along with factory management, on questions of the allocation of such

52. F. M. Rudich, *O sochetanii gosudarstvennykh i obshchestvennykh nachal v upravlenii proizvodstvom,* Kiev, 1968, p. 77.

53. Ibid., p. 76.

54. Ia. E. Stul' and I. O. Tishchenko, "Social-Psychological Principles of Management," in V. G. Afanas'ev, *Nauchnoe upravlenie obshchestvom,* No. 6, 1970, p. 276.

55. G. Kh. Popov and G. A. Dzhavadov, *Upravlenie i problema kadrov,* Moscow, 1972, p. 17.

56. N. I. Alekseev and I. A. Riazhskikh, "The Highest Organ of the Collective," in V. G. Afanas'ev ed., *Nauchnoe upravlenie obshchestvom,* no. 6, p. 151.

funds.[57] It is also clear, however, that violations of collective agreements by management often go unpunished, and that it is not difficult for management to obtain the agreement of the union committee's chairman to the former's views on the proper forms of expenditure of incentive funds.[58] Nonetheless at least the principle of joint decision-making is recognized as appropriate here, and examples of management obtaining union "permission" for specific uses of incentive funds have been publicized as models of "collective management."[59]

The case is quite different, however, with respect to other forms of union "participation." In the drafting of production plans, capital investment plans, and in the choice of new technology, the union has only a "consultative" role. Its proposals are in no sense binding on management, and there is no pretense of joint decision-making.[60] The same is true of any recommendations made by the plant's production conferences, most of whose participants are manual workers. The purely "consultative" or "advisory" status of their recommendations in these areas means that their influence on managerial decisions hardly adds up to effective participation in management. This is readily admitted in the more serious Soviet literature on the role of unions:

> Today our chief weakness in the sphere of participation of the working people in the management of the production affairs of the enterprise is the frequent nonfulfillment of the recommendations of the trade union committee and the production conference.[61]

It is against this background that two recent proposals made in the name of extending "production democracy" assume some significance. One of these calls for extending the principle of "parity rights" of unions to areas in which they have previously exercised only a "consultative" role—in particular to the adoption of plans for the introduction of new technology and to production plans generally. The other proposal calls for the decisions adopted on these matters by production conferences of workers and employees to be treated as "juridically obligatory" for management.

> Since workers and employees at the enterprise have the obligation of fulfilling the plan, they should have a deciding voice in formulating it.[62]

There is nothing to indicate that such proposals will soon be formally implemented, or that if they are the typical worker (as distinct from the union official) will experience a heightened sense of involvement in important decisions at the plant. But such proposals (as well as the short-lived proposal for election of managers) imply a readiness to consider restricting the still-sacred principle of one-man management in favor of more "collegial" forms. What is

57. N. I. Alekseev, I. I. Kravchenko, and E. G. Plimak, "The Myth of 'Statism' and Socialism without Myths," *Voprosy filosofii,* 1971, no. 5, p. 49; S. A. Ivanov, *Trudovoe pravo i nauchno-tekhnicheskii progress,* Moscow, 1974, pp. 400–1; N. I. Alekseev and I. A. Riazhskikh, pp. 149–50.

58. S. A. Ivanov, p. 398. N. I. Alekseev and I. A. Riazhskikh, p. 150.

59. Ibid., p. 145.

60. S. A. Ivanov, pp. 407–8.

61. Ibid., p. 414.

62. Ibid., pp. 415–17.

most striking here is that the participatory rhetoric (if not the practice of participation) has been extended to a significant new area—the choice of production technology. The idea that the choice of technology must be justified "not only on technical and economic grounds but on social grounds as well," and that this requires "joint decisions" of management and the work collective, is a rather recent one in Soviet discussions.[63] The Soviet source on which we rely here does not spell out the "social grounds," but the latter obviously refer to the impact of new technology on work satisfaction and job skills.[64] The introduction of such ideas into the literature on "production democracy," rather than any tangible changes in the distribution of decision-making power, is probably the chief consequence thus far of proposals for extending the role of unions at the enterprise.

Efforts to extend "production democracy" appeared in a very different guise in agriculture than in industry. They were associated with a movement, which initially emerged in the early 1960s, to rely increasingly on the small, self-managing work team *(beznariadnoe zveno)* as the basic unit of work organization on the farm rather than on the more traditional large work brigades of several hundred members requiring close managerial supervision. The work teams were assigned their "own" plot of land and complement of machinery for more or less extended periods. The conflict between adherents and opponents of the work-team method deserves a separate study which we shall not undertake here. The issue raised was that of "internal" control (by the work group itself) versus "external" control (by farm administrators standing apart from the "direct producers") over the peasant's work activity. Little wonder that some published accounts of the movement reported that it generated a "social struggle" in the countryside. Our examination of a short-lived experiment which not only incorporated the idea of self-managing work teams but also a most unusual form of farm administration and leadership selection should make clear the importance of this issue. Suffice it to say for the moment that this experiment constituted a radical challenge to traditional Soviet management philosophy and organization. It projected the vision of a highly equalitarian and participatory form of economic organization.

### The Akchi Experiment

This experiment is probably the most important illustration of recent efforts to devise less authoritarian forms of organization in economic enterprises. The precise period covered by the experiment is uncertain, but it is apparent that it was in effect at least during the years 1968–70. Although it directly concerned only a single state grain farm, it embodied a management ideology that departed so drastically from prevailing management principles that it could not have been authorized except by high-ranking levels of political authority. The only materials at our disposal which describe the experiment are a few journalistic ac-

---

63. Ibid., p. 414.

64. A. Yanov in *Molodoi kommunist,* 1972, no. 2, pp. 64–69, explicitly urged that choices among alternative technologies be guided, at least in part, by the opportunities they created for higher skill levels. Yanov's article, however, was primarily concerned with the functions of the industrial sociologist rather than the trade union at the plant.

counts in 1969–72 and a brief *post-mortem* comment in a sociological journal in 1974.[65] The experiment was inspired—or at least explicitly justified—by an aspect of the Leninist heritage that is almost never cited in the voluminous management literature of recent years.[66] We refer to Lenin's remarks in *State and Revolution* that socialism will create

> an order in which the functions of control and accounting—becoming more and more simple—will be performed by each in turn, will then become a habit, and will finally die out as the special functions of a special stratum of the population. . . .
>
> Under socialism all will govern in turn and will soon become accustomed to no one governing.[67]

There is nothing unusual about a particular industrial plant or farm being singled out in Soviet press reports for achieving levels of economic performance substantially in excess of the norm. This was true in the case of the experimental farm at Akchi in Kazakstan. Its economic performance as measured by the usual indicators of labor productivity, production costs, and profits per worker was reported to be vastly superior to that of the typical farm in its region. What was unusual was that its success apparently had nothing to do with high levels of mechanization, long hours of work, or the high quality of the educational and practical work of the farm's Party organization. In the words of the leader of the experiment, it reflected the ability to create a form of work organization in which "the functions of production and management were not divided" between different occupational strata.

In the brief description of the experiment which follows we are less interested in the details of the farm's organization—these are reported rather sketchily and in somewhat idealized terms in the press accounts—than in the ideas on authority and participation it articulated. The basic structural units were the small work teams referred to earlier, the members of which were paid from the proceeds of the team's "final output" (grain available for delivery to the state). Unlike the system prevailing on most farms, no individual output norms and piece rates were established. No payments were based on tilled or sown area, only on the team's harvest of grain. Work activities of team members were coordinated from "within" by team leaders who worked in the field. The team's income was distributed equally among its members, although there was no separate accounting of the amount of work done by individual members. "Conscience," the pressure of the team's "internal control," was relied on to maintain work discipline.

The most striking aspects of the farm's organization concerned the structure

---

65. *Iskusstvo kino*, 1972, no. 11, pp. 93–96; *Literaturnaia gazeta*, May 21, 1969; *Molodoi kommunist*, 1970, no. 2, pp. 62–68; *Sotsiologicheskie issledovaniia*, 1974, no. 2, pp. 186–87. All quotations in the text concerning the experiment are drawn from these sources. The author is grateful to Alexander Yanov for calling some of these sources to his attention.

66. The only recent reference we have found to Lenin's remarks, cited below, other than in the accounts of the Akchi experiment, appears in *Voprosy filosofii*, 1971, no. 5, p. 56.

67. The first part of the quotation is given in the translation appearing in V. I. Lenin, *Selected Works*, Vol. VII (New York: International Publishers, 1943), p. 48. The second part is from V. I. Lenin, *The State and Revolution* (Peking: Foreign Languages Press, 1973), p. 140. In each case we have selected the translation which seems to us to best fit the original Russian.

and functions of its management staff. The latter consisted of a "coordinating team" of only two individuals: the farm director and the bookkeeper-economist. The mode of payment, the absence of individual output norms, and the moral authority of the work teams over their members all presumably operated to reduce the need for "external" (managerial) sources of supervision and authority. The functions of the managerial staff were described in unusual terms. Such functions were, in part, "diplomatic" (maintaining "external" relations with the government ministry and supply organizations) and, in part, "educational" (providing instruction in the new mode of work organization). The decision to reduce to a minimum the number of individuals who were not "direct producers" reflected the views of the experiment's organizer that the excessive administrative staffs of most farms created attitudes of "dependence" among workers—a feeling that "the authorities know best"—and simply added unnecessarily to overhead costs.

In the words of the experiment's organizer, "it is important in our methodology that all people should manage in turn." Hence the principle of job rotation was to be applied to the positions of farm director and work-team leaders. The new director would be chosen from among team leaders, and the latter would be drawn from team members. The selections would be made by an "economic council" composed of the coordinating team, work-team leaders, and the farm's "social organizations" (clearly the Party and trade union).

The somewhat idyllic and undoubtedly oversimplified picture of a single farm's operations which emerges in these accounts should not obscure the significance of the Akchi experiment. Nor should the fact that the farm's staff was specially selected for experimental purposes and thus contained a larger proportion of skilled and experienced personnel than was typical on state farms. The decision to initiate the experiment, and perhaps even more important to publicize it, represented a challenge to the most sacred principles of management and to prevailing views concerning the requirements of effective work organization. It was obviously in conflict with the whole spirit of one-man management. It downgraded the need for a large social stratum of professional managers and "specialists." It denied that Soviet technological backwardness was the principal source of poor economic performance in agriculture. It affirmed the compatibility of an equalitarian income distribution (at last within work teams) with efficient work performance. It revived an aspect of the socialist heritage (reflected in the above citation from Lenin) long concealed by selective quotations from Engels on the need for authority and Lenin on the need for "unity of will" and subordination to a single leader. There was good reason for one of the published commentaries on Akchi to invoke the distinction between "juridical" socialization—long in effect—and the "real" change in relations of production which the experiment sought to institutionalize. Perhaps most important—and most threatening—the experiment left unclear just what useful role could be played by the Party organization in an economic enterprise modeled on the Akchi farm. Its "mobilizing" and "monitoring" role (its function of *kontrol'*) hardly seemed necessary here. The only reference to the Party organization in the accounts of the Akchi experiment concerned its participation in selecting the rotating incumbents of managerial positions. But this was hardly a structural requirement of the farm's mode of operation. In short, the Akchi experiment, by moving from the "juridical" socialization of property to its "collective management," projected a form of economic organization that could not help but raise serious questions about the prevailing distribution of power and rewards in the enterprise and in the society at large. This was undoubtedly the principle source of its undoing.

In 1974 a Soviet sociological journal reported that at a conference held the previous year on social and economic problems of the countryside, a number of speakers had argued that the principles of the Akchi experiment represented "the only promising path for the country's agricultural development"[68] The writer then presented what must be interpreted as the "official verdict" on the experiment, a verdict that in effect sealed its fate:

> As for the experiment at Akchi, . . . we must see two features of it: on the one hand an attempt to "drag" into being a communal form *(artel'nuiu formu)* of work collective— clearly in conflict with the collective and state farm forms—known in Russia since prerevolutionary times and representing a rudimentary form of organization of work collectives on democratic principles, and on the other hand a more or less successful form of organization of production utilizing value levers. The first clearly has no prospects for its development, but the second is being used and deserves wider application as an effective means of raising labor productivity in small work groups.[69]

Thus the only acceptable feature of the Achi experiment was judged to be a system of payment based on a work group's finished product ("value levers"). But its efforts to affirm the principle of collective management, to test the feasibility of rotating incumbents of leadership positions, and to reduce the role in the enterprise of privileged strata who were not "direct producers" were all dismissed as a throwback to "rudimentary" forms of democratic work organization. There is nothing to indicate that the experiment was ended because of poor economic performance. Although we cannot unravel all the elements in the "social struggle" obliquely referred to in the scanty published accounts, it seems much more likely that Akchi was aborted by the threat it posed to the power and privileges of "professional" managers, both in the economic and political spheres. Whatever the experiment's other features, one can readily imagine the resistance that such groups would offer to the apparently serious attempt to test the principle that "all should manage in turn."

Finally, we must not exaggerate the pressures for more participatory forms of organization in the enterprise or oversimplify the obstacles to their implementation. The chronically unsatisfactory performance of agriculture, the reliance on deeply rooted authoritarian methods of enterprise management, and the emergence of a more highly educated urban work force often dissatisfied with the limited content of available jobs are all part of the setting in which the issue of "production democracy" has been raised. But the various studies, proposals, and experiments reviewed here have not yet produced tangible changes in the hierarchical distribution of authority and influence at the factory or farm. Only

---

68. V. I. Vladimirov, "Problems and Prospects of Socioeconomic Development of the Countryside," *Sotsiologicheskie issledovaniia,* 1974, no. 1, p. 186.

69. Ibid., p. 187. It appears that the fate of the experiment's organizer has also been sealed. See the article by A. Yanov in the *New York Times,* December 31, 1975.

the Soviet version of "human relations" in management seems to be taking hold. As for the obstacles to worker participation, the whole structure of centralized economic administration continues to limit the scope for at-plant decisions (even on the use of incentive funds) and hence for worker participation in such decisions. But not all such obstacles can be reduced to the "power" considerations of economic and political authorities. The increased stress on the need for expertise in "scientific management"—presumaby beyond the capacity of most manual workers—is not only a cover for managerial privileges, although it certainly helps to maintain them. Thus Soviet authorities will undoubtedly find it easier to rely on the less disruptive social mechanism of short-range occupational mobility to mitigate the effects of hierarchy than to institute effective forms of worker participation in enterprise decision-making. Among other problems this would threaten too many entrenched interests, as the Akchi experiment did.

# · 30 ·

# Growth Strategy, Competing Interests, and the Soviet Occupational System

## Elizabeth Garnsey

## Introduction

In this paper some connections between the process of capital accumulation and the division of labour in the Soviet Union are explored. The Soviet occupational system was transformed as a result of decisions over resource allocation which were the outcome of a unique distribution of power. Those in control of the overall rate and direction of investment had, however, to deal with economic constraints, and the division of labour evolved in part through the economic forces generated by the Soviet growth strategy.[1] The planning authorities did not have unlimited power to determine the organization of work at the local level; incentives and sanctions affecting manning ratios have a certain autonomy; and conflicts of interest between planning authorities and managers, on the one hand, and managers and workers, on the other, exert their influence in various ways on the introduction of new methods of production and on the division of labour. A comprehensive study of these interacting causes is beyond the scope of a single paper; I propose to outline the broad features of change in

* Some of the material in this paper appeared in the author's 'Capital Accumulation and the Division of Labor in the Soviet Union', *Cambridge Journal of Economics,* Vol. 6, no. 1.

NOTE: The research on which this paper is based was supported by a grant from the S.S.R.C.

1. The term 'growth strategy' is not used to imply that all policies adopted were deliberately pursued as part of a coherent plan. Many of the measures which shaped the occupation system were pursued not for their own sake but as a consequence of other priorities. Nevertheless, a distinctively Soviet model of economic development can be identified (Ofer 1973).

the occupational system and trace some of the influences exerted by the Soviet pattern of capital accumulation on the occupational division of labour.

## The Division of Labour and Inequality

Most contemporary class analysis takes as its subject matter the inequalities associated with membership of various occupational groups and the implications of these inequalities for class conflict. In this paper an attempt is made to shift the focus of analysis; instead of taking the division of labour as given and considering the inequalities that proceed from it, we will try to ascertain how the Soviet occupational system evolved and why it is perpetuated in its present form. We accept that the division of labour[2] underlies inequalities of condition and opportunity in the Soviet Union as in other societies. But while the inequalities that obtain in the Soviet Union have been discussed at length in the Western literature, the evolution of the occupational system is, in comparison, still uncharted. Soviet occupational groups have been shown to differ in terms of the educational levels, income, consumption patterns and social attitudes of their members (Lane 1973). The question whether social groups identifiable through shared characteristics of this kind constitute classes in the Soviet Union and, if so, where the divisions between classes should be drawn has also received a good deal of attention but shows no signs of being resolved (Nove 1975). The aim of this paper is not to map out classes or trace class boundaries. However, some of the issues raised by this enterprise are relevant to our concerns and require brief consideration at this point.

For a variety of reasons the use of the term 'class system' raises difficulties in the Soviet context. Classes are usually defined in terms of relationship to the means of production, but where these are owned by the state all groups are similar in this respect. Bureaucratic office can provide a considerable degree of effective control over production and distribution, but this is not an advantage directly comparable to that available through inherited property in a class system of the kind described by Marx. Although there are inequalities in material circumstances and status as between occupational groups, with members of higher professional and administrative occupations enjoying significant advantages in these respects, there are no great concentrations of privately owned wealth such as prevail in market economies. Moreover, the absence of political alternatives to identification with the aims of the Party affects social attitudes in various ways. Class consciousness is not found in the same form as in market economies; instead social groups appear to have an awareness of prevailing inequalities and a sense of mutual or conflicting interest which is peculiar to Soviet society.[3] Conflict over the distribution of resources also takes on distinctive forms in the absence of collective bargaining and because of the organizational structure of the Soviet economy.

---

2. We can only deal with officially recognised paid employment in the present discussion. Illegal activities, forced labour and unpaid work in the household and community are important aspects of the division of labour which we cannot here consider.

3. In this area the evidence is inadequate and lends itself to conflicting interpretation; thus see the difference of opinion between Nove (1975) who maintains that there is a 'pervasive sense of Them and Us' in the Soviet Union and Lane (1978), who holds that members of Soviet occupational groups share a common outlook.

But there are respects in which the Soviet system of social stratification resembles that of other societies. There are processes at work in the Soviet Union generating and maintaining social inequalities through the family and through the division of labour, and there are conflicts of interest over production and distribution. It can be shown that, as in the West, the processes reproducing hierarchies of reward and authority operate through the interactions between power alignments, control over productive resources and the division of labour. In my view, as long as these factors remain central to the analysis, the terms used to describe the system of inequality which is found in the Soviet Union are immaterial.

In the Soviet Union labour allocation and payment structures are determined in part by market forces. (Hence, in terms of stratification theory, market situation is relevant to the benefits enjoyed by members of various occupational groups.) But skill scarcities are only one element in this process (Kirsch 1972) and, as in the West, though for different reasons, are not always reflected in the relative advantages obtained by groups of workers. It is, however, significant that scope has been allowed to market forces in the allocation of labour, in contrast with the policy of allocating capital and land by administrative procedure. Vested interests in the return to payment differentials in the Stalinist period cannot be discounted, though the move was justified in terms of the economy's requirements for rapid growth. Theories which explain labour allocation in the USSR in terms of the needs of economic efficiency cannot account for the actual range of reward differentials which have prevailed. Nor can they appraise the goal of economic efficiency or the means selected for its achievement; this depends on the time span selected and the value attached to an economy run along certain lines. The political context in which economic priorities were established (Lewin 1975) ultimately had a crucial effect on labour allocation.

## Two Views on the Soviet Occupational System

Certain similarities between the Soviet economy and Western economies in work organization and occupational trends have been widely recognized. The shift of labour out of agriculture into manufacturing and a gradual decline in the proportion of manual workers in the labour force have characterized industrialization in both types of economy. In both cases work is organized on a hierarchical basis, with specialization giving rise to relationships of authority and subordination. These shared characteristics have been interpreted in different ways by writers having conflicting perspectives. For some they serve to confirm that as industrialization proceeds similar trends are set in motion (Kerr et al. 1960; Treiman 1970; Lane and O'Dell 1978). For other writers these resemblances point to the adoption of a capitalist organization of production by the Soviet leadership (Braverman 1974; Marglin 1974; Crompton and Gubbay 1977). Neither approach provides a comprehensive analysis capable of identifying the distinctive features of change in the Soviet occupational system.

## The Neo-Marxist Analysis of the Soviet Division of Labour

The neo-Marxists do not hold identical positions, but they share an attempt to account for the nature of the Soviet labour process in terms of the drive to accumulation to which the economy has been geared. All societies need to divert some resources from consumption in order to maintain and expand productive capital. According to Marx, under capitalism this process involves the appropriation of surplus value or unpaid labour time and its conversion into physical capital concentrated in the hands of the owners of productive property.

The neo-Marxist writers have developed Marx's argument, and claim that technology, as it has evolved under the impetus of accumulation under capitalism, is designed to remove control over the labour process from the workers, partly by reducing the tasks they perform to routine operations. They go on to argue that this type of organization of labour was taken over by the Soviet leadership, who, according to Marglin, 'consciously and deliberately embraced a capitalist mode of production' (1974:15). We cannot here consider the detailed evidence (insofar as it is available) which would be required to substantiate this argument, nor assess the hypothetical alternatives it presents. But whether or not a dynamic and efficient industry could in principle be organized on a democratic basis, using autonomous and skilled labour, it is certainly true that the Soviet leaders did not think in these terms. They admired Western technology and did not conceive of technological change except as promoting specialization and hierarchy in the organization of work.

Similarities in the organization of work do not however justify statements describing the Soviet Union as a 'capitalist society with a division of labour on essentially the same principles as any capitalist enterprise' (Crompton and Gubbay 1977:135). The drive to rapid economic growth does not pre-determine the actual forms taken by the process of capital accumulation, since growth rates and investment rates do not have a one-to-one relationship. Growth is stimulated by high rates of investment but many forms of investment may not be growth-inducing, and too high a rate of accumulation may actually result in a lower rate of economic growth than could be achieved with higher rates of consumption and less social and economic dislocation (Brus and Laski 1965:201).

To describe the methods of production used in the Soviet Union as equivalent to a capitalist mode of production diverts attention from the actual ways in which the process of capital accumulation has affected the introduction and implementation of production methods.

## Marx's Account of Capital Accumulation and Soviet Experience

In considering the relationship between capital accumulation and forms of work organization adopted in the Soviet Union, it is important to note the following divergencies from the process described by Marx (*Capital* vol. I, Part 7, Ch. 23). (1) The unit carrying out the accumulation process in the Soviet Union is not the firm or corporation but the national planning authority. (2) Profit is not the criterion on the basis of which investment decisions are made, nor are shareholders' interests at stake. (3) The process is not stimulated by market competition. (4) The process does not create unemployment under the conditions of endemic shortage of industrial labour which have prevailed during the Soviet period.

The process of resource allocation embodied in capital accumulation takes place on a different basis in the Soviet Union as compared to Western market economies, even those having a large public sector. The alignment of interests and the structure of incentives and constraints guiding investment decisions which affect employment are quite distinctive in the Soviet system. Enterprise managers do not decide on the proportion of profits to plough back into their plants, nor do they determine the form of investment to be undertaken. The choice of new technologies to be introduced is not made at the enterprise level but by the relevant industrial ministries in negotiation with research organizations (Berliner 1976:114). The Soviet manager is frequently reluctant to introduce new technology, since innovation creates uncertainty, which throws into question the fulfillment of planning targets on which his performance is assessed (Berliner 1976; Halliday 1979). To the extent that managers can affect labour allocation, they tend to overstate their need for workers and technical staff to meet planning deadlines and swell the wage fund on the basis of which managers' bonuses are calculated. Full employment is an ideological tenet, and though low labour productivity may be a source of concern to the planning authorities, managers are not normally directly penalized for the size of their workforce. Attempts to provide incentives to reduce wage costs have not met with noticeable success. The divergence of interests between planning authorities and enterprise managers has indeterminate effects on employment. But in general the relentless drive to 'rationalize' the organization of work so as to minimize labour input and costs does not occur as it does in Western economies. The strategy adopted by the planning authorities has been based on achieving growth through maximum inputs of labour and capital, rather than by maximizing output for a given level of input (Kuznets 1963). The need to meet physical output targets specified by the planners makes Soviet managers tolerant of overmanning to an extent which is not possible in economies where profit criteria prevail. Determined efforts to raise labour productivity would require drastic changes in the organization of production in the Soviet Union and a marked realignment of interests.

According to the argument put forward by the neo-Marxist writers in their analysis of Western economies, the 'mode of production' cannot be explained without reference to the interests of those actually introducing new methods of production. These writers are therefore inconsistent in trying to explain the organization of work in the Soviet Union by reference to economic objectives at the national level, without identifying intervening factors which impinge on the division of labour.

## Advances in Technology as an Explanation of Soviet Occupational Patterns

The neo-Marxist approach can be contrasted with that adopted by those who argue that '. . . the Soviet occupational structure has evolved in a way not unlike that in capitalist societies' because of the effects of technological advance (Lane and O'Dell 1978:15). This argument takes up a theme of the convergence thesis (Ellman 1980) according to which similarities in occupational trends arise 'out of the uniformity of the basic technology itself' (Kerr et al. 1973:37). That occupational structure is linked to technological progress is indisputable. But the notion of technological advance is too imprecise to account for changes in work organization in particular industries. The intervening stages through which advances in technical knowledge come to affect occupational distribution need to be identified. Different forms of work organization and methods of production can coexist at any given level of technical knowledge (Brus and Laski 1965). The introduction of new methods of production in market economies depends on such factors as the state of demand for the products of the industry; it also depends on pressures deriving from the degree of competition and wage costs, on managers' willingness to innovate and on the state of labour relations. Some of these factors are at work in the Soviet economy, but the way they impinge on work organization is distinctive.

To explain changes in occupational distribution in Soviet plants and industries it is necessary to examine the degree to which Soviet technical knowledge has been applied to industrial use, the availability of Western technology and the rate of diffusion of new technology in industry. All three factors are influenced by planning priorities which govern the differential allocation of resources to the various industries; they are also affected by institutional rigidities in the organization and application of research and development (Halliday 1979; Berliner 1976). The Soviet equivalent of 'custom and practice' also has an influence on the organization of work. It is well attested that innovation is often resisted by Soviet managers; much less is known about ways in which Soviet industrial workers react to the introduction of new methods of production.

Technological factors do not suffice to explain the sectoral distribution of the labour force as between industries. This process involves more than the release of workers from a given sector through increasing mechanization. Not only the supply of, but also the demand for, industrial labour is a causal factor. Because of the centralization of investment in the hands of the planning authorities, the Soviet government could determine the rate of growth of employment in the various sectors. The causes of change in the occupational system operate at various levels, and a comprehensive explanation of occupational trends cannot leave economic policies outside the scope of the analysis.

## Dimensions of the Division of Labour

Many of the difficulties to which the accounts of the Soviet occupational system so far examined give rise are the result of the failure to specify clearly the aspect of the division of labour under discussion. Because they lack a clear framework for analysing changes in the division of labour, writers of both persuasions are led to put forward an explanation of one aspect of the occupational system in terms of factors which may not be relevant at that level.

Three aspects of the division of labour can be distinguished, of which the first and most specific is the organization of tasks and allocation of workers to sets of tasks or occupational roles in the workplace. The second aspect is the distribution of workers among the various branches of the economy. Together these determine the third or aggregate aspect of the occupational division of labour, which is reflected at any one time in the prevailing occupational structure of the society as a whole. The transformation of the occupational structure thus reflects two proximate sets of causes: the changing industrial structure, and changes in the occupational distribution within individual industries. It is through changes in the organization of work within industries that technological change impinges on the division of labour. Capital accumulation underlies both sets of proximate causes by increasing the productive capacity of industries and making possible the changes in output and productivity which accompany the relative expansion of employment in certain sectors and the changing skill-mix within industries.

In order to distinguish between general features of change in occupational systems in the course of industrialization and the distinctive features of Soviet experience, it is necessary to identify the main economic forces at work and the political context in which economic priorities were established.

## Investment, Consumption and the Sectoral Distribution of the Labour Force

The shifts of labour out of agriculture and into manufacturing and the service sectors, which facilitate and result from industrial expansion, took place in a distinctive way in the Soviet Union. The movement out of agriculture was rapid, but it occurred without the increase in agricultural productivity which made the migration to the cities possible in Western countries undergoing industrialization. The expansion of the manufacturing sector took place not as a result of rising per capita income and the growth of consumer demand for manufactured goods, as in the West, but through state demand for the products of heavy industry. Light industry did not provide the initial expansion of industrial employment, in contrast with the Western sequence of development.

As a result of government policies, an industrial labour force employed in industries using Western mass production techniques was created in the 1930s from a workforce of largely peasant origins. This workforce was further enlarged by the heavy use of labour in subsidiary and auxiliary processes organized along traditional lines. The craftsmen of Tzarist industry had been scattered during the years of disruption and workers were trained anew in the routines of the assembly line in a highly authoritarian setting (Granick 1967). The demise of trade union autonomy occurred before the implementation of the First Five Year Plans; workers' and unions' struggles against the harsh conditions imposed in the name of rapid industrialization are described by Carr and Davies (1969). A newly formed industrial labour force is likely to be vulnerable because lacking in organizational resources. With the social composition of the labour force undergoing rapid change, the heterogeneity of new recruits, who included large numbers of women, further weakened the position of workers in relation to managers. There were no longer relatively autonomous groups of skilled workers entrenched in established modes of custom and practice such as had formed in pre-Revolutionary times in Tzarist industry. The very rapid introduction of new methods of production in priority industries, and management strategies designed to ensure the allegiance of a number of key workers, rewarded for high productivity, also inhibited the improvement of the bargaining power of the bulk of the industrial workforce, despite shortages of skilled labour.

Meanwhile, the collectivization of agriculture completely undermined the ability of the peasants to influence the terms on which agricultural produce was made available to the authorities. Because of the expansion of heavy industry at the expense of light industry, manufactured consumer goods were not in any case available to induce the peasants to market more of their products.

The decision to invest in heavy industry without first raising productivity in agriculture or light industry was the ultimate cause of these developments. Neither collectivization nor national economic self-sufficiency had been envisaged by the economists who had earlier devised the strategy of economic growth which was pursued in the 1930s in a form distorted by Stalin's political priorities (Carr and Davies 1969). The policies embarked upon were in part the outcome of the isolation of Soviet Russia and the objective of 'Socialism in One Country', but they also appealed to Stalin because they involved a centralization of decisions over resource allocation which further concentrated power in his hands.

However, to fulfill (and overfulfill) the targets of the first Five Year Plans, control over the planning authorities was insufficient; it was also necessary to harness the vested interests of industrial ministries and the managers of large economic concerns (Kaser 1970:40). Industrial ministries vied with each other for priority in the allocation of capital funds and undertook a range of commitments in order to establish their claim to further investment funds. Labour and capital were tied up in long-term projects which diverted scarce resources from consumption and which did not invariably stimulate growth because of shortages and imbalances. Nevertheless, in these and other ways, constraints on any reduction in the level of accumulation were built into the growth process.

While social consumption in health and education was expanded to improve the performance of the labour force, personal consumption was depressed by low wages, the inflated prices of consumer goods and by curbs on employment in personal services. Employment in all services fell between 1928 and 1932, despite the expansion of the urban population (Eason 1963:82). In contrast with patterns in most market economies where a large proportion of the urban population were employed in trade and personal services in the early stages of industrialization, most new recruits to the cities were employed directly in industry. Essential services which were unavailable commercially had to be performed by unpaid labour, mainly by women, in the household, without the aid of manufactured consumer goods. State demand was the operative factor in the eventual rise in the proportion of the labour force employed in the service sector.

The diversion of resources from current to future use entailed by the growth strategy created a divergence of interests between planning authorities and consumers which, especially in the early period, affected the whole population. Among the privileges of the bureaucracy and of some other cadres the most valuable has been access to scarce consumer goods through the special distributive network. Frequently in a situation of acute shortages this has simply served to raise their standard of living nearer to the average level of the population in other Western nations. To some degree this situation still prevails; though excesses are reported (Matthews 1978), they are not condoned by the official ideology. Extravagant levels of consumption are not extolled as the prerogative of the successful, unlike the expenditure celebrated by the Western commercial media.

In recent years levels of personal income have no longer been the major constraint on consumer demand; under prevailing conditions, supply shortages have resulted in excesses in purchasing power over sales of consumer goods, and there are high levels of forced savings by the population. The consumer industries have been expanding, but employment in light industry is still determined by planning priorities, and there is still a great shortage of consumer goods. In 1975, 31% of Soviet G.D.P. was devoted to investment and 49% to personal consumption.[4] The Soviet economy continues to be geared to very high rates of accumulation.

## The Vertical Structure of Occupations

The Soviet occupational structure has altered along with changes in the sectoral distribution of the labour force. The proportion of manual workers has been declining since 1939 (Table 1), but is still high by Western standards. This is predictable from the large proportion of the labour force to be found in agriculture and the uneven introduction of mechanization in Soviet industry. Low initial levels of mechanization should in principle have made it possible to raise labour productivity rapidly as equipment was improved. Output per worker has risen, but the rate of increase in labour productivity has been unsatisfactory from the official viewpoint (Khachaturov 1979). One of the factors inhibiting rises in labour productivity is the high proportion of auxiliary and subsidiary workers in Soviet industry. We have seen that managers have an incentive to hoard labour, but this feature of Soviet employment may also be the outcome of union pressure. Soviet trade unions are primarily welfare agencies; they do not engage in collective bargaining (McAuley 1969). However, the official commitment to full employment gives Soviet unions scope to press for legal guarantees to work at equivalent pay levels for workers made redundant (Berliner 1976).

The effects of mechanization on craft skills cannot be clearly established. The introduction of mass production techniques in the 1930s involved the demise of jobs traditionally carried out by skilled craftsmen in such industries as metal fabricating (Granick 1967). The monotony of the assembly line is now recognized; more interesting jobs are said to be on the way as technology advances. However, lack of job satisfaction is reported among workers in high skill grades (Zdravomyslov 1970). Soviet writers are now acknowledging that even under advanced technology manual workers may have routine and repetitive tasks to carry out (Karpukhin and Oblomskaia 1980). The advantages still to be gained from mechanization can be seen from the fact that in 1979 over a

---

4. Figures supplied by Professor M. Kaser.

*Table 1.* **The Occupational Structure of the Gainfully Employed Population of the USSR, 1939, 1959, 1970 (in percentages)**

| OCCUPATIONAL GROUP | 1939 | 1959 | 1970 |
|---|---|---|---|
| Professional and Technical[1] | 5.35 | 9.25 | 14.50 |
| Administrative and Managerial[2] | 2.67 | 2.94 | 4.25 |
| Clerical[3] | 4.42 | 3.22 | 4.62 |
| Sales[4] | 1.69 | 1.72 | 2.00 |
| Other Non-Manual[5] | 3.40 | 3.38 | 1.93 |
| All Non-Manual[6] | 17.53 | 20.51 | 27.30 |
| Manual | 82.47 | 79.49 | 72.7 |
| TOTAL (%) | 100.00 | 100.00 | 100.00 |
| Total (millions)[7] | 78,811 | 99,130 | 115,204 |

Source: Calculated from Tsentral'noe Statisticheskoe Upravlenie SSSR, *Itogi vsesoiuznoi perepisi naselenie 1959 godu,* pp. 161–165; . . . *1970 godu,* pp. 14–23.

[1](a) Engineers, scientists, doctors of medicine, dentists, veterinary surgeons, agronomists, writers, journalists, performing artists, architects, legal personnel, teachers (all levels, including 'production education' but excluding sports). (b) Semi-professional, technical and other professional personnel not included under (a).

[2](a) Heads of departments and sub-units and their deputies at All-Union, republican, regional and city levels in state administration. (b) Heads of departments and sub-units and their deputies at the All-Union, republican, regional and city levels in Communist Party and social organizations (trade unions, Young Communist Organization, etc.). (c) Enterprise managers and deputies in industry, construction, agriculture and forestry. (d) Heads of departments and sub-units in communal services, cultural services (museums, libraries), heads of planning and accounts departments, planners, economists and statisticians, heads of medical educational and scientific establishments, heads of departments in trade and sales.

[3]Office workers (typists, stenographers, etc.), bookkeepers, accountants, office supervisors and inspectors in planning departments, agents and dispatchers.

[4]Excluding heads of trade and sales departments and retail establishments. Approximately 1 million workers classed as non-manual in the 1959 census volume were reclassed as manual in the 1970 presentation of the 1959 data. The discrepancy can be accounted for almost entirely by the reduced number of sales workers classed as non-manual in the 1970 reclassification of the 1959 totals. In table 1 an estimate based on the figures reported in 1959 is given; the 1970 figure is an estimate extrapolated from this. (See table note 6.)

[5]This residual includes workers in communications and some others who would be classed under manual categories in most Western occupational classifications. There is a disparity between the total figure reported in the source for those 'predominantly engaged in non-manual work' and the sum of the numbers in the occupational sub-categories provided in the same tables. This residual was no less than 2 million in 1939, 1.9 million in 1959 and 1.6 million in 1970. It may include career army officers and other defence personnel, diplomats and secret police.

[6]The non-manual figures for 1959 reflect the 1959 report for the sales category and is the same as that reported in 1959. The non-manual figure for 1979 has been retained and the residual (note 5) is accordingly diminished by the enlarged estimate for the sales category. This is unsatisfactory, but the reported 1970 sales (900,000) seem unrealistically small, even granted the extent of an alternative (illegal) economy in the USSR (Grossman 1978).

[7]The total overstates the size of the labour force by double-counting an unknown number of workers. The national statistical yearbooks give figures for sectoral labour shares based on annual average numbers of workers and employees; this understates the size of the labour force by averaging out numbers of days worked (Ofer 1973). The exact proportions for all the sub-categories are in doubt; only the order of magnitude of the occupational groups can be established with any certainty from the present table.

third of workers in industry were reported to be engaged in 'heavy physical labour' (Moskovich and Ananev 1979:66). In an economy in which heavy manual work is still common, the fact that these jobs are light and involve non-manual tasks is seen as an advantage in its own right.

In contrast, 'non-productive' routine clerical and sales work is viewed with disfavour. The proportion of sales and clerical workers is very low by international standards (Garnsey 1975). This follows from the sectoral distribution of the labour force and the small size of the trade and commercial branches in the economy. It also seems to be the result of the organization of work within industries; clerical staff are used less than in industry and government in the West (Nove 1964:269).

Table 1 shows a decline in administrative and clerical personnel between 1939 and 1959 and, by my classification of the census data, a rise again in the size of these categories by 1970.

Although other evidence is available on small office staffs, the census figures are unreliable on this score because of the overlap between clerical, administrative and professional-technical categories. The very large and fast-growing proportion of professional and technical workers include many employees carrying out administrative functions (Rapawy 1972). There have been repeated campaigns to reduce the numbers of 'unproductive' clerical and administrative workers since the 1930s. Some genuine reductions resulted from these efforts, as when the proportion of administrative and clerical workers in industry was reduced in the 1930s (Granick 1961:141–144). The size of the government sector was cut back after Stalin's death. But it is impossible to estimate the extent to which these reductions have been overstated because of the incentives at every level to under-report employment in these categories.

Despite these and other problems of evidence, the extent of polarization of skills in the Soviet occupational system as a whole is unmistakable. There is a large proportion of workers in heavy manual jobs, while the share of professionally qualified employees is as high as in any advanced Western economy. This situation reflects the massive opportunities for social mobility which have prevailed in the Soviet period. It also points to the obstacles now facing those who do not obtain the higher educational qualifications which are increasingly required for the finite number of professional and managerial positions.

In many countries, not least in the Third World, because of rewards attached to non-manual work there is pressure for the expansion of office employment in the government sector. The Soviet authorities appear to have countered such pressures, partly through the rapid expansion of professional and technical employment (Table 1), partly through pay differentials favouring manual as compared with clerical work. However, there appear to be no interests actively opposing the expansion of clerical employment and the growth of this category of occupations is to be expected if, as seems to be the case, Soviet administrative apparatuses are top-heavy and understaffed with clerical employees.

The alternative of a radical reshaping of the division of labour, with manual workers taking on managerial and administrative tasks in industry as envisaged by Lenin in the case of government administration (1917), is a remote one. The main justification for hierarchies of authority in industry and strict factory discipline in the early period was the need to ensure productivity from uneducated peasant recruits to industry. As educational levels have risen, this rationale for the hierarchical structure of authority has been undermined and a Soviet "Human Relations" approach to management has emerged (Yanowitch 1977). However, Lenin's approval of the precepts of Scientific Management is taken to sanction managerial authority and discretion over the organization of work (Lenin 1918:259).[5]

Gains in industrial democracy and job enlargement have been insubstantial in the West except in isolated instances. For different reasons there are forces militating against any such innovations in the Soviet economy, in which central planning imposes severe constraints on the autonomy of firms. Managers can to some extent influence the instructions they receive from the planning authorities by adjusting their preliminary statements of production needs, on which the planners base the targets they later establish for the firms concerned (Berliner 1976:15). Workers may therefore achieve some influence over production decisions and wages through local pressure on management. But a radical and unforeseeable shift in the balance of power would be required to alter the division of labour which is the basis of hierarchies of authority in industry. Any innovations affecting managerial authority would require the approval of policy-makers at the highest levels, and official support for such developments is not to be expected.

## Conclusion

A distinction can be drawn in principle between those who control or direct the accumulation process and those who submit to its consequences. But in practice control over accumulation is limited by economic constraints and overlaid by the conflicting interests to which the process gives rise. The drawing of a distinction of this kind is not the purpose of the present analysis. Our objective has been to examine how the Soviet occupational system evolved and why it is maintained in its present form.

We have been concerned with some of the policies and actions which have given rise to the division of labour with which hierarchies of authority and reward are associated in the Soviet Union. We have noted conflicts of interest between planning authorities and industrial ministries, between ministries and enterprise managers, between managers and workers, between consumers and producers. It is the official role of the Party to reconcile competition for resources of this kind, but in practice this means that the Party is involved in such conflicts at every level, from the determination of general investment priorities at the top echelons of government to the level of the factory where, for example, Party cadres may intervene to press for technological innovation opposed by managers (Hough 1969).

Conflicts between those attempting to exert their influence over production

---

5. There is a contrast between Lenin's account of the immanent demise of government bureaucracy in *The State and Revolution* (1917) and his acceptance of the manager's control function in industry (1918).

and distribution and the economic forces engendered by the Soviet growth strategy have together brought about the prevailing sectoral and occupational division of labour. The present hierarchical organization of work and rewards is likely to be maintained by the vested interests which have thereby been generated.

## References

Berliner, J. 1976, *The Innovative Decision in Soviet Industry*, Cambridge, Mass.: Harvard University Press.

Braverman, H. 1974, *Labor and Monopoly Capital, The Degradation of Work in the Twentieth Century*, New York: Monthly Review Press.

Brus, W., and K. Laski, 1972, 'Problems in the Theory of Growth Under Socialism' in *Socialist Economics*, ed. A. Nove and D. M. Nuti, Penguin Books.

Carr, E. H., and Davies, 1974, *Foundations of a Planned Economy 1926–1929*, Vol. 1, Harmondsworth: Penguin Books.

Crompton R., and J. Gubbay, 1977, *Economy and Class Structure*, London: Macmillan.

Eason, W. 1963, 'Labour Force', in *Economic Trends in the Soviet Union*, ed. A. Bergson, and S. Kuznets, Cambridge, Mass.: Harvard University Press.

Ellman, M. 1980, 'Against Convergence', *Cambridge Journal of Economics*, Vol. 4, No. 3, September.

Garnsey, E. 1975, 'Occupational Structure in Industrial Societies; Some Comments on the Convergence Thesis in the Light of Soviet Experience', *Sociology*, Vol. 9, No. 3, pp. 438–458.

———. 1981. 'The Rediscovery of the Division of Labour', *Theory and Society*.

Granick, D. 1961, *The Red Executive*, New York: Doubleday.

———. 1967, *Soviet Metalfabricating and Economic Development*, Madison: University of Wisconsin Press.

Grossman, G. 1977, "The Second Economy" *Problems of Communism*, Oct.

Holliday, G. 1979, *Technology Transfer to the USSR 1928–1937 and 1966–1975, The Role of Western Technology in Soviet Economic Development*, Boulder: Westview.

Hough, J. 1969, *The Soviet Prefects; The Local Party Organs in Industrial Decision-Making*, Cambridge, Mass.: Harvard University Press.

Karpukhin, D., and I. Oblomskaia, 1980, 'Social and Economic Problems of Labour in the Stage of Developed Socialism', *Planovoe Khoziaistvo*, No. 2, pp. 90–100; reprinted *Problems of Economics*, Oct. 1980, Vol. 13, No. 6.

Kaser, M. 1970, *Soviet Economics*, London: World University Library.

Khachaturov, T. 1979, 'Ways of Increasing the Effectiveness of Capital Investment', *Voprosy ekonomiki,* No. 7; reprinted *Problems of Communism,* Nov., Vol. 22, No. 7, pp. 52–69.

Kerr, C., et al. 1973 *Industrialism and Industrial Man,* Harmondsworth (British second edition).

Kirsch, L. 1972, *Soviet Wages,* Cambridge, Mass.: Harvard University Press.

Lane, D. 1971, *The End of Inequality? Stratification Under State Socialism,* Harmondsworth.

Lane, D., and F. O'Dell, 1978, *The Soviet Industrial Worker,* Oxford: Martin Robertson.

Lewin, M. 1975, *Political Undercurrents in Soviet Economic Debates.*

Lenin, V. I. 1917, 'The State and Revolution', *Collected Works,* Vol. 24, Moscow, 1964.

———. 1918, 'The Immediate Tasks of the Soviet Government', *Collected Works,* Vol. 27, Moscow 1965.

McAuley, M. 1964, *Labour Disputes in Soviet Russia 1957–1965,* Oxford: Oxford University Press.

Marglin, S. 1974, 'What Do Bosses Do?', in *The Division of Labour,* ed. A. Gorz, London: Harvester Press.

Marx, K. 1970, *Capital,* Vol. I, Moscow: Foreign Languages Publishing House.

Matthews, M. 1978, *'Privilege in the Soviet Union. A Study of Elite Life Styles under Communism',* London: Allen & Unwin.

Moskovich, V., and V. Anan'ev, 1979, 'The Occupational Skill Structure of Workers', *Voprosy ekonomiki,* No. 6, pp. 55–65; reprinted *Problems of Economics,* Nov., Vol. 22, No. 7, pp. 52–69.

Nove, A. 1964, 'Occupational Patterns in the USSR and in Great Britain', in *Economic Rationality and Soviet Politics,* New York: Praeger.

———. 1975, 'Is There a Soviet Ruling Class?', *Soviet Studies,* No. 4 (Oct.).

Ofer, G. 1973, *The Service Sector in Soviet Economic Growth,* Cambridge, Mass.: Harvard University Press.

Rapawy, S. 1972, 'Comparisons of U.S. and USSR Civilian Employment in Government 1950–1969', *International Population Reports,* Series P-65, No. 69, Washington D.C.: U.S. Government Printing Office.

Treiman, D. 1970, 'Industrialization and Social Stratification', *Sociological Inquiry,* 40, pp. 207–234.

Tsentral'noe Statisticheskoe Upravlenie, 1962, *Itogi perepisi naselenie 1959 godn,* Moscow: Ts S.U., 1973; *Itogi per naselenie 1970 godn,* Moscow.

Yanowitch, M. 1977, *Social and Economic Inequality in the Soviet Union,* London: Martin Robertson.

Zdravomyslov, A., et al. 1970, *Man and His Work,* New York: International Arts and Sciences Press.

# Selective Further Reading

Bahro, Rudolph, *The Alternative in Eastern Europe* (New York: New Left Books/Schocken, 1979).

Bauman, Zygmunt, 'Social Dissent in the East European Political System', *Archives européennes de sociologie* 12 (1971).

Berliner, J., *The Innovative Decision in Soviet Industry* (Cambridge, Mass.: Harvard University Press, 1976).

Bettleheim, Charles, *The Transition to Socialist Economy* (Hassocks, Sussex: Harvester, 1975).

Brus, W., *The Economics and Politics of Socialism* (London: Routledge & Kegan Paul, 1973).

Burns, Tom R., and Veljko Rus, eds., *Work and Power: The Liberation of Work and the Control of Political Power* (Beverly Hills: Sage, 1979).

Carlo, Antonio, 'The Socio-Economic Nature of the USSR', *Telos* 21 (1974).

Castoriadis, Cornelius, 'The Social Regime in Russia', *Telos* 22 (1974–1975).

Connor, Walter D., *Socialism, Politics, and Equality* (New York: Columbia University Press, 1979).

Crompton, R., and J. Gubbay, *Economy and Class Structure* (London: Macmillan, 1977).

Djilas, Milovan, *The New Class: An Analysis of the Communist System* (New York: 1957).

Faber, B. L., ed., *Social Structure in Eastern Europe* (New York: Praeger, 1975).

Feher, F., 'The Dictatorship over Needs', *Telos* 35 (1978).

Giddens, Anthony, *The Class Structure of the Advanced Societies,* 2nd ed. (London: Hutchinson, 1980).

Hegedus, Andras, *Socialism and Bureaucracy* (London: Allison & Busby, 1976).

Holubenko, M., 'The Soviet Working Class', *Critique* 4 (1974).

Kerr, C., et al., *Industrialism and Industrial Man* (Harmondsworth: Penguin, 1973).

Konrad, George, and Ivan Szelenyi, *The Intellectuals on the Road to Class Power* (New York: Harcourt Brace Jovanovich, 1979).

Krejci, Jaroslav, *Social Change and Stratification in Postwar Czechoslovakia* (London: Macmillan, 1972).

Lane, D., *The End of Inequality? Stratification Under State Socialism* (Harmondsworth: Penguin, 1971).

Lane, D., and F. O'Dell, *The Soviet Industrial Worker* (Oxford: Martin Robertson, 1978).

Lefort, Claude, *Éléments d'une critique de la bureaucratie* (Paris: Gallimard, 1979).

Marcuse, Herbert, *Soviet Marxism* (Boston: Beacon, 1964).

Matthews, M., *Privilege in the Soviet Union: A Study of Elite Life Styles Under Communism* (London: Allen & Unwin, 1978).

Nove, A., *The Soviet Economy* (Oxford: Oxford University Press, 1961).

Nove, A., and D. M. Nutti, eds., *Socialist Economics* (Harmondsworth: Penguin, 1972).

Parkin, Frank, *Marxism and Class Theory: A Bourgeois Critique* (London: Tavistock, 1979).

Rakovski, Marc, *Towards an Eastern European Marxism* (London: Allison & Busby, 1978).

Silnitsky, Frantisek, Larisa Silnitsky, and Karl Reyman, eds., *Communism and Eastern Europe* (London: Harvester, 1979).

Stoyanovíc, Svetozar, *Between Ideas and Reality* (New York: Oxford University Press, 1973).

Titken, H., 'Class Structure and the Soviet Elite', *Critique* 9 (1978).

Trotsky, L., *The Revolution Betrayed* (London: Faber, 1937).

Yanowitch, M., *Social and Economic Inequality in the Soviet Union* (London: Martin Robertson, 1977).

# Acknowledgements

For permission to reprint the texts contained in this volume the Editors wish to thank the following authors, copyright-holders and publishers:

Nicos Poulantzas      'On Social Classes', *New Left Review*.

Erik Olin Wright      'Class Boundaries and Contradictory Class Locations', from *Class, Crisis and the State*, New Left Books.

R. W. Connell      'A Critique of the Althusserian Approach to Class', *Theory and Society*, Elsevier Scientific Publishing.

Harry Braverman      'Capitalism and the Division of Labour' from *Labor and Monopoly Capitalism*, Monthly Review Press.

Anthony Giddens      'Class Structuration and Class Consciousness', from *The Class Structure of the Advanced Societies*, 2nd Ed., Hutchinson and Barnes and Noble.

Frank Parkin      'Social Closure and Class Formation', from *The Marxist Theory of Class: A Bourgeois Critique*, Tavistock Publications.

Maurice Zeitlen      'Corporate Ownership and Control: The Large Corporation and the Capitalist Class', *American Journal of Sociology*, University of Chicago Press.

Göran Therborn      'What Does the Ruling Class Do When it Rules?', *The Insurgent Sociologist*.

Claus Offe and Volker Ronge      'Thesis on the Theory of the State, *New German Critique*.

| Boris Frankel | 'On the State of the State: Marxist Theories of the State After Leninism', *Theory and Society*, Elsevier Scientific Publishing. |
|---|---|
| Stephen A. Marglin | 'What Do the Bosses Do? The Origins and Functions of Hierarchy in Capitalist Production,' *Review of Radical Political Economics*. |
| E. P. Thompson | 'Time, Work–Discipline, and Industrial Capitalism', *Past and Present: A Journal of historical studies*, The Past and Present Society. |
| David Stark | 'Class Struggle and the Transformation of the Labour Process: A Relational Approach', *Theory and Society*, Elsevier Scientific Publishing. |
| Jill Rubery | 'Structured Labour Markets, Worker Organisation, and Low Pay', *Cambridge Journal of Economics*. |
| David Lockwood | 'Sources of Variation in Working-Class Images of Society', *Sociological Review*. |
| Michael Mann | 'The Social Cohesion of Liberal Democracy', *American Sociological Review*, American Sociological Association. |
| Nicholas Abercrombie and Bryan S. Turner | 'The Dominant Ideology Thesis', *British Journal of Sociology*, Routledge and Kegan Paul. |
| Elizabeth Garnsey | 'Women's Work and Theories of Class and Stratification', *Sociology*. |
| Heidi Hartmann | 'Capitalism, Patriarchy, and Job Segregation by Sex', *Signs*, University of Chicago Press. |
| Jane Humphries | 'Class Struggle and the Persistence of the Working-Class Family', *Cambridge Journal of Economics*. |
| Robert Blauner | 'Colonised and Immigrant Minorities', from *Racial Oppression in America*, Harper and Row. |
| Erik Olin Wright | 'Race, Class and Income Inequality', *American Journal of Sociology*, University of Chicago Press. |
| David Harvey | 'Labour, Capital, and Class Struggle Around the Built Environment in Advanced Capitalist Societies', *Politics and Society*. |
| Frank Parkin | 'System Contradiction and Political Transformation', *Archives européennes de sociologie*. |
| Alec Nove | 'Is There a Ruling Class in the U.S.S.R?', *Soviet Studies*. |
| Murray Yanowitch | 'Work Hierarchy and Management "Participation" in the Soviet Union', from *Social and Economic Inequality in the U.S.S.R.*, M. E. Sharpe. |
| Elizabeth Garnsey | 'Growth Strategy, Competing Interests, and the Soviet Occupational System', *Cambridge Journal of Economics*. |